SPORT AND THE BODY:

A Philosophical Symposium

SPORT AND THE BODY:

A Philosophical Symposium

Edited and with Introductions and Bibliographies by

ELLEN W. GERBER, Ph.D.
Associate Professor
School of Physical Education
University of Massachusetts, Amherst

LEA & FEBIGER   Philadelphia · 1972

Health Education,
Physical Education, and
Recreation Series

Ruth Abernathy, Ph.D., Editorial Adviser,
Director, School of Physical and Health Education,
University of Washington, Seattle, Washington 98105

ISBN 0-8121-0388-2

Published in Great Britain by Henry Kimpton Publishers, London

Library of Congress Catalog Card Number: 72-175459

PRINTED IN THE UNITED STATES OF AMERICA

To Eleanor Metheny

humanist, scholar, teacher: the essence of a philosopher

Preface

The phenomenon of sport has been receiving increasing attention from academicians. Once the exclusive preserve of the strong, the hardy, the courageous, the competitive, and the leisured, it has now attracted those whose role in life is to contemplate and analyze. Observing that men and women have perennially been fascinated by sport, those who are equally fascinated with the behavior and institutions of men and women have sensed the fruitfulness of studying this enduring activity.

At first, particularly in times prior to the contemporary, those individuals who examined sport wrote primarily to describe its nature and values. More recently, in addition to those approaches, writers have attempted to investigate other aspects of the sport phenomenon. For example, the nature of the sport experience and its effect on the individual's growth as a human being have been described by a number of people.

Interest in the philosophy of the body is also a relatively new phenomenon, although philosophical treatises on the mind-body problem extend back to the ancient Greek thinkers. The new approaches to the subject, which relate directly to a theoretical consideration of sport, discuss the body as a mode of being-in-the-world. Examination of the experience of the body in sport has become a relevant philosophical topic.

Academic interest in sport and the body has led, inevitably, to the introduction in colleges and universities of appropriate courses. Although located primarily in departments of physical education, the discipline most concerned with the theory of sport, such courses have occasionally been taught by bold thinkers in departments of philosophy or cultural studies. It is my own experience teaching courses in sport philosophy to undergraduate and graduate students in physical education, that led me to assemble this work. In fact, it was in class that the following definition of sport was derived. For purposes of this book, sport is considered to be a human activity which involves specific administrative organization, a historical background of rules or customs which define the objective and limit the pattern of human behavior; it involves challenge and a definite outcome determined by physical skill.

My goals in developing this book were threefold. First, I wanted to organize the work in a way that would reflect valid philosophical approaches to any phenomenon. Thus, after a beginning and defining section on the nature of sport, there are sections on metaphysics, epistemology, ethics, and aesthetics—the traditional areas of philosophical study. However, I have specifically and deliberately attempted to stay away from problems which are internal to the discipline of philosophy and not particularly relevant to the study of sport. In this way, disagreements between branches of a philosophical school, or fine scholastic distinctions between various terms and methods, have been avoided. Sport is too live a phenomenon to be reduced to disputes akin to the question of how many angels can dance on the head of a pin. In the introductions to each section I have attempted to delineate the basic philosophical considerations appropriate to studying sport within the bounds of a specific philosophical framework.

The second aim was to bring together, in convenient form, what I considered to be the most significant philosophical writings on sport and the body. The major philosophers have rarely touched this subject in their writings, but whenever possible their brief comments have been included; it seemed appropriate to introduce students to the philosophical writings of some of the most respected thinkers of all time. Numerous selections in this book have come from scholars in the field of physical education, and a few articles have come from popular sources. In many cases only a portion of an article or chapter was included. This decision was made in order to permit the reader's acquaintance with the widest possible array of writers. It seemed more important to provide variety of approach rather than lengthy, in-depth studies—especially since the selections were obtained from widely scattered, often difficult to locate, sources. Decisions of what to include were based solely on my personal judgment of their worth and relevance. However the insightful reactions of my students played no small part in helping to make these determinations.

Finally, it was my intent to assist teachers and researchers of this topic by delineating some of the potential dimensions of a philosophical analysis of sport and the body. Therefore, in each introduction I have included a series of questions appropriate for considering specific aspects of the subject. In addition, I have suggested a number of topics which would probably be worthy subjects for research. Although there are cues to further reading in each introduction, the comprehensive bibliography located at the end of each section is an attempt to pinpoint the sources available for further study.

An explanation about the six bibliographies seems desirable. Their preparation was the hardest part of editing this book, for the choices of what to include and on which list to place the selected entries were very difficult to make. Of course I accept full responsibility for judging and classifying the relevance of each entry.

There are relatively few studies which have been undertaken primarily for the purpose of philosophically analyzing sport or some particular aspect of it. *Philosophers Index, Research Quarterly Index(es), Completed Research in Health, Physical Education and Recreation* were searched along with other journals and proceedings comprising the literature of the two fields. It was a frustrating experience for one seeking to identify articles on philosophy and sport. Therefore, many writings were included which come from the published works of other disciplines, particularly psychology, sociology, anthropology, art, and education. This multidisciplinary approach enabled me to locate many appropriate studies. The entries in this book's bibliographies are frequently articles which were written for some other purpose, but do include a philosophical treatment of sport. The main criterion I applied for selection was the presence of a reasonably full and germane discussion.

A second criterion used for selecting the bibliographical entries was that the primary subject matter had to be sport. Many articles which have the word play, game, recreation, or physical education in their titles were included because the context of the articles made it clear that the authors were actually writing about sport activities as I have defined them. Articles dealing with childhood play were excluded, as were those on game theory (in the von Neumann mode), board games and games of chance, physical education as a curricular entity, and general leisure or recreational activities.

Several entries seemed to have relevance for more than one section of the book and were therefore listed accordingly. The sections are so interrelated that, with articles not written to suit a philosophical framework, it was often difficult to make definitive judgments. For example, in the course of an article, the author might comment about the nature of sport, describe the meaning of sport to an individual's life, and delineate the general value of sport in society. In choosing which section, or sections, to place the entry (or the book's selections for that matter), I tried to determine what was the main point of the article—where the primary weight of the discussion fell. When in doubt I chose to duplicate the entry.

A work of this nature requires many acknowledgments. To Howard S. Slusher of the University of Southern California should go much credit for developing an approach to the philosophy of sport. His book, *Man, Sport and Existence,* was the first comprehensive attempt to discuss relevant questions. His classes, in which I participated as a doctoral student, were really original in that they developed a new structure for the study of sport. As a teacher in this area, I trace my conception of sport philosophy to his work.

I am also indebted to my colleagues in physical education who are interested in the theoretical aspects of sport. They are a small band of people, accomplished and generous in sharing the fruits of their studies. From them have come numerous ideas difficult to credit specifically, but for which I am nevertheless very grateful.

The authors included in this work should be acknowledged for their sagacity as well as their courtesy in permitting me to reprint their studies.

Finally, I reserve my greatest thanks to my friend and professional colleague, Pearl Berlin. She asks the right questions, insists on scholarly answers, cuts away the superfluous, edits my writings, and always inspires me to expend the extra effort that transforms the ordinary into something more valuable.

ELLEN W. GERBER

Amherst, Massachusetts

Contents

Sport and Aesthetics

THE NATURE OF SPORT

The Nature of Sport

INTRODUCTION

Fundamental to an examination of sport in its diversified and meaningful roles is an understanding of its nature as a phenomenon. There are numerous methods useful for discerning the nature of sport. Operating from the conviction that a given noun (e.g. sport) has a describable essence—an essentialistic philosophical position—a variety of techniques can be employed to analyze the phenomenon. These include definition, characterization, classification, and comparison.

Definition is basically an application of inductive reasoning. To define sport one might begin by listing all activities intuitively accepted as sport. If one rejects the personalism of intuition, convention or social agreement can be substituted as a better basis for constructing such a list. In either case, from this list of specific activities an all-embracing definition can be induced. The definition must be general enough to include all the activities one wishes to accept as sport and specific enough to exclude all activities which one rejects as non-sport. The articles "A Philosophy of Sport" by H. Graves and "What is a Game?" by Bernard Suits are excellent examples of this form of logic.

Characterization, although similarly beginning with an idea of the activities accepted as sport, is an example of deductive logic. From the generalized idea of what is sport (or from an accepted definition of sport), are deduced the characteristics of sport, viz. their common elements. The characteristics decided upon must be present in all activities accepted as sport and that precise combination of characteristics should not be found in activities not considered sport. "This 'Thing' Called Sport" by Eleanor Metheny, "Characteristics of Sport" by Howard S. Slusher, "The Nature of Play" by Johan Huizinga, and "Sport and Play: Suspension of the Ordinary" by Kenneth Schmitz all represent the application of deductive logic as the process used to ascertain the nature of sport.

At least since Aristotle, classification has been an important technique for delineating the essence of something. It can serve the purpose of clarifying the basic relationships that are inherent in sport activities. In many ways classification is similar to characterization because it groups subjects that have like elements. It may even be considered a secondary form of analysis because it is dependent upon the identification of common characteristics before grouping can be accomplished. Probably the most frequently cited model for classifying games was designed by Roger Caillois; it is presented here in the chapter called "The Classification of Games." John Loy expressed a somewhat different system in his article "The Nature of Sport: A Definitional Effort." A portion of Eleanor Metheny's article, "This 'Thing' Called Sport," also deals with categorizing in still a third manner.

The selection by Robert J. Fogelin represents a different kind of philosophical analytic technique. It is patterned after Wittgenstein who, in "Language-Games" (1958), provided a taxonomic model of linguistic analysis. The Positivist philosophers reject the idea that things have an essence; they assert, instead, that the subject (e.g. sport) is nothing more than the sum of its predicates (e.g. qualities, attributes) as these are evidenced by ordinary language usage. Thus, in "Sport: The Diversity of the Concept," Fogelin chose that which appears on the sports page of a newspaper as representative of ordinary language usage. Predicates relate to one another rather than to the subject sport, although they are found to be used in conjunction with the term sport. Thus sport has no nature—it is as language has used it.

The essentialist and analytic approaches to any philosophical issue are basically incompatible. Those who assume that there is a phenomenon—sport—with a describable essence, will not believe that sport is a conglomeration of the predicates used to describe sport in the course of ordinary language. This same dichotomy of views would be apparent if one were to attempt to approach the topic via an application of the principles advanced by each of the major philosophical systems. Idealism, realism and pragmatism assume the essential existence of things, though each differs in its belief as to what constitutes reality. Existentialism and the analytic philosophies refer the existence of things to the experience or verbalizations of individuals. No ultimate essence of any kind is assumed or understood.

In general, attempts to apply the technique of philosophical analysis to the nature of sport have been sparse. Most of the important writings on the subject are included in this book. The reader interested in pursuing further discussion of the topic is directed to the chapter "Play, Sport, and Game" in Weiss (1969) which offers a comparative analysis of all three activities, noting their similarities. Melvin (1960) does a good comparison between play, work and leisure. In their anthropological study on "Games in Culture," Roberts, Arth and Bush (1959) provide an interesting classification of games somewhat different from Caillois' version. Sutton-Smith (1959) offers an excellent analysis of game characteristics in an article on "game meaning." Approaching play as behavior, Avedon and Sutton-Smith construct a unique definition of play and games in the introduction to their new book (1971). Stone in his two articles (1957, 1969) presents the results of a sociological study which shows the varied meanings inherent in the symbolic term sport, to groups with different social characteristics. Such studies can be thought of as extensions of the analytic philosophical model. Ehrmann (1971) does a beautifully

presented criticism of the theories of Huizinga and Caillois. There is also a body of literature on games theory, which includes analyses of game characteristics, but the writings are too tangential to this book to be noted here.

Definitive answers to the question "What is the nature of sport and how does it differ from play and games?" have yet to be formulated. Discussion on the subject remains open-ended. What is an adequate definition of sport? What are the characteristics of sport, play and games? What is the concept of sport and how can it be distinguished from the practice of sport? How does the mode in which sport is practiced affect its qualities? In other words, are sandlot baseball, Little League, Lassie League, physical education class games, intramural games, varsity games, or professional baseball all the same activities having similar effects on the participants? Are field activities such as hunting and fishing regarded as sport (they were once the sole referents of the term)? Are activities not engaged in competitively, such as recreational skiing, sport? Can non-physical competitions like chess be considered sport? Are dog shows sport? Is professional sport really sport, or are paid performers really sportsmen? Are there yet undeveloped models for classifying sport? What is the relation of sport to play, games, work, and leisure, and is this a relationship which changes in time and varies across social groups?

Answers to these questions are of fundamental importance to physical educators, sport researchers or anyone else responsible for making decisions connected with sport. For example, sport financing and awards for performance are dependent upon the decision maker's philosophical position as to what constitutes sport. (Red Auerbach expressed shock at the selection of Arnold Palmer as the most outstanding athlete of the '60s, commenting that golf is a game, not a sport.) Karate, yoga and flycasting are among activities frequently excluded from school programs because they are not considered sport in the manner of basketball and tennis. Furthermore, curriculums are currently being balanced on an outdated model for classifying sports; new models may challenge the development of new curriculums. If professional sport is sport, a new frame of reference for the morality of sport should be delineated, which will affect the practice of high-powered collegiate and scholastic sport. If through comparison it is revealed that sport is not in opposition to work but has many factors in common, perhaps new attitudes toward it may be generated among the lay public. And lastly, new definitions, agreed-upon-characteristics and new classification models may yield renewed potential for research exploring factors such as individual motivation to participate, personality differences among sportsmen or the sociocultural roles of various activities and performers, to name but a few possibilities.

Classes in the philosophy of sport may need to agree on the (or their) definition of sport and its characteristics, as well as a basic classification system, before proceeding to further study about the phenomenon sport.

A Philosophy of Sport*

H. GRAVES

There are few words in the English language which have such a multiplicity of divergent meanings as the word sport. The dictionaries afford us very little help in arriving at a philosophic definition of the word—a definition common and essential to all its legitimate uses. Dr. Murray will perhaps come to our assistance when he works down to the later ages of the letter S, but in the meantime we must perforce have recourse to the "Century Dictionary" and its humbler rivals.

It seems at least certain, by the consensus of all the authorities, including Mr. Skeat, that sport is a shortened form of the old noun and verb disport, of which uses the latter survives as a more or less archaic word. Disport comes from the mediaeval *disportare*, to move from one place to another, transport, divert, distract. The reflexive *se disportare* means to distract, divert or amuse oneself, and a similar meaning of amusement, fun or recreation attaches to the word disport, and originally to the word sport. As a concrete noun "sport" means a mode of amusement. Thence the "Century" leads us to an arbitrarily restricted meaning of an "outdoor sport."

Similarly we learn from the same source a sportsman is "a man who sports," or specifically, "a man who practises field sports, especially hunting and fishing, usually for pleasure, and in a legitimate manner." But another and still narrower specific meaning is that of "one who bets, or is otherwise interested in field

sports, specially racing." For this use we are referred to Tom Brown, where we find the small boys who were mulcted of their scanty pocket-money for the Derby Sweepstake consoled by the reflection that "it was a pleasant thing to be called a gentleman sportsman."

An even lower connotation is attached by the "Century" to the expression "sporting man," who we learn is "one interested in field sports; hence in a bad sense a betting man, a gambler, a blackleg." The adjective sportsman-like is defined as "characteristic of or befitting a sportsman: hence legitimate from the point of view of the sportsman." The Encyclopaedic Dictionary covers much the same ground, giving us firstly "a game, pastime or amusement," secondly, "outdoor recreations such as grown-up men indulge in, especially hunting, shooting, fishing and the like," and in support of this restricted definition cites from Clarendon that "the king was excessively devoted to hunting and the sports of the field," though, as in the passage quoted, this meaning is only obtained by means of a qualifying expression, it by no means seems to clinch the matter. Thirdly, we have "a comprehensive term embracing all forms of athletics and games of skill in which prizes are competed for or money staked."

The other dictionaries do not open any fresh ground except Webster, who defines the verb "to sport" as meaning "to be given to betting, especially upon horse-racing."

This summary of the meanings of the word as given by the dictionaries will suffice to show the contradictory senses in which it is used.

* From *The Contemporary Review*, LXXVIII (December, 1900), 877-893.

Starting from the simple notion of sport as an amusement, we come down to the curiously specialized uses of the word which tie it down on the one hand to pursuits of killing and on the other to games in which a money stake is involved.

We may now test the dictionaries by comparison with the usages of modern conversational phraseology, especially as reflected in the newspapers, and at the same time try to trace any unity of idea which may underlie these discordant meanings.

To begin with, we find that one of the commonest meanings of the word is that of a physical, as distinct from a purely intellectual, recreation. In this sense it is held to cover such non-competitive recreations as hunting, fishing, mountaineering, and the like, together with such competitive recreations as horse-racing, running, cricket, football, in fact all outdoor games. But the words "physical recreation" will hardly serve as a definition of sport. For then we should be compelled to include amateur gardening, which I think no one would be sufficiently daring to class among sports, except, perhaps, in its competitive aspect at flower shows and the like—a form of gardening in which the physical aspect of the recreation is most subordinated to the intellectual. Nor do we get any nearer to a solution by adding the word "competitive" to one definition. For this would compel us to exclude hunting, fishing, and the like, none of which recreations are essentially competitive.

Indeed, as the dictionaries show, some sportsmen of the old school seem disposed to restrict the term sport to such non-competitive recreations as involve killing, thus restricting the term to hunting, fishing, shooting and so forth. But this definition brings us into worse bewilderment, for not only does it exclude cricket and football, to which most men would grant the title, but it reduces us to the necessity of regarding fox-hunting as coming within the boundary of sport and drag-hunting as falling outside it.

A further use of the word contrasts "sport" with "pastime." For instance, most writers on cycling make this distinction, treating of cycle-racing under the heading of sport and ordinary non-competitive cycling under that of pastime. This, however, brings us back to the definition of sport as "competitive physical exercise," which we have already rejected. Notwithstanding this, the heading "Sport and Pastime" is commonly used in our newspapers as a heading for descriptions of all manner of recreations, indoor and outdoor, apparently with the idea that the two words between them cover all modes of recreation, both competitive and non-competitive.

Another newspaper use of the word is in the form of "sporting intelligence," and, so far as I can gather, this expression is very commonly used to denote such recreations as are made the subject of betting—such in fact as can be expressed in odds, such for instance as horse-racing, coursing, professional sculling and pedestrianism, and the University boat race, though for some reason—probably the conservative instinct—the definition is stretched to include the ancient sports of killing, most of which involve the outlay of a considerable amount of money. So that we should be led to conclude that sport is a physical recreation which involves the passing of money. Far more popular outdoor games and competitions are very commonly placed under the separate heading of athletics, though this is sometimes amplified to athletic sports. This last expression makes yet another distinction which I have heard made between "sport" in the singular, which is taken to cover hunting, fishing, horse-racing, and so forth, and "sports" in the plural, which would include running and kindred competitions (indeed these are often spoken of as "sports" without further description), together with cricket, football and other games involving physical exercise.

If we are to enunciate any philosophy of sport, we must, I think, construct some definition which will cover all the pursuits which are distinguished as sport in any of these acceptations of the term. Now the one idea which seems to be essential to all of these is that they must be undertaken purely for the sake of recreation as distinct from business.

Whether sport is to be restricted to recreations of physical exercise must, I think, be left a matter for personal preference, and the exact import in which the word is used ought to be explicitly stated wherever it is not made clear from the context. For the purposes of this inquiry, however, I am inclined to think that such a restriction of the term would be unphilosophic, and would be somewhat of a hindrance to clear thought, especially in view of the difficulty in drawing a clear line between physical and non-physical recreations. There must, I think, be a code of ethics common to all branches of recreation, and applicable as such to card-playing equally with cricket. I propose, then, first to examine the logical consequences of defining sport as a recreation simply, without distinguishing between physical and non-physical, competitive and non-competitive forms, not with a view to proposing this as an adequate and final definition, but with the object of framing a code of ethics which shall be applicable to sport in its most comprehensive sense of recreation. We should then be able as we proceed to apply our general conclusions to the various sub-divisions of physical sport which are logically comprehended in this wider meaning.

In so far as a pursuit is followed as a means of livelihood it ceases to be sport, and becomes merely a matter of business. Sport is followed for no other end than to afford pleasure to those participating in it, and a sportsman follows sport for no other reason than to enjoy that pleasure.

Hence it happens that the object at which any particular sport ostensibly aims is often regarded as of less importance than the means employed to obtain it. The sportsman's ideal is not so much the retrospect of "something attempted, something done," as the present zest of a keen struggle, and in order to add to that zest he even fences in his sport with more or less artificial difficulties. Hence arises what we may term the conventionality of sport, which proposes for its object not to kill the bird, hook the fish, destroy the fox, win the match, but to derive, and perhaps afford to others, pleasure from the attempt to do so. If the object ostensibly aimed at be attained by a skipping of corners, by the use of illegitimate and unconventional means, by the maxim of "win, tie, or wrangle," in fact by any means which diminishes the pleasure to be gained from participation in the pursuit, then the result achieved is considered foreign to the nature of sport. Otherwise we should take guns to our foxes and poison to our fish. Our aim should be not so much to win as to play the game.

Consequently, sportsmanlike conduct would appear to lie in such practices as conduce to the pleasantness of a sport, and unsportsmanlike conduct in such actions as tend to spoil it by making it less pleasant. It is unsportsmanlike for a cricket eleven to try to save a lost match by wilful delays, sportsmanlike to consent to play extra time to bring it to an end. The action of a cyclist or oarsman who should refuse to take advantage of an accident to the machine or boat of his opponent would usually be referred to as sportsmanlike. To win a race by appeal against a foul is not usually regarded as the act of a sportsman. Again, when Cornell University, a year or two back, won their heat in the Grand Challenge Cup at Henley by taking advantage of a muddled

start, their conduct did not commend itself to public opinion. In all these cases the ground of our judgment would be found in the consideration whether the action complained of spoiled or tended to spoil the pleasantness of the sport. The unsportsmanlike player, over greedy for points, seeks to snatch advantage by committing acts which circumscribe the opportunities for good and legitimate play, and, in a word, spoil the game. The true sportsman plays for the love of the game, the sense of mastery, the sheer *joie de vivre* which he feels in playing a stroke well, and not for the mere honour, or still less the profit, of a victory. He would prefer to be fairly and squarely beaten by a superior opponent to scoring a win by a clever and unconventional jockeying of the rules.

These instances will perhaps serve to illustrate the spirit which governs sport as a recreation. But, side by side with this ideal, we have the opposite notion, very prevalent in the newspapers and in everyday conversation, that the word sport must connote the passing of money. I propose, therefore, to enquire into the actual reactions of sport and finance with a view of ascertaining how far these ideas of recreation and money-making are compatible.

The first consideration is, I think, the extent to which the making of profit from sport is legitimate and sportsmanlike.

The ideal sportsman, we have agreed, the sportsman "in reality," as Plato would have it, engages in sport purely for the love of the occupation. In so far as he is guided by other considerations he ceases to be a sportsman and becomes something else. The professional football player, for instance, may be a sportsman in so far as he plays for the love of the game and as a lover of it—even as Andrew Lang would sooner be "some poor player on scant hire" than buried from all god-like exercise at the noble game. But, in so far as he is a hireling, he is in the same position as the physician of Socrates and Thrasymachus—a physician to the extent to which he follows his art as a lover of it, and looking to its perfection, but a professor of the art of receiving pay, in so far as he looks to his fees. And just as the physician, having regard to the necessity of living himself, may be forced, or think himself forced, to humour the caprices of a valetudinarian, even to the sacrifice of the true well-being and dignity of his art, so the professional football player may, from the necessity of distinguishing himself and securing Press notices, sail very near the wind and adopt a style of play which would not commend itself to the ideal player or sportsman. In an approximately healthy atmosphere of public opinion, such as obtains in the case of cricket, the professional is saved from the necessity of deciding between his two selves. For sportsmanlike play is not only its own reward, but carries with it the applause of his employers. Here, too, not only is doubtful play a thing almost unknown, but the wisdom of the rulers has enacted that there shall be no trafficking in men, as when a footballer is hawked from one limited company to another, and the very patrons of the game engage their players as one buys stock and shares. Then the very example of the employers shows the players that the art of earning pay is the matter chiefly to be regarded.

In sports of individual competition the question assumes a somewhat different form. To begin with, the natural difficulties of giving all comers equal chances become more formidable when individual men and not teams are the units to be considered. Though sport be followed purely as a recreation, one man has more leisure than another to devote to perfecting his skill and bodily condition, or has greater resources from which to furnish himself with necessary equipment. In running and the like, the matter of equipment resolves itself into nothing but shoes and garments, but in other sports, such as cycling, the cost of machines and then upkeep involves a relatively heavy outlay. Hence the temptation to a needy man to secure assistance from makers who desire advertisement for their cycles or tyres.

Now a man may do this from the purest love of sport: he may wish nothing more than to fit himself so as to take the field on level terms with his competitors in point of equipment. But he may go further than this. He may accept money or maintenance from the makers so that he may extend his hours of training and thus compete on equal terms with more leisured opponents. Or, lastly, he may decide that he requires his whole time as leisure for training and may become wholly the servant of the makers.

I confess that the problem caused by the disparity in means and leisure of competitors is one difficult of solution. Anything like mutual disarmament is clearly out of the question, though I remember a suggestion to this effect was made to me early in 1891 by the late Professor Jowett. I was describing to him the way in which the introduction of pneumatic tyres had for the time being injured bicycle racing, how the man mounted on the new invention

was *caeteris paribus* bound to win if his tyres did not fail him, and how lamentably frequent and destructive of sport this occurrence was: for these were early days, and the tyres which were used would be to modern eyes inconceivably crude and unreliable. There was, too, the reluctance felt by the men of shorter purses to sink their scanty sovereigns in the doubtful invention. The Master's answer was emphatic. Pneumatic tyres ought to be barred from competition. As a matter of fact the possibility of doing this in the inter-University bicycle races was seriously considered by the clubs concerned. It was, however, felt that a policy of this kind would logically lead to such difficulties as to be untenable. There would be no end to allowances and penalties: in fact a handicap based on the merits of the machines ridden was the only really logical solution—and that an impossible one.

It may, then, be fairly assumed that it is impossible to eliminate the inequalities of birth and position, but it is very possible to draw a hard and fast line which shall prevent a man from deriving money or its equivalent from his participation in sport. It is not possible for a human judge to gauge the motives which in any given case lead a competitor to accept aid from improper sources, but it is quite clear that once we allow any measure of assistance from the makers, we cannot discriminate between the man who accepts money from sheer hunger of sport, and the man who follows sport from hunger of money. For this reason the National Cyclists' Union has with good logic professionalized the man who takes such help as stealing an unfair advantage from his competitors, and the Amateur Rowing Association has with still better logic professionalized all who are employed in or about boats.

The wisdom of this policy seems moreover to look beyond the immediate injustice which a competitor assisted from illegitimate sources inflicts upon his fellows. The "maker's amateur," as he is called, clearly seeks to steal an illicit advantage in point of leisure and outfit. But the evil goes further. Once the idea is imported into sport that a man's subsistence depends upon it, then the pleasantness of sport as a recreation ceases, and we import into it the bitterness of the world's struggle for existence. There are things which a man will do when his back is against the wall, and he feels that his own livelihood or that of his wife and children are dependent upon him, which he would not dream of doing if this feeling were removed. A man who is hard pushed to keep up his home, and sees his way to make money out of sport, is under a terrible temptation to sin against the gospel of sportsmanship. How, for instance, if the builder of boats or cycles offers assistance in return for advertisement, the sports promoter in return for the gate which he hopes to attract by a well-known name, or the bookmaker in return for the money of deluded backers betting on a race sold in advance? Is not the man whom I have described likely to yield to their solicitations? There is also the converse aspect of the case to be considered. With what feeling for instance would an amateur playing wholly for his own pleasure defeat a competitor whom he knew to be playing for his living, and whose happiness and well-being in life would be seriously lessened by ill success. Clearly he is faced by a most unpleasant dilemma—either to forego the pleasant stress of contest for which alone he follows the sport, or to deprive a fellow competitor of his bread. If sport is to be a recreation—a relief from the hard necessities of life—then the presence of a man who is competing with wholly different aims in mind is a menace to the sport of his fellows. This is no doubt a hard and pitiless conclusion, but it is that upon which the Amateur Rowing Association has built up its system of amateurism. It holds that a man whose financial and social position is such that he is likely to yield to the temptations which I have described, ought not in justice to himself and his competitors to be admitted to the sport. Moved by considerations such as these, that body has framed a definition of an amateur which excludes the mechanic, artisan or labourer, and persons who are or have been in a menial situation, and this has been done, not, I take it, from any sentiment of snobbishness or exclusiveness, but solely in the belief that this is the only way to keep the sport pure from the elements of corruption which I have named. It is argued, and with much show of truth, that the average workman has no idea of sport for its own sake. He cannot rise above the conception of "making a bit,"—his view of sport is that of the newspapers which reserve the title in its pre-eminence for those branches of competitive sport which are capable of being expressed in odds.

A typical and frequent case where the sportsman and the professor of the art of pay are inseparable is afforded by the Professional Blue. By this expression I mean the undergraduate who devotes himself to athletics with the idea of ultimately winning a livelihood by his strong right arm or leg, much as the scholar or exhibitioner hopes to attain the same end by the cultivation of his mighty brain. When scholastic agents make athletic distinctions a prominent item in the forms of application, and headmasters avowedly appoint their assistants from like considerations, it is fairly apparent that there must be a supply to meet this demand. Whether, from the point of view of instilling music and gymnastic into the young, this is a desirable state of things is a question beyond the scope of this enquiry, but it is difficult to resist the conviction that the undergraduate who looks to an appointment of this kind is practising the art of receiving pay, or, in plain English, is a professional athlete.

The question whether a sportsman may legitimately receive profit leads naturally to the problem of gate-money—the influence of which has completely altered the aspect of many forms of sport. Arguing from the premiss that sport is recreation as distinct from business, there is at least *primâ facie* ground for believing that any such consideration as gate-money is wholly alien to the sport. The best case that can be made out for its legitimacy is that certain games which demand for their practice a considerable outlay of capital, could hardly have boasted that excellence of play which distinguishes their best modern exponents without the assistance of the sightseer and his shilling. Grounds readily accessible from great cities, and therefore commanding a high rental, were not an element in the games of our forefathers: nor were the players of those days so exacting of the condition of their turf or the luxury of pavilions: most of all the growth of professionalism to which I have already referred has brought play to a higher point of excellence than had been seen before, and at the same time burdened the clubs with the maintenance of a crowd of retainers which would not in point of numbers have disgraced a feudal baron. Moreover, such sports as running, and, still more, cycling, call for very heavy outlay on tracks; and this, if club subscriptions are to be within the reach of middle-class youth, can hardly be reimbursed except by admitting spectators. A five-guinea subscription, such as that of Sheen House, would greatly restrict the field of competitors.

It may again be urged that the applause of a great crowd of spectators is exhilarating to the players, and not only raises their play to a higher level, but directly adds to the pleasure which they derive from the game. On the other hand, it may reasonably be held that this external stimulus to the players may in the end produce an ill rather than a good effect, leading them to take their pleasure less in the playing of the game than in the applause of the spectators, and thus to sacrifice the good of their side to pleasing the gallery. But the very important question of the effect on sport of this desire for individual distinction will be considered hereafter. Evils of this kind, however, would arise irrespective of whether the spectators pay for admission or not. But the necessity of enticing the paying public has had serious and definite effects upon many games, which have been modified with the express purpose of rendering them more attractive as spectacles.

The abolition of the spot-stroke in professional billiard matches is a case in point; this artificial restriction was introduced, not because the game is rendered any finer or pleasanter to the players, but because the public would not pay to see the "all in" game. Another instance is to be found in the modification of the rules of Rugby football by the Northern Union—a change which makes the game more dangerous and therefore less enjoyable to the players, but renders it brisker and more exciting to the man behind the ropes. The last visit of the Australian cricket team, too, was marked by very determined attempts on the part of the spectators to modify the style adopted by loudly expressed criticisms upon it. Whether or not the criticisms were well deserved, from the point of view of the sportsman, the recognition of the crowd as the arbiters of play is not likely to improve the tone of the game. The most striking case of all is the tinkering which has perplexed the rules of cycle-racing to prevent loafing in races. It may not be out of place to explain that if two riders of equal powers are competing, and one of them rides in front and makes the pace, he is bound to lose the race. Consequently, short distance races were ridden at a slow pace till the last hundred yards or so, the reason being that no man cared to risk his chance in order to make the pace for the others. The resulting races proved very monotonous to the public, who, in consequence, diverted their shillings to other purposes than visiting cycle tracks. Yet the competitors were acting quite rightly in riding each so that he might stand the best chance of winning. Therefore, purely in the interests of the gate, a new rule was made for the championships, that any race which was run in slower time than a fixed standard should be held void and the competitors disqualified—a foolish and unfair restriction, because, though each rider was supposed to take his turn in making the pace, it gave the victory, as has been remarked, "to the rider who most successfully evaded his obligations." Nor was the rule popular with the racing men, who justly objected that they took part in cycle-racing for their own recreation and not for that of the spectators.

But the chief evil arising from gate-money is the fatal facility which it affords for the employment of professionals, whether openly, as is the case with Association and Northern Rugby football, or with professional athletic sports or cycling, or secretly, as in the case of the "assisted" cricket amateur, or of amateur runners, jumpers, or cyclists who accept expenses, or even fees, from sports promoters. And the dangers to true sport inseparable from professionalism have already been discussed. It is said, with some truth, that the reason for the pre-eminent purity of amateur rowing lies in the fact that gate-money cannot form a factor in it.

Another obvious, and not less important, phase of the contact between sport and finance is to be found in organised betting. As we have learnt from the dictionaries—if reference to them were necessary—the idea that betting is an almost essential element in sport is exceedingly wide-spread. The questions for us, therefore, are, first, whether betting can itself be considered sport in its essential meaning of recreation; and, secondly, whether, allowing betting to be a form of sport, it is beneficial or hurtful to the healthy development of such sports as it may accompany. And in this enquiry it would seem legitimate to seek for analogies in other forms of gambling, and especially in gambling upon cards. For card games must certainly be considered of the nature of sport, inasmuch as they are pursuits followed for the sake of recreation. I do not mean to argue that card games could fairly be considered as sport in the ordinary acceptation of the term, for it is impossible to eliminate from sport the idea of an outdoor and more or less athletic pursuit, but in so far as card play and sport are both pursued for the sake of recreation, the same principles must, to this extent, be applicable to both.

The material for an answer to the first of the questions, whether betting is of the nature of sport, seems to have been already given. Sport is pursued as an end in itself, for the pure pleasure of playing the game, and independently of irrelevant considerations such as money-making. In so far as a man plays the game for the sake of the game he is a sportsman: in so far as he does it with a view to making a livelihood he is a huckster. Betting is obviously a matter of money; but we have to ask ourselves whether a man may not regard the making of bets as a sport in itself, to be pursued for the pleasure which it affords, and not as a means to a livelihood. For instance, of card games there are some, such as whist or picquet, which the sportsman might well play without money points, considering himself as well repaid by the intellectual exercise which they yield, or at all events considering that the practice of playing for money is a rule of hard necessity imposed to prevent slackness of play on the part of opponents less truly sportsmanlike than himself. But there are also games of cards which become meaningless without money stakes—such for instance as poker, baccarat or vingt-et-un—and yet these games are commonly played by gentlemen purely for the sake of amusement, and not with a view to making a livelihood out of them. It would seem, therefore, as if betting and gambling were in themselves somewhat of the nature of sport, and that a man might pursue them in a sportsmanlike spirit for the sake of recreation. What I mean is illustrated by the expression "a sporting bet," by which we mean a bet made with some degree of recklessness, and obviously for the pleasure of making it. There is a sportsmanlike and an unsportsmanlike way of playing cards. For instance, a man who in a purely gambling game plays an unduly cautious and safe game is not as a rule popular at the table, and perhaps rightly so. For in a game the sole *raison d'être* is to afford a pleasant opportunity for enjoying the excitement of chance; a man is clearly out of place whose play aims at eliminating the element of chance, and shows his thoughts to be centred on his domestic finances, and trembles when club law or jack pot is proclaimed. A player who renders such perfunctory and evasive homage to the goddess Fortune ought to have thought twice before he engaged at all in her rites. It is more straightforward and just to the table for the man whose means or inclinations are unequal to the game to refuse to play, and above all things it is imperative on the host not to over-persuade an unwilling guest to play a part so distasteful.

It would seem, therefore, that there is a sport of losing and winning money conforming to the general rules of sport which I have laid down, and really distinct from any of the sports with which it may happen to be associated. Thus a man may ideally be a sportsman of horse-racing or a sportsman of betting; or he may be both without injustice to either branch of sport, for all sport in the sense of recreation is governed by the same universal principles. But whether as a matter of fact the association of betting with other sports is harmful to them is a very different question. Ideally sport is confined to gentlemen: in real life it is also followed by hucksters who pervert it to the use of making a livelihood, removing it, as I have said before, from the realm of recreation, and importing into it the mercilessness and sordidness of the every-day struggle for bread. In no sport has betting become so highly organized a business as in horse-racing, and no other sport is accompanied by a fringe of such disreputable accessories. Granting that the Jockey Club, the most powerful of all the governing bodies of sport, manages to keep the higher circles of racing fairly free from notorious scandals, such scandals as have arisen are all due to the importation of the idea of money-making, while outside the enclosures the unfortunate state of our race-courses is too notorious to need comment—a condition of things due almost entirely to the gangs of welshers, touts and bullies attracted by the commercial side of horse-racing.

This conclusion is fortified by the fact that of all other sports those only are remarkable for the rough and undisciplined character of the crowds which they collect in which organised betting is a prominent feature. Professional pedestrianism and football, especially in the North of England, are cases in point. In fact, the mutual relation of these two factors form an excellent illustration of the logical method of agreement and difference.

Passing from the effects of betting upon sporting mankind in the mass to its effects upon the individual sportsman, it is easily possible to conceive cases—individual instances will arise in most minds—in which betting begun in a sportsmanlike spirit has ultimately resulted in the destruction of that spirit. I fail, as I have said, to detect any evil in betting provided it be conducted by gentlemen or, what for the purposes of sport is synonymous, by sportsmen. As a logical proposition this is true, for no sportsman would do an unsportsmanlike act. The difficulty is that a man may begin with betting as a recreation and may from recklessness or want of skill find that he has so compromised his financial position that his very means of livelihood are attacked. So that his sport ceases to be a recreation and becomes involved with the question of subsistence—a condition of things in which sport ceases to be sport. For now he aims οὐχ ἱερήιου οὐδὲ βοείην; the contest is for dear life, and the risk is great lest his necessity may drive him into some unsportsmanlike act.

I know nothing of Indian gymkhanas, but if it is permissible to place reliance upon the truthfulness of Anglo-Indian tales, betting there does not seem to make for straightness of running. In British professional running and rowing it is generally admitted that the race is not always to the swift, but it is not uncommonly predestined by the blessed gods who wield the pencil. But to dilate upon the corruption in sport which seems almost inseparable from organised betting is rather like flogging a dead horse: the best commentary upon it is the policy—not always, it is true, successful—strenuously followed by the governing bodies of amateur running and cycling to prohibit systematic betting upon their grounds.

Thus far, then, we have followed to its logical conclusions the doctrine that sport is essentially of the nature of recreation and ceases to be sport in so far as it is followed for livelihood. We have distinguished accordingly between the true amateur of sport and the huckster who follows sport otherwise than as a recreation. We have inferred that gate-money is not a consideration germane to true sport. We have found that betting, though it may have in it something of the nature of sport, is at best but a secondary or parasitic form of it, and, as is often the case with parasites, is in its over-developed forms harmful to the best interests of the parent sport. It would therefore appear that the claim of such branches of recreation as are associated with betting to be regarded as sport *par excellence* has hardly been maintained, and that the dictionaries are reflecting only a debased and arbitrary use of the word which can hardly have grown by legitimate development from its ancient signification.

We have now to consider another restricted use of the word, in the sense of a recreation for which prizes are offered, or in other words, in the sense of competitive sport. We must enquire whether the idea of competition is really essential to the notion of sport, and, failing that, whether it makes for the well-being of sport in its sense of recreation.

I have already referred to the two mutually exclusive schools which would restrict the word sport, the one to essentially noncompetitive sports of killing, such as might be classed under the convenient French term *la chasse*, the other to purely competitive recreations in sharp contrast to its antithesis of "pastime." There is ample literary authority for either use,

but I can see little philosophic reason for making this distinction. Both forms of sport are recreations, both are subject to conventional rules, both seem to present opportunities for sportsmanlike and unsportsmanlike conduct. If, for instance, I am trying by myself to see in how many strokes I can get round the golf links and conveniently omit one of the holes, if I shoot a bird sitting, it seems to me that my conduct is unsportsmanlike, even though I have no opponent but my own conscience. I propose, therefore, for the purpose of this enquiry, to include both competitive and noncompetitive recreations under the heading of sport, and if I be told that I shall thereby be compelled to include card patience among sports, I shall rejoin that to cheat at patience approaches as nearly as I can conceive to Plato's idea of the "lie in the soul."

Though this problem of definition has little more than an academic interest, the question of the extent to which it is legitimate and beneficial to carry competition in sport is one of considerable practical importance.

The desire for individual glory and notoriety, and the resulting stress of competition, have always been important factors in sport, but have acquired enhanced prominence during the present reign owing to the publicity granted by the Press, and to the facilities afforded by cheap and rapid travel which enable the sportsmen of distant localities to meet each other. This has resulted in a remarkable development in the organization of sport. The public desire is that the best man, the best team, the best performance shall be definitely hall-marked as such. Hence a profusion of championships, of athletic leagues, and the evolution of an endless series of records, together with all the paraphernalia of governing bodies of sport, official time-keepers, referees, umpires and what not. Now the idea of competition is essential to many forms of sport; it is in the keen encounter of strength and skill with a well-matched opponent that its chief pleasure resides. Notwithstanding this, there is a strong feeling among the more thoughtful lovers of sport that the competition of to-day is overdone, that the desire for individual distinction is carried to an excess which is harmful to sport, and that the complex organization thereby necessitated acts as an incubus, and, being too much of the nature of a business, robs sport of its natural character as a recreation.

If there be anything in these contentions, it would seem that competitive sport of all kinds carries within itself the seeds of its own decay.

For it would seem to tend naturally, in the course of time, to be strangled by that very spirit of competition to which it owes almost its existence, much as an excess of salt would be the ruin of a dish to which a moderate allowance would impart an agreeable flavour. It is for us, therefore, to enquire whether we cannot find some natural distinction between different manifestations of the combative spirit in sport, distinguishing those which are healthy and normal from those which are morbid and abnormal. Some clue to such a distinction may perhaps be found in the Greek idea that a gentleman will not wish to do a thing better than anyone else, but will be content to do it as well as its best exponents, much as Socrates, for example, in the Republic argues that the wise man will not wish to go beyond other wise men in matters of wisdom, but would be content to be their equal. This ideal is certainly one which does not come naturally to the combative British temperament, a temperament which, as Professor Cook Wilson remarked to me, can only be induced to interest itself in gymnastics by elaborately framing the sport into competitive form. Yet in this ideal we may perhaps find the means of drawing a generic distinction between healthy and unhealthy competition. Though he fight a game keenly, the ideal sportsman tempers his competition with something of generosity and unselfishness—unselfishness not only to his own side but also to his opponents. He feels and shows his sympathy with his opponent alike in victory or defeat, and would certainly not wish to raise himself to a class beyond all other competitors and so deny himself the true pleasures of sport.

A sportsman will take a keen pleasure in a contest with a well-matched opponent for the sheer joy of contest, wholly irrespective of whether the issue of the game be in his favour or not. So that the struggle be a game one, in which each side has tried its best, he will neither be unduly elated nor repine at the issue, preferring to lose a well-fought game than win in a walk over. Nor afterwards will he, if victorious, desire to write himself up as the superior of his opponent, and still less would he desire to have all players classed out after the manner of wranglers at Cambridge, with the title of champion for him who, by good play or good luck, comes out at the head of the list. Most men are agreed that truer sportsmanship is to be found among the adherents of the Rugby Union than among those of the Football Association, or still more of the Northern Union or of the Leagues.

There is something brutalizing in a competition which is bound to result in the expulsion of great and historic names from the ranks of "first-class" football. Such a system, moreover, attaches more importance to the victory than to the game itself, which is too often sacrificed to it. A notable example occurred, for instance, in the former qualifying competition of the Football League, in which the two last clubs of the first and the two first of the second division fought for the survival of the fittest. It so happened that two clubs had to play their last game of the series against each other, and the score so stood that if this game resulted in a draw both the combatants would save their places in the first division, if in a win for either team the other would lose its place. The result was, as the newspapers remarked, a farcical game, ending in a draw, a result which it was more than whispered was the result of previous negotiation. Again, at the end of last season, grave charges were made against a club which was in danger of being relegated to the second division, to the effect that it had attempted to bribe the opposing team to allow it to score a win. Whatever were the merits of the case, the very fact that such allegations are possible reflects unpleasantly on the character of League football. Surely a stronger instance could not be adduced of the evils of over-elaboration in sport.

The Cambridge tripos system of play, of carefully grading clubs and competitors in order of merit, has, moreover, evolved a curious class of spectators—men often incapable of appreciating the beauties of a fine game, yet inspired by the wildest enthusiasm for the success of the side which they "support," men who know nothing of the sport beyond the method of computation of the championship table, and are ready to mob a hostile team should they defeat their favourites. So far does the eagerness to score a mathematical win to the name of a town or club carry its members that they consider it worth while to fill their team with hired players, drawn from every place except the town which they purport to represent, club haggling with club over the exact sum to be paid for the transfer of a professional, much as a timid and unsportsmanlike card-player seeks to sell his deal. Nor can the crystallization into definite form of the County Cricket Championship be considered to have improved the tone of the game, for the subsidization of the professionals of poor counties to qualify by residence for rich ones seems to be growing far more frequent than of old.

Nor can the elaboration of the averages of public school cricket, by which the performances of each boy are scheduled in the almanacks with the same precision as the horse-power and tonnage of the ships in the Navy List, be regarded with unmixed satisfaction. The game tends to degenerate into business, boys calculating on their chances of blues much as on their prospects of scholarships, and for precisely similar reasons. One hears of pressure being brought to bear on fathers not to sacrifice the chances of a boy with a good average by denying him a University education, much as he might be entreated not to waste a potential scholar of Balliol upon the counting-house. I cannot but think that in this struggle to place his name above that of his fellows a boy seems rather to lose sight of the essential nature of sport as a recreation.

Much the same arguments hold good of the elaboration of records, and these derive additional weight from the artificial means which have in certain cases been employed, such as, for instance, when a long-distance cyclist rides over six hundred miles in the day behind great wind shields, which tow him by their suction almost as effectually as a piece of rope, or a short-distance man rides a record mile behind a railway engine. Much the same may be said of the enormous bags of game which are claimed as records by latter-day shooting men, bags which would be impossible without armies of beaters; and these are compared by the unthinking with the achievements of the less sophisticated sportsmen of hardier days.

This question of the elaboration of records leads naturally to that of the growth of spectacular sport in the affections of the public at the expense of their active participation in it. Whether or not it is a healthy symptom in the national life that our youth should read and talk of games instead of playing them is a matter rather outside the scope of this article. The question for us is whether a spectator as such can or cannot be considered a sportsman. We have admitted that betting contains the essential elements of sport, though but a parasitic one; the man who bets for amusement does thereby use certain of his active faculties for recreation, and has been shown to be capable of sportsmanlike or unsportsmanlike conduct. The spectator, however, exercises no active faculty, and so pale a reflection of reality as a "sport of sightseeing," if we can conceive the expression, seems hardly worthy the name

of a sport. Yet we do on occasion speak of spectators as sportsmanlike or the reverse. For instance, when Continental sightseers have hooted, and even mobbed, foreign cyclists who were so ill-starred as to win, or when a Northern mob has hustled a visiting team, we speak of their conduct as unsportsmanlike. As an instance of the contrary, on the recent visit of the German cyclist, Paul Albert, to England, his victory in the championships was acclaimed by the crowd even more heartily than if he had been an Englishman. Albert was surprised at his reception, which afforded so strong a contrast to what he would have expected in other foreign countries. The action of the spectators was considered sportsmanlike. But I think we must regard the use of the word as quite metaphorical, implying that their conduct was such as a sportsman would have approved, or would have displayed himself had he been a spectator, and not signifying that the spectator, as such, is a sportsman.

I am aware that the considerations which I have advanced cover but a small portion of what might be included in a philosophy of sport. We have not even arrived at a full definition of sport. The idea of recreation, though I believe it essential to everything which can be called sport does not go far enough. Our definition does not even succeed in eliminating such obviously non-sporting pursuits as chess or whist on the one hand, or gardening or carpentry on the other. Yet it is valid, so far as it goes, and it seems hardly possible to carry it further. If we wish to discuss sport we must first carefully limit the term by qualifying expressions so that the meaning intended is absolutely clear. Nor would it be within the scope of the present enquiry to frame a closer definition. If we admit the general and reasonable belief that sport must concern itself with physical exercise, we must, to compare the merits of various types of sport, enter into their effect on health and character; so that a discussion on the subject would encroach largely on the domains of physiology, hygiene, and ethics, and would require a portly volume for its inclusion. But it is upon these aspects of sport that there is least divergence of opinion, whereas those phases upon which I have touched, while they seem to open a wide field of controversy, have seldom or never been philosophically examined. While, therefore, I cannot hope to have said the last word upon this difficult subject, I may reasonably trust that I have indicated lines upon which legitimate controversy may proceed.

What Is A Game?*

BERNARD SUITS

By means of a critical examination of a number of theses as to the nature of game-playing, the following definition is advanced: To play a game is to engage in activity directed toward bringing about a specific state of affairs, using only means permitted by specific rules, where the means permitted by the rules are more limited in scope than they would be in the absence of the rules, and where the sole reason for accepting such limitation is to make possible such activity.

Prompted by the current interest of social and behavioral scientists in games, and encouraged by the modest belief that it is not demonstrably impossible for philosophers to say something of interest to scientists, I propose to formulate a definition of game-playing.

1. Game-Playing as the Selection of Inefficient Means. Mindful of the ancient canon that the quest for knowledge obliges us to proceed from what is knowable to us to what is knowable in itself, I shall begin with the commonplace that playing games is different from working. Games, therefore, might be expected to be what work, in some salient respect, is not. Let me now baldly characterize work as "technical activity," by which I mean activity in which an agent (as *rational* worker) seeks to employ the most efficient available means for reaching a desired goal. Since games, too, evidently have goals, and since means are evidently employed for their attainment, the possibility suggests itself that games

* From *Philosophy of Science*, 34 (June, 1967), 148-156.

differ from technical activities in that the means employed in games are not the most efficient. Let us say, then, that games are goal-directed activities in which inefficient means are intentionally (or rationally) chosen. For example, in racing games one voluntarily goes all around the track in an effort to arrive at the finish line instead of "sensibly" cutting straight across the infield.

The following considerations, however, seem to cast doubt on this proposal. The goal of a game, we may say, is winning the game. Let us take an example. In poker I am a winner if I have more money when I stop playing than I had when I started. But suppose that one of the other players, in the course of the game, repays me a debt of a hundred dollars, or suppose I hit another player on the head and take all of his money from him. Then, although I have not won a single hand all evening, am I nevertheless a winner? Clearly not, since I didn't increase my money as a consequence of playing poker. In order to be a winner, a sign and product of which is, to be sure, the gaining of money, certain conditions must be met which are not met by the collection of a debt or by felonious assault. These conditions are the rules of poker, which tell us what we can and what we cannot do with the cards and the money. Winning at poker consists in increasing one's money by using only those means permitted by the rules, although mere obedience to the rules does not by itself insure victory. Better and worse means are equally permitted by the rules. Thus in Draw Poker retaining an ace along with a pair and discarding the ace while retaining the pair are both permissible plays, although one is usually a better play than the other. The means for winning at poker, therefore, are limited, but not completely determined by, the rules. Attempting to win at poker may accordingly be described as attempting to gain money by using the most efficient means available, where only those means permitted by the rules are available. But if that is so, then playing poker is a technical activity as originally defined.

Still, this seems a strange conclusion. The belief that working and playing games are quite different things is very widespread, yet we seem obliged to say that playing a game is just another job to be done as competently as possible. Before giving up the thesis that playing a game involves a sacrifice of efficiency, therefore, let us consider one more example. Suppose I make it my purpose to get a small round object into a hole in the ground as efficiently as possible. Placing it in the hole with my hand would be a natural means to adopt. But surely I would not take a stick with a piece of metal on one end of it, walk three or four hundred yards away from the hole, and then attempt to propel the ball into the hole with the stick. That would not be technically intelligent. But such an undertaking is an extremely popular game, and the foregoing way of describing it evidently shows how games differ from technical activities.

But of course it shows nothing of the kind. The end in golf is not correctly described as getting a ball into a hole in the ground, nor even, to be more precise, into several holes in a set order. It is to achieve that end with the smallest possible number of strokes. But strokes are certain types of swings with a golf club. Thus, if my end were simply to get a ball into a number of holes in the ground, I would not be likely to use a golf club in order to achieve it, nor would I stand at a considerable distance from each hole. But if my end were to get a ball into some holes with a golf club while standing at a considerable distance from each hole, why then I would certainly use a golf club and I would certainly take up such positions. Once committed to that end, moreover, I would strive to accomplish it as efficiently as possible. Surely no one would want to maintain that if I conducted myself with utter efficiency in pursuit of this end I would not be playing a game, but that I would be playing a game just to the extent that I permitted my efforts to become sloppy. Nor is it the case

that my use of a golf club is a less efficient way to achieve my end than would be the use of my hand. To refrain from using a golf club as a means of sinking a ball with a golf club is not more efficient because it is not possible. Inefficient selection of means, accordingly, does not seem to be a satisfactory account of game-playing.

2. The Inseparability of Rules and Ends in Games. The objection advanced against the last thesis rests upon, and thus brings to light, consideration of the place of rules in games: they seem to stand in a peculiar relation to ends. The end in poker is not simply to gain money, nor in golf simply to get a ball into a hole, but to do these things in prescribed (or, perhaps more accurately, not to do them in proscribed) ways; that is, to do them only in accordance with rules. Rules in games thus seem to be in some sense inseparable from ends. To break a rule is to render impossible the attainment of an end. Thus, although you may receive the trophy by lying about your golf score, you have certainly not won the game. But in what we have called *technical activity* it is possible to gain an end by breaking a rule; for example, gaining a trophy by lying about your golf score. Whereas it is possible in a technical action to break a rule without destroying the original end of the action, in games the reverse appears to be the case. If the rules are broken the original end becomes impossible of attainment, since one cannot (really) win the game unless he plays it, and one cannot (really) play the game unless he obeys the rules of the game.

This may be illustrated by the following case. Professor Snooze has fallen asleep in the shade provided by some shrubbery in a secluded part of the campus. From a nearby walk I observe this. I also notice that the shrub under which he is reclining is a man-eating plant, and I judge from its behavior that it is about to eat the man Snooze. As I run across to him I see a sign which reads KEEP OFF THE GRASS. Without a qualm I ignore this prohibition and save Snooze's life. Why did I make this (no doubt unconscious) decision? Because the value of saving Snooze's life (or of saving a life) outweighed the value of obeying the prohibition against walking on the grass. Now the choices in a game appear to be radically unlike this choice. In a game I cannot disjoin the end, winning, from the rules in terms of which winning possesses its meaning. I of course can decide to cheat in order to gain the pot, but then I have changed my end from winning a game to gaining money. Thus, in deciding to save Snooze's life my purpose was not "to save Snooze while at the same time obeying the campus rules for pedestrians." My purpose was to save Snooze's life, and there were alternative ways in which this might have been accomplished. I could, for example, have remained on the sidewalk and shouted to Snooze in an effort to awaken him. But precious minutes might have been lost, and in any case Snooze, although he tries to hide it, is nearly stone deaf. There are evidently two distinct ends at issue in the Snooze episode: saving Snooze and obeying a rule, out of respect either for the law or for the lawn. And I can achieve either of these ends without at the same time achieving the other. But in a game the end and the rules do not admit of such disjunction. It is impossible for me to win the game and at the same time to break one of its rules. I do not have open to me the alternatives of winning the game honestly and winning the game by cheating, since in the latter case I would not be playing the game at all and thus could not, *a fortiori*, win it.

Now if the Snooze episode is treated as an action which has one, and only one, end— (Saving Snooze) ampersand (Keeping off the grass)—it can be argued that the action has become, just by virtue of that fact, a game. Since there would be no independent alternatives, there would be no choice to be made; to achieve one part of the end without achieving the other part would be to fail utterly. On such an interpretation of the episode suppose I am congratulated by a grateful faculty for my timely intervention. A perfectly appropriate response would be: "I don't deserve your praise. True, I saved Snooze, but since I walked on the grass it doesn't count," just as though I were to admit to kicking the ball into the cup on the fifth green. Or again, on this interpretation, I would originally have conceived the problem in a quite different way: "Let me if I can save Snooze without walking on the grass." One can then imagine my running as fast as I can (but taking no illegal short-cuts) to the Athletic Building, where I request (and meticulously sign out for) a pole vaulter's pole with which I hope legally to prod Snooze into wakefulness, whereupon I hurry back to Snooze to find him disappearing into the plant. "Well," I remark, not without complacency, "I didn't win, but at least I played the game."

It must be pointed out, however, that this example is seriously misleading. Saving a life and keeping off the grass are, as values, hardly on the same footing. It seems likely that the Snooze episode appears to support the contention at issue (that games differ from technical actions because of the inseparability of rules and ends in the former) only because of the relative triviality of one of the alternatives. This peculiarity of the example can be corrected by supposing that when I decide to obey the rule to keep off the grass, my reason for doing so is that I am a kind of demented Kantian, and thus regard myself to be bound by the most weighty philosophical considerations to honor *all* laws with equal respect. So regarded, my maddeningly proper efforts to save a life would not appear ludicrous but would constitute moral drama of the highest order. But since the reader may not be a demented Kantian, a less fanciful logically identical example may be cited.

Let us suppose the life of Snooze to be threatened not by a man-eating plant but by Professor Threat, who is found approaching the snoozing Snooze with the obvious intention of murdering him. Again I want to save Snooze's life, but I cannot do so (let us say) without killing Threat. However, there is a rule to which I am very strongly committed which forbids me to take another human life. Thus, although (as it happens) I could easily kill Threat from where I stand (with a loaded and cocked pistol I happen to have in my hand), I decide to try to save Snooze by other means, just because of my wish to obey the rule which forbids killing. I therefore run toward Threat with the intention of wresting the weapon from his hand. I am too late and he murders Snooze. This seems to be a clear case of an action having a conjunctive end of the kind under consideration, but one which we are not at all inclined to call a game. My end, that is to say, was not simply to save the life of Snooze, just as in golf it is not simply to get the ball into the hole, but to save his life without breaking a certain rule. I want to put the ball into the hole fairly and I want to save Snooze morally. Moral rules are perhaps generally regarded as figuring in human conduct in just this fashion. Morality says that if something can be done only immorally it ought not to be done at all. *What profiteth it a man, etc.* The inseparability of rules and ends does not, therefore, seem to be a completely distinctive characteristic of games.

3. Game Rules as Not Ultimately Binding. It should be noticed that the foregoing criticism requires only a partial rejection of the proposal at issue. Even though the attack shows that not all things which correspond to the formula are games, it may still be the case that all games correspond to the formula. This suggests that we ought not to reject the proposal, but that we ought first to try to limit its scope by adding to it an adequate differentiating principle. Such a differentia might be provided by noticing a striking difference between the two Snooze episodes. The efforts to save Snooze from the man-eating plant without walking on the grass appeared to be a game because saving the grass strikes us as a trifling consideration when compared with saving a life. But in the second episode, where KEEP OFF THE GRASS is replaced by THOU SHALT NOT KILL, the situation is quite different. The difference may be put in the following way. The rule to keep off the grass is not an ultimate command, but the rule to refrain from killing is. This suggests that, in addition to being the kind of activity in which rules are inseparable from ends, games are also the kind of activity in which commitment to these rules is never ultimate. For the person playing the game there is always the possibility of there being a non-game rule to which the game rule may be subordinated. The second Snooze episode is not a game, therefore, because the rule to which the rescuer adheres, even to the extent of sacrificing Snooze for its sake, is, for him, an ultimate rule. Rules are lines that we draw, but in games the lines are always drawn short of a final end or a paramount command. Let us say, then, that a game is an activity in which observance of rules is part of the end of the activity, and where such rules are non-ultimate; that is, where other rules can always supersede the game rules: that is, where the player can always stop playing the game.

However, consider the following counter-example. Suppose an auto racer. During a race a child crawls out on the track directly in the path of his car. The only way that he can avoid running over the child is to turn off the track and by breaking a rule disqualify himself. He chooses to run over the child, because for him there are no rules of higher priority than the rules of the game. I submit that we ought not, for this reason, to deny that he is playing a game. It no doubt strikes us as inappropriate to say that a person who would do such a thing is (only) playing. But the point is that the driver is not playing in an unqualified sense, he is playing a *game*. And he is evidently playing it more whole-heartedly than the ordinary driver is prepared to play it. From his point of view a racer who turned aside instead of running over the child would have

been playing *at* racing; that is, he would not have been a dedicated player. But it would be paradoxical indeed if supreme dedication to an activity somehow vitiated the activity. We do not say that a man isn't really digging a ditch because his whole heart is in it.

However, the rejoinder may be made that, to the contrary, that is just the mark of a game: it, unlike digging ditches, is just the kind of thing which cannot command ultimate loyalty. That, it may be contended, is just the force of the proposal about games under consideration. And in support of this contention it might be pointed out that it is generally acknowledged that games are in some sense essentially non-serious. We must therefore ask in what sense games are, and in what sense they are not, serious. What is believed when it is believed that games are not serious? Not, certainly, that the players of games always take a very light-hearted view of what they are doing. A bridge player who played his cards randomly might justly be accused of failing to take the game seriously; indeed, of failing to play the game at all just because of his failure to take it seriously. It is much more likely that the belief that games are not serious means what the proposal under consideration implies: that there is always something in the life of a player of a game more important than playing the game, or that a game is the kind of thing that a player could always have reason to stop playing. It is this belief which I would like to question.

Let us consider a golfer, George, so devoted to golf that its pursuit has led him to neglect, to the point of destitution, his wife and six children. Furthermore, although George is aware of the consequences of his mania, he does not regard his family's plight as a good reason for changing his conduct. An advocate of the view that games are *not* serious might submit George's case as evidence for that view. Since George evidently regards nothing in his life to be more important than golf, golf has, for George, *ceased to be a game*. And this argument would seem to be supported by the complaint of George's wife that golf is for George no longer a game, but a way of life.

But we need not permit George's wife's observation to go unchallenged. The correctness of saying that golf for George is no longer merely a form of recreation may be granted. But to argue that George's golf playing is for that reason not a game is to assume the very point at issue, which is whether a game can be of supreme importance to anyone. Golf, to be sure, is taking over the whole of George's life. But it is, after all, the game which is taking over his life, and not something else. Indeed, if it were not a game which had led George to neglect his duties, his wife might not be nearly as outraged as she is; if, for example, it had been good works, or the attempt to formulate a definition of game-playing. She would no doubt still deplore such extra-domestic preoccupation, but to be kept in rags because of a game must strike her as an altogether different order of deprivation.

Supreme dedication to a game, as in the cases of the auto racer and George, may be repugnant to nearly everyone's moral sense. That may be granted; indeed, insisted upon, since our loathing is excited by the very fact that it is a game which has usurped the place of ends we regard as so much more worthy of pursuit. Thus, although such behavior may tell us a good deal about such players of games, I submit that it tells us nothing about the games they play. I believe that these observations are sufficient to discredit the thesis that game rules cannot be ultimately binding on game players.[1]

4. Means, Rather than Rules, as Non-Ultimate. I want to agree, however, with the general contention that in games there is something which is significantly non-ultimate, that there is a crucial limitation. But I would like to suggest that it is not the rules which suffer such limitation. Non-ultimacy evidently attaches to games at a quite different point. It is not that the rules which govern a game must be short of ultimate commands, but that the means which the rules permit must be short of ultimate utilities. If a high-jumper, for example, failed to complete his jump because he saw that the bar was located at the edge of a precipice, this would no doubt show that jumping over the bar was not the over-riding interest of his life. But it would not be his refusal to jump to his death which would reveal his conduct to be a game; it would be his refusal to use something like a ladder or a catapult in the attempt. The same is true of the dedicated auto racer. A readiness to lose the race rather than kill a child is not what makes the race a game; it is the refusal to, *inter alia*, cut across the infield in order to get ahead of the other contestants. There is, therefore, a sense in which games may be said to be non-serious. One could intelligibly say of the high jumper who rejects ladders and catapults that he is not serious about getting to

[1] The author has argued for the possibility that life itself is a game in "Is Life a Game We Are Playing?" *Ethics.* Vol. 77, No. 3, April 1967.

the other side of the barrier. But one would also want to point out that he could be deadly serious about getting to the other side of the barrier *without* such aids; that is, about high-jumping. But whether games as such are less serious than other things would seem to be a question which cannot be answered solely by an investigation of games.

Consider a third variant of Snooze's death. In the face of Threat's threat to murder Snooze, I come to the following decision. I choose to limit myself to non-lethal means in order to save Snooze even though lethal means are available to me and I do not regard myself to be bound by any rule which forbids killing. (In the auto racing example the infield would *not* be filled with land mines.) And I make this decision even though it may turn out that the proscribed means are necessary to save Snooze. I thus make my end not simply saving Snooze's life, but saving Snooze's life without killing Threat, even though there appears to be no reason for restricting myself in this way.

One might then ask how such behavior can be accounted for. And one answer might be that it is unaccountable, that it is simply arbitrary. However, the decision to draw an arbitrary line with respect to permissible means need not itself be an arbitrary decision. The decision to be arbitrary may have a purpose, and the purpose may be to play a game. And it seems to be the case that the lines drawn in games are not actually arbitrary at all. For not only *that* the lines are drawn, but also *where* they are drawn, has important consequences not only for the type, but also for the quality, of the game to be played. It might be said that drawing such lines skillfully (and therefore not arbitrarily) is the very essence of the gamewright's craft. The gamewright must avoid two extremes. If he draws his lines too loosely the game will be dull because winning will be too easy. As looseness is increased to the point of utter laxity the game disappears altogether, since there are then no rules proscribing available means. Thus a homing propellant device could be devised which would insure a golfer a hole in one every time he played. On the other hand, rules are lines that can be drawn too tight, so that the game becomes too difficult. And if a line is drawn very tight indeed the game is squeezed out of existence. Suppose a game in which the goal is to cross a finish line. One of the rules requires the contestants to stay on the track, while another rule requires that the finish line be located at a position such that it is impossible to cross it without leaving the track. The present proposal, therefore, is that games are activities in which rules are inseparable from ends (in the sense agreed to earlier), but with the added qualification that the means permitted by the rules are smaller in scope than they would be in the absence of the rules.

5. Rules are Accepted for Sake of the Activity They Make Possible. Still, even if it is true that the function of rules in games is to restrict the permissible means to an end, it does not seem that this is in itself sufficient to exclude things which are not games. When I failed in my attempt to save Snooze's life because of my unwillingness to commit the immoral act of taking a life, the rule against killing functioned to restrict the means I would employ in my efforts to reach a desired end. What then distinguishes the case of the high jumper and of the auto racer from my efforts to save Snooze morally, or the efforts of a politician to get elected without lying? The answer lies in the reason for obeying rules in the two types of case. In games I obey the rules just because such obedience is a necessary condition for my engaging in the activity such obedience makes possible. But in other activities—e.g., in moral actions—there is always another reason, what might be called an external reason, for conforming to the rule in question; for a moral teleologist, because its violation would vitiate some other end, for a deontologist because the rule is somehow binding in itself. In morals conformity to rules makes the action right, but in games it makes the action.

Further to illustrate this point, two other ways in which rules function may be contrasted with the way in which rules function in games. Rules can be directives to attain a given end (If you want to improve your drive, keep your eye on the ball), or they can be restrictions on the means to be chosen to a given end (Do not lie to the public in order to get them to vote for you). In the latter way morals, for example, often appear as limiting conditions in a technical activity, although a supervening technical activity can also effect the same limitation (If you want to get to the airport in time, drive fast, but if you want to drive safely, don't drive too fast). Consider a ruled sheet of paper. I conform to these rules, when writing, in order to write straight. Now suppose that the rules are not lines on a sheet of paper, but paper walls which form a labyrinth, and while I wish to be out of the labyrinth, I don't wish to damage the walls. The walls are limiting conditions on my coming to be out. Returning to games, consider a third

case. Again I am in the labyrinth, but now my purpose is not to *be* outside (as it might be if Ariadne were waiting for me), but to *get* out of the labyrinth, so to speak, labyrinthically. What is the status of the walls? Clearly they are not means for my coming to be outside the labyrinth because it is not my purpose to (simply) be outside. And if a friend suddenly appeared overhead in a helicopter I would decline the offer of a lift, although I would accept it in the second case. My purpose is to get out of the labyrinth only by accepting the conditions it imposes. Nor is this like the first case. There I was not interested in seeing whether I could write a sentence without breaking a rule (crossing a line), but in using the rules so that I could write straight.

We may therefore say that games consist in acting in accordance with rules which limit the permissible means to a sought end, and where the rules are obeyed just so that such activity can take place.

6. Winning Is Not the End with Respect to which Rules Limit Means. There is, however, a final difficulty. On the one hand to describe rules as operating more or less permissively with respect to means seems to conform to the ways in which we invent or revise games. But on the other hand it does not seem to make sense at all to say that in games there are means for attaining one's end over and above the means permitted by the rules. Consider chess. The end sought by chess players is, it would seem, to win. But winning means putting a chess piece on a square in accordance with the rules of chess. But since to break a rule is to fail to attain that end, what other means are available? It was for just this reason that the first proposal was rejected: using a golf club in order to play golf is not a less efficient, and thus alternative, means for seeking the end in question; it is a (logically) indispensable means.

The objection can be met, I believe, by pointing out that there is an end in chess analytically distinct from winning as an end. Let us begin again, therefore, from a somewhat different point of view and say that the end in chess is, in a very restricted sense, to place one of your pieces on the board in a position such that the opponent's king is, in terms of the rules of chess, immobilized. Now, without going outside the game of chess we may say that the means for bringing about this state of affairs consist in moving the chess pieces. The rules of chess, of course, state how the pieces may be moved; they distinguish between legal and illegal moves. Since the knight, for example, is permitted to move in only a highly restricted manner, it is clear that the permitted means for moving the knight are of less scope than the possible means for moving him. It should not be objected at this point that other means for moving the knight—e.g., along the diagonals—are not really possible on the grounds that such use of the knight would break a rule and thus not be a means to winning. For the present point is not that such use of the knight would be a means to winning, but that it would be a possible (though not permissible) way in which to move the knight so that he would, for example, come to occupy a square such that, according to the rules of chess, the king would be immobilized. A person who made such a move would not, of course, be playing chess. Perhaps he would be cheating at chess. By the same token I would not be playing a game if I abandoned my arbitrary decision not to kill Threat while at the same time attempting to save Snooze. Chess, as well as my third effort to save Snooze's life, are games because of an "arbitrary" restriction of means permitted in pursuit of an end.

The chief point is that the end here in question is not the end of winning the game. There must be an end distinct from winning because it is the restriction of means to this other end which makes winning possible, and also defines, in any given game, what it means to win. In defining a game we shall therefore have to take into account these two ends and, as we shall see in a moment, a third end as well. First there is what might be called the end which consists in a certain state of affairs: a juxtaposition of pieces on a board, saving a friend's life, crossing a finish line. Then, when a restriction of means for attaining this end is made with the introduction of rules, we have

a second end, winning. Finally, with the stipulation of what it means to win, a third end emerges: the activity of trying to win; that is, playing the game. It is noteworthy that in some cases it is possible to pursue one of these ends without pursuing the others and that in some cases it is not. Thus, it is possible to pursue the end of getting as many tricks at bridge as you can without pursuing the end of winning, since you may seek this goal, and also achieve it, by cheating. But it is impossible to seek to win without seeking to take a certain (relative) number of tricks, nor is it possible to seek to play without seeking both of the other ends.

7. The Definition. My conclusion is that to play a game is to engage in activity directed toward bringing about a specific state of affairs, using only means permitted by specific rules, where the means permitted by the rules are more limited in scope than they would be in the absence of the rules, and where the sole reason for accepting such limitation is to make possible such activity.[2,3]

[2] Additional work on the subject of games by the author includes "Games and Paradox" *Philosophy of Science.* Vol. 34, No. 3, September, 1969; "Can You Play a Game Without Knowing It?" *Studies in Philosophy and in the History of Science,* Coronado Press, 1970.

[3] In a paper titled "The Elements of Sport" presented to the Third International Symposium on the Sociology of Sport, the author presented a revised version of the definition advanced in the present article: To play a game is to attempt to achieve a specific state of affairs, using only means permitted by rules, where the rules prohibit use of more efficient in favour of less efficient means, and where such rules are accepted just because they make possible such activity. Or, for short: Playing a game is the voluntary attempt to overcome unnecessary obstacles.

This "Thing" Called Sport*

ELEANOR METHENY

A generation ago many theories of play rested on Johann Huizinga's widely quoted definition of "play," as presented in *Homo Ludens* (Man the Player):

Play is a voluntary activity or occupation executed within certain fixed limits of time and place, according to rules freely accepted and absolutely binding, having its aim in itself and accompanied by a feeling of tension, joy and consciousness that it is "different" from "ordinary life." (Beacon Press paperback edition, p. 28)

Then, as you will remember, Huizinga speculated at length about various manifestations of "the play element" in many forms of behavior, including those he called "sport and athletics." But while he noted that "the old play-factor has undergone almost complete atrophy" in contemporary "sport and athletics," he did not attempt to make a categorical distinction between the activities he called sport and those he called by various other names. So Huizinga's widely quoted theory of play is not particularly useful to the current generation of theorists interested in the significance of the activities designated by the term "sport."

Now that sport has become a subject for research—now that theorists of many disciplines are attempting to generalize about the personal and cultural significance of man's

* From American Association for Health, Physical Education, and Recreation: *Journal of Health, Physical Education, and Recreation*, 40 (March, 1969), 59-60.

involvement in something they all call sport, there would seem to be much need for a categorical definition of this term—if only so the theorists can tell the rest of us precisely what they are theorizing about. And so, from time to time, I have asked groups of students to undertake the formidable task of trying to make a categorical distinction between "activities commonly called sport" and "activities commonly known by some other descriptive name."

Each group began with a long list of activities which answer to the name sport. In composing these lists, we settled all arguments about whether or not a given activity was worthy of this name by using the criterion of "common usage." Thus, any activity which anyone might refer to as a sport was eligible for inclusion in this master list.

Then, with much sorting, fitting, and trying, we eventually succeeded in identifying one set of characteristics which were common to *all* of these "sport-type activities," and several sets of characteristics which were common to *many* but not to all.

No two groups of students ever wholly agreed with each other—or with me—about the wording to be used in describing these characteristics in terms applicable to all of the samples studied. So I must take full responsibility for the phrasing of the description which follows.

As commonly used today, the term sport refers to a diverse set or category of *activities* or *organizations of human behavior* in which:

One or more persons, designated as *performers,* move about within an *environmental setting,* which may be described in terms of *time, space, and terrain,* performing *actions* which are directed toward an attempt to induce or bring about a series of *observable changes* in the *location* and/or *configuration* of certain specified *objects, animals,* and/or *persons.*

While the performers are pursuing this *objective,* their actions are governed by the provisions of a set of *man-made rules* or *personal agreements.* These rules also identify the *procedures* to be utilized in *evaluating* the achievement of the *objective* or the extent to which the objective was achieved by each performer or set of performers.

Characteristically, after each series of attempts to achieve the objective has been completed, all persons involved in that series of attempts *return* to their *initial location/configuration;* and all objects and animals utilized in that series of attempts are either *returned* to their *initial location/configuration* or *replaced* by similar objects/animals before the next series of attempts is initiated.

Characteristically, each *performance* of a sport or sport-type activity is conducted within the context of a specified *pattern of organization,* which is known to and accepted by all persons involved in that particular performance.

Typically, some performances are organized by individual performers or sets of performers who plan, conduct, and evaluate the outcomes of that performance in accordance with the provisions of a set of personal or mutual agreements about the objective and about the actions which may be performed during each attempt to achieve the objective. For purposes of classification, this *type* of performance may be identified as a *personally-organized* or *individually-organized performance.*

Further, many performances are organized as *contests* in which two or more performers or sets of performers openly *compete with each other* in their attempts to achieve a common objective. Such *contests* are usually governed by a commonly accepted set of operational rules, based on, but not necessarily identical with, some recognized set of standard or official rules.

Typical *contest patterns* may be classified as:

Individual performances in which each personal or individual performance is rated or judged by another person, who compares his conception of that performance with a conceptual model or standard

Side-by-side performances in which the performers move either simultaneously or sequentially, and each individual performance yields objective evidence of the extent to which the performer has achieved the objective

Comparative parallel performances in which all performers move simultaneously and in the same direction, attempting to out-distance each other

Face-to-face oppositional performances in which two performers or two sets of performers attempt to move in opposing directions as they contend with each other in their attempts to achieve the objective

Frankly, many students who worked on this project objected to this cold-blooded, impersonal, objective, scientifically oriented attempt to describe the characteristics of the organizations of behavior commonly called sport. They said this description reduced sport to the status of a "thing." They said it ignored and ruled out the human element which endows that thing with significance. They said it obliterated all traces of the *values* a person might find in the personal experience of participating in, or involving himself in, this behavioral thing. And of course they were quite right on every count.

Nonetheless, as they worked at the task of trying to describe the characteristic structure and composition of the activities commonly called sport, they became less disposed to make sweeping generalizations about such humanly defined values, and they became increasingly critical of many of the theories of sport which are now appearing in our professional literature.

And so they began to say: When I say this, I am not generalizing about sport-in-general; I am theorizing about the significance of certain face-to-face oppositional types of performance which involve bodily contact between opposing performers. Or they said: I am now theorizing about certain individually-organized types of performance in which the performer uses this kind of an implement in this way. Or they said: I am now talking about bull fighting, and I am comparing it with ice hockey. Or: The values I find in sport performances that involve the act of "hitting a ball" are different from those I find in the act of "hitting a person."

Thus, they came to recognize our professional need for a comprehensive taxonomic classification of sport-type behaviors—but time did not permit us to undertake the enormous task of composing one.

Sport and Play:
Suspension of the Ordinary*

KENNETH L. SCHMITZ

Sport and play are familiar, but their meaning is not obvious. Play is perhaps as old as man himself, and some will say older. Sport has undergone a remarkable development in some civilizations. It is pursued today by millions in the highly technological societies. Sport is sometimes firmly distinguished from play, and it certainly contains other factors. Nevertheless, the following reflection will suggest that sport is primarily an extension of play, and that it rests upon and derives its central values from play. On this basis it will be maintained that a generous acceptance of the play element in sport is essential for the full realization of this latter form of human behaviour.

The variety of play poses a grave difficulty in understanding it. Its very unity is problematic. Is there a single phenomenon of play which has sufficient unity to be called a special form of human behaviour? The present reflection moves within the context of certain uses not exclusive to English in which the word "play" occurs. Children play in the yard, waves play on the beach, lovers engage in erotic play, an actor plays a part, a musician plays an instrument, a footballer plays a game, a bettor plays the horses, and the gods play with men.

The meanings are various; some are peripheral, extended or metaphorical uses. I think, however, that a central core of meaning remains which points towards an indeterminate yet coherent form of human behaviour. This complex structure I call the phenomenon of play.

Wittgenstein poses the difficulty when he lists a wide range of uses of the word "game." He thinks that the variety shows that there is no essence common to all games but only a family resemblance which permits a chain of different uses. I sympathize with much of what Wittgenstein says about the search for a common essence at all costs. Nevertheless, I think that he assumes too strong a doctrine of essence and too exacting a conception of language before he goes on to his refutation. He seems to tie the doctrine of essence to the doctrine of substance. Now this is an understandable conjunction in the light of much of traditional philosophy, but I do not think it is a necessary or a wise one. It might be said that I set out here to clarify the "essence" of play, but I certainly do not think that I will have established a "substance" of play. I have mentioned a "central core" and a "structure," but it may be more helpful to bear in mind more fluid and dynamic metaphors than the traditional figure of a static structure, idea or form. Gabriel Marcel often speaks of a phenomenon as present in varying degrees along a continuum.[1] Or we might even picture an element as more or less present and more or

* Presented at the annual meeting of the American Association for the Advancement of Science, Dallas, Texas, December, 1968.

[1] For example, G. Marcel, *The Mystery of Being* (Gifford Lectures, 1949-50), Regnery, Chicago, 2 vols., n.d.

less pure in a series of chemical solutions.[1] But these are only metaphors.

Nor should we be surprised if the same word is extended to activities which do not share an important central meaning. Ordinary usage is the usage of ordinary men, and not that of scientists or philosophers. Family resemblances suffice. It is enough in ordinary speech that one important similarity hold between a clear instance of play, such as children's frolic, and an extended usage, such as piano playing. Thus we speak of ball-players and easily transfer the vocabulary of play and sport to events such as war-games where the factor of contest so heavily weighs. Although the usage is clear enough, further thought may uncover reasons for the frequent association of contest with play but not its necessity for all forms of play. Then, too, the contest in war-games may prove alien in meaning and psychological tone to the contest which occurs in sporting games.

When reflective analysis seeks to isolate the phenomenon of play it must recognize still other hazards. The difficulty of bringing play to reflective clarity is a difficulty which all immediate and obvious phenomena share. Just as in emotion, for example, so too in play, we live under the spell of peculiar immediacy. We throw ourselves into the spirit of the frolic or game, and when reflection itself becomes an ingredient in playfulness it takes on the character of immediacy, serving the values and objectives of the game. Moreover, play compounds the difficulty by revealing itself in a way that is secretive and shy. It can dodge the determined attentions of reflection by encouraging an amused contempt for it, or by permitting itself to be banished to the years of growing-up. An adult and work-oriented thought finds it easy to neglect or to misrepresent it, as though it were not worthy of "serious" attention. It resists analysis and preserves its essential meaning by turning our accounts of it away from itself to some alien value. Of course, we must recognize the biological and psychological value of play, in relaxation and escape, in rest and exercise, in education and character-formation. But unless play is nothing but these functions, we cannot understand them fully without understanding *it*. The present intent, then, is to clarify the spirit of play, to determine its appropriate forms, and to characterize the element of play in sport.

There is a thicket of other difficulties, too. Play hides obscurely within a host of very complex phenomena and behaviours and is subtle enough to be easily confused with other forms. For a full analysis, it would be necessary to say what play is not. It seems easiest to see that play is not work, and yet it may call sometimes for very great effort. War may highlight the difference, for like work, war is serious, but like play it is non-productive. The words "conquest" and "victory" belong to the vocabulary of war. The first is said easily enough of work, and the second of play. Some forms of play also resemble war in having the element of contest in them; but the essence of war is deadly contest, it is heavy with death. The grave risk of life is not excluded from play, but if life is risked for some alien value, no matter how high, or if death is certain, the spirit of play is extinguished. There is a certain lightness about play which it shares with other forms of leisure. To be sure, play is not the same as good humour, for although it may be fun, it is not necessarily funny. G. K. Chesterton caught the mood when he remarked that certain affairs were too important to be taken seriously. Play consists in what we may call "non-serious" importance. Still, it cannot be equated simply with pleasure or amusement. Indeed, a full analysis of play would have to make room within it for ingredients of pain and discomfort. It would have to be asked, too, whether a high degree of cruelty, as in the ancient bear-baiting or the gladiatorial games, crushes, perverts or merely tempers the spirit of play.

Such an extended analysis of play is not appropriate here, and I turn instead to sketch out, briefly and tentatively, the positive character of this elusive blithe spirit.

The Varieties of Play. Play can be considered under four general varieties: frolic, make-believe, sporting skills and games. The least formal play is simple spontaneous frolic, and this is associated especially with the very young. It is that aspect of play which is found also in young animals, and its occasional appearance in adult humans seems to manifest the feature of neoteny so pronounced in man. Such play among kittens and puppies, or something very like play, may well be a kind of training along with a desire to satisfy curiosity and to express plain high spirits. It is usually intense and brief and tends to dissipate itself with the outburst of energy that makes it possible. It is an immediate and unreflecting expression of a kind of animal joy, a kicking off of the normal patterns of behaviour, purposeless and without constraint. "Horsing around" illustrates the manner in which the play-world can erupt for a brief moment. A practical joke can trigger a spontaneous display. Someone from the group splashes cold water upon the others lying at leisure in sun and sand, and an impromptu "battle" begins, with little or no declared object and with fluid changing of sides. It is a quicksilver form of play, dashing off now in one direction, now in another, fragmenting and rejoining forces in new combinations for new momentary objectives.

A second more or less informal variety of play is that of make-believe or "just pretending." This, too, is commonest with children but not exclusive to them. There is, of course, daydreaming, a sort of playing with images, roles and situations, though this tends to diminish with adult life or is translated into artistic creativity. Among adults the carnival such as the Mardi Gras, the parade such as the Santa or homecoming parade, and costume parties are examples of this variety of play, intermixed with elements of frolic. It is interesting that some form of the mask or costume is used as a means by which the adult can enter the play-world. In its secular shape as in its religious origin, the mask is a device for suspending the everyday world. The child, on the other hand, needs no such device and with nothing at all can create for himself the world which his playful imagination gives to him. There are usually no well-defined and explicit rules for pretending games, though the roles assumed determine a rough and approximate fittingness. One child is quick to tell another that she is out of character, and the adult who goes to a ball dressed as Bugs Bunny will find his part already somewhat defined for him. Such playfulness, however, is quite different from a theatrical role in which the part is already drawn *a priori* and the actor is expected to interpret and manifest it by using the words and situations provided beforehand by the playwright. What is uppermost in the play of the theatre is representation, whereas in play itself a rough approximation serves merely to suggest and maintain the illusion proper to it. On stage the play is for the sake of presentation, whereas in make-believe the representation is for the sake of play. More generally, it may be said that art and aesthetic experience centre upon the embodiment and expression of meaning, whereas play is for the sake of a certain form of action. In the ballet, for example, action is subordinated to gesture, but in genuine play, mimicry and expression are either incidental or for the sake of the action.

The more formal varieties of play take two styles: skills and games. The first style includes surfboarding, sailing, horse-riding, mountain-climbing, hiking and similar play activities. It calls for knowledge, skill and a certain endurance; so, at least in an elementary way, does the bouncing of a ball, jumping with a pogo stick, yawing a Yo-Yo and skipping rope. The final style of play is completely formal, such as the games of baseball, card-playing and the like. Both styles of play are contests. The former require the mastery of a skill in conformance with natural forces, such as the behaviour of wind and water or the motion of ball and rope. They may even have rudimentary rules. In the truly formal games, however, rules predominate, and although they are determined by agreement, they are held as absolutely binding. Even in solitaire one cannot actually *win* the game if he cheats. Cheating in play is the counterpart of sin in the moral order. It seeks the good of victory without conforming to the spirit of the game and the rules under which alone it is possible to possess it. In the flowery language of a bygone era: the crown of victory sits hollow upon the head of a cheat, who has excluded himself from the values of the game-world and can only enjoy the incidental fruits that sometimes attend a victory. This is quite apart from any moral do's or don'ts, and is written into the very texture of the game-world. In any case, the rules of play differ from those of morality. We can take up the game or leave it, but the rules of morality oblige without any conditionality. Moral rules apply within a context of human action and values that is not that of play and that may touch directly upon the issues of life and death.

In each of these four varieties of play different features predominate: in the frolic the aspect of spontaneous celebration, in imaginative pretense the aspect of creativity, in skill and game the aspect of contest. These aspects are met with in non-play situations too: celebration in worship, creativity in art and contest in work and war. It remains, therefore, to mark out their peculiar quality in the play-world and to indicate its ontological character.

Play as Suspension of the Ordinary World.[2] The spirit of play may be carried over into many activities and even subordinated to other purposes, but it is manifested and realized most perfectly in the four varieties distinguished above. The essence of play comes into existence through the decision to play. Such a constitutive decision cannot be compelled and

[2] See Eugen Fink, *Spiel als Weltsymbol*, Kohlhammer, Stuttgart, 1960.

is essentially free. Through it arises the suspension of the ordinary concerns of the everyday world. Such a decision does not simply initiate the playing but rather constitutes it. That is, it does not stand before the playing as winding a mechanical toy stands before its unwinding performance, but rather it underlies and grounds the entire duration of play. This duration may be interrupted or ended at any time, and in this sense the play-world is fragile, ceasing to be either because of the intrusion of the natural world of ordinary concerns, the loss of interest on the part of the players, or the completion of the play-objective. Devices are sometimes used for entrance into and maintenance of the play-spirit, but they are subordinate to the essential demands of play. In a prevalent adult form of contemporary play, nightclubbing, which intends to resemble the frolic, alcohol is almost methodically used to make the transition from the ordinary world somewhat easier. The constant threat of the price tag at the end of the evening naturally makes the suspension of ordinary concerns rather more difficult. It goes without saying that too much alcohol brings about the demise of play, as do drugs, for play seems to demand a deliberate maintenance of itself in keeping with the voluntary character of its founding decision. Play may be a kind of madness, but it is self-engendered and self-maintained.

Inasmuch as the play-decision suspends ordinary concerns, it breaks open a new totality. The world of play with its own non-natural objectives and formalities may be said to transcend the natural world and the world of everyday concern. Of course, it must reckon with natural laws and cannot suspend their real effective impact. Players tire and drop out of the game or are injured; or there just isn't time for a last set of tennis or bridge; or the little girls playing house are called in for supper. Moreover, some forms of play, such as surfboarding or mountain-climbing, deliberately set for their objectives the conquest of natural forces. What is common to these and all forms of play is that natural processes do not determine the significance of the play. The player does not follow natural forces as such. Whereas the worker often follows them in order to redirect them as in cultivation, the player may resist them, ignore them as far as possible or create a new order of significance whose elements are non-natural, as in word-games. The surfer follows them in order to wrest from them a carefree moment of exhilarating joy; the archer takes them into account in order to hit a target of his own proposing; and the chess-player moves within a set of spatial possibilities that are ideal in themselves and only indicated by the board and chessmen.

Religion, art and play are rightly spoken of as ways of transcending the strictly natural world. Religion, however, does not suspend the world of nature. Quite the contrary, in its historical forms, it turns back from a sacred and alien distance towards nature in order to reawaken and restore it to its original freshness and creativity. Art and aesthetic experience transcend the natural world in the embodiment and expression of concrete, symbolic meaning. Art suspends the natural and puts it out of play when it gives ultimate value to trans-natural objectives. Kant, of course, speaks of a certain detachment or disinterestedness. The sign of the transcendence of play over the natural world is manifest by a certain excess which characterizes its spirit. There is in it an uncalled-for exhilaration, a hilarity in the contest and in the mood of celebration. Like art and religion, play is not far from the feast, for art celebrates beauty and religion celebrates glory, but play celebrates the emergence of a finite world that lies outside and beyond the world of nature while at the same time resting upon it.

The Play-world as a Distinctive Order. The space and time of play are not contiguous with natural space and time. The little child creates an area in the room in which battles are fought, seas sailed, continents discovered, in which animals roam and crops grow. Adults create the playing field which is a space directed according to the objectives and rules of the game. A ball driven to the right of a line is "foul," another landing beyond a certain point is "out of play." In chess the knight alone can jump and the bishop can only move diagonally. Play-space is not at all relative in most games and to the extent to which arbitrary rules are invented to that extent the space becomes more determinate and more absolute. Players hold willingly to the rules or those who do not have officials to encourage them in the most formal sports. This maintenance of the absolutely binding force of the rules is a free acceptance flowing out of and essentially one with the play-decision, and with the suspension of the natural ordinary world and the substitution of a new order. The laws of natural forces are put to use in an extraordinary way within an extraordinary world inspired by a motive that has suspended the ordinary interests of everyday life.

The structured order of play-space is especially evident in those games in which a single or double point in the play-space is the key to the contest, the privileged space of the goals, target or finishing-line. So, too, play-time is not contiguous with ordinary time, though it must frequently bow to it. In ice hockey sixty minutes of play-time are not sixty minutes of clock-time, and in baseball play-time is simply nine innings or more. Of course, natural space and time are the alien boundaries that ring about and mark the finitude of human play, but the play has its own internal boundaries set by the objectives and rules of the game. When a ball is out of bounds in many games the game-time stops also. Men set the objectives and rules of play and yet there is a certain sense in which the play-objective, freely chosen, sets its own basic rules. Play seems to begin by abandoning forms of everyday behaviour, but it maintains that abandonment in a positive and determinate way by creating a new space and time with new forms and rules of behaviour that are not determined by or functional within the everyday world but which nevertheless have a positive meaning of their own. Within its boundaries and objectives the play-world exhibits a totality of meaning and value that is strikingly complete and perfect. Play reveals itself as transnatural, fragile, limited perfection.

The suspension of the natural world and its subordination to the game or its sublimation into the play context can be described as the suppression of the real, where "reality" is restricted to the natural and ordinary world. Play then builds an illusion. Huizinga notes that the Latin word for play (*ludus*) is closely related to the word for illusion (*inlusio*).[2] The "inactuality" of play is most evident in the imaginative play of make-believe. This suspension of the "real" world by means of a play-decision releases a world of "unreality" which needs no justification from outside itself. It is a self-sealed world, delivering its own values in and for itself, the freedom and joy of play. As a piece of fine art needs no other defence than itself, and as the feast need exist for no other reason than its own values, so too play, though its claims must be balanced within the whole man against those of "reality," receives justification only through and in itself. As colour cannot validate its existence and meaning except to one who sees, so play cannot vindicate itself except to one who plays. To

anyone else it appears superfluous. The stern Calvin Coolidge, it is said, once snorted that going fishing was childish, which only proved to fishermen that he was absurd. Play has its own built-in finality. It is in this sense objectless; it has no other object than itself.

Nevertheless, an adequate philosophy can free the mind from an exclusive preoccupation with the natural world and open it out onto all the modes of being. Each is seen to have its value. Like religion and art, play embodies a significance that is not fully grasped in clear concepts. As an analysis does not replace a poem or a painting, so a description of its rules is no substitute for play. But an analysis may open the mind to the genuine reality of play. The proper vehicle of meaning in play is action and in this it is much closer to ritual and myth than to scientific concepts. Play is meaning embodied in action; it is "significant form"[3] precisely as human behaviour. The world which opens out through the play-decision is a world of possibilities closed off from the natural and ordinary world. Measured against the ordinary world the world of possibility opened up by play seems inactual and illusory; but measured in terms of being itself, it is a radical way of being human, a distinctive mode of being. It is a way of taking up the world of being, a manner of being present in the world in the mode of creative possibility whose existential presence is a careless joyful freedom.

I suggest, then, that there is a phenomenon of play which is an indeterminate yet coherent mode of human behaviour. It comes to be through a decision which does not simply initiate or occasion play, but which founds and underlies it. It is a decision which is freely taken and maintained, either spontaneously or deliberately. It is a decision which seeks to secure certain values for human consciousness and human existence, a certain meaning and a certain freedom. It may be called an activity of maintaining an illusion, if we speak in terms which still give primacy to the natural world. But it may also be called an activity of suspension, whereby the natural forces while not abrogated are dethroned from their primacy. More positively, it may be called an activity of constitution, which breaks open distinctive possibilities of meaning, freedom and value. It has no other essential objective than those implicit in the founding decision. It has its own time and space, boundaries and objectives, rewards and penalties. It is a distinctive way, voluntary and finite, of man's being-in-the-world. Playing in the world, man recovers himself as a free and transcendent being.

The Play-element in Sport. Two factors

---

[2] *Homo Ludens: a study of the play element in culture,* (1944), Beacon, Boston, 1955, p. 36. See also Fink, *op. cit.,* pp. 66 ff.

[3] Huizinga, *op. cit.,* p. 4.

are especially prominent in sport: the first is the emphasis on good performance, and the second is the element of contest. If sport consisted simply of performance and contest, however, scholarship examinations would be reported in the sporting pages. Examinations are liable to be deadly serious and to be related directly to educational objectives which are part of the natural and social world.

Sport may be carried on at various levels of competence and preparedness, from the unplanned street game to the carefully planned amateur or professional sporting event. In the former, natural ability and past experience determine the proficiency of the maneuvers. Planned events are usually preceded by exercises for general conditioning and precise training. These preparations are directed towards the performance of activities within a non-natural space and time and in accord with more or less formally specified rules. The excellence of the performance is judged within a matrix of values that flow from the decision to play this or that kind of game.

The performance, moreover, is for the sake of the contest, either against natural forces, such as in the high jump, or against other players, as in track meets. In some sports, there is only one contestant, as in hunting; but in most, as in team games, a contestant pits himself also against other players. The performance is tested by the contest of player against player, and the verdict is sealed by the victory.

It may seem that the play element is not essential to sport. Thus, for example, the sport of hunting lies very close to the natural needs of man. Moreover, it has little of formal rules. The various game laws are not to be confused with sporting rules, for they are meant to conserve the natural supply of game as a condition for further hunting. They are laws, not rules. Of course, if two huntsmen vie with each other for the largest or the quickest bag, we say that they have made a game out of it. Here again, they have imposed upon the natural value, namely, the food procured, a game-value, the prize of victory. Such a contest, however, is to be distinguished from the contest of bucks seeking a mate or tycoons seeking a fortune. It is imaginable that the latter might be taken up in a *spirit* of play, but it is not properly playful in its *form*. We see here a distinction between the forms of play and the spirit which inhabits them. This spirit can sometimes animate certain other forms of behaviour. Thus a man may bet in order to win and pay off the mortgage, or he

may bet in order to risk something valuable to him. Only the latter is animated by a spirit of play. Even it is no longer play if it is compulsive, for it may then be the sublimation of the wish to totter between life and death.

In addition to good performance and contest, then, spontaneous creative freedom is inherent in play. This suggests that sport can be carried out without the spirit of play. Nevertheless, in the life of individuals and in the history of the race, sport emerges from play as from an original and founding existential posture. Sport is free, self-conscious, tested play which moves in a transnatural dimension of human life, built upon a certain basis of leisure. Sport is in its origin and intention a movement into transcendence which carries over from the founding decision to play and which builds upon that decision an intensified thrust towards the values of self-consciousness tested through performance, competition and victory. There is certainly a return to seriousness in the discipline of formal sport. There is training, performance and competition. But the objectives of sport and its founding decision lie within play and cause sport to share in certain of its features—the sense of immediacy, exhilaration, rule-directed behaviour, and the indeterminacy of a specified outcome.

Sport can be demanding, but its essence is as delicate as any perfume and can be as readily dissipated. There are three abuses which can kill the spirit of play within sport and reduce sport to something less than its fullest human possibilities.

The first abuse is the exaggeration of the importance of victory. I do not refer to the will to win, which must be strong in any highly competitive sport. Still, such a will must be situated within a more generous context—the desire to perform as well as it is humanly possible. Many factors not under the control of players or judges may determine the ultimate victor. Such an awareness does not tarnish the prize, but situates it properly within a limited and qualified texture. Victory in sports is not absolute, and it should not be allowed to behave like the absolute. The policy of winning at all costs is the surest way of snuffing out the spirit of play in sport. The fallout of such a policy is the dreary succession of firings in college and professional sport. Such an emphasis on victory detaches the last moment from the whole game and fixes the outcome apart from its proper context. It reduces the appreciation of the performance, threatens the proper disposition towards the rules and turns the contest into a naked power struggle. The upshot is a brutalization of the sport. And so, the sport which issued from the play-decision, promising freedom and exhilaration, ends dismally in lessening the humanity of players and spectators.

The second abuse stems from the rationalization of techniques within a sport when the rationalization is promoted by an exaggerated sense of the value of efficiency. Good performance is important and the best performance is a desirable ideal. A coach has always to deal with a definite group of individual players. He must assess their potential for the game, combining firmness with good judgment and enthusiasm with restraint. Hard coaching is to be expected, but under pressure of competition it is tempting to let moderation give way to an uninterrupted drive for limitless proficiency. An abstract tyranny of the possible may drive players beyond what they should be asked to give, compelling them to spend what they neither have nor can afford. Driven beyond their natural capacities, they lose the spirit of play, and the values which are supposed to be the initial and perhaps even the paramount reason for taking up the sport. There is a subtle and difficult difference between such tyrannic proficiency and the will to excel which every competitor must have and which leads him to pit his body and personality with and against others. There is a difference between a tyrant and a coach who rightly demands the best his players can put forth. There is a difference, too, between a rationalization which sacrifices everything to technical competence and a reasonable improvement of techniques of training and performance which lift a sport to new accomplishments. Such a merely technical drive is more than likely in our age which tends to over-rationalize all life in the name of technical perfection. The deepest problems in our technological society centre about salvaging, promoting and developing truly human possibilities. Sport stands in a very sensitive position. It can be part of the drive to dehumanization, or in a very direct and privileged way, to the recapture of human values and human dignity. An ultimate and limitless demand for proficiency forced upon players and sport at the cost of all other values including those of play will diminish all who participate—players, staff and spectators.

The first and second abuses are internal threats which arise from detaching victory or performance from the context of play. The third abuse arrives from outside what is essential to sport. It arises with the presence of spectators and threatens to alienate the sport from its play-objectives and values. Such an alienation becomes even more likely when the commercial possibilities of a sport are exploited. The genuine essence of play cannot be present when it is play only for the spectators, as in the gladiatorial contests of the Roman circus in which contestants were often compelled against their wishes to face wild beasts or even one another. One of the requirements is that the participants also take up the activity in a spirit of play. In commercial sport, the spectators usually attend the game in a spirit of play, though some attend simply with friends or to be seen. The players, on the other hand, are under contract, though it is under contract precisely "to play." It seems an oversimplification, however, to discount professional sport as play merely because the players are paid. We do not call a work of fine art non-art simply because it is commissioned. Moreover, the distinction between amateur and professional is a social one, distinguishing those who pursue a vocation from those who pursue an avocation. Olympic sport claims to reflect the time when some games were part of the culture of a "gentleman." Amateurs today are of three kinds: the occasional players who are not very serious in their pursuit of the sport; those who, like many bowlers or curlers, are serious devotees of the sport but not under contract to play it; and those would-be pros who are not yet skilled enough to play the sport under contract. On the side of the professional player what threatens the purity of the spirit of play is the compulsion implied in the contractual obligation to render services at given times, to practise in order to maintain and improve skills, and to participate in games as required. But these demands are intrinsic to many games. The threat lies even more in the nature of the binding force. In professional sport it does not lie in interest in the game itself but rather is reinforced and ultimately enforced by values not intrinsic to the game. Perhaps the clearest distinction is between the wage the pro earns and the win or loss of the game. Win or lose, for a time at least he is paid a wage for services delivered; but he gets the victory only when "the gods of the game" smile upon him. Play ceases when the primary reasons for undertaking it are alien to the values of the play-world itself. Values intrinsic to the play-world include not letting down one's own teammates in team games, not begging off the contest because of personal discomfort, taking pleasure in performing activities within the rules of the game, prizing the victory and its symbols. Values that lie outside the play-world include agreement to deliver services for wages earned, abiding by a contract because of fear of being sued, playing out games in order not to be barred from further league participation, finishing out a sports career in order to achieve social and economic standing upon ceasing to play. These motives are not unworthy; they are simply not motives of play. A player may respect the values of play without directly experiencing them, as when he finishes out his sports' career as ably as possible in order to fulfill the possibilities of the game and thereby allow other participants and spectators to share in the values of the game. Heroism in sport often arises through the determination of a player to maintain the importance of the play-world even in the face of disturbances from the "real" world, such as painful injuries, private worries, physical exhaustion, or even fading interest, although the fan tends to look upon the latter as a betrayal. On the side of the spectator in professional and even in other organized sport, what threatens the purity of the spirit of play is the reduction of the players to hirelings, and the game to something which is expected to deliver to the spectator a period of pleasure for money paid. The commercialization of sport can, of course, be a way of seeing that the quality and abundance of playing is increased; but it can and often does simply pervert sport into just another profitable pleasure industry. Many things give pleasure. Some of them can be bought. The play-world is not one of them. Over-commercialization of sport disillusions the spectator and risks defeating the objectives of commercialization.

The play-world in general offers itself to anyone who wishes to enter it, either as participant or as spectator. But to receive the gift of play he must take up the values of the game as important in and for themselves. He may get angry with "his" team when it plays badly and boast of it when it plays well; but he will not view the players simply as objects employed to give him a pleasurable spectacle. This is a purely objectivist viewpoint and a form of reductionism. It is easy for a spectator to drift into this attitude, because his relation to the game is only partial. He bears no responsibility, and he lives the risks and thrills, defeats and victories in a moving but not a completely involved way. The player is committed with his body and plunges in as one

participant; the spectator participates as the whole team, but indirectly. Nevertheless, play calls for and can achieve a vantage point which undercuts the distinction of the purely subjective and the purely objective, in which I am here and they are there. The fan enjoys a special complicity with his team and easily transfers the symbolic value of the victory to himself and his group. He feels himself in some sense one with the participants of the game. What unites them is the particular form of the play-world, and the importance of its objectives and values.

In sum, then, sport can nourish the spirit of objectivity, for it contains a native generosity with which it seeks excellence of form and action in obedience to conventional rules and submits freely to the award of victory or defeat according to those rules. In so doing, sport manifests a distinctive mode of human life, combining creative freedom with disciplined order for the sake of skilled competition and earned victory. In the engagement the player must encounter his opponent not as an enemy in war but as one whose excellence challenges him and makes possible his own best performance. Players and spectators discover in a new dimension the significance of competitors, team and fans. The sharp difference of subject and object is bridged by the common context and objectives. A fan may surprise himself applauding an exceptionally fine play against his own team, or at least unhappily admiring it. At a race-meet fans from several schools spontaneously urge on the front runner who seems able to beat the existing record, even though he will beat their own runners. It is a victory of man against time and space and himself. Of course, the spectator can be treated as one who needs bread and circuses, but wiser sports managers will try to transform an appetite for constantly renewed sensations into an experience of community. The radical breaking-down of more traditional ties has seen the rise of massive spectator sports. Is it not possible that the attraction of sport for non-players lies in the invitation to experience freedom, meaning and excellence in the context of a free community of individuals bound together by a common appreciation for the values of the game? In that experience of free community men discover new possibilities of human excellence and reach out to recover a fuller meaning of themselves.

Characteristics of Sport*

HOWARD S. SLUSHER

When I initially formulated the proposal for this work I was almost certain that I could define sport. Without being unnecessarily pedantic I could assume that baseball was a sport while sleeping was not. In my own mind, this book was to deal with activities such as football, race car driving, hunting, fishing, tennis, etc. It was not to consider board games such as Monopoly, checkers or even chess (which is often found within the general classification of sport). Somehow I *knew* what sport was but I did not know how to define it.

I began to ask questions of myself. What is this experience I call sport? What differentiates sport activities from other activities of life? When is an activity considered sport and when does it lose the qualities that make it sport? To be sure, these are searching questions of deceptive simplicity.

In attempting to respond to these queries one could easily "beg" the question. My first impulse was to rely on traditionally accepted classifications. When this became inappropriate, I turned my attention to "working definitions." But again this did not answer the fundamental problem. What *is* this book's concern? What are the characteristics of sport?

Certainly it is necessary to inform the reader what I am including and, of equal import, what I am excluding from the analysis. This is not an easy task. I am certain no formulation could encompass the many divergent activities commonly located within the province

* From *Man, Sport and Existence*. Philadelphia: Lea & Febiger, 1967.

of sport. But my initial attempts had to follow the structure of deductive analysis. I asked myself what are the activities I consider as sport. Secondly, what identifying factors were inherent in these activities. No doubt this systematized attempt creates both errors of omission and commission; however, it allows the reader a scope within which meaningful discussion can be localized. Certainly the characteristics put forth are not meant to be definitive.

As previously indicated, my initial attempts were localized in the identification of factors inherent in sport. After repeated frustration I have come to realize that I can best describe sport by simple reference to theoretical constructs that are located within sport. Initial reaction by the reader, to this method of abstraction of traits, might appear unorthodox and perhaps even limiting. But, in truth, it provides a structure within which the reader can focus his attention. Thus, the stated theories are *not* meant to be (and certainly are not) all-inclusive elements found in *one* sport or localized in *all* sports. However, they are constructs that *are* located within that which I call the *spirit of the concept of sport.*

Contention of Interest. All activities so designated as *sport,* within this analysis, possess a quality which indicates that within the activity the participants, whether teams or individuals, contend differing interests and desires. Philosophically, those individuals writing in "game theory" have called this "conflict of interest." More commonly the term competition is used. However, the phrase *contention of interest* implies a *directed commitment* that is perhaps not as strongly implied in the term competition. In other words, in sport man overtly, through obvious thought, has an interest that is contended by either man, animal or nature. The participant may be able to regulate some of the variables in determination of outcome; however, he never, during the process or proceedings of the event, can manage to control the situation completely. Generally, it is easy to locate obvious preferences. Tennis player A desires to hit the ball to player B's side of the net. On the other hand B's contention of interest is to hit the ball to A's side of the net.

Outcomes are a direct extension of the theory of contention of interest. The desired results, accruing from "play," may be quite varied. Dependent upon the orientation of the activity, victory, reward, death are all "dictated" by the sport. In professional sports, the rules are such that they demand superior performance toward victory and assumed monetary rewards. Development of values such as sportsmanship is utterly naive and really not within the *real* rules of the game. Frequently, an "ethic" might be present but, more often than not, this is founded on "survival."

Thus, sport outcomes are in part based on *knowledge*. That is, each player must be completely aware of the *form* of the sport. He must know the rules and the interest of each player. He assumes, by social contract, the agreement of role contention—or else there is chaos.

Consistency of Role. A characteristic related to the construct of contention of interest is germane to potential "outcomes." It appears that toward the given "end," a consistent pattern of preferences is always maintained by the performers. The tennis player has a consistent and structured pattern relative to his "preferences." He always desires the same over-all end, and thus maintains a consistency of role expectation.

This characteristic carries with it the need for *choice*. The problem is placed in the forefront by the performer. What choice should I make in order that my partial influence over the outcomes benefits me the most?[1] That is to say, given a specific set of conditions (that may or may not change), we could ascertain, one way or another, what choice the player should make. This point must be stressed. The

[1] R. D. Luce and H. Raiffa. *Games and Decisions.* (New York: John Wiley & Sons, 1957), p. 6.

dilemma of *individual decision making* is crucial to sport. Where this characteristic is not found—sport does not exist.

The thesis of decision-making, as applied to sport, must be conceived in two categories: (1) decisions made by the individual, and (2) decisions made by the group. However, if the decision of the group is one of complete agreement, it should really be thought of as an individual decision. Frequently, in so-called "team-sports" such as field hockey, football, basketball, etc., we assume the decision depicts *unitary* interest but, in truth, it might be little more than segmented groups' decisions. This could be a contributing factor in the apparent lack of consistency in predicting *outcomes*. We assume the team is making decisions as a group, with mutual interests, when in reality many individual decisions may be ones of conflicting interest. To achieve efficient "productivity" the individualized interests must be resolved or adjusted. So often this is the job of the coach or manager—to mold a group of individuals into a team.

Utilization-Actualization. This characteristic in sport is relevant to maximization of individual effort toward utilitarian ends. This point could be quickly misinterpreted if not clarified.

One could easily argue that in many sport events the participants participate without any overt attempts toward actualization. They might be engaging in "recreational" activity with no intent to better their ability. However, upon closer inspection, one will have to admit that if "sport" is the engagement, actualization might not be the intended purpose but it is always within the context of the media. Secondly, the participants perform with a utility function present. Utilization-Actualization theory does not imply an agreement with traditional ends, nor does it assume the participant knows the functions that others in the sport are attempting to fulfill. Although one has to admit this is usually general knowledge.

Variable Predictability. Related to the theory of contention of interests is the problem of variables. In the sport situation the variables which contribute to possible outcomes are *not* completely specified. It is possible to "program" all the possible "moves" in one given chess game. However, it is *not* possible *absolutely* to program all the chances that could occur in one tennis game. *Realistically* this might be possible, but absolutely **it** is not. It is this characteristic that, in part, eliminates all forms of dice games, roulette, bingo, etc., from sport. In each case it is potentially possible to predict the chance variability of a given situation. One cannot enter into a football contest with a mathematically determined coefficient of variable predictability. In games the controlling variables, hypothetically, can be predicted. In sport they cannot.

If this premise is accepted, we proceed to the next applied assumption; namely, that when the choices evolving from outcomes are based on knowledge, a specific player will select the choice yielding the most desirable result perceived. This might appear to be obvious; however, it is this premise, within the presented development of sport, that attempts to explain the difference in preferences relative to empirical results as opposed to non-rational preferences.

Perhaps the point can be better illustrated in the *game* of poker. The fascination in this game is the element of chance which, in turn, is interwoven by human decision. "Bluffing" is of course prevalent in many "sporting" events, but in poker this element is not "unique" as much as it is a basic skill and fundamental to the game. Poker is not so much a game of cards as it is a game of self-fulfillment. One can test his strength against his opponents. In the long run the cards are not important and thus man can make his own destiny. Poker involves *people*. It is inherently human. Perhaps this is one of the reasons it played such an important role in the settlement of our country, especially the west. Fortunes and territories were won and lost at the poker table. Unlike chess or even bridge, poker cannot be played against an IBM machine.[2] The game has rules but they are so diversified that man has broad interpretational limits. This suits man just fine. For he has the security of boundary but also the excitement afforded by the presence of freedom. The *will of man* determines the rules and these rules are often changed, depending upon the specific conditions or the desire of the man in control. The dealer indeed does more than just hand out cards. He makes a prime choice. His choice

of game indicates his perception of personal success.

The chance elements in sport and games are what appeal to modern man. In sport man pits himself against that which is fated. In a time of computer science and logical positivistic forms of analysis, the element of chance is all the more appealing to the man who would like to make room for emotion in a world that is perhaps a little too rational. Man has reason to hope. And after there is always a chance the underdog will be victorious.

The western world often fuses thought and practice. Man's choice and will are believed predominant to the elements of *chance*. It is therefore not surprising that when man takes part in sport, especially when the activity is "recreative," his attentions turn to an activity that combines these elements. The "national pastime," baseball, is a case in point. It combines both skill and chance, with the emphasis on the latter.

Theoretically, the batter has one main purpose, namely, to hit the ball "where the opposition ain't." But in truth, the *prevailing* manner, even with the most skilled players, is to swing the bat in hopes of getting a "piece of the ball." To be sure, players try to "place" the ball; however, the majority of efforts can be described as a "swing and a hope." A hope, not only that the ball will hit the bat, but that it will *fortunately* avoid the glove of any of the nine opponents. The element of chance is great. To be certain the variables are so large that man must indeed be fortunate. Certainly, the element of chance operates in all sports. The basketball player might aim at the rim of the basket and score by hitting the backboard. The quarterback might complete a deflected pass. Or the soccer goalie might be saved not so much by his ability as by the goal post. Just a fraction of an inch will often make the difference between success and failure. It is difficult to avoid the element of chance; however, few sports possess the infinite and consistent elements of chance in the degree that is localized in baseball. It is not surprising that the "common" man, seeking some form of "hope," turns to baseball as an American pastime. It gives him a *chance!*

[2] J. Lukas. "Poker, An American Character," *Horizon*, 5 (1963), p. 57.

The Classification of Games*

ROGER CAILLOIS

The multitude and infinite variety of games at first causes one to despair of discovering a principle of classification capable of subsuming them under a small number of well-defined categories. Games also possess so many different characteristics that many approaches are possible. Current usage sufficiently demonstrates the degree of hesitance and uncertainty: indeed, several classifications are employed concurrently. To oppose card games to games of skill, or to oppose parlor games to those played in a stadium is meaningless. In effect, the implement used in the game is chosen as a classificatory instrument in the one case; in the other, the qualifications required; in a third the number of players and the atmosphere of the game, and lastly the place in which the contest is waged. An additional over-all complication is that the same game can be played alone or with others. A particular game may require several skills simultaneously, or none.

Very different games can be played in the same place. Merry-go-rounds and the diabolo are both open-air amusements. But the child who passively enjoys the pleasure of riding by means of the movement of the carousel is not in the same state of mind as the one who tries as best he can to correctly whirl his diabolo. On the other hand, many games are played without implements or accessories. Also, the same implement can fulfill different functions,

depending on the game played. Marbles are generally the equipment for a game of skill, but one of the players can try to guess whether the marbles held in his opponent's hand are an odd or even number. They thus become part of a game of chance.

This last expression must be clarified. For one thing, it alludes to the fundamental characteristic of a very special kind of game. Whether it be a bet, lottery, roulette, or baccara, it is clear that the player's attitude is the same. He does nothing, he merely awaits the outcome. The boxer, the runner, and the player of chess or hopscotch, on the contrary, work as hard as they can to win. It matters little that some games are athletic and others intellectual. The player's attitude is the same: he tries to vanquish a rival operating under the same conditions as himself. It would thus appear justified to contrast games of chance with competitive games. Above all, it becomes tempting to investigate the possibility of discovering other attitudes, no less fundamental, so that the categories for a systematic classification of games can eventually be provided.

After examining different possibilities, I am proposing a division into four main rubrics, depending upon whether, in the games under consideration, the role of competition, chance, simulation, or vertigo is dominant. I call these *agôn, alea, mimicry,* and *ilinx,* respectively. All four indeed belong to the domain of play. One *plays* football, billiards, or chess (*agôn*); rou-

* Reprinted with permission of The Macmillan Company from *Man, Play, and Games* by Roger Caillois, translated by Meyer Barash. Copyright © 1961 by The Free Press of Glencoe, Inc.; and with permission of © Editions Gallimard.

lette or a lottery (*alea*); pirate, Nero, or Hamlet (*mimicry*); or one produces in oneself, by a rapid whirling or falling movement, a state of dizziness and disorder (*ilinx*). Even these designations do not cover the entire universe of play. It is divided into quadrants, each governed by an original principle. Each section contains games of the same kind. But inside each section, the different games are arranged in a rank order of progression. They can also be placed on a continuum between two opposite poles. At one extreme an almost indivisible principle, common to diversion, turbulence, free improvisation, and carefree gaiety is dominant. It manifests a kind of uncontrolled fantasy that can be designated by the term *paidia*. At the opposite extreme, this frolicsome and impulsive exuberance is almost entirely absorbed or disciplined by a complementary, and in some respects inverse, tendency to its anarchic and capricious nature: there is a growing tendency to bind it with arbitrary, imperative, and purposely tedious conventions, to oppose it still more by ceaselessly practicing the most embarrassing chicanery upon it, in order to make it more uncertain of attaining its desired effect. This latter principle is completely impractical, even though it requires an ever greater amount of effort, patience, skill, or ingenuity. I call this second component *ludus*.

I do not intend, in resorting to these strange concepts, to set up some kind of pedantic, totally meaningless mythology. However, obligated as I am to classify diverse games under the same general category, it seemed to me that the most economical means of doing so was to borrow, from one language or another, the most meaningful and comprehensive term possible, so that each category examined should avoid the possibility of lacking the particular quality on the basis of which the unifying concept was chosen. Also, to the degree that I will try to establish the classification to which I am committed, each concept chosen will not relate too directly to concrete experience, which in turn is to be divided according to an as yet untested principle.

In the same spirit, I am compelled to subsume the games most varied in appearance under the same rubric, in order to better demonstrate their fundamental kinship. I have mixed physical and mental games, those dependent upon force with those requiring skill or reasoning. Within each class, I have not distinguished between children's and adults' games, and wherever possible I have sought instances of homologous behavior in the animal world. The point in doing this was to stress the very principle of the proposed classification. It would be less burdensome if it were perceived that the divisions set up correspond to essential and irreducible impulses.

Fundamental Categories

Agôn. A whole group of games would seem to be competitive, that is to say, like a combat in which equality of chances is artificially created, in order that the adversaries should confront each other under ideal conditions, susceptible of giving precise and incontestable value to the winner's triumph. It is therefore always a question of a rivalry which hinges on a single quality (speed, endurance, strength, memory, skill, ingenuity, etc.), exercised, within defined limits and without outside assistance, in such a way that the winner appears to be better than the loser in a certain category of exploits. Such is the case with sports contests and the reason for their very many subdivisions. Two individuals or two teams are in opposition (polo, tennis, football, boxing, fencing, etc.), or there may be a varying number of contestants (courses of every kind, shooting matches, golf, athletics, etc.). In the same class belong the games in which, at the outset, the adversaries divide the elements into equal parts and value. The games of checkers, chess, and billiards are perfect examples. The search for equality is so obviously essential to the rivalry that it is reestablished by a handicap for players of different classes; that is, within the equality of chances originally established, a secondary inequality, proportionate to the relative powers of the participants, is dealt with. It is significant that such a usage exists in the *agôn* of a physical character (sports) just as in the more cerebral type (chess games for example, in which the weaker player is given the advantage of a pawn, knight, castle, etc.).

As carefully as one tries to bring it about, absolute equality does not seem to be realizable. Sometimes, as in checkers or chess, the fact of moving first is an advantage, for this priority permits the favored player to occupy key positions or to impose a special strategy. Conversely, in bidding games, such as bridge, the last bidder profits from the clues afforded by the bids of his opponents. Again, at croquet, to be last multiplies the player's resources. In sports contests, the exposure, the fact of having the sun in front or in back; the wind which aids or hinders one or the other side; the fact, in disputing for positions on a circular track, of finding oneself in the inside or outside lane constitutes a crucial test, a trump or disadvantage whose influence may be considerable. These inevitable imbalances are negated or modified by drawing lots at the beginning, then by strict alternation of favored positions.

The point of the game is for each player to have his superiority in a given area recognized. That is why the practice of *agôn* presupposes sustained attention, appropriate training, assiduous application, and the desire to win. It implies discipline and perseverance. It leaves the champion to his own devices, to evoke the best possible game of which he is capable, and it obliges him to play the game within the fixed limits, and according to the rules applied equally to all, so that in return the victor's superiority will be beyond dispute.

In addition to games, the spirit of *agôn* is found in other cultural phenomena conforming to the game code: in the duel, in the tournament, and in certain constant and noteworthy aspects of so-called courtly war.

In principle, it would seem that *agôn* is unknown among animals, which have no conception of limits or rules, only seeking a brutal victory in merciless combat. It is clear that horse races and cock fights are an exception, for these are conflicts in which men make animals compete in terms of norms that the former alone have set up. Yet, in considering certain facts, it seems that animals already have the competitive urge during encounters where limits are at least implicitly accepted and spontaneously respected, even if rules are lacking. This is notably the case in kittens, puppies, and bear cubs, which take pleasure in knocking each other down yet not hurting each other.

Still more convincing are the habits of bovines, which, standing face to face with heads lowered, try to force each other back. Horses engage in the same kind of friendly dueling: to test their strength, they rear up on their hind legs and press down upon each other with all their vigor and weight, in order to throw their adversaries off balance. In addition, observers have noted numerous games of pursuit that result from a challenge or invitation. The animal that is overtaken has nothing to fear from the victor. The most impressive example is without doubt that of the little ferocious "fighting" willow wrens. "A moist elevation covered with short grass and about two meters in diameter is chosen for the arena," says Karl Groos.[1] The males gather

[1] Karl Groos. *The Play of Animals.* English translation. New York: D. Appleton & Co., 1898, p. 151.

there daily. The first to arrive waits for an adversary, and then the fight begins. The contenders tremble and bow their heads several times. Their feathers bristle. They hurl themselves at each other, beaks advanced, and striking at one another. *Never is there any pursuit or conflict outside the space delimited for the journey.* That is why it seems legitimate for me to use the term *agôn* for these cases, for the goal of the encounters is not for the antagonist to cause serious injury to his rival, but rather to demonstrate his own superiority. Man merely adds refinement and precision by devising rules.

In children, as soon as the personality begins to assert itself, and before the emergence of regulated competition, unusual challenges are frequent, in which the adversaries try to prove their greater endurance. They are observed competing to see which can stare at the sun, endure tickling, stop breathing, not wink his eye, etc., the longest. Sometimes are the stakes more serious, where it is a question of enduring hunger or else pain in the form of whipping, pinching, stinging, or burning. Then these ascetic games, as they have been called, involve severe ordeals. They anticipate the cruelty and hazing which adolescents must undergo during their initiation. This is a departure from *agôn,* which soon finds its perfect form, be it in legitimately competitive games and sports, or in those involving feats of prowess (hunting, mountain climbing, crossword puzzles, chess problems, etc.) in which champions, without directly confronting each other, are involved in ceaseless and diffuse competition.

Alea. This is the Latin name for the game of dice. I have borrowed it to designate, in contrast to *agôn,* all games that are based on a decision independent of the player, an outcome over which he has no control, and in which winning is the result of fate rather than triumphing over an adversary. More properly, destiny is the sole artisan of victory, and where there is rivalry, what is meant is that the winner has been more favored by fortune than the loser. Perfect examples of this type are provided by the games of dice, roulette, heads or tails, baccara, lotteries, etc. Here, not only does one refrain from trying to eliminate the injustice of chance, but rather it is the very capriciousness of chance that constitutes the unique appeal of the game.

Alea signifies and reveals the favor of destiny. The player is entirely passive; he does not deploy his resources, skill, muscles, or intelligence. All he need do is await, in hope and trembling, the cast of the die. He risks his stake. Fair play, also sought but now taking place under ideal conditions, lies in being compensated exactly in proportion to the risk involved. Every device intended to equalize the competitors' chances is here employed to scrupulously equate risk and profit.

In contrast to *agôn, alea* negates work, patience, experience, and qualifications. Professionalization, application, and training are eliminated. In one instant, winnings may be wiped out. *Alea* is total disgrace or absolute favor. It grants the lucky player infinitely more than he could procure by a lifetime of labor, discipline, and fatigue. It seems an insolent and sovereign insult to merit. It supposes on the player's part an attitude exactly opposite to that reflected in *agôn*. In the latter, his only reliance is upon himself; in the former, he counts on everything, even the vaguest sign, the slightest outside occurrence, which he immediately takes to be an omen or token—in short, he depends on everything except himself.

Agôn is a vindication of personal responsibility; *alea* is a negation of the will, a surrender to destiny. Some games, such as dominoes, backgammon, and most card games, combine the two. Chance determines the distribution of the hands dealt to each player, and the players then play the hands that blind luck has assigned to them as best they can. In a game like bridge, it is knowledge and reasoning that constitute the player's defense, permitting him to play a better game with the cards that he has been given. In games such as poker, it is the qualities of psychological acumen and character that count.

The role of money is also generally more impressive than the role of chance, and therefore is the recourse of the weaker player. The reason for this is clear: *Alea* does not have the function of causing the more intelligent to win money, but tends rather to abolish natural or acquired individual differences, so that all can be placed on an absolutely equal footing to await the blind verdict of chance.

Since the result of *agôn* is necessarily uncertain and paradoxically must approximate the effect of pure chance, assuming that the chances of the competitors are as equal as possible, it follows that every encounter with competitive characteristics and ideal rules can become the object of betting, or *alea*, e.g. horse or greyhound races, football, basketball, and cock fights. It even happens that table

stakes vary unceasingly during the game, according to the vicissitudes of *agôn*.[2]

Games of chance would seem to be peculiarly human. Animals play games involving competition, stimulation, and excess. K. Groos, especially, offers striking examples of these. In sum, animals, which are very much involved in the immediate and enslaved by their impulses, cannot conceive of an abstract and inanimate power, to whose verdict they would passively submit in advance of the game. To await the decision of destiny passively and deliberately, to risk upon it wealth proportionate to the risk of losing, is an attitude that requires the possibility of foresight, vision, and speculation, for which objective and calculating reflection is needed. Perhaps it is in the degree to which a child approximates an animal that games of chance are not as important to children as to adults. For the child, play is active. In addition, the child is immune to the main attraction of games of chance, deprived as he is of economic independence, since he has no money of his own. Games of chance have no power to thrill him. To be sure, marbles are money to him. However, he counts on his skill rather than on chance to win them.

Agôn and *alea* imply opposite and somewhat complementary attitudes, but they both obey the same law—the creation for the players of conditions of pure equality denied them in real life. For nothing in life is clear, since everything is confused from the very beginning, luck and merit too. Play, whether *agôn* or *alea*, is thus an attempt to substitute perfect situations for the normal confusion of contemporary life. In games, the role of merit or chance is clear and indisputable. It is also implied that all must play with exactly the same possibility of proving their superiority or, on another scale, exactly the same chances of winning. In one way or another, one escapes the real world and creates another. One can also escape himself and become another. This is *mimicry*.

Mimicry. All play presupposes the temporary acceptance, if not of an illusion (indeed

[2] For example, in the Balearic Islands for jai alai, and cockfights in the Antilles. It is obvious that it is not necessary to take into account the cash prizes that may motivate jockeys, owners, runners, boxers, football players, or other athletes. These prizes, however substantial, are not relevant to *alea*. They are a reward for a well-fought victory. This recompense for merit has nothing to do with luck or the result of chance, which remain the uncertain monopoly of gamblers; in fact it is the direct opposite.

this last word means nothing less than beginning a game: *in-lusio*), then at least of a closed, conventional, and, in certain respects, imaginary universe. Play can consist not only of deploying actions or submitting to one's fate in an imaginary milieu, but of becoming an illusory character oneself, and of so behaving. One is thus confronted with a diverse series of manifestations, the common element of which is that the subject makes believe or makes others believe that he is someone other than himself. He forgets, disguises, or temporarily sheds his personality in order to feign another. I prefer to designate these phenomena by the term *mimicry*, the English word for mimetism, notably of insects, so that the fundamental, elementary, and quasi-organic nature of the impulse that stimulates it can be stressed.

The insect world, compared to the human world, seems like the most divergent of solutions provided by nature. This world is in contrast in all respects to that of man, but it is no less elaborate, complex, and surprising. Also, it seems legitimate to me at this point to take account of mimetic phenomena of which insects provide most perplexing examples. In fact, corresponding to the free, versatile, arbitrary, imperfect, and extremely diversified behavior of man, there is in animals, especially in insects, the organic, fixed, and absolute adaptation which characterizes the species and is infinitely and exactly reproduced from generation to generation in billions of individuals: e.g. the caste system of ants and termites as against class conflict, and the designs on butterflies' wings as compared to the history of painting. Reluctant as one may be to accept this hypothesis, the temerity of which I recognize, the inexplicable mimetism of insects immediately affords an extraordinary parallel to man's penchant for disguising himself, wearing a mask, or *playing a part*—except that in the insect's case the mask or guise becomes part of the body instead of a contrived accessory. But it serves the same purposes in both cases, viz. to change the wearer's appearance and to inspire fear in others.

Among vertebrates, the tendency to imitate first appears as an entirely physical, quasi-irresistible contagion, analogous to the contagion of yawning, running, limping, smiling, or almost any movement. Hudson seems to have proved that a young animal "follows any object that is going away, and flees any approaching object." Just as a lamb is startled and runs if its mother turns around and moves toward the lamb without warning, the lamb trails the man, dog, or horse that it sees moving away. Contagion and imitation are not the same as simulation, but they make possible and give rise to the idea or the taste for mimicry. In birds, this tendency leads to nuptial parades, ceremonies, and exhibitions of vanity in which males or females, as the case may be, indulge with rare application and evident pleasure. As for the oxyrhinous crabs, which plant upon their carapaces any alga or polyp that they can catch, their aptitude for disguise leaves no room for doubt, whatever explanation for the phenomenon may be advanced.

Mimicry and travesty are therefore complementary acts in this kind of play. For children, the aim is to imitate adults. This explains the success of the toy weapons and miniatures which copy the tools, engines, arms, and machines used by adults. The little girl plays her mother's role as cook, laundress, and ironer. The boy makes believe he is a soldier, musketeer, policeman, pirate, cowboy, Martian,[3] etc. An airplane is made by waving his arms and making the noise of a motor. However, acts of mimicry tend to cross the border between childhood and adulthood. They cover to the same degree any distraction, mask, or travesty, in which one participates, and which stresses the very fact that the play is masked or otherwise disguised, and such consequences as ensue. Lastly it is clear that theatrical presentations and dramatic interpretations rightly belong in this category.

The pleasure lies in being or passing for another. But in games the basic intention is not that of deceiving the spectators. The child who is playing train may well refuse to kiss his father while saying to him that one does not embrace locomotives, but he is not trying to persuade his father that he is a real locomotive. At a carnival, the masquerader does not try to make one believe that he is really a marquis, toreador, or Indian, but rather tries to inspire fear and take advantage of the surrounding license, a result of the fact that the mask disguises the conventional self and liberates the true personality. The actor does not try to make believe that he is "really" King Lear or Charles V. It is only the spy and the fugitive who disguise themselves to really deceive because they are not playing.

Activity, imagination, interpretation, and

[3] As has been aptly remarked, girls' playthings are designed to imitate practical, realistic, and domestic activities, while those of boys suggest distant, romantic, inaccessible, or even obviously unreal actions.

mimicry have hardly any relationship to *alea*, which requires immobility and the thrill of expectation from the player, but *agôn* is not excluded. I am not thinking of the masqueraders' competition, in which the relationship is obvious. A much more subtle complicity is revealed. For nonparticipants, every *agôn* is a spectacle. Only it is a spectacle which, to be valid, excludes simulation. Great sports events are nevertheless special occasions for *mimicry*, but it must be recalled that the simulation is now transferred from the participants to the audience. It is not the athletes who mimic, but the spectators. Identification with the champion in itself constitutes *mimicry* related to that of the reader with the hero of the novel and that of the moviegoer with the film star. To be convinced of this, it is merely necessary to consider the perfectly symmetrical functions of the champion and the stage or screen star. Champions, winners at *agôn*, are the stars of sports contests. Conversely, stars are winners in a more diffuse competition in which the stakes are popular favor. Both receive a large fan-mail, give interviews to an avid press, and sign autographs.

In fact, bicycle races, boxing or wrestling matches, football, tennis, or polo games are intrinsic spectacles, with costumes, solemn overture, appropriate liturgy, and regulated procedures. In a word, these are dramas whose vicissitudes keep the public breathless, and lead to denouements which exalt some and depress others. The nature of these spectacles remains that of an *agôn*, but their outward aspect is that of an exhibition. The audience are not content to encourage the efforts of the athletes or horses of their choice merely by voice and gesture. A physical contagion leads them to assume the position of the men or animals in order to help them, just as the bowler is known to unconsciously incline his body in the direction that he would like the bowling ball to take at the end of its course. Under these conditions, paralleling the spectacle, a competitive *mimicry* is born in the public, which doubles the true *agôn* of the field or track.

With one exception, *mimicry* exhibits all the characteristics of play: liberty, convention, suspension of reality, and delimitation of space and time. However, the continuous submission to imperative and precise rules cannot be observed—rules for the dissimulation of reality and the substitution of a second reality. *Mimicry* is incessant invention. The rule of the game is unique: it consists in the actor's fascinating the spectator, while avoiding an error that

might lead the spectator to break the spell. The spectator must lend himself to the illusion without first challenging the décor, mask, or artifice which for a given time he is asked to believe in as more real than reality itself.

Ilinx.   The last kind of game includes those which are based on the pursuit of vertigo and which consist of an attempt to momentarily destroy the stability of perception and inflict a kind of voluptuous panic upon an otherwise lucid mind. In all cases, it is a question of surrendering to a kind of spasm, seizure, or shock which destroys reality with sovereign brusqueness.

The disturbance that provokes vertigo is commonly sought for its own sake. I need only cite as examples the actions of whirling dervishes and the Mexican *voladores*. I choose these purposely, for the former, in technique employed, can be related to certain children's games, while the latter rather recall the elaborate maneuvers of high-wire acrobatics. They thus touch the two poles of games of vertigo. Dervishes seek ecstasy by whirling about with movements accelerating as the drumbeats become ever more precipitate. Panic and hypnosis are attained by the paroxysm of frenetic, contagious, and shared rotation.[4] In Mexico, the *voladores*—Huastec or Totonac—climb to the top of a mast sixty-five to one hundred feet high. They are disguised as eagles with false wings hanging from their wrists. The end of a rope is attached to their waists. The rope then passes between their toes in such a way that they can manage their entire descent with head down and arms outstretched. Before reaching the ground, they make many complete turns, thirty according to Torquemada, describing an ever-widening spiral in their downward flight. The ceremony, comprising several flights and beginning at noon, is readily interpreted as a dance of the setting sun, associated with birds, the deified dead. The frequency of accidents has led the Mexican authorities to ban this dangerous exercise.[5]

It is scarcely necessary to invoke these rare and fascinating examples. Every child very well knows that by whirling rapidly he reaches a

[4] D. Depont and X. Coppolani. *Les Confréries religieuses musulmanes* (Algiers, 1887), pp. 156-159, 329-339.

[5] Description and photographs in Helga Larsen. "Notes on the Volador and Its Associated Ceremonies and Superstitions," *Ethnos*, 2, No. 4 (July, 1937), 179-192, and in Guy Stresser-Péan. "Les origines du volador et du comelagatoazte," *Actes du XXVIII Congres International des Américanistes*, Paris, 1947, 327-334. . . .

centrifugal state of flight from which he regains bodily stability and clarity of perception only with difficulty. The child engages in this activity playfully and finds pleasure thereby. An example is the game of teetotum[6] in which the player pivots on one foot as quickly as he is able. Analogously, in the Haitian game of *maïs d'or* two children hold hands, face to face, their arms extended. With their bodies stiffened and bent backward, and with their feet joined, they turn until they are breathless, so that they will have the pleasure of staggering about after they stop. Comparable sensations are provided by screaming as loud as one can, racing downhill, and tobogganing; in horsemanship, provided that one turns quickly; and in swinging.

Various physical activities also provoke these sensations, such as the tightrope, falling or being projected into space, rapid rotation, sliding, speeding, and acceleration of vertilinear movement, separately or in combination with gyrating movement. In parallel fashion, there is a vertigo of a moral order, a transport that suddenly seizes the individual. This vertigo is readily linked to the desire for disorder and destruction, a drive which is normally repressed. It is reflected in crude and brutal forms of personality expression. In children, it is especially observed in the games of hot cockles, "winner-take-all," and leapfrog in which they rush and spin pell-mell. In adults, nothing is more revealing of vertigo than the strange excitement that is felt in cutting down the tall prairie flowers with a switch, or in creating an avalanche of the snow on a rooftop, or, better, the intoxication that is experienced in military barracks—for example, in noisily banging garbage cans.

To cover the many varieties of such transport, for a disorder that may take organic or psychological form, I propose using the term *ilinx*, the Greek term for whirlpool, from which is also derived the Greek word for vertigo (*ilingos*).

This pleasure is not unique to man. To begin with, it is appropriate to recall the gyrations of certain mammals, sheep in particular. Even if these are pathological manifestations, they are too significant to be passed over in silence. In addition, examples in which the play element is certain are not lacking. In order to catch their tails dogs will spin around until they fall down. At other times they are seized by a fever for running until they are exhausted. Antelopes, gazelles, and wild horses

are often panic-stricken when there is no real danger in the slightest degree to account for it; the impression is of an overbearing contagion to which they surrender in instant compliance.[7]

Water rats divert themselves by spinning as if they were being drawn by an eddy in a stream. The case of the chamois is even more remarkable. According to Karl Groos, they ascend the glaciers, and with a leap, each in turn slides down a steep slope, while the other chamois watch.

The gibbon chooses a flexible branch and weighs it down until it unbends, thus projecting him into the air. He lands catch as catch can, and he endlessly repeats this useless exercise, inexplicable except in terms of its seductive quality. Birds especially love games of vertigo. They let themselves fall like stones from a great height, then open their wings when they are only a few feet from the ground, thus giving the impression that they are going to be crushed. In the mating season they utilize this heroic flight in order to attract the female. The American nighthawk, described by Audubon, is a virtuoso at these impressive acrobatics.[8]

Following the teetotum, *maïs d'or*, sliding, horsemanship, and swinging of their childhood, men surrender to the intoxication of many kinds of dance, from the common but insidious giddiness of the waltz to the many mad, tremendous, and convulsive movements of other dances. They derive the same kind of pleasure from the intoxication stimulated by high speed on skis, motorcycles, or in driving sports cars. In order to give this kind of sensation the intensity and brutality capable of shocking adults, powerful machines have had to be invented. Thus it is not surprising that the Industrial Revolution had to take place before vertigo could really become a kind of game. It is now provided for the avid masses by thousands of stimulating contraptions installed at fairs and amusement parks.

These machines would obviously surpass their goals if it were only a question of assaulting the organs of the inner ear, upon which the sense of equilibrium is dependent. But it is the whole body which must submit to such treatment as anyone would fear undergoing, were it not that everybody else was seen struggling to do the same. In fact, it is worth watching people leaving these vertigo-inducing machines. The contraptions turn people pale and

---

[6] [*Toton* in the French text. M.B.]

[7] Groos, *op. cit.*, p. 208.

[8] *Ibid.*, p. 259.

dizzy to the point of nausea. They shriek with fright, gasp for breath, and have the terrifying impression of visceral fear and shrinking as if to escape a horrible attack. Moreover the majority of them, before even recovering, are already hastening to the ticket booth in order to buy the right to again experience the same pleasurable torture.

It is necessary to use the word "pleasure," because one hesitates to call such a transport a mere distraction, corresponding as it does more to a spasm than to an entertainment. In addition, it is important to note that the violence of the shock felt is such that the concessionaires try, in extreme cases, to lure the naive by offering free rides. They deceitfully announce that "this time only" the ride is free, when this is the usual practice. To compensate, the spectators are made to pay for the privilege of calmly observing from a high balcony the terrors of the cooperating or surprised victims, exposed to fearful forces or strange caprices.

It would be rash to draw very precise conclusions on the subject of this curious and cruel assignment of roles. This last is not characteristic of a kind of game, such as is found in boxing, wrestling, and in gladiatorial combat. Essential is the pursuit of this special disorder or sudden panic, which defines the term vertigo, and in the true characteristics of the games associated with it: viz. the freedom to accept or refuse the experience, strict and fixed limits, and separation from the rest of reality. What the experience adds to the spectacle does not diminish but reinforces its character as play.

The Nature of Sport: A Definitional Effort*

JOHN W. LOY, JR.

Sport is a highly ambiguous term having different meanings for various people. Its ambiguity is attested to by the range of topics treated in the sport sections of daily newspapers. Here one can find accounts of various sport competitions, advertisements for the latest sport fashions, advice on how to improve one's skills in certain games, and essays on the state of given organized sports, including such matters as recruitment, financial success, and scandal. The broad yet loose encompass of sport reflected in the mass media suggests that sport can and perhaps should be dealt with on different planes of discourse if a better understanding of its nature is to be acquired. As a step in this direction we shall discuss sport as a game occurrence, as an institutional game, as a social institution, and as a social situation or social system.

I. SPORT AS A GAME OCCURRENCE

Perhaps most often when we think of the meaning of sport, we think of sports. In our perspective sports are considered as a specialized type of game. That is, a sport as one of the many "sports" is viewed as an actual game occurrence or event. Thus in succeeding paragraphs we shall briefly outline what we consider to be the basic characteristics of games in general. In describing these characteristics we shall continually make reference to sports in particular as a special type of game. A game we define as any form of playful competition

* From *Quest*, X (May, 1968), 1-15.

whose outcome is determined by physical skill, strategy, or chance employed singly or in combination.[1]

IA. "Playful." By "playful competition" we mean that any given contest has one or more elements of play. We purposely have not considered game as a subclass of play,[2] for if we had done so, sport would logically become a subset of play and thus preclude the subsumption of professional forms of sport under our definition of the term. However, we wish to recognize that one or more aspects of play constitute basic components of games and that even the most highly organized forms of sport are not completely devoid of play characteristics.

The Dutch historian Johan Huizinga has made probably the most thorough effort to delineate the fundamental qualities of play. He defines play as follows:

> Summing up the formal characteristics of play we might call it a free activity standing quite consciously outside "ordinary" life as being "not serious," but at the same time absorbing the player intensely and utterly. It is an activity connected with no material interest, and no profit can be gained by it. It proceeds within its own proper boundaries of time and space according to fixed rules and in an orderly manner. It promotes the formation of social groupings which tend to surround themselves with secrecy and to stress their differences from the common world by disguise or other means (Huizinga, 1955, p. 13).

Caillois has subjected Huizinga's definition to critical analysis (Caillois, 1961, pp. 3-10) and has redefined play as an activity which is free, separate, uncertain, unproductive, and governed by rules and make-believe (*Ibid.*, pp. 9-10). We shall briefly discuss these qualities ascribed to play by Huizinga and Caillois and suggest how they relate to games in general and to sports in particular.

IA1. *"Free."* By free is meant that play is a voluntary activity. That is, no one is ever strictly forced to play, playing is done in one's free time, and playing can be initiated and terminated at will. This characteristic of play is no doubt common to many games, including some forms of amateur sport. It is not, however, a distinguishing feature of all games, especially those classified as professional sport.

IA2. *"Separate."* By separate Huizinga and Caillois mean that play is spatially and temporally limited. This feature of play is certainly relevant to sports. For many, if not most, forms of sport are conducted in spatially circumscribed environments, examples being the bullring, football stadium, golf course, race track, and swimming pool. And with few exceptions every form of sport has rules which precisely determine the duration of a given contest.

IA3. *"Uncertain."* The course or end result of play cannot be determined beforehand. Similarly, a chief characteristic of all games is that they are marked by an uncertain outcome. Perhaps it is this factor more than any other which lends excitement and tension to any contest. Strikingly uneven competition is routine for the contestants and boring for the spectators; hence efforts to insure a semblance of equality between opposing sides are a notable feature of sport. These efforts typically focus on the matters of size, skill, and experience. Examples of attempts to establish equality based on size are the formation of athletic leagues and conferences composed of social organizations of similar size and the designation of weight classes for boxers and wrestlers. Illustrations of efforts to insure equality among contestants on the basis of skill and experience are the establishment of handicaps for bowlers and golfers, the designation of various levels of competition within a given organization as evidenced by freshman, junior varsity, and varsity teams in scholastic athletics, and the drafting of players from established teams when adding a new team to a league as done in professional football and basketball.

IA4. *"Unproductive."* Playing does not in itself result in the creation of new material goods. It is true that in certain games such as poker there may occur an exchange of money or property among players. And it is a truism

that in professional sports victory may result in substantial increases of wealth for given individuals. But the case can be made, nevertheless, that a game *per se* is non-utilitarian.[3] For what is produced during any sport competition is a game, and the production of the game is generally carried out in a prescribed setting and conducted according to specific rules.

IA5. *"Governed by rules."* All types of games have agreed-upon rules, be they formal or informal. It is suggested that sports can be distinguished from games in general by the fact that they usually have a greater variety of norms and a larger absolute number of formal norms (i.e., written prescribed and proscribed norms).[4] Similarly, there is a larger number of sanctions and more stringent ones in sports than in games. For example, a basketball player must leave the game after he has committed a fixed number of fouls; a hockey player must spend a certain amount of time in the penalty box after committing a foul; and a football player may be asked to leave the game if he shows unsportsmanlike conduct.

With respect to the normative order of games and sports, one explicit feature is that they usually have definite criteria for determining the winner. Although it is true that some end in a tie, most contests do not permit such an ambivalent termination by providing a means of breaking a deadlock and ascertaining the "final" victor. The various means of determining the winner in sportive endeavors are too numerous to enumerate. But it is relevant to observe that in many sport competitions where "stakes are high," a series of contests is held between opponents in an effort to rule out the element of chance and decide the winner on the basis of merit. A team may be called "lucky" if it beats an opponent once by a narrow margin; but if it does so repeatedly, then the appellations of "better" or "superior" are generally applied.

IA6. *"Make-believe."* By the term make-believe Huizinga and Caillois wish to signify that play stands outside "ordinary" or "real" life and is distinguished by an "only pretending quality." While some would deny this characteristic of play as being applicable to sport, it is interesting to note that Veblen at the turn of the century stated:

Sports share this characteristic of make-believe with the games and exploits to which children, especially boys, are habitually inclined. Make-believe does not enter in the same proportion into all sports, but it is present in a very appreciable degree in all (Veblen, 1934, p. 256).

Huizinga observes that the " 'only pretend-ing' quality of play betrays a consciousness of the inferiority of play compared with 'serious-ness' " (Huizinga, 1955, p. 8). We note here that occasionally one reads of a retiring pro-fessional athlete who remarks that he is "giving up the game to take a real job"[5] and that several writers have commented on the es-sential shallowness of sport.[6] Roger Kahn, for example, has written that:

The most fascinating and least reported aspect of American sports is the silent and enduring search for a rationale. Stacked against the atomic bomb or even against a patrol in Algeria, the most exciting rally in history may not seem very im-portant, and for the serious and semi-serious people who make their living through sports, trivi-ality is a nagging, damnable thing. Their drive for self-justification has contributed much to the de-velopment of sports (Kahn, 1957, p. 10).

On the other hand, Huizinga is careful to point out that "the consciousness of play being 'only pretend' does not by any means prevent it from proceeding with the utmost serious-ness" (Huizinga, 1955, p. 8). As examples, need we mention the seriousness with which duffers treat their game of golf, the seriousness which fans accord discussions of their home team, or the seriousness that national govern-ments give to Olympic Games and university alumni to collegiate football?[7,8]

Accepting the fact that the make-believe quality of play has some relevance for sport, it nevertheless remains difficult to empirically ground the "not-ordinary-or-real-life" charac-teristic of play. However, the "outside-of-real-life" dimension of a game is perhaps best seen in its "as-if" quality, its artificial obstacles, and its potential resources for actualization or pro-duction.

IA6(a). In a game the contestants act as if all were equal, and numerous aspects of "ex-ternal reality" such as race, education, occupa-tion, and financial status are excluded as rele-vant attributes for the duration of a given contest.[9]

IA6(b). The obstacles individuals encounter in their workaday lives are not usually pre-determined by them and are "real" in the sense that they must be adequately coped with if certain inherent and socially conditioned needs are to be met; on the other hand, in games obstacles are artificially created to be overcome. Although these predetermined ob-stacles set up to be conquered can sometimes attain "life-and-death" significance, as in a dif-ficult Alpine climb, they are not usually es-sentially related to an individual's daily toil for existence.[10]

IA6(c). Similarly, it is observed that in many "real" life situations the structures and pro-cesses needed to cope with a given obstacle are often not at hand; however, in a play or game situation all the structures and processes necessary to deal with any deliberately created obstacle and to realize any possible alternative in course of action are potentially available.[11]

In sum, then, games are playful in that they typically have one or more elements of play: freedom, separateness, uncertainty, unproduc-tiveness, order, and make-believe. In addition to having elements of play, games have com-ponents of competition.

IB. "Competition." Competition is defined as a struggle for supremacy between two or more opposing sides. We interpret the phrase "between two or more opposing sides" rather broadly to encompass the competitive relation-ships between man and other objects of nature, both animate and inanimate. Thus competitive relationships include:

1. competition between one individual and another, e.g., a boxing match or a 100-yard dash;
2. competition between one team and an-other, e.g., a hockey game or a yacht race;
3. competition between an individual or a team and an animate object of nature, e.g., a bullfight or a deer-hunting party;
4. competition between an individual or a team and an inanimate object of nature, e.g., a canoeist running a set of rapids or a mountain climbing expedition; and finally,
5. competition between an individual or team and an "ideal" standard, e.g., an individ-ual attempting to establish a world land-speed record on the Bonneville salt flats or a basket-ball team trying to set an all-time scoring record. Competition against an "ideal" standard might also be conceptualized as man against time or space, or as man against himself.[12]

The preceding classification has been set forth to illustrate what we understand by the phrase "two or more opposing sides" and is not intended to be a classification of competi-tion *per se*. While the scheme may have some relevance for such a purpose, its value is limited by the fact that its categories are neither mutually exclusive nor inclusive. For instance, an athlete competing in a cross-country race may be competitively involved in all of the following ways: as an individual against another individual; as a team member against members of an opposing team; and as an individual or team member against an "ideal" standard (e.g., an attempt to set an individual and/or team record for the course).[13]

IC. "Physical skill, strategy, and chance." Roberts and Sutton-Smith suggest that the various games of the world can be classified

. . . on the basis of outcome attributes: (1) games of *physical skill,* in which the outcome is determined by the players' motor activities; (2) games of *strategy,* in which the outcome is determined by rational choices among possible courses of action; and (3) games of *chance,* in which the outcome is determined by guesses or by some uncontrolled artifact such as a die or wheel (Roberts and Sutton-Smith, 1962, p. 166).

Examples of relatively pure forms of competitive activities in each of these categories are weight-lifting contests, chess matches, and crap games, respectively. Many, if not most, games are, however, of a mixed nature. Card and board games, for instance, generally illustrate a combination of strategy and chance. Although chance is also associated with sport, its role in determining the outcome of a contest is generally held to a minimum in order that the winning side can attribute its victory to merit rather than to a fluke of nature. Rather interestingly it appears that a major role of chance in sport is to insure equality. For example, the official's flip of a coin before the start of a football game randomly determines what team will receive the kickoff and from what respective side of the field; and similarly the drawing of numbers by competitors in track and swimming is an attempt to assure them equal opportunity of getting assigned a given lane.

ID. "Physical prowess." Having discussed the characteristics which sports share in common with games in general, let us turn to an account of the major attribute which distinguishes sports in particular from games in general. We observe that sports can be distinguished from games by the fact that they demand the demonstration of physical prowess. By the phrase "the demonstration of physical prowess" we mean the employment of developed physical skills and abilities within the context of gross physical activity to conquer an opposing object of nature. Although many games require a minimum of physical skill, they do not usually demand the degree of physical skill required by sports. The idea of "developed physical skills" implies much practice and learning and suggests the attainment of a high level of proficiency in one or more general physical abilities relevant to sport competition, e.g., strength, speed, endurance, or accuracy.

Although the concept of physical prowess permits sports to be generally differentiated from games, numerous borderline areas exist. For example, can a dart game among friends, a horseshoe pitching contest between husband and wife, or a fishing contest between father and son be considered sport? One way to arrive at an answer to these questions is to define a sport as any highly organized game requiring physical prowess. Thus a dart game with friends, a horseshoe pitching contest between spouses, or a fishing contest between a father and son would not be considered sport; but formally sponsored dart, horseshoe, or fishing tournaments would be legitimately labelled sport. An alternative approach to answering the aforementioned questions, however, is to define a sport as an institutionalized game demanding the demonstration of physical prowess. If one accepts the latter approach, then he will arrive at a different set of answers to the above questions. For this approach views a game as a unique event and sport as an institutional pattern. As Weiss has rather nicely put it:

A game is an occurence; a sport is a pattern. The one is in the present, the other primarily past, but instantiated in the present. A sport defines the conditions to which the participants must submit if there is to be a game; a game gives rootage to a set of rules and thereby enables a sport to be exhibited (1967, p. 82).

II. SPORT AS AN INSTITUTIONALIZED GAME

To treat sport as an institutionalized game is to consider sport as an abstract entity. For example, the organization of a football team as described in a rule book can be discussed without reference to the members of any particular team; and the relationships among team members can be characterized without reference to unique personalities or to particular times and places. In treating sport as an institutionalized game we conceive of it as distinctive, enduring patterns of culture and social structure combined into a single complex, the elements of which include values, norms, sanctions, knowledge, and social positions (i.e., roles and statuses).[14] A firm grasp of the meaning of "institutionalization" is necessary for understanding the idea of sport as an institutional pattern, or blueprint if you will, guiding the organization and conduct of given games and sportive endeavors.

The formulation of a set of rules for a game or even their enactment on a particular occasion does not constitute a sport as we have conceptualized it here. The institutionalization of a game implies that it has a tradition of past exemplifications and definite guidelines for future realizations. Moreover, in a concrete game situation the form of a particular sport need not reflect all the characteristics represented in its institutional pattern. The more organized a sport contest in a concrete setting, however, the more likely it will illustrate the institutionalized nature of a given sport. A professional baseball game, for example, is a better illustration of the institutionalized nature of baseball than is a sandlot baseball game; but both games are based on the same institutional pattern and thus may both be considered forms of sport. In brief, a sport may be treated analytically in terms of its degree of institutionalization and dealt with empirically in terms of its degree of organization. The latter is an empirical instance of the former.

In order to illustrate the institutionalized nature of sport more adequately, we contrast the organizational, technological, symbolic, and educational spheres of sports with those of games. In doing so we consider both games and sports in their most formalized and organized state. We are aware that there are institutionalized games other than sports which possess characteristics similar to the ones we ascribe to sports, as for example chess and bridge; but we contend that such games are in the minority and in any case are excluded as sports because they do not demand the demonstration of physical prowess.

IIA. "Organizational sphere." For present purposes we rather arbitrarily discuss the organizational aspects of sports in terms of teams, sponsorship, and government.

IIA1. "Teams." Competing sides for most games are usually selected rather spontaneously and typically disband following a given contest. In sports, however, competing groups are generally selected with care and, once membership is established, maintain a stable social organization. Although individual persons may withdraw from such organizations after they are developed, their social positions are taken up by others, and the group endures.[15]

Another differentiating feature is that as a rule sports show a greater degree of role differentiation than games do. Although games often involve several contestants (e.g., poker), the contestants often perform identical activities and thus may be considered to have the same roles and statuses. By contrast, in sports involving a similar number of participants (e.g., basketball), each individual or combination of just a few individuals performs specialized activities within the group and may be said to possess a distinct role. Moreover, to the extent that such specialized and differentiated activities can be ranked in terms of some criteria, they also possess different statuses.

IIA2. "Sponsorship." In addition to there being permanent social groups established for purposes of sport competition, there is usually found in the sport realm social groups which act as sponsoring bodies for sport teams. These sponsoring bodies may be characterized as being direct or indirect. Direct sponsoring groups include municipalities which sponsor Little League baseball teams, universities which support collegiate teams, and business corporations which sponsor AAU teams. Indirect sponsoring groups include sporting goods manufacturers, booster clubs, and sport magazines.

IIA3. "Government." While all types of games have at least a modicum of norms and sanctions associated with them, the various forms of sport are set apart from many games by the fact that they have more—and more formal and more institutionalized—sets of these cultural elements. In games rules are often passed down by oral tradition or spontaneously established for a given contest and forgotten afterwards; or, even where codified, they are often simple and few. In sports rules are usually many, and they are formally codified and typically enforced by a regulatory body. There are international organizations governing most sports, and in America there are relatively large social organizations governing both amateur and professional sports. For example, amateur sports in America are controlled by such groups as the NCAA, AAU, and NAIA; and the major professional sports have national commissioners with enforcing officials to police competition.

IIB. "Technological sphere." In a sport, technology denotes the material equipment, physical skills, and body of knowledge which are necessary for the conduct of competition and potentially available for technical improvements in competition. While all types of games require a minimum of knowledge and often a minimum of physical skill and material equipment, the various sports are set apart from many games by the fact that they typically require greater knowledge and involve higher levels of physical skill and necessitate more material equipment. The technological aspects of a sport may be dichotomized into those which are intrinsic and those which are extrinsic. Intrinsic technological aspects of a sport consist of the physical skills, knowledge, and equipment which are required for the conduct of a given contest *per se*. For example, the intrinsic technology of football includes: (a) the equipment necessary for the game—field, ball, uniform, etc.; (b) the repertoire of physical skills necessary for the game—running, passing, kicking, blocking, tackling, etc.; and (c) the knowledge necessary for the game—rules, strategy, etc. Examples of extrinsic technological elements associated with football include: (a) physical equipment such as stadium, press facilities, dressing rooms, etc.; (b) physical skills such as possessed by coaches, cheer leaders, and ground crews; and (c) knowledge such as possessed by coaches, team physicians, and spectators.

IIC. "Symbolic sphere." The symbolic dimension of a sport includes elements of secrecy, display, and ritual. Huizinga contends that play "promotes the formation of social groupings which tend to surround themselves with secrecy and to stress their difference from the common world by disguise or other means" (1955, p. 13). Caillois criticizes his contention and states to the contrary that "play tends to remove the very nature of the mysterious." He further observes that "when the secret, the mask or the costume fulfills a sacramental function one can be sure that not play, but an institution is involved" (1961, p. 4).

Somewhat ambivalently we agree with both writers. On the one hand, to the extent that Huizinga means by "secrecy" the act of making distinctions between "play life" and "ordinary life," we accept his proposition that groups engaged in playful competition surround themselves with secrecy. On the other hand, to the extent that he means by "secrecy" something hidden from others, we accept Caillois's edict that an institution and not play is involved.

IIC1. The latter type of secrecy might well be called "sanctioned secrecy" in sports, for there is associated with many forms of sport competition rather clear norms regarding approved clandestine behavior. For example, football teams are permitted to set up enclosed practice fields, send out scouts to spy on opposing teams, and exchange a limited number of game films revealing the strategies of future opponents. Other kinds of clandestine action such as slush funds established for coaches

and gambling on games by players are not always looked upon with such favor.[16]

IIC2. A thorough reading of Huizinga leads one to conclude that what he means by secrecy is best discussed in terms of display and ritual. He points out, for example, that "the 'differentness' and secrecy of play are most vividly expressed in 'dressing up'" and states that the higher forms of play are "a contest *for* something or a representation *of* something"—adding that "representation means display" (1955, p. 13). The "dressing-up" element of play noted by Huizinga is certainly characteristic of most sports. Perhaps it is carried to its greatest height in bullfighting, but it is not absent in some of the less overt forms of sport. Veblen writes:

It is noticeable, for instance, that even very mild-mannered and matter-of-fact men who go out shooting are apt to carry an excess of arms and accoutrements in order to impress upon their own imagination the seriousness of their undertaking. These huntsmen are also prone to a histrionic, prancing gait and to an elaborate exaggeration of the motions, whether of stealth or of onslaught, involved in their deeds of exploit (1934, p. 256).

A more recent account of "dressing-up" and display in sports has been given by Stone (1955), who treats display as spectacle and as a counterforce to play. Stone asserts that the tension between the forces of play and display constitute an essential component of sport. The following quotation gives the essence of his account:

Play and dis-play are precariously balanced in sport, and, once that balance is upset, the whole character of sport in society may be affected. Furthermore, the spectacular element of sport, may, as in the case of American professional wrestling, destroy the game. The rules cease to apply, and the "cheat" and the "spoilsport" replace the players.

The point may be made in another way. The spectacle is predictable and certain; the game, unpredictable and uncertain. Thus spectacular display may be reckoned from the outset of the performance. It is announced by the appearance of the performers—their physiques, costumes, and gestures. On the other hand, the spectacular play is solely a function of the uncertainty of the game (p. 98).

In a somewhat different manner another sociologist, Erving Goffman, has analyzed the factors of the uncertainty of a game and display. Concerning the basis of "fun in games" he states that "mere uncertainty of outcome is not enough to engross the players" (1961, p. 68) and suggests that a successful game must combine "sanctioned display" with problematic outcome. By display Goffman means that "games give the players an opportunity to exhibit attributes valued in the wider social world, such as dexterity, strength, knowledge, intelligence, courage, and self-control" (*Ibid.*). Thus for Goffman display represents spectacular play involving externally relevant attributes, while for Stone display signifies spectacular exhibition involving externally non-relevant attributes with respect to the game situation.

IIC3. Another concept related to display and spectacle and relevant to sports is that of ritual. According to Leach, "ritual denotes those aspects of prescribed formal behavior which have no direct technological consequences" (1964, p. 607). Ritual may be distinguished from spectacle by the fact that it generally has a greater element of drama and is less ostentatious and more serious. "Ritual actions are 'symbolic' in that they assert something about the state of affairs, but they are not necessarily purposive: i.e., the performer of ritual does not necessarily seek to alter the state of affairs" (*Ibid.*). Empirically ritual can be distinguished from spectacle by the fact that those engaged in ritual express an attitude of solemnity toward it, an attitude which they do not direct toward spectacle.

Examples of rituals in sport are the shaking of hands between team captains before a game, the shaking of hands between coaches after a game, the singing of the national anthem before a game, and the singing of the school song at the conclusion of a game.[17]

IID. "Educational sphere." The educational sphere focuses on those activities related to the transmission of skills and knowledge to those who lack them. Many if not most people learn to play the majority of socially preferred games in an informal manner. That is, they acquire the required skills and knowledge associated with a given game through the casual instruction of friends or associates. On the other hand, in sports, skills and knowledge are often obtained by means of formal instruction. In short, the educational sphere of sports is institutionalized, whereas in most games it is not. One reason for this situation is the fact that sports require highly developed physical skills as games often do not; to achieve proficiency requires long hours of practice and qualified instruction, i.e., systematized training. Finally, it should be pointed out that associated with the instructional personnel of sport programs are a number of auxiliary personnel

such as managers, physicians, and trainers—a situation not commonly found in games.

III. SPORT AS A SOCIAL INSTITUTION

Extending our notion of sport as an institutional pattern still further, we note that in its broadest sense, the term sport supposes a social institution. Schneider writes that the term institution

. . . denotes an aspect of social life in which distinctive value-orientations and interests, centering upon large and important social concern . . . generate or are accompanied by distinctive modes of social interaction. Its use emphasizes "important" social phenomena; relationships of "strategic structural significance" (1964, p. 338).

We argue that the magnitude of sport in the Western world justifies its consideration as a social institution. As Boyle succinctly states:

Sport permeates any number of levels of contemporary society, and it touches upon and deeply influences such disparate elements as status, race relations, business life, automotive design, clothing styles, the concept of the hero, language, and ethical values. For better or worse it gives form and substance to much in American life (1963, pp. 3-4).

When speaking of sport as a social institution, we refer to the sport order. The sport order is composed of all organizations in society which organize, facilitate, and regulate human action in sport situations. Hence, such organizations as sporting goods manufacturers, sport clubs, athletic teams, national governing bodies for amateur and professional sports, publishers of sport magazines, etc., are part of the sport order. For analytical purposes four levels of social organization within the sport order may be distinguished: namely, the primary, technical, managerial, and corporate levels.[18] Organizations at the primary level permit face-to-face relationships among all members and are characterized by the fact that administrative leadership is not formally delegated to one or more persons or positions. An example of a social organization associated with sport at the primary level is an informally organized team in a sandlot baseball game.

Organizations at the technical level are too large to permit simultaneous face-to-face relationships among their members but small enough so that every member knows of every other member. Moreover, unlike organizations at the primary level, organizations at the technical level officially designate administrative leadership positions and allocate individuals to them. Most scholastic and collegiate athletic teams, for example, would be classified as technical organizations with coaches and athletic directors functioning as administrative leaders.

At the managerial level organizations are too large for every member to know every other member but small enough so that all members know one or more of the administrative leaders of the organization. Some of the large professional ball clubs represent social organizations related to sport at the managerial level.

Organizations at the corporate level are characterized by bureaucracy: they have centralized authority, a hierarchy of personnel, and protocol and procedural emphases; and they stress the rationalization of operations and impersonal relationships. A number of the major governing bodies of amateur and professional sport at the national and international levels illustrate sport organizations of the corporate type.

In summary, the sport order is composed of the congeries of primary, technical, managerial, and corporate social organizations which arrange, facilitate, and regulate human action in sport situations. The value of the concept lies in its use in macro-analyses of the social significance of sport. We can make reference to the sport order in a historical and/or comparative perspective. For example, we can speak of the sport order of nineteenth-century America or contrast the sport order of Russia with that of England.

IV. SPORT AS A SOCIAL SITUATION

As was just noted, the sport order is composed of all social organizations which organize, facilitate, and regulate human action in sport situations. Human "action consists of the structures and processes by which human beings form meaningful intentions and, more or less successfully, implement them in concrete situations" (Parsons, 1966, p. 5). A sport situation consists of any social context wherein individuals are involved with sport. And the term situation denotes "the total set of objects, whether persons, collectivities, culture objects, or himself to which an actor responds" (Friedsam, 1964, p. 667). The set of objects related to a specific sport situation may be quite diverse, ranging from the elements of the social and physical environments of a football game to those associated with two sportniks[19] in a neighborhood bar arguing the pros and cons of the manager of their local baseball team.

Although there are many kinds of sport situations, most if not all may be conceptualized as social systems. A social system may be simply defined as "a set of persons with an identifying characteristic plus a set of relationships established among these persons by interaction" (Caplow, 1964, p. 1). Thus the situation represented by two teams contesting within the confines of a football field, the situation presented by father and son fishing from a boat, and the situation created by a golf pro giving a lesson to a novice each constitutes a social system.

Social systems of prime concern to the sport sociologist are those which directly or indirectly relate to a game occurrence. That is to say, a sport sociologist is often concerned with why man gets involved in sport and what effect his involvement has on other aspects of his social environment. Involvement in a social system related to a game occurrence can be analyzed in terms of degree and kind of involvement.

Degree of involvement can be assessed in terms of frequency, duration, and intensity of involvement. The combination of frequency and duration of involvement may be taken as an index of an individual's "investment" in a sport situation, while intensity of involvement may be considered an index of an individual's "personal commitment" to a given sport situation.[20]

Kind of involvement can be assessed in terms of an individual's relationship to the "means of production" of a game. Those having direct or indirect access to the means of production are considered "actually involved" and are categorized as "producers." Those lacking access to the means of production are considered "vicariously involved" and are categorized as "consumers." We have tentatively identified three categories of producers and three classes of consumers.

Producers may be characterized as being primary, secondary, or tertiary with respect to the production of a game. (1) "Primary producers" are the contestants who play the primary roles in the production of a game, not unlike the roles of actors in the production of a play. (2) "Secondary producers" consist of those individuals, who while not actually competing in a sport contest, perform tasks which have direct technological consequences for the outcome of a game. Secondary producers include club owners, coaches, officials, trainers, and the like. It may be possible to categorize secondary producers as entrepreneurs, managers, and technicians. (3) "Tertiary producers" consist of those who are actively involved in a sport situation but whose activities have no direct technological consequences for the outcome of a game. Examples of tertiary producers are cheerleaders, band members and concession workers. Tertiary producers may be classified as service personnel.

Consumers, like producers, are designated as being primary, secondary, or tertiary. (1) "Primary consumers" are those individuals who become vicariously involved in a sport through "live" attendance at a sport competition. Primary consumers may be thought of as "active spectators." (2) "Secondary consumers" consist of those who vicariously involve themselves in a sport as spectators via some form of the mass media, such as radio or television. Secondary consumers may be thought of as "passive spectators." (3) "Tertiary consumers" are those who become vicariously involved with sport other than as spectators. Thus an individual who engages in conversation related to sport or a person who reads the sport section of the newspaper would be classified as a tertiary consumer.

In concluding our discussion of the nature of sport we note that a special type of consumer is the *fan.* A fan is defined as an individual who has both a high personal investment in and a high personal commitment to a given sport.

NOTES

1. This definition is based largely on the work of Caillois (1961) and Roberts and others (1959). Other definitions and classifications of games having social import are given in Berne (1964) and Piaget (1951).
2. As have done Huizinga (1955), Stone (1955), and Caillois (1961).
3. Cf. Goffman's discussion of "rules of irrelevance" as applied to games and social encounters in general (1961, pp. 19-26).
4. E.g., compare the rules given for games in any edition of Hoyle's *Book of Games* with the NCAA rule book for various collegiate sports.
5. There is, of course, the amateur who gives up the "game" to become a professional.
6. For an early discussion of the problem of legitimation in sport, see Veblen, 1934, pp. 268-270.
7. An excellent philosophical account of play and seriousness is given by Kurt Riezler (1941, pp. 505-517).
8. A sociological treatment of how an individual engaged in an activity can become "caught up" in it is given by Goffman in his analysis of the concept of "spontaneous involvement" (1961, pp. 37-45).
9. For a discussion of how certain aspects of "reality" are excluded from a game situation, see Goffman's treatment of "rules of irrelevance." Contrawise see his treatment of "rules of transformation" for a discussion of how certain aspects of "reality" are permitted to enter a game situation (1961, pp. 29-34).
10. Professional sports provide an exception, of course, especially such a sport as professional bullfighting.
11. Our use of the term "structures and processes" at this point is similar to Goffman's concept of "realized resources" (1961, pp. 16-19).
12. Other possible categories of competition are, of course, animals against animals as seen in horse racing or animals against an artificial animal as seen in dog racing. As noted by Weiss: "When animals or machines race, the speed offers indirect testimony to men's excellence as trainers, coaches, riders, drivers and the like—and thus primarily to an excellence in human leadership, judgment, strategy, and tactics" (1967, p. 22).
13. The interested reader can find examples of sport classifications in Hesseltine (1964), McIntosh (1963), and Sapora and Mitchell (1961).
14. This definition is patterned after one given by Smelser (1963, p. 28).
15. Huizinga states that the existence of permanent teams is, in fact, the starting-point of modern sport (1955, p. 196).
16. Our discussion of "sanctioned secrecy" closely parallels Johnson's discussion of "official secrecy" in bureaucracies (1960, pp. 295-296).
17. For an early sociological treatment of sport, spectacle, exhibition, and drama, see Sumner (1960, pp. 467-501). We note in passing that some writers consider the totality of sport as a ritual; see especially Fromm (1955, p. 132) and Beisser (1967, pp. 148-151 and pp. 214-225).
18. Our discussion of these four levels is similar to Caplow's treatment of small, medium, large, and giant organizations (Caplow, 1964, pp. 26-27).
19. The term sportnik refers to an avid fan or sport addict.
20. Cf. McCall and Simmons (1966, pp. 171-172).

REFERENCES

Berne, Eric. *Games People Play,* New York: Grove Press, 1964.

Beisser, Arnold R. *The Madness in Sports.* New York: Appleton-Century-Crofts, 1967.

Boyle, Robert H. *Sport—Mirror of American Life.* Boston: Little, Brown, 1963.

Caillois, Roger. *Man Play and Games,* tr. Meyer Barash. New York: Free Press, 1964.

Caplow, Theodore. *Principles of Organization.* New York: Harcourt, Brace and World, 1964.

Fromm, Erich. *The Sane Society*. New York: Fawcett, 1955.

Goffmann, Erving. *Encounters*. Indianapolis: Bobbs-Merrills, 1961.

Hesseltine, William B. "Sports," *Collier's Encyclopedia*, 1964.

Huizinga, Johan. *Homo Ludens—A Study of the Play-Element in Culture*. Boston: Beacon Press, 1955.

Johnson, Harry M. *Sociology: A Systematic Introduction*. New York: Harcourt, Brace, 1960.

Kahn, Roger. "Money, Muscles—and Myths," *Nation*, CLXXXV (July 6, 1957), 9-11.

Leach, E. R. "Ritual," in *A Dictionary of the Social Sciences*, ed. Julius Gould and William L. Kolb. New York: Free Press, 1964.

Lüschen, Gunther. "The Interdependence of Sport and Culture." Paper presented at the National Convention of the American Association for Health, Physical Education and Recreation, Las Vegas, 1967.

McCall, George J., and J. L. Simmons. *Identities and Interactions*. New York: Free Press, 1966.

McIntosh, Peter C. *Sport in Society*. London: C. A. Watts, 1963.

Piaget, Jean. *Play, Dreams and Imitation in Childhood*, tr. C. Gattegno and F. M. Hodgson. New York: W. W. Norton, 1951.

Riezler, Kurt. "Play and Seriousness," *The Journal of Philosophy*, XXXVIII (1941), 505-517.

Roberts, John M., and others. "Games in Culture," *American Anthropologist*, LXI (1959), 597-605.

————, and Brian Sutton-Smith. "Child Training and Game Involvement," *Ethnology*, I (1962), 166-185.

Sapora, Allen V., and Elmer D. Mitchell. *The Theory of Play and Recreation*. New York: Ronald Press, 1961.

Schneider, Louis. "Institution," in *A Dictionary of the Social Sciences*, ed. Julius Gould and William L. Kolb. New York: Free Press, 1964.

Smelser, Neil J. *The Sociology of Economic Life*. Englewood Cliffs, N. J.: Prentice-Hall, 1963.

Stone, Gregory P. "American Sports: Play and Display," *Chicago Review*, IX (Fall 1955), 83-100.

Sumner, William Graham. *Folkways*. New York: Mentor, 1960.

Torkildsen, George E. "Sport and Culture." M.S. thesis, University of Wisconsin, 1957.

Veblen, Thorsten. *The Theory of the Leisure Class*. New York: Modern Library, 1934.

Weiss, Paul. "Sport: A Philosophic Study." Unpublished manuscript, 1967.

The Nature of Play*

JOHAN HUIZINGA

First and foremost . . . all play is a voluntary activity. Play to order is no longer play: it could at best be but a forcible imitation of it. By this quality of freedom alone, play marks itself off from the course of the natural process. It is something added thereto and spread out over it like a flowering, an ornament, a garment. Obviously, freedom must be understood here in the wider sense that leaves untouched the philosophical problem of determinism. It may be objected that this freedom does not exist for the animal and the child; they *must* play because their instinct drives them to it and because it serves to develop their bodily faculties and their powers of selection. The term "instinct", however, introduces an unknown quantity, and to presuppose the utility of play from the start is to be guilty of a *petitio principii*. Child and animal play because they enjoy playing, and therein precisely lies their freedom.

Be that as it may, for the adult and responsible human being play is a function which he could equally well leave alone. Play is superfluous. The need for it is only urgent to the extent that the enjoyment of it makes it a need. Play can be deferred or suspended at any time. It is never imposed by physical necessity or moral duty. It is never a task. It is done at leisure, during "free time". Only when play is a recognized cultural function—a rite, a

* From *Homo Ludens*. London: Routledge & Kegan Paul, 1950. Copyright 1950 by Roy Publishers. Reprinted by permission of Beacon Press and Routledge & Kegan Paul Ltd.

ceremony—is it bound up with notions of obligation and duty.

Here, then, we have the first main characteristic of play: that it is free, is in fact freedom. A second characteristic is closely connected with this, namely, that play is not "ordinary" or "real" life. It is rather a stepping out of "real" life into a temporary sphere of activity with a disposition all of its own. Every child knows perfectly well that he is "only pretending", or that it was "only for fun". How deep-seated this awareness is in the child's soul is strikingly illustrated by the following story, told to me by the father of the boy in question. He found his four-year-old son sitting at the front of a row of chairs, playing "trains". As he hugged him the boy said: "Don't kiss the engine, Daddy, or the carriages won't think it's real". This "only pretending" quality of play betrays a consciousness of the inferiority of play compared with "seriousness", a feeling that seems to be something as primary as play itself. Nevertheless, as we have already pointed out, the consciousness of play being "only a pretend" does not by any means prevent it from proceeding with the utmost seriousness, with an absorption, a devotion that passes into rapture and, temporarily at least, completely abolishes that troublesome "only" feeling. Any game can at any time wholly run away with the players. The contrast between play and seriousness is always fluid. The inferiority of play is continually being offset by the corresponding superiority of its seriousness. Play turns to seriousness and seriousness to play.

Play may rise to heights of beauty and sublimity that leave seriousness far beneath. Tricky questions such as these will come up for discussion when we start examining the relationship between play and ritual.

As regards its formal characteristics, all students lay stress on the *disinterestedness* of play. Not being "ordinary" life it stands outside the immediate satisfaction of wants and appetites, indeed it interrupts the appetitive process. It interpolates itself as a temporary activity satisfying in itself and ending there. Such at least is the way in which play presents itself to us in the first instance: as an intermezzo, an *interlude* in our daily lives. As a regularly recurring relaxation, however, it becomes the accompaniment, the complement, in fact an integral part of life in general. It adorns life, amplifies it and is to that extent a necessity both for the individual—as a life function—and for society by reason of the meaning it contains, its significance, its expressive value, its spiritual and social associations, in short, as a culture function. The expression of it satisfies all kinds of communal ideals. It thus has its place in a sphere superior to the strictly biological processes of nutrition, reproduction and self-preservation. This assertion is apparently contradicted by the fact that play, or rather sexual display, is predominant in animal life precisely at the mating-season. But would it be too absurd to assign a place *outside* the purely physiological, to the singing, cooing and strutting of birds just as we do to human play? In all its higher forms the latter at any rate always belongs to the sphere of festival and ritual—the sacred sphere.

Now, does the fact that play is a necessity, that it subserves culture, or indeed that it actually becomes culture, detract from its disinterested character? No, for the purposes it serves are external to immediate material interests or the individual satisfaction of biological needs. As a sacred activity play naturally contributes to the well-being of the group, but in quite another way and by other means than the acquisition of the necessities of life.

Play is distinct from "ordinary" life both as to locality and duration. This is the third main characteristic of play: its secludedness, its limitedness. It is "played out" within certain limits of time and place. It contains its own course and meaning.

Play begins, and then at a certain moment it is "over". It plays itself to an end. While it is in progress all is movement, change, alternation, succession, association, separation. But immediately connected with its limitation as to time there is a further curious feature of play: it at once assumes fixed form as a cultural phenomenon. Once played, it endures as a new-found creation of the mind, a treasure to be retained by the memory. It is transmitted, it becomes tradition. It can be repeated at any time, whether it be "child's play" or a game of chess, or at fixed intervals like a mystery. In this faculty of repetition lies one of the most essential qualities of play. It holds good not only of play as a whole but also of its inner structure. In nearly all the higher forms of play the elements of repetition and alternation (as in the *refrain*), are like the warp and woof of a fabric.

More striking even than the limitation as to time is the limitation as to space. All play moves and has its being within a play-ground marked off beforehand either materially or ideally, deliberately or as a matter of course. Just as there is no formal difference between play and ritual, so the "consecrated spot" cannot be formally distinguished from the play-ground. The arena, the card-table, the magic circle, the temple, the stage, the screen, the tennis court, the court of justice, etc., are all in form and function play-grounds, i.e. forbidden spots, isolated, hedged round, hallowed, within which special rules obtain. All are temporary worlds within the ordinary world, dedicated to the performance of an act apart.

Inside the play-ground an absolute and peculiar order reigns. Here we come across another, very positive feature of play: it creates order, *is* order. Into an imperfect world and into the confusion of life it brings a temporary, a limited perfection. Play demands order absolute and supreme. The least deviation from it "spoils the game", robs it of its character and makes it worthless. The profound affinity between play and order is perhaps the reason why play, as we noted in passing, seems to lie to such a large extent in the field of aesthetics. Play has a tendency to be beautiful. It may be that this aesthetic factor is identical with the impulse to create orderly form, which animates play in all its aspects. The words we use to denote the elements of play belong for the most part to aesthetics, terms with which we try to describe the effects of beauty: tension, poise, balance, contrast, variation, solution, resolution, etc. Play casts a spell over us; it is "enchanting", "captivating". It is invested with the noblest qualities we are capable of perceiving in things: rhythm and harmony.

The element of tension in play to which we have just referred plays a particularly important part. Tension means uncertainty, chanciness; a striving to decide the issue and so end it. The player wants something to "go", to "come off"; he wants to "succeed" by his own exertions. Baby reaching for a toy, pussy patting a bobbin, a little girl playing ball—all want to achieve something difficult, to succeed, to end a tension. Play is "tense", as we say. It is this element of tension and solution that governs all solitary games of skill and application such as puzzles, jig-saws, mosaic-making, patience, target-shooting, and the more play bears the character of competition the more fervent it will be. In gambling and athletics it is at its height. Though play as such is outside the range of good and bad, the element of tension imparts to it a certain ethical value in so far as it means a testing of the player's prowess: his courage, tenacity, resources and, last but not least, his spiritual powers—his "fairness"; because, despite his ardent desire to win, he must still stick to the rules of the game.

These rules in their turn are a very important factor in the play-concept. All play has its rules. They determine what "holds" in the temporary world circumscribed by play. The rules of a game are absolutely binding and allow no doubt. Paul Valéry once in passing gave expression to a very cogent thought when he said: "No scepticism is possible where the rules of a game are concerned, for the principle underlying them is an unshakable truth. . . ." Indeed, as soon as the rules are transgressed the whole play-world collapses. The game is over. The umpire's whistle breaks the spell and sets "real" life going again.

The player who trespasses against the rules or ignores them is a "spoil-sport". The spoil-sport is not the same as the false player, the cheat; for the latter pretends to be playing the game and, on the face of it, still acknowledges the magic circle. It is curious to note how much more lenient society is to the cheat than to the spoil-sport. This is because the spoil-sport shatters the play-world itself. By withdrawing from the game he reveals the relativity and fragility of the play-world in which he had temporarily shut himself with others. He robs play of its *illusion*—a pregnant word which means literally "in-play" (from *inlusio, illudere* or *inludere*). Therefore he must be cast out, for he threatens the existence of the play-community. The figure of the spoil-sport is most apparent in boys' games. The little community does not enquire whether the spoil-sport is guilty of defection because he dares not enter into the game or because he is not allowed to. Rather, it does not recognize "not being allowed" and

calls it "not daring". For it, the problem of obedience and conscience is no more than fear of punishment. The spoil-sport breaks the magic world, therefore he is a coward and must be ejected. In the world of high seriousness, too, the cheat and the hypocrite have always had an easier time of it than the spoil-sports, here called apostates, heretics, innovators, prophets, conscientious objectors, etc. It sometimes happens, however, that the spoil-sports in their turn make a new community with rules of its own. The outlaw, the revolutionary, the cabbalist or member of a secret society, indeed heretics of all kinds are of a highly associative if not sociable disposition, and a certain element of play is prominent in all their doings.

A play-community generally tends to become permanent even after the game is over. Of course, not every game of marbles or every bridge-party leads to the founding of a club. But the feeling of being "apart together" in an exceptional situation, of sharing something important, of mutually withdrawing from the rest of the world and rejecting the usual norms, retains its magic beyond the duration of the individual game. The club pertains to play as the hat to the head. It would be rash to explain all the associations which the anthropologist calls "phratria"—e.g. clans, brotherhoods, etc.—simply as play-communities; nevertheless it has been shown again and again how difficult it is to draw the line between, on the one hand, permanent social groupings—particularly in archaic cultures with their extremely important, solemn, indeed sacred customs—and the sphere of play on the other.

The exceptional and special position of play is most tellingly illustrated by the fact that it loves to surround itself with an air of secrecy. Even in early childhood the charm of play is enhanced by making a "secret" out of it. This is for *us*, not for the "others". What the "others" do "outside" is no concern of ours at the moment. Inside the circle of the game the laws and customs of ordinary life no longer count. We are different and do things differently. This temporary abolition of the ordinary world is fully acknowledged in child-life, but it is no less evident in the great ceremonial games of savage societies. During the great feast of initiation when the youths are accepted into the male community, it is not the neophytes only that are exempt from the ordinary laws and regulations: there is a truce to all feuds in the tribe. All retaliatory acts and vendettas are suspended. This temporary suspension of normal social life on account of the sacred play-season has numerous traces in the more advanced civilizations as well. Everything that pertains to saturnalia and carnival customs belongs to it. Even with us a bygone age of robuster private habits than ours, more marked class-privileges and a more complaisant police recognized the orgies of young men of rank under the name of a "rag". The saturnalian licence of young men still survives, in fact, in the ragging at English universities, which the *Oxford English Dictionary* defines as "an extensive display of noisy and disorderly conduct carried out in defiance of authority and discipline".

The "differentness" and secrecy of play are most vividly expressed in "dressing up". Here the "extra-ordinary" nature of play reaches perfection. The disguised or masked individual "plays" another part, another being. He *is* another being. The terrors of childhood, open-hearted gaiety, mystic fantasy and sacred awe are all inextricably entangled in this strange business of masks and disguises.

Summing up the formal characteristics of play we might call it a free activity standing quite consciously outside "ordinary" life as being "not serious", but at the same time absorbing the player intensely and utterly. It is an activity connected with no material interest, and no profit can be gained by it. It proceeds within its own proper boundaries of time and space according to fixed rules and in an orderly manner. It promotes the formation of social groupings which tend to surround themselves with secrecy and to stress their difference from the common world by disguise or other means.

Sport: The Diversity of the Concept*

ROBERT J. FOGELIN

Where do we begin in developing a philosophy of sports? What methodology is appropriate? What data are appropriate? And, finally, what is such an inquiry intended to establish? To borrow a phrase from someone else, these are large questions to which I can give only small answers. (1) Where should we begin? I suppose that just about anywhere will do, for if sports constitutes an area capable of philosophical investigation, it will form a more or less tight network, and wherever we begin, eventually we will be led over the entire terrain. (2) Methodology? Again I think that almost anything goes provided that we do not engage in *a priori* empiricism. *A priori* empiricism can operate in at least two ways: we can make up our minds about how things *are* without bothering to look, and, more dangerously, we can make assumptions about how things *must be* and thus make looking quite beside the point. Later in this paper I shall say quite a lot about this second form of *a priori* empiricism. (3) Finally, I think that the philosopher can avail himself of any kind of data, provided that he does not mix things up. As I now see it, philosophy is largely an investigation into conceptual relationships. To give this a nominalistic turn, our data will then be the natural, honest, and serious talk about sports. Here the nominalism is not essential, for we could also investigate the natural, honest,

and serious *thought* about sports. I am assuming, of course, that our speech is *normally* an expression of our thought. I cannot here defend this assumption, but if anyone wishes to deny it, it will be interesting to hear his reasons for thinking that others will understand him.

To state matters in a technical way: a conceptual analysis will concern the set of truths that remain invariant concerning a body of discourse regardless of the truth or falsity of the individual claims themselves. Since this is not a familiar idea, let me illustrate it by analogy with a conceptual analysis of Newtonian Mechanics. Such a conceptual analysis will show how physical reality is *represented* in that framework, but since it is about the framework that we are talking, our investigation will not tell us anything about the way in which the world is in fact situated. A philosopher of science is not a super scientist, and in the same way a philosopher of sports should not be a super-coach or super-sports writer.

To begin to get down to work, I shall hazard a first definition of sports:

Sports is the sort of thing written about on sports pages. Here you may doubt my seriousness, but let me say at once that I am perfectly serious. First of all, the definition is not, as some may think, circular. You can find the sports page without knowing in advance what sports is; you need only look in the index. The definition is a bit too wide, for other things, (e.g., advertisements) also appear on sports pages. Since it will not cause any trouble, we can simply let this defect ride. Finally, the

* Unpublished paper presented at the annual meeting of the American Association for the Advancement of Science, Dallas, Texas, December, 1968.

expression 'sort of thing' makes the definition extremely vague. I do not take this as a defect in the definition, for the concept of sports *is* extremely vague and vague in interesting ways. (It is not generally known that vagueness can be interesting.)

The correct criticism of my definition is that it is completely external; it is rather like defining theoretical physics as the sort of thing that Einstein spent his life working on. In fact, all that our definition does is to point us in the direction where an answer to our questions can be found, for sports pages give us a rich source of natural, honest, and serious talk concerning sports. Very well, what sort of things do we find on sports pages? Here it would be a mistake to rush to certain paradigm cases: (in America) baseball, football, basketball, and the like. Reversing the standard Platonic procedure, we should, instead, look for occurrences and omissions that are somehow surprising. We should wonder at the fact that horse races and dog shows (of all things) are typically reported on the sports pages, whereas bridge and chess competitions are not. This should seem remarkable, for football, say, seems to have more in common with chess than with a dog show. (I have heard sports announcers describe football as one great game of chess, but never as one great dog show.)

If we use the notion of a contest broadly enough (i.e., if we stretch it to suit our abstract purposes), we can say that sports usually involve some sort of contest. But bridge and chess are contests, and we have already seen that our natural instincts are against calling them sports. To put matters simply, bridge and chess seem somehow too cerebral to count as sports. A sport, it seems, must be a contest involving the exhibition of physical strength, speed, endurance, or other forms of prowess. If we dwell upon the physical aspect of sports, we then see why horse racing is closely connected with, say, tennis in a way that chess is not. This brings to the fore a fact that we can easily overlook; a sport need not exhibit the physical prowess of a *human* body. (I know that there is a temptation here to say that the contest is *really* between the owners or the jockeys. This is only half right, and the temptation to think that it is all right is the mark of an *a priori* prejudice. But more on this later.)

Dog shows are worth studying *just because* they constitute a peripheral or intermediate case. It seems to me that if dog shows were simply canine beauty contests, they would not appear on sports pages. As it is, the principles

of conformation still bear at least a remote connection to the physical prowess of the animal. Thus we find two elements that we have associated with sports: (1) the idea of a contest, and (2) in a degenerate form, the exhibition of physical prowess. It is just because the second criterion is met in only a degenerate way that we feel uneasy about calling a dog show a sporting event at all. There is a moral to be drawn from this simple case: a proper conceptual analysis of sports will not simply divide the world up into two neat compartments—those things that are sports and those things that are not sports. It will also represent intermediate cases *as* intermediate by exhibiting the principles that give them this status. This goes quite beyond the glib assertion that the term "sports" is vague, for it suggests that it is just in this area of so called vagueness that we can get our clearest insights into the conceptual structure of the notion under investigation.

It will help to represent these ideas schematically. Borrowing an idea from Wittgenstein, we can say that many of our natural concepts do not mark out an area of things sharing a common essence, but instead, they collect together a family of things sharing a system of overlapping features. It might look something like this:

S_1	S_2	S_3	S_4	S_5
A	B	C	D	D
B	C	D	E	A
C	D	E	F	B

Here there is no common feature running through all these cases, but for all that, they are not grouped together under no principles at all. Now it will not help to say that there *is* a common feature running through all these cases, i.e., a disjunctive common feature. Given any two things, they will share a common disjunctive feature, so this kind of shared feature does not preserve the notion of an essence.

This simple diagram will allow us to illustrate some of the standard ways of going wrong in carrying out a conceptual analysis. (a) We can, contrary to fact, assume that there must be a common feature running through all the cases. This can lead to a willful disregard of actual cases, and even to a flight beyond the empirical altogether. What we cannot find in this world we will posit in a better world next door. (b) More often, we become captivated by special cases that we set up as paradigms. Thus if we hit upon S_1 as a true exemplar, S_2, S_3, and S_5 will make it as sports, but S_4 will be rejected as not *really* being a sport. (Thus we want to say that a dog show is not really a sporting event.) Of course, if we hit upon S_4 as our exemplar our decision will be completely different. Thus if you pick one exemplar and I pick another, we can get into seemingly irreconcilable debates about the nature of sports for, in fact, each of us is confusing a decision that we have made, with an essential feature of the subject matter. This is one source of *a priori* empiricism. (c) If we drop S_1 from our list, we get a new case: there is something common, i.e., D, running through all the cases, and we might then say that this is an essential property of sports. But the idea of something being essential is used in two ways that can easily be confused. By an essential feature we might just mean a common feature, and then again we might mean an important feature. There is no reason to believe that something which is essential in one way is also essential in the other. Thus we might be able to construct a "correct" definition that is perfectly unilluminating. My own earlier definition, even if suitably adjusted, would fall into this class. Or again, we might find certain features that are essential for understanding sports that cannot be made part of its definition.

The last point demands elaboration. It is far from incidental that sporting events are typically staged before the public, that they involve *teams* with an enduring identity, that these teams often *represent* communities or nations, that players and teams have followings, that people are sometimes paid to engage in them, that they involve training and regimentation, etc., etc., etc. If we look at this list of items, we will immediately see that no one of them is indispensable, and thus if we are obsessed with the demand for getting at what is common to all sports we will have to do one of two things: (1) let these items go by the board and thus divest ourselves of a whole range of interesting subjects, or (2) simply legislate out of existence all those things that stand as counter-examples to what we want to say. Of course, we do not have to do either of these things, for the demand for something essential is not itself essential for intelligent inquiry. It is not even a damned shame that the concept of sports constitutes a diverse system of overlapping notions; it is precisely this fact that makes it more interesting, say, than the concept of a prime number.

By now some of you, perhaps all of you, are anxious to hear the point of all this. I can well imagine you saying something like this: "Why not stop gassing about the language of sports, and talk about sports itself?" I shall try to give a direct answer to this reasonable question. We can imagine a three-tiered structure:

The Analysis of the Language of Sports
The Language of Sports
Sports

Sports finds its instantiation in concrete happenings that we observe or engage in. The language of sports provides us with means of representing, either truly or falsely, these concrete happenings. Finally in the analysis of the language of sports, we attempt to categorize and understand the conceptual system that makes up the language of sports. Thus far I have only made the modest, but still important, point that this inquiry should be freed of the essentialist prejudices that are still inculcated by introductory logic texts. I shall now take you into deeper waters by trying to show you that I am absolutely correct not to talk about sports directly.

To put matters another way, the analysis of the language of sports concerns the *convention* that we use when speaking (and thinking) about sports. Now when people hear the word "convention" they usually think of arbitrariness, and thus talk about conventions seems to be talk about the arbitrary and thus hardly worth hearing. (I think that this is the underlying source of the prejudice against linguistic analysis.) But this is a very misleading way of viewing the matter. The truth is this: if we look at conventions from the outside they do appear arbitrary, but when we speak from within a system of conventions, they take on a kind of necessity. They are rules that *govern* our discourse; they are ways that we have to speak in order that our talk (or thought) can form a coherent system. Of course no particular convention is necessary (this is witnessed by the fact that they change over time); what is necessary, is that at any given time our discourse (and thought) confers to some conventions.

But now to come to the point. One of the standing dangers in any form of reflection is to project these necessities of discourse into the subject matter itself. I think that this move demands a name; I shall call it the Fallacy of Conflation. What happens is this: we *tacitly* collapse the three-tiered structure I have previously sketched into a two-tiered structure:

The Philosophy of Sports
Sports

We now blend empirical claims about sports with conceptual claims about the language of sports, and this gives rise to the following picture: contained within each instance of a sport there is a deep structure—a necessary structure—which is the framework upon which everything empirical hangs. This deep structure is transcendental (I am not abusing this word) and thus becomes the special subject matter for philosophy. The social scientist may study the empirical characteristics of this or that sport, and if he raises his sights, he may even study the empirical character of the entire institution of sports with a culture. But it takes the philosopher to answer the really important questions: what is the fundamental structure of sports and what is the fundamental role of sports with the basic structure of a culture?

It is precisely this way of thinking (and this style of philosophizing) that I wish to reject!

My reason for this high-handed attitude is that this style of thought rests upon a mistake: it mixes things up. Furthermore, it is a mistake

that has serious practical consequences. If we project the necessity of our rules into the subject matter itself, then we dislocate empirical investigation. If something has to be the case, then no empirical investigation can dislodge it. If something cannot be the case anything that seems contrary to it must be written off as illusion (wild data, experimental error, etc.). It is now a commonplace that every theory has both a conceptual and empirical dimension, and that what we call revolutions in science involve a fundamental shift in the conceptual component of theories. With such a shift, a whole new range of data becomes accessible, relevant, and ultimately intelligible. Perhaps the time will come when theorists will find it easy to control their conceptual apparatus, but my hunch is that Kant was right and that there is a natural tendency of human beings to abuse their conceptual apparatus in an attempt to make it yield substantive truth. I have tried not to do this in this paper, and that is why I have nothing profound to tell you.

BIBLIOGRAPHY ON THE NATURE OF SPORT

Blumenfield, Walter. "Observations Concerning the Phenomenon and Origin of Play." *Philosophy and Phenomenological Research*, I (June, 1941), 470-478.

Bowen, Wilbur P. and Mitchell, Elmer D. "The Philosophy of Play" in *The Theory of Organized Play*. New York: A. S. Barnes, 1927.

Browne, Evelyn. "An Ethological Theory of Play." *Journal of Health, Physical Education, and Recreation*, 39 (September, 1968), 36-39.

Caillois, Roger. "Unity of Play; Diversity of Games." *Diogenes*, 19 (Fall, 1957), 92-121.

————, "Play and the Sacred" in *Man and the Sacred*. Translated by Meyer Barash. Illinois: Free Press of Glencoe, 1959.

————, *Man, Play, and Games*. Translated by Meyer Barash. New York: Free Press of Glencoe, 1961.

Carlisle, R. "The Concept of Physical Education." *Proceedings of the Annual Conference of the Philosophy of Education Society of Great Britain*. Vol. III, January, 1969.

Chase, Stuart. "Play." *Whither Mankind*. Edited by Charles A. Beard. New York: Longmans, Green and Company, 1928.

Cox, Harvey. "Faith as Play" in *The Feast of Fools: A Theological Essay on Festivity and Fantasy*. Cambridge: Harvard University Press, 1969.

Dearden, R. F. "The Concept of Play." *The Concept of Education*. Edited by R. S. Peters. London: Routledge & Kegan Paul, 1967.

Fogelin, Robert J. "Sport: The Diversity of the Concept." Unpublished paper presented at the annual meeting of the American Association for

the Advancement of Science, Dallas, Texas, December, 1968.

Giddens, A. "Notes on the Concept of Play and Leisure." *Sociological Review*, 12 (March, 1964), 73-89.

Graves, H. "A Philosophy of Sport." *Contemporary Review*, LXXVIII (December, 1900), 877-893.

Grazia, Sebastion de. *Of Time, Work, and Leisure*. New York: Twentieth Century Fund, 1962.

Groos, Karl. *The Play of Man*. New York: D. Appleton, 1901.

Gulick, Luther Halsey. "Psychological, Pedagogical, and Religious Aspects of Group Games." *Pedagogical Seminary* [now *Journal of Genetic Psychology*], 6 (1899), 135-151.

————. *A Philosophy of Play*. New York: Charles Scribner's Sons, 1920.

Huizinga, Johan. *Homo Ludens*. London: Routledge & Kegan Paul, 1950.

Jolivet, Régis. "Work, Play, Contemplation." Translated by Sister M. Delphine. *Philosophy Today*, V (Summer, 1961), 114-120.

Kaplan, Max. "Games and Sport as Leisure" in *Leisure in America: A Social Inquiry*. New York: John Wiley & Sons, 1960.

Keating, James W. "Sportsmanship as a Moral Category." *Ethics*, LXXV (October, 1964), 25-35.

————. "The Urgent Need for Definitions and Distinctions." *Physical Educator*, 28 (March, 1971), 41-42.

Kleinman, Seymour. "Toward a Non-Theory of Sport." *Quest*, X (May, 1968), 29-34.

Krug, Orvis. "The Philosophical Relationship Between Physical Education and Athletics." Unpublished Ed. D. dissertation, New York University, 1958.

Loy, John Jr. "The Nature of Sport: A Definitional Effort." *Quest,* X (May, 1968), 1-15.

Manser, Anthony. "Games and Family Resemblances." *Philosophy,* XVII (July, 1967), 210-255.

Melvin, Bruce L. "Play, Recreation, and Leisure Time." *Proceedings of the Sixty-Third Annual Meeting of the College Physical Education Association.* Washington, D.C., 1960.

Metheny, Eleanor. "This 'Thing' Called Sport." *Journal of Health, Physical Education, and Recreation,* 40 (March, 1969), 59-60.

Miller, David L. *Gods and Games: Toward a Theology of Play.* New York: World Publishing Company, 1970.

Neale, Robert E. *In Praise of Play.* New York: Harper & Row, 1969.

Patrick, G. T. W. "The Play of a Nation." *Scientific Monthly,* 13 (October, 1921), 350-362.

Petrie, Brian Malcom. "Physical Activity, Games, and Sport: A System of Classification and an Investigation of Social Influences Among Students of Michigan State University." Unpublished Ph.D. dissertation, Michigan State University, 1970.

Potter, Stephen. "The Game Itself" in *The Theory and Practice of Gamesmanship.* New York: Bantam Books, 1965. (First published New York: Holt, Rinehart and Winston, 1948.)

Roberts, John M., Arth, Malcom J. and Bush, Robert R. "Games in Culture." *American Anthropologist,* 61 (August, 1959), 597-605.

Rossi, Ernest Lawrence. "Game and Growth: Two Dimensions of our Psychotherapeutic Zeitgeist." *Journal of Humanistic Psychology,* 7 (Fall, 1967), 139-154.

Roszak, Theodore. "Forbidden Games." Wayne State University Graduate *Comment,* X (1967), 25-34. (Reprinted in *Sport in the Socio-Cultural Process.* Edited by M. Marie Hart. Dubuque, Iowa: Wm. C. Brown, 1972.)

Sapora, Allen V. and Mitchell, Elmer D. "Definitions and Characteristics of Play and Recreation" in *The Theory of Play and Recreation.* Third Edition. New York: Ronald Press, 1948.

Schmitz, Kenneth L. "Sport and Play: Suspension of the Ordinary." Unpublished paper presented at the annual meeting of the American Association for the Advancement of Science, Dallas, Texas, December 28, 1968.

Slusher, Howard S. *Man, Sport and Existence.* Philadelphia: Lea & Febiger, 1967.

Steinbeck, John. "Then My Arm Glassed Up." *Sports Illustrated,* 23 (December 20, 1965), 94-102.

Stone, Gregory P. "Some Meanings of American Sport." College Physical Education Association. *Proceedings of the 60th Annual Meeting.* Columbus, Ohio, 1957. (Reprinted in *Sport and American Society.* Edited by George H. Sage. Massachusetts: Addison-Wesley, 1970).

————. "Some Meanings of American Sport: An Extended View." *Aspects of Contemporary Sport Sociology.* Proceedings of C.I.C. Symposium on the Sociology of Sport. Edited by Gerald S. Kenyon. Illinois: The Athletic Institute. 1969.

Suits, Bernard. "What is a Game?" *Philosophy of Science.* 34 (June, 1967), 148-156.

Sutton-Smith, Brian. "A Formal Analysis of Game Meaning." *Western Folklore,* XVIII (January, 1959), 13-24.

VanderZwaag, Harold J. "Sport: Existential or Essential?" *Quest,* XII (May, 1969), 47-56.

————. "Sports Concepts." *Journal of Health, Physical Education, and Recreation,* 41 (March, 1970), 35-36.

Vernes, Jean-René. "The Element of Time in Competitive Games." Translated by Victor A. Velen. *Diogenes,* 50 (September, 1965), 25-42.

Weiss, Paul. *Sport: A Philosophic Inquiry.* Carbondale: Southern Illinois University Press, 1969.

Wittgenstein, Ludwig. "Language Games" in *Philosophical Investigations.* Second Edition. Translated by G. E. M. Anscombe. Oxford: Basil Blackwell, 1958.

SPORT AND METAPHYSICAL SPECULATIONS

Sport and Metaphysical Speculations

INTRODUCTION

Metaphysical considerations of sport can appropriately proceed in two dimensions. The reality of sport as a phenomenon is one consideration and the effect of the sport encounter on the individual's existence is another. Philosophically, the terms existence, reality and being are very close in meaning, although there are fine differences which various philosophers have carefully distinguished within their writings. It will, however, be sufficient for the purposes of this work if they are considered interchangeable; therefore, metaphysics or the study of existence shall not be differentiated from ontology or the study of reality.

No agreement has been reached on what constitutes the ultimate nature of reality. Traditional philosophers have exposited theories ranging from the view of reality as consisting of real, substantial entities which exist whether they are known or not (some forms of realism or materialism), to a view of reality as pure mind or idea, independent of the material world (idealism). Both of those essentialist views have in common the belief that there is some predetermined world order. In these views man does not make reality—he comes to know it through perception and coherent reasoning. A third point of view (pragmatism or experimentalism) describes reality as related to the experience of humans. This position sees reality as a kind of interaction between man and the material world, neither predetermined nor entirely individualized.

The importance of these distinctions within the realm of philosophical inquiry has greatly diminished in recent years. The existential philosophers have approached the question from an entirely new position. Interested primarily in human existence, they view ultimate reality as grounded in the subjective human experience. Man, who has no nature, attains being by accruing a history of experiences. In other words, though existence is a given, essence is to be developed. The focus of the existential metaphysic, therefore, is upon man's quest for being or essence.

In contrast to the existentialists whose main concern is ontology, the analytic philosophers are primarily epistemological. In fact, they totally reject metaphysical speculation. They are interested in the methodological analysis of a proposition, not its being. Finally, one might consider phenomenology to be a bridge between the existential and analytic schools in that the phenomenologist does a methodological analysis (reduction or description) of a subjective experience.

Although not much attention has been given to speculation about the metaphysical reality of sport, the first paper in this section, "Arguments on the Reality of Sport" by Ellen W. Gerber, deals directly with this issue and uses criteria drawn from traditional and existential schools of thought. In "Games: The Extension of Man" by Marshall McLuhan, the metaphysical reality of sport is acknowledged in somewhat different terms. Games are described as objectifications of inner reality, social reality and cosmic reality. Their reality is therefore derivative, but at the same time they are assumed to attain independent existence. "The Ontology of Play" by Eugen Fink is probably the only published study which directly attempts to discuss systematically this particular aspect of thought. Fink analyzes the existence of play and clarifies its relationship to human existence and to unreality. He, too, assumes that play is self-sufficient, has an internal end and possesses a complete and firmly established meaning—all philosophical conditions of reality.

The nature of the reality of sport is a problem of interest largely to those who are interested in philosophy *qua* philosophy. It is a subject most appropriate to the disciplines of the traditional philosophies that are willing to use things or ideas rather than man as the point of reference. The more interesting issue is the one that is the central concern of existentialism: the nature of man's existence. More specifically, in the papers collected in this book, the relationship between sport and the attainment of being or selfhood is examined.

The selection, "Athletic Angst: Reflections on the Philosophical Relevance of Play" by Drew Hyland clearly establishes the single human experience as the central referrant of sport: Hyland analyzes the playing of the game as a meaningful act of being-in-the-world. Jean-Paul Sartre's work on "Play and Sport" deals with the appropriation of being-in-itself through sport; thus the goal of sport is the attainment of self. In "Man Alone" William A. Harper is concerned with still another aspect of self— the awareness of one's existence, the realization through sport of one's unique identity.

"Play, the Game, and the Generalized Other" by George Herbert Mead, "Identity, Relation and Sport" by Ellen W. Gerber, and "Play: A Basic Human Structure Involving Love and Freedom" by William A. Sadler, Jr., each examine the development of one's identity, of self, through the meaningful encounter with others in a sport situation. While Mead's work speaks of personality and social conditions in terms familiar to readers of the literature of psychology, the articles by Gerber and Sadler reflect the existentialist ideas, particularly those of Martin Buber, on being through relation.

Freedom as a metaphysical condition is another central concern of philosophy. The article by Sadler examines the concept of freedom as it is experienced in a sport situation.

The excerpt from Karl Jasper's work, "Limits of the Life-Order: Sport," is a statement on the human condition enriched by sport. The final selection in this section, "The Great Doctrine of Archery" by Eugen Herrigel, relies on Zen philosophy to describe the transcendence of the human into oneness with universe, as represented by the bow, arrow and target in archery.

Thus this section entitled "Metaphysical Speculations" moves from a consideration of the reality of sport itself, to examining sport in relation to individual man's existence, to sport and the human condition, and finally to the transcendence of man through sport. The reader is confronted by numerous questions, including the key one: what is one's own belief about the nature of ultimate reality? How does this belief affect one's conceptions of sport and/or physical education? Do those associated with sport deal more with perceptual reality than with symbolic reality? Would the athlete disagree with the most famous statement of existence, Descartes' *cogito ergo sum*? Does the search for fitness versus pleasure through sport reflect differing views of reality? Is the play world different from the real world? Does the physical educator's belief about reality affect the selection of curriculum and teaching methodology? Does the reality of sport differ for each participant? If the sport experience is to be a profound encounter with one's being, does that imply certain levels of skill or involvement? Does the structure of sport affect the individual? Does one really experience freedom in sport? What is the real nature of the human relations encountered in sport?

Those interested in further study of this topic will find several other works available which touch upon metaphysical questions. Huizinga (1950), and Reizler, in his article in the section on "Sport as a Meaningful Experience," write about the separation of play from the real world. Froebel (1900), on the other hand, sees playthings as the symbolic representation of the universe and playing, therefore, as an experiencing of the inner and external unity of the world. A viewpoint similar to McLuhan's, but one which places a greater balance on the interaction of sport and human beings to produce the special reality of sport, is advanced by Felshin in her paper presented in this book's section on "Sport as a Meaningful Experience."

Like Hyland, Harper (1971) and Thomson (1967) are interested in a phenomenological analysis of the sport experience. Both have written dissertations which are extensive analyses of aspects of the human condition in a specific sport situation. The search for being through the sport experience is the focus of

Slusher's book (1967) and is considered in a closing chapter entitled "A Metaphysical Excursus" in Weiss' work (1969).

The most comprehensive work on sport and relation is Kretchmar's dissertation (1971) in which he extensively analyzes the "other" in sport. Slusher (1967) offers the only other direct philosophical treatment of the subject, though it runs as a theme throughout the writings of John Dewey. The process of socialization through sport is extensively treated in both the sociological and psychological literature. However, since this context is not central to this book's subject, those works have not been listed.

Similar views on freedom in sport are presented by Felshin (1969) and Metheny in her article in this book on "The Symbolic Power of Sport." Slusher (1967) and Coutts (1968) also examine this concept.

The symbolic reality of sport is comprehensively dealt with by Metheny (1968a). Desmonde (1952) has an interesting account of the bullfight as a religious ritual. In a primarily psychoanalytic manner, Stokes (1956) and Childe Herald [Ferril] examine the symbolism in football, cricket and other ball games.

Another interesting article on the human condition vis à vis sport was written by Axelos (1971). In its spiritual connotations it calls to mind the fine works by Rahner (1967), Caillois (1959), Neale (1969), and Cox (1969), each of which deals with the concept of play in relation to the spirit of man. Lastly, another Zen-type work, in which man in sport is an exemplification of man himself, is the ancient Chinese writing "She I, or The Meaning of the Ceremony of Archery."

These metaphysical speculations on man in sport have only begun to approach the issue. Topics relating sport to aspects of man's ontological condition await examination or more extensive explication: hope, freedom, death, the ability to transcend, relation, and despair are some examples of such concerns. The symbolic nature of sport, its ritualistic elements, the affect of natural forces and of nature itself on man in sport are significant subjects which warrant investigation. Time and space modalities are two conditions of sport which would make superb topics for consideration.

It is hardly necessary to justify study of this subject to those connected with sport. Each teacher, coach, athlete who has been extensively involved in sport knows that it touches on his or her own sense of being-in-the-world. To understand who one is, to enhance self-awareness is, by extension, to increase one's ability to communicate.

Arguments on the Reality of Sport

ELLEN W. GERBER

Those who love sport—players, teachers, coaches, researchers, spectators—regard it as "special." In fact, they tend to view it as something apart from the ordinary rhythms of life, of working and studying and doing the countless chores associated with daily existence. In other words, they consider sport *not* to be a part of real life.

This position is widely reflected in the literature on sport and play.[*] In *Homo Ludens,* perhaps the most comprehensive and highly regarded study on play, Huizinga states specifically that "play is not 'ordinary' or 'real' life. It is rather a stepping out of 'real' life into a temporary sphere of activity with a disposition all of its own." (1955, p.8) Another well-known sociologist, Caillois lists as one of play's characteristics: "*Make-believe:* accompanied by a special awareness of a second reality or of a free unreality, as against real life." (1961, p. 10) The physical education literature in general follows the definitions and characteristics of play as set forth by Huizinga and Caillois. A good example of this occurs in Ulrich's book, *The Social Matrix of Physical Education,* in which she states: "Play is never a real-life situation, although it may imitate real life or it may have implications of real life within its makeup." (1968, p.101) Loy questions the appropriateness of "accepting the fact that the make-believe quality of play has . . . relevance

[*] Although the words sport and play are obviously not identical, the authors cited in this work use the term play in its broadest connotations, thereby including games and sport.

for sport." (1968, p.4) However, he does accept the notion of the two sociologists with caution. The philosopher Eugen Fink seems unique in his belief that "play itself is a fundamental phenomenon of existence, just as original and basic in itself as death, work and domination." (1960, p.101)

The grounds for the widely held conviction that play is not real seem to be based upon play's essential frivolity or lack of productivity; it is what Sutton-Smith refers to as the "triviality" factor. (1970) Old, puritan notions still pervade modern thinking, causing the belief that anything not productive is not a part of real life. The traditional (and certainly outmoded) dichotomy of work and play resolves itself to a parallel dichotomy of real-life and . . . what? Semantically, the opposite of real is unreal or fake? Can such a thing as "fake" life exist? Is there a moment in time when a person's participation in life is "unreal"? This appears to be an ontological impossibility. It is, however, the hidden assumption upon which has been constructed a complete syndrome of ideas relating to the uses to which sport can be put to *produce* learnings suitable for use in real life—thus justifying its existence and popularity. Such an assumption creates a two-headed monster, first because it corrupts the agreed-upon idea that sport by definition is non-productive; and second, because it denies the availability of sport or play as a meaningful experience in and of itself.

Philosophers differ on the criteria of ultimate reality, but an examination of the usual ontological considerations reveals that sport and play are real by any measure. They have perceptual reality to the participant and spectator. Sport can be seen; the game as a whole can be witnessed and its various parts seen as smaller wholes. It can be heard; the sound of a ball bouncing, a man running, a player calling "mine," are identifying auditory elements of sport. The ball, the field, the wave, the ski slope, the sweat, the clothing, the other player, are some of the components associated with the perception of feeling. Not only does the player use perceptions in order to play, but sport is itself an action that can be perceived.

Sport and play exist as ideas. Attempts at definition of the terms differ, but all are based upon the assumption that the potential for definition exists. In other words, there is an idea that can be described. Furthermore, sport and play form the nucleus of a coherent system of concepts generating from, and attached to, the "mother" construct. Ideas of order, of boundary, of motion, of competition, and of limits are some which are inextricably connected with sport, as are the endless details of the individual games such as rules, routines and strategies. As with perception, players hold independent constructs of sport and play, but these may themselves be examined and studied by observers.

Perhaps more fundamental than either the perceptual or ideational reality of sport, is its metaphysical existence as an experience. Man, who assumes himself to be real, plays; ergo, play is real. All that man does, all that is present to him in his daily encounters with a limited world, he takes to be real by extension of his own reality. Sport is something in which man participates; he experiences it in time, in space, in communication with people and objects; it exists in his day, in his thoughts, in his past, present and future; it is part of his

life; it is an extension of him. He is real, his life is real, so sport must be real. Furthermore, his involvement with the sports pages and television, attendance at games, exposure to art, poetry, literature, and drama in which sport is described, indicate that it is equally real or a part of the experience of others.

Sport considered as a reality fulfills a different role in man's life than it could as an unreality or irreality. As an entity it can be assigned values, can be studied with the tools of philosophy, science or art. Most important, it can be chosen by man as a legitimate, real-life activity in which to engage, to spend his time, or even to be a mode of living. As a nonentity, it can serve only as a medium for the fulfillment of other purposes, because the meaning derived from fantasy is severely limited and possibly distorted by transference to real life.

It is clear to the writer, that despite the contentions of some individuals that sport is unreal and separate from real life, their studies and writings have treated it otherwise. They have rightfully accorded it the status of an important human experience, a part of the unfolding self-creating, self-renewing life of the individual.

REFERENCES

Caillois, Roger. *Man, Play, and Games.* Translated by Meyer Barash. New York: Free Press of Glencoe, 1961.

Huizinga, Johan. *Homo Ludens.* Boston: Beacon Press Edition, 1955. (First published 1950: Routledge & Kegan Paul.)

Loy, John, Jr. "The Nature of Sport: A Definitional Effort." *Quest,* (May, 1968), 1-15.

Sutton-Smith, Brian. "The Psychology of Childlore: The Triviality Barrier." *Western Folklore,* 29 (1970), 1-8.

Ulrich, Celeste. *The Social Matrix of Physical Education.* New Jersey: Prentice-Hall, 1968.

Games: The Extension of Man*

MARSHALL McLUHAN

Alcohol and gambling have very different meanings in different cultures. In our intensely individualist and fragmented Western world, "booze" is a social bond and a means of festive involvement. By contrast, in closely knit tribal society, "booze" is destructive of all social pattern and is even used as a means to mystical experience.

In tribal societies, gambling, on the other hand, is a welcome avenue of entrepreneurial effort and individual initiative. Carried into an individualist society, the same gambling games and sweepstakes seem to threaten the whole social order. Gambling pushes individual initiative to the point of mocking the individualist social structure. The tribal virtue is the capitalist vice.

When the boys came home from the mud and blood baths of the Western Front in 1918 and 1919, they encountered the Volstead Prohibition Act. It was the social and political recognition that the war had fraternalized and tribalized us to the point where alcohol was a threat to an individualist society. When we too are prepared to legalize gambling, we shall, like the English, announce to the world the end of individualist society and the trek back to tribal ways.

We think of humor as a mark of sanity for a good reason: in fun and play we recover the integral person, who in the workaday world or in professional life can use only a small

sector of his being. Philip Deane in *Captive in Korea,* tells a story about games in the midst of successive brainwashings that is to the point.

> There came a time when I had to stop reading those books, to stop practising Russian because with the study of language the absurd and constant assertion began to leave its mark, began to find an echo, and I felt my thinking processes getting tangled, my critical faculties getting blunted. . . . then they made a mistake. They gave us Robert Louis Stevenson's *Treasure Island* in English. . . . I could read Marx again, and question myself honestly without fear. Robert Louis Stevenson made us lighthearted, so we started dancing lessons.

Games are popular art, collective, social *reactions* to the main drive or action of any culture. Games, like institutions, are extensions of social man and of the body politic, as technologies are extensions of the animal organism. Both games and technologies are counter-irritants of ways of adjusting to the stress of the specialized actions that occur in any social group. As extensions of the popular response to the workaday stress, games become faithful models of a culture. They incorporate both the action and the reaction of whole populations in a single dynamic image.

A Reuters dispatch for December 13, 1962, reported from Tokyo:

BUSINESS IS A BATTLEFIELD

Latest fashion among Japanese businessmen is the study of classical military strategy and tactics in order to apply them to business operations. . . .

It has been reported that one of the largest advertising companies in Japan has even made these books compulsory reading for all its employees.

Long centuries of tight tribal organization now stand the Japanese in very good stead in the trade and commerce of the electric age. A few decades ago they underwent enough literacy and industrial fragmentation to release aggressive individual energies. The close teamwork and tribal loyalty now demanded by electrical intercom again puts the Japanese in positive relation to their ancient traditions. Our own tribal ways are much too remote to be of any social avail. We have begun retribalizing with the same painful groping with which a preliterate society begins to read and write, and to organize its life visually in three-dimensional space.

The search for Michael Rockefeller brought the life of a New Guinea tribe into prominent attention in *Life* a year ago. The editors explained the war games of these people:

The traditional enemies of the Willigiman-Wallalua are the Wittaia, a people exactly like themselves in language, dress and custom. . . . Every week or two the Willigiman-Wallalua and their enemies arrange a formal battle at one of the traditional fighting grounds. In comparison with the catastrophic conflicts of "civilized" nations, these frays seem more like a dangerous field sport than true war. Each battle lasts but a single day, always stops before nightfall (because of the danger of ghosts) or if it begins to rain (no one wants to get his hair or ornaments wet). The men are very accurate with their weapons—they have all played war games since they were small boys—but they are equally adept at dodging, and hence are rarely hit by anything.

The truly lethal part of this primitive warfare is not the formal battle but the sneak raid or stealthy ambush in which not only men but women and children are mercilessly slaughtered. . . .

This perpetual bloodshed is carried on for none of the usual reasons for waging war. No territory is won or lost; no goods or prisoners seized. . . . They fight because they enthusiastically enjoy it, because it is to them a vital function of the complete man, and because they feel they must satisfy the ghosts of slain companions.

These people, in short, detect in these games a kind of model of the universe, in whose deadly gavotte they can participate through the ritual of war games.

Games are dramatic models of our psychological lives providing release of particular tensions. They are collective and popular art forms with strict conventions. Ancient and non-literate societies naturally regarded games as live dramatic models of the universe or of the outer cosmic drama. The Olympic games were direct enactments of the *agon,* or struggle of the Sun god. The runners moved around a tract adorned with the zodiacal signs in imitation of the daily circuit of the sun chariot. With games and plays that were dramatic enactments of a cosmic struggle, the spectator role was plainly religious. The participation in these rituals kept the cosmos on the right track, as well as providing a booster shot for the tribe. The tribe or the city was a dim replica of that cosmos, as much as were the games, the dances, and the icons. How art became a sort of civilized substitute for magical games and rituals is the story of the detribalization which came with literacy. Art, like games, became a mimetic echo of, and relief from, the old magic of total involvement. As the audience for the magic games and plays became more individualistic, the role of art and ritual shifted from the cosmic to the humanly psychological, as in Greek drama. Even the ritual became more verbal and less mimetic or dancelike. Finally, the verbal narrative from Homer and Ovid became a romantic literary substitute for the corporate liturgy and group participation. Much of the scholarly effort of the past century in many fields has been devoted to a minute reconstruction of the conditions of primitive art and ritual, for it has been felt that this course offers the key to understanding the mind of primitive man. The key to this understanding, however, is so swiftly and profoundly re-creating the conditions and attitudes of primitive tribal man in ourselves.

The wide appeal of the games of recent times—the popular sports of baseball and football and ice hockey—seen as outer models of inner psychological life, become understandable. As models, they are collective rather than private dramatizations of inner life. Like our vernacular tongues, all games are media of interpersonal communication, and they could have neither existence nor meaning except as extensions of our immediate inner lives. If we take a tennis racket in hand, or thirteen playing cards, we consent to being a part of a dynamic mechanism in an artificially contrived situation. Is this not the reason we enjoy those games most that mimic other situations in our work and social lives? Do not our favorite games provide a release from the monopolistic tyranny of the social machine? In a word, does not Aristotle's idea of drama as a mimetic reenactment and relief from our besetting pressures apply perfectly to all kinds of games and dance and fun? For fun or games to be welcome, they must convey an echo of workaday life. On the other hand, a man or society without games is one sunk in the zombie trance of the automation. Art and games enable us to stand aside from the material pressures of routine and convention, observing and questioning. Games as popular art forms offer to all an immediate means of participation in the full life of a society, such as no single role or job can offer to any man. Hence the contradiction in "professional" sport. When the games door opening into the free life leads into a merely specialist job, everybody senses an incongruity.

The games of a people reveal a great deal about them. Games are a sort of artificial paradise like Disneyland, or some Utopian vision by which we interpret and complete the meaning of our daily lives. In games we devise means of non-specialized participation in the larger drama of our time. But for civilized man the idea of participation is strictly limited. Not for him the depth participation that erases the boundaries of individual awareness as in the Indian cult of *darshan,* the mystic experience of the physical presence of vast numbers of people.

A game is a machine that can get into action only if the players consent to become puppets for a time. For individualist Western man, much of his "adjustment" to society has the character of a personal surrender to the collective demands. Our games help both to teach us this kind of adjustment and also to provide a release from it. The uncertainty of the outcomes of our contests makes a national excuse for the mechanical rigor of the rules and procedures of the game.

When the social rules change suddenly, then previously accepted social manners and rituals may suddenly assume the stark outlines and the arbitrary patterns of a game. The *Gamesmanship* of Stephen Potter speaks of a social revolution in England. The English are moving toward social equality and the intense personal competition that goes with equality. The older rituals of long-accepted class behavior now begin to appear comic and irrational, gimmicks in a game. Dale Carnegie's *How to Win Friends and Influence People* first appeared as a solemn manual of social wisdom, but it seemed quite ludicrous to sophisticates. What Carnegie offered as serious discoveries already seemed like a naïve mechanical ritual to those beginning to move in a milieu of Freudian awareness charged with the psychopathology of everyday life. Already the Freudian patterns of perception have become an outworn code that begins to provide the cathartic amusement of a game, rather than a guide to living.

The social practices of one generation tend to get codified into the "game" of the next. Finally, the game is passed on as a joke, like a skeleton stripped of its flesh. This is especially true of periods of suddenly altered attitudes, resulting from some radically new technology. It is the inclusive mesh of the TV image, in particular, that spells for a while, at least, the doom of baseball. For baseball is a game of one-thing-at-a-time, fixed positions and visibly delegated specialist jobs such as belonged to the now passing mechanical age, with its fragmented tasks and its staff and line in management organization. TV, as the very image of the new corporate and participant ways of electric living, fosters habits of unified awareness and social interdependence that alienate us from the peculiar style of baseball, with its specialist and positional stress. When cultures change, so do games. Baseball, that had become the elegant abstract image of an industrial society living by split-second timing, has in the new TV decade lost its psychic and social relevance for our new way of life. The ball game has been dislodged from the social center and been conveyed to the periphery of American life.

In contrast, American football is nonpositional, and any or all of the players can switch to any role during play. It is, therefore, a game that at the present is supplanting baseball in general acceptance. It agrees very well with the new needs of decentralized team play in the electric age. Offhand, it might be supposed that the tight tribal unity of football would make it a game that the Russians would cultivate. Their devotion to ice hockey and soccer, two very individualist forms of game, would seem little suited to the psychic needs of a collectivist society. But Russia is still in the main an oral, tribal world that is undergoing detribalization and just now discovering individualism as a novelty. Soccer and ice hockey have for them, therefore, an exotic and Utopian quality of promise that they do not convey to the West. This is the quality that we tend to call "snob value," and *we* might derive some similar "value" from owning race horses, polo ponies, or twelve-meter yachts.

Games, therefore, can provide many varieties of satisfaction. Here we are looking at their role as media of communication in society as a whole. Thus, poker is a game that has often been cited as the expression of all the complex attitudes and unspoken values of a competitive society. It calls for shrewdness, aggression, trickery, and unflattering appraisals of character. It is said women cannot play poker well because it stimulates their curiosity, and curiosity is fatal in poker. Poker is intensely individualist, allowing no place for kindness or consideration, but only for the greatest good of the greatest number—the number one. It is in this perspective that it is easy to see why war has been called the sport of kings. For kingdoms are to monarchs what patrimonies and private income are to the private citizen. Kings can play poker with kingdoms, as the generals of their armies do with troops. They can bluff and deceive the opponent about their resources and their intentions. What disqualifies war from being a true game is probably what also disqualifies the stock market and business— the rules are not fully known nor accepted by all the players. Furthermore, the audience is too fully participant in war and business, just as in a native society there is no true art because *everybody* is engaged in making art. Art and games need rules, conventions, and spectators. They must stand forth from the over-all situation as models of it in order for the quality of play to persist. For "play," whether in life or in a wheel, implies *interplay*. There must be give and take, or dialogue, as between two or more persons and groups. This quality can, however, be diminished or lost in any kind of situation. Great teams often play practice games without any audience at all. This is not sport in our sense, because much of the quality of interplay, the very medium of interplay, as it were, is the feeling of the audience. Rocket Richard, the Canadian hockey player, used to comment on the poor acoustics of some arenas. He felt that the puck off his stick rode on the roar of the crowd. Sport, as a popular art form, is not just self-expression but is deeply and necessarily a means of interplay within an entire culture.

Art is not just play but an extension of human awareness in contrived conventional patterns. Sport as popular art is a deep reaction to the typical action of the society. But high art, on the other hand, is not a reaction but a profound reappraisal of a complex cultural state. Jean Genet's *The Balcony* appeals to some people as a shatteringly logical appraisal of mankind's madness in its orgy of self-destruction. Genet offers a brothel enveloped by the holocaust of war and revolution as an inclusive image of human life. It would be easy to argue that Genet is hysterical, and that football offers a more serious criticism of life than he does. Seen as live models of complex social situations, games may lack moral earnest-

ness, it has to be admitted. Perhaps there is, just for this reason, a desperate need for games in a highly specialized industrial culture, since they are the only form of art accessible to many minds. Real interplay is reduced to nothing in a specialist world of delegated tasks and fragmented jobs. Some backward or tribal societies suddenly translated into industrial and specialist forms of mechanization cannot easily devise the antidote of sports and games to create countervailing force. They bog down into grim earnest. Men without art, and men without the popular arts of games, tend toward automatism.

A comment on the different kinds of games played in the British Parliament and the French Chamber of Deputies will rally the political experience of many readers. The British had the luck to get the two-team pattern into the House benches, whereas the French, trying for centralism by seating the deputies in a semicircle facing the chair, got instead a multiplicity of teams playing a great variety of games. By trying for unity, the French got anarchy. The British, by setting up diversity, achieved, if anything, too much unity. The British representative, by playing his "side," is not tempted into private mental effort, nor does he have to follow the debates until the ball is passed to him. As one critic said, if the benches did not face each other the British could not tell truth from falsehood, nor wisdom from folly, unless they listened to it *all*. And since most of the debate must be nonsense, it would be stupid to listen to all.

The form of any game is of first importance. Game theory, like information theory, has ignored this aspect of game and information movement. Both theories have dealt with the information content of systems, and have observed the "noise" and "deception" factors that divert data. This is like approaching a painting or a musical composition from the point of view of its content. In other words, it is guaranteed to miss the central structural core of the experience. For as it is the *pattern* of a game that gives it relevance to our inner lives, and not who is playing nor the outcome of the game, so it is with information movement. The selection of our human senses employed makes all the difference say between photo and telegraph. In the arts the particular mix of our senses in the medium employed is all-important. The ostensible program content is a lulling distraction needed to enable the structural form to get through the barriers of conscious attention.

Any game, like any medium information, is

an extension of the individual or the group. Its effect on the group or individual is a re-configuring of the parts of the group or individual that are *not* so extended. A work of art has no existence or function apart from its *effects* on human observers. And art, like games or popular arts, and like media of communication, has the power to impose its own assumptions by setting the human community into new relationships and postures.

Art, like games, is a translator of experience. What we have already felt or seen in one situation we are suddenly given in a new kind of material. Games, likewise, shift familiar experience into new forms, giving the bleak and the blear side of things sudden luminosity. The telephone companies make tapes of the blither of boors, who inundate defenseless telephone operators with various kinds of revolting expressions. When played back this becomes salutary fun and play, and helps the operators to maintain equilibrium.

The world of science has become quite self-conscious about the play element in its endless experiments with models of situations otherwise unobservable. Management training centers have long used games as a means of developing new business perception. John Kenneth Galbraith argues that business must now study art, for the artist makes models of problems and situations that have not yet emerged in the larger matrix of society, giving the artistically perceptive businessman a decade of leeway in his planning.

In the electric age, the closing of the gaps between art and business, or between campus and community, are part of the overall implosion that closes the ranks of specialists at all levels. Flaubert, the French novelist of the nineteenth century, felt that the Franco-Prussian War could have been avoided if people had heeded his *Sentimental Education*. A similar feeling has since come to be widely held by artists. They know that they are engaged in making live models of situations that have not yet matured in the society at large. In their artistic play, they discovered what is actually happening, and thus they appear to be "ahead of their time." Non-artists always look at the present through the spectacles of the preceding age. General staffs are always magnificently prepared to fight the previous war.

Games, then, are contrived and controlled situations, extensions of group awareness that permit a respite from customary patterns. They are a kind of talking to itself on the part of society as a whole. And talking to oneself is a recognized form of play that is indispensable to any growth of self-confidence. The British and Americans have enjoyed during recent times an enormous self-confidence born of the playful spirit of fun and games. When they sense the absence of this spirit in their rivals, it causes embarrassment. To take mere worldly things in dead earnest betokens a defect of awareness that is pitiable. From the first days of Christianity there grew a habit, in some quarters, of spiritual clowning, of "playing the fool in Christ," as St. Paul put it. Paul also associated this sense of spiritual confidence and Christianity play with the games and sports of his time. Play goes with an awareness of huge disproportion between the ostensible situation and the real stakes. A similar sense hovers over the game situation, as such. Since the game, like any art form, is a mere tangible model of another situation that is less accessible, there is always a tingling sense of oddity and fun in play or games that renders the very earnest and very serious person or society laughable. When the Victorian Englishman began to lean toward the pole of seriousness, Oscar Wilde and Bernard Shaw and G. K. Chesterton moved in swiftly as countervailing force. Scholars have often pointed out that Plato conceived of play dedicated to the Deity as the loftiest reach of man's religious impulse.

Bergson's famous treatise on laughter sets forth the idea of mechanism taking over life-values as the key to the ludicrous. To see a man slip on a banana skin is to see a rationally structured system suddenly translated into a whirling machine. Since industrialism had created a similar situation in the society of his time, Bergson's idea was readily accepted. He seems not to have noticed that he had mechanically turned up a mechanical metaphor in a mechanical age in order to explain the very unmechanical thing, laughter, or "the mind sneezing," as Wyndham Lewis described it.

The game spirit suffered a defeat a few years ago over the rigged TV quiz shows. For one thing, the big prize seemed to make fun of money. Money as store of power and skill, and expediter of exchange, still has for many people the ability to induce a trance of great earnestness. Movies, in a sense, are also rigged shows. Any play or poem or novel is, also, rigged *to produce an effect*. So was the TV quiz show. But with the TV effect there is deep audience *participation*. Movie and drama do not permit as much participation as that afforded by the mosaic mash of the TV image. So great was the audience participation in the quiz shows that the directors of the show were prosecuted as con men. Moreover press and radio ad interests, bitter about the success of the new TV medium, were delighted to lacerate the flesh of their rivals. Of course, the riggers had been blithely unaware of the nature of their medium, and had given it the movie treatment of intense realism, instead of the softer mythic focus proper to TV. Charles Van Doren merely got clobbered as an innocent bystander, and the whole investigation elicited no insight into the nature or effects of the TV medium. Regrettably, it simply provided a field day for the earnest moralizers. A moral point of view too often serves as a substitute for understanding in technological matters.

That games are extensions, not of our private but of our social selves, and that they are media of communication, should now be plain. If, finally, we ask, "Are games mass media?" the answer has to be "Yes." Games are situations contrived to permit simultaneous participation of many people in some significant pattern of their own corporate lives.

The Ontology of Play*

EUGEN FINK

In an age characterized by the noise of the machine, the role of play in the structure of human life becomes more and more apparent. Not only the expert analysts of civilization, educators and specialists in anthropology as well are agreed on this point. Modern man himself has become aware of the importance of play. Contemporary literature and the passionate interest in games and sports are evidence enough. For modern man play is a vital-impulse with its own value and sphere of activity, participated in for its own sake. It is a kind of reward for the unpleasantness that goes with material progress in modern technocracy. It is also seen as a means of rejuvenating one's inner vitality, a return to the morning freshness of life at its origin, to the source of one's creative powers. In human history there have certainly been times a good deal more gay, more relaxed, more given to play than our own; when there was more play, when men had more leisure and were more familiar with the Muses. However, no other age has had so many possibilities and occasions for play. Never has there been such a systematic exploitation of life on a grand scale. Playfields and stadiums are in the original plans of cities. Games in vogue in different countries are brought to international com-

* From *Philosophy Today*, 4 (Summer, 1960), 95-110. English translation by Sister M. Delphine from *Oase des Glucks Gedanken zu einer Ontologie des Spiels*. Freiburg in Br.: Alber-Verlag, 1957.

petitions. Playing materials are mass-produced. But it is still in question whether our age has reached a deep understanding of the nature of play. Can we evaluate the many meanings of the term or thoroughly penetrate the aspect of being in the phenomenon-play? Do we know what constitutes play and specifies it from the philosophic point of view?

We want to consider that strange and very particular mode of being that characterizes the play of man, to conceptualize the elements that make up its being and give rough draft of the speculative concept of play. To some this subject may seem dry and abstract. We would surely prefer something of the very atmosphere of play with a lightness of touch in treating the subject, stressing its creative fullness, its overflowing richness and its inexhaustible attraction. A brilliant essay could be written, a game with the reader discovering the hidden sense of words and ideas through the surprise effect of a play on words; something pertaining to a literary *genre* rather than a treatise on play. In using a serious approach there is the feeling of betraying the very nature of play. Philosophy, as with Plato, has made contributions poetic-wise in the domain of speculative thought. A consideration of play in the same vein might achieve the same end, since the subject itself is provocative of a sublime play of the spirit. But such a treatment demands something of the Attic wit. Our consideration, therefore, will be simple, with no pretence to poetry. It will be in three parts: a preliminary characterization of the phenomenon-play; the analysis of its structure; the relation of play and being.

I.

Play is a vital fact which each of us knows subjectively. Everyone has taken part in play and can speak of it from experience. It is hardly necessary to make it the subject of scientific research to discover it and to disengage it from other phenomena. Play is universally known. Each of us understands it in its many forms. Our experience is all the evidence we need. Each of us has been a player. Moreover, familiarity with play is more than individual. It is a public act in which all can participate. Play is an accepted and ever recurring fact of the social world. We live through abandon[ing] ourselves to it, we recognize it as an ever possible act. Through play we find ourselves no longer imprisoned and isolated on our own individuality. In play we are assured of a social contact of particular intensity. All play, even that which seems to turn in upon oneself, such as that of the solitary child, has a social dimension. The fact that we actually live ourselves into the act of play, approaching it as something interior to ourselves, makes man as the subject of the attribute-play. However does man alone play? Can we say that animals play, the vitality of each living creature expressing itself exteriorly in a sort of joy of living? Biology, it is true, presents us with some interesting cases of animal behavior which occasionally resemble the play of human beings. It would be a mistake, however, to consider these on the same plane in terms of constituent elements, as if surface resemblance presupposes identity in mode of being. We can certainly formulate a biological concept of behavior in play which would link man and animal from the point of view of animality. But this would say nothing about the mode of being behind the exterior manifestations which resemble each other. We cannot proceed with the discussion from this point of view until the question of the ontological mode of being of man and animal is clarified. In our opinion human play possesses a meaning and exclusiveness of its own. Only a halting metaphor can be used to apply it to the case of either animals or the ancient gods. In the final analysis, what is important is the way in which the term "play" is applied, the fullness of meaning attributed to it, its delimitation in terms of reference, the conceptual penetration we give it.

We propose the question of human play,

beginning with the fact such as moments of play, we are freed by it, we understand it in our daily experience. Play does not enter into our lives as simply as vegetative processes. It is always a process that has a meaning, a lived experience. All our life consists in enjoying this act (which does not require reflexive consciousness). Generally, if we give ourselves over to play, we are far from reflection. And yet, all play presupposes the awareness of our own activity. There is a current and rather pedestrian view of play, a sort of vulgar interpretation: that play is nothing more than a phenomenon on the margin of human life, a peripheral fact, an occasional sort of thing. The more important moments of our existence lie elsewhere. We consistently hear it opposed to the serious occupations of life that are filled with a sense of responsibility; it is referred to as "recreation," "relaxation," and "diversion." It is claimed that life finds its fulfillment in the difficult pursuit of knowledge, in moral excellence or a professional attitude of mind, in prestige, in dignity and honor, in power, prosperity and similar goals. Play, on the other hand, seems to be like an occasional break, a pause that highlights the more genuine and serious aspects of life, like a dream opposed to being awake. From time to time, it is argued, man should slip from under the yoke of slavery, free himself from the shame of always starting over, lift the weight of the daily grind, quit watching the clock—for a more leisurely pace, perhaps even squandering time. In the economy of life "tension" alternates with "relaxation," business with leisure. We prescribe for ourselves "weeks of hard work" and "holidays for merry-making." Thus play seems to have a legitimate but quite restricted place in the vital rhythm man has set himself. Play is an *ergänzung*, a supplementary thing, a recreative pause, a surcease from burdens, a ray of light over the darker and severe landscape of life. By force of habit we limit play by contrasting it to the seriousness of life, to an attitude of moral commitment, to work—to all the prosaic things of reality. We identify it with frolic, with flight toward the regions of imagination, away from the hard realities of life to dreams and utopia. It exists just to keep man from succumbing to the modern world of work, from forgetting how to laugh amid moral rigorism, from becoming the prisoner to duty. Analysts of civilization recommend play to ward off disasters. It takes on a therapeutic value against the ills of the soul. But the question is, how does such advice understand the very nature of play? As a peripheral phenomenon in contrast to the serious? Can we never look at it except in terms of work, of a drive against odds? Is there not within us a little of that divine detachment of spirit, of the joyous buoyancy of play that joins us to the "birds of the air" and the "lilies of the field?" Is play only for preventing psychic disorders that trouble men in the modern world? As long as we accept such implications, "play and work," "play and the realities of life," play cannot be thought of in its proper sense and in its true ontological dimensions. It remains in the shadow of phenomena seemingly opposed to it, which obscure and deform it. It is considered as the non-serious, the non-obligatory, the non-authentic, as mere idleness. It is precisely by the very way in which its salutary effects are praised that we prove our estimation of it as a marginal phenomena, a peripheral counterbalance or as a sort of ingredient adding flavor to the insipidity of our existence.

It is even doubtful that such a view gives an adequate understanding of play as phenomenon. It is true that the behavior of adults shows less and less of the grace natural to play. Too often their games are nothing more than an organized escape from boredom. An adult seldom plays naturally. But for a child, play is the undisturbed center of existence. It is the very stuff of child-life. As age forces him to leave this center, the rude storms of life get the upper hand. Duty, care and work use up the vital energies of the adolescent. As the serious side of life asserts itself, the importance of play diminishes. We usually consider how we can educate the child to pass smoothly from a being who plays into one that works. We present work to the child under the aspect of play, as a methodical and disciplinary game where the burden becomes unnoticeably heavier little by little. The point is to keep a maximum of spontaneity, imagination and initiative as in play, to create a kind of joy in work. This well-known pedagogical experience is based on the general conviction that while play is inherent in man, especially during childhood, it occupies a less conspicuous place with the advancement of age. The play of the child shows more freely certain traits characteristic of human play. It is more ingenuous, less equivocal and dissimulating than the play of adults. The child knows little about the seduction of masquerading. It plays in all innocence. But how much hidden play is disguised in the serious affairs of the adult world, in honors, social conventions; how much hidden drama in the meeting of lovers. Everything considered, perhaps we would not want to say that ideal play is that of the child. The adult can also play, but in a different way that is more furtive, more masked. If we take our notion of play from the world of the child alone, we misunderstand its nature, fall into equivocation. In fact, the domain of play extends from the little girl's playing with a doll to the tragedy. Play is not only a peripheral manifestation of human life, it is not a contingent phenomenon that emerges upon occasion. In essence, it comes under the ontological dispositions of human existence. It is a fundamentally existential phenomenon. It is not derived from any other manifestation of life. To oppose play to any other phenomenon is to risk misunderstanding it. On the other hand, we must recognize that the fundamental phenomena which are decisive in human existence are all interlaced and intertwined. They never appear isolated or juxtaposed against one another. They interpenetrate, interinfluence. Each has a hold over the whole of man. To throw light upon the reciprocal influence of the moments of existence, the tensions and harmonies, is the task of an anthropology not limited to the description of biological, psychic and intellectual facts, but which penetrates by intuition the paradoxes of lived existence.

Man, at every stage of existence, is marked by the all-pervasive proximity of death, inescapable. And in so far as he has a body and sensitive life, he is affected by his relations to the earth which both resists him and yields its riches. The same is true of domination and love, all his dealings with his fellowmen. In his essence man is mortal; by nature he works, he struggles, and by the same count, he plays. Death, work, domination, love and play, these are the elements of the patterns which we find in human existence, so enigmatic and ambiguous. And if Schiller says, ". . . A man is whole only when he plays," it is also true to say that he is whole only when he works, struggles, opposes death and loves. We cannot draw up principles for an interpretation of human existence without referring to these fundamental phenomena. It will be sufficient to say in passing, though, that all of them are manifested in changing, enigmatically and ambiguous ways. The principal reason is that man is exposed and abandoned and at the same time watched over and protected. He is not completely carried along by instinct like the animal, nor is he as free as the immaterial angel. His is a freedom in the midst of a nature which binds him to an obscure tendency which permeates his being. And he simply integrates it into his knowledge of his own existence. On the other hand, free acts completely control his life. Because of this mingling of self-expression and repression, his existence is a continual tension within the self. We live within ourselves constantly preoccupied with ourselves. Only the vital being, of whom it can be said that "into his being he goes with his own being," can die, work, struggle, love and play. Only such a being is in touch with surrounding reality and the total environment—the world. To be related to self, to understand being and to reveal oneself to the world, this triple moment is known perhaps less easily in play than in the other fundamental phenomena of human existence.

But that is why play exists. It is act in its spontaneity, acting in its very activity, the living impulse. Play is life that moves within its own orbit. However, the moving forces of play do not coincide with the other forces of human life. For in all action other than play—whether it be the simple "praxis" which has its end in itself or the production of the artist (*poiesis*) where the end is the work—there is essentially implied a tendency toward the end of man, toward beatitude, toward *Eudaimonía*. We are busy finding the virtuous path to the fullness of life. For us life is a "task." Consequently, at no moment can we be said to have a place of rest. We are aware of the fact that we are "travelers." The violence of our vital project constantly lifts us out of the established moment to carry us toward a life of virtue and happiness. Thus we are compelled to attain *Eudaimonía,* though we are not in agreement as to what it is. We are not only moved by aspirations that uplift us, we are not at rest until we can give the one and only "interpretation" of this happiness. It is one of the paradoxes of human existence that in the incessant pursuit of *Eudaimonía* we never attain it; we cannot be happy in the sense of perfect achievement in this life. While we breathe, our life is caught in a vertiginous cascade. We are carried forward by the desire to perfect and complete our fragmentary being. We live in terms of the future. We experience the present moment as a preparation, as a stage, as a passing phase. This strange "futurism" of man's life is bound up with his fundamental character. We are not a simple fact like plants and animals. We force ourselves to find a "meaning" in our existence. We must understand the reason for our life on earth. It is a demon-like urge which drives man to search for an interpretation of his earthly journey, a passion of the soul. Something with-

in makes man search for the source of his grandeur as well as his misery. No other creature is troubled in his very being by the question of the mysterious meaning of his existence. The animal cannot and God has no need to ask the question. All human response to the question of the meaning of life means that man has an end which will finally be attained. With most men the position is not explicit, but their conduct is directed by the basic idea which they form of the "supreme good." The different ends which permeate our daily life are ordered in terms of a principle which harmonized their oppositions and indicates the final end. Particular ends are linked to what the community considers the absolute end of man.

Within this architectonic ordering of ends all human work is carried on. The serious side of life is developed, authentic attitudes are produced and confirmed. But the tragic element in man's situation is that he cannot guarantee in any absolute sense his final end by his own efforts. When the major question of his existence is brought up, he gropes in the night unless a superhuman power comes to his aid. That is why the confusion of Babel reigns among men as soon as we ask what can be the true end, the destination, the true happiness of human nature. This is also why unrest, anxiety and uncertainties are characteristic of human life.

But play fits into this situation in a way quite different from any other human activity. It stands out in remarkable relief to all that characterizes life teleologically. It cannot be expressed in terms of the architectonic complex of ends. It does not fall under the final end as do other actions. Its activity is not disturbed by the fundamental uncertainties which we take into account in interpreting happiness. If we compare play to the rest of life with its impetuous dynamism, its provoking orientation toward the future, play appears as a serene "presence" with a meaning sufficient to itself. It is like an oasis of happiness found in the desert of our questing, which in itself recalls the punishment of Tantalus. Play enraptures us. During play we are momentarily freed from the daily grind and, as it were, magically transported to another planet where life seems more light, more carefree, more happy. We often hear that play is a gratuitous activity, without finality. This is not exactly the case. Considered as a whole, play is determined by an internal end and we will discover in its different stages the particular ends which form a whole. However, the immanent end of play directed as that of the other activities man toward the supreme end. The activity of play has only internal finalities which do not transcend it. This brings to mind that particular form of play that is seen in terms of its physical attraction: military formation. For the sake of our well being, play is here found in an adulterated form, an activity in view of an end other than its own. Play is here in terms of ends extraneous to its nature and it is not easy to see just how much value comes from it as play. It is precisely because play in an unadulterated form is self-sufficient that it possesses a complete and firmly established meaning which makes it possible for man to find in it an asylum in time where time itself is no longer that torrent which carries us forward. It is rather a respite with a spark of eternity in it. It is apparently the child, therefore, who plays best. Again it is the child who knows that relation to time most intimately of which the poet Rilke speaks:

O childhood hours, behind whose make-believe
Was hid more than the past and before us lay
No future to contend. Though we dreamed, 'tis true
Of growing up and were perhaps in haste to be well grown,
More was it for the love of being those
Who had no other merit than being grown.
While yet not hid from life, we tasted joy
Which gives repose and were suspended thence
In an interval between the universe and play, a place,
From all eternity, chosen for the pure event.
(Rilke, *Duineser Elegien—*
Vierte Elegie)

For the adult, play is a strange oasis, a place of rest filled with dreaming along the relentless, pressing course of life. Play gives us a "presence." But it does not reach into the silent depths of the soul where we listen to the eternal breathing of the universe and contemplate pure images in the stream of passing things. Play is activity, creative force, and still it is near what is unchangeable and eternal. Play breaks the continuity of life's course, its coherence which determines the final end. It cuts across the groove in which life ordinarily runs. It sees things "at a distance." However, in seeming to subtract from the unified current of life, it sets up a relation in a meaningful manner: the representation which it gives of it. When, as is the custom, we do not restrict play by relating it to work, to reality, to the serious, to the authentic, we commit the fault of not placing it with the other phenomena of

existence. For play is itself a fundamental phenomenon of existence, just as original and basic in itself as death, work and domination. Only it is not linked to the other fundamental phenomena in a common pursuit of the ultimate end. It confronts them, as has been pointed out, to use them representationally. We play with the serious, the authentic, the real. We play with work and struggle, love and death. We even play with play.

II

Let us look at the matter a little more closely. In making the initial step in understanding this valuable concept of play, we must examine the articulations and the structure of the whole of play just as it is.

We can indicate at first sight, as an essential element of play, that it is a passion of the soul. We can say that all man is and does is colored by either one or the other states of the soul— joy, sadness or the gray tone of indifference. Play, at least in its source, has the coloring of joy. Joy reigns in it as undisputed master at each moment, carrying it forward and giving it wings. As soon as the joy is gone, the action disappears. This does not mean that throughout the duration of play we must be gay and in good humor. The joy arising from play is a singular pleasure, difficult to put your finger on. It does not resemble the pleasures of the senses in the relaxation of the body or the physical intoxication with speed. On the other hand, neither is it a purely spiritual delight, sheer intellectual joy. It is a joy rooted in a most special creative activity, open to many interpretations. It can include a profound sadness, a tragic suffering. It can embrace the most striking contraries. The pleasure which accompanies tragic action from one end to the other draws its power of ecstasy and emotion, mixed with terror and rapture, from the reign of the dreadful. The representation of horror is the source of the pleasure. Play transfigures even the mask of the Gorgon.

What is that strange pleasure which drastically mixes contraries, overlapping one with the other, leaving joy in the first place? However moved to tears we may be, we smile at the comedy and tragedy which are our life and which the play represents to us. Does the pleasure of play include the suffering and grief thus presented to us in this evocation because the action refers to past afflictions and time has softened them? Or is it that the turning back of the wheel of time alleviates the living bitterness, the sorrows formerly so real? By no means. In play we do not experience "real pain"—and, yet, the emotion of play gives rise to a strange type of pain which, actually but not really, moves us, seizes us, touches us, shakes us. The sorrow is only played, but even modified by play it is still a power that moves us. It has this capacity only because the delights of play include it. This delight is indispensable to the activity of play. We cannot compare it to other known forms of functional pleasure. It is true that we always feel a sense of well-being unrelated to any object whenever we do not submit our life passively but offer our being with spontaneous initiative, direct it in assuming responsibilities and mold it in creative processes. The creative quality of existence is in itself a "surge forward." But the fulfillment of play is accompanied by a pleasure which we cannot compare with the joys experienced in any other action or psychic urge. The pleasure in play is grounded not only in the element of creative spontaneity— it is also the ecstasy which accompanies our entry into any "universe," into the objective world. It is not only the pleasure experienced in playing, but a joyous attitude with regard to play as well.

A second step in studying the structure of play is to point out the meaning play establishes. Each type of play, as far as we can see, establishes a certain meaning. But purely physical movement, exercising arms and legs by repeating certain rhythms is not play in the strict sense of the word. It is simply confusing to call play such behavior as that of relaxing indulged in by young animals and children. These movements bring no meaning whatsoever to their author. We can speak of play only when the meaning of a specific end creatively accompanies such movements. Furthermore, in a particular game, we must distinguish between the intrinsic meaning of play —the meaningful bond between things, actions and played relations—and the external meaning, the meaning of play for those who initiate it and take part in it, as well as the meaning it is supposed to have for the spectators. It is evident that there are games which include spectators as spectators (such as games at the circus), and games which exclude them.

We might mention a third element in play: the community element. Play is a fundamental possibility of social life. To play is to play together, to play with others; it is a deep manifestation of human community. Play is not, as far as its structure is concerned, an individual and isolated action; it is open to our neighbor as partner. There is no point in underlining the fact that we often find solitary players playing alone at personal games, because the very meaning in play includes the possibility of other players. The solitary player is often playing with imaginary partners. The community of play does not necessarily require real persons present. It is enough for a real player to have a real game and not merely an imagined one.

Another essential element is that of the rule in play. Play is established by a commitment and bound to it; it is limited by whatever concerns the arbitrary modification of any action. It is not entirely free. There is no play without a commitment agreed upon and accepted. However, the rule of play is not a law; the commitment is not irrevocable. Even in the course of play, we can change the rule with the permission of partners. However, then the modified rule holds and fixes the course of what can be done by either. We all know the difference between traditional games where we adopt rules already formulated and the improvised games that are just made up. The community of play has to come to an agreement about the rules of the latter. We might expect these improvised games to be the most popular, since they leave the field open to imagination and permit the development and free reign of pure possibilities. But this is not necessarily the case. The act of being bound to a pre-established rule is often a positive experience with its own delights. This may seem strange, but it is explained by the fact that traditional games are often bound up with collective imagination, with self-commitments rooted in the deep primordial patterns of common experience. A number of children's games, which may seem naive, are in fact rudiments of certain magical practices of antiquity.

Each type of play demands equipment. Each of us knows about playthings, but it is still hard to define them. We do not have to enumerate all possible types, but we must know their nature or at least recognize that here is a problem. Playthings do not make up a definite world of their own, as is the case with things that are made. According to nature (in the larger sense of that which exists in itself), these are not artificial objects if man has not made them. It is only by his own work that man produces artificial things. He is the artisan (*technités*) of a human environment. He cultivates the earth, tames the animals, makes tools. A tool is an artificial thing that human work has formed. We can distinguish artificial things from natural things, but they are one and the same in being on the plane of the same universal reality which includes them all.

Though a plaything can be an artificial object, it is not necessarily so. Just a piece of wood, a fallen branch, can function as a doll. The hammer, which, by its very form, is the will of man imposed on an assemblage of wood and iron, belongs just as the wood, the iron, and the man himself, to one and the same order of reality. It is not so with playthings. Seen from the exterior, that is from the point of view of those who do not play, it is evidently a fragmentary object of the real world. It is simply something that holds a child's attention. The doll is a product of the toy industry, it is a mannequin made up of material and a piece of wire or of plastic. We can buy it at a certain price; it is merchandise. But seen with the eyes of a little girl who plays, the doll is a child and the small girl is its mother. Perhaps it is not as though the child thought the doll were actually a living child, for she is not under a false impression nor apt to confuse the nature of things. She possesses, on the contrary, a simultaneous knowledge of the doll as such and its meaning in play. The child who plays lives in two worlds. What makes a thing a toy—gives the essence of toy— is something rather magical. It endows an everyday thing with a kind of mysterious being. It is then infinitely more than a simple means of amusement, more than a thing which one must put together and keep in hand. Human play has need of playthings. Above all, in his specifically human actions, man is not free to bypass things. He needs them. He cannot ignore the hammer in his work, the sword for conquest, the couch for love, the lyre if he be a poet, an altar for religion— and playthings for play.

Each plaything symbolizes the totality of real things. To play is to take an explanatory attitude toward being at all times. Reality is concentrated in the plaything in the form of a single thing. All play is an attempt to have the plaything yield to the vital energy of man so that he might test symbolically the totality of the resistance of being. But human play not only comes under the magical intimacy with playthings. We must look a little closer at the notion of the player, for we are in the presence of a very particular type of "schizophrenia," of the duality of man; which of course is not pathological. The player who engages in play performs a precise action in terms of the real world, quite recognizable. However, as to the meaning and intrinsic context of play he assumes a role. It then becomes

necessary to distinguish between the real man who "plays" and the man charged with a role within the context of play. There is a real basis for saying that the player loses himself in his role. He lives his role with a very particular intensity and, for that reason, not in the manner of an hallucination where we cannot distinguish "reality" from "illusion." The player can renounce his role. Even at times he is necessarily engrossed, the consciousness of his double existence does not abandon him. He lives in two worlds, but not through distraction or want of concentration. The duality belongs to the very nature of play.

The structural elements we have thus listed are all present in the fundamental concept, "the world of play" (Spiel welt). All play is a magical creation in the world of play. It is here that the player assumes a role, that the community of play alternately distributes the roles, that the rules of play are imposed and that the plaything takes on meaning. The world of play is an imaginary sphere. It is a difficult problem, therefore, to clarify its essential structure. We play in the world which we call real, but in so doing, we create for ourselves another world, a mysterious one. This is not just nothing and still it is not something real either. In the world of play we act according to our role; but in this world imaginary persons live, as the "child" which takes on body and life, but which is nothing more than a doll or even a piece of wood in reality. In projecting a world of play, the player disguises himself as a creature of that "world," losing himself in the project, becoming that person whose role he has assumed and moving, for the present, in the midst of things and among partners who belong to such a world of play. Confusion might arise here for in imagination we think of things of the world of play in themselves as "realities" and even the distinction between reality and illusion can frequently be re-adjusted.

But it does not follow that the real things in our daily world are veiled or even masked by the superimposition of the world of play to the point that we no longer recognize them. This is not at all the case. The world of play does not interpose a wall between us and being that surrounds us. Strictly speaking, the world of play has neither place nor duration but operates in interior space and time proper to it. However when we play we use real time and have real space besides. But we do not pass by continuous transition from the space of the world of play to that we ordinarily occupy. The same holds for time. The strange interlacing of spheres of the world of reality and that of play cannot be explained by any other example known of spatial-temporal proximity. The world of play is not suspended in a domain of pure imagination. It always possesses a real theatre. However, it is never a real thing among other real things. But real objects are indispensable to it as props. This is to say that the imaginary character of the world of play cannot be reduced to purely subjective illusion, nor defined as fancy not affecting us except interiorly and unable to make its appearance in the world of real things.

We come now to the fundamental characteristics of play. Human play is a creation through the medium of pleasure of a world of imaginary activity. It is the singular joy of "appearances" (*Freud am Schein*). Play is always characterized by an element of representation. This element determines its meaning. It then effects a transfiguration; life becomes peaceful. We are freed little by little, and we eventually discover that we have been redeemed from the weight of real life. Play lifts us from a situation of fact, from an imprisonment depressing by nature, and by means of fantasy helps us enjoy passing through a multitude of "possibilities," without imposing on us the necessity of making a choice. In playing man lives out two extremes of existence. One puts man at the peak, gives him an almost unlimited power of creation, establishes a freedom that is impossible in reality. The player feels himself master of his own creations, play becomes a possibility scarcely limited by human freedom. At the highest point in play freedom prevails. But we also find in play the contrary of freedom (a facet of being taken perhaps from the real world) which can bring about a sort of alienation from enchantment, even to the point of coming under the demonical power of the mask. Play can conceal the Appolonian clarity of free ipseitas as well as the Dionysian inebriation which accompanies a certain abandonment of human personality.

Man's relationship to the enigmatic "appearances" of the world of play, to the sphere of the imaginary, is ambiguous. Play is a phenomenon for which we cannot easily find adequate categories. It is perhaps a dialectic much concerned with not reducing paradoxes to a dead level, which would let us for that very reason experience the tantalizing ambiguity of dialectic. The great philosophers have insisted on the eminent meaning of play. If common sense does not recognize this it is because play means nothing more to it than a lack of seriousness and authenticity, because it sees in play only pointless activity. Hegel, however, said that in its indifference and extreme lack of seriousness, play is the unique and most sublime expression of true seriousness. And Nietzsche in *Ecce homo*: "I do not know of any other method than play for facing the most important tasks."

Can play be explained if it is not seen purely and simply as an anthropological phenomenon? Could it be that our consideration has gone beyond man? Does this mean that we must study the behavior of play as it involves other creatures also? The problem is really that of knowing whether or not we can understand play in its ontological structure without limiting it by paying attention to the sphere of the imagination. Whether play is something man alone can do is a question which remains open and depends on whether man the player is still bound to the human world or if he has entered a superhuman world.

From the beginning, play is a symbolic act of representation, in which human life interprets itself. The most ancient games are magical rites, the principal liturgical cultures of primitive man, expressing his being-in-the-world in which he represents his destiny, commemorates the events of birth and death, weddings, war, the chase and work. The manner of symbolic representation in magical games draws its elements from the simple world around men just as he draws upon the nebula world of the imagination. In primitive times, play was not practiced so much as an act in its pleasure-giving aspect as is the case for those isolated individuals or groups, who periodically detach themselves from the social group to inhabit their own little isle of passing happiness. Originally, play was the strongest unifying force. It found a community quite different, it is true, from that of the living and the dead, the governing and governed, and even from that based on the family. The community of play of primitive man included all the forms and structures of common life that we have enumerated and it is called forth a reliving of all the elements of life. This reached its high point with the community keeping festival. The ancient feast was more than a popular form of rejoicing. It was reality itself —hoisted to the world of magic—the reality of human life in all its relations. It was a liturgical spectacle where man experienced the proximity of the gods, heroes, the dead, and where he found himself in the presence of all the beneficent and dreadful powers of the universe. Primitive play had deep contacts with religion. The community *en fête* included the spectators, the mysteries and epics; here the exploits and sufferings of the gods and man were passed in review. What was represented was nothing less than the whole universe.

III

In attempting to reduce the structure of play to a certain number of fundamental concepts, such as the climate of play, community of play, rule of play, plaything, and the world of play, we often used the word "imaginary." An equivalent of this word would be "appearing-to-be." However, in this term is concentrated a remarkable intellectual aporia, a dead end. We understand the term "appearing-to-be" in its strictest sense when it operates in concrete determined situations. But it is still a difficult and complicated matter to say precisely what we mean by it. The most important philosophic questions and considerations are involved in the most everyday things and words. The concept "appearing-to-be" is altogether as obscure and indefinable as that of "being." And the two concepts are related to each other in an intricate, perplexing and even inextricable manner; they interpenetrate and intermingle in their application. In thinking all this out we get further and further into the labyrinth of being.

With the question of the "appearing-to-be," in so far as it is related to the domain of human play, we ask a truly philosophic problem. Play is a "creative producing." Its effect, that is in the world of play, is exercised in the sphere of the "appearing-to-be," a field in which we can hardly expect consistency. The "appearing-to-be" of the world of play cannot be dismissed simply by calling it nothingness. We actually move within it when we play. We live in it at times, certainly, a life that is as free and fanciful as that of a dream, but sometimes we give ourselves over to it with genuine zeal. At times such an "appearing-to-be" has a presence and suggestive force more powerful and impressive than the everyday affairs which are quite banal in their very seriousness. What then is the imaginary? Where should we locate this strange "appearing-to-be," what is its condition? On the determination of that place and condition depends, in great part, the understanding of the ontological nature of play.

We are in a habit of speaking of "appearings-to-be" in various acceptations of the term. For example we think of the exterior appearance of things, of their superficial aspect, of their frontal aspect, and the like. That which "appears-to-be" pertains to what is represented as the shell pertains to the nut and as the substance to its manifestation. More often we speak of an "appearing-to-be" as in the case of a subjective fallacious interpretation, of an erroneous opinion, of a confused representation. In this case, we who interpret reality poorly have within us a semblance of that which resides in the subject. But there is also a subjective "appearing-to-be" with a legitimate place within us. It is a product of the imagination and does not relate to the categories of truth and error as does the representation and objects represented. With these abstract distinctions we can formulate our question. Which "appearing-to-be" is in the world of play? The outer appearance of things? A fallacious representative? A phantasm produced within us? We cannot deny that in play as a whole imagination manifests itself and unfolds in a particular manner. However, is the world of play nothing more than a product of the imagination? We might find an easy way out by saying that the imaginary universe that is the world of play exists uniquely in the human imagination and cite accordingly the case of hallucination and individual imaginary occurrences which have been united into collective hallucination or "intersubjective fantasy." To play, however, is always to use playthings. Anyone who considers the nature of a plaything will attest that play does not come into our life only in a purely interior manner, for it cannot escape being related to the objective exterior world. The world of play consists in both subjective elements of the imagination and objective ones or real ones. The imagination is known as the psychic power. We recognize the dream as such, as well as interior percepts and various imaginary contents. But what is the significance of the objective or real "appearing-to-be"? It exists in the reality of curious things which, without doubt, are in themselves something of reality and yet contain an element of un-reality. This may seem both singular and astounding. However, this is commonly known, though we ordinarily do not speak of it in terms so involved and abstract. All that is needed is simply images presented objectively, as a poplar on the shore of a lake projecting its reflection over the mirroring surface of the water. The reflections themselves make up part of the whole of the optic phenomenon, which consists of real things and the light which envelops them. Things exposed to light project their shadows. The trees on the bank are reflected in the lake, a smooth and highly polished metal surface reflects the objects around it. What is reflected? As an image it is real; it is a real reproduction of a real tree, its source. But it is "in" (or "as") image that the tree is represented. It appears to be on the surface of the water, but in such a way that it springs from the medium of the reflection and is not there in reality. An "appearing-to-be" of that nature is a kind of being apart. As a constituent element of its reality it possesses a specifically unreal element. It resides on the surface of another being which is simply real. The reflection of the poplar does not hide the surface of the water which it covers and which serves it as a mirror. The reflections of the poplar are there as reflection, a real thing known in itself and an unreal poplar in the sphere of reflection. This may seem sophistic; however, this fact is in everyone's experience and easily distinguished, for it is of daily occurrence. The doctrine of being of Plato, which has profoundly influenced western philosophy, takes as a model at decisive moments in his elucidation, the notion of image in terms of shadow and reflection and thus interprets the structure of the universe.

There is more than a simple parallel between the real "appearing-to-be" (reflection and the like), and the work of play. The real "appearing-to-be" is by priority counted as a structural element in the world of play. To play is real behavior, which includes what we call a "reflection," the attitudes which the world of play portions out according to the roles one takes in it. When all is taken together, the possibility that a man might construct a real "appearing-to-be" proper to a world of play depends, in a great measure, on the fact that such already exists in nature. Man not only knows how to make artificial objects generally, but he knows how to produce things which properly belong to an "appearing-to-be-that-is." He projects imaginary worlds of play. The little girl raises the body of material composition, doll, to the sphere of her "living child" by an act of the imagination, and with it herself to the role of "mother." Real things are always involved in the world of play; but they take on the character of a real "appearing-to-be"; sometimes even they are related to a subjective "appearing-to-be" which comes from the human spirit. Play is a creation with limited possibilities in the magical world of appearances.

The problem of explaining how the real and unreal interlace in human play requires untiring effort. The ontological determination of play leads us into the chief questions of philos-ophy, to being and nothingness, to the "appearing-to-be" and becoming. We see that the expression, "the unreality of play," is both hasty and superficial, unless we understood in terms of the enigmatic world of the imaginary. But we ask, what human and what cosmic meaning does the imaginary have? Is it a limited sphere in the midst of real things? Is the strange country of the unreal that exalted place where we call upon the presence of the "essences" of all things? In the magical reflection which operates in the world of play, it is not important which isolated object (for instance the plaything) becomes *symbol*. It represents another thing. Human play (even if we no longer recognize it as such after a while) is the symbolic action which puts us in the presence of the meaning of the world and of life.

The ontological problems which play poses for us do not exhaust the questions which have been brought up concerning the mode of being of the world of play and the symbolic value of playthings or of the action of play. In the history of thought, there have been those who have not only tried to conceive of the being of play, but also have dared an unheard of inversion of the process, concluding that the meaning of being springs from play. This is what I would call the speculative concept of play. In short, speculation is the characterization of the nature of being which takes for its point of departure the metaphorical consideration of a being. It is a conceptual formula of the essence of the world developed from a model within that world. The philosophers have used and perhaps abused models of this kind: Thales, of water; Plato, of light; Hegel, of the spirit; and the like. But the clarifying force of these models do not depend on the arbitrary choice of each of these thinkers. It is important, above all, to know whether or not the whole of being can be found in reflection in a single isolated being. In the measure in which the cosmos reproduces itself metaphorically in something which makes up part of the world in terms of structure and imprint, a key-phenomenon of philosophy can be discovered from which a speculative formula of the world can be developed.

As far as that goes, the phenomenon of play is a manifestation distinguished by the fundamental character of symbolic representation. Could it be then that play is a spectacle which might represent the whole as in parable, producing a clarifying and speculative metaphor of the world? One philosopher has had the courage or rather the temerity to think so. At the dawn of European thought, Heraclitus had formulated the sentence: "The course of the world is a child who plays at moving his pawns —a kingship of childhood." (Frg. 52, Diels.) And about twenty-five centuries later in the history of thought, we find in Nietzsche: "Becoming and disappearing, constructing and destroying, without moral imputation, with an eternally childlike innocence, behold what is reserved in the world for the souls that play, those of the artist and the child." "The world is Zeus' play . . ." (*Die Philosophie im tragischen Zeitalter der Griechen.*)

The depth of such a concept has its danger and its power of seduction, for it impels one to an esthetic interpretation of the world. But the strange formula of the world through which the totality of being is viewed as a game could be made to bear out the fact that play is not an anodyne, a peripheral or even puerile phenomenon, that we mortals are oriented to play in a mysteriously fundamental sense, precisely because we can produce magically things that testify to our creative power and our glory. If the essence of the world were thought of as play, it would follow that man is the only being with the immensity of the universe who can understand the infinity of the whole and respond accordingly. This is nothing more than recovering for himself the sense of the infinite, that eludes him, that he might be able to reach to the source of his being.

The opening up of human existence to the abyss of being by means of play, to being as a whole, which is also a form of play, is a theme that has inspired the poet Rilke:

So long as you merely catch, what you yourself
Toss up—'tis only skill of a minor range.
Only when you suddenly catch the ball
Thrown by your eternal Companion of play
Against your center, in a perfect gesture,
In one of the arcs, traced against the great bridge of God
Does knowing how to seize it really count—
Not for yourself, but for the world. And if, perchance,
You had the force and courage to return it—
Why then, 'tis no miracle;
But if lacking the strength and courage, you still
Have thrown it, as the Year throws the birds,
The south ward seeking birds to the Young Warmth
Of the land beyond the seas—then first
In such a feat do you really play the game.
Do not bother to throw again.
Be not disturbed. Out of your hands it springs
Like a Meteor and settles in its proper sphere.
(Translation of Fritz Klatt in *Rainer Maria Rilke,* p. 79.)

When philosophers and poets stress the power and meaning of play as a profound human reality, perhaps we should remember the words that warn us that we will not enter into the kingdom of heaven unless we become like little children.

Athletic Angst:
Reflections on the Philosophical Relevance of Play

DREW A. HYLAND

But yield who will to their separation,
My object in living is to unite
My avocation and my vocation
As my two eyes make one in sight.
Only where love and need are one
And the work is play for mortal stakes,
Is the deed ever really done
For Heaven and the future's sakes.
ROBERT FROST: "Two Tramps in Mud Time"

An acquaintance of mine once said to me, in a state of considerable inebriation, "The trouble with women is they've never been out on the football field, back on their own two yard line, where they had to hold the line or lose the game." There is probably a kernel of truth in this, not about women but about being on one's own two-yard line. For my own experience with athletics has suggested to me that many athletic contexts function in part as writ large images of life itself.[1] That is, many of the recurring themes and issues of life are magnified and made explicit in the exigencies of a contest. This occurs on several levels. On a fairly obvious level, one finds the element of competition, so integral an aspect of human being, brought forth as the urgent issue that it truly is. Similarly with such themes as working with others, being a good winner and loser, staying in good physical health, all the reasons usually and rightfully offered by proponents of athletics every day. But on a somewhat less obvious level, this same phenomenon occurs, this same magnification and making explicit of

the issues of life itself. To suggest just one example: I believe we could say that athletics offers something which, on the aesthetic level, all great art offers, and which may be one of the ultimate sources of appeal to human being of both art and athletics: a suggestion of a completed theme in a life characterized by the most radical and decisive partiality. It should be obvious how art accomplishes this. I am concerned here with athletics. It could be said that our day-to-day lives are shot through with incompleteness—jobs left undone, aspirations unfulfilled, human frustrations everywhere. In the midst of this partiality, athletics, by the very fact that the game has a time limit, impose a momentary if arbitrary possibility of completeness, a theme of life begun and brought to fulfillment. This completeness, even if arbitrary, may bring to focus that which is obscured by the seeming interminableness of our day-to-day lives. Part of my intention in this paper, then, is to offer some suggestions as to the relevance of athletic games to an understanding of man.

In this regard, it is worth noting that the various "movements" in contemporary philosophy have been notably silent on this theme, possibly because of their confidence that anything like athletics could in principle have nothing to do with the "serious" pursuit of philosophy, possibly also because their conception of philosophy makes them incapable of dealing with such a concrete aspect of human experience. In the case of at least one such "movement," however, "existential phenomenology" so-called, such silence is, unnecessary. For I believe that existential phenomenology, specifically of the sort which Heidegger employs in *Being and Time,* can reveal much about the meaning of athletics for human being. For that reason, I propose to adopt a basically Heideggerian framework in my analysis of athletics.

At the same time, I believe we shall discover in the Heideggerian mode, that the Heideggerian-phenomenological method itself both reveals and conceals, that while the method is certainly capable of revealing much, it also necessarily conceals certain aspects of experience. However, since I myself am not an existential phenomenologist (nor, to be sure, a positivist) I shall not hesitate to make a value judgment on this revealing-concealing of phenomenology. Instead of suggesting that it is a necessary consequence of the revealing-concealing happening of Being in the 20th century, I shall suggest that it constitutes an inadequacy in the Heideggerian-phenomenological method. I hope that my effort will be both play-ful and ser-ious.

One of the most common dissatisfactions with *Being and Time* (indeed with many works in existential phenomenology) is that notwithstanding its claim to analyze concrete human experience, it is an immensely abstract work. In an effort to overcome this objection, I propose to begin by taking as my material for analysis the most concrete possible experience, the last few minutes of a particular basketball game in which I played. An analysis of the structure of that experience will, I hope, be fruitful; but first, it will be necessary to describe in some detail that experience.

Basketball has long had a deep effect on my life, from my first game in junior high school, when I was sick with nervousness the whole day of the game, through high school, when on those occasions when we lost or I had not played well, I refused to attend school the following day, to my years on the basketball team at Princeton University, where the increase in my own maturity and the people with whom I played gave the game an even deeper, yet less obsessive meaning than it had had before. The particular experience I wish to relate involves the last basketball game I played for Princeton, in fact the last four minutes of that game. We had won the Ivy League all three years, but this was the best team on which I had ever played. After winning the League Championship, we had been

invited to play in the N.C.A.A. Championship tournament, and had surprised everyone except ourselves by winning the first game. We were now in the Eastern quarter-finals, against St. Joseph's College, a team which was ranked among the top ten teams in the country and which was heavily favoured to beat us. The game was played in the Coliseum in Charlotte, North Carolina, a large fieldhouse with 13,500 seats, all filled, of whom most of the occupants were cheering for us, probably because we were such underdogs. The game had gone much as expected. St. Joseph's, bigger and stronger, had gradually pulled away from us until, with about five minutes left in the game, they had about a fifteen point lead. I had been in and out of the game several times, alternating with my brother, Art, who, although only a sophomore, was already bigger and a much better player than me. With about five minutes left, Artie committed a foul, and the coach sent me in to take his place. I reported to the scorer and knelt along the sideline, awaiting a pause in the game so that I could go in. As I waited, the pressure relaxed a bit, and my thoughts wandered, not definitely, but vaguely, over my whole experience of basketball that year, and all years.

It had been an eventful and meaningful year. As a team, we had developed a closeness both on and off the court which is rare, and which probably added to our success. We were all clubmates in the same eating club. Three of the members of the team were also my roommates, a fourth, my brother. We had, through temperament and interest, I suppose, developed a friendship, a rapport, such as I had never known before, nor have I experienced since.

Early in the season, our coach, "Cappy" Cappon, whom we all respected in deep measure, suffered a severe heart attack, and we had won the league championship largely by remembering all that he had previously taught us. Coupled with that loss, Don Swan, the captain of the team and one of my roommates, had been nearly killed in the first tournament game two nights before when he had taken a spill and landed on his head. He was in a hospital in New York City.

I reflected, vaguely as I say, on these people, and on this game, as I awaited a pause. These reflections, and especially this game, were given a deeper sense of urgency and meaning by the realization that the four remaining minutes were probably to be the last four minutes I was to play with this team, these people. Yes, I would continue to live with them, probably know some of them all my life, even play basketball with them in pickup games; but not like this; not with the peculiar unity and closeness that had gone with playing on an organized team, where more, it seemed, was at stake. If I had had time to continue reflecting, I might have become sad; but the whistle blew, and I entered the game.

Even as Heidegger speaks of becoming "lost" in the world of the everyday[2]—and one must hope, despite his protestations, that he speaks here pejoratively—so one can speak of becoming "lost" in a game—but here most emphatically *not* pejoratively. In the game about which I am speaking I became "lost" in the game in the sense that my involvement was total. One thinks here of Spinoza's discussions of the unity of one's own power of activity with the power of activity of nature. All the activity of my mind, indistinguishable now from the activity of my body, became involved in, yet determinative of, the rhythm and flow of the game. I became part of it in a way that is not expressed by saying that *I* was a participant *in* the game. Such language draws too arbitrary a dichotomy between my own activity and the game. Perhaps foremost among the characteristics of these moments of total involvement is the extraordinary experience of time. The "hour" is irrelevant; so too is the arbitrary fact that a game happens to last forty minutes. Rather, time has its meaning almost exclusively in terms of past, present, and future. But what was "past" was only what I had done in the game so far, and it was all encompassed into what I did right now, and what I did now was wholly directed towards what was to happen in the next play. The past, present, future were all drawn into my activity, into the action of the game. I remember that we began to catch up, that we stole the ball again and again, scoring each time, so that the pandemonium of the spectators made more forceful still the excitement of knowing that we were catching up. I stole the ball twice, scored both times, told myself to push harder in effort. We kept coming on, driven by the intensity of the game itself, intensified still further by the indefinite but pervasive roar of the crowd. As St. Joseph's was coming down the court I ran to deflect a pass, turned to throw the ball to a teammate alone for an easy shot, when the referee's whistle blew. When I had hit the ball in the air and run to retrieve it, he called me for an "air dribble." St. Joseph's was awarded the ball. I looked at the scoreboard for the first time since I had entered the game. There were twelve seconds left. We were losing by one point, one point which, if the referee had not blown his whistle, would have been our margin of victory instead of defeat.

It was not really sadness that pervaded the locker room as we sat there, mostly glancing at each other and back to the floor. Nor was it depression, bitterness, anger. There was something simple, a sense of oneness between us all, which both had to terminate, yet would always be; a silent calmness that bespoke a deep realization; something had come to an end.

II

Let me begin my Heideggerian analysis of this experience with two of the most obviously relevant issues, space and time. To take space first; it is immediately clear, and commensurate with the phenomenological view, that what is not of primary relevance here is my so-called "objective" location in the world, that I happened to be in Charlotte, North Carolina (instead of, say, Durham), that the game was played in *this* gym (rather than some other) even that the size of the floor on which the game was played was some one hundred feet by fifty. Rather, the space that was relevant *was* relevant in terms of the game itself. In the game, I "experienced" space in terms of how tired I got running from one end to the other, whether a teammate was close enough to me to throw an accurate pass, whether I was close enough to the basket to take a good shot, and most significantly, in terms of the boundary lines, outside of which the game no longer continued. To be sure, at any given moment of the game I happened to be so many feet or inches from the basket, the boundaries, my teammates. But that was not the criterion in terms of which I decided to shoot or not, in terms of which the game took on its meaning. Far more relevant was whether I was across the half-court line, whether my teammate had a better opportunity for a shot. One can even go into some of the details of Heidegger's discussion of spatiality and note such factors as the "de-severing" character of my participation in the game and the "directionality" involved. What better examples could be given of the de-severing character of Dasein's spatiality than that of a basketball player dribbling up a court, looking to see what teammates are open for a shot, or whether an opening is developing for him to take a shot himself? Similarly, the directionality involved in the space of the game was understood in terms of which basket I was defending, which attacking, on which side of the court most of my teammates happened to be, whether the basket was to my right or left. It never occurs to any basketball player to determine that the "objective" direction of the basket he is defending is south-southwest. The space involved in this or any basketball game, then, reaffirms Heidegger's conviction that to the space which is experienced by Dasein in his being, "present-at-hand" "objective" space is often largely irrelevant. The space, the "Da" in which I found meaning was determined by the exigencies of the game itself.

Closely related to the spatiality of the game is what Heidegger would call the ready-to-hand character of the equipment used. An "objective" observer might note that the circumference of all regulation basketballs is 22 inches, that every basket is 10 feet high, that every regulation basketball floor is made of wood. But because of the nature of the game every basketball player is sensitive to a whole range of factors which an objective observer might consider insignificant and perhaps even unnoticeable. The relative resilience of the floor, the "feel" of the backboard, the lighting in the gym, the slipperiness of the ball take on great importance only because of the nature of the game. One's "circumspective concern" in the game determines the "meaning" of the equipment we employ, and indeed of our environment. Basketball, or any game, exemplifies this clearly.

It is equally clear that the phenomenological account of time is relevant to my basketball experience. As I indicated earlier, anything like "objective" time cannot possibly account for my experience of time in the game. The game must have taken about two hours to play. Of what relevance is that? In that game, the past, present, and future were not disjuncted and understood as something separate from *me*. Rather, past, present, and future were understood as gathered together in a unity which was the unity of the game, and of my activity in the game. The "past" of the game was brought into the present as what I was doing *now*. My particular activity now *was* only as the action of the game *was*, and the action of the game always culminated in the present. Likewise, the future was gathered into the present in that all my activity was directed fully to the future, but to the *future* of the *game*, and of my continued activity in that game. Any athlete knows what I mean here. As I played, I played always *toward*

what was to be next, not any definite shot or act, but toward any possibility that the game—and I—would realize. But all this direction, *to* what was to be, out of what had been, was gathered into my playing as I was playing *now*. Thus, I did not, so to speak, pause and calculate my next move, I *played*, and my play was the game and what was to be the game. At the same time, in broader terms, I had a "history," a past which included my long interest in basketball, which had contributed to my being in that situation, in that game. Still, and in keeping with Heidegger's analysis, it was the future toward which my being in the game was primarily oriented. This phenomenon corresponds clearly, to that future orientation of Dasein which Heidegger calls "Being-ahead-of-itself."

Heidegger's notion of "Being-ahead-of-itself" clarifies another aspect of my experience, which he would refer to as possibility. He characterizes human being as ahead-of-itself in terms of its possibilities for being, possibilities which are *definite* possibilities for being what we are. This very sense of Being-ahead-of-itself in terms of possibility pervaded my basketball experience. All my playing was ahead-of-itself because it was directed towards the possibilities of my activity, which would in turn be the possibilities of the game. These possibilities were definite, definite because I was playing *basketball*, in this place, with *this* team. They were not definite in the sense of a calculated "next I will take a jump shot," which would have been, in terms of the basketball game, an inauthentic experience. Yet the experience that I described was not *just* in terms of the four minutes of the game, but included my reflections before I entered, and afterwards, in the locker room. On this level too, possibility was essential to my experience. For as I knelt along the sideline, although my reflections were of what had been (e.g., my coach's heart attack, my teammates), these reflections were occasioned by and directed to the future. They served to intensify my awareness of what was about to happen, intensify my awareness of the possibilities, definite possibilities for being, which lay immediately before me. At the same time they centered on one possibility which was in a way the most definite of all, that it might be the last time I played on this team, with these people. My reflections centered on the impending finality of the game I was about to play, and this sense of finality gave my playing a sense of urgency and importance which it had rarely had before. On a slightly different level, within the game itself, all my activity was directed and determined by one ultimate possibility, that the game would end. This, clearly, is the ultimate possibility of any game, but it is only in moments of genuine involvement that one becomes aware of its importance.

Both these levels of possibility have close affinities with what Heidegger calls the ultimate possibility of authentic being, Being-towards-death. It was Heidegger's remarks on Being-toward-death that clarified for me the overpowering sense of urgency that I found in that basketball game. For authentic Dasein, Being-toward-death is the ultimate possibility, the possibility that *that* Dasein might not be. This possibility is certain, yet indefinite as to the "when" it might become actual. Likewise in my experience, the possibility of *not* playing on that team, *not* playing that game, was certain, yet indefinite, in the same way. Similarly, the fact that the game had an imminent end gave it the meaning it had. A game without an end would be no game. The same may be true with life. And this brings us to the closely related issue of finitude.

One of the most important aspects of Being-toward-death as Heidegger elucidates it is its revelation of Dasein's radical finitude. Heidegger's remarkable suggestion is that our lives take on the meaning they do precisely *because* we are finite, not in spite of that fact. This finitude has two basic modes, first, that Dasein dies, second, that Dasein is always situated, always in a "place," and so never in all places. Again, the basketball game reflects and magnifies both forms. The finitude of the situation is manifested, for example, in the boundaries of the court. When I or the ball move outside the boundaries, the game stops. The court is the basketball player's "world." Its meaning *is* within the bounds. Similarly my own limitations had a special meaning in that situation. At 5'9", I necessarily was a backcourt man rather than a center or forward. My possibilities in the game were therefore oriented *toward*, say, playmaking, and so *not* toward, say, rebounding. The finitude of death is reflected in the fact that the game has an end, and that the end is that *toward* which, in a sense, the game is always oriented. It is nowadays fashionable to congratulate such men as Sartre and Camus for their sunburst that because we die, life is absurd. The basketball game suggests precisely the reverse. The end makes the game rational. Death enables life to take on meaning. It offers us a stake.[3]

It should now be obvious that the kind of involvement that I had in that game was a mode of what Heidegger calls Being-in-the-world.[4] I suggested in my description of the game that the relation between my own being and that of the game was much too close to say simply that *I* played *in* the game. Such a distinction suggests too radical a separation between *my* being as one *playing* the game and the game itself. *My* being *was* in terms of my being part of the game, and the game took on *its* being in part, through my participation. To suggest that that game, or any game, was nothing more than the activity of each of the players would be inadequate; equally so to suggest that the game would have had the same meaning, or any meaning, *without* those particular players in that particular situation. Heidegger takes pains to show that the existentiale of Being-in-the-world undercuts the traditional subject-object dichotomy, that such a dichotomy can only inadequately characterize Dasein's relation to world. He is surely right.

There remains to discuss the importance in that game of the other players involved, both my own teammates and those against whom I was competing. The relevant Heideggerian existentiale here is of course "Being-with" as "solicitude" (Fürsorge). I indicated in my descriptive section that the friendships that had developed on our team contributed to the deep meaning that the game had for me. If we had not been so close, the game undoubtedly would not have had the same meaning, much less if I had been playing with strangers in a pickup-game. Similarly, my orientation toward the St. Joseph players was a mode of solicitude. I did not, could not, comport myself toward them as I did toward, say, the ball and the basket. They were other human beings, some of whom, in fact, I had come to know personally in other encounters. Yet here we were playing against them, in competition with them. It would be easy but entirely wrong to identify this encounter in competition as alienation. For even in this "important" game, as in all genuine play, the competition is never alienation. If it were, cheating, trying to hurt the opposing players, in short doing *anything* to overcome the opposition, understood, supposedly, as a threat to my freedom, would be the rule. Instead, even though both teams wanted to win, rules were still obeyed; the competition was in a context of sportsmanship. It is not too much to say that the sportsmanlike competition in athletics offers to man an image of an encounter with others, even in the context of opposition, which avoids the alienation on which Heidegger and the other existentialists dwell so endlessly, and about which I shall presently have more to say.[5]

III

By now I hope these two broad theses have been established: that reflection on play *is* relevant to a philosopher's effort to "know thyself" and that the Heideggerian phenomenological framework is indeed insightful in such a reflection. In establishing these theses, it might also have come to pass that play itself was established as a worthwhile enterprise, even if only to offer material for phenomenological investigations. But to paraphrase Heidegger, "revealing and concealing are the same," and so it is necessary to observe that the Heideggerian phenomenological method does not seem to adequately "save the phenomena." Let us begin with a more thorough discussion of "Being-with."

It is important to note that Heidegger includes his discussion of Being-with and solicitude in his analysis of Dasein's "everydayness,"[6] and that when he turns to a consideration of "authenticity" all Dasein's relations to other Dasein become utterly irrelevant as, with anticipatory resoluteness, he faces up alone to his ultimate possibility.[7] The strong implication is that all of one's dealings with others, either positive or negative, are part of the mode of "Fallenness," when one is lost in the world of "The They." When one is "Angst-voll" and authentic, one is *alone*. This attitude, even more forcefully maintained by Sartre, contributes to the excessive emphasis in existentialism on individuality, and the accompanying conviction that the most fundamental stance that man takes toward "the other" is one of *alienation*. But my basketball experience suggests quite the contrary.[8] It is fair to say that that experience, indeed my whole experience with basketball, has been deeply meaningful, meaningful in good measure because it led me to precisely that experience—a recognition of one's kind of being—which the existentialists call authentic. Yet that meaning occurred in such a way that possibly the most decisive "existentiale" was Being-with. The meaning of that game arose in terms of positive modes of Being-with, both the close kinship with my teammates and the sportsmanlike competition with the opposition. This is confirmed by a consideration of the ways in which these positive modes can on occasion break down in athletic competition. Fights occasionally break out; but when such explicit modes of alienation arise, the game is ruined, it is not a game

at all. Similarly, we have all known and been frustrated by teammates who would seem to play with anticipatory resoluteness; for them their teammates pale into irrelevance; not how the team fares but how *they* do is what counts. They play alone, no matter how many men are on the team. But interestingly, we would likely label this mode of participation inauthentic. The Heideggerian account reverses itself. The basketball game situation suggests that meaning of the sort that leads to authentic awareness of one's human being can occur in a context of encounter, an encounter which can even be a kind of opposition.[9] Perhaps the most obvious of all instances of this is love. But what we call love is one manifestation of what Plato called Eros. It has been noted,[10] and it is true enough, that Eros is Plato's word for Care (Sorge). But in substituting the "value-less" phenomenologically descriptive term Care for Plato's Eros, Heidegger apparently neglected to remember that the intentional character of human being means that man's most primordial mode of being is encounter, and that that encounter can be, and often is, with other men.

But possibly the most conspicuous absence from my Heideggerian analysis has been the all-important mood of Angst. There was no sense of being in a nothing in which I no longer had anything to hold onto for support. To be sure, my orientation was toward the possibility of the end of the game and of an experience—I have already related this to Being-toward-death—but I was hardly "Angst-voll." There was no calling into question of my whole being, no placing it in a void where it would be forced to take on itself or else fall back into the tranquillity of "The They." An essential characteristic of Angst as Heidegger describes it is uncanniness (Unheimlichkeit), a feeling of "no longer being at home." Yet in that experience playing basketball—and to judge from my own experience, in all play situations—I *was* at home in a way that I rarely feel at other times. Playing first reveals to man the true meaning of home.

And yet, if "authenticity" as the term is used by the existentialists signifies something like self-knowledge, a coming to explicit awareness of one's own being and one's place in "world," then my experience with basketball, my experience with play generally, has been "authentic." I hope I have documented this. If so, then it looks as if "Angst" is not the only stance out of which authenticity can emerge. Two questions then arise; what is there about the play experience which can occasion self-knowledge, and why might Heidegger have overlooked it? I have already adumbrated my answer to the first question. Certainly *one* of the primary qualities of my experience which contributed to its having meaning was what Heidegger calls Being-with, or what I have called encounter. That game—all games—offered a variety of encounters which were revelatory of the kind of encounter possible in life, and so revelatory of one of the primary modes of human being. While many aspects of that experience closely fit Heidegger's framework, it now appears that Angst was replaced by encounter. And this is possible, again, because both Angst and encounter are manifestations, one "positive," one "deficient," of what Plato called Eros.

If so, why does Heidegger overlook this possibility? I believe we can now suggest the following. Interpreters of Heidegger, both pro and con, invariably follow the master in making the mood of Angst the core of any discussion about "authenticity." But it now seems that Angst is derivative of a far more basic position of Heidegger's. I refer to the fact that, by placing his prior discussion of Being-with in his analysis of "Everydayness" and so in *contrast* to authenticity, Heidegger has closed off in advance the possibility of encounter as a path to authenticity. I have already related this to an excessive concern with individuality on the part of Heidegger and the existentialists generally. Once encounter has been closed off as an occasion for authenticity, Heidegger is thrown back on the individual as the sole source of insight into himself. And what is that mood in which we are literally most individual? It is *loneliness,* which comes close to being a synonym for Angst. Thus the crucial reason for the centrality of Angst in Heidegger's analysis—and at the same time, as the play experience reveals, his decisive mistake—is the prior rejection of encounter as one other possible occasion for that self-knowledge in which we truly become "our own selves" (eigentlich).[11]

IV

Heidegger rightly characterizes genuine self-awareness, as man's mode of transcendence. And it is transcendence, precisely the finite transcendence of self-awareness, that breaking free from the unreflective wallowing in our everyday lives, that man seeks and sometimes precariously achieves. No doubt Angst can occasion that transcendence. But I believe I have documented another occasion for a similar transcendence in my analysis of one experience in a basketball game. In play, we break out of the rut of our ordinary lives. Play thus adumbrates a deeper way of breaking out of the everyday, of achieving transcendence through encounter. Perhaps this is what Plato had in mind when he has the Athenian Stranger say in the *Laws* (803[e]ff)

I say that it is necessary to be serious with the serious, but not with the not serious. God is worthy of all seriousness, but man is constructed as a plaything of the gods, and this is the best part of him. All of us then, men and women alike, must live accordingly and spend our lives making our play as beautiful as possible . . . We should pass our lives playing certain games—sacrifice, song, and dance—so that we will be able to propitiate the gods . . .

In play man comes close to the gods. No wonder, then, that Socrates characterizes all writing about the highest things, poetry and even philosophy as the playfulness of the most intelligent men (*Phaedrus,* 276[d]ff, 277[e]ff). The Platonic reaction to Heidegger and the other Angst-voll existentialists might well be: "These men are playing; but not playfully."

FOOTNOTES

1. But like all images, both similar and different, and so doubly instructive.
2. Heidegger, Martin, *Sein und Zeit,* Tubingen: Max Nemeyer Verlag, 1963, e.g. pp. 126, 127.
3. Death, obviously enough, does not guarantee meaning. My point is that only within a context of finitude is it *possible* for meaning to emerge.
4. I believe one could go further, and characterize my being in that game as "ahead-of-itself-Being-already-in (the world) as Being-alongside (entities encountered within-the-world)" or Care (*Sein und Zeit,* e.g. p. 192—Marquarrie and Robinson translation, p. 237).
5. It is tempting to close by noting an analogue to Heidegger's distinction between authenticity and inauthenticity, namely, that many, indeed most of my basketball experiences were not as meaningful as this one, although others were. But I suspect the primary difference, in such a non-intellectual activity as basketball was one of intensity of immersion. To be sure, "authentic" experiences, for Heidegger, are probably more intense than the "tranquilizing" placidness of the everyday. But to characterize intensity as the *essential* difference between authenticity and inauthenticity would be to commit the same mistake as those who claim that because, under conscious-expanding drugs, colors, sounds, and feelings are more intense, they are therefore more authentic. That view is vulgar, even if not always hedonism.

6. Heidegger, *Sein und Zeit*, p. 113 ff.

7. *Ibid.*, p. 235 ff, p. 305 ff, et al.

8. Others have generalized this, I believe rightly, to all play. Cf. Wm. Sadler, "Play: A Basic Human Structure Involving Love and Freedom," in *Review of Existential Psychology and Psychiatry*, Volume VI, No. 3, Fall, 1966, p. 242. One might argue that the play situation is irrelevant because not as real, not as important as our "working" lives, when we are *serious* (and grim). I hope my discussion has already refuted this. But in any case, such a concession to the Protestant Ethic hardly becomes the Neo-Paganism of our post-Christian "happening."

9. Gabriel Marcel has brought home forcefully a similar point against Sartre, but in a different way. Cf. "Existence and Human Freedom" in *The Philosophy of Existentialism*, New York: Citadel Press, pp. 46-90.

10. Rosen Stanley, "Heidegger's Interpretation of Plato" in *The Journal of Existentialism*, Volume VII, No. 28, Summer, 1967, p. 279.

11. In this regard, it is instructive to consider Socrates, whose explicit and constant endeavor was to know himself, but who nevertheless spent his life talking to—and loving—other people. From the absence of Angst from my basketball experience, the absence of such concomitant themes as "guilt" and "anticipatory resoluteness" becomes understandable.

Play and Sport*

JEAN-PAUL SARTRE

There remains one type of activity which we willingly admit is entirely gratuitous; the activity of *play* and the "drives" which relate back to it. Can we discover an appropriative drive in sport? To be sure, it must be noted first that play as contrasted with the spirit of seriousness appears to be the least possessive attitude; it strips the real of its reality. The serious attitude involves starting from the world and attributing more reality to the world than to oneself; at the very least the serious man confers reality on himself to the degree to which he belongs to the world. It is not by chance that materialism is serious; it is not by chance that it is found at all times and places as the favorite doctrine of the revolutionary. This is because revolutionaries are serious. They come to know themselves first in terms of the world which oppresses them, and they wish to change this world. In this one respect they are in agreement with their ancient adversaries, the possessors, who also come to know themselves and appreciate themselves in terms of their position in the world. Thus all serious thought is thickened by the world; it coagulates; it is a dismissal of human reality in favor of the world. The serious man is "of the world" and has no resource in himself. He does not even imagine any longer the possibility of *getting out of* the

* Reprinted by permission of Philosopical Library, Inc. from *Being and Nothingness* by Jean-Paul Sartre, translated by Hazel E. Barnes, © Copyright, 1956, by Philosophical Library Inc., New York.

world, for he has given to himself the type of existence of the rock, the consistency, the inertia, the opacity of being-in-the-midst-of-the-world. It is obvious that the serious man at bottom is hiding from himself the consciousness of his freedom; he is in *bad faith* and his bad faith aims at presenting himself to his own eyes as a consequence; everything is a consequence for him, and there is never any beginning. That is why he is so concerned with the consequences of his acts. Marx proposed the original dogma of the serious when he asserted the priority of object over subject. Man is serious when he takes himself for an object.

Play, like Kierkegaard's irony, releases subjectivity. What is play indeed if not an activity of which man is the first origin, for which man himself sets the rules, and which has no consequences except according to the rules posited? As soon as a man apprehends himself as free and wishes to use his freedom, a freedom, by the way, which could just as well be his anguish, then his activity is play. The first principle of play is man himself; through it he escapes his natural nature; he himself sets the value and rules for his acts and consents to play only according to the rules which he himself has established and defined. As a result, there is in a sense "little reality" in the world. It might appear then that when a man is playing, bent on discovering himself as free in his very action, he certainly could not be concerned with *possessing* a being in the world. His goal, which he aims at through sports or pantomime or games, is to attain himself as a certain being, precisely the being which is in question in his being.

The point of these remarks, however, is not to show us that in play the desire to *do* is irreducible. On the contrary we must conclude that the desire to do is here reduced to a certain desire to be. The act is not its own goal for itself; neither does its explicit end represent its goal and its profound meaning; but the function of the act is to make manifest and to present to *itself* the absolute freedom which is the very being of the person. This particular type of project, which has freedom for its foundation and its goal, deserves a special study. It is radically different from all others in that it aims at a radically different type of being. It would be necessary to explain in full detail its relations with the project of being-God, which has appeared to us as the deep-seated structure of human reality. But such a study can not be made here; it belongs rather to an *Ethics* and it supposes that there has been a preliminary definition of nature and the role of purifying reflection (our descriptions have hitherto aimed only at *accessory* reflection); it supposes in addition taking a position which can be *moral* only in the face of values which haunt the For-itself. Nevertheless the fact remains that the desire to play is fundamentally the desire to be.

Thus the three categories "to be," "to do," and "to have" are reduced here as everywhere to two; "to do" is purely transitional. Ultimately a desire can be only the desire *to be* or the desire *to have*. On the other hand, it is seldom that play is pure of all appropriative tendency. I am passing over the desire of achieving a good performance or of beating a record which can act as a stimulant for the sportsman; I am not even speaking of the desire "to have" a handsome body and harmonious muscles, which springs from the desire of appropriating objectively to myself my own being-for-others. These desires do not always enter in and besides they are not fundamental. But there is always in sport an appropriative component. In reality sport is a free transformation of the worldly environment into the supporting element of the action. This fact makes it creative like art. The environment may be a field of snow, an Alpine slope. To see it is already to possess it. In itself it is already apprehended by sight as a symbol of being.[1] It represents pure exteriority, radical spatiality; its undifferentiation, its monotony, and its whiteness manifest the absolute nudity of substance; it is

[1] See section III.

the in-itself which is only in-itself, the being of the phenomenon, which being is manifested suddenly outside all phenomena. At the same time its *solid* immobility expresses the permanence and the objective resistance of the In-itself, its opacity and its impenetrability. Yet this first intuitive enjoyment can not suffice me. That pure in-itself, comparable to the absolute, intelligible plenum of Cartesian extension, fascinates me as the pure appearance of the not-me; What I wish precisely is that this in-itself might be a sort of emanation of myself while still remaining in itself. This is the meaning even of the snowmen and snowballs which children make; the goal is to "do something out of snow"; that is, to impose on it a form which adheres so deeply to the matter that the matter appears to exist for the sake of the form. But if I approach, if I want to establish an appropriative contact with the field of snow, everything is changed. Its scale of being is modified; it exists bit by bit instead of existing in vast spaces; stains, brush, and crevices come to individualize each square inch. At the same time its solidity melts into water. I sink into the snow up to my knees; if I pick some up with my hands, it turns to liquid in my fingers; it runs off; there is nothing left of it. The in-itself is transformed into nothingness. My dream of appropriating the snow vanishes at the same moment. Moreover *I do not know what to do* with this snow which I have just come to see close at hand. I can not get hold of the field; I can not even reconstitute it as that substantial total which offered itself to my eyes and which has abruptly, doubly collapsed.

To ski means not only to enable me to make rapid movements and to acquire a technical skill, nor is it merely to *play* by increasing according to my whim the speed or difficulties of the course; it is also to enable me to *possess* this field of snow. At present *I am doing something to it.* That means that by my very activity as a skier, I am changing the matter and meaning of the snow. From the fact that now in my course it appears to me as a slope to go down, it finds again a continuity and a unity which it had lost. It is at the moment connective tissue. It is included between two limiting terms; it unites the point of departure with the point of arrival. Since in the descent I do not consider it in itself, bit by bit, but am always fixing on a point to be reached beyond the position which I now occupy, it does not collapse into an infinity of individual details but is *traversed toward* the point which I assign myself. This traversal is not only an activity of movement; it is also and especially a synthetic activity of organization and connection; I spread the skiing field before me in the same way that the geometrician, according to Kant, can apprehend a straight line only by drawing one. Furthermore this organization is marginal and not focal; it is not for itself and in itself that the field of snow is unified; the goal, posited and clearly perceived, the object of my attention is the spot at the edge of the field where I shall arrive. The snowy space is massed underneath implicitly; its cohesion is that of the blank space understood in the interior of a circumference, for example, when I look at the black line of the circle without paying explicit attention to its surface. And precisely because I maintain it marginal, implicit, and understood, it adapts itself to me, I have it well in hand; I pass beyond it toward its end just as a man hanging a tapestry passes beyond the hammer which he uses, toward its end, which is to nail an arras on the wall.

No appropriation can be more complete than this instrumental appropriation; the synthetic activity of appropriation is here a technical activity of utilization. The upsurge of the snow is the matter of my act in the same way that the upswing of the hammer is the pure fulfillment of the hammering. At the same time I have chosen a certain point of view in order to apprehend this snowy slope: this point of view is a determined *speed,* which emanates from me, which I can increase or diminish as I like; through it the field traversed is constituted as a definite object, entirely distinct from what is would be at another speed. The speed organizes the ensembles at will; a specific object does or does not form a part of a particular group according to whether I have or have not taken a particular speed. (Think, for example, of Provence seen "on foot," "by car," "by train," "by bicycle." It offers as many different aspects according to whether or not Béziers is one hour, a morning's trip, or two days distant from Narbonne: that is, according to whether Narbonne is isolated and posited for itself with its environs or whether it constitutes a coherent group with Béziers and Sète, for example. In this last case Narbonne's *relation to the sea* is directly accessible to intuition; in the other it is denied; it can form the object only of a pure concept.) It is I myself then who give form to the field of snow by the free speed which I give myself. But at the same time I am acting upon *my matter.* The speed is not limited to imposing a form on a matter given from the outside; it *creates* its matter. The snow, which sank under my weight when

I walked, which melted into water when I tried to pick it up, solidifies suddenly under the action of my speed; it supports me. It is not that I have lost sight of its lightness, its non-substantiality, its perpetual evanescence. Quite the contrary. It is precisely that lightness, that evanescence, that secret liquidity which hold me up; that is, which condense and melt in order to support me. This is because I hold a special relation of appropriation with the snow: *sliding.* This relation we will study later in detail. But at the moment we can grasp its essential meaning. We think of sliding as remaining on the surface. This is inexact; to be sure, I only skim the surface, and this skimming in itself is worth a whole study. Nevertheless I realize a synthesis which has depth. I realize that the bed of snow organizes itself in its lowest depths in order to hold me up; the sliding is action *at a distance;* it assures my mastery over the material without my needing to plunge into that material and engulf myself in it in order to overcome it. To slide is the opposite of taking root. The root is already half assimilated into the earth which nourishes it; it is a living concretion of the earth; it can utilize the earth only by making itself earth; that is, by submitting itself, in a sense, to the matter which it wishes to utilize. Sliding, on the contrary, realizes a material unity in depth without penetrating farther than the surface; it is like the dreaded master who does not need to insist nor to raise his voice in order to be obeyed. An admirable picture of power. From this comes that famous advice: "Slide, mortals, don't bear down!" This does not mean "Stay on the surface, don't go deeply into things," but on the contrary, "Realize syntheses in depth without compromising yourself."

Sliding is appropriation precisely because the synthesis of support realized by the speed is valid only for the slider and during the actual time when he is sliding. The solidity of the snow is effective only for me, is sensible only to me; it is a secret which the snow releases to me alone and which is already no longer true *behind my back.* Sliding realizes a strictly individual relation with matter, an historical relation; the matter reassembles itself and solidifies in order to hold me up, and it falls back exhausted and scattered behind me. Thus by my passage I have realized that which is unique *for me.* The ideal for sliding then is a sliding which does not leave any trace. It is sliding on water with a rowboat or motor boat or especially with water skis which, though recently invented, represent from this point of view the ideal limit of aquatic sports. Sliding on snow is already less perfect; there is a trace behind me by which I am compromised, however light it may be. Sliding on ice, which scratches the ice and finds a matter already organized, is very inferior, and if people continue to do it despite all this, it is for other reasons. Hence that slight disappointment which always seizes us when we see behind us the imprints which our skis have left on the snow. How much better it would be if the snow re-formed itself as we passed over it! Besides when we let ourselves slide down the slope, we are accustomed to the illusion of not making any mark; we ask the snow to behave like that water which secretly it is. Thus the sliding appears as identical with a continuous creation. The speed is comparable to consciousness and here symbolizes consciousness.[2] While it exists, it effects in the material the birth of a deep quality which lives only so long as the speed exists, a sort of reassembling which conquers its indifferent exteriority and which falls back like a blade of grass behind the moving slider. The informing unification and synthetic condensation of the field of snow, which masses itself into an instrumental organization, which is *utilized,* like the hammer or the anvil, and which docilely adapts itself to an action which understands it and fulfills it; a continued and creative action on the very matter of the snow; the solidification of the *snowy mass* by the sliding; the similarity of the snow to the water which gives support, docile and without memory, or to the naked body of the woman, which the caress leaves intact and troubled in its inmost depths—such is the action of the skier on the real. But at the same time the snow remains impenetrable and out of reach; in one sense the action of the skier only develops its *potentialities. The skier makes it produce* what it can produce; the homogeneous, solid matter releases for him a solidity and homogeneity only through the act of the sportsman, but this solidity and this homogeneity dwell as properties enclosed in the matter. This synthesis of self and not-self which the sportsman's action here realizes is expressed, as in the case of speculative knowledge and the work of art, by the affirmation of the right of the skier over the snow. It is *my* field of snow; I have traversed it a hundred times; a hundred times I have through my speed effected the

birth of this force of condensation and support; it is *mine.*

To this aspect of appropriation through sport, there must be added another—a difficulty overcome. It is more generally understood, and we shall scarcely insist on it here. Before descending this snowy slope, I must climb up it. And this ascent has offered to me another aspect of the snow—resistance. I have realized this resistance through my fatigue, and I have been able to measure at each instant the progress of my victory. Here the snow is identical with *the Other,* and the common expressions "to overcome," "to conquer," "to master," etc. indicate sufficiently that it is a matter of establishing between me and the snow the relation of master to slave. This aspect of appropriation which we find in the ascent, exists also in swimming, in an obstacle course, etc. The peak on which a flag is planted is a peak which has been *appropriated.* Thus a principal aspect of sport—and in particular of open air sports—is the conquest of these enormous masses of water, of earth, and of air, which seem *a priori* indomitable and unutilizable; and in each case it is a question of possessing not the element for itself, but the type of existence in-itself which is expressed by means of this element; it is the homogeneity of substance which we wish to possess in the form of snow; it is the impenetrability of the in-itself and its nontemporal permanence which we wish to appropriate in the form of the earth or of the rock, etc. Art, science, play are activities of appropriation, either wholly or in part, and what they want to appropriate beyond the concrete object of their quest is being itself, the absolute being of the in-itself.

Thus ontology teaches us that desire is originally a desire *of being* and that it is characterized as the free lack of being. But it teaches us also that desire is a relation with a concrete existent in the midst of the world and that this existent is conceived as a type of in-itself; it teaches us that the relation of the for-itself to this desired in-itself is appropriation. We are, then, in the presence of a double determination of desire: on the one hand, desire is determined as a desire to be a certain being, which is the *in-itself-for-itself* and whose existence is ideal; on the other hand, desire is determined in the vast majority of cases as a relation with a contingent and concrete in-itself which it has the project of appropriating.[3]

---

[2] We have seen in Part Three the relation of motion to the for-itself.

[3] Except where there is simply a *desire to be*— the desire to be happy, to be strong, etc.

Man Alone*

WILLIAM A. HARPER

Of late it has become increasingly difficult for man to become aware of his unique existence. He is constantly being categorized, functionalized, labeled, and numbered. He is a passive witness to the demise of his own uniqueness and to the extinction of his own being. Man is handing over his personal identity in exchange for the comfort and security afforded him in the Heideggerian *they*. It is this notion of personal identity with which I am here concerned, a notion that can be likened to asking the question: "Who am I, really?" It is the intention of this article to demonstrate that because the asking of the question "Who am I?" presupposes *that I am*, it is first necessary to become aware of my existence (that I am) before I can consider answering the proposed question of personal identity. And it will be suggested that man's relative aloneness in sport can provide an opportunity for seizing upon the awareness of one's own unique existence.

The surrendering of one's self can be no better explicated than by reference to the "official dossier" as characterized by Marcel,[4] in which the essence of a human being is reduced to a few pages of paper: pages indicating his name, his address, his financial standing, his vocation, and his physical characteristics:

The point here is not only to recognize that the human, all too human, powers that make up my life no longer sustain any practical distinction

between myself and the abstract individual all of whose "particulars" can be contained on the few sheets of an official dossier, but that this strange reduction of a personality to an official identity must have an inevitable repercussion on the way I am forced to grasp myself. . . . What does a creature who is thus pushed about from pillar to post, ticketed, docketed, labeled, become, for himself and in himself?[4:36]

The submerging of the individual identity attains an even more crucial position in the metaphysics of Heidegger,[2] where I (*Dasein*) am absorbed and hiding in the everyday world of the *they*. *Dasein* is captive in the everyday through the phenomena of idle talk, curiosity, and ambiguity whereby I tend to seek anonymity in holding the public values and championing the everyday knowledge:

In utilizing public means of transport and in making use of information services such as the newspaper, every Other is like the next. This Being-with-one-another dissolves one's own Dasein completely into the kind of being of the "Others," in such a way, indeed, that the Others, as distinguishable and explicit, vanish more and more. In this inconspicuousness and unascertainability, the real dictatorship of the "they" is unfolded. We take pleasure and enjoy ourselves as *they* (man) take pleasure; we read, see, and judge about literature and art as *they* see and judge; likewise we shrink back from the "great mass" as *they* shrink back; we find "shocking" what *they* find shocking.[2:164]

The I is lost in the averageness of the *they*, in the publicness of the Other. And this public-

* From *Quest*, XII (May, 1969), 57-60.

ness controls the way in which everything (both the world and I) is interpreted; it is never wrong. For Heidegger, "everyone is the other, and no one is himself."

And still another voice adding support to the case for the "surrendering of self" and the difficulty in maintaining one's personal identity, is that of Jean-Paul Sartre.[3] The everyday man, according to Sartre, who is in a state of self-deception (bad faith) by public demand, abandons his own unique individuality in fulfilling a particular function:

Let us consider the waiter in a cafe. His movement is quick and forward, a little too precise, a little too rapid. He comes toward the patrons with a step a little too quick. He bends forward a little too eagerly; his voice, his eyes express an interest a little too solicitous for the order of the customer. Finally there he returns, trying to imitate in his walk the inflexible stiffness of some kind of automaton while carrying his tray with the recklessness of a tight-rope walker by putting it in a perpetually unstable, perpetually unbroken equilibrium which he perpetually reestablishes by a light movement of the arm and hand. All his behavior seems to us a game. He applies himself to chaining his movements as if they were mechanisms, the one regulating the other; his gesture and even his voice seem to be mechanisms; he gives himself the quickness and pitiless rapidity of things. He is playing; he is amusing himself. But what is he playing? We need not watch long before we can explain it: he is playing *at being* a waiter in a cafe.[3:255-256]

For Sartre, society (Heidegger's *they*) demands that he fulfill his function and that he limit himself to his function. Self-deception is maintained when man is not what he is.

Since the common denominator in the three aforementioned descriptions of the abrogation of the self is a state of being whereby man is as others wish him to be, it must now be relatively apparent that to seek an answer to the question "Who am I, really?" is a project guided by uncertainty, ambiguity, and mystery. The man who seeks an answer is condemned to struggle, sentenced to tentativeness. And yet the search goes on. Men want to know. Therefore, it would seem that the initial undertaking is by far the most crucial: man must *become aware* of his unique existence (that he is). Man must realize *that he is* before he can attempt an understanding of *who he is*. And it is in a state of aloneness, a state of solitary presence within-one's-self, that one may realize his uniqueness. Being alone is not dependent upon physical isolation. I can be "with others" while locked in a closet, and I can be with myself in a room full of people.

Being alone is, in a sense, a oneness; a singularity; a unity within one's self. And in being aware of this whole or total state one can truly understand *that he is*.

Man is alone in sport. When he is actively involved, his personal success or failure depends solely upon him. The man in sport cannot shirk being alone; he cannot defer this state in preference for a public substitution. His only choice is to play or not to play. If he chooses the former, he is condemned to solitude. However, an awareness of this single state is by no means guaranteed. True, the realization of his isolation belongs only to the participating man himself, but this awareness is not a cognitive, predetermined choice. The feeling is not easy to come by. Many times this revealing understanding comes about when a man does not fulfill his expected potential, an experience more than merely isolating:

For Manager Brown, getting along is making do with the material at hand—of which the best is schizophrenic Snoopy, who sometimes imagines he is an alligator but steals second base like a lion. A second worthy principle is tolerance. It is horrible, sure, to see easy fly balls muffed, but horribler yet to muff them yourself.[7:46-51]

Only those who are less than perfect in the athletic endeavor can understand what it means to drop a fly ball, miss an easy lay-up, double fault on set point, or pull a six-inch birdie putt. The experience is indeed individualizing.

Many other times it may be the acceptance of personal responsibility which opens one up to knowing that he is. And it is the *awareness* of this personal responsibility which characterizes the man who really knows he is alone in the sport experience. In his aloneness the obligation to himself distinguishes his sport experience from the "other" determined experiences of the everyday world. And it is this reliance upon his own special capabilities and potentials, and not the public panaceas, that allows the sport participant to realize his unique individuality. In an awareness of his personal responsibility, Rick Barry, a professional basketball player, says the following:

"There are a lot of guys who work hard at defense, they play you close and they make you work for every shot. But it all comes down to whether you can put them in or not. In the final analysis, it is not them stopping you but *you* missing it." He kept talking in the second person, but as he went on and expanded, the "you" seemed to contract more and more from the general to the personal.[1:32-35]

In short, the occasion of this awareness may be any immediate happening. It may be the loneliness of the cross-country bicyclist; the suffering of the long distance runner; the pain and agony of the mile runner; the physical beating taken by the boxer; or the frequent "hits" received by participants in contact sports. It may also be the elation in winning; the deep despair of losing; the nervous tension and excitement before a competition; the fear of an opponent; the battle against nature; the freedom of movement; or the frightening realization of one's mortality that comes in facing death:

Auto racers, they defy death. I stare it right in the face. I believe we were born dead. I did not ask to be put on earth. I have accepted the fact that dying is a part of living.[5:60-70]

Evel Knievel, the motorcycle jumper who plans to jump the Grand Canyon on a jet propelled bike, went on to say, "My thing is a serious thing. . . . I'm awful nervous . . . [but] I'm really doing what I'm doing."

The occasions are many; the feeling is real. It is for man himself, in the end, to realize himself as man, to shake himself loose from his death grip on the averageness of the everyday, and to *be*. In the aloneness of sport man is potentially able to realize that he is— that he is unique—that there is no other person like him in the world. He is, and that in itself is important. One must imagine that Don Schollander, captain of the Yale swimming team and winner of four gold medals in the 1964 Olympics, has loosened his grip on publicness, when, in rejecting functionalization, he describes well the task before each man:

I don't call myself a swimmer at all. I'm a person who happens to swim. . . . Before you decide how you want to live your life, you must look at yourself and *attempt* to know yourself. I look at myself as a person who is trying to develop as an individual. It's been important to me throughout my life to be much more than a student, to be much more than an athlete, to be much more than anything.[6:24-34]

Whether he is hurling a javelin, soaring off a ski-jump, performing a double back flip off a diving board, or screaming towards earth in a free fall sky dive, man is alone. He is beyond the world of public determinations; of official identities; of functions; of self-deceptions and of everydayness. And in the solitary state of oneness, man can meet himself. Whether he meets a friend or a complete stranger, he very suddenly knows *that he is*.

REFERENCES

1. Deford, Frank. "Razor-cut Idol of San Francisco," *Sports Illustrated,* February 13, 1967, 32-35.
2. Heidegger, Martin. *Being and Time,* translated by J. Macquairre and E. Robinson. New York: Harper and Brothers, 1962.
3. Kaufmann, Walter. *Existentialism from Dostoevsky to Sartre.* Cleveland: World Publishing Co., 1956.
4. Marcel, Gabriel. *The Mystery of Being:* Volume I, *Reflection and Mystery.* Chicago: Henry Regnery and Co., 1950.
5. Rogin, Gilbert. "He's Not a Bird, He's Not a Plane," *Sports Illustrated,* February 5, 1968, 60-70.
6. Rogin, Gilbert. "Is Schollander a Swimmer?," *Sports Illustrated,* April 1, 1968, 24-34.
7. Schulz, Charles. "The Woes of a Peanut Manager," *Sports Illustrated,* June 20, 1966, 46-51.

Play, the Game, and the Generalized Other*

GEORGE HERBERT MEAD

We were speaking of the social conditions under which the self arises as an object. In addition to language we found two illustrations, one in play and the other in the game, and I wish to summarize and expand my account on these points. I have spoken of these from the point of view of children. We can, of course, refer also to the attitudes of more primitive people out of which our civilization has arisen. A striking illustration of play as distinct from the game is found in the myths and various of the plays which primitive people carry out, especially in religious pageants. The pure play attitude which we find in the case of little children may not be found here, since the participants are adults, and undoubtedly the relationship of these play processes to that which they interpret is more or less in the minds of even the most primitive people. In the process of interpretation of such rituals, there is an organization of play which perhaps might be compared to that which is taking place in the kindergarten in dealing with the plays of little children, where these are made into a set that will have a definite structure or relationship. At least something of the same sort is found in the play of primitive people. This type of activity belongs, of course, not to the everyday life of the people in their dealing with the objects about them—there we have a more or less definitely developed self-consciousness—but in their attitudes toward the forces about them, the nature upon which they depend; in their attitude toward this nature which is vague and uncertain, there we have a much more primitive response; and that response finds its expression in taking the rôle of the other, playing at the expression of their gods and their heroes, going through certain rites which are the representation of what these individuals are supposed to be doing. The process is one which develops, to be sure, into a more or less definite technique and is controlled; and yet we can say that it has arisen out of situations similar to those in which little children play at being a parent, at being a teacher—vague personalities that are about them and which affect them and on which they depend. These are personalities which they take, rôles they play, and in so far control the development of their own personality. This outcome is just what the kindergarten works toward. It takes the characters of these various vague beings and gets them into such an organized social relationship to each other that they build up the character of the little child.[1] The very introduction of organization from outside supposes a lack of organization at this period in the child's experience. Over against such a situation of the little child and primitive people, we have the game as such.

The fundamental difference between the game and play is that in the latter the child must have the attitude of all the others involved in that game. The attitudes of the other players which the participant assumes organize into a sort of unit, and it is that organization which controls the response of the individual. The illustration used was of a person playing baseball. Each one of his own acts is determined by his assumption of the action of the others who are playing the game. What he does is controlled by his being everyone

* From *Mind, Self and Society from the Standpoint of a Social Behaviorist.* Edited by Charles W. Morris. Chicago: University of Chicago Press, 1959. Copyright © 1934 by the University of Chicago. All rights reserved, published December, 1934. Reprinted by permission of the University of Chicago Press.

[1] "The Relation of Play to Education," *University of Chicago Record,* I (1896-97), 140 ff.

else on that team, at least in so far as those attitudes affect his own particular response. We get then an "other" which is an organization of the attitudes of those involved in the process.

The organized community or social group which gives to the individual his unity of self may be called "the generalized other." The attitude of the generalized other is the attitude of the whole community.[2] Thus, for example, in the case of such a social group as a ball team, the team is the generalized other in so far as it enters—as an organized process or social activity—into the experience of any one of the individual members of it.

If the given human individual is to develop a self in the fullest sense, it is not sufficient for him merely to take the attitudes of other human individuals toward himself and toward one another within the human social process, and to bring that social process as a whole into his individual experience merely in these terms: he must also, in the same way that he takes the attitudes of other individuals toward himself and toward one another, take their attitudes toward the various phases or aspects of the common social activity or set of social undertakings in which, as members of an organized society or social group, they are all engaged; and he must then, by generalizing these individual attitudes of that organized society or social group itself, as a whole, act toward different social projects which at any given time it is carrying out, or toward the various larger phases of the general social process which constitutes its life and of which these projects are specific manifestations. This getting of the broad activities of any given social whole or organized society as such within the experiential field of any one of the individuals involved or included in that whole is, in other words, the essential basis and prerequisite of the fullest development of that individual's self: only in so far as he takes the attitudes of the organized social group to which he belongs toward the organized, co-operative social activity or set of such activities in which that group as such is engaged, does he develop a complete self or possess the sort of complete self he has developed. And on the other hand, the complex co-operative processes and activities and institutional functionings of organized human society are also possible only in so far as every individual involved in them or belonging to that society can take the general attitudes of all other such individuals with reference to these processes and activities and institutional functionings, and to the organized social whole of experiential relations and interactions thereby constituted—and can direct his own behavior accordingly.

It is in the form of the generalized other that the social process influences the behavior of the individuals involved in it and carrying it on, i.e., that the community exercises control over the conduct of its individual members; for it is in this form that the social process or community enters as a determining factor into the individual's thinking. In abstract thought the individual takes the attitude of the generalized other[3] toward himself, without refer-

---

[2] It is possible for inanimate objects, no less than for other human organisms, to form parts of the generalized and organized—the completely socialized—other for any given human individual, in so far as he responds to such objects socially or in a social fashion (by means of the mechanism of thought, the internalized conversation of gestures). Any thing—any object or set of objects, whether animate or inanimate, human or animal, or merely physical—toward which he acts, or to which he responds, socially, is an element in what for him is the generalized other; by taking the attitudes of which toward himself he becomes conscious of himself as an object or individual, and thus develops a self or personality. Thus, for example, the cult, in its primitive form, is merely the social embodiment of the relation between the given social group or community and its physical environment—an organized social means, adopted by the individual members of that group or community, of entering into social relations with that environment, or (in a sense) of carrying on conversations with it; and in this way that environment becomes part of the total generalized other for each of the individual members of the given social group or community.

[3] We have said that the internal conversation of the individual with himself in terms of words or significant gestures—the conversation which constitutes the process or activity of thinking—is carried on by the individual from the standpoint of the "generalized other." And the more abstract that conversation is, the more abstract thinking happens to be, the further removed is the generalized other from any connection with particular individuals. It is especially in abstract thinking, that is to say, that the conversation involved is carried on by the individual with the generalized other, rather than with any particular individuals. Thus it is, for example, that abstract concepts are concepts stated in terms of the attitudes of the entire social group or community; they are stated on the basis of the individual's consciousness of the attitudes of the generalized other toward them, as a result of his taking these attitudes of the generalized other and then responding to them. And thus it is also that abstract propositions are stated in a form which anyone—any other intelligent individual—will accept.

ence to its expression in any particular other individuals; and in concrete thought he takes that attitude in so far as it is expressed in the attitudes toward his behavior of those other individuals with whom he is involved in the given social situation or act. But only by taking the attitude of the generalized other toward himself, in one or another of these ways, can he think at all; for only thus can thinking—or the internalized conversation of gestures which constitutes thinking—occur. And only through the taking by individuals of the attitude or attitudes of the generalized other toward themselves is the existence of a universe of discourse, as that system of common or social meanings which thinking presupposes at its context, rendered possible.

The self-conscious human individual, then, takes or assumes the organized social attitudes of the given social group or community (or of some one section thereof) to which he belongs, toward the social problems of various kinds which confront that group or community at any given time, and which arise in connection with the correspondingly different social projects or organized co-operative enterprises in which that group or community as such is engaged; and as an individual participant in these social projects or co-operative enterprises, he governs his own conduct accordingly. In politics, for example, the individual identifies himself with an entire political party and takes the organized attitudes of that entire party toward the rest of the given social community and toward the problems which confront the party within the given social situation; and he consequently reacts or responds in terms of the organized attitudes of the party as a whole. He thus enters into a special set of social relations with all the other individuals who belong to that political party; and in the same way he enters into various other special sets of social relations, with various other classes of individuals of each of these classes being the other members of some one of the particular organized subgroups (determined in socially functional terms) of which he himself is a member within the entire given society or social community. In the most highly developed, organized, and complicated human social communities—those evolved by civilized man—these various socially functional classes or subgroups of individuals to which any given individual belongs (and with the other individual members of which he thus enters into a special set of social relations) are of two kinds. Some of them are concrete social classes or subgroups, such as political parties, clubs,

corporations, which are all actually functional social units, in terms of which their individual members are directly related to one another. The others are abstract social classes or subgroups, such as the class of debtors and the class of creditors, in terms of which their individual members are related to one another only more or less indirectly, and which only more or less indirectly function as social units, but which afford or represent unlimited possibilities for the widening and ramifying and enriching of the social relations among all the individual members of the given society as an organized and unified whole. The given individual's membership in several of these abstract social classes or subgroups makes possible his entrance into definite social relations (however indirect) with an almost infinite number of other individuals who also belong to or are included within one or another of these abstract social classes or subgroups cutting across functional lines of demarcation which divide different human social communities from one another, and including individual members from several (in some cases from all) such communities. Of these abstract social classes or subgroups of human individuals the one which is most inclusive and extensive is, of course, the one defined by the logical universe of discourse (or system of universally significant symbols) determined by the participation and communicative interaction of individuals; for of all such classes or subgroups, it is the one which claims the largest number of individual members, and which enables the largest conceivable number of human individuals to enter into some sort of social relation, however indirect or abstract it may be, with one another —a relation arising from the universal functioning of gestures as significant symbols in the general human social process of communication.

I have pointed out, then, that there are two general stages in the full development of the self. At the first of these stages, the individual's self is constituted simply by an organization of the particular attitudes of other individuals toward himself and toward one another in the specific social acts in which he participates with them. But at the second stage in the full development of the individual's self that self is constituted not only by an organization of these particular individual attitudes, but also by an organization of the social attitudes of the generalized other or the social group as a whole to which he belongs. These social or group attitudes are brought within the individual's field of direct experience, and are included as elements in the structure or constitution of his self, in the same way that the attitudes of particular other individuals are; and the individual arrives at them, or succeeds in taking them, by means of further organizing, and then generalizing, the attitudes of particular other individuals in terms of their organized social bearings and implications. So the self reaches its full development by organizing these individual attitudes of others into the organized social or group attitudes, and by thus becoming an individual reflection of the general systematic pattern of social or group behavior in which it and the others are all involved—a pattern which enters as a whole into the individual's experience in terms of these organized group attitudes which, through the mechanism of his central nervous system, he takes toward himself, just as he takes the individual attitudes of others.

The game has a logic, so that such an organization of the self is rendered possible: there is a definite end to be obtained; the actions of the different individuals are all related to each other with reference to that end so that they do not conflict; one is not in conflict with himself in the attitude of another man on the team. If one has the attitude of the person throwing the ball he can also have the response of catching the ball. The two are related so that they further the purpose of the game itself. They are interrelated in a unitary, organic fashion. There is a definite unity, then, which is introduced into the organization of other selves when we reach such a stage as that of the game, as over against the situation of play where there is a simple succession of one rôle after another, a situation which is, of course, characteristic of the child's own personality. The child is one thing at one time and another at another, and what he is at one moment does not determine what he is at another. That is both the charm of childhood as well as its inadequacy. You cannot count on the child; you cannot assume that all the things he does are going to determine what he will do at any moment. He is not organized into a whole. The child has no definite character, no definite personality.

The game is then an illustration of the situation out of which an organized personality arises. In so far as the child does take the attitude of the other and allows that attitude of the other to determine the thing he is going to do with reference to a common end, he is becoming an organic member of society. He is taking over the morale of that society and is becoming an essential member of it. He be-

longs to it in so far as he does allow the attitude of the other that he takes to control his own immediate expression. What is involved here is some sort of an organized process. That which is expressed in terms of the game is, of course, being continually expressed in the social life of the child, but this wider process goes beyond the immediate experience of the child himself. The importance of the game is that it lies entirely inside of the child's own experience, and the importance of our modern type of education is that it is brought as far as possible within this realm. The different attitudes that a child assumes are so organized that they exercise a definite control over his response, as the attitudes in a game control his own immediate response. In the game we get an organized other, a generalized other, which is found in the nature of the child itself, and finds its expression in the immediate experience of the child. And it is that organized activity in the child's own nature controlling the particular response which gives unity, and which builds up his own self.

What goes on in the game goes on in the life of the child all the time. He is continually taking the attitudes of those about him, especially the rôles of those who in some sense control him and on whom he depends. He gets the function of the process in an abstract sort of a way at first. It goes over from the play into the game in a real sense. He has to play the game. The morale of the game takes hold of the child more than the larger morale of the whole community. The child passes into the game and the game expresses a social situation in which he can completely enter; its morale may have a greater hold on him than that of the family to which he belongs or the community in which he lives. There are all sorts of social organizations, some of which are fairly lasting, some temporary, into which the child is entering, and he is playing a sort of social game in them. It is a period in which he likes "to belong," and he gets into organizations which come into existence and pass out of existence. He becomes a something which can function in the organized whole, and thus tends to determine himself in his relationship with the group to which he belongs. That process is one which is a striking stage in the development of the child's morale. It constitutes him a self-conscious member of the community to which he belongs.

Such is the process by which a personality arises. I have spoken of this as a process in which a child takes the rôle of the other, and said that it takes place essentially through the use of language. Language is predominantly based on the vocal gesture by means of which co-operative activities in a community are carried out. Language in its significant sense is that vocal gesture which tends to arouse in the individual the attitude which it arouses in others, and it is this perfecting of the self by the gesture which mediates the social activities that gives rise to the process of taking the rôle of the other. The latter phrase is a little unfortunate because it suggests an actor's attitude which is actually more sophisticated than that which is involved in our own experience. To this degree it does not correctly describe that which I have in mind. We see the process most definitely in a primitive form in those situations where the child's play takes different rôles. Here the very fact that he is ready to pay out money, for instance, arouses the attitude of the person who receives money; the very process is calling out in him the corresponding activities of the other person involved. The individual stimulates himself to the response which he is calling out in the other person, and then acts in some degree in response to that situation. In play the child does definitely act out the rôle which he himself has aroused in himself. It is that which gives, as I have said, a definite content in the individual which answers to the stimulus that affects him as it affects somebody else. The content of the other that enters into one personality is the response in the individual which his gesture calls out in the other.

We may illustrate our basic concept by a reference to the notion of property. If we say "This is my property, I shall control it," that affirmation calls out a certain set of responses which must be the same in any community in which property exists. It involves an organized attitude with reference to property which is common to all the members of the community. One must have a definite attitude of control of his own property and respect for the property of others. Those attitudes (as organized sets of responses) must be there on the part of all, so that when one says such a thing he calls out in himself the response of the others. He is calling out the response of what I have called a generalized other. That which makes society possible is such common responses, such organized attitudes, with reference to what we term property, the cults of religion, the process of education, and the relations of the family. Of course, the wider the society the more definitely universal these objects must be. In any case there must be a definite set of responses, which we may speak of as abstract, and which can belong to a very large group. Property is in itself a very abstract concept. It is that which the individual himself can control and nobody else can control. The attitude is different from that of a dog toward a bone. A dog will fight any other dog trying to take the bone. The dog is not taking the attitude of the other dog. A man who says "This is my property" is taking an attitude of the other person. The man is appealing to his rights because he is able to take the attitude which everybody else in the group has with reference to property, thus arousing in himself the attitude of others.

What goes to make up the organized self is the organization of the attitudes which are common to the group. A person is a personality because he belongs to a community, because he takes over the institutions of that community into his own conduct. He takes its language as a medium by which he gets his personality, and then through a process of taking the different rôles that all the others furnish he comes to get the attitude of the members of the community. Such, in a certain sense, is the structure of a man's personality. There are certain common responses which each individual has toward certain common things, and in so far as those common responses are awakened in the individual when he is affecting other persons he arouses his own self. The structure, then, on which the self is built is this response which is common to all, for one has to be a member of a community to be a self. Such responses are abstract attitudes, but they constitute just what we term a man's character. They give him what we term his principles, the acknowledged attitudes of all members of the community toward what are the values of that community. He is putting himself in the place of the generalized other, which represents the organized responses of all the members of the group. It is that which guides conduct controlled by principles, and a person who has such an organized group of responses is a man whom we say has character, in the moral sense.

It is a structure of attitudes, then, which goes to make up a self, as distinct from a group of habits. We all of us have, for example, certain groups of habits, such as the particular intonations which a person uses in his speech. This is a set of habits of vocal expression which one has but which one does not know about. The sets of habits which we have of that sort mean nothing to us; we do not hear the intonations of our speech that others hear unless we are paying particular attention to them. The habits of emotional expression which belong to our speech are of the same sort. We may know that we have expressed ourselves in a joyous fashion but the detailed process is one which does not come back to our conscious selves. There are whole bundles of such habits which do not enter into a conscious self, but which help to make up what is termed the unconscious self.

After all, what we mean by self-consciousness is an awakening in ourselves of the group of attitudes which we are arousing in others, especially when it is an important set of responses which go to make up the members of the community. It is unfortunate to fuse or mix up consciousness, as we ordinarily use that term, and self-consciousness. Consciousness, as frequently used, simply has reference to the field of experience, but self-consciousness refers to the ability to call out in ourselves a set of definite responses which belong to the others of the group. Consciousness and self-consciousness are not on the same level. A man alone has, fortunately or unfortunately, access to his own toothache, but that is not what we mean by self-consciousness.

I have so far emphasized what I have called the structures upon which the self is constructed, the framework of the self, as it were. Of course we are not only what is common to all: each one of the selves is different from everyone else; but there has to be such a common structure as I have sketched in order that we may be members of a community at all. We cannot be ourselves unless we are also members in whom there is a community of attitudes which control the attitudes of all. We cannot have rights unless we have common attitudes. That which we have acquired as self-conscious persons makes us such members of society and gives us selves. Selves can only exist in definite relationships to other selves. No hard-and-fast line can be drawn between our own selves and the selves of others, since our own selves exist and enter as such into our experience only in so far as the selves of others exist and enter as such into our experience also. The individual possesses a self only in relation to the selves of the other members of his social group; and the structure of his self expresses or reflects the general behavior pattern of this social group to which he belongs, just as does the structure of the self of every other individual belonging to this social group.

Identity, Relation and Sport*

ELLEN W. GERBER

I

Psychiatrists, sociologists and educators, in particular, have noted the phenomenon of sport as being a part of every culture that has ever existed. At one time or another participants have included every age group from children to the aged, and every stratum of people within a society. The attempts to explore the reasons for this phenomenon have led to the development of a whole set of Freudian symbols connected to sport; to theories concerning the diversion of the Darwinian-designated instincts for survival to competition on the field of play; to the idea of sport as preparation for life; and to the concept that sport is a way for man to demonstrate his ability to control his environment. Each of these approaches appears to have validity as it is applied to different people at different times. This article seeks to explore another possible dimension as answer to the questions of why people participate in sport—what satisfaction they gain from it, what meaning it has for them.

This approach may be expressed by the following hypothesis: When people are engaged in the act of competing in a sport they are essentially engaged in a dialogue between themselves and the other players. The relationship of the players to each other is basically an I-Thou relationship, thus making sport a medium for self-definition and the creation of man's essential being (or being of essence).

* From *Quest*, VIII (May, 1967), 90-97.

The ontological question has been studied by philosophers since the beginning of philosophical thought, but new questions focusing on the differences between the being of existence, the primeval life force, and the being of essence—man as the sum total of his individual experiences—have been the focus of thinkers in the mid-twentieth century. The crucial relevance of this question was not to the philosophers alone, but to the artists, poets, dramatists, theologians, novelists, and readers as well. Exploration of the question became loosely systematized into the formal philosophy of existentialism, but writers who did not necessarily consider themselves existentialists explored the nuances of the problem in tangential ways. Among these was the philosopher-theologian Martin Buber.

Buber's concern was with existential meaning, particularly how and where man finds meaning and how this relates to the development of his own being. William Barrett, author of *Irrational Man,* a study in existential philosophy, commented:

Buber is one of the few thinkers who has succeeded in the desperate modern search for roots, a fact with which his work continuously impresses us. . . . At first glance his contribution would seem to be the slenderest of all the Existentialists, to be summed up in the title of his most moving book, *I and Thou.* . . . But this one thought—that meaning in life happens in the area between person and person in that situation of contact when one says *I* to the other's *Thou*—is worth a lifetime's digging.[1:16-17]

Unlike Sartre, Buber believed that man is not doomed to live alone and alienated, finding himself only in a confrontation with his own non-Being. In *I and Thou* he theorizes that man finds himself, man becomes, man is, only in relation to his Thou. Through relation, through the encounter of the I with the Thou, through the dialogue, man finds himself, his meaning and his roots.

As Buber discussed and explored this concept of relation he indicated that unfortunately it is the exception, rather than the rule in man's life. Man is more likely to meet man not as a Thou, but as an It. It is more likely that he will experience another than that he will stand in relation to him.

Man travels over the surface of things and experiences them. He extracts knowledge about their constitution from them: he wins an experience from them. He experiences what belongs to the things.[3:5]

Man meeting an It is not an unimportant happening. As man grows in his ability to experience and to use, he transmits this knowledge from generation to generation, so that in each succeeding culture the world of objects and the manipulation of Its becomes more extensive. But (and this is the dilemma of the whole cybercultural revolution), the development of the real man, the essential man, striving for meaningful life, can occur only through the I-Thou relation.

All things have within them the disposition to be Thous, however briefly, however rarely. In fact Buber emphasizes that only God never becomes an It. Man, animals, natural objects, inanimate objects, all move in and out of true relation with each other, move from the I-It stand to the I-Thou, to the I-It, living the I-Thou encounter sometimes briefly, sometimes lengthily.

But when one that is alive arises out of things, and becomes a being in relation to me, joined to me by its nearness and its speech, for how short a time is it nothing to me but Thou! It is not the relation that grows feeble, but the actuality of its immediacy.[3:98-99]

The value, the tremendous importance of the I-Thou encounter, is that ". . . Without *It* man cannot live. But he who lives with *It* alone is not a man."[3:34] Man finds himself and defines himself, not by his experience with "Its," but by his relationships with "Thous." "That essence of man which is special to him can be directly known only in a living relation."[6:205]

II

The I-Thou relationship is the dialogue between man and man. "I-Thou is the primary word of relation. It is characterized by mutuality, directness, presentness, intensity and ineffability."[8:57] An examination of the attributes of this special relationship as they may occur when playing a sport, follows in this article. Any sport might be used in demonstration, for the basic structure of competition to score points against opposition within defined areas and under defined rules, is present in all sports where players compete connectedly.[*] From among the possibilities, tennis doubles was selected because it is a sport played by both men and women; is the same game for both; is sometimes played by both at the same time; and has the situation of having both opponents and teammate.

The level of competition is an important factor affecting the entire discussion, because the extent of the individual's involvement is crucial to the whole subject of relation. It is assumed that the degree of involvement will depend upon what is at stake to the individual participant at the moment of the game, and this may range from one end of a continuum to another. Hidden psychological need for status or overt desire for a high grade could make a simple class contest a very important event to a student. The important point is that the potential for relationship exists and the degree to which it occurs is dependent upon the player's level of involvement.

Mutuality. The meaning of the word "mutuality," perhaps the most crucial of all the words describing relation, is the most difficult to comprehend. Buber considers that man lives in a two-fold world, in accordance with his two-fold attitude. In the one world man is an object among objects, perceiving and experiencing the qualities of things and events around him; in the other world man lives as an authentic being—the world lives neither within him (as the idealists would say) nor outside of him (as the realists would say)—but rather they take their stand in mutual relation to each

[*] This arbitrarily excludes sports where players compete separately, such as weight lifting, or field events, but it is acknowledged that it might be possible to uncover the elements of an I-Thou relationship in these sports also—especially with regard to man and his implement. However, in the last of Buber's books, *The Knowledge of Man,* he deliberately attempts to distinguish the *I-Thou* as a dialogue between man and man, excluding the relationship between man and objects in nature that had been included in earlier writings.

other. "Only when a structure of being is independently over against a living being (*Seiende*), an independent, opposite, does a world exist."[4:61]

The implications of mutuality make the point particularly crucial. It must be asked: "*Who* is this I, this man, who can take his stand in relation?" This is the basic question of Being that existentialism is so concerned with.

This human being is not *He,* or *She,* bounded from every other *He* or *She,* a specific point in space and time within the net of the world; nor is he a nature able to be experienced and described, a loose bundle of named qualities. But with no neighbour, and the whole in himself, he is *Thou* and fills the heavens.[3:8]

He is "whole in himself"; he is independent, therefore, for dependency cannot exist concurrently with wholeness; and he accepts the wholeness, independence and authenticity of the Thou. When two beings take their stand in mutual relation to the other each chooses and is chosen, and in so doing affirms and is affirmed.

But the speaker does not merely perceive the one who is present to him in this way; he receives him as his partner, and that means that he confirms this other being, so far as it is for him to confirm.[4, p.85]

Whether the players in a tennis match perceive each other as objects or take their stand in mutual relation to each other, can now be considered. The ball is put into play and the four players move about the court:

But what is it that motivates my* movements? It is you—both my opponents and my teammate; it is not a quality of you, not your strength, or beauty, or known skill that I consider and move in response to. Rather it is you as a totality. I quite literally move in relation to you. My own movement is at once a response and an instigation. During the course of play there is no thought, no examination, no experiencing, but simply the response of my being to that of yours, and vice-versa. Before play, or after play, or perhaps during a pause, this mutuality slips away and the object "I" very much evaluates the object "you." I may consider your ability to place your fore-

---

* The choice was made to use first person when demonstrating the I-Thou relationship situationally. It is believed that this will make clearer the realities of the dialogue by enabling the reader to enter the situation in a more personal way.

---

hand; the relative strength of your backhand; your short serve; your tired physical condition; your sense of humor; your sportsmanship—I can examine any one of a number of qualities in this "it." My partner is better than I and we carefully consider this as we arrange ourselves on the court; your service is stronger and we decide that you shall serve our first game, but when play begins, or resumes, these examinations, these considerations melt away and we play with a wholeness of self that cannot be taken apart. Your grace or lack of it goes unnoticed; I see you, but I do not look at you. I summon the totality of my powers; in the deepest recesses of my being I know that your presence is there. I send the ball across—the ball that is now part of me because it too has stood in relation to my effective power—and you step forth to meet this ball that is part of our mutual relation. And in the act of my sending the ball across I affirm your presence. And in the act of meeting it and returning it, you affirm my presence. We stand in mutual relation to each other.

Directness. There are two connotations to the word "direct" when used in connection with relation. The first is that:

No system of ideas, no foreknowledge, and no fancy intervene between *I* and *Thou.* . . . No aim, no lust, and no anticipation intervene between *I* and *Thou.* . . . Every means is an obstacle. Only when every means has collapsed does the meeting come about.[3:11-12]

And the second is that "In face of the directness of the relation everything indirect becomes irrelevant."[3:12]

In the first instance Buber expresses an essential phenomenological approach. In the light of the I-Thou there is nothing but the real, the essential *I* and the essential *Thou,* uncluttered by the distortions that man habitually places upon objects as he looks at them in terms of how he may use them or what they can mean and do for him. When one meets a *Thou* directly there is no use, no need, no plan, no temporizing and therefore, no distortion. In the words of Paul: "For now we see in a glass darkly, but then face to face. Now I know in part; then I shall understand fully, even as I have been fully understood."[10:I Cor.13:12]

Probably nowhere more than in a sport situation is this concept clearly demonstrated. The naked clarity of self-distortion superimposed upon the other stands out in this type of action situation where all judgments are acted upon and returned with immediate results.

In our tennis game I am continually confronted with the fact that you are where you are, rather than where I might have thought you to be. I can place the ball down the alley and score a point if you truly cannot get to the ball; however, if I theoretically believe you cannot get there, and you do, you can return the ball. The evidence is always there. There are many times though when the habit of manipulation becomes too strong and I will try to play the shots as they come to me, and also to manipulate your future shots—perhaps by forcing you to set-up a ball to me. In these instances, when I am playing my own game *and* yours, I fall back into an I-It relationship.

The second instance is also demonstrated with especial clarity in the context of sports. My concern, my relation, on the tennis court is with the others, with the balls, and with the racquet. I must face all of these directly—and if I do so the world drops away, becomes irrelevant. When the game is over and the directness slips into indirectness, there is the sudden realization that it's late; that I have an aching blister on my hand; that I am hot and thirsty; that my partner did not play well, etc. In the face of direct relation all these became irrelevant. In direct relation I accept all that is around me as it is and respond as I am. In sport this is greatly facilitated by the constant pattern of action and response that in its immediacy exposes illusion.

Presentness. "The real filled present exists only in so far as actual presentness, meeting, and relation exist."[3:12] When Buber talks of the "real filled present" he distinguishes between the use of the word present in ordinary concepts of time, and the word present (perhaps it should have a capital P) that signifies the illuminated now, when both past and future come together. T. S. Eliot, the poet, expressed this perfectly when he said:

At the still point of the turning world. Neither flesh nor fleshless; Neither from nor towards; at the still point, there the dance is, But neither arrest nor movement. And do not call it fixity, Where past and future are gathered. . . .[7:119]

Presentness is a condition of relation, but relation is also a condition of presentness. To Buber, "True beings are lived in the present, the life of objects is in the past."[3:13] "Its" and things find meaning only in the completed action, or the examined quality, because only afterward can they be related to other things which are useful and have meaning. But the men in dialogue find their meaning *within*

the encounter, *within* the relation, and thus know the "real filled present."

As I face the others in our tennis game, the past and the future coalesce into the present moment. Whatever you mean to me, you mean now, at this moment, because our actions recognize the reality of each other. From this recognition comes our meaning, and from this meaning comes our recognition. The present moment is affirmed in your movement of response to me, in your act of sending the ball—of sending yourself to me, in my act of receiving, and in my partner's racing to be by my side at the net. There is no past and no future to be considered; in our relation is presentness.

Intensity. What is meant when one speaks of a human being as intense, or a human relationship as an intense relationship? In the mechanical world degrees of heat can be measured, but in the human world there is no such gauge. Instead, intensity refers to degree of involvement. In an I-Thou relationship the involvement of the individual must be total and undivided. "Every real relation with a being or life in the world is exclusive. Its *Thou* is freed, step forth, is single, and confronts you."[3:78] "What then do we know of *Thou?*—Just everything. For we know nothing isolated about it any more."[3:11] When one speaks of degree of involvement in the context of intensity it does not mean that the whole person is involved to greater or lesser degree, but that more and more of the person is involved, concentration and perceptions are more singly focused, until finally *all* of the person's powers are involved, and then it can be said that there is total involvement and intensity.

When I enter into our game of tennis I am more fully I than just before we have begun. The difference lies here: as I play—run, swing, lunge, push myself to limits of physical giving and endurance—I am involving that part of me which is only rarely called forth, the strength and swiftness of my body. You call this forth from me—you demand the response that involves *all* my powers. If I am to really play, really compete, the only way in which I can respond is with total involvement. I have to gather together all my forces and expend them totally in the single swinging thrust of hitting the ball. Sometimes I do not; sometimes you do not ask for all of me; sometimes the demand is not there and I can return the ball, or not return it, with only partial involvement—with no intensity. But other times in the magic of a well placed shot you ask me for everything. And in that moment there is a heightened, very real intensity between us.

Ineffability. Ineffability is the summing up characteristic of relation; all the other factors are inherent in the meaning of the term. With utterance, directness and intensity and presentness would fall away, for the demands of speech call forth examination, which in turn sends one back into the past and breaks up unity; it sets up barriers between people as they strive to understand the meaning of the utterances. For a relationship to be ineffable does not mean that it must be silent, though in such a relationship much silent communication takes place, but it means that it must be silent about itself.

As my partner and I move up and down the court together we do not need to discuss where we are or should be—we are simply there together, moving in concert. As I hit the ball and cause you to respond by bringing your whole being to its meeting, there is no speech between us or even within us singly. The meaning of the dialogue between us would be changed by speech; it would be destroyed by analysis—as indeed it does become when later we talk of "why" and "when" and "how." At that time we may argue, accuse, reject, criticize, suggest. But earlier, in the silence of our dialogue, there was only acceptance. Relation is ineffable.

III

"And in all the seriousness of truth, hear this: without *It* man cannot live. But he who lives with *It* alone is not a man."[3:34] Man finds himself and defines himself, not by his experiences with "Its," but by his relationships with "Thous." The I-Thou relationship is characterized by being mutual, direct, present, intense, and ineffable. When the kind of relationship that exists between the players in a game of tennis is examined, it is evident that it exhibits the characteristics of an I-Thou relationship. It must be understood that this does not happen every moment of every game, but rather it does happen, or can happen, in the circumstances described. The importance of this may be suggested by the final quotation:

But the *I* that steps out of the relational event into separation and consciousness of separation, does not lose its reality. Its sharing is preserved in it in a living way. In other words, as is said of the supreme relation and may be used of all, "the seed remains in it."[3:63]

The nature of the game, and of sports in general, is such that this kind of relationship tends to occur. Thus, through the medium of the game man approaches his fellow players as *Thous,* and finds meaning in his own *I.*

REFERENCES

1. Barrett, William. *Irrational Man.* New York: Doubleday Anchor Books Edition, 1962.
2. Buber, Martin. *Between Man and Man.* New York: Macmillan Paperbacks Edition, 1965.
3. ————. *I and Thou.* New York: Charles Scribner's Sons, 1923.
4. ————. *The Knowledge of Man.* New York: Harper Torchbooks Edition, 1965.
5. ————. *The Way of Man.* Pennsylvania: Pendle Hill Pamphlet 106.
6. ————. *Two Types of Faith.* New York: Harper Torchbooks Edition, 1961.
7. Eliot, Thomas Stearns. *The Complete Poems and Plays, 1909-1950.* New York: Harcourt, Brace and Company, 1952.
8. Friedman, Maurice S. *Martin Buber: The Life of Dialogue.* New York: Harper Torchbooks Edition, 1960.
9. Howe, Reuel L. *The Miracle of Dialogue.* Connecticut: The Seabury Press, 1963.
10. *New Testament,* Revised Standard Version I Corinthians 13:12.

Play: A Basic Human Structure Involving Love and Freedom*

WILLIAM A. SADLER, JR.

While it is increasingly being realized that play is a significant form of behavior, it is nevertheless a phenomenon which puzzles and confounds many who study it, as evidenced by a general inability to define it. What is play? Why do people play? What does it mean to them?

From an adult point of view it would appear to be the opposite of work—a mode of being in the world whereby the work-a-day world with its sense of gravity and urgency is left behind. In the moment of play the serious cause-effect order of work is forgotten as one finds himself "freed" from the confinements of ordinary concerns. Play is obviously a form of freedom, yet it has rarely been understood as such. Many older psychological theories have attempted to explain play in terms of energy. It has been seen to be the result of an exuberance of energy; or in the opposite direction, it has been viewed as a compensating form of behavior when one is not really up to serious work. Some theories have even considered play to be a kind of pre-exercise, a preparatory behavior to work wherein one learns to develop new skills. Many of the theories of play have been in terms of observed effects without focusing upon the actual content of it. Current psychological approaches have shifted from mere observation of effects,

* From *Review of Existential Psychology and Psychiatry*, 6 (Fall, 1966), 237-245. Also incorporated in William A. Sadler, Jr., *Existence and Love: A New Approach in Existential Phenomenology*. New York: Charles Scribner's Sons, 1969 and 1970.

which were then combined with hypotheses regarding inferred causes, to empirical studies of the actual play of children.

One of the most illustrious modern theories is that put forth by Piaget, in which play is seen as part of the whole realm of infantile dynamics. As he studied children, Piaget came to conclude that play is a stage in a child's thinking about reality. He postulated two basic existential modes: one, to adapt reality to what one already knows; the other, to adapt oneself to what is encountered. An infant's play begins when he becomes somewhat familiar with his environment, and it continues as behavior directed toward that which is familiar. Accordingly, play is behavior which bends reality to what the individual already knows. It is also closely associated with dreams and fantasy. As Piaget theorizes, play will tend to drop in importance as one progresses toward consistent adaptation to reality. Yet because it continues to bring pleasure and serves the purpose of learning to adapt to new situations or to find compensations for unfulfilled longings, an element of play will be still found in adults(1).

Aside from the naive naturalistic presuppositions upon which this theory is apparently based, this kind of approach fails to distinguish the various possibilities of play as seen from an existential viewpoint. It does not see play from its own frame of reference but from a supposedly adult world of work. Thus it fails to see play in its actual situation as a form of existential encounter, which is to say, a specific

113

mode of freedom. Much more illuminative of the significance of play is the multi-directional approach of Erik Erikson. He also focuses upon the play of children, particularly the play of disturbed children; and he, too, studies it primarily as a phenomenon within childhood development. Yet he insists that it is much more than a way of finding refuge from new aspects of reality or of seeking pleasure; indeed he maintains it is an essential and constructive mode of behavior. Like Sigmund Freud, and even more, his daughter Anna, Erikson sees children's play as a way of dealing with anxiety by attempting to decrease and eventually dissolve it (2, pp. 216-217, 3). Yet a shortcoming of a strictly Freudian approach was that it concentrated upon the phenomenon of a solitary child's acting out of his fears and wishes; his play was seen to be a dramatic concretization of his fantasy. In studying children's play in a specific situation (2, p. 219), Erikson has discovered that a child frequently enters into play with a precarious sense of his own time-space, and that play gives him an opportunity to develop his own field of significance, his own world (2, p. 100; p. 220). Erikson's particular theory is that play is a function of the ego to synchronize the child's bodily and social processes. Much children's play expresses the need of an ego to master various areas of life where the child senses himself to be wanting, that is, where he confronts anxiety (2, p. 211). A neurotic individual is one who falls prey to over-identification with certain limited aspects of his situation; his play is often a way of breaking loose to find his own identity. Erikson's definition of play is limited because it is too centered upon childhood in anxious situations; he proposes the theory that "the child's play is the infantile form of the human ability to deal with experience by creating model situations and to master reality by experiment and planning" (2, p. 222). Though restricted in scope, Erikson has made the valuable suggestion that play is a mode of creating a world. It will thus best be seen as a distinct form of encounter; and, as such, it must be seen not from a detached observational viewpoint but through participation which reaches into and opens up its intentional structure.

In his classic work, *Homo Ludens,* which sees play as an essentially indispensable mode of human existence, Johan Huizinga goes far beyond the view of play as infantile or juvenile activity and concentrates upon play as a cultural rather than a solely individual phenomenon. As a cultural historian, he is aware that any attempt to understand man as a cultural being which neglects play, would be hopelessly jejune. Inspired by Plato's eloquent statement, that play is the form of activity in which man most nearly approaches the similitude of the gods (4, pp. 211-212), he argues for play as the cultural phenomenon upon which man's highest spiritual accomplishments are based. Life to be human must be lived as play. Though eschewing neat definitions of play, he nevertheless concentrates upon its specific content, as evidenced in numerous cultures, both primitive and highly civilized. In summarizing his analysis, he illumines certain fundamental characteristics of play:

> . . . a free activity standing quite curiously outside "ordinary" life as being "not serious," but at the same time absorbing the player intensely and utterly. It is an activity connected with no material interest, and no profit can be gained by it. It proceeds within its own proper boundaries of time and space according to fixed rules, and in an orderly manner. It promotes the formation of social groupings which tend to surround themselves with secrecy and to stress their difference from the common world by disguise or other means (4, p. 13).

Though some fine points of this summary might be challenged, there are basic structures upon which we can agree. First, play is seen as an act of freedom expressing itself. Secondly, this act of freedom consists in stepping outside ordinary life in the work-a-day world and discovering its unique significance within its own intentional structure. Thirdly, as distinct from ordinary life in the world, play constitutes its own form of encounter, charts a unique direction in the world, and creates its own space-time reality. Finally, though it divorces itself from the common world of work, it nevertheless can create another form of "common world," such as indicated by the term "a play community." To clarify its unique intentional order, he points out that play has two universal functions: it is a contest *for* something and it is a representation *of* something (4, p. 13). We can immediately suggest, and Huizinga's detailed historical-phenomenological study substantiates this, that play is freedom geared toward the appropriation of important existential significance, or of meaningful existential possibility. In a contest man seeks to excel so as to be considered better; thus he seeks to be honored and esteemed, to achieve prestigious existence (4, p. 50). Cheating is such a foul crime in the play world because it breaks down the special order and value sought for in play.

As a basic form of existence, play in Huizinga's eyes is linked to man's need to live in beauty (4, p. 63). Whether such a need can be demonstrated is questionable. Yet he does substantiate play as a creative form of encountering the world, one which makes the significance of a man's being-in-the-world more apparent to him. It is through "playing that society expresses its interpretation of life and the world" (4, p. 46). Culture is not merely based on play; rather, culture plays out through us as we attempt to express how we feel about being in the world and where we think the truth of our existence lies. Play begins with childhood, and he insists that "really to play, a man must play like a child." That is, he must fully engage himself in this particular mode of being in the world (4, p. 199). Yet the childlike character of play should not lead, as in some theories, to its disparagement; for, play is an essential factor in the whole cultural process. To summarize this entire work which is deserving of careful study, he wrote:

> It has not been difficult to show that a certain play-factor was extremely active all through the cultural process and that it produces many of the fundamental forms of social life. The spirit of playful competition is, as a social impulse, older than culture itself and pervades all life like a veritable ferment. Ritual grew up in sacred play; poetry was born in play and nourished on play; music and dancing were pure play. Wisdom and philosophy found expression in words and forms derived from religious contests. The rules of warfare, the conventions of noble living were built upon play-patterns. We have to conclude, therefore, that civilization is, in its earliest phases, played. It does not come *from* play like a babe detaching itself from the womb: it arises *in* and *as* play, and never leaves it (4, p. 173).

Like many other students of our culture, Huizinga feels that contemporary civilization faces a crisis. His theory suggests that the cause is to be discovered not in a breakdown of reason but in modern man's misunderstanding of and disparagement of play. As civilization grows more complex, it becomes more serious and assigns a secondary place to playing (4, p. 75). In our era we have lost the spirit of play, engaging in pursuits which are similar to it, but really constitute false play. Indeed a contemporary psychoanalytic interpretation of play has been presented in terms of a game theory which sees the playing of games from a purely negative viewpoint, as a "basically dishonest"

form of interpersonal behavior (5, p. 48). (This author's theory is that "a game is an ongoing series of complementary ulterior transactions progressing to a well defined, predictable outcome. . . . a series of moves with a snare, or 'gimmick.' "Thus, they are moves interposed between our possibilities of obtaining genuine interpersonal relations and authentic cultural expressions. It is highly regrettable that this author does not also see games from the positive viewpoint of play as presented by Huizinga.)

To illuminate play as a basic form of existential encounter, expressing a genuine form of freedom, helps us to see the play phenomenon as it really is, in terms of its intentional and essential content. It also suggests immediately to us that we have to do here with a form of transcendence which sounds remarkably similar to that discoverable in the phenomenon of love. Play is a form of being-in-the-world which is nevertheless beyond the world of concern. Certainly play is a realization of genuine human freedom, not merely individual but also social, and especially cultural. It is truly an historical phenomenon in the full sense of that term. Yet how is it related to love, if at all? We shall see the relation more clearly if we ask the question: How is it possible for man really to play as a child, fully to engage himself positively in play?

Immense insight in this direction comes from a Swiss psychiatrist, Gustav Bally, who made a study of freedom as play. Bally emphasizes that freedom is not a possession of man; rather it is a dynamic process of becoming, an ordering of being-in-the-world, as we would put it (6, p. 5, ff.). Thus, freedom has its boundaries; and its meaning is to be discovered in terms of the extent of its boundaries. We shall look upon freedom not merely in terms of what man is free from but what he is free for; or perhaps better expressed, what he is free *towards*. First, let us recognize that play is a different form of activity than ordinary behavior. This is noticeable even in animals, whose behavior seems to be largely under the domination of instincts directed toward specific objects. Yet when animals, particularly the young, have received sufficient nourishment and are sure of security, a new behavior appears which is not aimed at the procuring of some external object. Rather this behavior seems to end where it begins; it has no immediate aim other than itself. Such behavior is termed play (6, p. 59).

Man is in this respect different from animals. His play does not occur on the periphery of his involvement in the world. Rather he plays his whole life, and his play has to do with his search for a sense of historical identity in a human world (6, p. 67-74). Play is essential to him if he is to gain a perspective of the becoming world in which his existence is geared to realize genuine human possibilities. If inner forces prevent him from playing and thus finding significance, human development is severely retarded and/or distorted. A child must find the play room in which to grow to be a man; and as a man he must continually play so as to discover and formulate the significance of his being in the world. The task of society is to keep man open to his genuine possibilities. Man needs the openness of the freedom which arises within play so as to lead his life within the world rather than to be led through it by anxiety, pressures, and deceptions (6, p. 76).

Man as being-in-the-world is engaged in a problematic situation. Upon confronting his freedom, he is aware of his limitations and the possibility of his non-existence. Thus the awareness of freedom as an isolated individual is a process which constricts the boundaries of freedom. Man stands in a world bounded by dark shadows of failure and death. The task of playing man is to learn to play while standing on the very boundaries of his freedom. Yet how is this possible? To face the naked horror of possible non-existence leads man to be serious, to face his death resolutely or to escape from the fearful spectre of his existential possibilities. Yet in the phenomenon of play there may be a presentiment of a reality which is beyond merely individual possibilities. It may be a presentiment of God, as Bally suggests (6, p. 103, ff.); or it may be the feeling that one is at home in the world with another being who addresses him as Thou. Bally discovered that as animals must have a sense of security really to play, so men must have a sense of being loved. In the heart of man there is a longing for loving encounter in which one's freedom will be acknowledged and affirmed. In order to play most creatively one needs to develop a sense of trust not merely in himself or in the other, but basically in the world which opens before him. This is precisely the world which love provides. Love gives man a home in which it is safe to play.

In line with Bally, Ludwig Binswanger discovered that freedom arises out of the gift of love rather than from a confrontation with anxiety. As clinical studies indicate, a strong dose of anxiety will "paralyze" a child, preventing him from playing (see 1, 2). Play is one form of overcoming relatively mild forms of anxiety; but in confronting such anxiety the child needs to find trust in himself by virtue of being trusted. In adults Binswanger discovered essentially the same facts. In psychotherapy the doctor confronts often massive anxiety which imprisons the patient; the latter finds his liberation through the love of a therapist who communicates presence and makes the patient feel at home in his world. Whereas Heidegger's analysis of existence maintained that freedom emerged as a freedom toward one's ground as one faced his own negation of being, Binswanger found that freedom emerges within the boundaries of love (7, p. 139-142). The ground upon which human freedom emerges is not that of the isolated self, but the ground of loving duality—the personal reality of "we." We have said that human freedom arises within boundaries, and that it needs a definite space in which to play itself out. Phenomenological investigations indicate that the playground of freedom is love. Real love is not a force which imprisons a person. It is a gift of trust, an embrace which affirms the significance of the individual and the importance of becoming himself in a common world. Freedom does not die in love; it is born there. As Binswanger has shown, the boundaries within the household of love are infinite; the space of love gives ample enough room for freedom to express itself in historical growth towards man's fullest possibilities.

Further insight into the significance of play as a form of freedom grounded in love will emerge from phenomenological investigations of play within the structure of interpersonal relations. The emphasis of much play study has been on the isolated individual; but the significance of play can better be seen when we focus upon the world-making phenomenon of people playing together, which is surely the richest and happiest form of play. As people play together we have a paradigm of interpersonal freedom creating its own meaningful boundaries and its own form of communication. Play as genuine communication can clearly be seen in much play of children with children or with their parents. A small child calling, "Daddy, come and play with me," is making a bid for an encounter in a new world of play, a world grounded in love and open to possibilities for existence not possible when he was alone. Playing together, the child and parent construct a world which is not fantasy or subjective; it is the world of love in which they find a limitless home and a moment of time in which to be themselves.

The play of love actualizes a new mode of responsive freedom.

Such may also be the case in what we commonly refer to as love-play. In the play between lovers a time of trust is established where they can speak intimately. In playful caresses, they define a common space in which they become sure of each other. Their histories interpenetrate in mutual presence as they come to feel at home with each other. In true love-play the difference between love and attempts at seduction become clear. The latter is an effort to possess another, which would rob the other of his freedom. Love, on the other hand, reaffirms the unique being of the other so as to continue in the special moment of loving encounter. The "moment" lasts so long as in reciprocal presence each other's freedom is affirmed. Once the freedom of the other is downgraded or denied, the game of love is over, and a game of the suppression of authentic existence ensues.

To play with another within the bounds of love is to give another courage to be himself. As we are well aware, playing with loved ones where we feel at home often inspires us to very individual actions. We do things, sometimes silly or daring, that we would never do in front of strangers. Our spirits and bodies soar in play as we jump, skip, kick up our heels, or swing through the air. Play in love is the most spontaneous of activities and the most unpredictable. The poet Schiller was more right than perhaps even he suspected when he wrote: "*Der Mensch ist nur Mensch wenn er spielt*—Man is only fully a man when he plays." To stop playing is not to grow up; it is to cease living authentically. Man is by nature a playing creature. When playing he is not being like an animal; rather, he is most like himself, as man is meant to be. To speak again in terms of intentionality, play is what man is made *for*. In play, as it is grounded on love, man reaches into his fullest possibilities as an individual sustained and liberated by another in a truly personal world. In this modern era, which still suffers from a hangover of the Puritan suspicion that somewhere someone might be having a good time, and in which the ethic of work has been absolutized as that activity where man proves his worth, we are dangerously close to losing our awareness of the vital importance of play for authentic existence. To become human, to find the meaning of life, we must learn to play—to play not merely alone but more basically to play together in the ecstatic, boundless, carefree, riotous world of love. Play is not an optional activity to be reserved for occasional moments of leisure, as though these are moments of escape from the real business of living. As Zorba told us, a man must have a little madness or else he will not be free (8, pp. 300-301). The madness that is essential is constituted by the transport of love—the dual reality of "we" and is attained as persons are inspired to dance together, to laugh together, to play together until their hearts are content (9, p. 148).

REFERENCES

1. See the study by J. Barnard Gilmore, "Play: A special behavior," *Current Research In Motivation*, Haber, Ralph N. ed. New York: Holt, Rinehart and Winston, 1966. See also J. Piaget. *Play, Dreams, and Imitation in Childhood.* London: William Heinemann, 1951.
2. Erikson, Erik H. *Childhood and Society.* New York: W. W. Norton & Co., 1963 (Revised Edition).
3. Freud, Anna. *The Ego and the Mechanisms of Defence.* New York: International Universities Press, 1946.
4. Huizinga, Johan. *Homo Ludens.* Boston: The Beacon Press, 1955.
5. Berne, Eric. *Games People Play.* New York: Grove Press, 1964.
6. Bally, Gustav. *Vom Ursprung und Von Den Grenzen Der Freiheit: Eine Deutung Des Spiels Bei Tier Und Mensch.* Basel: Benno Schwabe & Co., 1945.
7. Binswanger, Ludwig. *Grundformen und Erkenntnis Menschlichen Daseins.* Zürich: Max Niehans Verlag, 1953 (2nd Edition).
8. Kazantzakis, N. *Zorba The Greek.* New York: Simon and Schuster, 1959.
9. A strong argument for the essential place of playful, imaginative love in the development of man in society is presented by Herbert Marcuse in his *Eros and Civilization.* Boston: The Beacon Press, 1955. He argues provocatively against the exaltation of what Freud called the performance principle, so that culture might have the chance to regain genuine "forms of freedom and happiness."

Limits of the Life-Order: Sport*

KARL JASPERS

The self-preservative impulse as a form of vitality finds scope for itself in sport; and as a vestige of the satisfaction of immediate life, finds scope for itself in discipline, versatility, adroitness. Through bodily activities subjected to the control of the will, energy and courage are sustained, and the individual seeking contact with nature draws nearer to the elemental forces of the universe.

Sport as a mass-phenomenon, organised on compulsory lines as a game played according to rule, provides an outlet for impulses which would otherwise endanger the apparatus. By occupying their leisure, it keeps the masses quiet. It is the will to *vitality*, in the form of movement in the fresh air and sun, that leads to this communal enjoyment of life; it has no contemplative relationship to nature as a cipher to be elucidated, and it makes an end of fruitful solitude. The exercise of the combative instinct or of the desire to excel in sport demands the utmost skill, each competitor wishing to establish his superiority over the others. For those animated by this impulse, the all-important thing is to make a record. Publicity and applause are essential. The necessity of observing the rules of the games establishes an obedience to good form, thanks to which in the actual struggle of life rules are likewise observed which facilitate social intercourse.

The venturesome doings of individuals show forth what is unattainable by the masses, but

* From *Man in the Modern Age*. Translated by Eden and Cedar Paul. Garden City, New York: Doubleday, 1957. Reprinted with permission of Routledge & Kegan Paul Ltd.

what the masses admire as heroism and feel they would themselves like to do if they could. Such exemplars stake their lives as mountain-climbers, swimmers, aviators, and boxers. These, too, are victims, at the sight of whose achievements the masses are enthused, alarmed and gratified, being inspired all the while with the secret hope that they themselves, perhaps, may become enabled to do extraordinary things.

A collaborating factor in promoting a delight in sport may, however, be that which, in classical Rome, unquestionably helped to attract crowds to the gladiatorial shows, namely the pleasure that is felt in witnessing the danger and destruction of persons remote from the spectator's own lot. In like manner the savagery of the crowd is also manifested in a fondness for reading detective stories, a feverish interest in the reports of criminal trials, an inclination towards the absurd and the primitive and the obscure. In the clarity of rational thought, where everything is known or unquestionably knowable, where destiny has ceased to prevail and only chance remains, where (despite all activity) the whole becomes insufferably tedious and absolutely stripped of mystery—there stirs among those who no longer believe themselves to have a destiny establishing ties between themselves and the darkness, the human urge towards the alluring contemplation of eccentric possibilities. The apparatus sees to it that this urge shall be gratified.

Even so, the activities of modern man in

sport are not made fully comprehensible through an understanding of what such mass-instincts as the aforesaid can make out of sport. Looming above sport as an organised enterprise wherein the human being forced into the labour mechanism seeks nothing more than an equivalent for his immediate self-preservative impulse, we discern, we feel, in the sport movement, something that is nevertheless great. Sport is not only play and the making of records; it is likewise a soaring and a refreshment. To-day it imposes its demands on every one. Even a life that is over-sophisticated gives itself up to sport under stress of natural impulse. Some, indeed, compare the sport of contemporary human beings with that of classical days. In those times, however, sport was, as it were, an indirect participation of the extraordinary man in his divine origin; and of this there is no longer any thought to-day. But even contemporary human beings wish to express themselves in one way or another, and sport becomes a philosophy. They rise in revolt against being cabined, cribbed, confined; and they seek relief in sport, though it lacks transcendent substantiality. Still, it contains the aforesaid soaring element—unconsciously willed, though without communal content—as a defiance to the petrified present. The human body is demanding its own rights in an epoch when the apparatus is pitilessly annihilating one human being after another. Modern sport, therefore, is enveloped in an aura which, though the respective historical origins differ, makes it in some ways akin to the sport of the antique world. Contemporary man, when engaged in sport, does not indeed become a Hellene, but at the same time he is not a mere fanatic of sport. We see him when he is engaged in sport as a man who, strapped in the strait-waistcoat of life, in continuous peril as if engaged in active warfare, is nevertheless not crushed by his almost intolerable lot, but strikes a blow in his own behalf, stands erect to cast his spear.

But even though sport imposes one of the limits upon the rationalised life-order, through sport alone man cannot win to freedom. Not merely by keeping his body fit, by soaring upward in vital courage, and by being careful to 'play the game', can he overcome the danger of losing his self.

The Great Doctrine of Archery*

EUGEN HERRIGEL

"The right art," cried the Master, "is purposeless, aimless! The more obstinately you try to learn how to shoot the arrow for the sake of hitting the goal, the less you will succeed in the one and the further the other will recede. What stands in your way is that you have a much too willful will. You think that what you do not do yourself does not happen."

"But you yourself have told me often enough that archery is not a pastime, not a purposeless game, but a matter of life and death!"

"I stand by that. We master archers say: one shot—one life! What this means, you cannot yet understand. But perhaps another image will help you, which expresses the same experience. We master archers say: with the upper end of the bow the archer pierces the sky, on the lower end, as though attached by a thread, hangs the earth. If the shot is loosed with a jerk there is a danger of the thread snapping. For purposeful and violent people the rift becomes final, and they are left in the awful center between heaven and earth."

"What must I do, then?" I asked thoughtfully.

"You must learn to wait properly."

"And how does one learn that?"

"By letting go of yourself, leaving yourself and everything yours behind you so decisively that nothing more is left of you but a purposeless tension."

* From *Zen in the Art of Archery*, by Eugen Herrigel, translated by R. F. C. Hull. Copyright 1953 by Pantheon Books, Inc. Reprinted by permission of Pantheon Books/A Division of Random House, Inc. and by permission of Routledge & Kegan Paul Ltd.

. . . .

In order to slip the more easily into the process of drawing the bow and loosing the shot, the archer, kneeling to one side and beginning to concentrate, rises to his feet, ceremoniously steps up to the target and, with a deep obeisance, offers the bow and arrow like consecrated gifts, then nocks the arrow, raises the bow, draws it and waits in an attitude of supreme spiritual alertness. After the lightning release of the arrow and the tension, the archer remains in the posture adopted immediately following the shot until, after slowly expelling his breath, he is forced to draw air again. Then only does he let his arms sink, bows to the target and, if he has no more shots to discharge, steps quietly into the background.

Archery thus becomes a ceremony which exemplifies the "Great Doctrine."

Even if the pupil does not, at this stage, grasp the true significance of his shots, he at least understands why archery cannot be a sport, a gymnastic exercise. He understands why the technically learnable part of it must be practiced to the point of repletion. If everything depends on the archer's becoming purposeless and effacing himself in the event, then its outward realization must occur automatically, in no further need of the controlling or reflecting intelligence.

. . . .

Then, one day, after a shot, the Master made a deep bow and broke off the lesson. "Just then 'It' shot!" he cried, as I stared at him bewildered. And when I at last understood what he meant I couldn't suppress a sudden whoop of delight.

"What I have said," the Master told me severely, "was not praise, only a statement that ought not to touch you. Nor was my bow meant for you, for you are entirely innocent of this shot. You remained this time absolutely self-oblivious and without purpose in the highest tension, so that the shot fell from you like a ripe fruit. Now go on practicing as if nothing had happened."

Only after a considerable time did more right shots occasionally come off, which the Master signalized by a deep bow. How it happened that they loosed themselves without my doing anything, how it came about that my tightly closed right hand suddenly flew back wide open, I could not explain then and I cannot explain today. The fact remains that it did happen, and that alone is important. But at least I got to the point of being able to distinguish, on my own, the right shots from the failures. The qualitative difference is so great that it cannot be overlooked once it has been experienced. Outwardly, for the observer, the right shot is distinguished by the cushioning of the right hand as it is jerked back, so that no tremor runs through the body. Again, after wrong shots the pent-up breath is expelled explosively, and the next breath cannot be drawn quickly enough. After right shots the breath glides effortlessly to its end, whereupon air is unhurriedly breathed in again. The heart continues to beat evenly and quietly, and with concentration undisturbed one can go straight on to the next shot. But inwardly, for the archer himself, right shots have the effect of making him feel that the day has just begun. He feels in the mood for all right doing, and, what is perhaps even more important, for all right not-doing. Delectable indeed is this state. But he who has it, said the Master with a subtle smile, would do well to have it as though he did not have it. Only unbroken equanimity can accept it in such a way that it is not afraid to come back.

. . . .

The Master proceeded to give us a demonstration of target-shooting: both arrows were embedded in the black of the target. Then he bade us perform the ceremony exactly as before, and, without letting ourselves be put off by the target, wait at the highest tension until the shot "fell." The slender bamboo arrows flew off in the right direction, but failed to hit even the sandbank, still less the target,

and buried themselves in the ground just in front of it.

"Your arrows do not carry," observed the Master, "because they do not reach far enough spiritually. You must act as if the goal were infinitely far off. For master archers it is a fact of common experience that a good archer can shoot further with a medium-strong bow than an unspiritual archer can with the strongest. It does not depend on the bow, but on the presence of mind, on the vitality and awareness with which you shoot. In order to unleash the full force of this spiritual awareness, you must perform the ceremony differently: rather as a good dancer dances. If you do this, your movements will spring from the center, from the seat of right breathing. Instead of reeling off the ceremony like something learned by heart, it will then be as if you were creating it under the inspiration of the moment, so that dance and dancer are one and the same. By performing the ceremony like a religious dance, your spiritual awareness will develop its full force."

I do not know how far I succeeded in "dancing" the ceremony and thereby activating it from the center. I no longer shot too short, but I still failed to hit the target. This prompted me to ask the Master why he had never yet explained to us how to take aim. There must, I supposed, be a relation of sorts between the target and the tip of the arrow, and hence an approved method of sighting which makes hitting possible.

"Of course there is," answered the Master, "and you can easily find the required aim yourself. But if you hit the target with nearly every shot you are nothing more than a trick archer who likes to show off. For the professional who counts his hits, the target is only a miserable piece of paper which he shoots to bits. The 'Great Doctrine' holds this to be sheer devilry. It knows nothing of a target which is set up at a definite distance from the archer. It only knows of the goal, which cannot be aimed at technically, and it names this goal, if it names it at all, the Buddha." After these words, which he spoke as though they were self-evident, the Master told us to watch his eyes closely as he shot. As when performing the ceremony, they were almost closed, and we did not have the impression that he was sighting.

Obediently we practiced letting off our shots without taking aim. At first I remained completely unmoved by where my arrows went. Even occasional hits did not excite me, for I knew that so far as I was concerned they were only flukes. But in the end this shooting into the blue was too much for me. I fell back into the temptation to worry. The Master pretended not to notice my disquiet, until one day I confessed to him that I was at the end of my tether.

"You worry yourself unnecessarily," the Master comforted me. "Put the thought of hitting right out of your mind! You can be a Master even if every shot does not hit. The hits on the target are only the outward proof and confirmation of your purposelessness at its highest, of your egolessness, your self-abandonment, or whatever you like to call this state. There are different grades of mastery, and only when you have made the last grade will you be sure of not missing the goal."

. . . .

I seated myself opposite him on a cushion. He handed me tea, but did not speak a word. So we sat for a long while. There was no sound but the singing of the kettle on the hot coals. At last the Master rose and made me a sign to follow him. The practice hall was brightly lit. The Master told me to put a taper, long and thin as a knitting needle, in the sand in front of the target, but not to switch on the light in the target-stand. It was so dark that I could not even see its outlines, and if the tiny flame of the taper had not been there, I might perhaps have guessed the position of the target, though I could not have made it out with any precision. The Master "danced" the ceremony. His first arrow shot out of dazzling brightness into deep night. I knew from the sound that it had hit the target. The second arrow was a hit, too. When I switched on the light in the target-stand, I discovered to my amazement that the first arrow was lodged full in the middle of the black, while the second arrow had splintered the butt of the first and plowed through the shaft before embedding itself beside it. I did not dare to pull the arrows out separately, but carried them back together with the target. The Master surveyed them critically. "The first shot," he then said, "was no great feat, you will think, because after all these years I am so familiar with my target-stand that I must know even in pitch darkness where the target is. That may be, and I won't try to pretend otherwise. But the second arrow which hit the first—what do you make of that? I at any rate know that it is not 'I' who must be given credit for this shot. 'It' shot and 'It' made the hit. Let us bow to the goal as before the Buddha!"

The Master had evidently hit me, too, with both arrows: as though transformed over night, I no longer succumbed to the temptation of worrying about my arrows and what happened to them. The Master strengthened me in this attitude still further by never looking at the target, but simply keeping his eye on the archer, as though that gave him the most suitable indication of how the shot had fallen out. On being questioned, he freely admitted that this was so, and I was able to prove for myself again and again that his sureness of judgment in this matter was no whit inferior to the sureness of his arrows. Thus, through deepest concentration, he transferred the spirit of his art to his pupils, and I am not afraid to confirm from my own experience, which I doubted long enough, that the talk of immediate communication is not just a figure cf speech but a tangible reality. There was another form of help which the Master communicated to us at that time, and which he likewise spoke of as immediate transference of the spirit. If I had been continually shooting badly, the Master gave a few shots with my bow. The improvement was startling: it was as if the bow let itself be drawn differently, more willingly, more understandingly. This did not happen only with me. Even his oldest and most experienced pupils, men from all walks of life, took this as an established fact and were astonished that I should ask questions like one who wished to make quite sure. Similarly, no master of swordsmanship can be moved from his conviction that each of the swords fashioned with so much hard work and infinite care takes on the spirit of the swordsmith, who therefore sets about his work in ritual costume. Their experiences are far too striking, and they themselves far too skilled, for them not to perceive how a sword reacts in their hands.

One day the Master cried out the moment my shot was loosed: "It is there! Bow down to the goal!" Later, when I glanced towards the target—unfortunately I couldn't help myself—I saw that the arrow had only grazed the edge. "That was a right shot," said the Master decisively, "and so it must begin. But enough for today, otherwise you will take special pains with the next shot and spoil the good beginning." Occasionally several of these right shots came off in close succession and hit the target, besides of course the many more that failed. But if ever the least flicker of satisfaction showed in my face the Master turned on me with unwonted fierceness. "What are you thinking of?" he would cry. "You know already that you should not grieve over bad shots; learn now not to rejoice over the good ones. You must free yourself from the buffetings of pleasure and pain, and learn to rise above them in easy equanimity, to rejoice as though not you but another had shot well. This, too, you must practice unceasingly—you cannot conceive how important it is."

During these weeks and months I passed through the hardest schooling of my life, and though the discipline was not always easy for me to accept, I gradually came to see how much I was indebted to it. It destroyed the last traces of any preoccupation with myself and the fluctuations of my mood. "Do you now understand," the Master asked me one day after a particularly good shot, "what I mean by 'It shoots,' 'It hits'?"

"I'm afraid I don't understand anything more at all," I answered, "even the simplest things have got in a muddle. Is it 'I' who draw the bow, or is it the bow that draws me into the state of highest tension? Do 'I' hit the goal, or does the goal hit me? Is 'It' spiritual when seen by the eyes of the body, and corporeal when seen by the eyes of the spirit— or both or neither? Bow, arrow, goal and ego, all melt into one another, so that I can no longer separate them. And even the need to separate has gone. For as soon as I take the bow and shoot, everything becomes so clear and straightforward and so ridiculously simple. . . ."

"Now at last," the Master broke in, "the bow-string has cut right through you."

More than five years went by, and then the Master proposed that we pass a test. "It is not just a question of demonstrating your skill," he explained. "An even higher value is set on the spiritual deportment of the archer, down to his minutest gesture. I expect you above all not to let yourself be confused by the presence of spectators, but to go through the ceremony quite unperturbed, as though we were by ourselves."

Nor, during the weeks that followed, did we work with the test in mind; not a word was said about it, and often the lesson was broken off after a few shots. Instead, we were given the task of performing the ceremony at home, executing its steps and postures with particular regard to right breathing and deep concentration.

We practiced in the manner prescribed and discovered that hardly had we accustomed ourselves to dancing the ceremony without bow and arrow when we began to feel uncommonly concentrated after the first steps. This feeling increased the more care we took to facilitate the process of concentration by relaxing our bodies. And when, at lesson time, we again practiced with bow and arrow, these home exercises proved so fruitful that we were able to slip effortlessly into the state of "presence of mind." We felt so secure in ourselves that we looked forward to the day of the test and the presence of spectators with equanimity.

We passed the test so successfully that the Master had no need to crave indulgence of the spectators with an embarrassed smile, and were awarded diplomas on the spot, each inscribed with the degree of mastery in which we stood. The Master brought the proceedings to an end by giving two masterly shots in robes of surpassing magnificence. A few days later my wife, in an open contest, was awarded the master title in the art of flower arrangement.

From then on the lessons assumed a new face. Contenting himself with a few practice shots, the Master went on to expound the "Great Doctrine" in relation to the art of archery, and to adapt it to the stage we had reached. Although he dealt in mysterious images and dark comparisons, the meagerest hints were sufficient for us to understand what it was about. He dwelt longest on the "artless art" which must be the goal of archery if it is to reach perfection. "He who can shoot with the horn of the hare and the hair of the tortoise, and can hit the center without bow (horn) and arrow (hair), he alone is Master in the highest sense of the word—Master of the artless art. Indeed, he is the artless art itself and thus Master and No-Master in one. At this point archery, considered as the unmoved movement, the undanced dance, passes over into Zen."

BIBLIOGRAPHY ON SPORT AND METAPHYSICAL SPECULATIONS

Axelos, Kostas. "Planetary Interlude." *Game, Play, Literature.* Edited by Jacques Ehrmann. Boston: Beacon Press, 1971.

Bouet, Michel. "The Function of Sport in Human Relations." *International Review of Sport Sociology,* 1 (1966), 137-140.

Caillois, Roger. *Man, Play, and Games.* Translated by Meyer Barash. New York: Free Press of Glencoe, 1961.

Coe, George Albert. "A Philosophy of Play." *Religious Education,* LI (May-June, 1956), 220-222.

Coutts, Curtis A. "Freedom in Sport." *Quest*, X (May, 1968), 68-71.

Cox, Harvey. "Faith as Play" in *The Feast of Fools: A Theological Essay on Festivity and Fantasy*. Cambridge: Harvard University Press, 1969.

Ehrmann, Jacques, Ed. *Game, Play, Literature*. Boston: Beacon Press, 1971. (First published 1968: Yale French Studies.)

Fink, Eugen. "The Ontology of Play." *Philosophy Today*, 4 (Summer, 1960), 95-110.

Froebel, Friedrich. *Pedagogics of the Kindergarten*. Translated by Josephine Jarvis. New York: D. Appleton and Company, 1900.

Genasci, James E. and Klissouras, Vasillis. "The Delphic Spirit in Sports." *Journal of Health, Physical Education, and Recreation*, 37 (February, 1966), 43-45.

Gerber, Ellen W. "Identity, Relation and Sport." *Quest*, VIII (May, 1967), 90-97.

Gregg, Jearald Rex. "A Philosophical Analysis of the Sports Experience and the Role of Athletics in the Schools." Unpublished Ed. D. dissertation, University of Southern California, 1971.

Harper, William A. "Man Alone." *Quest*, XII (May, 1969), 57-60.

————. "Human Revolt: A Phenomenological Description." Unpublished Ph.D. dissertation, University of Southern California, 1971.

Herald, Childe [Thomas Hornsby Ferril]. "Freud and Football." *Reader in Comparative Religion: An Anthropological Approach*. Second Edition. Edited by William A. Lessa and Evon Z. Vogt. New York: Harper & Row, 1965.

Herrigel, Eugen. *Zen in the Art of Archery*. Translated by R. F. C. Hull. New York: McGraw-Hill, 1964. (First published 1960, New York: Pantheon Books.)

Horkheimer, Max. "New Patterns in Social Relations." *International Research in Sport and Physical Education*. Edited by E. Jokl and E. Simon. Illinois: Charles C Thomas, 1964.

Huizinga, Johan. *Homo Ludens*. London: Routledge & Kegan Paul, 1950.

Hyland, Drew. "Athletic Angst: Reflections on the Philosophical Relevance of Play." Unpublished paper, 1970.

Jaspers, Karl. "Sport" in *Man in the Modern Age*. Translated by Eden and Cedar Paul. Garden City, New York: Doubleday, 1957.

Jolivet, Régis. "Work, Play, Contemplation." Translated by Sister M. Delphine. *Philosophy Today*, V (Summer, 1961), 114-120.

Keating, James W. "Sartre on Sport and Play." Unpublished paper presented at the annual convention of the American Association for Health, Physical Education, and Recreation, Chicago, Illinois, March, 1966.

Kretchmar, Robert Scott. "A Phenomenological Analysis of the Other in Sport." Unpublished Ph.D. dissertation, University of Southern California, 1971.

Kretchmar, R. Scott and Harper, William A. "Why Does Man Play?" *Journal of Health, Physical Education, and Recreation*, 40 (March, 1969), 57-58.

McLuhan, Marshall. "Games" in *Understanding Media: The Extensions of Man*. New York: A Signet Book, 1964.

Mead, George H. "Play, the Game, and the Generalized Other" in *Mind, Self and Society from the Standpoint of a Social Behaviorist*. Edited by Charles W. Morris. Illinois: University of Chicago Press, 1959.

Metheny, Eleanor. *Movement and Meaning*. New York: McGraw-Hill, 1968.

Neale, Robert E. *In Praise of Play*. New York: Harper & Row, 1969.

Orringer, Nelson Robert. "Sport and Festival: A Study of Ludic Theory in Ortega y Gasset." Unpublished Ph.D. dissertation, Brown University, 1969.

Rossi, Ernest Lawrence. "Game and Growth: Two Dimensions of our Pyschotherapeutic Zeitgeist." *Journal of Humanistic Psychology*, 7 (Fall, 1967), 139-154.

Sadler, William A., Jr. "Play: A Basic Human Structure Involving Love and Freedom." *Review of Existential Psychology and Psychiatry*, 6 (Fall, 1966), 237-245.

————. "Creative Existence: Play as a Pathway to Personal Freedom and Community." *Humanitas*, V (Spring, 1969), 57-79.

Sartre, Jean-Paul. "Doing and Having" in *Being and Nothingness*. Translated by Hazel E. Barnes. New York: Philosophical Library, 1956.

"She I, or the Meaning of the Ceremony of Archery." in Woody, Thomas. *Life and Education in Early Societies*. New York: The Macmillan Co., 1959. (Reprinted from Muller, F. M., Ed. *The Sacred Books of the East*. Volume XXVIII. Oxford: Clarendon Press, 1879-1910.)

Slovenko, Ralph and Knight, James A., Eds. *Motivations in Play, Games and Sports*. Illinois: Charles C Thomas, 1967.

Slusher, Howard S. "Sport and Existence: An Analysis of Being." Unpublished paper presented at the History and Philosophy Section of the American Association for Health, Physical Education, and Recreation, Chicago, Illinois, March 21, 1966.

————. *Man, Sport and Existence*. Philadelphia: Lea & Febiger, 1967.

Stokes, Adrian. "Psycho-Analytic Reflections on the Development of Ball Games, Particularly Cricket." *International Journal of Psychoanalysis*, 37 (1956), 185-192.

————. "The Development of Ball Games." *Motivations in Play, Games and Sport*. Edited by Ralph Slovenko and James A. Knight. Illinois: Charles C Thomas, 1967.

Thomson, Patricia. "Ontological Truth in the Game of Golf." Unpublished Ph.D. dissertation, University of Southern California, 1967.

Van Den Berg, J. H. "The Human Body and the Significance of Human Movement." *Psychoanalysis and Existential Philosophy*. Edited by Hendrik M. Ruitenbeck. New York: E. P. Dutton, 1962.

Walsh, John Henry. "A Fundamental Ontology of Play and Leisure." Unpublished Ph.D. dissertation, Georgetown University, 1968.

Weiss, Paul. *Sport: A Philosophic Inquiry*. **Carbondale: Southern Illinois University Press, 1969.**

THE BODY AND BEING

The Body and Being

INTRODUCTION

Thinkers who believe that man is a unified being, an integrated whole, nevertheless often resort to dualistic terminology. Thus one often reads that man is composed of mind, body and spirit, or that there are physical and mental aspects of man's functioning. For example, the early physical educators in America assumed their role to be the fostering of body development to parallel the mental development occurring in academic classes. Luther Halsey Gulick conceived of the symbol of the inverted triangle, the spirit upheld by mind and body, encircled to represent unity. Jesse Feiring Williams insisted that all activities taught should have mental and spiritual values, as well as physical benefits.

These beliefs have been reflective of the ideas advanced by philosophers who have wrestled with the problem of defining the relationships between body, mind and soul. The question of the relative value of each dimension is also inherent in the problem, and opinions range from those who accord greatest importance to the soul, to those who think that mind is the essential quality of man. Few philosophers have contended that the body has greatest value, though the seventeenth-century sense empiricists did establish the importance of the body to man's ability to know. In so doing, they clearly rejected the earlier idealistic rationalism, based upon Descartes' assertion that he is not a bodily man, but a thinking man who knows through pure "intellection" and not through sensation.

Descartes' position is similar to, but more extreme than, the influential description of the body-soul relationship* detailed in Plato's *Phaedo.* In the excerpt presented on later pages, Plato clearly indicates a separation of the body and soul, and a denigration of the kinds of knowledges available from the senses. In fact, his attitude towards the body is quite negative, a position doubtless derived from his personal struggles with bodily passions coupled with his intense belief in the values of harmony, balance and moderation. (Plato's negative opinions about the body should not be confused with his positive approach to sport, a position clearly delineated in *The Republic* and *The Laws.*) Descartes extends the concept of the dualism of mind and body to the point where he states that "we clearly perceive mind, that is, thinking substance, without body, that is to say, extended substance . . .; and conversely, body without mind . . ."† In the selection included in this book, René Descartes examines the relation between mind and body.

A whole body of philosophical literature has

* Plato's use of the term soul is to be taken as having the broad connotations of spirit and mind —the enduring, essential quality of the individual.

† From the "Second Replies to Objections" as quoted in T. V. Smith and Marjorie Grene, *Philosophers Speak for Themselves* (Chicago: University of Chicago Press, 1957), p. 124. However, in a persuasive discussion Stuart F. Spicker demonstrated that Descartes' position was really not as extreme as appears. He concluded that Descartes himself would have rejected what has come to be known as Cartesian dualism. See *The Philosophy of the Body* (Chicago: Quadrangle Books, 1970), pp. 8-18.

been created in modern times which continues in the tradition of Cartesian dualism. Seeking to clarify the relationship of mind and body, a branch of philosophy known as "philosophy of mind" has evolved. Because the primary stress is on mind, works of these philosophers have not been included in this book, but some of the more pertinent articles have been listed in the bibliography.

Theologians have been among the most vehement of dualists, not only viewing the body as distinct from the soul, but actually regarding it as antagonistic. The literature of the Christian church, especially, has been replete with works which condone asceticism, denial, abstinence, in a word, subjugation of the flesh. When not condemning the body, official Christian doctrine has generally placed a low value upon it. Warren Fraleigh, in a provocative article, presents the modern Christian view of the body-soul relation, one which emphasizes the unity of man, with body as a dimension of that unity. The excerpt from Jacques Sarano deals with the spiritual implications which arise from the body-subject existing in the universe.

The most interesting approaches to the study of the body have been those made by contemporary phenomenologists. They have completely broken from the dualistic Cartesian thinking and have, instead, worked from the point of view that the body is the primary self. In other words, the body is not an instrument of the mind, nor is it connected to it; it is not a vehicle for directed sensation, nor is it a devilish antagonist to the spirit. The body is you; you are your body. Your body is your mode of being-in-the-world. The body as object—to be perceived, studied, analyzed by self or others—is a different mode of being, called by Sartre being-for-others. The selection by Calvin O. Schrag describes the general parameters of the phenomenologist's approach to a consideration of the body. The short excerpts from Jean-Paul Sartre and Gabriel Marcel both illuminate the dimensions of the two approaches to the body: as self and as object. In "The Analytic of the Lived Body," Alphonse de Waelhens clearly delineates the essential considerations revolving around the concept of the body as being-in-the-world.

Strangely, those who have been interested in sport and/or physical education, have shown little interest in the philosophy of the body. They have treated the body as an object to be trained, trimmed, studied in a laboratory, or made a cause célèbre. In the first quarter of the twentieth century when the physical educators became satisfied with the idea of unity of mind and body, they ceased to speculate about it in any meaningful way. The four articles in this book, by Paul Weiss, Esar Shvartz, Eugene Kaelin, and Seymour Kleinman, represent a major portion of the articles existent from any discipline which attempt to philosophize about the body in physical activity.

What are the connections between sport and the body? What can be learned about oneself, and what experiences of being-in-the-body can occur in the sport experience? What affects these experiences? How does the experience of self differ if the body is trained and if it is untrained? What can be learned by studying the body as an object and determining such factors as its strength and agility? What effect does it have on the sport experience if the body is treated as an object? How much does deliberate concentration and/or reflection about the body contribute to the experience of the body in sport? Is it important to know the limitations of the body? If so, why?

Numerous books and articles have been published on the philosophy of the body. One of the best is a collection of readings edited by Stuart F. Spiker (1970). *Humanitas*, II (Spring, 1966) is a publication devoted entirely to "The Human Body." A number of its articles, however, fall into the psychological realm, particularly the area of "body image." Although the subject of body image is important and has captured the interest of many physical educators as well as psychologists, it was not included in this book because it really is tangential to a study of the philosophy of the body. Although only a short selection by Jacques Sarano (1966) could be included in this book, the reader will find the entire work interesting. Zaner (1964) presents a beautiful and comprehensive study of the phenomenology of the body.

Some of the significant articles on the radical reality (i.e., the roots or grounds of reality) include Hengstenberg (1963), Kwant (1966) and Jonas (1965). Books on existential phenomenology, such as Luijpen and Dondeyne (1960) usually include one or more chapters on the body.

Studies which analyze the body in movement situations, include the excellent chapter by Van Den Berg (1962), and articles by Beets (1964) and Wenkart (1963).

Some of the analytic writings about the body which might be of interest include Long (1964), Köhler (1960) and Shaffer (1965). Volume II of the Minnesota Series is an important collection in this area (Feigl, Maxwell and Scriven, 1958). *Body and Mind,* subtitled "A History and Defense of Animism," an early work by McDougall which was reprinted in 1961 includes an insightful historical account of its subject.

The philosophy of the body is a fascinating subject. It is one that those who are interested in sport and/or physical education would find highly relevant. Thus far the focus from people with such interests has been primarily on the body-for-others—in other words, the body as object. Some persons have been interested in the dysfunctional body, and some have focused their attention on the relation between body image and personality. However, a concern crucial to sport is the body as being-in-the-world—or the body as subject. A particularly important area for research is the possible difference experienced by the lived body in a sport situation, as opposed to a situation which is not marked by physical effort. It would also be significant to know the difference between experiences in various sports demanding different modes of body action; for example, the body as attacker (as a tackler in football) may provide a different experience of self than the body as strategic and skillful stroker (as in tennis). The body experience in different media also bears examination—in the air, in the water and on land. Finally, the differences between the body acting alone as opposed to acting in concert with others might be analyzed. The challenge to those who wish to undertake such studies definitely includes the development of philosophical techniques which reliably attempt the most difficult task of analyzing someone's subjective experience. Most likely this will involve a detailed study of the philosophy of phenomenology which has deliberately attempted to develop methods for just this purpose.

The Separation of Body and Soul*

PLATO

Do we believe death to be anything?

We do, replied Simmias.

And do we not believe it to be the separation of the soul from the body? Does not death mean that the body comes to exist by itself, separated from the soul, and that the soul exists by herself, separated from the body? What is death but that?

It is that, he said.

Now consider, my good friend, if you and I are agreed on another point which I think will help us to understand the question better. Do you think that a philosopher will care very much about what are called pleasures, such as the pleasures of eating and drinking?

Certainly not, Socrates, said Simmias.

Or about the pleasures of sexual passion?

Indeed, no.

And, do you think that he holds the remaining cares of the body in high esteem? Will he think much of getting fine clothes, and sandals, and other bodily adornments, or will he despise them, except so far as he is absolutely forced to meddle with them?

The real philosopher, I think, will despise them, he replied.

In short, said he, you think that his studies are not concerned with the body? He stands aloof from it, as far as he can, and turns toward the soul?

* From Plato: *Phaedo*, translated by F. J. Church, copyright © 1951, by The Liberal Arts Press, Inc., reprinted by permission of the publisher, The Bobbs-Merrill Company, Inc.

I do.

Well, then, in these matters, first, is it clear that the philosopher releases his soul from communion with the body, so far as he can, beyond all other men?

It is.

And does not the world think, Simmias, if a man has no pleasure in such things, and does not take his share in them, his life is not worth living? Do not they hold that he who thinks nothing of bodily pleasures is almost as good as dead?

Indeed you are right.

But what about the actual acquisition of wisdom? If the body is taken as a companion in the search for wisdom, is it a hindrance or not? For example, do sight and hearing convey any real truth to men? Are not the very poets forever telling us that we neither hear nor see anything accurately? But if these senses of the body are not accurate or clear, the others will hardly be so, for they are all less perfect than these, are they not?

Yes, I think so, certainly, he said.

Then when does the soul attain truth? he asked. We see that, as often as she seeks to investigate anything in company with the body, the body leads her astray.

True.

Is it not by reasoning, if at all, that any real truth becomes manifest to her?

Yes.

And she reasons best, I suppose, when none of the senses, whether hearing, or sight, or pain, or pleasure, harasses her; when she has dismissed the body, and released herself as far as she can from all intercourse or contact with it, and so, coming to be as much alone with herself as is possible, strives after real truth.

That is so.

And here too the soul of the philosopher very greatly despises the body, and flies from it, and seeks to be alone by herself, does she not?

Clearly.

And what do you say to the next point, Simmias? Do we say that there is such a thing as absolute justice, or not?

Indeed we do.

And absolute beauty, and absolute good?

Of course.

Have you ever seen any of them with your eyes?

Indeed I have not, he replied.

Did you ever grasp them with any bodily sense? I am speaking of all absolutes, whether size, or health, or strength; in a word, of the essence of real being of everything. Is the very truth of things contemplated by the body? Is it not rather the case that the man who prepares himself most carefully to apprehend by his intellect the essence of each thing which he examines will come nearest to the knowledge of it?

Certainly.

And will not a man attain to this pure thought most completely if he goes to each thing, as far as he can, with his mind alone, taking neither sight nor any other sense along with his reason in the process of thought, to be an encumbrance? In every case he will pursue pure and absolute being, with his pure intellect alone. He will be set free as far as possible from the eye and the ear and, in short, from the whole body, because intercourse with the body troubles the soul, and hinders her from gaining truth and wisdom. Is it not he who will attain the knowledge of real being, if any man will?

Your words are admirably true, Socrates, said Simmias.

. . . .

Let us assume then, he said, if you will, that there are two kinds of existence, the one visible, the other invisible.

Yes, he said.

And the invisible is unchanging, while the visible is always changing.

Yes, he said again.

Are not we men made up of body and soul?

There is nothing else, he replied.

And which of these kinds of existence should we say that the body is most like, and most akin to?

The visible, he replied; that is quite obvious.

And the soul? Is that visible or invisible?

It is visible to man, Socrates, he said.

But we mean by visible and invisible, visible and invisible to man; do we not?

Yes; that is what we mean.

Then what do we say of the soul? Is it visible or not visible?

It is not visible.

Then is it invisible?

Yes.

Then the soul is more like the invisible than the body; and the body is like the visible.

That is necessarily so, Socrates.

Have we not also said that, when the soul employs the body in any inquiry, and makes use of sight, or hearing, or any other sense—for inquiry with the body means inquiry with the senses—she is dragged away by it to the things which never remain the same, and wanders about blindly, and becomes confused and dizzy, like a drunken man, from dealing with things that are ever changing?

Certainly.

But when she investigates any question by herself, she goes away to the pure, and eternal, and immortal, and unchangeable, to which she is akin, and so she comes to be ever with it, as soon as she is by herself, and can be so; and then she rests from her wanderings and dwells with it unchangingly; for she is dealing with what is unchanging. And is not this state of the soul called wisdom?

Indeed, Socrates, you speak well and truly, he replied.

Which kind of existence do you think from our former and our present arguments that the soul is more like and more akin to?

I think, Socrates, he replied, that after this inquiry the very dullest man would agree that the soul is infinitely more like the unchangeable than the changeable.

And the body?

That is like the changeable.

Consider the matter in yet another way. When the soul and the body are united, nature ordains the one to be a slave and to be ruled, and the other to be master and to rule. Tell me once again, which do you think is like the divine, and which is like the mortal? Do you not think that the divine naturally rules and has authority, and that the mortal naturally is ruled and is a slave?

I do.

Then which is the soul like?

That is quite plain, Socrates. The soul is like the divine, and the body is like the mortal.

New tell me, Cebes, is the result of all that we have said that the soul is most like the divine, and the immortal, and the intelligible, and the uniform, and the indissoluble, and the unchangeable; while the body is most like the human, and the mortal, and the unintelligible, and the multiform, and the dissoluble, and the changeable? Have we any other argument to show that this is not so, my dear Cebes?

We have not.

The Real Distinction Between the Mind and Body of Man*

RENÉ DESCARTES

First, since I know that all the things I conceive clearly and distinctly can be produced by God exactly as I conceive them, it is sufficient that I can clearly and distinctly conceive one thing apart from another to be certain that the one is distinct or different from the other. For they can be made to exist separately, at least by the omnipotence of God, and we are obliged to consider them different no matter what power produces this separation. From the very fact that I know with certainty that I exist, and that I find that absolutely nothing else belongs necessarily to my nature or essence except that I am a thinking being, I readily conclude that my essence consists solely in being a body which thinks or a substance whose whole essence or nature is only to think. And although perhaps, or rather certainly, as I will soon show, I have a body with which I am very closely united, nevertheless, since on the one hand I have a clear and distinct idea of myself in so far as I am only a thinking and not an extended being, and since on the other hand I have a distinct idea of body in so far as it is only an extended being which does not think, it is certain that this "I"—that is to say, my soul, by virtue of which I am what I am—is entirely and truly

* From René Descartes: *Meditations on First Philosophy,* translated by Laurence J. Lafleur, copyright © 1951, 1960, by The Liberal Arts Press, Inc., reprinted by permission of the publisher, The Bobbs-Merrill Company, Inc.

distinct from my body and that it can be or exist without it.

Furthermore, I find in myself various faculties of thinking which each have their own particular characteristics and are distinct from myself. For example, I find in myself the faculties of imagination and of perception, without which I might no doubt conceive of myself, clearly and distinctly, as a whole being; but I could not, conversely, conceive of those faculties without me, that is to say, without an intelligent substance to which they are attached or in which they inhere. For in our notion of them or, to use the scholastic vocabulary, in their formal concept, they embrace some type of intellection. From all this I reach the conception that these faculties are distinct from me as shapes, movements, and other modes or accidents of objects are distinct from the very objects that sustain them.

I also recognize in myself some other faculties, such as the power of changing location, of assuming various postures, and other similar ones; which cannot be conceived without some substance in which they inhere, any more than the preceding ones, and which therefore cannot exist without such a substance. But it is quite evident that these faculties, if it is true that they exist, must inhere in some corporeal or extended substance, and not in an intelligent substance, since their clear and distinct concept does actually involve some sort of extension, but no sort of intelligence whatsoever.

Furthermore, I cannot doubt that there is in me a certain passive faculty of perceiving, that is, of receiving and recognizing the ideas of sensible objects; but it would be valueless to me, and I could in no way use it if there were not also in me, or in something else, another active faculty capable of forming and producing these ideas. But this active faculty cannot be in me, in so far as I am a thinking being, since it does not at all presuppose my intelligence and also since those ideas often occur to me without my contributing to them in any way, and even frequently against my will. Thus it must necessarily exist in some substance different from myself, in which all the reality that exists objectively in the ideas produced by this faculty is formally or eminently contained, as I have said before. This substance is either a body— that is, a corporeal nature—in which is formally and actually contained all that which is contained objectively and by representation in these ideas; or else it is God himself, or some other creation more noble than the body, in which all this is eminently contained.

. . . .

To begin this examination, I first take notice here that there is a great difference between the mind and the body, in that the body, from its nature, is always divisible and the mind is completely indivisible. For in reality, when I consider the mind—that is, when I consider myself in so far as I am only a thinking being— I cannot distinguish any parts, but I recognize and conceive very clearly that I am a thing which is absolutely unitary and entire. And although the whole mind seems to be united with the whole body, nevertheless when a foot or an arm or some other part of the body is amputated, I recognize quite well that nothing has been lost to my mind on that account. Nor can the faculties of willing, perceiving, understanding, and so forth be any more properly called parts of the mind, for it is one and the same mind which as a complete unit wills, perceives, and understands, and so forth. But just the contrary is the case with corporeal or extended objects, for I cannot imagine any, however small they might be, which my mind does not very easily divide into several parts, and I consequently recognize these objects to be divisible. This alone would suffice to show me that the mind or soul of man is altogether different from the body, if I did not already know it sufficiently well for other reasons.

I also take notice that the mind does not receive impressions from all parts of the body directly, but only from the brain, or perhaps even from one of its smallest parts—the one, namely, where the senses in common have their seat. This makes the mind feel the same thing whenever it is in the same condition, even though the other parts of the body can be differently arranged, as is proved by an infinity of experiments which it is not necessary to describe here.

I furthermore notice that the nature of the body is such that no one of its parts can be moved by another part some little distance away without its being possible for it to be moved in the same way by any one of the intermediate parts, even when the more distant part does not act. For example, in the cord A B C D which is thoroughly stretched, if we pull and move the last part D, the first part A will not be moved in any different manner from that in which it could also be moved if we pulled one of the middle parts B or C, while the last part D remained motionless. And in the same way, when I feel pain in my foot, physics teaches me that this sensation is communicated by means of nerves distributed through the foot. When these nerves are pulled in the foot, being stretched like cords from there to the brain, they likewise pull at the same time the internal part of the brain from which they come and where they terminate, and there produce a certain movement which nature has arranged to make my mind feel pain as though that pain were in my foot. But because these nerves must pass through the leg, the thigh, the loins, the back, and neck, in order to extend from the foot to the brain, it can happen that even when the nerve endings in the foot are not stimulated, but only some of the intermediate parts located in the loins or the neck, precisely the same movements are nevertheless produced in the brain that could be produced there by a wound received in the foot, as a result of which it necessarily follows that the mind feels the same pain in the foot as though the foot had been wounded. And we must make the same judgment about all our other sense perceptions.

Finally, I notice that since each one of the movements that occurs in the part of the brain from which the mind receives impressions directly can only produce in the mind a single sensation, we cannot desire or imagine any better arrangement than that this movement should cause the mind to feel that sensation, of all sensations the movement is capable of causing, which is most effectively and frequently useful for the preservation of the human body when it is in full health. But experience shows us that all the sensations which nature has given us are such as I have just stated, and therefore there is nothing in their nature which does not show the power and the goodness of the God who has produced them.

Thus, for example, when the nerves of the foot are stimulated violently and more than is usual, their movement, passing through the marrow of the backbone up to the interior of the brain, produces there an impression upon the mind which makes the mind feel something—namely, pain as though in the foot—by which the mind is warned and stimulated to do whatever it can to remove the cause, taking it to be very dangerous and harmful to the foot.

It is true that God could establish the nature of man in such a way that this same brain event would make the mind feel something quite different; for example, it might cause the movement to be felt as though it were in the brain, or in the foot, or else in some other intermediate location between the foot and the brain, or finally it might produce any other feeling that can exist; but none of those would have contributed so well to the preservation of the body as that which it does produce.

In the same way, when we need to drink, there results a certain dryness in the throat which affects its nerves and, by means of them, the interior of the brain. This brain event makes the mind feel the sensation of thirst, because under those conditions there is nothing more useful to us than to know that we need to drink for the conservation of our health. And similar reasoning applies to other sensations.

From this it is entirely manifest that, despite the supreme goodness of God, the nature of man, in so far as he is composed of mind and body, cannot escape being sometimes faulty and deceptive. For if there is some cause which produces, not in the foot, but in some other part of the nerve which is stretched from the foot to the brain, or even in the brain itself, the same effect which ordinarily occurs when the foot is injured, we will feel pain as though it were in the foot, and we will naturally be deceived by the sensation. The reason for this is that the same brain event can cause only a single sensation in the mind; and this sensation being much more frequently produced by a cause which wounds the foot than by another acting in a different location, it is much more reasonable that it should always convey to the

mind a pain in the foot rather than one in any other part of the body. And if it happens that sometimes the dryness of the throat does not come in the usual manner from the fact that drinking is necessary for the health of the body, but from some quite contrary cause, as in the case of those afflicted with dropsy, nevertheless it is much better that we should be deceived in that instance than if, on the contrary, we were always deceived when the body was in health; and similarly for the other sensations.

And certainly this consideration is very useful to me, not only so that I can recognize all the errors to which my nature is subject, but also so that I may avoid them or correct them more easily. For knowing that each of my senses conveys truth to me more often than falsehood concerning whatever is useful or harmful to the body, and being almost always able to use several of them to examine the same object, and being in addition able to use my memory to bind and join together present information with what is past, and being able to use my understanding, which has already discovered all the causes of my errors, I should no longer fear to encounter falsity in the objects which are most commonly represented to me by my senses.

And I should reject all the doubts of these last few days as exaggerated and ridiculous, particularly that very general uncertainty about sleep, which I could not distinguish from waking life. For now I find in them a very notable difference, in that our memory can never bind and join our dreams together one with another and all with the course of our lives, as it habitually joins together what happens to us when we are awake. And so, in effect, if someone suddenly appeared to me when I was awake and afterward disappeared in the same way, as do images that I see in my sleep, so that I could not determine where he came from or where he went, it would not be without reason that I would consider it a ghost or a phantom produced in my brain and similar to those produced there when I sleep, rather than truly a man.

But when I perceive objects in such a way that I distinctly recognize both the place from which they come and the place where they are, as well as the time when they appear to me; and when, without any hiatus, I can relate my perception of them with all the rest of my life, I am entirely certain that I perceive them wakefully and not in sleep. And I should not in any way doubt the truth of these things if, having made use of all my senses, my memory, and my understanding, to examine them, nothing is reported to me by any of them which is inconsistent with what is reported by the others. For, from the fact that God is not a deceiver, it necessarily follows that in this manner I am not deceived.

But because the exigencies of action frequently oblige us to make decisions and do not always allow us the leisure to examine these things with sufficient care, we must admit that human life is very often subject to error in particular matters; and we must in the end recognize the infirmity and weakness of our nature.

A Christian Concept of the Body-Soul Relation

WARREN FRALEIGH

There is a kind of duality in more recent Christian thinking regarding the body-soul relation. The different sense of duality [different in that it is not a metaphysical duality] is founded in man's phenomenological awareness of a "twoness" of body and soul.[5-373] This different sense of duality is recognition of man's continuing sensing that those qualities of his being which are "soulish" are somehow different from but, at the same time, intrinsically involved in those qualities of his being which are bodily. Conversely this different duality attempts to recognize that the "bodily" qualities of man's being are different from but, again at the same time, intrinsically involved in the "soulish." To reiterate here, Christian anthropology refuses to engage in the reductionism of explaining either body or soul as an emanation of one from the other as would materialist or Idealist abstract metaphysical monisms.[3-392] Thus, it is stated, "Ontologically man is a unity, phenomenologically, mind and nature, and especially mind and body, are to be strictly distinguished."[5-373] Much contemporary Christian theology views the unity of body and soul as indissolvable. Indeed, to talk ". . . of body or soul in reference to man, then, is to speak of abstractions."[7-37] For to speak of either body or soul is to verbalize about a totality (man) from only one side of the totality. But how can we hope to understand a totality which is a unity without examining what is being unified? In short, it becomes necessary to speak of the abstractions "body" and "soul" before we can speak meaningfully of their unity as man—analysis becomes the necessary prerequisite to synthesis.

What name shall be given to these two perspectives from which we view the totality? "Parts" and "levels" both seem to carry the meaning of independent and distinct substances which are "pasted" together to make the unity. "Factors" seems too impersonal in talking of man. Perhaps "dimensions" is the best English word since it seems to imply a perfect fusion of body and soul but, at the same time, has a disadvantage of connoting a static quality.[7-34] Henceforth, to speak of body or soul means to discuss the unity which is man from the perspective of one of the dimensions of the dynamic being of the unity itself.

The Bodily Dimension. The bodily side of man as unity of body and soul may be understood at the personal level by recognizing the functions of that dimension in relating man to the created world.

The bodily dimension is the openness of man to the world.[3-418] As openness, the body has a special relation to the awareness side of man's perception in that it allows the "other" to come *to* man. [3-401] In bringing the "other" *to* man, the bodily dimension lays the basis for communion with the "other." In turn, communion with the "other" makes possible the revelation of God's Word through the world.[4-63,8-154]

Further, man's bodily dimension functions

both ways, that is, by doing as well as by perceiving, by outward manifestation as well as "bringing to" man. One type of doing is that of man re-presenting himself, i.e., man as unity expressing himself.[4–62,8–41] Such bodily expression makes man available to the perceptual apparatus of the "other" and, by means of reciprocal expression, communication between men takes place. In turn, communication forms the basis of community and, consequently, human society.[8–154] Perhaps a more obvious kind of doing is understood by recognizing that man's bodily dimension is his shaper of matter[5–108] by allowing him to realize ideas concretely.[4–63]

But man as bodily dimension is to be understood in ways which go beyond perceiving and doing. Certain combinations of perceiving and doing bring meanings to man of somewhat greater depth. The bodily tells man of his common bond with all people in that, ". . . irrespective of individual differences," we are all ". . . in life's bundle together."[16–29] The intimate bond of man to man finds clear expression in his dependence upon others in the indispensable relations of procreation and birth.[5–108] And indeed of great significance to man is his awareness of bondage to the transitory and mortal—to the power of death—and this comes to him by the bodily.[5–388] This awareness of death, in conjunction with the bodily reality of bondage to the same necessities of the created world as all animals, is the sign to man of his "creaturely" character, i.e., he himself, man, is not the Creator—he is not God.[4–62;5,107–08]

The bodily dimension of man may also be expressed as object, that is, the body is the outer and peripheral moment of man as unity.[3–19] As the outer and peripheral moment —the bodily dimension, "*Man is called soma* [body] *in respect to his being able to make himself the object of his own action. . .*"[6–195] This is to say, man in his unity, he himself, does something *to* body (his objectivity) not he does something *with* body. Nonetheless, the idea of body as object must not be interpreted to mean that the body may be spoken of "in terms of a machine." The magnificence of the created living body cannot be explained in the same terms as a machine which has been invented and understood by man.[5–379] Further, the idea of body as object does not mean that "it" is a tool or instrument in man's "hand" which may be discarded ". . . when no longer wanted or needed. . . ."[7–38]

A key concept of the bodily dimension of man, which will be an important basis for later discussion, is that it is that which is man's involvement in finitude (space), temporality (time) and necessity.[7–35] This idea from Kierkegaard[11,1–2] means that man is *objectively* involved in the same kind of space-time determinism as are all other creatures in the created order and it is in the "givenness" of man's nature to be so.

The Soulish Dimension. The word soul seems to carry a whole cargo of conceptions. Current Christian thinking seems to evidence a general effort to explain soul in ways which are comprehensible to the modern mind. Perhaps the first necessity here is to approach directly what is *not* meant by soul in this present exposition.

It must be made clear that to talk of soul is not to speak of some ethereal substance which is capable of existence *sans* body. Neither must soul be considered as ". . . a *part* of God's Spirit, nor God's Spirit dwelling in man, nor God coming to consciousness in man."[7–75,15–167,17–99] Logically, the former concept above would necessitate either the development of an abstract metaphysical monism or an abstract metaphysical dualism. The latter idea above obviously makes man's soul only an emanation of God and, consequently, divests man of any individual, personal uniqueness and integrity of being. In this discussion it is hoped that both of these ideas are clearly rejected as inadequate to explain the soul of man.

Speaking in the positive vein about soul, while rejecting the two concepts above, it may be said "Rather we are trying to isolate the uniqueness of that configuration of life which we call "human," which is integrally fleshly or somatic."[7–59] The most general meaning of the word soul which is derived from the Hebraic Biblical tradition is that soul is "life." This means that any thing or any being which is has soul and life, or it is not. But this does not say anything in particular about the kind of life which whatever is possesses. Therefore, to speak of *human* soul is to speak of the *form* of life which is distinctly man's and, consequently, distinguishes man in his uniqueness from all other forms of being.[7,54–60] With this in mind it is now appropriate to discuss particular *qualities* of the human *form* of life, i.e., man's soul.

One way of "sorting out" the soulish dimension of man as unity is by use of spatial metaphors. In differentiation from the bodily dimension which is man's outer and peripheral openness to the world, the soulish is the inner and central dimension.[3,397–98] If the body brings the "other" *to* man, the soulish decides whether or not the "other" will come *into* man.[3,401-02]

Human soul is integrally fleshly or somatic. Soul as life is the difference between material body, i.e. not alive, and physical body, i.e. living. Man as unity *is* ". . . as his material body is *alive* and therefore physical body" (besouled), and, at the same time, he *is* ". . . as his *material body* is alive" (embodied).[3-350]

The soulish also stands for man's given capacity to desire in a way distinct from the common animate desires such as food and sex. Man in unity has ability ". . . to formulate ideas or images of what his soul (his total life) needs in order to be strong and full. . . . these images are his desires." These desires are a self-projection beyond the realized self—the ideal self as over against the realized self.[7-63] It is in this "gap" between the two selves that man becomes self-conscious, that is, he is aware of an "I" who exists ". . . in this tension between an awareness of what I am and an awareness of what I ought and long to be. . . ." Further, consciousness of this "I" arising in the tension between the projected self and the realized self makes man aware of his present inadequacy and perversion of his life. Thus, ". . . the Biblical conception of human desiring stands for the capacity of man to achieve self-consciousness through the act of self-projection or self-transcendence."[7,63-4]

Man's soulish dimension can be designated by the term "heart" when it connotes his being as a unified personal subject in distinction from heart as a material part or organ. "Heart," in its soulish connotation, means the basic thrust or direction of man in his unity. "Heart" means the unified thinking and willing person. But the soulish idea of "heart" is not to be confused with only a highly rationalistic, logical decision-type process since the rational (thinking) and the volitional (willing) are intimately involved in each other. They are not distinct, separable human "faculties." Indeed, a man's "heart" is his whole "organismic" thrust, "it" is ". . . the whole cumulative tendency or direction of his life. A man *is* his heart."[7,67-8] To use another word, which hopefully at this point has been divested of unwarranted connotations, a man's "heart" is his entire characteristic "spirit."

In the attempt to integrate several understandings regarding man's soul as his "heart" the following is appropriate:

By this unifying shaping capacity, man receives the formative imprint of those realities to which he turns his attention and to which he opens the sensitivities of all his avenues of experience; by it, he projects the image of the desirable self as over against the self as already formed by realities admitted into the soul; by it, man investigates, appropriates, and shapes those practical ideas which will lead to the "right result"; and as such a being, man moves into the appropriate event.[7-69]

Thus, the heart of man which directs his attention to and admits certain realities, projects desirable self images and investigates and shapes his practical concerns, results from the human unity of the bodily and soulish.

A final key understanding of the soulish from Kierkegaard (which will be an important basis for later discussion) is that it is that which involves man *subjectively* in infinity, eternity and freedom.[7-35] The soulish is that in the givenness of man's nature which makes him a subject in the image of God but not in the sense of ". . . pure divine spirituality. If the latter were true, man would not *be* subject (spirit) but would only *have* Subject (the divine Spirit. . . .")[7,88-9]

Man As Unity of the Bodily and Soulish Dimensions.[*] Now that the two dimensions of the human unity have been clarified by analysis it is possible to synthesize several meanings into a deeper understanding of the unity itself.

Man exists as a realized indissolvable unity of the bodily and soulish dimensions. This indissolvable unity is "I" or, to use contemporary language, self or person—or, to use contemporary Christian anthropological language, spirit.[7-37] This "I," this self or person, this spirit ". . . transcends either the bodily or the soulish in isolation. . ." and ". . . arises within the relation of the two, so that, apart from that unique relation wherein the two have continuing significance, the human self, or spirit, or person can have no life or reality."[7-37] In effect then, to speak of man as "I," self, person, or spirit is to speak of a unique "entity" who arises within the unity of the bodily and soulish, who is not himself only bodily or soulish, but is a transcendent "entity" who is neither one nor the other but both at the same time. It is this "I" (self, person or spirit) who speaks of "his body" or "his soul" and recognizes the constituent reality of these two dimensions of his own existence. This is the "I" who is conscious of his own

[*] Appreciation is here expressed to Dr. Arnold B. Come, President, San Francisco Theological Seminary for his reactions to the material included in this section of this paper.

consciousness, i.e., aware of a self-transcendence. This is the "I" who is aware of himself
as a unity in duality or dual unity.[7-75] This
phenomenon of man's sensing of his unitary
"twoness" is, perhaps, the meaning intended
by Brunner[5-373] when he states, "Ontologically
man is a unity ["I," self, person or spirit],
phenomenologically, mind and nature, and
especially mind and body [Kierkegaard's
soulish and bodily dimensions?], are to be
strictly distinguished.*

Although man's bodily dimension is that
which involves man in the temporal, in the
finite and in necessity, such involvement includes man's whole nature as the "entity" who
arises within the unity, the "I" (self, person
or spirit). Thus, man's bodily objectivity is
distinct from other animals and, consequently,
is not to be investigated and understood only
in the same way as other animals, i.e., via
strict naturalism. Conversely, although man's
soulish dimension is that which involves man
in the infinite and in freedom, such involvement also includes his whole nature as the
"entity" who arises within the unity, the "I"
(self, person or spirit). Thus, man's soulish
subjectivity is distinct from God (although in
His image) and, consequently, is not to be
investigated and understood only via spiritual-
ism. Man as "I" (self, person or spirit) exists
as man then objectively as a subject. That is,
because man's bodily dimension involves him
as "I" integrally in animal creatureliness he is
like all animals but still not pure animality
because the eternal, infinite and free dimension
of "I" (the soulish) allows the "I" transcendence over the animal. Also, because man's
soulish dimension involves him as "I" integrally
in the image of God he is like God but still
not "pure divine spirituality" because the
temporal, finite and necessity dimension of "I"
(the bodily) gives the "I" distinctness from
God and from other "I's". Man as "I," then, is
objectively a subject, that is, his objectivity
lies in his being like an animal but transcendent to same and like God but distinct from
God and other men and, further, being self-
conscious of his dual unity.[7,88-9]

In these ways, man is objectified in himself,
he is neither wholly animal nor wholly God
but like both. Man is thus objectified in himself
as a being in dual dependence for his very
objectivity of being. Man is not *either* bodily
or soulish but *both/and*—and it is this objectivity of being which makes man *man* and not
some other kind of being.

* Material in brackets is that of the present
writer.

"This unity in duality comprises man's
uniqueness and his greatness. But it also brings
about a dilemma for man that is unique to
his kind of life."[7-75] This dilemma is the problem of attaining *authentic human* selfhood
when existing as a unity of the temporal and
eternal, of the finite and infinite, of necessity
and freedom. To attempt to actualize one set
of these factors with consequent negligence
of the opposite set is, for man, to attempt to
be completely animal or completely a god
depending upon which set man attempts to
actualize. Further, such attempted actualization results in a fundamental denial of human
selfhood (a self-denial) who is uniquely constituted as a being who is objectively a subject.
True human selfhood (authentic human spirit,
human personality, human subjectivity) becomes a reality when the unitary relationship
of the bodily and soulish dimensions is self-
affirming, that is, when the "I" arising within
the relationship *freely, willingly* and *joyfully*
acknowledges the nature of his own givenness.
For man to acknowledge the nature of his own
givenness requires the following: the achieved
self of man (the realized indissolvable unity
of the bodily and the soulish) projects an
image of the ideal self and, in so doing, becomes "self" conscious (aware of the "I" who
arises within the relationship of the bodily
and soulish); this self-conscious being is aware
of his dual dependence upon the bodily and
the soulish *to be;* also, this self-conscious being
is aware of the potentiality of his freedom to
attempt to actualize either the bodily or the
soulish; then, if the self-conscious being chooses
to attempt to actualize either the bodily or the
soulish he destroys his true self since he has
denied one or the other bases of his own dual
unity (he attempts to be either animal or a
god); if, however, he attempts to actualize
both the bodily and the soulish bases of his
being he is affirming himself (accepting his
givenness as a unity of the bodily and soulish);
but he himself is not the author of the unitary
relationship of the bodily and soulish—in fact
the *power* which allows him to be self-project-
ing and thus self-conscious is not something he
gives himself but which is given to him in his
soulish dimension; further, the potentiality of
freedom to affirm his own givenness arises also
from his being in the image of God; therefore,
the *authentic* self-conscious being (the true
human self) comes into being when man not
only acknowledges the dual dependence of his
unity but also affirms that the very possibility
of his own awareness of his own unity is given

by Another.* Finally then, man comes to authentic human selfhood ("I," person or spirit) only when he freely affirms the bases of his own dual unity as well as fully acknowledging the Source of his own possibility of being aware of his own unity. Only man who freely loves his own nature is at one with himself, i.e., authentically human and not either an animal or a pseudo-god.

* There should be no concern at this point regarding any possible conflict between evolution and creationism. The point here is that man did not, and cannot, give himself the basic conditions from which he is now aware of his "manliness."

BIBLIOGRAPHY

1. Bair, Donn E. "Identification of Some Philosophical Beliefs of Influential Leaders in American Physical Education," *The Research Quarterly* 28: 315-320, December, 1957.
2. Ballou, Ralph. "An Analysis of the Writings of Selected Church Fathers to A.D. 394 to Reveal Attitudes Regarding Physical Activity." Unpublished Doctoral thesis, University of Oregon, Eugene, 1965.
3. Barth, Karl. *The Doctrine of Creation.* Vol. III, Part 2 of *Church Dogmatics.* Edited by G. W. Bromiley and T. F. Torrance. 4 vols. Edinburgh: T. & T. Clark, 1960.
4. Brunner, Emil. *The Christian Doctrine of Creation and Redemption.* Vol. II of *Dogmatics.* Edited by Olive Wyon. 3 vols. Philadelphia: The Westminster Press, 1952.
5. ————. *Man in Revolt* (A Christian Anthropology). Trans. Olive Wyon. Philadelphia: The Westminster Press, 1947.
6. Bultmann, Rudolf. *Theology of the New Testament.* Vol. I. Trans. Kendrick Grobel. 2 vols. New York: Charles Scribner's Sons, 1951.
7. Come, Arnold B. *Human Spirit and Holy Spirit.* Philadelphia: The Westminster Press, 1959.
8. De Wolf, L. Harold. *A Theology of the Living Church.* Revised edition. New York: Harper and Brothers, Publishers, 1960.
9. Gavin, Frank. *Some Aspects of Contemporary Greek Orthodox Thought.* New York: American Review of Eastern Orthodoxy, 1923.
10. Gilkey, Langdon. *Maker of Heaven and Earth.* Garden City, N.Y.: Doubleday and Co., Inc., 1959.
11. Kierkegaard, Soren. *The Sickness Unto Death.* Trans. Walter Lowrie. Garden City, N.Y.: Doubleday and Co., Inc., 1954.
12. Morland, Richard B. "A Philosophical Interpretation of the Educational Views Held by Seven Leaders in American Physical Education," *62nd Annual Proceedings, College Physical Education Association.* Washington, D.C.: American Association of Health, Physical Education and Recreation, 1959. pp. 125-130.
13. Niebuhr, Reinhold. *Human Nature.* Vol. I of *The Nature and Destiny of Man.* 2 vols. New York: Charles Scribner's Sons, 1945.
14. ————. *Human Destiny.* Vol. II of *The Nature and Destiny of Man.* 2 vols. New York: Charles Scribner's Sons, 1945.
15. Owen, Derwyn Randolph Grier. *Body and Soul: A Study of the Christian View of Man.* Philadelphia: The Westminster Press, 1956.
16. Robinson, John A. T. *The Body, A Study in Pauline Theology.* Studies in Biblical Theology No. 5. London: S C M Press, Ltd., 1952.
17. Stump, Joseph. *The Christian Faith.* Philadelphia: Muhlenberg Press, 1942.
18. Swain, Joseph Ward. "The Hellenic Origins of Christian Asceticism." Unpublished Doctoral Thesis, Columbia University, New York, N. Y., 1916.
19. Thomas, Owen C. "Psychology and Theology and the Nature of Man." *Pastoral Psychology,* 13: 41-46, February, 1962.

The Lived Body as a Phenomenological Datum *

CALVIN O. SCHRAG

Phenomenology, as a methodological principle, designates a disciplined attempt at a descriptive analysis and interpretive explication of the data of immediate experience. Husserl's formula *Zu den Sachen Selbst!* has become normative for all phenomenological enquiry. Heidegger, Scheler, Sartre, Merleau-Ponty, and others, have taken over Husserl's formula and applied it to various regions of man's lived experience. The differences among the phenomenologists are due primarily to variegated applications of the phenomenological method rather than to disputes concerning the nature of the phenomenological principle itself. My present task is not that of a historical examination of the similarities and differences between the different phenomenologists. Such an undertaking would indeed be helpful toward a further clarification of what is meant by phenomenology as a philosophical method, but the pursuit of this task would lead us too far afield. The specific purpose of this essay is that of developing a phenomenological analysis of the lived body. The phrase "the lived body" denotes a structure of human subjectivity. It indicates the experience of my body as it is disclosed to me in my immediate involvements and concerns. Sartre, Marcel, and Merleau-Ponty have given studied attention to the phenomenon of the lived body; but their descriptions are often fragmentary and singularly impoverished on rather decisive issues. Heideg-

* From *The Modern Schoolman*, XXXIX, (March, 1962), 203-218.

ger, on the other hand, has virtually nothing to say about the body. His *Dasein* appears to be a disembodied *Existenz* who moves about in his world of care in an abstracted unawareness of his bodily engagements and orientations. As Hegel, in his *Science of Logic,* had viciously abstracted reason from its context in man's lived historical existence, so it would seem that Heidegger comes perilously close to abstracting *Existenz* from its concrete bodily involvement. What is sorely needed as a corrective to the Heideggerian's neglect of the body is another Feuerbach to call us to an awareness of the bodily dimension of human existence, and another Nietzsche to remind us that life is lost in the moment that man no longer remains faithful to the earth.

In the following discussion I will seek to analyze and describe the datum of the lived body as it evinces a fourfold expression: (1) the lived body as self-referential, (2) the lived body in reference to other, (3) the lived body and human space, and (4) the lived body and human time.

I. THE LIVED BODY AS SELF-REFERENTIAL

I experience my body as uniquely and peculiarly my own. My body is so intimately related to what and who I am that the experience of selfness is indissolubly linked with the existential projects which radiate from my body as it is actually lived. My body is immediately experienced and initially disclosed as my concrete mode of orientation in a world of practical and personal concerns. The phenomenon in question is *my* body as *concretely lived*. The body as immediately apprehended is not a corporeal substance which is in some way attached to, or united with, another substance, variously called in the tradition a "soul," "mind," or "self." The body thus conceptualized is a later abstraction and objectivization, which is phenomenologically eviscerated and epistemologically problematic. I experience my body first as a complex of life-movements which are indistinguishable from my experience of selfness. My primordial experience is one of engagement in a world of concrete projects—projects which receive their significance through my body as the locus of concern. The distinctions between soul and body, or mind and body, as they have been formulated in the tradition (particularly by Descartes), are reified and objectivized distinctions, foreign to man's experience as it is immediately lived. Thus, the body as *concretely lived* must be consistently contrasted with the body as *objectively known*. The body as objectively known is a proper datum to be sure, but it is a scientific datum for the investigations of the anatomical and physiological sciences. The body as objectively known is a corporeal entity, properly defined as a complex of brain waves, neural pathways, endocrinal discharges, and muscular fibres. This is the body as it exists for the physiologist and the physician. But this is not the body which I experience in my lived concreteness and which I apprehend as being indelibly and uniquely my own. The body as an item for the special sciences, in which all data necessarily are objectivized, is an abstracted and general body which applies to everyone but characterizes no one in particular. It becomes a body conceptualized in its objectivized mode of being-for-another. No one can "know" his pituitary gland or his cerebral cortex as it is known objectively by the brain surgeon. To be sure, I can infer from my knowledge of cadavers that I have the same anatomical structures and the same physiological functions as have other bodies; but this is a level of knowledge in abstraction from the experience of my body as concretely lived.

The lived body, I have suggested, signifies a mode of orientation rather than a conceptualized entity. This mode of orientation is part and parcel of man's preobjective world. Merleau-Ponty has made the notion of a preobjective world central not only to his phenomenology of perception, but to his philosophy as such.[1] Being in the world, as a primordial experience, is a global structure of interrelating practical projects and not a conceptualization of a world schematized through the objectivizing categories of substance, quantity, and abstract quality. The world is initially disclosed as an instrumental world in which tools are accessible for the realization of my practical concerns, and a social world in which I already find myself concretely related to other selves. A putty knife, in the primitive and subjective experience of my world, is a utensil with which I seal the window pane to keep out the wintry draft. The putty knife *as object*, although still the same putty knife, is a thematized and conceptualized entity to which I attach certain abstract qualities of weight, shape, and solidity. The former movement discloses my preobjective world; the later is a construction of my objective world. Now it is in this preobjective world that the lived body makes its appearance. Preobjectively understood, the lived body is always related to an environment and social horizon, but in this relational complex it always appears as that which refers to itself as the locus of this relatedness. The lived body is self-referential.

It is through the orientation of my lived body that the personal meanings of my preobjective being in the world are disclosed, established, and broadened. The hand plays a privileged role in this disclosure and creation of meanings in my world orientations. It is through the use of my hand that I project meanings by pointing and touching, by writing and counting, by striking and stroking, by giving and taking. It is through the use of the hand that I create new worlds and refashion the old. The hand makes man a creator. Clocks and microscopes are works of the hand which express man's creativity and his power over the given. The lived body creates meanings by refashioning that which is simply given. Man becomes a maker of tools and a creator of values through the use of his hand. So also

[1] See particularly *Phénoménologie de la perception* (Paris: Gallimard, 1945), Part I, "Le Monde Perçu," and Part II, "L'Etre-pour-soi et l'être-au-monde." Also pertinent to the topic is his book *La Structure du comportement* (Paris: Presses Universitaires, 1953), especially Chap. 3: "L'Ordre physique, l'ordre vital, l'ordre humain." Gabriel Marcel points to the same phenomenon when he speaks of the world being initially presented as a confused and global experience: "What is given to me beyond all possible doubt is the confused and global experience of the world inasmuch as it is existent" (*Metaphysical Journal* [Chicago: Henry Regnery Co., 1952], p. 322).

it is through the use of my hand that the personal meanings in my relations with others are established and expressed. In the handshake and in the gesture, complexes of meaning are at once created and revealed. Karl Jaspers in his illuminating discussion of the hand in *Von der Wahrheit* has concretely defined man as that being who makes use of his hands. Man is *homo faber* as well as *homo sapiens*. It is this existential quality which differentiates man from the animal. An animal is bound to its environment and must accommodate itself to it; man modifies his environment through the use of his hand, which determines the application and use of his thought. One of the fateful errors of philosophy, continues Jaspers, is the vicious separation of doing and thinking. All activity involving the use of the hand already discloses thought as inextricably intertwined with the activity, and it is through the activities of the hand (*Handtätigkeiten*) that the activities of thought (*Denktätigkeiten*) are explicated.[2] The body in its lived concreteness expresses a concomitant upsurge of thought and activity through which I both grasp and shape the meaning of my incarnated being-in-the-world.

The self-referential quality of the lived body is most directly disclosed in my experience of my body as that which individualizes me. The body confers upon me my existential identity. The tradition was right in viewing the body as a principle of individuation but erred in objectivizing the individuating principle as an abstract *materia signata quantitate* which individuates the particular by somehow uniting with form. Particularly in the Aristotelian tradition does individuation remain abstract and objective, with the result that individuation never *individualizes*. Only when I apprehend my body in the particularity of its lived concreteness is it disclosed as a factor of individuation. The body individuates me in that it signifies the projects which are peculiarly my own—my hand grasping the pen with which I write, my head nodding to the person with whom I converse, my anticipation of the death which I alone must die. Sartre has clearly expressed this notion in stating that the body "represents the individualization of my engagement in the world."[3] I apprehend myself as

being marked off from other selves, and from objects and things, in the moment that I apprehend my lived body in its concrete involvements, referring to projects that are peculiarly and uniquely my own.

The lived body is not a *something*, objective and external to the self, which when attached to the self individuates it and marks it off from other selves. This external view of the body transforms it into an objectively conceptualized material substance. But on the level of the preobjective experience of the body as mine no such material substance can be found. Marcel elucidates this when he writes: "In the fact of *my body* there is something which transcends what can be called its materiality, something which cannot be reduced to any of its objective qualities."[4] Further clarification on the distinction between the objective and the preobjective understanding of the body is forthcoming in Marcel's distinction between "having" and "being." Viewed as an objective determinant of individuation, the body is understood as something that the self *has*. The self has a body analogous to the way in which the courthouse has a goldplated dome. The body, in such a view, is adventitious or external to the self. On the other hand, the body preobjectively understood as the *lived body* is not something which I *have*; rather it signifies who I *am*. I am my body or I exist as body. Immediate experience testifies to the fact that the body is not something which I possess and consequently use in one way or another as an instrument or a utensil. As formulated by Marcel: "I do not *make use of* my body, I *am* my body. In other words, there is something in me that denies the implication that is to be found in the purely instrumentalist notion of the body that my body is external to myself."[5] I am not related to my body in an external way. It is not a possession which I have and use. The lived body makes use of instruments and utensils in its world orientations, but the body is not itself an instrument. The body is myself in my lived concreteness. It is *who I am*, and indicates the *manner in which I am*. The lived body refers to my personal manner of existing, and the meanings attached to this manner of existing, in a world in which I experience presence.

II. THE LIVED BODY IN REFERENCE TO OTHERS

My body is lived in an existential immediacy and is apprehended as uniquely my own. But

---

[2] "Wie sehr alles Tun mit der Hand schon ein Denken in sich schliesst, ist daran zu bemerken, dass Denktätigkeiten durch Handtätigkeiten ausgedrückt werden" (*Von der Wahrheit* [München: Piper, 1947], p. 329).

[3] Sartre, *Being and Nothingness*, trans. Hazel Barnes (New York, Philosophical Lib.), p. 310.

[4] Marcel, *Metaphysical Journal*, p. 315.

[5] *Ibid.*, p. 333.

my body is also lived in such a manner that it is apprehended by the other. The lived body is not an isolated phenomenon. It is intentionally related to a world—a world which emerges in one's preobjective experience as a phenomenon in which various regions of concern are manifested. A most fundamental region of concern in one's primordial experience of being in the world is the region of interacting and interdependent selves. I apprehend my body in a communal context in which other selves are disclosed as already being there. This communal context adds another aspect to the experience of my body in its lived concreteness. A phenomenological analysis and description of this communal aspect will disclose a structure of experience in which there are two separable moments of awareness—the body of the other as known by me and the reapprehension of my body as known by the other. The experience of my body as mine is always coextensive with my experience of the body of the other and the consequent reappraisal of myself as existing in the world of the other. These two moments of consciousness can and must be separated for purposes of analysis, but it must not be forgotten that in man's immediate experience they are simultaneously given. The postanalytic fallacy, in which there is a reification and separation of analyzed components read out of a situation of prior relatedness, must be judiciously avoided. The engagements of the lived body always proceed within a self-other correlation. I seek to realize the projects of my lived body through a continuing encounter with the body of the other. The other is disclosed as part of my situation. His body is a factor in my world. It arises in my world either as an obstacle to be overcome (a coefficient of adversity, as Sartre would say), or as an instrument which I can use (coefficient of utility), or as an occasion for authentic communication and mutual fulfillment (the possibility of the latter would seem to be denied by Sartre). In any case, I must reckon with the incarnated other. I must assume some kind of existential attitude toward him.

After being thrust into the presence of the other I seek to apprehend his lived body as I seek to apprehend my own. Now what kind of knowledge is rendered possible through my encounter with the other? Quite clearly, I can never "know" the body of the other as he lives it. The interior of the projects of the other never becomes fully transparent to me. The movements of his body and the projects which they intend are always in some sense clothed with opaqueness and mystery. To be sure, I can describe empirically some of the obvious characteristics relative to his pigmentation, bone structure, eye color, texture of the hair, and the like; but in the specification of all these empirical determinants one can hardly attest that the lived body of the other has been comprehended. There is, however, a reality element which is disclosed in my encounter with the lived body of the other. His body is revealed as a unity of life movements which expresses a world orientation of its own. The body of the other constitutes *his* project of being in the world. I cannot penetrate this project as lived by the other, but I can apprehend and describe the project as it exists for me. In this apprehension I always apprehend a totality. Sartre makes this point when he says that the body of the other "appears within the limits of the situation as a synthetic totality of life and action."[6] There is the simple corporeal unity of arms, legs, thorax, and head disclosed as a living complex. We never experience the arm or the foot or the eyes of the other in isolation. To experience them thus would be to experience them as lifeless appendages or parts of a material composite but not as expressions of a living unity. We perceive the other as kicking his leg, raising his arm, squinting his eyes. In each of these perceptions a project or a complex of products of the other as a living whole becomes apparent. We find a negative testimony of this *Gestalt* character in the perceptual shock which occurs when one sees staring eyes which are not localized in a head, or fingers severed from a hand. Sartre in *Being and Nothingness* reminds us of the horror which we feel when we see an arm which looks as if it did not belong to any body, and perceive a hand (when the arm is concealed) crawling like a spider up the side of a doorway.[7] All these instances point to a structural life-unity which characterizes the lived body of the other as it is apprehended by me.

In my encounter with the lived body of the other there is thus the structural moment of the other as known by me. But equally a part of the situation of encounter is the structural moment of the reapprehension of my lived body as known by the other. When I emerge in the world I find that I am already looked at. My body is perceived by the other and exists for the other. The other, in formulating and executing his projects, sucks me into the orbit of his concerns and transforms me into

[6] *Being and Nothingness*, p. 346.
[7] *Ibid.*

an item for his world. I then reapprehend myself in the mode of being apprehended by the other. I become aware that the other has a certain image of my lived body and makes an appraisal of it, either tacit or explicit. I can take over this image and appraisal made by the other and seek to shape my life in accordance with them. I can also reject the formulated images and appraisals, and seek means of changing them or seek to affirm my individuality and my freedom in spite of them. In any case, whatever my particular response may be, my life and action are defined in reference to the other. The other is inescapable. He constitutes an irreducible element in my world orientations. He is responsible for my situation being one in which I stand before the other—in fear, anger, shame, and love. It is only in the presence of the other that I can experience these existential moods. These are revelatory moods, in the guise of preobjective intentional disclosures, which reveal my lived body as a body viewed and appraised by the other.

We have seen that the lived body in reference to the other involves at the same time an apprehension of the other and a being apprehended by the other. This structure of intersubjectivity or being with the other exhibits two possible existential qualifications— alienation and communication. I alienate myself from the other either by objectivizing his lived body and thus transforming it into an object or a thing, or by apprehending it solely as an instrument which I can use and manipulate for my own private ends. I thus deprive his lived body of its life quality—that is, its unique existential freedom—by dissolving his world of projects. Indeed, I seek to remove the other as lived body by transforming him into material for my self-actualization. But this can never fully succeed because I confront resistance through the counter projects of the other. I do not constitute the other; I encounter him. And in my encounter with the other I not only apprehend the other, but I experience myself as apprehended by the other. The other seeks to absorb me into his world of projects and divest me of my subjectivity, just as I seek to render him into an item for my projects. Alienation is the dialectical movement of perceiving and being perceived, acting and being acted upon, using and being used. Sartre has formulated an engaging elucidation of this dialectical movement in his chapter "The Look" in *Being and Nothingness*. The other decentralizes my world through his look and divests me of my freedom by transforming

me into a "being as object" or a "being as seen by another." The "fall" of man for Sartre comes about through the emergence of the other.[8] Sartre's dialectical analysis and description of the resistance of the other in the movement of alienation or estrangement seems to draw heavily from the insights of Hegel's teaching on the "unhappy consciousness" and the master-servant polarity. The master, which is self-consciousness striving for purity, actualizes himself by transforming the other into a servant. The master exercises his power over his servant by demanding various services. Thus the servant is dependent upon the master. But in the moment that the servant becomes conscious of himself as servant he drives toward independence and elevates himself above the status of a servant. Only through the servant can the master enjoy the services which are provided. The master now becomes dependent upon the servant. This is the structure of dialectical movement toward the unhappy or alienated consciousness.

All the movements of the lived body in its intersubjective field express various forms of alienation or estrangement. There is, however, another existential quality, equally important, which defines the relations of selves. This is the drive toward communion. It is on this point that Sartre's analysis remains singularly impoverished. Alienation, for Sartre, plays the trump card. Jaspers, Marcel, and Merleau-Ponty, on the other hand, have made the theme of communion central to their philosophies and thus established a counter-thrust to the alienating egocentrism of Sartre's existentialism. Marcel has formulated a doctrine of intersubjectivity in which the other can be encountered as a nonobjectivized presence. Communion is made possible only when the other is acknowledged as a subject with whom I experience a copresence in such a manner that our individual freedoms are mutually acknowledged. Communion involves communication. If I am to exist in communion with the other I must be able to communicate the meanings which are disclosed in the projects of my immediate concerns. The lived body

[8] *Ibid.*, p. 263. Cf. p. 267: "Thus being-seen constitutes me as a defenseless being for a freedom which is not my freedom. It is in this sense that we can consider ourselves as 'slaves' insofar as we appear to the Other. But this slavery is not a historical result—capable of being surmounted—of a *life* in the abstract form of consciousness. I am a slave to the degree that my being is dependent at the center of a freedom which is not mine and which is the very condition of **my being**."

plays a significant role in this communication of meanings. The projects of my lived body are intrinsically communicative. My lived body is an *act of communication*. This is to say more than to say that the body is simply a vehicle of communication. To speak of the body as a vehicle is already to externalize it and make it adventitious to the communication process itself. Merleau-Ponty has described the body as "expression and speech" in one of the chapters in his book *Phénoménologie de la perception*.[9] I convey meanings to the other through the gestures and movements which constitute my body as a living synthetic unity. The smile and the frown, the wink and the stare, the caress and the kiss, the handshake and the slap, are all modes of speech which disclose meanings in the world of my concrete lived experience. Merleau-Ponty elucidates this point when he refers to speech as a gesture which intends or signifies a world ("la parole est un geste et sa signification un monde").[10] Speech is a mode of orientation through which one discloses to others the world of one's projects. The gesture-complex of the lived body is an example of speech thus understood. Ordinary language gives clear evidence of such an apprehension of the lived body: "he speaks with his hands"; "her eyes reveal her inmost feelings;" "he uses the language of love." All these phrases bear testimony to a lived body as expression and speech. Any phenomenology of experience, which seeks to remain true to the data as they show themselves, will need to give disciplined attention to this form of communication.

III. THE LIVED BODY AND HUMAN SPACE

Spatiality is an existential quality of the lived body. The concept of space, in both the history of philosophy and the history of science, has fallen heir (or victim) to widely differing interpretations. Some have argued that space is infinite; others have argued that it is finite. Some have maintained it is absolute; others have maintained that it is relative. Some have asserted that it is to be identified with matter; others have persuasively denied its materiality. It becomes evident upon investigation that such arguments pro and con presuppose space to be some kind of externally observable entity or state which can be objectively defined. It may indeed be that Kant

has demonstrated in his transcendental dialectic once and for all that space as a unifying condition in one's objective view of the cosmos remains for ever unknowable. In any case, the spatiality which qualifies the lived body is not an objective space. It is *human space*, or what Merleau-Ponty has appropriately called "espace orienté." The space in which I live and in which I apprehend my lived body is articulated in and through my practical and personal projects, and as such must be consistently contrasted with the quantitative and measurable space which defines my objective world as an extensive continuum. Mathematical space, as an instance of quantifiable space, is properly defined as an abstract extensive continuum constituting a region of points. Whether this space is Euclidean or non-Euclidean, three-dimensional or multi-dimensional, is at this point irrelevant. The point which is relevant is that mathematical space is isotropic —that is, all the dimensions have the same value—and it is precisely this which makes it measurable in terms of spatial co-ordinates. Human or oriented space, which qualifies the lived body, is what Henri Ellenberger has called "anisotropic," having dimensions of different specific values and thus being contrasted with the abstract space of mathematics. The dimensions (or what might preferably be called "directions") of oriented space take on different values relative to the situation in which the lived body actualizes its projects. Merleau-Ponty has contributed the distinction between "spatiality of position" (*spatialité de position*) and "spatiality of situations" (*spatialité de situation*). The former characterizes the abstract space of mathematics, the latter the concrete oriented space of the lived body.[11]

Human space has three directional axes. The primary axis is the horizontal axis of front and back, or before and behind. In this primary axis the existentially proximate direction is that of frontward or forward. For the most part I spatialize my world in a forward direction. I face the table on which I write; I face the mountain which I must surmount; I face the person to whom I speak. In each of these projects an existential distance is already disclosed. The table is near when it is accessible for the writing of my book; it is too far away when it makes difficult the task of writing, producing a coefficient of adversity. Utensils become most readily accessible on the horizontal axis of front and back; and the concrete movements of my body, such as actualizing a proj-

[9] See Part I, Chap. 6: "Le Corps comme expression et la parole."
[10] *Phénoménologie de la perception*, p. 214.

[11] *Ibid.*, p. 116.

ect by walking, proceed for the most part on this axis. But there is also the directional axis of right and left. The hammer with which I pound the tack is to my left. Its place in my field of concerns is not some abstract locus geometrically defined relative to an extensive continuum of points, but rather that place where it belongs so as to be accessible for the realization of my project. It is near when it is in its right place—within reach—and thus can be spatially distinguished from other utensils, which, although metrically nearer, are existentially remote from the lived body. For example, at the same time that I reach for the hammer there may be a garden spade to my right which is six inches closer to me than the hammer. But the garden spade, in the context of my situation, remains exterior to my projects and thus existentially remote. Human space, and the value of its directions, varies with the situation. Human space is anisotropic. It is indissolubly linked with the projects of human concern. A proper phenomenological use of language, therefore, would refer to the body not as something which is *in* space but rather as a field of concern which *lives* its space.

The third directional axis is the vertical axis of up and down. I also live my space in the upward and downward direction. In standing up and sitting down, in raising and lowering my arm, in perceiving what is above and what is below, I express a concrete movement along this vertical axis. These various directional axes disclose themselves through the concrete movements of the lived body. The task of phenomenology is that of describing the phenomena as they show or disclose themselves. Hence any phenomenology which seeks to return to the data of immediate experience must pay due attention to the reality of human or oriented space. Ellenberger states the case clearly when he writes: "We know that the horizon and the celestial dome are not scientific concepts; but for our daily experience and for phenomenology, they are very important entities."[12]

IV. THE LIVED BODY AND HUMAN TIME

Phenomenology discloses not only the spatiality of the lived body but also its temporality. These two phenomena are disclosed simultaneously in the fundamental project of the body as a living synthetic unity. The concrete movements of the body always occur within a correlated complex of lived space and lived time. My body is immediately and preobjec-

tively revealed as coming from a past and moving into a future. Just as there is a spatial directionality, so also there is a temporal directionality. I will describe this temporal directionality in terms of a retentional protentional axis (categories already used by Husserl). The lived body is qualified by its past, indicating a retentional mode. My lived body is constituted by that which I have been. Hence my body *is* its past. To speak of the body as *having* a past is to externalize the past and violently abstract the body from its concrete temporalization. The past which qualifies the lived body is never left behind so long as the body exists. My past projects and the environmental and social complex in which these projects were defined are continuing determinants of my lived body. To be sure, my environmental and social world are no longer objectively present, but they remain *subjectively real*. The past is still a living reality, and it is lost in the moment that it is objectivized as a series of discrete nows which have somehow "passed by" and become divested of reality. The lived body is not an objectivized instant within an objectively measured time. The categories of quantitative or objectively measured time are inapplicable to the lived time of human experience. Human time is qualitatively unique. Quantitative time is an abstracted and objectivized time, which transforms the temporal unity into an infinite succession of nows correlated with geometrical points. Quantitative time co-ordinates time and space by postulating an abstract spatio-temporal continuum. Human time, or the time of immediate experience, remains concealed so long as time is understood as a succession of abstracted nows which precede each other in an objective order of coming to be and passing away. Quantitative time severs the past from

[12] R. May, E. Angel, and H. Ellenberger (eds.), *Existence: A New Dimension in Psychiatry and Psychology* (New York: Basic Books, 1958), p. 110. It is interesting to note that Ludwig Binswanger has made extended use of the phenomenological concept of oriented space in his existential psychotherapy. In its psychological expression oriented space becomes what he calls "attuned space" (*gestimmter Raum*), space conditioned by one's emotions and feelings. Space thus becomes allied with a psychological mood. One's mood determines space as being full or empty, expanding or constricting. For example, love is "space-binding" in that it produces a feeling of nearness to the beloved, even though the metrical distance may be great. Happiness expands attuned space, sorrow constricts it, and despair makes it empty (*ibid.*, pp. 110 ff.).

the future and both from the present. Human time has a past which is still present and a future which is already present. The directions of time are integrated in a synthetic unity of the body as concretely lived. Only for the anatomical biologist and the physiologist does the body become a lifeless object which somehow rests within an order of objective time. The lived body has time within itself. It does not *occur in time;* it *exists as time.* All of its projects or orientations are permeated with temporality. This temporality has both a retentional and a protentional direction. The lived body is temporalized retentionally in that at every moment it is a synthetic unity of its past projects, which includes its past environmental and social influences. This is what Heidegger and Sartre have called the *facticity* of human existence; that is, existence as qualified by pastness. But human existence is also qualified by futurity. The lived body is temporalized protentionally as well as retentionally. It is this protentional directionality which constantly reopens my past and keeps it from being solidified into a series of objectivized nows. It rescues my past from the determinism of an empirical necessity. In any given moment I can remember my past lived body as a burden—as an occasion for regret or remorse.[13] But this past, for human time, is not irrevocably closed or finally fixed. It can be translated into an existential possibility through the acknowledgment of futurity. The past can be retrieved and changed through the adoption of a new attitude toward it. That which weighs upon me as a burden can be transformed into a burden to be overcome—into a creative possi-

[13] Minkowski has differentiated regret and remorse in terms of different retentional values. The zone of remorse is the zone of the immediate past. The zone of the regretted is the zone of the mediate past. Finally, there is the zone of the obsolete which corresponds to the remote past. See his book *Le Temps vécu* (Paris: D'Artre, 1933).

bility. The memory of my lived body as a body whose projects have been limited by a withered arm can be translated into a future possibility of reappraisal.

The phenomenon of the lived body thus shows itself in immediate experience as a body qualified by temporality—qualified retentionally in that it is a body which has already become that which it is, defined by itself, its environment and other selves; but also it is qualified protentionally in that it is a body which has not yet lived out its projects. It is protended into a future and confronted with the task of appraising the meaning of its past as this past is translated into possibility. In this protentional directionality a final limit to the projects of the lived body is disclosed. This limit is death or the total dissolution of my being in the world. The unity of the lived body as a synthetic whole is achieved only when this final limit is interiorized and taken up in the present projects of the existing subject. Heidegger has elucidated this in his existential concept of *Sein-zum-Tode,* which means that death is a mode of existence qualifying man's being as soon as he is and so long as he is. (However, it is not clear in what sense death, in the Heideggerian analysis, has a bodily reference.) Death is not simply an empirical factuality apprehended only in the instant. This would comically place death outside experience insofar as when it would occur the lived body would no longer be there. Death is a mode of existence which involves the task of assuming some kind of existential attitude toward one's final limit. Death can become the occasion for cowardly retreat, poetic melancholy, martyrdom or dying for a cause, or resolute and courageous acceptance of it as the irrevocable limit of existence. The final meaning of the lived body as a synthetic unity of past and future is thus achieved in the taking over of one's death as the final possibility of the body. Death itself is interiorized and translated into subjectivity.

The Body*

JEAN-PAUL SARTRE

The problem of the body and its relations with consciousness is often obscured by the fact that while the body is from the start posited as a certain *thing* having its own laws and capable of being defined from outside, consciousness is then reached by the type of inner intuition which is peculiar to it. Actually if after grasping "my" consciousness in its absolute interiority and by a series of reflective acts, I then seek to unite it with a certain living object composed of a nervous system, a brain, glands, digestive, respiratory, and circulatory organs whose very matter is capable of being analyzed chemically into atoms of hydrogen, carbon, nitrogen, phosphorus, etc., then I am going to encounter insurmountable difficulties. But these difficulties all stem from the fact that I try to unite my consciousness not with *my* body but with the body *of others*. In fact the body which I have just described is not *my* body such as it is *for* me. I have never seen and never shall see my brain nor my endocrine glands. But because I who am a man have seen the cadavers of men dissected, because I have read articles on physiology, I conclude that my body is constituted exactly like all those which have been shown to me on the dissection table or of which I have seen colored drawings in books. Of course the physicians who have taken care of me, the surgeons who have operated on me, have been able to have

* Reprinted by permission of Philosophical Library, Inc. from *Being and Nothingness* by Jean-Paul Sartre, translated by Hazel E. Barnes, © Copyright, 1956, by Philosophical Library, Inc., New York.

direct experience with the body which I myself do not know. I do not disagree with them, I do not claim that I lack a brain, a heart, or a stomach. But it is most important to choose the *order* of our bits of knowledge. So far as the physicians have had any experience with my body, it was with my body *in the midst of the world* and as it is for others. My body as it is *for me* does not appear to me in the midst of the world. Of course during a radioscopy I was able to see the picture of my vertebrae on a screen, but I was outside in the midst of the world. I was apprehending a wholly constituted object as a *this* among other *thises*, and it was only by a reasoning process that I referred it back to being *mine*; it was much more my *property* than my being.

It is true that I see and touch my legs and my hands. Moreover nothing prevents me from imagining an arrangement of the sense organs such that a living being could see one of his eyes while the eye which was seen was directing its glance upon the world. But it is to be noted that in this case again I am the *Other* in relation to my eye. I apprehend it as a sense organ constituted in the world in a particular way, but I can not "see the seeing;" that is, I can not apprehend it in the process of revealing an aspect of the world to me. Either it is a thing among other things, or else it is that by which things are revealed to me. But it can not be both at the same time. Similarly I see my hand touching objects, but do not *know* it in its act of touching them. This is the fundamental reason why that famous "sensation of effort" of Maine de Biran does not really exist. For my hand reveals to me the resistance of objects, their hardness or softness, but not *itself*. Thus I see my hand only in the way that I see this inkwell. I unfold a distance between it and me, and this distance comes to integrate itself in the distances which I establish among all the objects of the world. When a doctor takes my wounded leg and looks at it while I, half raised up on my bed, watch him do it, there is no essential difference between the visual perception which I have of the doctor's body and that which I have of my own leg. Better yet, they are distinguished only as different structures of a single global perception; there is no essential difference between the doctor's perception of my leg and my own present perception of it. Of course when I touch my leg with my finger, I realize that my leg is touched. But this phenomenon of double sensation is not essential: cold, a shot of morphine, can make it disappear. This shows that we are dealing with two essentially different orders of reality. To touch and to be touched, to feel that one is touching and to feel that one is touched—these are two species of phenomena which it is useless to try to reunite by the term "double sensation." In fact they are radically distinct, and they exist on two incommunicable levels. Moreover when I touch my leg or when I see it, I surpass it toward my own possibilities. It is, for example, in order to pull on my trousers or to change a dressing on my wound. Of course I can at the same time arrange my leg in such a way that I can more conveniently "work" on it. But this does not change the fact that I transcend it toward the pure possibility of "curing myself" and that consequently I am present to it without its *being me* and without my *being it*. What I cause to exist here is the *thing* "leg;" it is not the leg as the *possibility which I am* of walking, running, or of playing football.

Thus to the extent that my body indicates my possibilities in the world, seeing my body or touching it is to transform these possibilities of mine into dead-possibilities. This metamorphosis must necessarily involve a complete *thisness* with regard to the body as a living possibility of running, of dancing, etc. Of course, the discovery of my body as an object is indeed a revelation of its being. But the being which is thus revealed to me is its *being-for-others*. That this confusion may lead to absurdities can be clearly seen in connection with the famous problem of "inverted vision." We know the question posed by the physiol-

ogists: "How can we set upright the objects which are painted upside down on our retina?" We know as well the answer of the philosophers: "There is no problem. An object is upright or inverted in relation to the rest of the universe. To perceive the whole universe inverted means nothing, for it would have to be inverted in relation to something." But what particularly interests us is the origin of this false problem. It is the fact that people have wanted to link *my* consciousness of objects to the body of the Other. Here are the candle, the crystalline lens, the inverted image on the screen of the retina. But to be exact, the retina enters here into a physical system; it is a *screen* and only that; the crystalline lens is a *lens* and only a lens; both are homogeneous in their being with the candle which completes the system. Therefore we have deliberately chosen the physical point of view—i.e., the point of view of the outside, of exteriority—in order to study the problem of vision; we have considered a dead eye in the midst of the visible world in order to account for the visibility of this world. Consequently, how can we be surprised later when consciousness, which is absolute interiority, refuses to allow itself to be bound to this object? The relations which I establish between the Other's body and the external object are *really* existing relations, but they have for their being the being of the for-others; they suppose a center of intra-mundane flow in which knowledge is a *magic* property of space, "action at a distance." From the start they are placed in the perspective of the Other-as-object.

If then we wish to reflect on the nature of the body, it is necessary to establish an order of our reflections which conforms to the order of being: we can not continue to confuse the ontological levels, and we must in succession examine the body first as being-for-itself and then as being-for-others. And in order to avoid such absurdities as "inverted vision," we must keep constantly in mind the idea that since these two aspects of the body are on different and incommunicable levels of being, they can not be reduced to one another. Being-for-itself must be wholly body and it must be wholly consciousness; it can not be *united* with a body. Similarly being-for-others is wholly body; there are no "psychic phenomena" there to be united with the body. There is nothing *behind* the body. But the body is wholly "psychic." We must now proceed to study these two modes of being which we find for the body.

If I am my Body*

GABRIEL MARCEL

October 24th, 1920

I am not at all sure about the soundness of the observations I made yesterday. This is the point I thought I had reached: if *I am my body* only means "my body is an object of actual interest for me" we have nothing that can confer on my body a real priority in relation to other objects. This is not so if "my body" is regarded as the necessary condition for an object to become a datum for my attention. But in that case the attention which is brought to bear on my body presupposes the exercise of this mediating element which itself falls outside the realm of the knowable. Only by an arbitrary step of the mind as in (*b*) can I identify the body-as-object with the body-as-mediator.

But what are we to think of the idea of a primary instrument of the attention (whether or not it coincides with what I habitually call my body)? From what I pointed out yesterday it emerges that no idea of a mediating principle by which the attention can be exercised is possible for me. But is that which can in no way be an object for me by that very fact incapable of being an object for anyone? Can we not conceive a type of organic structure and optics of the intellect that are different from ours so that from their standpoint the problem would collapse?

We must first of all delve deeper into the nature of the instrumental relation. Funda-

* From *Metaphysical Journal.* Translated by Bernard Wall. Chicago: Henry Regnery Company, Publishers, 1952.

mentally it seems to me that every instrument is a means of extending or of strengthening a "power" that we possess. This is just as true as regards a spade as regards a microphone. To say that these powers themselves are instruments would be merely playing with words; for we would need to determine what these powers themselves really prolong. There must always be some community of nature between the instrument and the instrumentalist. But if I look on my body as my instrument am I not yielding to a sort of unconscious illusion by which I give back to the soul the very powers which are merely prolonged by the mechanical dispositions to which I have reduced my body? It must be noted, moreover, that if I deny that the body is entirely thinkable, I am contesting that it can be treated as an instrument, since an instrument is essentially that of which an idea is possible, indeed that which is only possible through this idea of it.

Under such conditions the initial question changes its appearance. When I insisted on the necessity of a mediation for the attention to be concentrated on any object, had I not the impression that I was speaking of an instrument? And on the other hand when I said that, strictly speaking, I could not form an idea of that mediation, was I not implicitly denying that it was an instrument? I appear to be involved in a whole network of contradictions. All this should be taken up in detail.

If I think of my body as instrument I thereby attribute to the soul, whose tool it is, the potentialities which are actualised by means of this instrument. Nor is that all. I furthermore convert the soul into a body and in that way become involved in regression without end. To suppose on the other hand that I can become anything whatever, that is to say, that I can identify myself with anything whatever, by the minimum act of attention implied by an elementary sensation without the intervention of *any mediation whatsoever,* is to undermine the very foundations of spiritual life and pulverise the mind into purely successive acts. But I can no longer conceive this mediation as being of an instrumental order. I will therefore call it "sympathetic mediation." Is the idea of such mediation possible for an intelligence that is different from ours? Once again we need to make a roundabout approach. Instrumental mediation and sympathetic mediation seem to be bound up together and even unthinkable apart. But what exactly does their bond imply?

All that I can say from the standpoint which I have so far attained is that telepathy, for example, is doubtless only a particular case of a general mode of mediation which is alone capable of making instrumental mediation possible. But obviously we will not get an inch nearer the solution of the problem I have stated by interposing an unknown occult body between spiritual activity and the visible body. Moreover, the expression "spiritual activity" does not satisfy me. Things must be considered on a higher level. To say that the attention cannot be exercised directly on an object is to refuse to regard the attention as an independent reality. Could we not say that attention is always attention to self and inversely that there is only self where there is attention? Besides it is quite clear that to pay attention to something is always to pay attention to oneself as a feeling being. Yet we need to grasp that this *self* still *falls short* of all objectivity. Here we come back to the criticism that I made earlier of formalistic doctrine of the ego (as object that has nothing objective about it, that is neither a *what* nor a *who*).

I am unable to appear to myself otherwise than as an attentive activity bound up with a certain *"this"* on which it is exercised and without which it would not be itself. But have I not said that no idea of this *"this"* is possible? Whereas must it not at every moment be a

given *such,* that is to say, must it not be determined? (I would not like to insist here on the problem regarding time that we will come up against soon enough). The *this* of which I am speaking is not an object, but the absolute condition for any object whatever to be given to me as datum. I wonder whether I would be betraying the thought I am trying to "bring to birth" at this moment if I said that there is no attention save where there is at the same time a certain fundamental way of feeling that cannot in any way be converted into an object, that is in no way reduced to the Kantian *I think* (since this is not a universal form) and without which the personality is annihilated. To sum up, this fundamental sensation is confounded with attention to self (the self being no more than absolute immediacy treated as mediation).

But we must grasp clearly that this *Urgefühl* can in no way be felt, precisely because it is fundamental. For it could only be so in function of other sensations—but by that very fact it would lose its priority. But is it not conceivable that for other beings placed on another plane, this fundamental quality can on the contrary be felt? . . .

When I re-read the bulk of the foregoing reflections I think I can see a "hole" in my argument. Can I not be reproached for having taken as a sort of self-evident postulate that this fundamental quality cannot be identified with my body? Whereas I am really unable to identify the object and the condition of objectivisation.

Nor are we at the end of our difficulties. If my body is not to be identified with this mediating quality, how does it happen that my body appears to me as being *more* than an object amongst other objects? I think the answer is that for sympathetic mediation to take place, there must also be instrumental mediation. Hence, for there to be a medium there must also be a knowable instrument—i.e., a body.

The kind of antinomy involved in all this is essentially bound up with the very nature of personal life, because were all instrumental mediation lacking, we would be in the realm of pure diversity, of that which cannot be grasped.

The Analytic of the Lived Body[*]

ALPHONSE DE WAELHENS

We have shown that the different fragments utilized by experimental psychology will not serve to elaborate a response to the *philosophical* problem of the body, because these fragments (sensation, association, perception, etc.) are indetachable from the naturalist ontology of common sense, which is unable to think this problem without immediately vitiating it with a definite contradiction. This does not constitute an intrinsic criticism of experimental psychology but an effort made with a view to specifying its scope. Experimental psychology is what it is. Its evolution, its problems, the data it has chosen to gather and to question, are predetermined by a method whose scientific fecundity is beyond question, but which is forbidden by its presuppositions —perhaps unconscious—to explain our *lived* experience of the body.

So be it. It is still advisable to state exactly the meaning of this lived experience. That is what we would like to attempt now.

The problem of the relation between consciousness and the body declares itself inextricable, the moment it sets itself to unifying a *subjectivity* and a *thing*, the moment it aspires

* From "The Phenomenology of the Body." Translated by Mary Ellen and N. Lawrence in Nathaniel Lawrence and Daniel O'Connor, Eds., *Readings in Existential Phenomenology*, © 1967. Reprinted by permission of Prentice-Hall, Inc., Englewood Cliffs, N.J. First published in *la Revue philosophique de Louvain*, Volume 48, 3rd series, no. 19 (August, 1950), "La phénoménologie du corps, II: L'analytique du corps propre" (pp. 383-397).

to attach together the *I* who thinks, feels, suffers, loves, and desires to *a* body described in anatomical and physiological treatises. For such a body is a pure object, that is to say, a reality defined by the identity in which it is offered to the perception of *all* men; exactly as the City Hall of Brussels is a *thing* described in manuals of architecture, the *whole* entity set in the Grand'place being in a position to verify the exactitude of this description and to reproduce it. For it is precisely this possibility of awakening universal accord, from the level of perception, concerning what it is and the manner in which it is presented, that defines this monument as a thing-*object*. The difficulty about the body is that, if it appears *also* to be a thing (it does not matter who may put himself in a position to state that I am 1.70 meters tall, that I am blond, left-handed, lame, or diabetic), it is not that as *my* body, which is to say, not as it is felt, manipulated, possessed. So it is about this last aspect, and only about this last aspect, that our problem is concerned. The body it is appropriate to unite to my consciousness (if this already strongly suspect language may be permitted us) is not the one *you* see but the one *I* feel. How could it be that *I am* this hair you see blowing in the wind, this finger you see grasping a spoon, this stomach which the radiologist sees on the negative? The response is simple: there is no problem because *I am not these things*. This hair, these viscera, are *objects of perception for you* (and eventually for me, when, taking someone else's point of view I look at myself in a mirror or, at the cinema, look at my own picture). For you they are as they appear to a witness, not as *I* feel them as mine. And, as I have just said, I shall not be able to correct this displacement of perspective by placing myself opposite me in another's place: if I have a migraine headache and I look at myself in a mirror, the cranium which appears to me is not seen as suffering.

Quibbles, someone will say. For it certainly is I myself who will be operated on and who will be healed according to the directions of the radiologist. Certainly, I shall not pretend I am well if the negative shows an ulcer. But it is one reality to "present the objective symptoms of an ulcer" and another, *of an altogether different type,* to feel the discomforts and burning sensations which caused me to consult the doctor. The two phenomena are of a different order: I show the one and am the other.[2] But it's all the same, you say. The same for whom? For the person who could be at the same time me and a third-person spectator, which is to say, no one, since never will the two points of view be identical. For if I have looked at the negative of *a* stomach showing certain anomalies perceptible to all, I have not seen the piercing pain from which at certain moments I cannot detach myself, this lack of appetite, these periods of sleeplessness which cause my no longer being "fit." Let us understand it thoroughly and repeat it: I do not deny that treatment instituted on the basis of objective records and universal rules ("whoever has an ulcer should be made to rest and put on a milk diet") will put an end to "my" discomforts and cure them. It is maintained only that these are not the anatomical and physiological bases which constitute *in themselves my corporeality.* Doubtless they form, *compared with a certain plan of exploration,* the ingredients of it, just as my worktable becomes on a more distant scale, a system of molecules and atoms, but ceases then to be a table, which is to say, a utensil which I encounter on my perceived experience and which will not, within this experience be explainable by elements which do not form a part of it. Fleshly matter does not become *my* body until it is *assimilated,* and this "appropriation" (to use Jaspers' vocabulary), far from being reducible to a mere means of coupling the ob-

jectivity recordable to a subjectivity lived, is on the contrary our way of existing as incarnate subjectivity, which excludes all possibility of distinguishing either a body, or a consciousness as radically separate. This possibility only appears where what is in reality nothing more than a composite from some other place and not *formally mine,* is unduly considered as *my* body.

The true solution of our problem must thus be sought in the extension of the descriptions which reveal me as a felt subjectivity, intrinsically and immediately plunged into the heart of a reality which it doubtless exceeds, but remains all the while basically and to the depths of its nature *in it.*

* * *

If an existing human being is truly "a being-in-the-world," no one will ever succeed in describing his experience correctly in these "cinematographic" terms for which idealism and sometimes Bergson have a fondness (notably in the celebrated first page of his *Matter and Memory*). It will never be possible to reduce this experience to a pure succession of "images" or "representations" which subjectivity contemplates more or less actively without being in any sense part of them. The world does not appear as a collection of "givens" or of pictures of which we will have to take stock and which therefore we may look at again and dispose of as we please. On the contrary, experience is characterized by facticity, by fundamental perspectivism. Experience is always engaged: which means that I am constantly "here" and not "there," that I am born irrevocably healthy or weak, in a certain social position, in one word, that nothing is offered to me except from a *certain point of view.* It will never be possible to see the front and back of a passerby, live in Brussels and Sydney at the same time, be poor and taste an ample life free from material cares. So each of these facticities directs not necessarily all my future life, (for I may pass by the walker, move from Brussels, become rich or impoverished) but necessarily and at least, the way in which total reality will present itself to me in the immediate future. At every moment of our lives we carry with us, we are, a certain perspective—insurmountable in the instant where it appears—*from which basis* everything begins to present itself to us. It is true that I can change this perspective—but that will be substituting another for this; it is true that I may cross all spatiotemporal

---

[2] Moreover, we do not deny that the conciliation in one being of these antinomic aspects poses a difficult problem. But we do not have to resolve it today because it is not identical with the lived experience of my body. This is our main thesis.

limits for myself in my imagination; wherever I am, I can see before my eyes the Brussels City Hall; certainly, but it is necessary that I have already seen it, and it is seen in only one attitude, and even today, in Calcutta, when I attempt such an act of imagination, still it is an act of a "situated" spirit: it is true that by means of my intellectual activities I transcend the "here" and the "now" (it will be eternally true that a little while ago I pronounced some valid judgment), but this act happened "here" and "now." I can change my social condition but will never change it except from the point of view of someone who has known another: I will be rich who have been poor, and if, as a bourgeois, I decided to become a working man, I will become only a working man who has chosen to be one, which means that I will never penetrate the core of the misery of the working existence: that one finds it in himself without any reason, that one is "thrown into it" and that from the first glimmer of consciousness the misery was "already there."

And so there is always, for everyone, on all levels of experience, an "already there" which is important to remember. If, on principle, all points of view may be modified to some extent, still it is not possible to escape the necessity of a perspective.

For me, the perspective is being an engaged-subjectivity, having a body. We have deliberately spread our examples quite beyond corporeality in the current sense. That is because phenomenology tends to describe under this name all that is matter of fact in me. Moreover, I have not distinguished between what is definitely and what is momentaneously irrevocable. In reality, it is proper to show that all factual elements are at the same time binding and perpetually called into question. As past facts, clinging to me, they are unavoidably me myself. Nothing more can affect what I am or have been: Belgian or stateless, tubercular or healthy, son of a clerk or a doctor, in brief such determinations as innumerable facts have imprinted on me. But on the other hand these determinations, and here is the essential point, are, if I dare to say it, continually taken in hand again, and in this sense they are revocable. Concretely, if I am infirm, I will have to choose, constantly, the way in which I will be my infirmity; and that is the my-infirmity-for-me. To be paralyzed: that is to feel oneself incapable of certain things, and one only feels incapable of something one has definitely planned to do. Who among us feels incapable of climbing Mont Blanc? As a matter of fact at every moment I form projects with

regard to which my facticity constitutes an obstacle or an aid, a brake or a forward impulse, a handicap or an advantage. This infirmity, according to the projects I involve myself with, may promote them or hamper them. And as these projects are chosen freely, they are, in reality, a constant assumption of attitude toward my infirmity, a constantly new fashion of bearing it and of defining it. It is not only for a Christian life that a malady is an ordeal, it is one in a basic sense, and all facticity with it. Who does not see, for example, that the life of Roosevelt is that of a man who decided every day that he was not a paralytic, that the life of Amiel is that of a man who decided every day that he was a "failure." In such a way each of us carries ceaselessly with him his whole past, the humiliations he has felt and the successes he has won, his health or his illness; all his facticity; and by each of these projects gives to himself a new direction and one always to remake. And so we "forget" nothing? Yes, but forgetting is a perfectly possible behavior, a manner of assuming a position. A man who constantly forgets that he was a thief is not comparable to one who constantly remembers a theft committed, nor is he comparable to someone who has never stolen.

Our existence is indissoluble facticity and overcoming. It can only overcome itself because it is facticity, but inversely facticity takes meaning only in overcoming. To exist was, for Roosevelt, being paralyzed, to form plans which denied his paralysis: but this gigantic effort of negation constituted, each moment, the reality which was the paralysis of Roosevelt-for-himself. To exist was for Amiel, as a neurasthenic, to plan projects deliberately unrealizable; but by this continual setback was formed the reality which Amiel's neurasthenia was for him.

❂   ❂   ❂

Let us analyze more precisely what bodily facticity is in the narrow sense. First, the body is the facticity of my present position in the world of experience, the fact that I am always "here" and that this ecce-icity locates me at every moment in a new way. I occupy, every moment, a particular place, whence the real is ordered according to a particular perspective; and though I can change this place, I will never be able to free myself from the necessity of occupying some place; no more will I ever succeed in occupying the same place as another man. By this mode of facticity each of us draws in the world, for himself and for others, an appropriate perspective at the same time he acquires a point of view, or more exactly a mode of participation *sui generis* in existing reality.

From this "position," this "situation" which I necessarily occupy, it is permissible for me to discover in it various modalities corresponding to what are ordinarily called the various sensory domains. According to what has already been said, it is in no way possible to attach each of these to a precise physiological organ. Physiological organs do not belong to a body-for-me: if I can see my eye, it is not at all insofar as it sees, but insofar as it is an exterior object I look at by taking the point of view of another with regard to the body-object. One does not see himself in a mirror the way he feels himself alive, but as other people see us. This does not prevent the distinction of sensory fields from corresponding to an experience of *mine*, since the total of my real experience is susceptible to decomposing into sections which are not necessarily coexistent. The verbs *see, hear, touch, taste, smell* indicate the differentiations of experience, differentiations whose fields of appearance are not inescapable taken together. It even happens that some of them are definitively removed from our experience: we become deaf, blind, etc.

How may these differentiations in the perspective of lived experience be characterized? Let us say immediately, it is in vain that they are factually incontestable (no one confuses hearing a symphony with looking at the score, no one contests that this difference is *irreducibly given*), they remain nonetheless inaccessible to the knowledge which is called *thematic*. Each of us knows what is meant by *seeing* and *hearing*; yet I see only objects and never the act of seeing them; I only hear sounds but cannot hear their being heard. Said another way: to hear, to see, to touch, etc., are *lived* acts, inseparable from an intentionality which directs them outside of themselves; they are not susceptible of being grasped themselves for an intention or for a theme. This is what is meant by declaring them inaccessible to *thetic* knowledge. Certainly they are known to us, but, hoping that this apparently contradictory vocabulary may be excused, only within a *side immediacy*: I know the act of seeing directly and from having lived it, but I only feel this experience through the seen thing. One sees only the spectacle but, by means of it, one acquires the thetic experience of the spectacle and the nonthetic experience of seeing. One never hears himself hearing. Will someone object that to touch is an exception

and that, by clasping my hands, I perceive the touched and the touching at the same time? This would deceive us. We are here the victims of several confusions. To begin with, it is not a question of seeing what one touches. In the second place, looking at my clasped hands, I adopt the point of view of a third person. I see objects in contact as they appear to anyone; I do not see the interior experience which I have of touching or of being touched, which moreover constitutes only one single observable knowledge, and not an observable knowledge and its reflection in the observable (this being a pure absurdity).

But may we nevertheless describe, in however small a way, this nonthetic experience? Yes, to just the extent that there appears in it an intelligible structure which, as Jean Nogue has shown, is susceptible to being abstracted and reflected upon.[3] Indeed, each perceptible thing has its own structure, a system in which every datum is found integrated *a priori* as soon as it is announced to us as an object that is *visible, audible, tactile*, etc. The facticity belonging to each sense is the characteristic system-structure within which each object, in order to be of such or such a type, must perforce manifest itself.

Let us consider the simplest case, vision. It is essential to every visible object that it appear in a horizon of other visible objects. "When I see an object, I always feel that there is more being than I actually see" (Merleau-Ponty, *The Phenomenology of Perception*). One does not see the visible except among the visible. It is impossible to imagine a unique visible object. Let us notice that this principle, essential to a certain system (which we call the order of vision) is not valid for all such systems. It is perfectly conceivable to hear a sound which would not call up another. Secondly, no visible object is likely to be offered to us according to a perspective which appears as the only possible one; one sees the obverse *or* the reverse of a coin; the tableau is seen in the open air or in the context of a play. Each visible object appears as the inaccessible center of a series of "taking points of view" which is never complete. On the contrary, each sound is for itself a whole which is exhausted in its manifestation. Thirdly, visible objects show themselves as a group structured relatively to a center which is precisely myself. There is

[3] One sees thus that it is a question of a description by the formal and *a priori* characteristics of the act's intentional object and hence, in a sense, indirect; not a noetic description of the act, which is impossible in the case of sensory knowledge.

no visible object which is not situated to the left, to the right, in front of or behind, above or below me. As for sounds, they do not *necessarily* form an orderly whole (think of the cacophony emitted by a radio that is out of order), and if they form one, the principles of organization are of a nature different from that of the spatiality lived through sight. I will end these examples, which a phenomenology of the senses would have to develop, by saying: (1) There exists a series of systems, each one having its own laws, capable of defining in each case a differentiated sensory field, or, according to the language we have adopted, a sense. The problem of knowing how each of these systems is put into correspondence with an organ of the one public body (the eye, the ear, etc.) is external to this perspective. (2) These systems appear as the modalities of *one* fundamental system which is exactly *my-body*, as an insertion in the world. This last point, which is very important, is a result of the general fact that *every object from any system whatsoever* implies a reference to one beyond which does not necessarily belong to the same system. If a sound or a taste (by contrast to a seen object) can appear without relation to another object of their order, they cannot manifest themselves as islets of absolute experience. Every lived event, every perception is inserted by itself into a system of other lived events which make up *my* experience, *my* life. It was last night, while I was resting in my bed, that I heard an isolated fire alarm which broke a silence of several hours. One cannot think of a perception which would be the last in my life (although I *can* imagine perfectly, for example, that the fire alarm, having made me totally deaf, will be the last sound I would perceive).

Here again facticity and indetermination appear to be basically linked, each throwing light upon the other. Each one of us carries in himself in the capacity of a fact, perceptible systems and the system of these systems. I can change nothing of the *fact* that what is visible for me is all appearance structured after the manner of what has just been summarized above. Neither can I change anything of the fact that my experience is ordered within a system of all the systems equally characterizable in a certain way and which I call my body. These different facticities are, moreover, common to all men and are part of the human condition. Furthermore, each one of these systems and their total system have already received in me a characteristic, and in one sense irrevocable, orientation: it is, if you will, a

particular facticity. For example, it consists of the fact that everything I will ever see will inevitably be linked up with what I am seeing now, my study where I am writing, my back to the window. Very probably I will see the Place Rogier again, but I cannot do so without crossing in some way the distance which separates me from it. If I see it again some day, it is unavoidable that first a scene will take place for me which also unavoidably will not take place in the self-same way for my friend Pierre who is right now about to emerge opposite the Gare du Nord. I have or I do not have a musical, artistic disposition, and this facticity will inevitably affect everything I will ever see or hear in the way of pictures or music, at any rate, *differently* than if I did not have this facticity. Nothing prevents me from riding a bicycle, but my facticity, as it exists now, of having already ridden a bike, or of never having done so, will determine in this case an inevitably different behavior.

And so, I carry with me, both for each sensory system and for the total of these systems, an incalculable and directed facticity. But that facticity is also constantly susceptible to being informed and modified by my projects. Nevertheless, the particular facticity of such a determinate existing human being, which is dependent on the individual history and not on philosophy, interests us less than the structure of the body-for-me as it universally lets itself be disengaged.

One of the essential elements of this last facticity is that the totality of the data depending on a partial sensorial system is never able to be perceived *uno intuitu*: there is always more to see, to hear, to touch than what I see, hear, or touch at this moment.[4] And so all phenomena are submitted to the law of successive appearances. The organization of this order differs as to its principles for each sense and its application to facts is contingent on each one of us: the structure of succession is not exactly, for vision, what it is for hearing and, on the other hand, what I perceived by these senses has followed an order of fact which has never been duplicated in any other man. Which amounts to saying, in abandoning psy-

[4] This does not contradict what was said above, namely, that for certain sensorial systems like that of hearing, it is not necessary to think that a datum relative to this sense will be perforce followed by an *ulterior* datum relative to the same order. We affirm here that no idea in any system will ever appear as the *first* of its type and, again, that none will resemble absolutely all which have preceded it.

chological language, that being-in-the-world implies that all existing things are defined by an original and irreducible point of view.

The sum of these data is gathered and organized, however, relative to a center of global reference. As little similar as are the actions of touching and seeing, or, better, the things touched and seen, these things, because they appear in my visual field or tactile field, refer to a common point of origin from which they set out again: my body. The center of global reference is the body-for-me insofar as it is the system of systems. As each type of datum is organized relative to a partial center which is exactly the sense-for-me ("my eye" is the point on which all things visible are constructed), so the total of these types is organized around an absolute center: my body.

The question, then, is one of knowing what relations I maintain with this center. Put this way, the problem becomes insoluble because, as we said in the first part, I have no position for withdrawal, no means of getting away from this center, in order to ask myself what it is with relation to a me which would not be confused with it. It is impossible for me to *look at* the system while it unfolds: I am-the-system being unfolded. One does not see himself walking, dressing, striking, working, in brief, constituting that perspective in which everything manifests itself for me. I constitute it at every moment in unfolding the new relations which I am; each of my actions opens for itself new possibilities whose realized and never achieved totality continually constructs this world as it is manifested for me more precisely and relatively to an identical center. Each of my gestures engenders the foreseen promise of another gesture, falls into facticity by outlining a project. To grasp the handle of a cup is already a little bit of bringing it to one's mouth, and the digestion of this hot liquid which burns my palate is ushered in by the movement which brings it to my lips. And so everything "gathers itself" around a center which I am, which at every moment establishes a situation of fact whence all future acts must "depart" (no matter what I do, I will not be in Sydney in five minutes), but depart by surpassing it. All facticity is an invitation to perceive, to act, to project. It will never be possible to consider the body as my instrument; it is, on the contrary, at once the constantly moving and constantly irrevocable manner in which I insert myself in reality. If it is true that I am at every moment the thing which gives orientation to the real (the tree is on my left, the tramway is before me and

must be caught on the run, etc.), "I" will never be able to orient myself with regard to my own orientation, nor back off from it; at least insofar as I am a perceiving I. An instrument supposes a physical handling. Who is going to control my body "physically"? The question is absurd, and if it were not, its solution would suppose a regression to the infinite, also absurd: for the instrument with which "I" will control my body postulates another, thanks to which "I" will be able to control it and so on. An I which would have nothing in common with the body would not be able, without contradiction, to "live in" it.

And so, in the realm of perception, I am my body because *I am presence to the world.* But this presence produces itself in a twofold manner. It implies, in effect, that on the one hand I occupy at the heart of reality a factually irreducible situation (one cannot be-in-the-world without necessarily being *here* or *there*) and on the other hand, that this situation is a constant tendency toward new determinations, that in a single word, it is also a *project.* If it were not at least the sketch of a project, my situation would be comparable to the inert localization of a chair or a rock and, because of that, would cease to be truly a situation. And so my body is always both unsurpassable and the surpassed or, if you prefer, my fatality and my *élan.* Let us try to clarify this idea.

The body is my permanent possibility for going out toward objects. To perceive is to act. All grasping of things, because it is for us a participation, contains in itself an invitation to modify them: at every moment what I see or what I hear shapes the program of my actions; this program is my body for me. I am about to write; each of the words I write on the paper calls up others, and the movement I made in order to write "progra," while it comes to an end, calls up and outlines the one which will create the final *m.* The same goes for all our actions and all our perceptions which, actually, are never separable. My body is this situation which develops; my hand for me is this necessity to trace the final *m* on "program" at the same time that it is the fact which I can fulfill thereby. In this form, my body is this "always future hole" which is spoken of in the *Cimetière marin,* cited by Sartre, the unsurpassable, because it is itself the surpassing.

But on the other hand, the body is the pure surpassed (*dépassé*), that radical facticity which is the necessary starting point for all our projects, and which it is almost impossible to bring to light because any act of consciousness focused on the body takes place in the middle of a project which orients the body in leaving it behind that act. Seen thus, the body-for-me is this inertia, this weight, this brake which prevents me from being everything all at once and which I see only when I rush toward an end, thus specifying it with respect to that end. We cannot grasp bare facticity, apart from our projections, inasmuch as it forms the point of absolute departure for these projections. To do this would be a kind of contradiction; only the beginnings of it can be felt in certain experiences of bodily affectivity, such as physical pain or, according to the descriptions of Sartre, *Nausea*. As the analysis of an example will show, these "affections" should not be confused with what are properly called feelings, whose significance is quite different.

Take, for instance, this example. Let us imagine that important business obliges me to move from one place to another, something I can only do on foot. So I set out, completely intent, projected, toward what constitutes the motive for my journey: this journey which I must end in a nearby village and on which depends the re-establishment of my fortune. But the route is long, difficult, and I'm hardly in the habit of hiking. After a certain time I feel tired, and eventually I "drag my feet"; soon I endure positive pain. I realize that I have hurt my foot and that to walk farther will become torture. I persevere all the same because I must get there; I try to overcome my pain by realizing the importance of my trip. I try to forget my weary body and even the road it travels. I anticipate constantly: "When I get as far as that bend I see already, only one more hour of walking will remain." If I have the courage to hold out, in three hours the sale will be over and my financial situation restored; consider "what I shall then be." As long as pain and fatigue remain bearable, my body is present only implicitly, alongside, and as though through a veil, because the project which occupies me is the sole thematic object of my consciousness and because all the rest is, with reference to it, only a background lived "in an undertone," or more exactly, in counterpoint. Soon, however, the thematic objects themselves reveal my pain to me; it is the road which is causing me pain and this sale, the immediate object of my journey, becomes more distant, a painful, dreadful undertaking which in perhaps a minute will be *impossible*. Finally, the rubbing of my shoe against the foot itself disappears as an object capable of being fixed and from which, in a sense, I can still distinguish myself: from now

on I am altogether this shooting, throbbing pain; as Sartre puts it, "I exist my pain." And from that time on, in pain I reveal myself to myself as pure facticity, as a pure "this" which must constantly be overcome in the projects which give rise to me. And so there is a pain which is totally me myself in its infinite lack, but short of a certain paroxysm "the" pains do not admit of blending: a violent attack of toothache, an acute case of conjunctivitis, a finger caught in a door are pains which I can, if need be, describe differently and which at all events I shall not mistake for one another. However, is it always the same facticity which they signal? Yes and no. Because, as we already know, facticity is an unvarying alteration and these are different aspects of it which these pains disclose. The pain I feel in the eye, the finger, the tooth, is actually the *eye*, the *finger*, or the *tooth-for-me*, that is to say, in their pure facticity for me and cut off from their role of instrument by which I recognize that they are inserted into my projects (for then the eye for me is the possibility of reading the book which is waiting on my table; the finger, the possibility of pulling from between my lips the cigarette burning there; the tooth, the possibility of chewing my food). In pain, my "organs" are no longer the way in which I unfold my projects, but a particular fashion of existing as my facticity. And as such the pain is not immediately related to this "thing," seen on the body of another, this "thing" called the finger, the tooth, the eye. Different pains are for me diverse modalities of myself insofar as I exist them.

But the pure test of facticity is only a limit. The project, which will take over everything, is not far. As Sartre says, "pain-consciousness is a project toward a further consciousness which would be empty of all pain" (*Being and Nothingness*, p. 333). One must hurry to close the irritated eye, to withdraw the finger caught in the door, to put the tongue between the tooth and the piece of sugar. Already I flee facticity in these projects which have as a correlative a consciousness which will no longer be a painful one. One flees pain by the project of enduring it no longer. But one flees pain as facticity, equally, if, giving up trying to escape it, one wants to *reflect* it. For a reflected pain is constituted as an object, it becomes an illness (Sartre, *op. cit.*, p. 335). By reflecting my pain, I detach myself from it; it ceases to be me myself in order to become a process *in* me. I imagine it as the passive resistance I oppose to the action of mechanical, chemical, physiological, and so forth, causes on my organism. This resistance is at once me myself ("Oh! I am sick!") and not me myself ("I know that sickness; it has bothered me before").

Pain as a form of my pure facticity is thus a limit-phenomenon subject by definition to all the threats of envelopment, since, precisely, I am not pure facticity, and because *pure* facticity could not be anything but an abstraction for my real experience.

◦   ◦   ◦

Such, stated briefly, are some of the perspectives which a phenomenology of the body would have to explore systematically. It does not appear at all doubtful to us that they will open the way for more fruitful researches since for the first time in the history of modern philosophy they pose the problem in its proper light.

It is true that, at least where J.-P. Sartre is concerned, these data are apparently integrated into an unacceptable metaphysical position. However, we do not believe that they are altered by this context. We have, on the contrary, intentionally tried to loosen these bonds. It is possible that they will have to undergo one or another modification of details. It would remain only to prove that these modifications are unfavorable to them.

The Meaning, or Dimension, of the Body*

JACQUES SARANO

Our attitude regarding the body, the meaning of our body, the dimensions of our body: these are three expressions of one and the same choice, which determines our status as persons.

Does my body possess a reality other than that which my attitude toward it confers on it?[1] Does it have a reality other than its meaning for me? When all is said and done, we have the body that we *merit*, the body that we are fitted for.

This is why I said that the body-object is the body *objectified*, that is, in some way *chosen* as object; and the body-subject means the body *chosen* as subject. The body-object and the body-subject express respectively a body assumed or nonassumed by me. It is an either-or proposition: either the body will be completely taken in charge, *chosen* by the incarnated spirit, or, on the contrary, my body will be, for me, this limited reality that my spirit does not integrate (the cuticle or the skin of the spirit, or, as Bergson said, that part of the spirit which has fallen back into matter, has precipitated, has solidified).

* From *The Meaning of the Body* by Jacques Sarano, translated by James H. Farley, The Westminster Press. Copyright © MCMLXVI, W. L. Jenkins. Used by permission.

[1] To say "it" regarding my body already betrays my thought and sacrifices once more to dualistic language, against which it is necessary to guard constantly.

The truth which hopefully will come out of my account is that our attitude regarding our body, thus polarly schematized, *reflects and expresses our attitude regarding the entire world*, and that, in and through our bodies we ultimately witness to that which we are and to that which we want in our most profound verity. It is in and through my body that I bear witness. It is through the body that one sees the man.

There is what I would call a *depreciatory idealism of the body* that is strangely confused with a depreciatory idealism of the *human condition* in general. We all know this from experience, and we all have lived it at certain times in our life, in the adolescence of our life (there are some who remain adolescents all their lives).

An essential moment of our progressive maturation toward adulthood is characterized by an ensemble of reactions: the rejection of bodily and social conditioning, which is more than a contempt of conformity; the search for a surrealist escapism that shatters the structure of the body as well as cultural structures; a curious and paradoxical mixture of iconoclastic detestation and of idolatry of the body and of the human condition.

As an adolescent rebels violently against his parents and his environment, as a new people reveals itself aggressively nationalistic (which is quite understandable), so does this idealism of which I am speaking affirm the spirit only in reaction to and disparagement of the body and the human condition. It affirms the *I* only in conflict with and resentment against the world. Idealism and solipsism are combined in affirmation of absolute and theoretical freedom, sometimes to the extreme of theoretical suicide (in the manner of the Kirillovian nihilists[2]). Nothing is of significance to me, nothing exists but me, nothing exists in me but the spirit, which repudiates all shackles. Now, he who denies the universe in order to exist will, in turn, consider himself as the world in his own bodily existence. His exclusive affirmation of self ends by excluding himself from his affirmation. It is one and the same thing to deny the universe and to deny oneself as body, as an existent in the universe. *For the body is the symbol of the human condition.*

Our civilization is presently in the adolescent stage of unsatisfied technical exuberance. It is in the uncertain, intermediate, ambiguous stage of the disparagement-idolatry of the body (i.e., of the human condition). In the final analysis, disparagement and idolatry of the body are the same thing. But how is this so?

For some, the technical idolatry is combined with a disembodying and dehumanizing idealism, which aims to subdue animal conditioning and, in place of the real body, to substitute another entirely synthetic body born of electronic genius. The superman of Nietzsche was a hero; ours is a robot. Lunar rockets and test-tube babies and the dictatorship of man by robots are combined with Huxley's "best of worlds" in the dreams of our modern neurotics.

For others, this same technolatry, far from being disembodied in the coldness of the laboratory, is admirably suited to a certain frenetic materialism that scorns spiritual values and aids the seductions, pleasures, and frenzied immediacies of the body (consider, for example, certain modern dances, which only superficially achieve the spirit of African dances). Adolescence has two faces, especially when it is forty years old.

This possibility of the perfectly contradictory interpretation of the individual's attitude as well as of the mentality of our adolescent civilization, seems to me to be understandable when one becomes aware of the *profound complicity that obtains between the contempt for the body and idolatry of the body.*

Contempt and idolatry are two forms of ma-

terialism or of idealism (which come down to the same thing), for both have restricted our body to the petty limits of the individual body.[3] Both make the body fall back to the level of the body-object. The idolatry of the body, in fact, has made it an idol-body, which is a body-object, since it is not *recovered* in a significant or, if I dare say so, a sacramental intention. This idolatry of the body limits it to the individual body by excluding or being ignorant of the surrounding world into which the body is incorporated. Inversely, idealism, which turns away from the body, succeeds only in completing the same negative and nihilistic operation. The two misappreciate the body by seeing in it only a body, which is adored by one and abhorred by the other.

On the contrary, this same body, when it is *recovered* in a meaningful intention, then responds at one and the same time to two interdependent operations: (1) of the negation (surpassing) of the body-object or idol; (2) of the breaking forth of the individual body into a world.

The affirmation of the body-subject and the affirmation of the world body (that of human relationships, the Christic body) are really one and the same affirmation.

Our technical civilization participates, then, contradictorily and simultaneously in an idolatry of the body and in a disrespect for the body. Materialism and idealism, these hostile brothers, are more similar to each other than we think. They characterize the dualist or *critical* moment of our development. Now, we must undoubtedly come to this critical moment, but we must also go beyond it in order to reach a "new childhood." This new childhood will not be precritical, but *post-critical.* It will rediscover the salt of the earth, the communion of things, and something like the flavor of our body, namely, the absurd privilege of our corporeality and our incarnation.

When idealism yields to the disincarnational current, it does not take account of the extent to which its scorn for materialism is materialistic, since it treats as material a body that is not such.

But idealism will understand this later, when, as a prodigal son, it returns to this house, to this body which is the house and native

---

[2] *Translator's Note:* Alexey Kirillov, in Dostoevsky's *The Possessed*, is a revolutionary obsessed with the desire to commit suicide, thereby asserting his freedom of will.

[3] The same contempt is sometimes held regarding God. Believers who, with the best intentions, reduced God to some disembodied ideal or some idol, are no different from the atheists who (with some reason) reject this idol or this ideal. Atheism and deism, under opposite appearances, have missed the true face of the living God.

country of the spirit, of which a diabolical angelism meant to deprive it. Yet for the present this idealism indicts our body with all the resignations of the spirit, as one shifts the guilt to a scapegoat. In a cowardly manner, it accuses the body and escapes. It is like a hit-and-run driver, and leaves the scene of the accident.

Idealism is Manichaean. It makes the body the *locus* of egoism, so as to reserve for the spirit the privilege of interaction and love. But the truth is, however, that as body-spirit *we make an unambiguous choice*, for egoism or for love. As body-spirit, we remain entirely enclosed within ourselves or we turn fully open to the world of men. We are completely *flesh* or spirit.

The Pauline term "flesh" expresses something quite different from topography or an anatomy. It expresses the orientation of the whole man, of his spirit, that is, the spirit in which he lives and which will manifest itself either as anti-Spirit spirit or as spirit that is docile to the Spirit.

This is what I attempted to express previously in saying that our body is the locus of our individuation *and* of its surpassing. In reality, it is as *incarnated* beings that we are either *flesh* (individual) or spirit (person). We are soul-body for better or for worse, for spirit or for flesh. And it is in the body that we will be judged.

The dividing line is not located between the body and the soul, as is too often believed. Rather, it comes between the flesh and the spirit, which is quite a different thing. For it does not involve "regions" of man, but rather, an attitude and a fundamental choice of man. The opposition resides in the choice that I have made, and not in the parts of which I am composed in the eyes of abstract analysis (body, soul).

Certain "spiritualists" have only disdain for "materialism," without realizing that true "ma-terialism" (in the pejorative sense) does not come from matter, but from the spirit that rejects it as such, that is, from this dualist spirit that engenders, at the same time the two symmetrical twins idealism and materialism. Both harmonize in the same "materialism" of matter.[4] The true distinction lies elsewhere: it is in my attitude, my spirit, my total orientation that I reveal myself as "materialist" (i.e., *individualist* and narcissistic—and how many idealists are materialists in this respect) or "spiritualist," to use customary terminology (by "spiritualist" is meant, turned toward men, open to right relationships between men, in other words, *person*).

These contradistinctions of various formulas are not blind windows. They are intended to reveal the extent to which my body is wrapped in my choice, the extent to which my attitude regarding the body (which is an unavoidable dualist way of expressing it) furnishes the characteristic manifestation of this *choice*. One cannot conclude a "spiritualist" pact with the spirit by scorning and hating the body or by rejecting it as an encumbering object. On the contrary, this is an attitude of flight, a disguised or unconscious materialism.

In a word, it is absolutely necessary to overcome the Manichaean dualism that would place *body-egoism-individual* on one side and *spirit-love-person* on the other side. This is an error of perspective, and how illusory and dangerous it is for the health of man and of the world! Man is *one,* for better or for worse, for the flesh or for the spirit, for death or for life. And it is our corporeality that makes us workers for salvation or for anti-salvation, for our freedom or for our alienation. "Man is saved with his body and not from it."[5]

[4] "Nothing is more materialistic than to scorn a pleasure because it is truly material" (Chesterton).

[5] Mounier, *Traité du caractère* (Paris: Seuil, 1947), p. 121n.

Being in the Body*

EUGENE F. KAELIN

Il n'y a pas d'autre manière de le comprendre que de le regarder, mais alors il dit tout ce qu'il veut dire. Sa signification est la trace d'une existence, lisible et compréhensible pour une autre existence. — Maurice Merleau-Ponty, *La Phénoménologie de la perception*, p. 371.

I

One of the funniest lines ever written by a philosopher is found in the life of Plotinus, by his respectful student, Porphyry. In translation it reads, "Plotinus, the philosopher, our contemporary, seemed ashamed to be in the body." Porphyry himself, I would presume, had no difficulty understanding this sentence, and anyone familiar with the context of Plotinus' philosophy would, after some study, be able to give a reasonable interpretation of it. I once tried to do so to a group of students, and their immediate reaction to my explication was a raucous belly laugh. That was how I discovered the sentence is funny. The students grasped immediately something which I had not yet understood, and concerning which I should like to come to an understanding today. After all, why do people listen to philosophers or read their books, and sometimes pay them magnificent sums of money, if it is not in the hope that the philosophers in question will be of some help in the attempt to solve the problems of everyday life?

Philosophical beliefs usually turn up in any

* From National Association for Physical Education of College Women. *Report of the Ruby Anniversary Workshop.* Interlochen, Michigan, 1964.

organized attempt to control and direct human behavior, and when they do, it is in disguise as unexamined presuppositions about the nature of human beings, the ends it is good or possible for them to achieve, and the available means for achieving them. Since they are in disguise and unexamined, such beliefs which are also erroneous can do much harm. Starting out as attitudes on the part of teachers, for example, they become ingrained as habits within the responsive patterns of students, who as usual suffer most from the errors of their teachers. I do not know whether it is more difficult to shuck off a bad habit or to take on a good one. Each learning process, however, is difficult in its own way, so the strain of each may be incommensurate with that of the other. Nevertheless, habitual actions are engaged in without thought, and may continue in spite of thought, whereas the difficulty of initiating the habit we know to be good demands reflection upon the goodness of the proposed manner of behaving, as well as upon the means available for inducing it in ourselves or others. It is not enough to repeat the classical dictum, *mens sana in corpore sano;* we must come to know what these words mean in the conduct of our lives. Critical reflection on such ideals as this is, and has always been, the concern of philosophical inquiry.

Unfortunately, however, it is not always clear whose problems the philosopher is trying to solve. Plotinus, for example, seems to have had some problems of his own: where was he when he was not in the body? and what was it

165

like to be there? The answer to one of these questions is funny-ha-ha; to the other, only funny-odd. I do not propose to tell you which is which, for that would be to give away my game before it is time to do so. Perhaps the best I can do is to put the two questions back into their original form by asking, Who was Plotinus? And one answer to that question is "the philosopher who seemed ashamed to be in the body," a man, obviously who was confused as to who and where he was. The life and the biography of such a man eminently qualify for being both funny-odd and funny-ha-ha.

People interested in, and dedicated to, educational theory and practice are well situated to understand the oddity and the humor of Porphyry's words concerning Plotinus' feelings in the body. But perhaps it should be said, in order to escape the predicaments of Plotinus and his student, that your own interests as members of the National Association for Physical Education of College Women are better described as "the theory of educational practice and the practice of educational theory." Certainly we do not want to pursue a theory for its own sake. If it is to be any good at all, a theory must stem from, and result in improved, practice. Moreover, the theory and practice of physical culture for women, if qualified as anything but educational, might be interpreted to invite pleasantries which on this occasion would be out of place, if not in direct violation of taste. When I was a school boy—my mother always referred to me as a "college man"—the dandies of the day called the coeds who elected physical education as their major, "sweat socks," to distinguish them from their masculine counterparts, called by another name. By any other name, each would have smelled as sweet; or perhaps, as in Chinese cuisine, it would be better here to introduce the notion of the sweet and sour.

As you can see, the pendulum of my thought has returned full swing, back to the physics of the matter at hand. If Plotinus' idealism allowed him to separate mind from matter, or soul from body, and to find his ideals only in the realm of mind or soul, the realists among you have sometimes been criticized by your humanistic colleagues for acting as if the bodies you are training had no minds at all. You would be hard put, if pushed, to indicate any ideal or aim of your activities outside the development of motor skills. You will be shocked, I hope, to hear that the rationale of your own educational postures is equally as funny—odd and ha ha—as those of your ideal-

istic opponents. In what follows I hope to make this clear and to suggest one way of removing the oddity and the humor continuously associated with the concept of physical education.

As a start, my major contention is: minds and bodies, like theories and practice, cannot be separated from the context of direct human involvement in the processes of life. Neither are they substances, capable of being weighed in a balance or precisely measured by any instrument of quantitative analysis. Any insistence upon quantitative precision at this stage of our inquiry would merely serve to falsify our result, which should be an adequate conception of mind and body, of mind-body, as a relational system coming into existence and passing away in a single, indeterminate environment I shall here refer to as a phenomenal field. Much of this work has already been performed by philosophers and psychologists on the continent of Europe, and I shall be making almost exclusive use of two studies by Maurice Merleau-Ponty, the only French existentialist who was also a reputed academic philosopher.

These studies, *La Structure du comportement* and *La Phénoménologie de la perception*, have recently been translated, and there already exists a running commentary on their contents.[1] I shall select only those parts of Merleau-Ponty's philosophy that are relevant to my thesis. The business of philosophy is the criticism of an on-going social institution; when this job is not done, by a philosopher or someone else, none of our social behavior is minded or intelligent in the fullest sense of the word, that is, fully self-conscious. You will see then that I am not posing as a scientist, who must record, hypothesize, and predict; that is the work which must follow what I am about to do. As a philosopher, my present task is to evaluate, and what I shall be evaluating is the adequacy of the concepts used by scientists and educators in their descriptions and direction of the educational process. If you did not think such a project is possible, you would not have invited a philosopher to address your convention, and if I did not think it possible, I should not have accepted your kind invitation to be here.

II

When asked to justify the theory and practice of physical education, teachers have sometimes responded with ideas of great generality and widespread social approval. Physical education has been said to "teach character," or to "develop leadership potential," or to make its adepts "better citizens, in a democratic sort of way." The trouble with such answers as these is that no one, not even those who offer them as justification for their educational policies, believes them. No one believes them because no one can.

We cannot teach character to our athletes while insisting that they win at all costs or by turning them into underpaid professionals. Leadership in any field other than athletics has little to do with physical strength, endurance, or skill—President Franklin D. Roosevelt led this country admirably for more than twelve years from the restricted confines of a wheel chair. Better citizens need more qualities than teammanship. To work with others in pursuit of a common goal is precisely that quality instilled in the fanatical German populace by a power-mad dictator. The essence of democracy is another habit—that of considering in concert the desirability of a proposed common goal and maintaining respect for those who cannot acquiesce in the choice to pursue one goal rather than another.

Each of these so-called justifications of physical education is conceived from an external point of view, and each is grafted onto the actual practice of education in virtue of an extraneous, albeit tangential, relationship to the development of the human personality by physical means. One might as well argue, within the restricted framework of physical education for women, that the end of our educational program is the development of more physically fit wives and mothers. If this is truly the case, then perhaps we have been working on the wrong sets of muscles.

The corrective to these abortive attempts to justify physical education is a return to the phenomena of our physical existence. We cannot, like Plotinus, continue to feel ashamed to be in the body; we cannot, like some physical educators, continue to cover over our shame by espousing the ideals of mind, character, or social utility as justifications of our interest in educating the body. It is true, of course, that in some sense we are aiming to educate the "whole person" and not just the body or the mind, but if this is so, we must, in order to convince our skeptical opponents, be able to show how the intrinsic development of the human personality follows naturally from what we do to it in our efforts to educate it. In other words, if we are to break down the false separation of minded activity from bodily activity, we must show the continuity of physical responses and intelligent responses to the set of stimuli playing upon the human personality by virtue of its relationship to an environment—physical, biological, and social—in which goals are first perceived, evaluated, and pursued in the business of continued life. And this is another description of what I have previously referred to as the "phenomenal field" of human existence.

Education of whatever sort must take place within this field, and its purpose is the enrichment of the lives of the individuals capable of this kind of existence. Education must start with individuals at a level of development where they are found; they are to be led out of their narrow pre-occupation with self; they are to be put in a position to conceive and to build a newer environment of ever receding horizons, always working with what is given and, within the limits of possibility, changing what is given into what is desirable, the significant into something more significant because it is more satisfying, and, not least, the personal creation of men. The range of education therefore covers the full extent of human expression: from seeking an object at a distance, to feeling ashamed to be in the body; from the facts man constructs by his habit of seeing, to the values he conceives—and with luck turns into new facts—by his habit of feeling anything at all.

Existentialist philosophers refer to this enlargement of the horizons of human experience as "transcendence," and if education is to mean anything at all, it should help man transcend the limits placed upon his development by the raw facts of nature. He can do this, I am convinced, because within the structures of his experience, or existence if you prefer, he is capable of taking on a second nature; he can and does develop habits of conduct we loosely refer to as intelligent, meaning thereby a comparative or superlative degree of adaptability to the conditions of an environment. The term being compared is, I suggest, "significant," a delightfully ambiguous word used to qualify any fact possessing a meaning to some organism for its continued life process, or transcendence. I need only add here that significance is not properly speaking something we "understand"; it is, however, always, whether understood or not, something which we feel and with respect to which we must act. Since perception of significance starts with the body, and the body must be oriented to perform an action, it is no mystery why education must start with the body. Any further development of experience will likewise have reference to the body in that further significance will be constituted by other, varying ways in which the body may comport itself.

Continuity between body and mind is thus one of the facts of human existence. The question arises, however, as to the best manner of expounding this relationship, and here we have a choice. Phenomenological (or existential) philosophers are fond of saying that we can take the "natural attitude," or the "phenomenological." We can assume the guise of physical or natural scientists, abstracting completely from our own feelings or values, and describe in total objectivity what takes place in the area of our concern; then, relating this area to others, we will eventually have described everything that is true of the natural world, including the artifacts of men, moving from quality, to fact, to law, and finally to the law of laws or nature itself. The difficulty that goes along with this attitude is not merely one of knowing where and how to find our facts or of achieving the degree of objectivity necessary to describe the facts as they happen independently of our own deliberate intervention; our frustration goes much deeper than this. It is of a theoretical sort in that the natural attitude itself dissimulates the nature of the enterprise we should be investigating every time man and his behavior are the subject of investigation. In matters of education, we cannot be "objective" in the sense that our own values would make no difference for the outcome of our inquiry; our own values are part and parcel of the very process of education, and to abstract from them is to emasculate the experience it is our business to inculcate in our subjects (even if they are women).

The alternative to the natural attitude is the phenomenological. According to the latter, a phenomenon appears when a given subject is undergoing some kind of experience, which of course may later be described. An art critic, for example, allows the experience of a work of art to take place; he allows the work to engage his attention as completely as it might. In a very real sense, the work must happen first, and then it may be described according to the manner in which it has controlled the critic's experience. Edmund Husserl, who invented the method, called this technique "pure description." In order for it to work, the subject must "bracket the world," that is, suspend belief in the reality of the real, physical world and hold in check the propensity to appeal to facts or laws of the sciences describing the real world. Our belief in a real world, and our appeals to the physical conditions of having an **experience** of it, are merely two ways of prej-

udicing the experience we should be describing. Instead of recounting what has happened in the phenomenal occurrence, we appeal to what should have happened according to known or supposed scientific prescriptions. To proceed phenomenologically, then, we let ourselves go to the experience and, in a moment of reflection, describe what has happened to us as it has occurred. As a sculptor friend of mine once wrote, men were lovers long before they became gynecologists, and all the results of the most sophisticated kind of gynecology has had no bearing at all upon their capacity as lovers.[2] On the contrary, the abstractions of the gynecologist may very well have impeded that capacity. To get out of such a predicament, our scientist friend must reassume the phenomenological attitude.

This is what Martin Heidegger meant, in *What is Metaphysics?* when he snidely remarked that if you ask a scientific question you are likely to get a scientific answer. The pejorative he intended has never been understood by many Anglo-American philosophers who have been seduced by the scientism of our own age. The fact of the matter is that education is not a science at all, not even an applied science; it is an art, one of the useful arts, which, of course, may well use the technological results of any science, but which does so in the pursuit of a specified human value. To show that the phenomenological attitude is a necessary part of a viable educational procedure, I shall in what follows describe the human body first in "natural" and then in "phenomenological" terms. My guide is, again, Merleau-Ponty.

III

Within the natural attitude, the body can be considered in its most simple form as a purely physical entity. As physical, the body possesses mass and occupies space and its matter is convertible into energy. Mass is the constant we know relatively as weight, which, like the space the body occupies, can achieve enormous and unhealthy proportions. The function of the mind is to keep this from occurring; of themselves, bodies can only continue to occupy space, each part related to every other part contiguously and coextensively. Like stones, chairs and tables, and marble statues, the human body has a contour and is bounded into a shape which cuts its figure into "objective" space, the three dimensional container of all physical existents; like stones and chairs, the human body, if it were nothing but physical, could not move unless it were moved by another thing. Plato was so struck with this last thought that he used it to establish both the existence and the immortality of the soul.[3] After all, the human body does move, and not necessarily by the action of another physical thing. Whence, the soul. The soul is not moved by another thing, so is self-moving. What is self-moving must be eternal, so the soul will never die, even when it has left the body and given it over to rot.

In our own day of psychological enlightenment we should be shocked to hear stories of the body and soul. Or would we? We often declare our passion "body and soul," but for what purpose is never clear. Like Socrates, who could not resist the physical charms of the young Phaedrus, we begin to discourse upon the soul whenever the body begins to feel uncomfortable at the sight of our beloved. And should we fail to communicate we could even use the same myth as that invented by Socrates to explain our misadventure: the wise charioteer and the good steed always find it difficult to control the evil but powerful steed rearing its ugly head. This was the reason Plotinus felt ashamed to be in the body, but legend has it that he succeeded in getting out of his body at least seven times in his career. To show that the myths of the ancients have not really been surpassed in our own time I need only refer to those instructors of dance who teach their students to express themselves, that is, to feel something and then to make the movements that will convey that feeling to a sympathetic audience.

Feeling, movement, feeling; what could be simpler—and more misguided? It should suffice to point out that self-expression and artistic expression are different concepts, that whereas the latter is always the former, the former only rarely attains to the latter. I am expressing myself now, as I write these words; I could do the same by scratching the back of my head, yelling at my wife, or shooting my mother-in-law. Each of these acts would be mine, but hardly a work of art. Walking across the street, kicking a ball, or dancing each engage roughly the same muscular structures of the human body; each may be preceded by an intention of the mind; all, if continued long enough, are capable of producing another feeling—extreme fatigue. The lesson to be learned is that the feeling I have before or after moving my body is not the feeling embodied in a dance.

Can we say, for this reason, that the feelings of the dance are unfelt and merely symbolized by the movements of the dancers, the patterns of which correspond to patterns of sentience,

as Suzanne Langer does?[4] If so, we must explain how the dance which is seen by an audience becomes translated into kinesthetic reactions, and how these present a feeling to be understood. Better, it would seem, to show that the feelings expressed in a dance *are* the movements of a body, felt in the first instance and only then by the dancers as they move, and by an audience which perceives the forms of the movements themselves. Such feelings are objective, or at least intersubjective, and can be described in terms of the spatial and temporal coordinates necessary to define the force expended by the body in movement. Let us then forget the romantic notion of expression for the moment and adopt the language of movement considered as spatial and temporal forms.

The dancer works with the body as instrument, creating a dance *in* space and time, the two ultimate realities of everything physical. Given a space and a time, we could calculate the force necessary to move from here to there; or given the force, the direction, and the destination, we could calculate the time, etc. This, I am told, is the way dance is taught in many institutions, and there is only one thing wrong with the approach: the dancer's body is not a billiard ball rolling down a polished inclined plane, nor is it freely falling from the leaning tower of Pisa. We shall see later that it is not even an instrument, for who would be using the instrument? the soul? the mind? or another body? And the space through which it moves, and the time it consumes? Are these given before the dance, before the body moves? Or, on the contrary, does the body, by moving, create a unique space and a unique time in creating the dance? We must be led to think so, lest we continue to be misled by our concepts of the soul as feeler of feelings to be expressed, and thus as mover of the body; of an instrument without instrumentalist; of space and time without life; and of consciousness without the body, whether in pride or shame. Of course, all this can be avoided; we have only to insist that the only person to come into contact with the human body as a physical object is an undertaker. And only that profession is interested in embalming and burying its objects.

To move from physics to physiology is an interesting step. The phenomenon of movement no longer plagues us, the soul is dispatched to limbo or some other place, and the mind is explicable in terms of the reflex arc or conditioned reflexes.

The reflex arc poses a simple model: stimulus-organism-response, the incoming (afferent) nervous impulses transmitted to the central nervous system where connections are made and transferred into effective action of the body by means of the out-going (efferent) paths. Stimuli, it is supposed, can be controlled and overt behavior can be observed, and measured. Lights, sounds, and pressures can be increased or decreased, reactions noted, and thresholds established. With all this scientific precision, what could go wrong? What, indeed, except the precision itself? Our figures may be exact, but what do they represent? Are stimuli the causes of responses? If so, they should have the same effect at least upon the same subject. But they don't. Even discounting fatigue, reactions to the "same" stimulus differ when that stimulus is presented along with another stimulus of the same kind. There seems to be no absolute significance to any given form of stimulation.

Aestheticians have known this for a long time: an identical red presented contiguously with an equally intense and saturated green is seen as a space tension, and no longer as a red plus the green. And what are we to make of the connections in the central nervous system? Are they made there as in a switchboard, a dialing system, or a transformer? All the mechanical models used to explain the arc of the reflex system fail to account for the fact that each species and each subject, to some extent at least, interpret what is to count for them as a stimulus. The attempt to construct complex patterns of behavior in terms of additive functions of simpler reflex connections is to reduce the rhythm of life to the hygienic conditions of a laboratory, where all the selection of stimuli is made by the experimenting animal, the psychologist himself. Under these conditions the experimental animal always comes off as sick, pathologically related to an unreal environment. But we have made a gain: in the physicist's universe, you will recall, he was pronounced dead and ready for burial.

The learning of complex behavioral patterns by the conditioning of responses takes away some of the pathology, even if it introduces some theoretical problems of its own. One of Pavlov's dogs, you may remember, exhibited what Pavlov himself referred to as the "freedom reflex,"[5] an expression he used to cover the case where an observed response was a rejection, on the part of an overstimulated dog, of the whole experimental situation. How human of the dog, and how cynical (or canine) of the little boy who, if not allowed to pitch, picks up his ball and goes home!

Conditioning allows for the transference of a response proper for one stimulus to another. It can and does take place under conditions of control and in the ordinary life processes of living beings working out solutions of problems by trial and error. The transference of reactions to different stimuli allows the physiologist further to suppose a general law of irradiation, according to which any reaction whatever might follow upon any given stimulus—whence, the superiority of the conditioning process over the simple connections of the reflex arc.

But whence, too, comes the necessity to suppose some kind of limit on irradiation? If, in the life of lower animals, anything can become a stimulus to any kind of response theoretically, then there must be some further law operative in order to explain the specific responses of some species. A toad, for example, will not snap at anything but a moving prey and will continue to do so even if it butts its head against an invisible screen. It will even overcome any inhibition one would expect from having successfully nipped off a piece of moving paper and go on to other trials following this error. Obviously, then, excitation, conditioning, and/or inhibition do not successfully explain all the learning behavior of animals even of a lower order, even though experimenters have succeeded in conditioning reflexes of animals having no cortex, such as fish.

Enough has been said, perhaps, to understand that the doctrine of conditioned reflexes is not "scientific," in any but an extended sense of the term. Since one might always appeal to the law of conditioning to explain any positive results, and to that of conditioned inhibition to explain any negative, the theory is unassailable; but this means that it can be neither confirmed nor disconfirmed. Moreover, since the term "physiological fact" properly speaking is used for the observed processes of the nervous system, the so-called "laws of conditioning, irradiation, and inhibition" are not physiological facts in the same sense. They are theoretical concepts supposed by the experimenter to exist, and then imposed upon the facts of observed behavior.

Rightfully speaking, then, physiological laws are facts of the observer's symbolic behavioral reactions. How otherwise to explain the continued pursuit of many errors in the behavior of experimental animals? or the fixation of one successful trial as the reflex response to a given experimental situation? As in the simple reflex-arc behavior, the character of the stimulus is after all determined by what is meaningful to the organism being tested. This is why the toad continues on its merry way in spite of our efforts to condition his behavior. Some stimuli, moreover, seem to change character. Animals have been noted to react positively to two negative (inhibitory) stimuli when they are presented simultaneously. He who would count on a double, or reinforced inhibition is sadly mistaken. All behavioral responses are *forms* of behavior, and all are occasioned by *forms* of stimuli which are detached from the environmental situation by the animal responding. This evaluation of a situation by an organism is of another order than the physiological and leads us forward to descriptions purely psychological. At this stage, even if the reflexes are gone, Mehitabel could still sing in her characteristic manner, "Whatthehell, archie, *toujours gai;* there's a dance in the old dame yet."

The psychology of formal behavioral structures was pushed to its highest development in the work of the gestaltists. It is tempting to indicate that the failures of physiological explanation of perception, even in lower animal orders, stemmed from the inherent difficulty of describing the full nature of a complex physical stimulus. There seems to be no way of compounding simple stimuli. If colors in juxtaposition appear as spaces, and two inhibiting stimuli presented simultaneously fail to inhibit response because when presented as a whole they constitute a qualitatively different sort of stimulus, the least perceptible element in human perception is contrast, a most elementary kind of formal relationship. No contrast, no light—and we are in the dark of night, where, Hegel has pronounced, all cows are black.

The gestaltists concluded that all reactions are to forms, defined as a complex stimulus having a character different from any of its components in isolation. A change in any one of the components radically changes the total quality of the stimulus, whereas total transposition of the complex into another which maintains the relative values of the components fails to change the character of the whole: a change in key does not destroy the unity of a melody. There seems moreover to be no physical explanation of this phenomenon. The structure of any stimulus can be known only through the structure of responses to it. Hence, any attempt to explain the structure of a given response by reference to the structures of the stimulus is obviously an explanatory circle. Whatever description can be given to structured responses must therefore be phenomenological in character: the experience must first

be had, and then described as it has occurred.

Whether the behavioral forms are "syncretic," that is determined by the "rhythm of the organism's life" and tied to a specific characteristic of its environment, as in the spider's reaction to a vibration of its web; or whether they are "mutable," that is transferable from one situation to another, as in conditioned reflexes; or, finally, whether they are truly "symbolic" and capable of expression in the absence of any correlative stimulus—these responses take place within the organism in reaction to the things and other organisms found in its environment. The relationship between organism and environment thus defines the field in which phenomena make their appearance.

I shall maintain that walking across the street, playing a game, or creating a dance are merely continuous modifications of the phenomenal field. The modification is achieved by abstraction from "assigned" significance to "conventional" significance, and from there to "auto-significance." I shall not maintain, however, that only humans dance; if my account is correct, if I have not been misled by Merleau-Ponty, only those organisms dance which are capable of responding in symbolic forms.

. . . .

V

In order to show in what manner the human species transcends any limitation set upon it by the conditions of its physical and even biological environment by creating for itself a cultural and social environment, I shall once more follow the lead of Merleau-Ponty, whose metaphysics is sometimes called a "philosophical anthropology," centered around the notion of continuity. Educators have always pursued continuity in theory and practice out of fidelity to experience which exhibits a continuous gradation between lower and higher animals and, within the behavioral patterns of the higher, between the life of the organism and the processes of art. Theory and practice cannot be separated because art and life cannot be separated. Art and life cannot be separated because, in living, certain organisms have achieved an order of response of unique significance, an order of response no longer dedicated to the sheer purpose of continued life, but to that of enriching life by suffusing existence with human qualities—those which only a man can feel, only a man express. All this, to be sure, is already well known; what is not so well known is that man has achieved the heights of expression, not because he has a mind, but because he has learned to use his body in significant ways and in an increasing order of complexity. Whether physical or mental, conduct is intelligent when it is ordered to an end.

Consideration of the kinds of ends a man can intend will afford a means of measuring the degree of significance our species may import into its life. In a word, the more significance man achieves, the more intelligent is his behavior. If it is the purpose of education to inculcate the higher, more significant behavioral patterns of human conduct, it cannot pursue this end by derogating the less significant or by supposing that the higher have no relation to the lower. Indeed, a closer inspection of human existence reveals a continuity between man and nature, between mind and bodily response. Each higher order of response is the "mind" with respect to those responses of lower order immediately surpassed. The creation of a human, cultural environment is a product of a body having transformed its signals into symbols, but the signalizing responses are themselves mind with respect to the reflex behavior of immediate response, and reflex behavior is mind with respect to the action and reaction of the physical body within the system of universal gravitation.

We must learn to trace the ascent of man from corpse to living thing and from signalizer to symbolizer much in the same way as Plato and Plotinus envisaged the ascent of the soul. Their most grievous error seems to have been the supposition that the soul continues to ascend when it once has lost contact with the body. It matters little that the one imagined the ascent to be directed toward the Good, while the other saw the process as a return to the One. These notions are themselves symbols for the highest ideals of mankind, and ironically, understandable only in terms of the continuity between matter and life and expression.

For all his intelligence, and no matter how absent-minded, man cannot lose contact with his body. These very words call up imagery of infancy, in which the organism is notoriously incapable of controlling either end of its anatomy. The child's sucking reflex fails to lose its significance in adulthood and even gains for having been transported into the ceremony of love. Muscular contraction and expansion, along with the action and reaction between foot and pavement, permit locomotion to both children and adults. But even our locomotion may achieve an added significance, as when we send our young ladies to finishing schools to "learn how to walk"—that is, in style or with grace. The grossest kind of coquette does nothing basically different. She may slink, swing, jiggle, or bounce; every movement of her body added to the strict necessity of getting from here to there announces the advent of art. Engaged in one kind of activity, the walker holds out a promise of still another, richer and more rewarding for signalizing an intent not bound to the limits of our physical space. Those actions which are so bound, the syncretic forms of human response, are usually taken for granted. We all know how to walk, or have learned to, and so forget the triumph of our infancy when we first stood erect, pulling ourselves up on a chair or our mother's knee. An injury or a virus may well cause us to have to relearn.

But even walking is not our first encounter with space. That occurred when we first saw an object, at a distance or near, a rattle or a hand, both our own, and what a joy to touch! Seeing, reaching, touching; consummation; the thing was ours, wedded to our corporeal structure. Our physical education, it can be supposed, began with the synchronization of these formal perceptual responses. A figure on a ground relative to me; a perceived space tension, coordination of muscle and movement; a kinesthetic trajectory toward that fascinating object, contact and caress; the object yields over its form.

Thus, the bodily schema at this very low order of organization already contains three coordinated structures: visual reaction, anticipated tactile consummation, and kinesthetic synthesis of the body in motion. In a higher order, each of these may become symbolic of the other; here each is linked to the other by the necessity of life. The significance of the syncretic responses, then, are assigned, either by the structure of the organism or the nature of the environment. As the spider will approach anything that sets up a vibrating motion of its web in search of a fly, a child is attracted to what it sees. What it can see, of course, depends upon the objects in its environment, those making their appearance in its phenomenal field. How it propels itself toward the object depends upon the structure of its anatomy. Imagine, if you can, the woman capable of throwing an overhand fast ball; she can't. But she can learn to walk in the most seductive of manners, throwing the most insidious kind of curve.

When she does, her responses have already left the realm of the syncretic and entered the mutable. Freed from the necessity of getting from there to here, she has room to play with her own responses. Her game is conventional, and its end is arbitrarily set up for a purpose of her own. In making this move, she has performed a kinesthetic abstraction. Since the end (or significance) is no longer strictly dictated by the limits of her own structure or that of her environment, she has abstracted the movements for the sake of what they represent or suggest. Seeing her at a distance, I can note her style visually, kinesthetically, or in the other manner; but if I should do that, I will be playing her game, since that is what she intends.

Organized sports, again, are not basically different from this mode of significance. A terrain is set up arbitrarily; goals and movements ordered to the achievement or frustration of attaining the goals within the conventional terrain are likewise regulated by arbitrary decision. Just as above, where some affairs can be illicit, some pitches are illegal and some blows, foul. Since the achievement of the goal measures the significance of the act, all niceties of movement over and above those necessary to achieve the goal are for the form. A pitcher winds up to prepare his muscles for the delivery of his pitch; his goal is to throw the ball past the batter—preferably in the strike zone; his follow-through is for balance and power or break—all action intending an object. Yet some pitchers have style, and others lack form. Warren Spahn's overhand left-handed delivery and Robin Roberts' fluid side-arm right-handed motion are prodigies of human grace; both cases are not unakin to the slower motion grace of a cat stalking a bird.

A further abstraction puts all the significance of the movement into this characteristic of the kinesthetic-visual phenomenon. Diving, skiing, skating, and the like are judged for excellence in form, the figure of the body moving through space as a dynamic configuration. And at this level of abstraction (from locomotion) we are at the approaches of fine art. All that remains for the sport to become art is the symbolic response to the kinesthetic form, that is, for the visual form to call out the kinesthetic feeling. When this occurs, movement is dance. The significance at this last level of locomotor abstraction is created by the movements themselves, by the dancer in motion. It is for this reason that I have referred to the rhythms of dance as "auto-significant." The dance means only itself.

A last point may be made by comparing this scheme to the dance theory of Suzanne K. Langer. For her, too, the dance is symbolic of a pattern of sentience. The symbolism is explained by the dancer's activity of abstracting physical movements, describable in terms of space, time, and force, into a dynamic image of virtual power, which appears only to the attentive consciousness. Her theory runs aground, however, since the pattern of feeling cannot be ascribed to any one person, either to the dancer who composes the image or the audience who perceives its structure. If the feeling is not felt, it is said to be "understood," both by the dancer and his audience.

This theoretical appeal to the understanding of the dancer poses all the old problems of mind and body that have been the bane of philosophy and psychology since the inception of each. Her model for the explanation of mental behavior—a transformer—is as mechanical and as inadequate as the switchboard of the physiologists. To suggest that a dancer first understands a feeling, and then translates it into kinesthetic imagery, is to suggest that a dancer dances before dancing. Since the counters (she says "elements") of the dance medium are movements, the dancer must already have made the movements in order to have gained his or her "idea." Outside of the notion of a locomotor motif, which can be taken from any ordinary life situation and which must be developed in context as an element of the total dance image, the word "idea" has no application in the dance art— unless it be a reference to the finished dance itself. But this must be perceived to be believed. Like her model for the mind, her model for creative communication via works of art is seriously defective. The dancer communicates through her finished product, and she can "understand" its "import" only by making the movements presenting the image of a virtual power.

The same kinds of shortcomings are apparent on the other side of the communication process. If the dancer makes the dance kinesthetically, the audience must take in the dance visually. The "form" of a figure skater or water skier fails to fulfill all the requirements of balletic expression because the athlete is perceived visually, and only visually. The configuration of the athlete's motion outlines a dynamic image in physical space; it may even achieve the status of a virtual power; but the connection between what we see and the feeling expressed remains a theoretical surd. What Mrs. Langer lacked in order to have achieved the most significant interpretation of the dance is a working concept of the bodily schema, of a body which "understands" before a mind has had the time to function.

It is not uncommon for dancers to respond to the question, "How does this dance feel?" by making an appropriate balletic gesture. It feels like this. They are not inviting us to make an overt expression of our own physical bodies in order to understand what "this" means. And they don't have to. We see how the dance feels because the feeling is the global kinesthetic image, a modification of the dancer's bodily schema, and when we respond visually our bodily schemata undergo a similar kinesthetic modification. This is possible because within the bodily schema seeing and feeling and moving are correlative structures of a single system, of a single human existence in transcendence:

> Vision and movement are specific manners of relating ourselves to objects; and if, by all these experiences, a unique function is expressed, it is the unfolding of an existence which does not suppress the radical diversity of its contents. For, it relates whatever contents it has not by

placing them under the strict control of an "I think" (that such and such must be the case), but by orienting them towards the intersensorial unity of a "world."[6]

And this is how, by modifying her world, the dancer succeeds in modifying mine, for as long as I attend to her dance I am inhabiting her world. All the significance of the dance is to be found in this experience.

REFERENCES NOTES

1. Kaelin, E. F., *An Existentialist Aesthetic* (Madison: University of Wisconsin Press, 1962).
2. Steppat, Leo, commenting on "The University and the Creative Arts," by McNeil Lowry, *Arts in Society* (II, 1963, no. 3, p. 35).
3. This account is culled from the *Phaedrus*.
4. Langer, Suzanne K. *Feeling and Form* (New York: Charles Scribner's Sons, 1953, *passim*).
5. Cited in Merleau-Ponty, *La Structure du comportement* (Paris: Presses Universitaires de France, 1942), p. 134.
6. Merleau-Ponty (*ibid.*, p. 160, translation by author).

The Significance of Human Movement: A Phenomenological Approach*

SEYMOUR KLEINMAN

It is rather ironic that those activities which are most intimately concerned with body are precisely the ones which physical educators choose to ignore or pay only a minimal amount of attention to. Those activities which explore movement with great scope and depth appear to be studiously avoided. For a long period of time gymnastics was almost a dirty word in this profession. And the discipline which encompasses all aspects of movement, the dance, is almost completely alienated from physical education. In men's physical education, dance is practically nonexistent. It appears that in our pursuit of and subservience to game and sport, the body almost acts as an obstacle which must be overcome in order that the ends of sport and games be achieved. We have come to regard the body as a thing to be dealt with rather than as an existent presence or mode of being. The body and its movement is viewed as the means to attain the ends of a game. We seek neither significance nor meaning to human movement. The game has become the thing. We have become uneasy about body and movement. Witness our testy attitude toward the emphasis on fitness and our embrace of the impersonal scientific analysis of human activity. We have divorced the body from experience and we do not attempt to understand it as it operates in the life world.

* From National Association for Physical Education of College Women. *Report of the Ruby Anniversary Workshop.* Interlochen, Michigan, 1964.

Rather, we attempt to explain it as a physiological organism. We don't look at it as it is but as we conceptualize it scientifically.

To understand one's body as one lives with it is foreign to us, but not to the phenomenologist. For the phenomenologist, to understand the body is to understand its existential being in the world. This is different from viewing the body as an object for study the way one would study a thing. Merleau-Ponty held that such a view of the body is a secondary meaning of bodily being. He wanted to penetrate into a primordial meaning of the human body. Probably the best and most widely noted illustration of this is Jean-Paul Sartre's description of the three dimensions of the human body. An understanding and awareness of these dimensions will help us understand from whence human movement derives its significance. I will use Sarte's example as described by Van Den Berg in an essay from the book *Psychoanalysis and Existential Philosophy.*[1]

A mountaineer about to set out to achieve a difficult peak makes careful plans and pays careful attention to things like his ropes, his shoes, his pitons, and other items of equipment. He concerns himself with the preparation of his body for the task. He is cognizant and actively aware of his body. However, as soon as he begins the climb, all these thoughts vanish. "He no longer thinks of his shoes to which a short time ago he gave such great attention; he forgets the stick that supports him while he climbs . . . he 'ignores his body' which he trained for days beforehand. . . . For only by forgetting, in a certain sense, his body, will he be able to devote himself to the laborious task that has to be performed." What remains, what *is*, is only the mountain. He is absorbed in it, his thoughts are completely given to it. And it is *because* he forgets his body that the body can realize itself as a living body. "The body is realized as *landscape*"; its length is demonstrated by the difficulties which must be faced from hand hold to hand hold. "Fatigue shows itself first as the changed aspect of the landscape, as the changed physiognomy of the objects." The rocks, the snow-fields, the summit appear more hostile.

"The qualities of the body: its measurements, its efficiency and vulnerability can only become apparent when the body itself is forgotten, passed over in silence for the landscape." *It is only the behavior, the act, the movement that explains the body.* In this dimension the landscape is where the significance lies. It is to the landscape that the movement is directed and there in the landscape is where the movement is furnished with significance. Knowing one's body is not revealed by scientific analysis or observation. We just do not come to know our bodies in this way. Wolff discovered that on the average only one out of ten persons can recognize his hand when shown a series of photographs which includes a likeness of his own hand. And yet in fact we *do* know our bodies. It "is that which is most our *own* of all conceivable things, which is least opposed to us, least foreign and so, least antagonistic."[2]

"The second dimension of the body comes into being under the eyes of his fellow man. In the first dimension, remember, the mountaineer in order to accomplish his task transcended his body, 'passed beyond' it in silence." The only change introduced into the second dimension is that the mountaineer unknown to him is being watched by another. The viewer in this dimension concentrates on the very thing that the climber has transcended. He sees the boots, the movements, the bruises. He sees the *body*. The viewer's landscape is centered in this moving body—this object. That which holds least significance to the climber contains the most significance for the hidden viewer. It is this recognition of another as a functioning organism which makes anatomical and physiological analysis possible. And it has been with this dissectable thing—the body— that psychology has been until recently solely concerned. Also physical education has been

content to limit its study of movement to this dimension. We have embraced physiological and anatomical analysis with such vigor and tenacity that it has become the only dimension of being in the world which we recognize. We regard man as a moving organismic thing—an object, capable of being completely understood by means of stimulus-response conditioning, laws of learning, transfer of training, and neurological brain wave analysis. But I shall return to this point later.

The third dimension of the body comes into being when the mountaineer becomes aware that he is being watched. For Sartre, this dimension of being is destructive. It destroys the "passing beyond." The climber becomes annoyed, uncomfortable. He feels vulnerable and defenseless. He miscalculates, he stumbles, he becomes ashamed. For Sartre, the look of the other always results in alienation. Van Den Berg disagrees. "Sartre's look is the look from behind, the malicious look of an unknown person. There is (on the other hand) the look of understanding, of sympathy, of friendship, of love. It may impart a happiness far exceeding in value any solipsistic satisfaction."

The significance of the movements on this dimension lies *in the look.* The somewhere where the movements take place also lies in the look. Under the gaze of the other, whether it be one of approval or disapproval, my body, my movements, my being is out there at the gaze, at the look. This dimension has great meaning and implication for teachers.

Now it is important to note that only one of these three dimensions of being attributes and suggests significance to movement as we physical educators generally regard it. Our profession's approach to movement has been by means of the mechanical, the kinesiological, the physiological, and the anatomical. The psychologically and sociologically oriented people in our field who attempt to study and predict cultural patterns and behavior strive to operate on this same kind of scientific level. During the course of experimentation and observation the individual comes to be regarded as an organism capable of being manipulated. He becomes a thing or an object in the eyes of the other. Analysis and explanation of human movement results but not real understanding.

To the phenomenologist, to understand the body is to see the body not in terms of kinesiological analysis but in the awareness and meaning of movement. It's to be open to gestures and action; it's the grasping of being and acting and living in one's world. Thus movement becomes significant not by a knowledge about the body but through an awareness of the self—a much more accurate term.

What are the implications of this view for physical education? From the phenomenological view it becomes the purpose of the physical educator to develop, encourage, and nurture this awareness of and openness to self—this understanding of self.

I suggest that this will not be accomplished if we continue to equate physical education with sports and games. Games provide satisfactions and fulfill a need to play and compete, but I contend that it is not the function of physical education to take as its responsibility the teaching and playing of games, especially when there is so much more that can be done in the way of enhancing fulfillment and realization through movement.

Thus the objectives of physical education become the following:

1. To develop an awareness of bodily being in the world.
2. To gain understanding of self and consciousness.
3. To grasp the significations of movements.
4. To become sensitive of one's encounters and acts.
5. To discover the heretofore hidden perspectives of acts and uncover the deeper meaning of one's being as it explores movement experiences.
6. To enable one, ultimately, to create on his own an experience through movement which culminates in meaningful, purposeful realization of the self.

This last I feel is the stage of true freedom, ultimate existence, and being. Its result is the attainment of the truly, independent spirit, and this should be the goal of all education.

Needless to say this is not the purpose or function of sports and games. Nor should it be! I am not here to deprecate games. But somehow back in its earlier days this profession reacted against the stultifying discipline of gymnastics and equated play with democracy and freedom. Our readiness to accept and encourage the concept of sport and physical education as being one and the same has brought us to this present state of uneasiness and dissatisfaction—a profession in search of a discipline. Nothing could be more shattering to a dedicated group of people such as we have in this field. It has resulted in a fantastic race to justify our existence and gain respectability by publishing nonbooks, nonarticles, and *non*sensical data by the score. This attempt to convert a field such as ours which operates on

a human experiential level into a science would be absurd were it not so tragically close to being accomplished. Physical education is an art, not a science. In our attempts to exhaustively analyze movement, exercise, fatigue, and the like we have moved farther and farther away from the experience as it is acted out—as it *actually* occurs.

This flight to science for respectability has turned many of our best people toward research in this area. But might I point out that whatever these people do in the sciences, be they behavioral or physical, they are not doing physical education. If they study muscle fatigue, they are doing physiology. If they study mechanics of movement, they are doing physics. If they study behavior, they are doing psychology. If they study games and sports, they are doing sociology. But these fields are disciplines in their own right. They are certainly not the discipline of physical education. In fact, I don't believe this profession knows that it means to *do* physical education.

How does one go about *doing* physical education? It is, I believe, our job to deal with the experience of movement, and it is our role to make this movement experience as highly significant as possible. The student must "enter into" the movement as completely as possible. And I am convinced that no other area in our field fills this need as successfully as the dance. Dance points toward this objective specifically and directly. The interesting thing about this is that most of the dancers and choreographers don't intellectualize and verbalize the experience to death. They just do it and it comes. The objective is attained in the experiencing of it.

Dance is the most demanding of all movement activities. It requires almost complete submissiveness to an iron discipline. And teachers of dance aren't known usually for the democratic spirit that exudes from their studio. Yet despite all of the "wrong" educational techniques the results are astonishing. Out of this experience emerges, not a slave, but a truly free individual—one who has such knowledge and command of his body that he is capable of experiencing movement at its highest and most significant level.

Although all participants in a dance may be performing exactly the same movements, the individual, if he is truly engaged in the act, knows nothing of others. He is completely absorbed in his landscape. He is acting only as *he* can act. He is deriving meaning and significance only in the way *he* is capable. He is aware of his movements as a creative art. It almost doesn't matter that he didn't design the move. He brings to it what he has to offer and what emerges is a noble experience, an enriching experience, a rewarding experience. Even the gaze of the other is transcended at this point. The audience becomes part of the landscape too. The spectators gain their rewards by what they as individuals bring to the experience.

Of course, all this happens if these movements—the dance—are good. So much of dance is extraordinarily poor. On these occasions both audience and dancers suffer. But dance, even when it fails, is by its nature concerned with significant movement.

Of the three dimensions of being outlined in this paper, those two, the first and third, which are most intimately related to physical education still await investigation and description. This is most unfortunate because it is here, in the phenomenological realm, where most of the work needs to be done. Gaining greater sensitivity and awareness of landscapes and their importance in contributing to significant movement is a task with which physical education must become intricately involved.

"Existence as a giver of meaning, manifests itself in all human phenomena, in the gestures of our hands, the mimicry of our face, the smile of the child, the creation of the artist, speech and work. . . The body is this power of expression. It gives rise to meaning; it makes meaning arise on different levels. . . ."[3] My contention is that for physical education the goal should be meaning and significance on the highest level of existence. I don't believe this can be achieved by a physical education as we know it today. Games and sports by their inherent nature do little toward achieving this goal at best and, in fact, often do much to keep us from it.

REFERENCES NOTES

1. J. H. Van Den Berg, "The Human Body and the Significance of Human Movement," *Psychoanalysis and Existential Philosophy*, H. M. Ruitenbeek, editor (F. P. Dutton & Co., New York, 1962, pp. 90-129).
2. F. J. J. Buytendijk, *General Theory of Human Carriage and Movement* (Utrecht, Spectrum, 1948).
3. R. C. Kwant, *The Phenomenological Philosophy of Merleau-Ponty* (Duquesne University Press, Pittsburgh, Pa., 1963, p. 57).

The Challenge of the Body*

PAUL WEISS

We men live bodily here and now. This is as true of the most ecstatic of us as it is of the most flat-footed and mundane. No matter what we contemplate or how passive we make ourselves be, we continue to function in a plurality of bodily ways. Whatever our mental state, throughout our lives our hearts beat, our blood courses through our arteries, our lungs expand and contract. Our bodies grow and decay unsupervised, and, in that sense, uncontrolled. Only a man intoxicated with a Cartesian, or similar, idea that he is to be identified with his mind will deny that he is a body too.

Some, with the brilliant Merleau-Ponty, think that man's body is unique, not to be compared with the bodies of other living beings. Most men, instead, follow Darwin and view the human body as a minor variant on the kind of body that primates have. Today a number are reviving La Mettrie's idea that the human body is only a machine. They, and sometimes some of the others, occasionally claim that a man is nothing more than a body. Since they have at least mind enough to think there is nothing more than a body, I have no mind to follow them. The body is, of course, a precondition for the exercise of some, and perhaps even all, mental functions. This fact is sufficient to make it desirable to cultivate the body, and to consider the body seriously in any attempt at understanding the nature of

* From *Sport: A Philosophic Inquiry* by Paul Weiss. Copyright © 1969 by Southern Illinois University Press. Reprinted by permission of Southern Illinois University Press.

man, without requiring us to suppose a man is only a body.

Everyone lives at least part of the time as a body. Occasionally our minds are idle, sometimes we sleep; we can spend much time in just eating and drinking. Though no one is merely a body, every one of us can be lost in his body for a time. Sooner or later, however, the minds in most of us awaken and we stray to the edges of reflection.

Even a dedicated sybarite has flashes of self-consciousness. Like the rest of us, he sometimes remembers and expects. He, too, looks to what lies beyond the here and now, and even beyond the whole world of bodily experience, to take account of ideals, if only to dismiss them. And sometimes, with poets and religious men, he deliberately detaches himself from his body and tries for a while to have a non-bodily career, occupied with fancies, myths, and transmundane beings.

He who gives himself to the life of the mind acknowledges as limits only what, if anything, is found to be beyond the reach of thought. But no one can totally identify himself with his mind. Bodily demands are imperious; the body's presence intrudes on consciousness. A man may escape the thrall of his body for a while, crush his desires, or focus on what is eternal, but sooner or later his body will show that it will not be gainsaid. It has needs and makes demands which must be met.

The life of thought proceeds at a different pace and pursues a different set of ends than that which concerns the life of the body. Each

179

exhibits in a special shape what man can possibly be and do. Neither is replaceable, though the full use of either at a given time precludes the full use of the other; a career devoted to one alone is possible to only half a man.

The body is voluminous, spread out in space. Through it we express tendencies, appetites, impulses, reactions, and responses. The mind, in contrast, is a tissue of implications, beliefs, hopes, anticipations, and doubts. It has no size, and cannot, therefore, be identified with a brain. But the two, body and mind, are not distinct substances, closed off from one another. They are linked by the emotions.

Emotions are at once bodily and mental, inchoate unifications of mind and body. A controlled expression of the emotions drains them of their confusion at the same time that it intensifies the unity which they provide for the mind and the body. That is why emotions should not be allowed to come forth unchecked and unguided. Because art and sport involve a controlled expression of emotions, making it possible for minds and bodies to be harmonized clearly and intensely, they offer excellent agencies for unifying man.

Never in full possession of their bodies, men are always more than they bodily reveal themselves to be. Their bodies can only partly reflect what they are; the fullest bodily life exhibits them as less than they can be and less than they ought to be. This remains true even when the mind is put at the service of the body. A more independent and freer exercise of the mind is desirable, for the controlled expression of the emotions is then given a greater role, thereby making possible the production of a more complete man.

These remarks summarize a vast literature, bypass discussions centuries old, and hide perhaps as much as they make evident. Our minds are mysteries. The interplay of mind with body is more a matter of supposition and speculation than of solid fact, unimpeachably evidenced. But if we stop here to make sure that all will be persuaded about that which all believe, we will lose our chosen topic. This is not the place to give full attention to the nature of the mind or the emotions, and the way they can and should relate to one another or to the body. Perhaps, though, enough has been said to make what follows not be as dogmatic as it may at first sound.

At the very beginning of life the mind's course is determined by what the body does and what it encounters. Soon the imagination, aided by language, the consciousness of error, self-awareness, and the unsatisfactoriness of what is available, begins to operate. The mind then turns, sometimes hesitantly but occasionally boldly, to topics which may have little relevance to what the body then needs, to what it may encounter, or to the ends it should serve.

One cannot live a life solely of the mind for very long. Its exercise is brought suddenly to a halt when the unsupervised body becomes mired in difficulty. To restrain, redirect, and protect the body, the mind must be forced back into the service of that body. But now it need no longer wait on bodily prompting. By itself it has learned a good deal about ideals, abstract categories, and logical consequences. Some of that knowledge it can now use to point the way the body ought to go. A mathematical notion will help clarify how this is done.

Mathematicians speak of a "vector" as a quantity having a direction and magnitude. The term has been adapted by astronomers and biologists for more special uses. I follow their lead and treat the bodily relevant mind as a vector, reaching from the present toward a future prospect. Normally that mind terminates at a bodily pertinent prospect, an objective for the body to be realized in subsequent bodily action. The mind in this way provides the body with a controlling future.

Far down in the scale of living beings, bodies are comparatively simple, but they still thrust vectorally, albeit not consciously, toward the future. What they do is triggered in good part by occurrences that are relevant to their welfare. As we go up the scale the bodies become more and more complex, and some impulses arise without any bearing on external occurrences. And some of the occurrences that elicit responses may do so at the wrong time and in the wrong way, leading the individual into disaster and maybe death.

Were there any completely unsupervised, complex bodies their health would be most precarious and their life span very short. Fortunately, the higher organisms embody an intelligence, at service to their bodies. Without effort, though, none embodies as much intelligence as it can.

The human body, like all others, on one side is part of an external world. It too is to be understood in terms of what the world offers and insists upon. To be fully a master of its body, a being must make it act in consonance with what that body not only tends to, but what it should, do. This is an accomplishment possible only to men. Only they can envisage what is really good for the body to be and to produce. Only men can impose minds on bodies. Those minds have many grades and functions, running from attention to commitment. Man uses his mind to dictate what the body is to do.

Literally, "attention" means "a stretching out" (of the mind). Since this implies a consciousness, he who is attentive evidently has a vectoral, conscious mind. By directing itself at bodily relevant prospects, that mind makes certain places and objects into attended referents for that body. Desire, intention, and commitment, as we shall see, build on this base.

The athlete comes to accept his body as himself. This requires him to give up, for the time being, any attempt to allow his mind to dwell on objectives that are not germane to what his body is, what it needs, and what it can or ought to do. But that to which he consciously attends is not always that which his body is prepared to realize. It becomes a prepared body only after he has learned how to make it function in accord with what he has in mind. Normally, he does this by habituating his body to go through a series of acts which, he has learned, will eventuate in the realization of the prospect to which he attends. Training—of which therapy is a special instance—is the art of correcting a disequilibrium between mind and body either by altering the vector, or, more usually, by adjusting the way in which the body functions until the body follows the route that the vector provides.

To function properly as a body, it is necessary for the athlete to correct the vectorial thrust, or to alter the body so that it realizes the prospect at which the vector terminates. Correction of the vectorial thrust is one with a change in attitude and aim, themselves presupposing some change in what the mind does. Alteration of the body demands a change in the bodily organization and activity. Both changes are involved at the very beginning of the process of making an athlete. To ignore the need to undergo these changes is to remain with a disaccord of body and mind, of present and future. It is to allow the body to react to what occurs, or to allow the mind to follow its own bent, without regard for what the body is to do. Most of us exhibit the disaccord too frequently in the first of these ways. It is a characteristic defect of the intellectual; in his occupation with the life of thought, he leaves his body insufficiently supervised and directed.

The correction of the direction of the vectorial thrust is promoted by the awareness of the inadequacy of a project, an appreciation of other goals, and a temptation to change. Men usually make this correction after listening to authorities. Coaches, teachers, and models help them to change their course so that they have an object of attention which they will bodily realize.

. . . .

A training program's central purpose is to make men well trained. By making them go through various moves and acts many times its aim is to get their bodies to function in accord with what those bodies are expected to do. Training helps them to be their bodies, to accept their bodies as themselves. It makes those bodies habituated in the performance of moves and acts while enabling them to function harmoniously and efficiently, and thereby be in a position to realize the projects at which the vectorial minds terminate.

Some men do not train. Their bodies proceed from beginning to end, often without needing to be redirected in the course of it. Eventually, it is hoped, he who trains by mastering distinct moves will reach this state too, though it is a question whether he will then ever do more than blur the checking points that his moves provided.

. . . .

No one is completely ripened, incapable of being improved through training. Whether young or old, all must learn not to yield to the body, not to allow its reactions and responses to determine what will be done. The body is to be accepted, but only as subject to conditions which make it function in ways and to a degree that it would not were it left to itself. He who refuses to do this is self-indulgent, almost at the opposite pole from the self-disciplined and controlled athlete. Men do not play well persistently unless they are well trained.

A man who is content to be successful in the perpetual adventure of withstanding or overcoming the world he encounters is hard to distinguish from a well-functioning animal. A man should do more. He should use his mind to quicken and guide his body. He should make his body a locus of rights and duties, and a source of acts, desirable and effective. Only if he so structures and directs this body will he have a body that is used and not merely worked upon by what is external to it. Only he who expresses his emotions through such a possessed and structured body can become well-unified and not be undone by what he feels.

Most men, a good portion of the time, are in control of their bodies. What they do part of the time, without much thought or concentration, the athlete does both persistently and purposively. It is tempting, therefore, to say that for the athlete the body has an exclusive role, in contrast with the intellectual for whom it serves only as a place in which, and perhaps as an avenue through which, he expresses what he has independently discovered. But no athlete lives entirely in his body, any more than a thinker has only thoughts that are entirely unrelated to what is going on somewhere in the physical world.

Athlete and thinker differ in the attention they give to improving their bodies and their bodies' performance. The former, but not the latter, pushes himself toward the state where he so accepts his body that he cannot, without difficulty, distinguish himself from it. Mind and body are united by both. In neither case are mind and body related as are hand and glove. Their connection is more like that of fingers to one another. They presuppose a self just as the fingers presuppose a hand.

. . . .

An athlete makes use of his good condition to vitalize moves and acts under restrictive rules, both in practice sessions and in actual contests and games. He prepares himself primarily to be ready to discover in the course of a genuine struggle how good he is in comparison with others. Until he meets that test, although he is fulfilled as well-trained, he is still unfulfilled as an athlete.

The good coach makes a preparation be more than an exercise and less than a game. He understands that the body offers a challenge to one who would achieve excellence through bodily acts, and that it must be structured, habituated, and controlled by the object of a vectorial mind. This makes it possible for him to see to it that his athletes are in fine condition, and that this condition enables them to perform well. No preparation can, of course, guarantee a fine performance. The circumstances may be untoward, or the athlete may be out of sorts at the time.

The art of training and coaching is the satisfying and dissatisfying of athletes at one and the same time. It is also part of the art of making men. That art comes to completion when the athlete makes himself be not merely a fine body, but a body in rule-governed, well-controlled action. Athletics is mind displayed in a body well made, set in particular situations, involved in struggles, and performing in games.

Nietzsche: A Philosopher of Fitness*

ESAR SHVARTZ

Questions of values have always handicapped the profession of physical education. Accumulating research during the last forty years has provided evidence concerning beneficial effects of sports and exercise on various physiological functions. Other studies have demonstrated the superiority of trained people in performing exhaustive tasks. Numerous articles have been written, speculating about the nonquantitative aspects of physical activities. However, the fact still remains that we are primarily dealing with normal individuals, living in a modern industrialized world. Outside of cases of emergency and wars, most people would continue to live normally if they did not participate in physical activities.

There is no question in the minds of most people about the importance of medicine, because medicine is aimed at curing the sick, bringing subnormal people back to a normal condition. But many people are not convinced that it is of importance to take perfectly normal people and make them super-normal in some forms of behavior and physiological functions. One way to arrive at an answer to this question is to go back to metaphysics, and among the great philosophers of modern times we find Nietzsche, whose teaching we have neglected to consider.

NIETZSCHE'S PHILOSOPHY

Nietzsche is considered as one of the great thinkers of any age, and his philosophy influ-

* From *Quest*, VIII (May, 1967), 83-89.

enced most of the great minds of the 20th century. He was born in Germany in 1844, and died in 1900. His teaching has been widely misinterpreted by people who have read him superficially. When read superficially, he seems to be an extremist, an anti-semite and a German nationalist. But for anybody who bothers to understand, his writings reveal that he was an anti-anti-semite, and anti-German nationalist and one of the most humane thinkers. There was hardly an aspect of life which he did not cover, developing a few lines of thought unique only to him.

Nietzsche was the major originator of existential thought, and he influenced later existential writers such as Jaspers, Heidegger and Sartre. Unlike the first two, but like Sartre, he practiced his teaching, that is, he carried out the existentialists' belief that one has to live and suffer the consequences of his ideas. He revolted against the hypocrisy and idealism of traditional philosophies and devoted his passion to the realities of life. Like other missionary thinkers, he was very concerned with honesty and integrity and applied them to his amazing psychological and philosophical analysis of art, literature and science from the Greeks to his days.

Being a philosopher of life, he accepted the irrational side of man as well as the rational one, along with the tragic and pessimistic aspects of life. But out of his metaphysical preoccupation with the realities of existence comes the most alive attitude toward life, a philosophy of action and self becoming similar to that of Sartre, and a doctrine of "live dangerously" which is unique only to him in his vision of the superman.

Nietzsche's optimism may seem strange at first, but it can be best understood in his own words, in his comments about Zarathustra, his superman: ". . . by thinking out pessimism to its extreme, his eyes were opened to the opposite ideal of the most exultant, alive, world-affirming man."[8:77] This expresses much of his thinking. Exhaustive exploration of the roots of ideas, man, values, arts, science, morals, and history led him to certain conclusions which he faced squarely. Passing through a period of romanticism (escape from reality), he later developed the most earthly philosophy by "un-romanticizing romanticism." He attacked the problems of anxiety, despair, hypocrisy, and laziness to which man led himself, and preached for self fulfillment, "become who you are," an individualistic doctrine. It is also a philosophy for the strong. In many of his writings, Nietzsche despises weakness of all kinds and expresses the manly aspects of life, a philosophy for the strong minded that knows no compromises. He went to the extremes on this point and developed his theory of the "Will to Power" as against the accepted theory of adaptation to the environment. This is humanism in its extreme, a doctrine of action, a refusal to surrender to human weaknesses and falsely human institutions, a call for excellence in every aspect of human endeavor.

Three of his major beliefs are of concern for the philosophy of fitness.

THE BELIEF IN THE BODY

Unlike traditional philosophers, Nietzsche took the body seriously. He saw it, as Rollo May put it, "not as a collection of abstracted substances or drives, but as *one mode of the reality of a person*."[3:26] He strongly denied the separation of body and mind and believed that the idea of "soul" was invented to undermine the body.[2:85] For Nietzsche the body is much more than an instrument of the mind:

The body is a great reason, a plurality with one sense, a war and a peace, a herd and a shepherd . . . behind your thoughts and feelings, my brother, there stands a mighty ruler, an unknown sage—whose name is self. In your body he dwells; he is your body. There is more reason in your body than in your best wisdom. And who knows why your body needs precisely your wisdom?[24:146]

It has been often said about Nietzsche that his philosophy cannot be separated from his

life. This may be true also concerning his concepts of the body. In his youth, he was healthy and experienced vigorous physical activities, but his health was ruined during the Franco-Prussian wars, and he experienced intense suffering in his later days, thus knowing the joys and agonies of existence. He attacked the despisers of the physical in many occasions: ". . . The belief in the body is more fundamental than the belief in the soul. The latter arose from the unscientific observation of the agonies of the body. . . ."[5:18] He demanded that matters of bodily health be taken much more seriously than what was suggested by idealists of his time. He placed matters of the physical in first priority in his criticism of morals that aimed at the cultivation of feelings and thoughts without consideration of the body.[2:199]

Being a psychologist, Nietzsche was also pre-occupied with scientific exploration of behavior. He describes how all observations begin and end in the body. The body and physiology are a starting point for every scientific endeavor and "with the clue to the body" he explains his psychological analysis of man.[5:18–20] Morgan explained Nietzsche's views on the subject:

. . . he characteristically subjects "external phenomenology" also to careful examination and qualification. The physical data described by science are a translation of an "internal process" into the sign language of visual and tactile sensations. What we ordinarily call "the body" is only the best metaphor for the real interplay of forces which composes our nature. . . . Thus Nietzsche uses the clue of the body to suggest a complex relational structure, something manifold and in perpetual flux, in short the hierarchical society already familiar to us from his theory of the living organism; the self or "subject" is simply the ruling oligarchy in this society. But the members of the society borrow from the "inner phenomenology"; they all in some sense "think," "feel," "will."[2:88–89]

Here is a philosopher who says: "We think with our bodies," who transfers bio-physical existence to a manifold significance.

THE WILL TO POWER

Nietzsche underestimates the influence of the environment. This is secondary for him. In his search for the secret life he developed the theory of "the will to power": life takes the initiative and adaptation is secondary. He applied this theory to the process of life and to human activities:

The will to power can manifest itself only against obstacles; it therefore goes in search of what resists it—this is the primitive tendency of the protoplasm when it extends its pseudopodia and feels about it. The act of appropriation and assimilation is, above all, the result of a desire to overpower, a process of forming, of additional building and rebuilding, until at last the subjected creature has become completely a part of the superior creature's sphere of power, and has increased the latter. . . .[5:130]

All living organisms follow the same line of development, there is "an ascent of the line of life" rather than self-preservation. This sounds like romantic humanism, but it represents Nietzsche's gay attitude toward life, throwing oneself into life in a grand fashion. A decline in the will to power means decay. "The invalid has the inclination of old age in advance."[2:76] The will to power extends to every corner of human existence, and happiness is one of them. In his magnificent discussion of human feelings he describes happiness as a "symptom of the feeling of power," it is "an accompanying, not an actuating factor."[4:162]

The ascending, rather than a horizontal outlook toward life, is also an intergral part of the over-man.

THE OVER-MAN

Nietzsche was the pioneer in the search for the origin of "bad conscious"—the alienation of man from his fellow men and from himself. He saw it as a process arising from drastic changes that occurred in human life when natural instincts were subjected to political and religious domination thus turned inward resulting in laziness, love of comfort, hypocrisy, mediocrity and fear. To this he responded with passionate individualism: "The secret of the greatest fruitfulness and the greatest enjoyment of life is to *live dangerously*. . . ."[6:97] What is needed is "superb health," strong minds that will restore to life its true biological existence. This will be accomplished by the over-man:

. . . But at some future time, a time stronger than our effete, self-doubting present, the true Redeemer will come, whose surging creativity will not let him rest in any shelter or hiding place, whose solitude will be misinterpreted as a flight from reality, whereas it will in fact be a dwelling on, a dwelling in reality—so that when he comes forth into the light he may bring with him the redemption of that reality from the curse placed upon it by a lapsed ideal. This man of the future, who will deliver us both from a lapsed ideal and from all that this ideal has spawned—violent loathing, the will to extinction, nihilism—this great and decisive stroke of midday, who will make the will free once more and restore to the earth its aim, and to man his hope; this anti-Christ and anti-nihilist, conqueror of both God and Unbeing— *one day he must come* . . .[7:229-230]

This is crucial to the understanding of Nietzsche. Being a philosopher of the earth, he faces tragedy squarely and turns romanticism upside down. The man of the future will not escape from life tragedies, but will be part of them; he will be reality itself, and this will allow him to enjoy existence through "self-overcoming." He will overcome fate and pity by courage, and will learn to live "beyond good and evil." This is his "*amor fati*," the love of fate which does not surrender to reality but faces it, and loves it. The man of the future will have that knowledge which he calls the "gay science" and will experience a feeling of gayness and lightness by overcoming the burdens of life through the affirmation of it.[2:309-315]

A PHILOSOPHY OF FITNESS

With Nietzsche's ideas in mind, we may be ready now for an existential interpretation of fitness. When one comes to consider the issue of fitness, he is faced with disagreements and problems of definition. Since the beginning of World War II, we have asked questions such as: "fitness for what?," "how much fitness?," etc., and we have made several statements about it. Two of the major statements have been that fitness is not only physical but also "social, emotional, and mental," and that one should seek a level of fitness which is between the physical culturists and the despisers of the body.

The above pragmatic and idealistic approaches to fitness do not help us much if we want to consider matters of significance and values. The word "fitness" connotes a state of good physical conditioning; everybody knows this very well. We also know that other professions are much better equipped than we are to deal with "other aspects of fitness," and they have, indeed, dealt with them for quite some time. Our task here is to find the significance of physical fitness.

A moment's reflection on the subject would first reveal an objective finding: research in fitness, training and related matters shows that we are talking about a state of being which is *above* normal in physiological functions and movement ability, and this fact is also recognized in medical research. Darwin's or Spencer's theories of adaptation to the environment could not possibly apply to physical fitness. This is where Nietzsche's theory of the "Will to Power" beautifully fits into the picture. What is physical fitness if not an avenue through which an individual achieves more power? A physically fit person does not adapt to our passive environment; he does not bother with a state of being by which "one can carry on his daily activities with undue fatigue," or with "fitness for a job." We have dealt with this essentialism for purposes of educational convenience. A physically fit person is only trying to do his best against internal resistances and against forces of the universe, like gravity and air resistance. We are dealing with an ascending line of biological phenomena, rather than with "fitness for everyday living" which is within the realm of medicine.

Another observation is a subjective one. Some athletes, at one time or another, may experience a sensation of power as if they are not controlled any more by outside forces. This "emotion of power" is an unexplored area in physiological psychology, even though it was recognized by the eminent psychologist Cannon forty years ago.[1:238] Future research in this area, like other research in physiological psychology, will have to rely on the body and physiology for objective assessment of this emotion. The emotion of power may arise from an enlarged heart which is capable of transporting blood to more than one human organism, from a hypertrophied skeletal muscular system or from changes in relationships between the mid-brain and the forebrain.

The emotion of power is many times experienced in connection with an activity which involves overcoming fear, danger, in an adventurous experience. Cannon, spending only one page on the subject, beautifully concluded:

> . . . And thus in the hazardous sports, in mountain climbing, in the hunting of big game, and in the tremendous adventures of war, risks and excitement and sense of power surge up together, setting free unsuspected energies, and bringing vividly to consciousness memorable fresh revelations of the possibilities of achievement.[1:239]

This has great existential significance. Unknowingly, Cannon touched on a point which has bothered mankind since the dawn of history. What should one do with his life in a world of no absolute values? An existential answer tends to be a yes-saying to life, and that of Nietzsche is yes in its extreme—"live dangerously." What one should do with his bio-physical being demands an explanation here. Bio-physical being is not an accumula-

tion of physical abilities or scores on a fitness test. It is, rather, the awareness that I possess these abilities which I may use to my advantage. The awareness of being is sharpened when one is confronted with non-being. This may happen in cases of injury, when one is aware of temporarily lacking a certain ability. Or it may be experienced in hazardous sports containing an element of fear. When fear is ignored, when we escape from it, our sense of being is dulled. But when we welcome it and learn to enjoy it we come closer to being part of a bio-physical reality. This is exactly what Nietzsche meant when describing his superman.

At this point, a question may be asked: why should anybody try to be physically fit if an improved state of fitness is not going to improve his health, and if he does not need to be fit for any practical purpose? The answer is that the process of being more physically fit is a fight against the *alienation of man from his bio-physical reality*. This is, using Nietzsche's words, a "pessimism of strength." Being optimistic about human bio-physical existence is a detachment from reality. We cannot escape facts such as physiological limits of performance, inescapable decrements due to old age, dangers of injury or death as a result of external forces, and above all—human tendency toward laziness. Why do we go back to strenuous sports during every fitness alarm? The obvious answer is that strenuous activities make you more fit. But this is only the essence of things, the applied part of human performance. We also go back to strenuous sports when we lose the sense of our bio-physical reality. What is then bio-physical reality? Bio-physical reality appears under any circumstances that limit our powers and arise our will for more power. The reader can immediately see that the overload principle is part of this reality, so is an aggressive opponent and extreme time and space factors. In the process of becoming fit, we deliberately create situations in which we become a part of a bio-physical reality. We become reality itself, an integral part of this earth.

When we succeed in becoming a part of reality, then we may experience the sensation of power, joy and lightness which Nietzsche talks about. The so-called "gentleman's sports" are not true representatives of our bio-physical reality. A golf ball or a tennis racket are only symbols of this reality. Participating in these sports is romanticism in its very last stages. Being part of a bio-physical reality requires an involvement in its fearful and exhaustive qualities. This is the existential answer to our tragic bio-physical existence: fitness for bio-physical self affirmation.

We cannot ignore the metaphysical significance of physical fitness. This would be a useless optimism. And indeed, when we say that through physical fitness we help to improve and maintain the vitality of this nation we are not fooling anybody. We are just fooling ourselves if we say it only half-heartedly.

REFERENCES

1. Cannon, Walter B. *Bodily Changes in Pain, Hunger, Fear and Rage.* New York: Harper and Row, 1963.

2. May, Rollo et al. *Existence; A New Dimension in Psychiatry and Psychology.* New York: Basic Books, 1958.
3. Morgan, George A. *What Nietzsche Means.* New York: Harper and Row, 1965.
4. Nietzsche, Friedrich. *Thus Spake Zarathustra.* New York: The Macmillan Company, 1916.
5. ———. *The Will to Power.* London: T. N. Foulis, 1913.
6. ———. *The Joyful Wisdom.* London: T. N. Foulis, 1910.
7. ———. *The Birth of Tragedy and the Genealogy of Morals.* Garden City, New York: Doubleday and Company, 1956.
8. ———. *Beyond Good and Evil.* London: T. N. Foulis, 1914.

BIBLIOGRAPHY ON THE BODY AND BEING

Aristotle. "De Anima." Translated by J. A. Smith. *Introduction to Aristotle.* Edited by Richard McKeon. The Modern Library. New York: Random House, 1947.

Barral, Mary Rose. "Merleau-Ponty: The Role of the Body in Interpersonal Relations." Unpublished Ph.D. dissertation, Fordham University, 1963.

Beets, N[icholas]. "The Experience of the Body in Sport." *International Research in Sport and Physical Education.* Edited by E. Jokl and E. Simon. Illinois: Charles C Thomas, 1964.

———. "Historical Actuality and Bodily Experience." *Humanitas,* II (Spring, 1966), 15-28.

Broekhoff, Jan. "Physical Education and the Reification of the Human Body." Presented at the Second Canadian Symposium on History of Sport and Physical Education. Windsor, Ontario, Canada, May 1-3, 1972.

Chryssafis, Jean E. "Aristotle on Physical Education." *Journal of Health and Physical Education,* 1 (January; February; September, 1930), 3-8, 50; 14-17, 46-47; 14-17, 54-53.

Cornman, James W. "The Identity of Mind and Body." *Journal of Philosophy,* LIX (August, 1962), 486-492.

Descartes, René. "Of the Existence of Corporeal Things and of the Real Distinction Between the Mind and Body of Man" in *Meditations on First Philosophy.* Translated by Laurence J. Lafleur. The Library of Liberal Arts. New York: Bobbs-Merrill, 1960.

Doherty, J. Kenneth. "Holism in Training for Sports." *Anthology of Contemporary Readings.* Edited by Howard S. Slusher and Aileene S. Lockhart. Iowa: Wm. C. Brown, 1966.

Duhrssen, Alfred. "The Self and the Body." *Review of Metaphysics,* 10 (September, 1956), 28-34.

Fairs, John R. "The Influence of Plato and Platonism on the Development of Physical Education in Western Culture." *Quest,* XI (December, 1968), 14-23.

Feigl, H., Maxwell, G. and Scriven, M., Eds. *Concepts, Theories, and the Mind-Body Problem.* Minnesota Studies in the Philosophy of Science, Vol. II. Minneapolis: University of Minnesota Press, 1958.

Fraleigh, Warren P. "A Christian Concept of the Body-Soul Relation and the Structure of Human Movement Experiences." Unpublished paper (mimeographed), 1968.

Gerber, Rudolph J., S. J. "Marcel's Phenomenology of the Human Body." *International Philosophical Quarterly,* IV (September, 1964), 443-463.

Hengstenberg, Hans-Eduard. "Phenomenology and Metaphysics of the Human Body." *International Philosophical Quarterly,* 3 (May, 1963), 165-200.

Holbrook, Leona. "A Teleological Concept of the Physical Qualities of Man." *Quest,* I (December, 1963), 13-17.

Hook, Sidney, Ed. *Dimensions of Mind.* New York: Collier Books, 1961.

Horne, Herman H. "The Principle Underlying Modern Physical Education [body-mind unity]." *American Physical Education Review,* XV (June, 1910), 433-439.

Jonas, Hans. "Life, Death, and the Body in the Theory of Being." *Review of Metaphysics,* 19 (September, 1965), 3-23.

Kaelin, Eugene F. "Being in the Body." National Association for Physical Education of College Women. *Report of the Ruby Anniversary Workshop.* Interlochen, Michigan, 1964.

Kelly, Darlene Alice. "Phenomena of the Self-Experienced Body." Unpublished Ph.D. dissertation, University of Southern California, 1970.

Kennedy, John F. "The Soft American" in *Background Readings for Physical Education.* Edited by Ann Paterson and Edmund C. Hallberg. New York: Holt, Rinehart and Winston, 1965.

Kleinman, Seymour. "The Significance of Human Movement: A Phenomenological Approach." National Association for Physical Education of College Women. *Report of the Ruby Anniversary Workshop.* Interlochen, Michigan, 1964.

————. "Will the Real Plato Stand Up?" *Quest*, XIV (June, 1970), 73-75.

Kohler, Wolfgang. "The Mind-Body Problem." *Dimensions of Mind*. Edited by Sidney Hook. New York: Collier Books, 1961.

Kwant, Remy. "The Human Body as the Self-Awareness of Being." *Humanitas*, II (Spring, 1966), 43-62.

Long, Douglas C. "The Philosophical Concept of a Human Body." *Philosophical Review*, 73 (July, 1964), 321-337.

Luijpen, William A. "The Body as Intermediary" in *Existential Phenomenology*. Pittsburgh: Duquesne University Press, 1960.

McDougall, William. *Body and Mind*. Boston: Beacon Press, 1961. (First published London: Methuen, 1911.)

Marcel, Gabriel. *Metaphysical Journal*. Translated by Bernard Wall. Chicago: Henry Regnery, 1952.

Nietzsche, Friedrich. "The Despisers of the Body" in *Thus Spake Zarathustra*. Translated by Thomas Common. The Modern Library. New York: Random House, n.d.

Peursen, C. A. Van. *Body, Soul, Spirit: A Survey of the Body-Mind Problem*. Translated by Hubert H. Hoskins. London: Oxford University Press, 1966.

Plato. *Phaedo*. Translated by F. J. Church. New York: The Liberal Arts Press, 1951.

Sarano, Jacques. *The Meaning of the Body*. Translated by James H. Farley. Philadelphia: Westminster Press, 1966.

Sartre, Jean-Paul. "The Body" in *Being and Nothingness*. Translated by Hazel E. Barnes. New York: Philosophical Library, 1956.

Schrag, Calvin O. "The Lived Body as a Phenomenological Datum." *Modern Schoolman*, XXXIX (March, 1962), 203-218.

————. "The Embodied Experiencer" in *Experience and Being. Prolegomena to a Future Ontology*. Evanston: Northwestern University Press, 1969.

Shaffer, Jerome A. "Recent Work on the Mind-Body Problem." *American Philosophical Quarterly*, 2 (April, 1965), 81-104.

————. "Persons and Their Bodies." *Philosophical Review*, XXV (January, 1966), 59-77.

Shvartz, Esar. "Nietzsche: A Philosopher of Fitness." *Quest*, VIII (May, 1967), 83-89.

Spicker, Stuart F., Ed. *The Philosophy of the Body*. Chicago: Quadrangle Books, 1970.

Staley, Seward C. "The Body-Soul Concept" in *The Curriculum in Sports (Physical Education)*. Illinois: Stipes Publishing Company, 1940.

Van Den Berg, J. H. "The Human Body and the Significance of Human Movement." *Psychoanalysis and Existential Philosophy*. Edited by Hendrik M. Ruitenbeck. New York: E. P. Dutton, 1962.

Waelhens, Alphonse de. "The Phenomenology of the Body." Translated by Mary Ellen and N. Lawrence. *Readings in Existential Phenomenology*. Edited by Nathaniel Lawrence and Daniel O'Connor. New Jersey: Prentice-Hall, 1967.

Weiss, Paul. *Nature and Man*. New York: Henry Holt, 1947.

————. *Sport: A Philosophic Inquiry*. Carbondale: Southern Illinois University Press, 1969.

Wenkart, Simon. "The Meaning of Sports for Contemporary Man." *Journal of Existential Psychiatry*, 3 (Spring, 1963), 397-404.

————. "Sports and Contemporary Man." *Motivations in Play, Games and Sports*. Edited by Ralph Slovenko and James A. Knight. Illinois: Charles C Thomas, 1967.

Zaner, Richard M. *The Problem of Embodiment. Some Contributions to a Phenomenology of the Body*. The Hague: Martinus Nijhoff, 1964.

————. "The Radical Reality of the Human Body." *Humanitas*, II (Spring, 1966), 73-87.

SPORT AS A MEANINGFUL EXPERIENCE

Sport as a Meaningful Experience

INTRODUCTION

An examination of the sport experience depends, first of all, upon an understanding of the term "experience." Experience as a subject lies in the philosophical realm of epistemology because ultimately all questions of truth or confirmation of knowledge relate to experience. It is one of the more complicated philosophical problems because it deals with the mysterious relationship between subject and object. In what manner does the experiencer experience the experienced? What is the nature of that experience? It is generally assumed by contemporary philosophers that "Experience is not restricted to so-called sense experience. There is . . . experience of relations, meanings, values, requiredness, other minds, social and cultural phenomena. Any kind of cognitive contact with particular data is an occasion for genuine experience."[1] In the articles which follow, the authors have explored many of these different kinds of experiences. However, they could not (as philosophers cannot) really define satisfactorily the way in which this happens—the connections between the external object of experience and the subjective knowing.

There are generally accepted universal characteristics of experience, which are, as summarized by Farber:[2] (1) experience is temporal in character, (2) has elements of organic,

physical and cultural relatedness, (3) involves the past, present and future, (4) has a space-time locus, (5) is always experience *of* some object or phenomenon, and (6) is of various types, such as perceptual, imaginative and conceptual.

Acceptance of the universality of the characteristics of experience, does not imply acceptance of the universality of *each* experience. In fact, it should be understood that each experience is peculiar to the experiencer. Individuals do not have identical perceptions, nor do they process their perceptions to the same conclusions. In other words, there is no such thing as a universal experience and, hence, no possibility of saying that the meanings inherent in an experience are universal. It can only be said that there are similar meanings experienced by different people. Theoretically, data could be gathered to support hypotheses relating to the high incidence of similarity of certain meanings occurring in the sport experience.

It is a general characteristic of the articles which attempt to describe the meaning of the sport experience, that they assume a certain universality of meaning. Although this, in some way, oversteps the bounds of philosophical precept, there is nevertheless some justification for believing in the similarity of meaning derived by many sport participants. Large numbers of books and articles written by sports participants, descriptive of their experiences, give evidence of similarity. However, there is also a certain homogeneity of condition among

[1] Herbert Spiegelberg, "Toward a Phenomenology of Experience," *American Philosophical Quarterly*, I (October, 1964), 327.

[2] Marvin Farber, *Basic Issues of Philosophy* (New York: Harper & Row, 1968), pp. 121-122.

these writers who recount their own sport experiences, despite their diversified sport activities. Most are people who have great involvement in their sport, have invested much of themselves in terms of time and effort, have attained a high level of skill, and have both the ability and desire to verbalize their experiences. Researchers who have attempted to generalize about the sport experience seem to have written primarily about people who fit the above description.

It is only recently that philosophers of sport have turned their attention to the question: Why does man play? In their article, R. Scott Kretchmar and William A. Harper set the question in historical context by showing that research relating to man and play essentially ignores this question. Furthermore, there has been an assumption that the action of playing has been rationally motivated and that this conscious motivation is somehow inherent in the activity. Although they do not attempt really to explore answers to their question, the authors' perspectives set the stage for the articles which follow.

In "Man, Nature and Sport," Jan Progen offers a unique analysis of the sport experience as it occurs in a natural, non-competitive setting. Kurt Riezler's article deals with one of the factors affecting the meaning of the sport experience: the player's attitude. The extensiveness of the effect of the experience is directly related to whether man "merely plays" or "seriously plays." The brief selection from Josef Pieper contradicts this point of view. Pointing out that play is, in itself, a way of acting, Pieper concludes that it is inherently meaningless. The articles by George Santayana, J. Kenneth Doherty, Mary Pavlich Roby and Eleanor Metheny, each using somewhat different emphases, examine the subjective meanings potentially derived from the sport experience. Each seems to assume that because sport demands a certain fullness of commitment and extended effort from its participants, it, in turn, extends to them a meaningful experience. The final selection, a brief excerpt from a story by J. B. Priestley, gives a flash of insight into the meaning of the spectator's sport experience.

"The Socialization of Sport" by Jan Felshin approaches the subject from a somewhat different context. In analyzing the relationship between the meaningfulness of sport to man and the structure of sport, she establishes an interactive effect of one upon the other. The structure of sport affects the meanings derived from it; the meanings affect the structure of sport.

Asking "Why do *I* play?" leads to questions about the potential similarity of meanings for any given particular sport population. For instance, are the meanings to be found in competitive sport different from those associated with non-competitive sport? Does the natural sport experience differ in meaning from the game-type experience? What external conditions affect the meaning of the sport experience? Can one have a meaningful sport experience in a physical education class? Does the teacher or coach have any role to play in enhancing or inhibiting the meaningfulness of the sport experience? What personal variables affect the experience? Does the spectator experience sport?

Attempts to analyze the meaningfulness of the sport experience have not been numerous. Slusher's book, *Man, Sport and Existence* (1967) is probably the most comprehensive attempt by a single philosopher of sport. *Motivations in Play, Games and Sport*, edited by Slovenko and Knight (1967), has many articles which treat meaningful aspects of the sport experience. Weiss (1969) offers some original ideas in a chapter titled "The Attraction of Athletics." Metheny's *Movement and Meaning* (1968) is an extended examination of the meaning of three movement forms: sport, dance and exercise. Felshin's fine article (1964) provides a basis for her work included in this section.

In general, writers have attempted to isolate one or more factors inherent in the sport experience which they have assumed engender meaning to the participant. Hout's discussion (1970) of the peak experience is a good example of this. Rupp (1958), in a paean to winning, assumes the inherent meaningfulness of victory, of success. Desmonde (1952) explores the meaning of a sport, the bullfight, as a religious ritual. In fact, numerous writers have examined the meaningfulness of play as a spiritual experience, including particularly Huizinga (1950), Rahner (1967) and Miller (1970).

Several articles offer theories which involve basic beliefs about the nature of man and the meaningfulness inherent in the satisfying of basic drives or needs: Blumenfield's article (1941) is typical of this approach. Beisser (1961) discusses at length the "psychodynamics" or psychological meanings in sport. Lorenz (1966), assuming man's basic aggressive nature, singles out the cathartic effect of sport. Another evolutionist, Lionel Tiger (1969), sees in sport the satisfaction of the need to engage in the hunting pattern, developed in man through evolution. Furlong (1969), Klausner (1968) and others contributing to his book, delineate the phenomenon of sport as a medium for stress-seeking through risk-taking. Neale (1969) sets forth an original theory of play as the *absence* of the usual inner conflict which results from man's need to discharge energy and to design experience.

And finally, Davis (1936), McMurty (1971) and Scott (1971) present some interesting comments relating to negative meanings potentially accruing from sport.

Researchers will find this aspect of sport philosophy a fruitful area of study. It would be interesting to explore the various kinds of experiences to see which are particularly relevant to sport. A model of various types of sport experiences could be developed to account for types of experience and levels or varieties of sport situations. This would make it possible to study the meaningfulness of sport in more diverse conditions than hitherto has been done. For such studies, available sources of data include the verbalized sport experience of individuals or groups (perhaps a class or team), as gained through interviews or published accounts such as are found in numerous autobiographies of sports figures. Certain kinds of experiences can also be analyzed from data collected by observation of the sporting event—either by being there, watching a telecast, or studying films. However, the latter two sources of data are contaminated by the cameraman's selectivity and judgments based, perhaps, on criteria irrelevant to the study. The methods of phenomenology seem particularly appropriate to an analysis of the meaning of the sport experience. Techniques of description or reduction are meant to provide rigorous tools for precisely this kind of analysis: the universalization of the subjective experience. Logically, the researcher's own sport experience will provide the primary data for this type of analysis.

Those interested in examining the meaningfulness of the sport experience, will find such analysis lends itself to a variety of nonverbal expressive forms. One's own statement of meaning can be conveyed through choreography of movement, through pictures, films, tapes, and verbal forms such as poetry and descriptive statements. Hopefully, attempts to understand the meaning of one's own experience will enhance the experience itself.

Why Does Man Play?*

R. SCOTT KRETCHMAR
WILLIAM A. HARPER

Why do you play? Is it for health, fun, or social relationship? Are you satisfied with these answers? Are there other possibilities? Do these reasons accurately explain your presence in sport? Why *do* you play?

Health, fun, and social contact, among other factors, are utilized by many as short but sufficient solutions to the question of "why I play." It is difficult to find individuals who do not have logical explanations for an activity; it seems that nearly everybody knows why he plays.

Historically, play (the term, for the purpose of this paper includes the traditional activities within sport and dance while eliminating the nonactivity games such as chess or cards) precedes any formalized teaching. It precedes compilation of a body of knowledge which might constitute a discipline. Children play. Aboriginal tribesmen play. Animals play. And they all play without any sophisticated notions of *why* they should. Play is a more primary category than play *for* education, than play *for* health and fitness, than play *for* social acquaintances.

Individually, the physical education professional person generally encounters the intrigue of play prior to coming to any decision to pursue a career in the field. Much of the fervor which is at times apparent in the actions of

the teacher usually stems from an exciting encounter, either past or present, with some form of play. The instructor knows this enjoyment to be a part of his own history, and he often continues to recreate the actual engagement of sport or dance throughout his active life.

Empirically, most of the research in physical education relates to play—how one can participate with greater skill or for a longer time; how one can train better and learn faster; or how one can play more safely. It seems then, that play is the cornerstone of the profession, of the professional man, and of the field's scientific research. Play precedes all of the superstructure which develops around it.

Given the significance of play for the field and the number of statements which purport to describe this relationship between man, play, and the profession, it is a curious fact that so little attention is *now* directed toward this issue. It is paradoxical that physical education, based on play should house several scientific and humanistic branches which at this time seem to consider themselves self-sufficient, intellectual disciplines apart from ties with actual activity. It seems that the end of research—an understanding of play in all of its parameters, both scientific and humanistic—has been forgotten and the means have become a new goal. Statistics are exciting; scientific research is a challenge; philosophical and historical study command a compelling interest. Yet the priority, play, remains forgotten in the background. Play, which initiated the profession, lies buried

* From American Association for Health, Physical Education, and Recreation: *Journal of Health, Physical Education, and Recreation,* 40 (March, 1969), 57-58.

under mounds of research and academic discussion. It remains the victim of its own children. Is the issue of the relationship between man and play dead?

But perhaps the question of demise is premature. Many of the traditional answers or "solutions" appear inadequate. Many physical educators begin their theorizing with two assumptions, that one can logically deduce "ought" statements from "is" descriptions and that man is rational. The discipline's philosophers articulate the various benefits which accrue to man through participation. They argue for the goals of increased longevity, safety, greater vigor, and increased opportunity for social interaction, among countless others. Both on scientific and sociological grounds the arguments for these objectives carry some weight, though they certainly lack verification.

For the purpose of this paper, let us assume that they are, in toto, true. It may be said these idealisms do occur in play. But it is the subsequent utilization of these "facts" which leads the theoreticians astray. From the fact that various goals *are* realized, they progress to the proposition that goals *should* be achieved and, further, to the notion that man will work actively toward these objectives once he is convinced of the validity of the proposition. It is these latter two extensions of logic which place the rationale for play on tenuous ground.

These difficulties can be clarified by means of examples. An instructor may lecture on the dangers of sky diving in an effort to discourage participation by any of his pupils. He begins with several statements of fact: (1) sky diving has a relatively high mortality rate and (2) man does not search out situations in which he has a great chance of dying. Given the fact that every student is a man, the teacher believes he is justified in concluding that the student *should not* sky dive. However, the instructor, when he initiates his argument with descriptive statements (the "is" facts), can conclude only in that same mood. There are no grounds for his leap from an "is" *description* to an "ought" *prescription*. The theoretician cannot logically state:

1. All men who do not want to die do not sky dive.
2. John is a man who does not want to die.

Therefore:
3. John *should not* sky dive.

All he is justified in stating is:
1. All men who do not want to die do not sky dive.

Therefore:
3. John *does not* sky dive.

The physical educators, then, have many facts relative to the outcome or benefits of play. They incorrectly suggest that mere availability of the facts leads to valid conclusions concerning why man *should* play. Given the various facts of play, such as fitness, health, vigor, and community, the instructors suggest that the student *should* play for these ends. What these instructors assume with such argumentation is that these entities are, in themselves, universal values. Fitness is not only a *value* but equally a *necessity!* Man should become fit! But common sense rebels against this reasoning. An object can remain a "good" without any obligation to achieve it. Fitness can intellectually be recognized as a value without deciding it is necessary for oneself.

It is clear then, that one who attempts to describe man's contact with play on logical grounds has major difficulties. For his account to be valid he must assume that the values of health, fitness, and vigor carry with them their own command for action. But even if one could agree on the values of play, it would still not be clear why man *should* strive for these ends.

It might be objected, at this point, that man does and must make value judgments, whether they be logical or not. In this light, all of the foregoing discussion becomes a wasted intellectual exercise. Who cares if a value judgment lies behind much of the profession's theory? Physical education is willing to stand behind its claims of value!

It might be maintained, then, that the instructor has no difficulty convincing the student of a specific "good." For example, a teacher may argue for the value of fitness, and the student may accept his discussion. The student intellectually agrees to the proposition that fitness is a worthy value and that his subsequent actions should reflect that conviction. The student has complete knowledge of the connections between fitness and play and has no qualms in accepting the value of the former.

However, is it not paradoxical that man, with some consistency, acts contrary to knowledge and commitment? Many people acknowledge the value of fitness while maintaining a sedentary existence. Many people who value their lives and who know that smoking may shorten the expected life span continue to smoke. Evidence shows that man often acts irrationally. Even the most disciplined individuals do inexplicably act against reason or the knowledge suggesting a singular mode of behavior.

The rationalists want to make play the result of consciously accepted goals and understandings. Though play may be a result in isolated situations, though an individual may initiate activity on rationalist grounds (i.e., "it is good for me"), he may continue to play in ignorance of benefits and in spite of potential detrimental effects.

Perhaps man intuits that play is somehow an irrational activity. He often plays for no good reason, yet he cannot, it seems, let himself live with this fact. Play becomes acceptable when man can explain his activity on rational grounds. The rational is superimposed upon the irrational. The absurd is made to conform to the reasonable. Does one not hide behind the rational facade because he fears, as an academician, the indeterminate, the unpredictable? Is it not more comfortable to have the ready answer and finite reply for the interrogator? But does not this disposition restrict the search for answers to a predetermined arena, that of the rational? By limiting the range of the quest does one not presuppose the nature of the answer, that it must be logical? What if the truth were to fall outside of his realm?

Clearly, it has been suggested that the solution does supersede the rational cause-and-effect motif. Man's intrigue and persistent relationship with play cannot be sufficiently explained through a rationalist method. Health, fitness, strength, relaxation, and other objectives probably accrue from play, but to suggest that these *explain* man's presence in play seems unfounded. To propose that man is in sport because he should be, or that he participates as a result of knowledge of and commitment to a value, vastly oversimplifies the situation. Man is in sport or dance on grounds independent of the practical or rational.

It was once asked what would happen to play if it were shown to have absolutely no beneficial results. Would play terminate? Once its useful ends were negated would its captivating effect on man likewise end? It is contended that play would not cease. It would, in fact, continue as before, perhaps with even more success because of its less artificial place in man's life.

The riddle of "why I play" has no simple answer. Man plays before he asks the question. He plays while continually ignoring the question. He plays in spite of known detrimental effects. Play and man seem bound together with reason or without it.

To explain the relationship between the phenomena of man and play on rational, cause-and-effect grounds is to render both man and play lifeless. The problem of "why I play" is equal and related to the incredible complexity of man. Man plays for many reasons, he plays for no reason at all. Man cannot be given an input of reasons and be expected to produce consistent, mechanical behavior. Man will act with spontaneity, irrationality, and abandon. The lived reality of this union between man and play defies all attempts to reduce it to a rationally explicable understanding.

Man, Nature and Sport

JAN PROGEN

There is a universal appeal in nature. Whether it be found in the magic of water, the magnetism of mountains, the beckoning of the sky or the power of an unknown world beneath the surface of the earth, the attraction is there and it is very real. The Homeric Greeks' love for the sea shows this interest to be deep-rooted in the history of man. The current ecological movement to save the natural environment from an affluent and over-productive society indicates a modern concern for nature as well as its great appeal expressed by increasing numbers of people seeking sports activities away from the cities and gymnasiums and in natural settings.

I see this trend toward natural sports not so much as an escape *from* daily life as an escape *to* nature: not so much to forget, but rather to remember.(23:9) For the surf, mountains, open sky, etc. have always provided a challenge to man, and the existence of challenge has always stimulated a response from him (13:57)—a desire to do the undone, to see the unseen, to push beyond the previous limitations of his abilities and accomplishments. This drive and need for adventure is unique to man.

To make a definition of sport which would be comprehensive enough to include games, with their highly structured, rule-orientated form and natural sports, with their free form, is not feasible. Therefore, a special definition of natural sport is offered for the purposes of this paper. Natural sports are activities which involve human participation as a response to the challenge offered primarily by the physical, natural world such as hills, air currents and waves. They are bounded by the personally constructed goals of the participant as, for example, to climb the mountain, explore the cave or ski down the hill. This paper explores the relationship of man to natural sports. Through the use of recorded commentary by parachutists, mountaineers, surfers, soarers, skiers, hikers, sailors, canoeists and spelunkers, the meaning of the natural sport experience is revealed and clarified.

The Aesthetic Experience. The primary motive for many who engage in natural sports is the sheer enjoyment of the beauty of nature. One mountaineer found a great pleasure in renewing his senses in the natural beauty of clean air, sparkling snow and brilliant sunsets and sunrises, and found it satisfying just to be surrounded by trees, grass, flowers and bare, honest rock.(12:631) There is an abundant amount of visual beauty in nature, and all that needs to be done is to open oneself up to it.

One aspect of beauty is the great pleasure and special thrill in being the first one to enter a cave.(6:160) One spelunker who found a virgin room in a new cave filled with tall, white stalagmite formations was not primarily impressed by the beauty of it all. "What really excited me was the floor of the room. There wasn't a print in the sand. I was the first human to ever set foot there."(28:54) Skiing more commonly provides this opportunity to touch "untouched" nature—to know it in a new

197

way. By making one's tracks in the snow, "this possibility of touching nature as the first person is provided since the evidence brought down by newly fallen snow precludes any contamination of this evidence of nature by anything else."(18:642) Styles sees this as a contribution to mankind: "He enlarges it [the mountain] by a first ascent, from a remote wedge of upheaved rock and ice into a field for the adventure and pleasure of other men; he adds it to the accessible delights of the human heritage." (25:3)

The sensation of being finite in the cosmos is also part of the aesthetic experience. Challenging the mighty forces of nature, a surfer with only a sliver seems very small. (20:130) Jim Whittaker's feelings on the top of Everest were very similar. "Not expansive. Not sublime. I felt like a frail human being."(27:78) In contrast to this, sport in nature has offered man an opportunity to feel alive, full and significant. "Who's afraid of the universe? It's midnight on the desert or the coast or high above the timberline; the Milky Way is close and the stars are singing. I tremble before the cosmos no more than a fish trembles before the tide."(23:109) But there is something beyond this expansive feeling. "The jumper has his brief moment of exhilaration, his fleeting illusion of omnipotence. But there is more. A man can find a sound and abiding satisfaction in jumping—perhaps a new and better sense of what he is."(5:669)

Challenge. But for numerous others, beauty is not the major reason. Overwhelming beauty can be viewed from easily attainable summits. (13:49) For some there must be something more, and this something is often challenge. Challenge is a concept which transcends competition. It is a personal response to one's environment, a willingness to test oneself within various contexts and media. While sometimes it takes the form of rivalry, it often has no element of strife, no need to declare victor or defeated. David Smith "paraswamdoveranbiked" in his own peace pentathlon of non-war, fun events to satisfy his need for challenge without competing against anyone else, and to make his statement about the absurdity of competition.(16:50-61)

Some spelunkers are driven to discovery, to put up with great physical and psychological ordeals, to brave the hardships and hazards of seemingly unscalable walls, deep abysses and steep and slippery slopes of caves like Schoolhouse in West Virginia and Neff Canyon Cave. The attraction is the many kinds of challenges offered there. (6:173,176) The names

of features in Schoolhouse Cave such as "Groan Box," "Sam's Struggle," "Nick of Time," and "Grind Canyon" express the essence of their activities.(6:173)

Houston recognized the constant striving of man to do the ultimate, to reach beyond his grasp, as a response to challenge and the primary motive for mountaineering.(12:633) John Hunt, leader of the first successful climb of the world's highest peak, stated: "There was the challenge, and we would lay aside all else to take it up."(15:231) Mallory spoke of self-knowledge, development and satisfaction in mountaineering and indicated that mountains, as all other natural elements, are not conquered or an enemy to battle against. "Whom have we conquered? None but ourselves. Have we won a kingdom? No—and yes. We have achieved the ultimate satisfaction, filled a destiny. To struggle is to understand, never the last without the other."(13:58) Houston also noted that "men do not conquer mountains any more than mountains conquer men, in the pursuit of what mountains offer, men find more than victory."(13:634)

> Mountaineering is more a quest for self-fulfillment than a victory over others or over nature. . . . The aim is to transcend a previous self. . . . A true mountaineer knows he has not conquered a mountain by standing on its summit for a few fleeting moments. Only when the right men are in the right places at the right time are the big mountains climbed, never are they conquered. (12:57)

Hunt also recognized man's need to respond to other challenges of nature and expressed his faith in the spirit of man to accomplish his goals:

> I also believe that we cannot avoid the challenges of other giants. Mountains scarcely lower than Everest itself are still "there," as Mallory said. They beckon us and we cannot rest until we have met their challenge too. And there are many other opportunities for adventure; whether they be sought among the hills, in the air, upon the sea, in the bowels of the earth, or on the bottom of the ocean bed. . . . There is no height, no depth, that the spirit of man, guided by a higher Spirit, cannot attain. (15:232)

There are many examples of men designing more intense challenges into those already proffered by nature. In mountaineering "to add to stress and its headiness, climbers now make ascents at night or in winter, alone, or deliberately in bad weather."(13:51) Participants of soaring, which is a sport like surfing and sailing in that the thrill is experienced by "harnessing" the energy of nature, find that "power flight isn't fun any more. The challenges are gone."(8:101) The challenge of accomplishing a difficult feat motivated ten men to jump from an airplane one after another and join hands in the form of a star—the first ten-man star ever made—before opening their parachutes. (10:66)

Stress-Risk. Many of the sports occurring in natural, non-competitive settings involve a relatively high degree of stress and risk in the spirit of adventure which provides a sense of thrill in danger, exhilaration, confidence, control and self-satisfaction in the participant. Voluntarily "the stress-seeker struggles under heavy baggage and against severe hardships to 'stretch his capacity' to do what few others can do—his capacity to bear the fear of falling and endure thirst, sunburn, frostbite, blisters, fatigue, and the effects of altitude where 'simple tasks become major struggles'."(13:49) But it must be made clear that these hardships are not the goal, and the mountaineer is not a masochist; rather, he accepts these hardships as part of the game in order that he might know the pleasures of mountaineering.(12:634)

Nor are the activities performed *because* of the risks. Alvarez pointed out that "what looks like absurd risk is usually quite different to the expert: it is justifiable control."(1:10) Comparing the degree of control in daily life to that of a skilled mountaineer, he stated:

> In America there are more daily risks and violence than mountain climbers see in a lifetime. I would rather commit myself ten times over to El Capitan than go alone into Harlem or Watts or try to cross Central Park after dark; on a mountain at least you have some control over disaster. (1:12)

Control is the key factor which separates the difficult from the dangerous:

> No true mountaineer ever courted danger for its own sake. The whole point of any sport is that it demands the acquisition of a special skill which cancels out the danger. It was the mountaineer's justification that he climb by routes where his skill in mountaincraft, supported by courage and resolution of no mean order, made him competent to ascend and descent safely. (25:129)

Houston distinguished between risk and danger giving a very clear example of the role of control. "Experienced climbers understand, enjoy, and seek risk because it presents a difficulty to overcome and can be estimated and controlled. He equally abhors danger because it is beyond his control."(13:52) Manageable risks that make a route difficult, such as difficult mountain faces or deep sea waters, attract participants; uncontrollable dangers such as are found in areas with a high incidence of avalanches or shark-infested waters, are not popular with sportsmen.

Speaking especially of the lonely, risky sports, Alvarez showed that "intentional, planned risk demands all the qualities most valuable in life: intelligence, skill, intuition, subtlety, control." (1:12) Robert Kennedy recognized the abilities characterizing the men with whom he climbed Mt. Kennedy as they "possessed qualities of the best mountain men: keen intelligence, an obvious willingness to undergo pain and discomfort for an objective, and a very high degree of courage. Theirs is not blind, inescapable, meaningless courage. It is courage with ability, brains, tenacity of purpose."(17:22)

Dr. Sol Roy Rosenthal introduced the idea that there is a specific reason, perhaps chemical, why people participate in risk-action sports. His thesis suggests that calculated risks as provided by these activities are necessary for daily well-being. He observed that the exhilaration and even euphoria resulting from risk-exercise is absent from the non-risk, gamelike sports such as tennis and golf, and he noted that the degree of exhilaration resulting varied with the competence of the individual and with the degree of difficulty of the sport, the more dangerous sports producing the greatest uplift in spirit.(7:52-53) Further, he stated that "the feeling, characteristic of many of the most demanding, risk-exercises, is so intense that you almost feel hooked. It is like being addicted, you feel you must go back and know it again."(7:53) This is supported by Robert Gannon's comment about soaring: "I'm hooked, and it seems for good. I look out my window and see a cloud hanging, beckoningly, over the distant mountains and I long to spread my wings and get under it to circle with the other hawks."(8:204) The tantalizing may be due to the fact that the experience, while usually satisfying, is not totally so. There are so many questions to be answered and aspects of the experience which could be perfected; the development of control is a slow and challenging one.

Another part of the reason for the addictive quality of these sports may be that they call forth "lost traces of strength and courage that daily life does not afford."(12:631) Sylvian Saudan established life-death situations in which he skied down 14,000-foot peaks in the Alps into the unknown, alone and without mountaineering equipment. He claimed that this gave him an opportunity not often found in normal life enabling him to dominate his fears and passions.(4:61,72) Such sports afford an attitude of "complete" living as the purpose is to escape death not life, for death is an accident in sport.(24:204-206) Alvarez stated that essentially all risky sports are "like a close up on your life, in which the essentials are concentrated and defined. You deliberately set up a situation in which, in order to survive, you must respond as fully as you know how to."(1:12)

Natural sports require total involvement and commitment. "It is like playing chess with your body, a sort of physical strength which demands not courage but sheer concentration." (1:10) Leydet showed his complete involvement in the description of his first run down the rapids of the Colorado River. "We were committed—there was no way to turn back or to try a different approach. And oddly enough with that realization my apprehension ceased, giving way to a feeling of aliveness and exhilaration."(19:38)

Freedom-Independence. The absence of organization and rules in such non-competitive sports as skiing and surfing allows for a very high degree of independence which is a great appeal, particularly to young people. "One of the greatest attractions of surfing is that it is an individual sport and you don't have to belong to anything to do it. Kids resent organization. In surfing you just pick up your board and go—no rules, no uniforms, no one you have to compete with."(22:108)

Concomitantly, in natural sports there is a great degree of freedom; "you take complete responsibility for your own life. You choose and are responsible."(1:12) Coutts claimed that "one basic underlying reason why man engages in sport is the sense of freedom which he finds there."(2:68) He pointed out that "non-game sports, such as mountain climbing, skiing, sky diving and scuba diving, allow for a greater feeling of being free in the sense of being dependent on self for survival or success and in providing for more creative expression through choices and action."(2:70) How many ways can a baseball player play right field? Certainly a mountaineer has much more freedom—more alternatives in how he engages in his sport, allowing for greater creativity.(24: 189) Perhaps the characteristic simplicity of

mountaineering, surfing and the like as compared to game and team sports enables this greater degree of freedom and creativity. Renny and Terry Russell found that in camping they had an opportunity to act rather than being acted upon:

> The elemental simplicities of the wilderness travel with thrills not only because of their novelty, but because they represent complete freedom to make mistakes. The wilderness gave them their first tastes of the rewards and punishments for wise and foolish acts. . . .

Slusher noted that "the surfer is endlessly free. . . he determines his own destiny. . . . Failure cannot be blamed on a sudden gust of wind or a strong current. This is part of the sport. In fact it is the sport. . . . Each and every encounter is new and fresh. Man stands on his own and faces the unstructured and unique forces of nature."(24:178)

Union with Self, Nature and Other Men. Responding to the question, "What is a National wave?" an Australian surfer gave this answer:

> A series of incidents that add, tie up to a tale, a being. One minute a pressure, then a cruise of ease, euphoria, next a calculus, finally, always, a satisfaction. One pure slice of existence. Being. (3:122)

Slusher established that "there is a certain feeling that comes to the body through involvement in sport that is a sense of being. In the straining and alteration from normal pursuits, man feels his body as he never knew it before."(24:36)

Slusher said that being is "a total expression of the wholeness of man."(24:12) This oneness is often expressed in sports of nature:

> Autonomy of existence can be achieved by the body *knowing* the object in a way that is not known by others or by other objects. Through the process of transcendence he no longer perceives the self as is. The skin diver becomes part of the sea, the skier part of the mountains . . . *In the body* and *by the body* man learns *existenz* as an exciting new way. (24:36)

As Nuuhiwa said, "you must try to blend into the wave, you match the wave's movements, you become part of it."(21:27) The peace pentathloner expressed a similar idea:

> The rhythm of movements. A relaxation of flow of the inner essence—continuity of being, moving through any movement, harmony. I run up the mountain. I flow down the mountain. In time with the moment. In pace with the universe. Watching from inside and out. Unity with all. (16:52)

In sport there is an I-thou relationship in which "man finds himself, man becomes, man is, only in relation to his thou" [possibly some element of nature].(9:90) It is a very personal and loving thing. Julius Kugy said, "I leaned on mountains as upon strong friends. They were so kind to me as to bring me comfort and restoration after grave earthly sorrow. Such is the love and trust with which I turn to them." (12:633) Ricky Grigg felt the same way about the sea. "The sea absorbs me and provides every passion I know. There's intense interest, excitment, love, fear, deep respect. . . the sea is very personal to me."(3:93)

No wonder natural sportsmen become addicted to their sport. It is not strange that they often experience a touch of sadness when their adventure is over, as Hillary did at the end of that Everest expedition.(11:248) Flying in the warmth of a plane over Canada's Back River, whose rapids he had just canoed down, Austin Hoyt stated that already he "had begun to miss the bite of the wind in his face and the fury of the river."(14:41)

Yet during those expeditions both of these men must have felt some anxiety in their freedom—an anxiety which assisted them in their efforts. It's like the surfer in relation to the wave who "while he needs to 'ride it in,'. . . would like nothing better than to relieve himself of his situation."(24:179)

Sometimes man finds a deep union with other men after sharing a sports experience in nature, particularly because man is dependent upon his fellow man and is depended on in a survival, life-death situation. Mountaineering provides a very vivid example. "Each man deliberately places his life in the hands of his companions. . . . After many or arduous climbs together, individuals feel deeply this kinship of the rope."(13:51)

Together two or three or four can do what is impossible for one to accomplish. Slusher noted that in sports like mountaineering there is both a quality of cooperation between the participants and a struggle for survival where man just wants to exist.(24:39) Teamwork is essential to ascents like Everest, and it provided John Hunt with one of the greatest sensations he had ever known. "Comradeship, regardless of race or creed, is forged among high mountains, through the difficulties and dangers to which they expose those who aspire to climb them, the need to combine their efforts to attain their goal, the thrill of a great adventure shared together."(15:231)

Contrast with Ordinary Life. Part of the beauty of sports occurring in natural settings is the marked absence of spectators, who dominate most of the game sports with their artificial standards and scores. Aloneness doesn't have to be the same as sheer loneliness. Sometimes it's good to be alone. Joseph Krutch recognized this when he asked the question: "How many more generations will pass before it will become nearly impossible to be alone even for an hour, to see anywhere nature without man's improvements upon her?"(19:30) Parachuting enables man to be very much alone. In fact, it's a very private thing to do. (26:85) The sportsman is in control of the situation of aloneness. Though he may be anxious, fearful or excited, he knows the reason for these emotions, which is often not the case in daily life where "floating" anxieties plague many. Being alone for the first time in soaring brought this reaction from Gannon: "It's a funny thing, but you just don't know the thrill, the real thrill of soaring—you never become lightheartedly alive with joy—until you're up there alone."(8:100)

Aloneness is only one of the sudden contrasts in natural sport. An exciting and strenuous 160-foot belay into a cave is very different from the utter calm and beauty discovered once inside it.(6:156) The quiet, motionless temperament of water is quite a contrast to the anxious exhilaration of the unknown just around the bend in the river.(14:40) Parachuting provides this contrast as well as a sense of freedom and a desire to make time and the world stand still, if for only an instant:

The physical sensations of the jump occur as sudden contrasts. From noise, vibration, immobility and confinement, the jump brings rapid motion, and suddenly, as the canopy opens, suspension in what seems for the moment an absolute quiet in endless time and space. The subjective release of tension with a surge of exhilaration. . . . You feel free when you jump. And when that old canopy opens, it's like the hand of God has caught you up. You look down on the world, and you think how nice it would be to stay up there. (5:663)

In man's exhilaration from the release of such earthly holds he recognizes himself as a complete and united being. Life is restored to him and man is important to himself. (24:10, 22)

By accepting and seeking the challenges of nature in the natural sports experience, the participant has the opportunity to know himself and the world in new ways. In an aesthetic sense, man can open himself up to great visual beauty, virgin experiences and the sensation of being finite in the cosmos. There is an opportunity to meet challenges which demand the development of control in risky and stressful situations not often found in ordinary life. Man has a chance to know freedom and to be dependent upon and responsible for himself. Ultimately, he has the unique opportunity to unite with himself, nature and other men in the world of natural sports.

BIBLIOGRAPHY

1. Alvarez, A. "I Like to Risk My Life." *Saturday Evening Post*, 240 (September 9, 1967), 10-12.
2. Coutts, Curtis A. "Freedom in Sport." *Quest*, X (May, 1968), 68-71.
3. Dixon, Peter. *Men Who Ride Mountains*. New York: Bantam Books Inc., 1969.
4. Edwards, Harvey. "Daredevil of the Alps: He Skis the Steepest." *Ski*, 34 (Spring, 1970), 61, 72.
5. Farrell, Dennis. "The Psychology of Parachuting." *Motivations in Play, Games and Sports*. Edited by Ralph Slovenko and James A. Knight. Springfield, Illinois: Charles C Thomas, 1967.
6. Folsome, Franklin. *Exploring American Caves*. New York: Collier Books, 1962.
7. Furlong, William. "Danger as a Way of Life." *Sports Illustrated*, 30 (January 27, 1969), 52-53.
8. Gannon, Robert. "Half-Mile Up Without an Engine." *Popular Science*, 192 (April, 1968), 98-101.
9. Gerber, Ellen W. "Identity, Relation and Sport." *Quest*, VIII (May, 1967), 90-97.
10. "Go and Make a Falling Star." *Esquire*, 70 (July, 1968), 66-67.
11. Hillary, Edmund. *High Adventure*. New York: E. P. Dutton & Company, Inc., 1955.
12. Houston, Charles S. "Mountaineering." *Motivations in Play, Games and Sports*. Edited by Ralph Slovenko and James A. Knight. Springfield, Illinois: Charles C Thomas, 1967, 626-636.
13. ———. "The Last Blue Mountain." *Why Men Take Chances*. Edited by Samuel Z. Klausner. Garden City, New York: Anchor Books, Doubleday & Company, 1968, 49-58.
14. Hoyt, Austin. "Down the Back to the Arctic." *Sports Illustrated*, 19 (August 26, 1963), 34-41.
15. Hunt, John. *The Ascent of Everest*. London: Hodder & Stroughton, 1953.
16. Jones, Robert F. "The World's First Peace Pentathlon." *Sports Illustrated*, 32 (May 11, 1970), 50-60.
17. Kennedy, Robert F. "Our Climb Up Mt. Kennedy." *Life*, 58 (April 9, 1965), 22-27.
18. Knight, James A. "Skiing." *Motivations in Play, Games and Sports*. Edited by Ralph Slovenko and James A. Knight. Springfield, Illinois: Charles C Thomas, 1967, 637-648.
19. Leydet, Francois. *Time and the River Flowing: Grand Canyon*. Edited by David Brower. San Francisco: Sierra Club & Ballantine Books, 1968.
20. Mitchell, Carleton. "The Fad and Fascination of Surfing." *Holiday*, 35 (May, 1964), 122-130.
21. Ottum, Bob. "The Charger Sinks the Dancer." *Sports Illustrated*, 25 (October 10, 1966), 26-29.
22. Rogin, Gilbert. "An Odd Sport and an Unusual Champion." *Sports Illustrated*, 23 (October 18, 1965), 94-110.
23. Russell, Terry and Russell, Renny. *On the Loose*. San Francisco: Sierra Club & Ballantine Books, 1967.
24. Slusher, Howard S. *Man, Sport and Existence*. Philadelphia: Lea & Febiger, 1967.
25. Styles, Stowell. *On Top of the World*. New York: The Macmillan Company, 1967.
26. "The Joys of Falling Through Space." *Saturday Evening Post*, 239 (June 18, 1966), 82-85.
27. Ullman, James Ramsey. "At the Top—and Out of Oxygen." *Life*, 55 (September 20, 1963), 68-92.
28. "Wonders of a Cave Find: A Big Spelunking Jackpot in the Ozarks." *Life*, 57 (December 18, 1964), 49-54.

I Like to Risk my Life*

A. ALVAREZ

When George Leigh-Mallory, the British schoolmaster who vanished near the peak of Mount Everest in 1924, was asked why in the world he wanted to climb the mountain, he replied, "Because it is there." No doubt the questioner was part belligerent, part offended, as though climbing were a personal affront to him, and so Leigh-Mallory took appropriate evasive action. I myself find counteraggression the best defense, and reply, when asked why I climb, "Because you're here." But an American mountaineer, faced with the same question, would be well advised to plead the Fifth Amendment. So should the American racing drivers, cave explorers, sky divers and skin divers, and all other devotees of lonely, dangerous sports. For there seems to be a firm belief in the United States that anyone who takes a deliberate risk for any reason except financial gain is indulging in an activity that is basically un-American.

Anyone who feels that way should go any Sunday to the Shawangunks, a long, low cliff just north of New York City. Every weekend the rocks are black with climbers, sweating, heaving, and straining, just as climbers regularly struggle with outcrops outside Paris and London and Munich. These are the risk addicts, geting their weekly fix. So far as the average American citizen is concerned, they seem somehow subversive. At a dinner party one recent evening in New York, for example, I mentioned that I had spent the day climbing

* From *Saturday Evening Post*, 240 (September 9, 1967), 10-12. Reprinted by permission of John Cushman Associates, Inc. and *The Saturday Evening Post*. © 1967 The Curtis Publishing Company.

that Shawangunk cliff. My hostess turned her stunning dark eyes on me. "What," she asked, "do you want to go and do a thing like that for?" She made me feel that I had just confessed to insanity.

Yet I suspect that if I had said that I played poker for a living, she would have been pleased. It is one of the oddities of modern America that you can gamble your future on stocks or in Las Vegas and gain nothing but approval. This would show that you are after more security, more goodies. But to take risks for their own sake is felt to be an attack on the social order.

Maybe it is, yet in my experience only Americans take it as a personal threat. A European may secretly think that mountaineers are out of their minds, but he will allow them a certain ambiguous respect. John Hunt got a knighthood out of leading the first expedition to climb Everest; Edmund Hillary, the New Zealander who was the first man to reach the actual peak, also was knighted; Italy's Walter Bonatti, England's Joe Brown, and the late Lionel Terray of France are all minor national heroes for their mountain-climbing skills. And there are advantages even for average performers like myself: In those Italian climbing huts, with action pictures of dead climbers on every wall, the caretaker allows you special rates, his daughter will wash your socks if you ask nicely, and after a big route the nonclimbing tourists buy you drinks and pump you for details.

It is different in the States. Last year I went out to Yosemite Valley, because the word is out that the greatest climbing area in the world is available there, on vast blank walls that rise thousands of feet. At Yosemite a handful of California mountaineers have revolutionized the techniques of climbing. I had always regarded a piton as a mere slug of metal that was hammered into a crack. At Yosemite a piton is an elegant chrome molybdenum instrument to be used with finesse, like a sculptor's chisel. The Yosemite climbers have made the valley into a way of life: They live there for months on a dollar a day, and have trained themselves to spend incredibly long periods—sometimes nine days on end—nailed to what one of them called "the enormous vertical desert" of the cliff faces, hauling their water after them and sleeping in nylon hammocks suspended from pitons over empty space.

In Europe their reputation is awesome; on their home ground they are treated like psychopaths. Admittedly, they are badly dressed and shockingly poor; but they are also devoted, retiring, and not in the least delinquent. For all the good it does them, they might as well be Hell's Angels. While I was there three friends of mine spent five days climbing the great Nose of El Capitan, over 3,000 feet of sheer and overhanging rock. On the last day I was watching them from the road at the foot of the cliff, among a cluster of tourists in Bermuda shorts. A car drew up and someone got out and joined the onlookers. It was hard to pick out the tiny specks far up on the dazzling cliff.

"It ain't right," he said. A murmur of approval went through the crowd.

"We ought to run those guys out of the valley," said a park ranger, reassuringly. "They're snarling up the traffic."

Such a promise to protect the American public from the spectacle of risk could be a healthy sign. Hero worship and its cult of bravery can be a nasty contagious disease, as Nazi Germany showed. But few people climb mountains, race cars or sky-dive simply to cut a figure. Would-be heroes are either incompetent or dead. On a hard route, if you pause to think, "How grand and operatic I must look, plastered on this unforgiving precipice," you will probably fall off. Instead, you are so utterly absorbed in tiny, localized details—problems of technique, balance, power, stamina, equipment—that you scarcely have time to look at the view. It is like playing chess with your body, a series of physical strategies which demand not courage but sheer concentration. The British racing driver Sterling Moss summed this up very well when he said, "It doesn't frighten me to go over the blind brow of a

hill at one hundred and sixty or seventy miles an hour. I know I shall make it. I say to myself, if I say anything, that I know how to do this. . . . What's the point of living if one's not able to do *one* thing?"

So what looks like absurd risk to the outsider is usually something quite different to the expert: It is justifiable, controlled. Yet the American public just does not seem to want to know the truth. Consider, for example, the curiously toned-down, "safe" image given the astronauts. They are, on any count, the bravest men since the first aborigine launched his coracle. You would never know it from official sources. The hero of space flight is not Shepard or Grissom or Glenn, in this official version; it is NASA, with all its marvelous technology. It is, in short, good old American know-how writ large and modern. The NASA public-relations campaign is devoted to proving that these men who actually orbit the planet are merely mature and adjusted, with wives and children and investments, just like you and me. A p.r. campaign like the one to which the astronauts are subjected acts as a kind of tranquilizer, and tranquilizers can be habit forming, and most American are hooked to an unprecedented degree. To a foreigner like myself, who has carried on a commuter's love affair with the States for years, it seems that Americans use their glimmering vision of the American Way of Life in order to sedate themselves and to forget the violent realities.

Consider the simple fact: The average American city dweller lives daily with more risk and violence than most mountaineers meet in a lifetime. I would rather commit myself 10 times over to El Capitan than go alone into Harlem or Watts or try to cross Central Park after dark; on a mountain at least you have *some* control over disaster. Even apart from the race riots and muggings, there is violence in the very tone of American life. Think of the casual, almost tender brutality that most New Yorkers take airily for granted. When I first arrived in the States in 1953—innocent, aghast, and 24—I had not been in the country more than an hour before I had been assaulted verbally by a customs officer, a taxi driver, a cop. And when I went into the subway at rush hour I emerged like some minor paranoid in a Dostoevski novel, feeling that I had been assaulted by the whole world. The average New Yorker, used to it all, simply does not notice anymore. Meanwhile, woe betide anyone who denies the illusion by facing up to risks on purpose.

"Those guys up there," announced one of the Bermuda shorters that day in Yosemite, "they're sick, real sick." I suppose this is the standard response. In a society where violence is as normal as the common cold is in England, everyone must automatically protect himself from exposure. To believe in security is the American equivalent of the Englishman's umbrella: an elementary protective mechanism which only a madman would ignore. Thus anybody who voluntarily takes a risk is, wherever it can be arranged, urged to undergo psychiatric treatment.

No doubt a massive, statistical society like the U.S. would simply not work without a great deal of placid adjustment. Hence all those socially acceptable outlets for aggression, ranging from movies and spectator sports to more complex exercises like hating the Communists or the Birchers or your mother-in-law. But too much enforced placidity, like all other evasions of reality, takes a psychic toll. After a certain point security provokes uneasiness. As Freud said, "Life loses in interest when the highest stake in the game, life itself, may not be risked."

The corollary, that risk somehow enhances life, can mean many things, most of them, alas, untrue. It is, for instance, not true that only the threat of death makes you realize how sweet life is. It is still less true that only when your hair is on end with fear are you really alive. Anyone who needs so violent a stimulus to break through his torpor is already half-dead, just as the people who talk most fervently about the beautiful emotions induced by drugs are those who have the most difficulty in feeling anything at all. But it is true, I think, that intentional, planned risk demands all the qualities most valuable in life: intelligence, skill, intuition, subtlety, control. These are precisely the qualities the good artist brings to his work, and they are also those called upon in the lonely, risky sports. On a cliff you must be intelligent, skillful, intuitive, subtle and controlled with your body. And the greater the risk you choose to take, the greater the reserves you must tap.

I found this out for myself the hard way in August, 1964. A companion and I spent 12 hours perched on a tiny ledge rather too small for both of us, 1500 feet up an overhanging rock wall in the Italian Dolomites. A storm had caught us; we had no food and no extra clothes and we had to sit it out while the stars glinted with cold and our outer clothing froze on us. The huge, folded landscape below us was blue and deep. Both of us were convinced we would freeze to death, though neither of us mentioned the fact for fear of demoralizing the other. Since sleep lowers the body temperature, it was important to stay awake; so we talked in a desultory way, swapped stories, recited limericks; we even tried singing. Occasionally we would slap each other about the back and chest—but tentatively, because of our precarious stance. Our minds like our bodies, were in suspension, neither frightened nor grieving, just blank.

The following morning we still had 500 feet of vertical and, by then ice-clad rock to climb. Difficult in the best conditions, it demanded then a concentration and effort that wrung us dry. As a poet once wrote of an artillery barrage, "It seemed disproportionate to the fragility of us." When we finally got back to the hut, swaying with exhaustion, ravenous, battered, we had reached the absolute end of our tether. But that in itself was something. After all, to know how much you can take is a form of self-knowledge. More important still were the other resources we had had to call on—the obscure doggedness that prevented us from simply giving up. At no point did we feel we were fighting the mountain; the battle was only with ourselves.

And that, finally, is what all the risky games are about. They are like a sharp close-up of your life, in which all the essentials are concentrated and defined. You deliberately set up a situation in which, in order to survive, you must respond as fully as you know how. The situation itself may be utterly artificial—on a mountain there is nearly always an easier way to the top—but the element of risk makes it terribly serious. The fascination for me is keeping the risk in complete control. Flirting with danger for kicks bores me; it is a form of exhibitionism, a vulgarity to one's self. I would no more climb or drive fast cars in order to hurt myself, then I would play poker to lose. The pleasure is in doing something difficult, something that extends your concentration and effort and resourcefulness without ever losing control.

Within the edgy terms they set up, the risky sports provide an area in which you must take complete responsibility for your own life; that is, they provide precisely the occasions for choice and responsibility that never quite arrive in clear, recognizable form in the routine world. However trivial the context—who, finally, cares about a piece of rock, or a big wave, or a racing record that will be broken next year?—the element of risk can turn a weekend hobby into a small-scale model for living, a life within a life. Perhaps what Leigh-Mallory really meant about his lonely sport was: "I take risk because, for better or for worse, I'm here."

Play and Seriousness*

KURT RIEZLER

We say: this is merely play; he is merely playing. We differentiate between play and something that is not merely play but is serious. What does this "merely" mean?

But is not the answer obvious? We say "merely playing" whenever we are not serious. We say we are not merely playing so far as we are serious though playing. Unfortunately, the simple answer does not get us very far. What, for heaven's sake, is serious, and why? The "merely" points to a deficiency, to something that is absent in playing. When we say "not merely play" we indicate that this something is present despite our playing. Thus explaining this something whose absence the "merely" asserts, the "not merely" denies, means explaining our seriousness. The question grows.

That seems to be an inquiry into the usage of a word. But the "merely," asserted or denied, accompanies all playing throughout the countries, ages, and languages. It tends to indicate something in man, the queer being, that is able to play and bound to be serious.

The "merely" or "not merely" resides in the attitude of man, not in things, matters, actions, that we could subsume under play and seriousness. The "merely" differentiates attitudes. Man may decide according to his own will or mood whether he should deal playfully or seriously with a person, a thing, a task, a situation, or a game. Man does not decide which attitude of his is playful and which

serious. Though man's mood can move things to and fro over the borderline between play and seriousness, he can not move the borderline itself, which demarcates attitudes, not things.

I begin with the most simple case. We play games such as chess or bridge. They have rules the players agree to observe. These rules are not the rules of the "real" world or of "ordinary" life. Chess has its king and queen, knights and pawns, its space, its geometry, its laws of motion, its demands, and its goal. The queen is not a real queen, nor is she a piece of wood or ivory. She is an entity in the game defined by the movements the game allows her. The game is the context within which the queen is what she is. This context is not the context of the real world or of ordinary life. The game is a little cosmos of its own.

We may call this little cosmos a world—the "playworld." The term, however, is misleading. "World" suggests certain features the playworld lacks. "World" means or should mean the totality of a something "in" which we live. We ourselves are part of this something. Though the world is always our world, it is intended to mean a world that is not and never will be ours. It means everyone's world. It embraces all other worlds of all other beings. So it is the real world.

We are free to play or not to play, to enter or to leave the "playworld." Our relation to the real world is of a different kind. We have been thrown into it willy-nilly; we can leave but never re-enter it. As the real world differs

* From *Journal of Philosophy*, XXXVIII, (September, 1941), 505-517.

from the playworld, so a real queen differs from the queen in chess. In the real world all things are connected with all things, every effect is a cause, every end a means. Not so in the playworld. Here the chains of causes and effects are thought of as having limits. Events within the game are separated from events in the real world. To the player the game is not a part of the real world. The "merely" may have to do with this separation.

In playing chess we can be more or less serious. A bridge player may be chided by his partner for lack of seriousness. She feels he is not paying sufficient attention to the game or that he does not live up to its spirit. Still, mere lack of seriousness should not be called a playful attitude toward the game. Play or playfulness is not a negative term. We could speak of a playful attitude if a player were to play a play within the game itself, whether by pursuing a goal of his own or by superimposing rules of his own on the rules of the game—replacing the spirit of the game by the caprices of his mood, which are at odds with the spirit of the game although not forbidden by its rules. For example, a bridge-player might try to get as many kings as possible in his tricks. He could be said to play with the play. We say that he merely plays so far as he substitutes demands of his own for the demands of the game. Here playfulness stresses the detachment of a sovereign mood—which in this case is detachment from the spirit of the game. Thus the "merely" seems to indicate a detachment from demands that seriousness commands us to respect.

The story of our playing has still other aspects. Though the playworld may be separated from the real world, the goal of the game can be connected with the real world, our ordinary life, our substantial interests. Money, honor, even life, may depend on our winning or losing. The gambler can raise his stakes to a point at which losing would mean serious harm. He has not much use for the "merely," though we might say that he deals seriously with the play but playfully with his money. It is he himself who links his serious interests with the play. To the football champion the victory of Lions over Tigers may be the only thing that matters. Glory, honor, career may depend on his success, according to the customs and codes of the society in which he lives. Since he has to submit to these codes, his football is not merely a play, perhaps no play at all—at least to him. It is an institution of the real world or ordinary life. The playful attitude, if there is any, is on the side of a society that connects a mere play with the glory, honor, and career of its members.

A fashionable gentleman trifles away his day and gambles at night. His gambling is his only seriousness. Here at least he faces the reality of life: fear and hope, risk, action, passion, need for caution and self-control. It may even be that the very thirst for real concern drives him to the gambling table—away from his day of non-committing trifles. Now play and seriousness exchange places. We may conclude: play can be serious, ordinary life need not be serious at all. The "real world" or "ordinary life" may be used to differentiate things belonging to play from those belonging to seriousness; they can not be used to differentiate a playful from a serious attitude.

There are, however, many games of another sort. In some the emphasis lies not on obeying but on inventing or changing rules. After all, chess and bridge also were invented in a playful mood. We might even dare to say that in the present American form, bridge has taken on the character of work by being fettered to so many elaborate rules and conventions that obedience to them threatens to suffocate the playful mood. We never enjoy a playful attitude more than when making or changing the rules or conventions to which we submit. We do it rarely, because we are lazy or lack inventiveness.

This is clear in the case of children's play. What they enjoy most is their own inventive activity. Long before they play games children play with or without toys. They invent and perform stories, determine the meaning of things, assume for themselves the rôle of a king or a queen. This chair is a mountain, the doll in the blue dress and with pink cheeks is Aunt Geraldine. The child disregards the fact that Aunt Geraldine has neither a blue dress nor pink cheeks. She enjoys her activities in determining the meaning of the doll or in forcing Aunt Geraldine to sit straight in her doll chair.

Grownups, watching the child, say: she plays. In their world the child's play is "merely" play. There may be, however, no "merely" for the child herself—no playful attitude, no "merely" that could hint at a deficiency. The distinction between play and seriousness is still in the making, the real and the imaginary world are not yet separated. For the child, things do not yet have their own definite meaning, which demands to be respected and is put aside when we merely play. Things, as separated from their meanings, are as yet unknown. They are what they mean. To children their little activity in playing seems to share in a seriousness in which, in between anxiety and curiosity, they discover the world and its things, themselves and their relation to the world, their power and its limitations. It is the share they enjoy, since in playing alone are they acting.

The "merely" enters the scene when children begin to be capable of, and granted, a first consistent activity in a consistent reality. Now the things of the real world begin to raise their voices, impose their demands, and be conceived in the horizon of an order in which things are no longer what you choose them to be. Now the doll and Aunt Geraldine, play and seriousness, part company. This process may take considerable time.

A four-year-old boy plays railroad with a series of chairs. He sits on the first chair and is the engine. His father enters the room and kisses him. "Don't kiss me," protests the boy, "the chairs could see it and forget that they are railroad cars." Huyzinga[1] [sic] uses the case to support his thesis that children realize that they merely play. The example, however, is dubious. It shows only how the real and the imaginary world still interpenetrate each other.

A girl, we say, plays around with the boys. Or this man merely plays with that girl. We may pity the girl who takes herself or her love seriously and demands to be not merely played with. The girl or the social group sets a standard of love to which this man should but does not conform. His merely playing means disregarding this standard. In some cases both the male and the female merely play. They play with each other a very old play, each knowing that the other merely plays and both enjoying the charm of the game. "Why not? After all, it is not so serious a matter." We say they merely play though they may pretend or even believe themselves to be serious. We say so if we know that neither would go a few steps out of his way for the other's sake. We set a standard of love to which intimate relations between a boy and girl should conform. The "merely" means that an obligation inherent in the relations between the sexes has been disregarded. In some languages, as older Low German and Dutch, the term for an illegitimate child is "playchild," suggesting that only marriage is serious. But play is not the mere negation of seriousness. A love affair that lacks seriousness need not even be play. The amorous life of societies that succeeded in bestowing some charm on love as a game tells another story. There are winners and losers,

[1] In his *Homo ludens.*

goals and rules. The two players may play with each other; the prize may be to be loved and not love. It may be mere vanity, honor, reputation, in a leisure class engaged in a collective battle against boredom. Or the lovers may play not only with each other but with the danger that at any moment one may commit him- or herself seriously and really fall in love. The game has its rules. These rules—the moral code of illicit love—tend to separate the game from ordinary life, its commitments, its interests, titles, rights, and its knowledge. The rules demand "discretion" in all the shades of the term, which range from separation through freedom to courtesy. It may happen that both players lose and really fall in love. Then they no longer merely play, though they may go on observing some rules of the game and try to isolate their love from ordinary life. Out of mutual respect for their self-defense they may even go on pretending to play, using the ruse of a playful attitude to cloak their seriousness.

In some Catholic countries of an old tradition a few weeks of carnival festivities put the relations between the sexes under the exceptional rules of a play. Visitors from countries without such a tradition usually assume that all they have to do is to rid themselves of an habitual restraint. Though nowadays the actual practice of the natives themselves does not quite live up to the idea, the natives still dislike these visitors because their failure to observe the rules spoils the game. Here a social code demands the playful attitude. You are in disguise, wearing a mask and a costume. You are not yourself. You play a rôle. No one is expected to ask or answer serious questions. The stories you tell, the promises you make, the love you profess need be true but for the moment—in a fictitious world. No consequences should be drawn, no obligations remembered, beyond Mardi Gras. The favors you may consummate give you no titles. They do not count in ordinary life. A really jealous husband who does not merely act the part of a jealous husband violates the rules of the play.

Here a society plays, watching in common agreement over rules meant to separate the game from the real world or ordinary life and its chains of causes and effects, ends and means.

The example of love is ambiguous—the ambivalence of love between play and seriousness being the charm of the game. Other examples are simpler.

A writer's cunning and skill may be remarkable. He forces the language to follow his moods. Yet we blame him for merely playing with the language. What do we mean? He only wants to display his skill, enjoys moving along the boundary of what is still allowed, startles us by his artifices. He is an acrobat, not an artist. He merely plays so far as he disregards, for purposes of his own mood, obligations that the correlation of subject-matter and language silently imposes.

We say that a conductor deals but playfully with a Beethoven symphony. We mean that the desire to show off his craftsmanship overpowers the devotion the work demands.

Statesmen, whose job it is to consider all sides of a situation, often complain of experts who isolate the interests of their fields. Once in a while they may sigh angrily; the generals or the diplomats are merely playing their game. The statesman may be right or wrong; he means that the diplomat, educated in the traditions of the European balance of power, the rules of diplomacy and its craftiness, looks at Europe as the playground of a diplomatic game that is an end in itself, and is unable to realize demands beyond his game or requirements of a situation that can not be mastered by his means, methods, or goals. In an analogous way the general, educated as a staff officer by playing war games on maps or in manoeuvres, regards the surface of the earth as a playground for moving armies and navies. Both separate a playworld from the real world, absolutize their own rules and goals, and disregard every horizon that is beyond the limited horizon of their game. Even in such cases play and its "merely" retain the shadow of their meaning. Such examples can be multiplied; the "merely" continues to accompany the playful attitude.

I venture a preliminary thesis. The diversity of our playing seems to suggest two ways of defining the "merely," the one starting from the player, the other from the play. In a playful attitude the manner of our being concerned has specific features, as has the object with which we are concerned. Since these two sorts of specificity correspond to each other the two ways of defining the "merely" converge; they explain each other.

In a playful attitude we are "not really" concerned. But it is just this "not really" that must be explained. Moreover, "not really" is wider than "merely playfully." We are "not really" concerned in many cases when there is no playfulness in our attitude. We may try to say: in a playful attitude things do not matter so much—we are only partly concerned, not with the whole of our interest. But this again is doubtful.

We are often partly concerned in matters of ordinary life, yet this our partial concern need not be playful. If "partial" is to be used this partialness must be of a peculiar kind. We are partly concerned but without linking this partial concern to other parts or to the whole of our concern. It does not count. In severing the link that connects this part with other parts we treat a "partial" concern as if it were no part of anything. Thus the part, not being conceived of as part, is not a part. In the seriousness of ordinary life all partial concern remains partial because it is connected with some of or all our other concerns. The "merely" in our playing seems to point not to a partial concern, but to a distinction in which our concern in playing is separated from our other concerns.

If we start from the game or from the object with which a playful attitude is concerned, a different aspect tells the same story. An area of playing is isolated by our sovereign whim or by man-made agreement. Things within this area mean what we order them to mean. They are cut off from their meanings in the so-called real world or ordinary life. No chains of causes and effects, means and ends, are supposed to connect the isolated area of play with the real world or ordinary life. If there still are such chains they are disregarded. So far as we do not disregard them our attitude is no longer merely playful. An area that under the aspect of ordinary life would be conceived of as only a part is regarded not as part of a wider area but as a cosmos of its own. Thus the two aspects tell the same story.

In merely playing we forget the "real world," our ends, our dependence on things. We often play only for the sake of diversion. At any rate, we disregard the context of ordinary life, the meaning of things, their demands, our obligations, and put in their place meanings, demands, and obligations of our own making. In playing we enjoy being our own masters.

Playing, if it is merely playing, is never a means. The goal of playing is part of the game. It is not an end to which our playing is the means—it serves only to direct our activity, to measure the skill, to differentiate between winner and loser. Playing, our activity in playing is its own end, though we are capable of linking the goal of the game to means and ends in our life outside the game. If we do, we usually drop the "merely." The chains of causes and effects, means and ends, are meant to be cut at the boundaries of the play. No more than causes from outside are allowed to interfere, lest they spoil the game, should consequences be drawn to the life outside the play.

So it seems that with respect to both the how and the what of our concern the "merely" could be explained as follows: things, in their relation to us, are surrounded by a horizon that depends on our attitude toward them. In different attitudes we see things in different horizons. The horizon makes things what they are to us. In the seriousness of our daily activity we look at things within the horizon of our interests in the various concatenations of causes and effects, means and ends. Here every horizon seems to be partial, pointing beyond itself, intended to mean something in connection with other things and other possible horizons. When in serious life we say that we are only partly concerned, we look at our own concern as but a greater or smaller part of our concernedness—in the horizon of something that is more than this part. In a playful attitude the horizon does not point at anything beyond itself, though it is the horizon of a limited area or of a limited concern that is not yet connected with, and not a part of, a wider area or a broader concern: the horizon of a play that is merely a play.

This thesis, however, is preliminary indeed. It may be of some service to differentiate playfulness from the average seriousness of our daily life. But it has no reason to offer why this kind of ordinary life should be serious at all. Why should or could a man not deal playfully with all the chains of means and ends in this dubious seriousness? The question grows out of the answer.

Ere I proceed, I permit an antithesis to speak and to sweep the thesis away in a burst of rage.

At last, so the argument runs, you seem to discover the shortcomings of a thesis that takes for granted the seriousness of ordinary life. In starting from the "merely" you presuppose a standard of seriousness that may be only the standard of the kind of society that thinks in terms of means and ends, in terms of business. It may be that the "merely" is only a habit of speaking. There need not be an absolute "merely" in playing as such—no deficiency. If there is deficiency it may be a deficiency not in play but in the man who utters the "merely" and thus shows that he can not rid himself of his puny sort of seriousness. Your start from the "merely" distorts the story of play.

There is no "merely"—rather an "even." Play is man's triumph—he, the greatest of all beings, can even play. Only the lowest animals do not play. All higher animals, wild or tame,

play. The reasons for which we call them higher or lower may account for their playing and not playing. We assume that worms do not play, though we can not know what movements, actions, things are to worms in their worm world, if there is such a thing. We think of worms as closely tied up with their actual environment at any given moment. They live in the dark. The demands they put upon and receive from their environment are dumb pressures. They can not detach themselves from their environment, change the meaning of things and their functions, as play implies. Dogs and cats, most higher animals, undoubtedly can. They can fight for the love of fighting and not "mean it seriously." They chase a ball, push it away and capture it again, for the fun of chasing; give it importance for a while and leave it as something that is of no interest. Their playing is detachment from the environment and its demands, a sort of freedom the worm seems to lack. The way from worm to cat is but the first and minor part of the way from slavery to freedom. From dog to man is another, and the history of man's culture is again another part. Man's playing is his greatest victory over his dependence and finiteness, his servitude to things. Not only can he conquer his environment and force conditions to comply with his needs and demands far beyond the power of any other animal. He can also play, i.e., detach himself from things and their demands and replace the world of given conditions with a play-world of his own mood, set himself rules and goals and thus defy the world of blind necessities, meaningless things, and stupid demands. Religious rites, festivities, social codes, language, music, art—even science—all contain at least an element of play. You can almost say that culture is play. In a self-made order of rules man enjoys his activities as the maker and master of his own means and ends. Take art. Man, liberated from what you call the real world or ordinary life, plays with a world of rhythms, sounds, words, colors, lines, enjoying the triumph of his freedom. This is his seriousness. There is no "merely."

The antithesis plays havoc with our preliminary thesis. If the shattered thesis is to survive, it must be reshaped in order to withstand the violent assault.

We must make a new start. The "merely" may be misleading. What about the "not merely"? There are cases in which play, though play, is not merely play; and not only because the result of the play is connected by agreement with means and ends in ordinary life, such as money or honor, but in itself, by its inherent seriousness, which is not the seriousness of the real world or ordinary life. But is there such a thing? Why is it serious?

Art is play, though not merely play. Some put the emphasis on play, others on the "not merely." To the artist, if he is a real artist, it is deadly earnest, as earnest as religion to the religious man. But what is art? If we define art as the class of things called art—by some minimum conditions to which the elements of this class must submit,—we find works of art that are not even play, others that are merely play, and again others that certainly are not merely play. In search of the "not merely" we can not start from a definition of minimum conditions. There is something—whatever it may be, call it quality or value,—by virtue of which a work of art is "real art" or "great" or more or less "good." Toward this something both the artist and the art connoisseur are looking, the one in creating, the other in judging, the work. Though both may be equally unable to say what this mysterious something is, they presuppose that there is some thing. Whoever honestly denies it is not an artist or an art connoisseur. Obviously the "not merely" refers to this mysterious something.

If we apply to art the standards of the preliminary thesis, art is merely play. It separates things from the real world, disregards their demands, puts things in an imaginary context, within which they mean what art orders them to mean. The artist is the creator of his own rules and laws, which are not the rules and laws of ordinary life and are conceived of as being severed from its endless chains of means and ends, causes and effects. Thus, he merely plays.

And yet he does not play. There is not and can not be a playful attitude, be it in the artist who creates or in the connoisseur who enjoys and judges a work of art. It seems even that this play can not be played in a playful attitude. There is, in art itself, a demand, an ultimate obligation, with which no artist plays. It is devotion to this demand and detachment from all other demands that makes him an artist. With respect to this detachment you may say that he merely plays; with respect to this devotion, he simply can not help being serious indeed. This obligation is there ere the artist becomes an artist and creates his particular style and his works. It is the supreme lead, taken on in reverence and obeyed in judging, choosing, rejecting. It is not man-made, not the creation of any arbitrary mood, not part of the rules of the play, but prior to

any rules. There is no such thing in playing games. Thus, art is not play. The "not merely" points at an unconditional obligation.

Here, however, we are likely to run into a peculiar difficulty. We use and certainly need the term "playful" to characterize a style, a work, the individuality of an artist. Mozart is more playful than Beethoven. Rafael sometimes seems to be; Michelangelo is never playful. The history of art abounds in examples. The term, used in this way within art, need not have any bearing on "good" or "bad"— there is no "merely" in this playfulness, no differentiation of any kind. We mean only an apparently effortless ease that makes creativity look like the play of a sovereign mood. Both *King Lear* and *Midsummer Night's Dream* are called plays, though the former is certainly less playful than the latter. We are tempted to say that compared with *King Lear Midsummer Night's Dream* is "merely" a play: it is a dream in a playworld that does not claim to represent the real world. But we certainly do not mean that Shakespeare's attitude toward his poetry and its inherent demands is merely playful.

In the *Merchant of Venice* the relation itself between play and seriousness is the core of the work. Hence its difficulties. In most performances the tragedy of Shylock is put to the fore as the center of the work framed by a playworld of love, fun, music, and sweetness. Such performances can hardly be convincing. If the relation is reversed the performance convinces—a world of play and love put to the fore against the background of a world in which Shylocks hate and suffer. The poet, however, does not deal playfully with the tension between play and seriousness or with human life, of which this tension is part, or with his poetry.

Whenever in the history of art artists not only seem to have but really have an attitude toward their art that could be called merely playful, this "merely" indicates decay, second-rate work, or the end of a style. Playfulness in art is "not merely" playful at the beginning and "merely" playful at the end of a stylistic period—not in all but in many cases.

Art, whether playful or not, is never merely play. If the mysterious something we call good or quality or value means an obligation that is unconditionally serious, this seriousness is certainly not the seriousness of ordinary life and its horizons of means and ends. If the lead of the term "horizon" is to be followed the "horizon" in art is of another kind.

Listen to a Beethoven symphony. You are

in a world of sounds—nowhere else. This world embraces you. It is present as a whole. There is nothing beyond. The "real world" or ordinary life with all its endless chains of aspects, causes, means, in which every step is finite and none the last, disappears. Something else appears—which can be grasped with your senses but not put into words. If unfortunately a philosophical context or a question that continues to grow compels you to describe it you search for words in a kind of despair. One of the words you are likely to hit upon is "horizon."

This horizon includes a whole. This whole seems present at whatever point we touch this horizon. It is just this that the term "horizon" suggests or should suggest. We apply the term to the sky: south or north, west or east—only one horizon borders the sky. It is the same horizon all around. Thus the term implies the oneness of a whole. Here "whole" does not mean completeness of several elements. It means a Gestalt, present in every part, and not only by virtue of the presence of all other parts. You look only southward and yet the horizon you see embraces a whole. In art the horizon of the whole can still be visible in a torso or a fragment.[2]

The horizon embracing a whole is an ultimate horizon. It does not limit a part as part. It is not a particular horizon, pointing beyond itself. If there is infinity this infinity is within the horizon—an inward infinity.

While you listen to the symphony you are not partly concerned—the whole of your being is listening, you are moved to the core, open to something the term "ultimate horizon" is intended to indicate. The term does not claim to answer the unanswerable question of the mysterious something by virtue of which a work of art is more or less good. Its only claim is descriptive power. We might say that Leonardo or Michelangelo or Shakespeare in their Mona Lisa or Adam or Caesar succeeded in making visible an ultimate horizon that forces the human cosmos as a whole to become transparent in the portrait of a lady, in the movement of a body, in verses uttered by actors that are not Caesars on the boards of a stage that is not the world.

Reformulating the preliminary thesis I may say: Man acts and is acted upon as a being directed in itself toward a "whither" whatever

this whither may be or at any given moment seems to be. He lives in a world on which he depends. His life is his relation to his world. The world, however, is not merely the sum total of the things in the world. Nor is our relation to our world the sum total of our relations to the things in the world. Single things are to us what they are in the context of our world as a whole. In all our meddling and wrestling with things we wrestle with and woo the world as a whole in a loud or mute give and take, understanding and misunderstanding, power and devotion. So far as we deal with single things, all our "whithers" are finite, though behind each stands another that again is finite—in an endless finiteness. So far as we relate single things to the whole of our being or to our world as a whole (we can not do the one without the other) an ultimate horizon and in it an ultimate whither become visible, which is not the next step. In fact, it is no step at all, not even the last one, because it is not an element of a sequence.

Art is but an example. Though nowadays registered under entertainment business, it was born as a child of religion and entrusted with making visible its ultimate horizon. Art could outlive any religious faith but never the ultimate horizon. The ultimate horizon is not a monopoly of either religion or art. You love someone. The ultimate horizon is present though your theories about love may prevent you from recognizing its presence. You are confronted with a cause you would fight for, whatever words you choose to use. It is by referring the cause to an ultimate horizon, embracing your world as a whole, that you would fight for it. You "evaluate." You do it in two ways: by relating single things or actions to other things or actions in the endless finiteness of your chains of means and ends; or by referring one thing to the whole of your world, to an ultimate horizon bordering this whole. In the second, you may happen to use the term "value." Again it does not matter which terms you use. Let us assume that a social scientist tries honestly to prove that there are no values, but only wants and desires that bring about valuations. He may even succeed. Yet he can not help either looking at his own honesty in an ultimate horizon or admitting that he is not serious.

An any moment any link in one of the endless chains of our ordinary life can be referred to an ultimate horizon of our world as a whole. Without such reference it need not be serious. None of our games that are merely play, such as bridge or chess, has an ultimate horizon;

[2] I refer to the logical tools of Gestalt psychology which realizes the insufficiency of a logic that starts from a multitude of elements and their relations.

nor have the endless chains of causes and effects, means and ends, in the so-called seriousness of our ordinary life, as far as you conceive of life as a linkage of chains in which any horizon is only particular and no end ultimate. Whenever an ultimate horizon grips the whole of our being our playing is no longer "merely" playing, ordinary life is bound to be serious, and our concern with whatever it is is really real concern.

It is the ultimate horizon that lets both our play and ordinary life be serious—as the one thing nobody can play with, unless it disappears.

Thus the preliminary thesis, reshaped, can deal with the antithesis. Play may be a triumph of freedom; culture may contain an element of play. Since, however, the very life of culture is nothing else than an ultimate horizon, made visible, this playing never acknowledges a "merely." But the question goes on growing and the thesis remains preliminary. Heracleitus, watching boys playing in the holy grove of the temple of the Ephesian Diana, said: "Aeon is a boy who plays and moves the pawns to and fro." Though you may think of the world as God's play, you are not God. What is "merely" to such a God is "not merely" to you.

Play: A Non-Meaningful Act*

JOSEF PIEPER

How can we visualize something that serves nothing else, that by its very nature has meaning only in its own terms?

Almost inevitably there comes to mind a notion that has been much discussed in anthropological literature of recent decades—although it has been the subject of considerable romantic speculation, as well as of sound analysis. I am referring to the concept of *play*. Does not play epitomize that pure purposefulness in itself, we might ask? Is not play activity meaningful in itself, needing no utilitarian justification? And should not festivity therefore be interpreted chiefly as a form of play?

Obviously, these are extremely complex questions which cannot be settled merely in passing. Nevertheless, we would hazard that the term *play* does not adequately define the distinguishing feature of free activity, let alone of festivity. To be sure, Plato closely associates the two ideas when he speaks of "the graciousness of play and festival." And if "seriousness," as Hegel says, "is work in relation to the need," then it does seem logical to equate play with festivity in similar fashion. In fact a real festival can scarcely be conceived unless the

ingredient of play—perhaps also, although here I am not so sure, the ingredient of playfulness —has entered into it. But all this has not answered the crucial question of whether the element of play makes an action meaningful in itself. Human acts derive their meaning primarily from their content, from their object, not from the manner in which they are performed. Play, however, seems to be chiefly a mere *modus* of action, a specific way of performing something, at any rate a purely formal determinant. Thus it is natural enough that people inevitably flounder in phantasms and unrealities when they try to regard all those human activities that are obviously not just work as play and nothing more: the work of the artist, too—of the writer, musician, painter —or even religious worship. For suddenly everything that was "meaningful in itself" slips through their fingers and becomes a game empty of all meaning. Significantly, one good argument against Huizinga's book on *homo ludens*, which represents the religious festivals of primitive peoples purely as play, is that this view is tantamount to saying that all sacred acts are meaningless. Incidentally, this objection has not been made by a theologian; the critic is an ethnologist, protesting against distortion of empirical observation.

The question, then, remains open: By what virtue does an act possess the inner quality of being meaningful in itself?

*From *In Tune With The World* by Josef Pieper, copyright © 1963 by Kösel-Verlag KG München; English translation by Richard and Clara Winston. New York: Harcourt, Brace & World, 1965. © by Kösel-Verlag GmbH & Co., München, and reprinted with their permission.

The Power of Sport*

MARY PAVLICH ROBY

History and art have recorded sport in words and beauty; science and philosophy are tugged-at by its means and meanings; but the soul of sport remains uncaptured.

Sport has its "flipside." It has been described as a phenomenon which demands complete relaxation and full effort; it provides physical exhaustion yet rehabilitates; it can be a casual diversion or a complete fulfillment; it shapes man and is shaped by man. Whatever else it is, sport is a "thing" of remarkable power.

In creating sport, man gave it its own meaning in time and space and enveloped it in a compelling ritual. Each individual who enters this realm of expression finds in it meanings which are in some instances shared and in other instances peculiarly his own. But, as man involves himself in this phenomenon, it becomes apparent that he has created something that was not only shaped by him but that seems to be infused with powers that would in turn help shape its creator. A state of affairs to which any person will attest who has felt himself, at times, a "sportsman" first and a man second.

The powers of sport are many—and the selection that follows must be limited to a few that seem to be explainable as ways in which sport might contribute to the development of its participants—although perhaps the most exciting powers are those which defy description.

Sport Allows Self-discovery. Few experi-ences have the impact that one finds in sport wherein participants have discovered the knowledge that body-mind-spirit is a longer hyphenated way of saying "me." There is no possible way to use one-third of one's self, for only as a totality can one become a sportsman.

In this totality one experiences challenge, effort, joy, frustration, patience, excitement. For some it is the experience of mastering skills that brings the participant into possession of himself and his powers. For truly, it is skill that makes the skier one with the terrain, never acknowledging the fact that there is any possibility that the skis which bind him to the slope might find a path different from his own for arriving at the bottom of the mountain. This same kind of skill tells a basketball player that the drive toward the basket and the ensuing shot will be a success. The sureness is no less than it might be if a giant hand swept his opponents off the court . . . for the player will not be stopped!

Sport Provides the Drama of Life. Sport is a part of life and, like drama, sport too wears the comedy-tragedy masks. It produces winners and losers, successes and failures. Tapped emotions may be short or long lived, but whatever the duration they are real, not superficial outbursts, but a vital aspect of life's feelings. To lose with nobility and win with humility is the acceptable way, but sport never guarantees the participant a way, only a choice. And upon these choices rest judgments of ability in skill, wit, self-discipline, determination, learning and outlook, for success and failure are to be measured in a myriad of ways.

* From *Arizona Journal of Health, Physical Education, Recreation,* 10 (Fall, 1966), 9-10.

215

Sport Reveals the Unseen. Sports research has extended our insights into the capabilities of the human body increasing our factual knowledge and enlarging our aesthetic perception. In a sense then, sports reveal the unseen by capturing the will and power of man to extend himself to limits beyond that which were thought possible. A semblance of that which sport has revealed is captured by the arts. The arts themselves become richer because of this revelation of the unseen and in turn the multitude of images the artists create about sport increase the sportsman's perception of things not at first apparent.

Sport Extracts Essence. Sport has the ability to render the "thingness" of things—the poise of balance, the smoothness of rhythm, the power of a leg leaping, the effort of a muscle taut with strain. No writer can quite describe in words a "second wind" in the completeness it occurs to the runner, sport therefore is not a representation of what is real and vital but rather is reality itself.

Sport involves the full spectrum of emotions from joy and excitement to sadness and despair. The threshold is reached during the game itself; once over the emotions may swiftly readjust to their normal state.

Sport Is Power Over the Elements. Man is entitled to wander in his native habitat, and perhaps to attempt to understand or master those parts of this earth, which at first may appear hostile to his very being.

Sport makes man one with the elements. Antagonism cannot exist between the surfer and the surf. A surfer becomes a part of the wave that breaks against the shore for only in their unity is it possible to experience the elements.

In other instances, sport may help man discover that he is, at least temporarily, master of the elements. The thrill of defying the force of gravity long enough to do a full twisting one-and-a-half dive is a feeling found in few activities outside of sport.

Sport Transcends Barriers. Historians tell us that breaches were created in ancient city walls to receive the victorious sports performers. This welcoming spirit has not been lost in the centuries that followed for sport continues to vault walls erected by people of differing cultures and ideologies. There is no more effective pass for the excitement of being a part of people and places than the magical ability of a skillful sportsman. It is a rare instance when the quality of the performance does not transcend all other characteristics of the performer.

Sport Captivates Souls. Because of the emotional elements of sports performance, such an experience is apt to burn deeply into the memory of the performer. When man chooses to become involved in sport, a chain reaction of factors and emotions is touched off if only for the duration of the activity. Skill, effort, grace, persistence, involvement, courage are all demanded. To those who do not give them freely, the experience falls short of what it might be. One need not be able to put into words the thing that happens; no matter, it has captivated his soul.

All these powers of sport: self-discovery, drama, revealing the unseen, extracting essence, cooperating with the elements, transcending barriers, captivating souls—those are all neutral forces in themselves. As man enters this realm, he alone selects the direction of this force. He gives it meaning. Sport, in and of itself, is an exciting experience. And as man has molded it, he must be very much aware that he can be molded by it. This resulting mold is not necessarily cast by the individual alone, but also by the society which calls for sport as a part of its life.

A greater insight as to how sport acts on human thought and spirit, as well as actions, might lead to a wiser response to all sports activities. But sport techniques have tended to advance much more rapidly than have insights into the aesthetic and psychological implications of those techniques. This is strange for in the long perspective of man's history one would think the understanding of, reasons for, and use of these structured activities would have been understood by men long ago. But that is not the way of sport. Its powers alone are great and when we combine them with the miracle of man, there is little wonder that an analysis cannot easily be made. Sport will continue to fascinate thinkers for years to come, for in the thousands of years of its existence many believe that we have only begun to understand the nature of sport.

Why Men Run*

J. KENNETH DOHERTY

Why do men run? The wisest answer would undoubtedly be given by a child, or by a runner, or by a Zen Master; without saying a word, they each would start running. Men do run. That may be the most penetrating reason of all as to why they run. It tells us, beyond all words and abstractions, they are made *for* running, and have been made as they are *by* running.

Why do men run? A physiologist might answer that they run because they have running bodies: running hearts, running lungs, running muscles, running bones. Without a long racial history of running, these would not be what they are.

Man is a land animal. His use of other land animals for transportation has been limited and part-time. His use of machines is a last-minute innovation. For untold ages he has had to depend upon himself whenever and wherever he wanted to go. Sometimes he wanted to go in a hurry. Thus, he ran, and by running he became a man-that-runs. Had he stuck to walking, he would not be as he is today. The maximum stroke volume of his heart would never have reached the 200 cc of blood, nor its effective number of beats the 180 or so per minute that a trained runner's heart puts forth. His muscles would have contained only a fraction of the current 317 billion blood capillaries.

A historian might explain that men run because running is deep in our social history. We are all familiar with the glorious run of Pheidippides from the battle ground of Marathon to

cry, "Victory!" in the market-place of Athens. All peoples have such tales of great running. Students of the ancient Inca civilization have become aware that the very extensive system of roads throughout the widespread Inca territory was entirely for foot travel, and more specifically, for running. They had no horses or other animals for rapid transportation. Messages were sent by relay runners, each of whom ran about a mile in distance, carrying knotted ropes by which to refresh their memories of the details they were to transmit by word of mouth. Much of this running was done at 9000 feet or more over the Andes mountains, so that training must have been a matter of studious concern. Other examples from other lands could be cited.

Why do men run? A sociologist might explain man's running on the basis of the strong awareness of need that modern nations have for running, and therefore of the high recognition they give to those who succeed in it. Running is the foremost activity of all the Olympic Games. It attracts more spectators, more worldwide attention, and more representatives from more nations than any other (8:62). The rising new nations of the world are keenly aware of this showcase and of society's tendency to accept the victory of even one man as proof of the virility of an entire nation (12:47). It has not been by chance that the 1960 Olympic marathon was won by an unknown from Ethiopia, or that most of the recent world-records in running have been made by men from Australia and New Zealand.

* From *Quest,* II (April, 1964), 61-66.

To understand why men run, a sociologist also might well turn to Finland where, between 1912 and 1952, a total of a mere four millions of people produced more Olympic champions in running than any other nation. A great social need and readiness, born out of Finland's struggle for independence from the heavy hand of Russia is in evidence. Our sociologist would find that it was individual achievement which turned this social readiness into widespread participation and dedication. The victories of Kohlemainen and Stenroos over the 1912 Olympic world excited the Finnish people tremendously. They made heroes of their runners. Villages even a hundred miles north of the Arctic circle set up running clubs and excellent running facilities.

Why do men run? Psychologists might answer that to run is satisfying to the individual, that it is a "natural" activity providing a sense of achievement for its own sake. Psychologists might quote Roger Bannister, M.D., who found in running—win or lose—". . . a deep satisfaction that I cannot express in any other way . . . . I sometimes think that running has given me a glimpse of the greatest freedom that a man can ever know, because it results in the simultaneous liberation of both body and mind" (1:229). Or they might quote a great coach of runners, Arthur Lydiard of New Zealand, who said of running, "It is a simply unalloyed joy to tackle yourself on the battlefield of your own physical well-being and come out the victor" (10:46).

Psychologists also may find great resources for study in the small-group dynamics of running. England's former mile champion, Bill Nankerville, has written (11:26) of a closely-knit group of non-school running enthusiasts who nourished each other toward international levels of performance. Such great Irish runners as R. M. N. Tisdall, Ron Delany, and Noel Carroll developed out of small running clubs and the leadership and energy of individuals such as Billy Morton of Dublin. The great Gunder Haegg of Sweden probably never would have run competitively if his own father and his friends had not been interested in running and in turn motivated him (6:14). Herb Elliott also has written of his father's passion for running fitness and of their jogs on the long sea beaches when Herb was but a boy of seven (5:9). Examples could be extended endlessly.

But even more endless would be the research to ferret out the cross-currents of racial inheritances, social customs and mores, institutional incentives, family expectations, encouragements of friends, as well as the personal aggressions, impulsions, insecurities, and frustrations that can and do motivate men to run.

One of the most discerning stories of long distance running is by Alan Sillitoe, *The Loneliness of the Long Distance Runner*. When the big race is about two-thirds over, the "hero's" impulsion to prove his worth forced him to pour it on, ". . . so by the haystack I decided to leave it all behind and put on such a spurt, in spite of the nails in my guts, that before long I'd left both Gunthorpe and the birds a good way off" (13:34). Yet his sense of what he called honesty and realness would not let him win; or rather, would not let his dishonest trainer-jailer win through his efforts. In full sight of the finish line and the crowd, he deliberately slowed down, waited for his opponent to break the tape, then finished with his back straight and his eyes looking disdainfully into those of his trainer.

Few readers will suffer or even understand the twisted life that produced such a twisted motivation, but many will run with a similar tangle of likes and dislikes, tenacity and weakness, of which they are quite unaware and certainly could never put into words.

When a boy first starts to run competitively, his motives tend to be of as low an order as are his performances: to win a medal or a varsity letter, to make the team, to be one of the gang, to get one's picture in the school paper or yearbook. At this stage he is likely to understand verbal motives that are only a short step beyond what he has already experienced. The coach who emphasizes only the deeply hidden satisfactions that lie in hard work and self-discipline will find his words wasted. Even such a sensitive person as Roger Bannister admitted that, as a boy, he took up running as an escape from the gibes of his school-mates so that he would be free to do what really interested him: to be active as a student, a musician, and an actor (1:35).

Some obstacle becomes a challenge to these boys, some annoyance becomes a hobby, some inspiration cries out, "Begin!" But inspiration produces only the first few steps. During early stages, the runner may need a sort of baby's walker to hold him erect, and a fatherly voice to give encouragement. Until he was sure Gunder could go it alone, Haegg's father devised endless ways, even falsifying times on one occasion, to develop his son's confidence and belief in his future as a runner.

In the later stages motivation emerges holistically in ways that remind us of Coghill's concept of individuation (4:19-20, 88). In fact, in a few instances, running becomes almost an inescapable way of life, and certainly the focus of life. In 1957, at the age of 68, Clarence DeMar competed in a 10-mile race, notwithstanding the presence of a surgical colostomy (2:81). In 1963, at the age of 65, Percy Cerutty of Australia offered to run from Los Angeles to New York simply to demonstrate the values of running (14:8).

Of course, some men, by body structure and chemistry, are better made for and by running than others. For these men, distance running is a challenge even when it is a hardship; play even when they slave at it; fun, even when they hate it. Cerutty wrote, "Running at its best is an outpouring, a release from tensions. . . . An hour, two hours of hard training slips away as so many minutes. We become tired, exhaustingly tired, but never unhappy. It is work but it seems only fun. Exhilarating, satisfying fun" (3:17).

We may understand this statement when we realize that such attitudes were developed at Camp Portsea, Australia, where men ran along the beautiful seacoast, up great sand dunes, across open country, sometimes nude, then back, following Cerutty's uninhibited methods, to plunge at last in the cold sea. It may be harder to understand the motivations of the Englishman, W. R. Loader, who has described his early training experiences through the sooty brick and stone deserts of Clyneside, Tyneside, and Merseyside, with their coke ovens, foundries, shipyards, blast furnaces, and machine shops. In one instance he had to run through a certain tough district of his town where the handicaps of terrain were as nothing compared with the derisive jeers of the onlookers, especially of the girls:

"Yah, look at the runner coming! . . . Mary Ann, look, it's a runner! He's got nae claes on!" Faces rose up all around, derisive, jeering, insulting. A scabby mongrel dog snapped at the heels, delighted for once to discover that someone else's life was being made a misery. Urchins sprinted alongside, mocking the runner's strides with their own exaggerated movements. It was a torment of the soul far more bitter than any torture of the body. And through it all one had to run with measured step, eyes fixed ahead as if unaware of the tumult, trying to abolish it by ignoring it. . . . But it is a hard thing for youth to set itself alone against spite and hostility. I did that run a number of times and never faced it without a premonitory chill of the spine. Having stood the jeers to the point where I could persuade myself I wasn't giving up through cowardice, I quietly abandoned the practice. (9:61)

Although Loader's experiences and his way of relating them may seem unusual, the hindrances and distractions of social environment often are deterrents to why men run, or better, why men continue to run. Herb Elliott was only 22 when he retired from running; his best running years potentially were still ahead of him. But following his world-record at Dublin in 1959, he was granted a three-year scholarship at Cambridge University and, along with his regular studies, had to cram a four-year Latin course into nine months. He met and married Ann Dudley and had a son and often found himself thinking of his family debts while listening to Cerutty's exhortations toward greater running efforts.

Percy and I weren't on the same wave-length . . . . It surely wasn't indolence that kept me from training. It was my realization that as a family man . . . training was not as important in my career . . . . Running was a job that had to be fitted in between my other activities. (5:88)

We must accept the fact, therefore, that the demands of vocation and family and everyday fun do limit the kind and amount of running that men do. That amateur running is avocational is an even more essential concept than that it must receive no material reward.

I began this article by saying that men, even modern men, are men-that-run, that their vital organs and systems and chemistry are as they are partly because man ran long before he became homo sapiens. To say that running is socially recognized or personally satisfying cheapens the argument, makes running an artificial action that waits upon cultural whims and gadgets. Running is not so much a tool of the new emerging nations as an inherent part of a man-society-nature interactions. Not to run, even to a modern man, is as unthinkable as not to eat, or not to sleep, or not to make love.

But try as I may, I shall never say it as well as did Brutus Hamilton, head coach of the University of California and the 1948 U.S. Olympic track team:

People may wonder why young men like to run distance races. What fun is it? Why all that hard, exhausting work? Where is the good of it? It is one of the strange ironies of this strange life that those who work the hardest, who subject themselves to the strictest discipline, who give up certain pleasurable things in order to achieve a goal, are the happiest of men. When you see 20 or 30 young men line up for a distance race in some meet, don't pity them, don't feel sorry for them. Better envy them instead. You are probably looking at the 20 or 30 best "bon vivants" in the world. They are completely and joyously happy in their simple tastes, their strong and well-conditioned bodies, and with the thrill of wholesome competition before them. These are the days of their youth, when they can run without weariness; these are their buoyant, golden days; and they are running because they love it. Their lives are fuller because of this competition and their memories will be far richer. That's why men love to run. That's why men do run. There is something clean and noble about it. (7:7)

REFERENCES

1. Bannister, Roger. *The Four Minute Mile.* New York: Dodd, Mead & Company, 1955.
2. Bock, Arlie V. "The Circulation of a Marathoner," *The Journal of Sports Medicine and Physical Fitness,* III (June-September, 1963).
3. Cerutty, Percy. "Running with Cerutty," *Track and Field News,* 1959.
4. Coghill, G. E. *Anatomy and the Problem of Behavior.* New York: Cambridge University Press, American Branch, 1929.
5. Elliott, Herb, as told to Alan Trengrove. *The Golden Mile.* London: Cassell & Company, Ltd., 1961.
6. Haegg, Gunder. *Gunder Haegg's Dagbook.* Stockholm: Tidens Forlag, 1952.
7. Hamilton, Brutus. "Why Men Like To Run," *Coaching Newsletter,* II (July, 1957).
8. Jokl, Ernst, et al. *Sports In The Cultural Pattern Of The World.* A paper prepared for the Institute of Occupational Health, Helsinki, 1956.
9. Loader, W. R. *Testament Of A Runner.* London: William Heinemann Ltd., 1960.
10. Lydiard, Arthur and Garth Gilmour. *Run To The Top.* London: Herbert Jenkins, Ltd., 1962.
11. Nankeville, Bill. *The Miracle Of The Mile.* London: Stanley Paul and Co., Ltd., 1956.
12. Natan, Alex. "Sport and Politics," *Sport And Society.* London: Bowes & Bowes, Ltd., 1958.
13. Sillitoe, Alan. *The Loneliness of the Long Distance Runner.* New York: New American Library of World Literature, 1959.
14. *Track and Field News,* September, 1963.

The Symbolic Power of Sport*

ELEANOR METHENY

For some years now I have been trying to enrich my own understanding of the educational potential of sport by talking with people who know much more about sport than I do. I have talked with football players who have told me that playing football is one of the most meaningful experiences of their lives. I have heard one lineman talk about "the explosion of joy" he experiences whenever he brings every ounce of his 240 pounds into play. "It's beautiful," he said; and then he added: "I've never said that word out loud before—but it is the right word, and I want to say it."

I have seen a gymnast's eyes grow bright with tears of genuine emotion as he talked about the feeling of wholeness he finds in doing a giant swing. And I have heard a ping pong player say: "Maybe this sounds silly—but somehow for me its the greatest—the most. I don't know how to say this, but somehow all of me is there when I knock that silly little ball back and forth across the table—and it is important in a way I can't describe."

I asked her if she knew Wallace Stevens' lines about an experience that was "like a flow of meanings with no speech—and of as many meanings as of men." She liked these lines, and she wrote them down, saying: "Yes, that's what ping pong is. Was Wallace Stevens a ping pong player?"

And again and again these men and women

* Presented at the Annual Convention of the Eastern District Association for Health, Physical Education and Recreation, Washington, D.C., April 26, 1968.

—and boys and girls—who have found such important meanings in sport competition said: "I've never said these things out loud before." And most of them said: "Thank you for giving me a chance to talk about these things." And one veteran coach said: "It is good to know that one physical educator understands and cares about sport in this way. How wonderful it would be if they could all stand up and 'tell it like it is' without yakking around about physical fitness and character building."

None of them quoted the poetry of Wallace Stevens to me—but many of them recognized this bit of verse as a statement of their own feelings about sport competition.

> I measure myself
> Against a tall tree.
> I find that I am much taller,
> For I reach right up to the sun
> With my eye. . .
>
> Nevertheless, I dislike
> The way the ants crawl
> In and out of my shadow.

Tonight I want to talk about some of the meanings I have found in my own experiences as a competitor on the symbolic field of sport, as a spectator, and as a physical educator. Much of what I shall say is a composite of what I have learned in many conferences with men and women who love sport as much as you do —and with the same ambivalence—and for the same reasons. So perhaps you may wish to validate some of my generalizations by ex-

221

ploring your own feelings about your own favorite form of sport competition as we go along.

No one knows how long men have been competing with each other on the rule-governed field of sport. No one knows when the first rule-governed sport contest was held. But certainly the custom of holding sport contests at funerals was well established by the time of the Trojan Wars—which were fought during the 12th century B.C. And fortunately for all historians, Homer did describe one of these symbolic contests in the *Iliad*—which was written some four hundred years later. So I shall start with this chapter in the long and always controversial history of sport.

As you probably remember, Patroclus was a nobleman, a warrior, and a hero who died on the bloody plains of Troy. In his brief lifetime, he had done well and gloriously all that the gods might expect of such a man; he had done well and gloriously all that such a man might expect of himself. And so, at his funeral, his companions thought it fitting to remind the gods of "the excellence of Patroclus" by re-enacting some of his glorious deeds on the man-made field of sport.

Thus, his companions threw javelins, hurled stones, drove horse-drawn chariots at full speed, ran as fast as they could run, and wrestled with each other in hand-to-hand combat. But they did not perform these actions in the same way that Patroclus had performed them in the heat of battle.

On the battlefield a warrior is not interested in demonstrating how far he can throw a spear. He is interested in killing his enemies, and in saving his own life. As he throws his spear at other men who may be running toward him with their own spears at the ready, he must adjust his aim and force to the requirements of the moment, and he must keep his own guard up to ward off the spears and arrows of the enemy. As he throws, other warriors may jostle him, his feet may slip in the muck, he may be off balance, or his throw may be hampered or hindered by any one of a dozen other circumstances. Thus, he seldom gets a chance to throw his spear as far as he can possibly throw it by giving it everything he has.

In the funeral competitions, the Greek warriors created this chance for themselves. They ruled out the hindering and hampering requirements of war by defining the act of spear throwing as a voluntary action, which a man might choose to perform for his own reasons. They abstracted the pattern of the spear throwing action from the confusion of warfare and described it as the inconsequential act of throwing a stick at empty space.

They specified when and where this action was to be performed by announcing a time for the competition and defining the boundaries of the field. They eliminated all need to debate about the motives and intentions of other men by imposing the same standards of conduct on all competitors—and by appointing an official judge who was empowered to enforce these man-made rules. And they answered all questions about how each man's performance might be evaluated by spelling out what "counted" in unequivocal terms.

Thus, as each man stepped up to the starting line on the rule-governed field of sport, he knew precisely what he was going to try to do; he knew how the outcomes of his efforts were to be evaluated—and by whom; and he knew that he had a fair chance to perform that action as well as he could perform it—a fair chance to exert his own utmost effort in the performance of one human action.

Freed of all the hampering effects of war, he was free to go all out, holding nothing back—free to focus all the energies of his being on one supreme attempt to hurl his javelin at the nothingness of empty space.

He was free to throw his stick as far as he could throw it. He was free to run as fast as he could run—to hit as hard as he could hit—to leap, to jump—as high, as far—as he could leap and jump. He was free to match his strength with the strength of other men in open combat. He was free to involve every fiber of his mortal being in the performance of one human action. He was free to focus all the forces of his being on one supreme attempt to impose his own man-made design on the universe of his existence.

The Greek warriors created this moment of freedom for themselves—and for all men—by devising the most restrictive set of rules men have ever made for themselves. They devised the prototype of the man-made rules that now govern all sport competition.

These rules are paradoxical. They restrict in order to free. They impose restrictions on human behavior, and they limit human action; but within those restrictions they offer every man an opportunity to know the feeling of being wholly free to go all out—free to do his utmost—free to use himself fully in the performance of one self-chosen human action.

These paradoxical rules create this man-made moment of freedom by ruling out the conditions and considerations of human reality, and by ruling in the pattern of an idealized world in which every man might be and do whatever he is capable of being and doing—an ideal world in which every man might be free to pursue his own interests—an ideal world in which every man might function at his best—an ideal world in which every man might make full use of all the energies of his mortal being, unhampered and unhindered by the demands imposed by the realities of his existence.

Or we might say, in the words of Wallace Stevens, the rules of sport propose

A new text for the world,
A scribble of fret and fear and fate,
From a bravura of the mind,
A courage of the eye . . .
A text of intelligent men
At the center of the unintelligible . . .

In the funeral competitions, the Greek warriors did not show the gods how well Patroclus had actually performed the actions of his life in the heat of battle. They showed the gods—and other men—how well each competitor actually did perform the empty action of throwing a javelin through space under ideal circumstances which offered each competitor a fair chance to do his utmost as a man among men.

Perhaps we would all like to think that the Greek warriors performed these symbolic actions with great dignity. Perhaps we would like to think that all men exhibit their best behavior on the symbolic field of sport. But Homer's description of the funeral games does not support this exalted theory. And neither do our own experiences.

So let it be said to the glory of the Greek warriors—and to the glory of all competitors from that day to this—that most of them did honor their own restrictive man-made rules. They did give every man who entered into the competitions a fair chance to function at his utmost. But they also argued with the officials and with each other. They boasted; they bragged; they belittled the powers of other men; they devised strategies that gave them advantage over other competitors; and some of them cheated when the officials were not looking. They were aggressive; they displayed their hostilities; and they revealed all their anxious doubts and fears about themselves, their gods, and other men on the symbolic field of sport.

The actions men perform in sport are indeed symbolic actions—but a sport contest is not a ritual. It is not a symbolic pageant. It is not a cool-headed philosophical debate about human motives and values. It is an emotional moment of commitment to the values of human action—and the emotions aroused by that commitment and those actions are powerful emotions.

In that moment of commitment to the values he attaches to his own human actions, no competitor has time to rationalize about his own feelings and his own motivations. In that moment of all-out action he must experience himself as he is, in all the complexity of his own feelings about himself, his gods, and other men who claim the right to share the universe of his existence.

Or, as the competitors in the early Olympic Games put it, on the symbolic field of sport "every man stands naked before his gods" and reveals himself as he is in the fullness of his own human powers. Stripped of all self-justifying excuses by the rules of sport, he must involve himself in the performance of one self-chosen task. Naked of all pretense, he must use himself as he is, and he must demonstrate his ability to use himself fully, under circumstances which permit him to function in the wholeness of his being as a man.

If he is a proud man, he must experience his own pride. If he is domineering man, he must experience his own need to dominate the lives of other men. So, too, a neurotic man must use sport to satisfy his own neurotic needs; a resentful man must know his own resentments; and an anxious man his anxieties. An idealistic man must recognize his ideals—and the conflicts he experiences as he tries to live up to those ideals; a loving man will reveal his love; and a fearful hating man will experience his own fearful hate.

Yes, a man may learn much about himself—and about all men—on the symbolic field of sport. In those self-revealing moments of commitment to the values of human action he may know himself at his best—but equally he must also know himself at his worst. And he cannot escape the implications of either image because this is what he is, this is how he feels, and this is what he does in a situation that offers him a fair chance to use himself fully in the performance of one self-chosen human action.

Yes . . .   I measure myself
Against a tall tree.
I find that I am much taller,
For I reach right up to the sun
With my eye . . .

Nevertheless, I dislike
The way the ants crawl
In and out of my shadow.

Many of the sport contests invented by the companions of Patroclus have endured for more than three thousand years—and most of them will be hotly contested in Mexico City come October. But human inventiveness in sport was not exhausted by the ingenuity of the Greeks.

During the Middle Ages, the kings and noblemen of feudal Europe found new ways to compete with each other in the colorful tournaments that symbolized their own excellence as warriors. They, too, took some of the practical and effective actions of their lives and redefined them as impractical and futile actions that produced nothing of material value. They, too, devised rules that gave every competitor a fair chance to use himself fully in the performance of one symbolic action.

For example, they converted the useful and necessary actions a nobleman might perform as he rode his horse into the thick of battle into a series of "knightly exercises;" and they competed with each other in the performance of these actions. In Mexico City, men and women will still compete with each other in terms of their ability to perform those twisting, turning, hanging, swinging, and vaulting actions—but they will not ride into the arena on the back of a spirited horse. Rather, they will perform those symbolic actions on the back of a stationary and leather-covered horse, and on other equally symbolic pieces of apparatus—familiar to all persons who have ever attended a gymnastic meet.

The hard-working peasants who tilled the fields of the feudal lords did not compete in their tournaments. In time of war they did not ride into battle on horseback. They slogged it out on foot, hurling huge rocks at the enemy, and pooled their strength in attempts to push heavy battering rams through the gates of neighboring strongholds.

Perhaps these hard-working peasants recognized the values of cooperative effort. Perhaps they recognized that men who are individually inconsequential can sometimes achieve their purposes by working together as a team. More probably they did not. But in either case, they did devise sport forms that exemplify this principle—for these hard-working peasants invented the prototype of all team sports.

Initially, these team competitions were little more than mass mayhem—because there were few rules and no officials in those days. One group of peasants tried to push a huge boulder in one direction; an opposing group tried to push it in the opposite direction; and surely every peasant worked out many of his frustrations, his aggressions, and his hostilities as he got into the act. But gradually, rules were defined, the boundaries of the field were marked out, and sticks were set up to represent the gates of the enemy's castle—and you may see those symbolic gates today on the goal lines of every soccer, football, and hockey field. Gradually, too, the heavy rock was reduced in size, and took on the shape of a sphere—and eventually this sphere-shaped ball became the object of contest in many different team sports.

Much has been written about the ball as a symbolic representation of our ball-shaped earth. Perhaps the peasants who threw and kicked such balls on the symbolic field of sport noticed this resemblance; more probably they were not consciously aware of it. But in either case it may be noted that the ball did become a familiar object of contest at about the time Columbus proved that the world of man's existence is indeed a sphere.

As feudal Europe was gradually reorganized into the more complex social patterns of the Renaissance, the old feudal lords were transformed into a new class of human beings called gentlemen. These gentlemen did not work with their hands; they did not maintain their social position by displays of muscular power. Rather, they prided themselves on their ability to deal with the world by using their wits—and by employing all manner of strategic devices.

These gentlemen exhibited little interest in the rough team sports of the muscular peasants. Rather, they developed new sport forms which symbolized their own ways of dealing with the forces of mass, space, and time.

In the sports that symbolized the actions of gentlemen—as exemplified by tennis and golf—each man performed alone, or perhaps with one partner, and his opponents were always men of equal social rank. The rules for these sports prohibited any bodily contact between players, and there was little direct contact with the object of contest. Rather, a light ball was manipulated with a device or implement which greatly extended the player's reach and force; and this implement was wielded with skill, dexterity, and strategy, rather than with the greatest possible muscular effort.

Did these gentlemen recognize the resemblance between their sport effort and their conception of themselves as gentlemen who manipulated the things of earth with ease, skill, and light implements? Probably not. But we may conjecture that they found satisfaction in these sports because they were consonant with their own self-image.

Moving now toward our own time, we may note that the invention of new ball games came to an end during the 19th century—with the invention of basketball in 1891 and the invention of volleyball in 1895. And we may note that the new sports of the 20th century exhibit very different patterns of organization.

Today, men have extended their concern for the earthly globe to a vision of the farthest reaches of the universe, and their expectations of exploring that universe are based on their mastery over complex machines and atomic sources of power. Both of these conceptions are reflected in the new sport forms that have been developed in recent years.

In sky diving, for example, the diver utilizes the man-made power of mechanical flight to carry himself to the heights of the sky—from which he descends with great skill, using his parachute only in the final moments of the dive. In scuba diving, the diver uses the discoveries of modern science and technology to equip himself for his descent into the depths of the sea. And in all forms of mechanized racing, men control the power of motorized vehicles on land, on sea, and in the air—even as they may use these vehicles in machine-to-machine combat in such events as the destruction derby.

These new sports symbolize "the excellence of Patroclus" in terms that reflect the hopes, dreams, and accomplishments of men now living in the latter days of the 20th century—and it seems likely that many men and women, boys and girls, are interested in them for that reason. But, equally, many other men and women, boys and girls, are interested in performing the symbolic actions that the Greek warriors performed three thousand years ago. So we must not try to account for the symbolic power of sport by describing it in terms of the work men do.

Perhaps a contestant may find a particular sport particularly meaningful because it does formulate his conception of himself as a man who performs certain kinds of work. Perhaps he may also choose a sport because it formulates the basic patterns of his own personality structure—as some psychologists and psychiatrists have suggested. Perhaps he finds a particular sport particularly interesting because his own physical being is so admirably designed for the performance of that action. Perhaps he chooses it because he was introduced to it at an early age and became in-

volved in the challenge it provided. Or perhaps he chooses it for the same reason a mountain climber may choose to scale Mt. Everest—simply because it is there.

Perhaps he chooses to ski because he likes the feeling of cold air as it stings his face, or because he likes the whiteness of snow and the blueness of the sky. Perhaps he chooses to swim because he likes the sensation of being supported by water—or the feeling of being engulfed by its oceanic depths. Perhaps he likes contact sports because he likes the feeling of slamming his body against the body of another person with all his force—or perhaps he avoids the contact sports for the opposite reason. Perhaps he likes the open air and sunlit greenness he finds on the golf course. Perhaps he likes the smell of sweat—or the feeling of being confined in a closed space. Perhaps, perhaps, perhaps . . . for who can account for all the likes and dislikes of human beings?

I think that all of these factors are relevant to the choices men may make in sport. I think all of them provide some insight into men's reasons for preferring one sport rather than another. But I also think they are secondary to men's interest in the symbolic power of sport, as such.

During the past ten years I have talked with many men and women, and many boys and girls, about the dimensions of their interest in the rule-governed competitions of sport. In those conversations, I have heard many explanations—but always, sooner or later, I have heard the word "freedom." Freedom to go all out, holding nothing back—freedom to focus all the energies of my own mortal being on the voluntary performance of one self-chosen human action—freedom to experience myself at my own utmost as a whole-hearted, fully motivated, fully integrated, and fully functioning human being.

Many of these performers testified that their all-out efforts in sport had improved their physiological functioning and made them more fit for the rigors of their daily lives. Others mentioned permanently damaged ankles, knees, hip joints, shoulder joints, necks and fingers. One was wearing a steel plate in his skull; another was wearing a back brace. But none of them told me that they had entered into competition for the purpose of becoming physically fit. Rather they had become more fit—or less fit—because they had engaged in competition for its own sake. (And in all truth, all of them knew that there are many quicker and easier and more efficient ways to develop muscular strength, flexibility, speed, and cardio-respiratory endurance.)

Yes, of course, the all-out effort of sport competition can improve physiological functioning—and I am interested in improving the physiological functioning of every school child. But this is not why I want to give every child a fair chance to compete on the symbolic field of sport during the school day.

The meanings I have found in my own involvement in sport are important meanings. I value them as I value the meanings I have found in my own involvement in poetry, drama, music, science, philosophy, history, mathematics, sculpture and dance. I value them with the most important meanings I have found in my own commitment to the values of human action. I value them as some of the most important meanings I have found in my own commitment to the values of education.

I think you do too. I think every member of the Eastern District Association for Health, Physical Education and Recreation values the meanings he has found in sport in this way.

And so I am doing my own utmost to persuade my colleagues in education—and particularly my colleagues in health education, physical education, and recreation—that sport is truly "a flow of meanings without speech"— and "of as many meanings as of men." I am telling my colleagues that they have been undervaluing the educational potential of sport for a long, long time. And I am urging them— as I am urging you—to re-examine the meanings they have found in their own glorious moments of all-out effort on the symbolic field of sport. And I am urging you, too, to stand up proudly in the forums of education and "tell it like it is."

The Socialization of Sport

JAN FELSHIN

Although the sources of sport meaning are personal, the modes by which meaning is fulfilled and understood are largely socialized. The structure of sport and meaningfulness of the sport experience, therefore, is a dual concept, and explicatory analysis depends upon some cognizance of the mutuality of personal sources and socialized modes of meaning. "Meaning," because it is derived only with reference to experiencing, is always personal. "Structure," however, is the means by which abstract concepts are rendered concrete and assured of a continuing existence; it achieves this function best when it is non-personal.

The effort to understand man-in-sport has focused on analysis of both man and sport. The hypothesis that the structure and reality of sport are particularly satisfying to human motivation is obviously valid. The problem is that the reality of structure is an objective, non-personal view, and human motivation is a personal construct. Both, however, are symbolically significant. Better understanding of man-in-sport depends upon clarifying concepts focused on the interactive nature of sport-experiencing; that is, the socialized aspects of meaning provided and affirmed by the structure of sport, and the structure itself as a framework for the description of the meaning of sport.

The "essence" of sport has been described in several ways: as its defining characteristics; as the "spirit" requisite to its conduct; as appropriate motivations, and even as structure. For the purposes of this discussion, the "essence" of sport is the descriptive expression of the most crucial characteristics of play, contest,

and performance. There are, of course, a host of related qualifying and enlarging concepts involved, but they do seem to emerge from these three features. The "structure" of sport, then, is simply the framework of rules that orders and controls its conduct, and these refer most specifically to the sport itself. Beyond the structure of any sport, however, there is a "context" within which it is carried on, and this, too, may be structured by rules and policies as well as a prevailing spirit. All sport organizations, for instance, are contexts for sport.

On the most obvious level, the structure of sport and of particular sports should evolve as refinements necessary to preserve and enhance the essence of sport; and, of course, it does. As players "beat" a game, a sport becomes less exciting, uncertain, or suspenseful, and the rules are changed. This development is obvious to all of us who have watched basketball players get taller, and "dunking" and goaltending rules emerge. Sport structures are rendered obsolete by technology, too, and rules are also changed to protect the essential spirit. As the substance and design of bows and arrows have become more and more sophisticated, the target faces have become smaller, and more precise refinements of scoring and shooting distance have emerged. Almost any rulechange in sport exemplifies the relationship of structure to the crucial characteristics of sport on this level. The thesis here accepts that the sport experience is understood best within a view of the structure of sport as the means by which man pursues and experiences the essence

227

of sport. Beyond that, however, it is suggested that the structure and contexts are modalities which define the essence of sport *at it has been socialized.*

To examine this assumption is to explore the structure of sport, in general or in particular, in relationship to its own crucial characteristics and to societal influences. The notion of "contest," for instance, is characteristic of all that is sport, but one contests one's own prior performance, or the abilities of others, or the potential forces and dangers of man, machine, or nature itself. Even chance can be contested as surely as time or energy. It is simplistic to conclude that somehow competition is meaningful to man and serves as a pervasive explanation of the continuing attraction of sport. Although the structures of sport affirm the characteristics of contest (by providing for an uncertain outcome and, wherever possible, equality of competition), the meanings that accrue to any individual may transcend the obvious outcome of "winning" or "losing." The construct of "striving" or of "mastery;" of "community" or "engagement;" of "dependence" or "singularity" may be the mode of meaning in competition. "Perseverance," "pain," and "sacrifice" are as clearly understood sport references as are "joy," "freedom," and "fulfillment." And the compatibility of the juxtaposed constructs is not clarified within considerations of only the structure and essence of sport itself.

Social dispositions provide modes which affect both the structure of sport and the way the essence of sport is conceived and experienced. The relationship of sport and society is an indisputable one. This relationship has been described in the consideration of sport as a social institution. Usually, however, it is only the various contexts of sport which have been considered. In that view, the society is seen as an important variable affecting such things as: what sports are popular; spectator and fan involvement; use of communications media; economic and commercial relationships, and perhaps socialization, social stratification and age and sex as sport elements. Attendant psychological concerns reflect the whole realm of questions which center around the human motivations which seem most crucial to the sport experience, and most appropriate in light of the social factors. Beyond these concerns, however, sport and society are inextricably related, *and the structure of sport describes and defines the refinement of its essence as a social modality.*

In subtle and unnoticed ways, then, social modes actually interact with the essential characteristics of sport and influence them. It is a complex process because in the United States, at least, the importance of sport and its connotations have led to wide symbolic usage. Sport reflects both "ideal" and traditional values; it reflects actual values, and it may reflect valuing which emerges from need or deficiency. "Contest" in our technological society still reflects our enduring value and pursuit of excellence of performance, but it also reflects our pursuit of the kind of control and mastery that are technical and mechanical. And the technological complexity with which the individual is hopelessly confronted in this society may serve to heighten his desire for such control.

It seems, then, that the notion of "contest" is still essential to the sport experience, but its modality may be a kind of non-personal mastery. If so, the essence of sport as a source of meaning is modified and socialized to define the spirit of "striving" and "contest" in changed ways. This hypothesis can be documented only by more intensive analysis of the changing structures of sport, but there is a great deal of evidence to suggest its validity. This relationship cannot be singular, of course, but neither is it logical to believe that individuals in a material, instrumental culture can experience the "joys" of competition as they have been understood in the past to express the essence of sport. It is more probable that the "joys" of competition now describe altered modes of experiencing joy, and the essence of sport has been modified.

However "play" is defined, it serves to represent a host of assumptions accepted as characteristic of sport. These assumptions describe sport as a structured reality of its own and differentiate between the seriousness of the "real" world and the seriousness of the "sport" world. Obviously, sport cannot be viewed as "trivial" within the bounds of its own domain, but, still, the domain itself is understood to be a land of "make-believe" wherein a player can both be and do his best. The realm of sport is available whenever men are appropriately dressed, equipped, and interested. And one enters the sport world as soon as he perceives turf and lime as a football field, black paint and hardwood floors as a basketball court, or even a creek in the woods as a fishing site. The essence of sport as play must contain dimensions of "let's pretend" as well as a kind of voluntary eagerness to participate.

The structure of both sport and its contexts has been defined to enhance the play-essence of sport. Why would one distinguish "amateurs" and "professionals" with contextual qualifications except on the assumption that one was more truly "sport"? The professional athlete obviously has committed himself to the essence of sport because he plays, but he has not separated himself from a "real" world insofar as money is a social and not an athletic symbol. If both motivation and reward are external to the world of sport, it cannot be defined as play. Societal pressures to succeed, to earn, to compare, and to evaluate means only with reference to ends has led sport to a kind of deadly earnestness and disregard for idealized behavior that is the antithesis of play. The fact of "players" as a category describing neither an amateur nor a professional tennis player; the accepted procedures by which schoolboy super-stars are courted, and the use of the Olympics as a commercial opportunity by the athletes themselves are only a few examples of the socialization of sport.

The "evils" and "exploitation" of athletics have been widely decried for a long time. And if the essence of sport is subordinated to motives and values with which it is not consistent, it is being exploited. In the larger view, however, if sport survives, it can be assumed that its essential features still exist. Even professional sport can be viewed as play if it is understood that play in the United States has come to be satisfying in its seriousness and obligatory aspects. The socialization of play has led away from notions of frolic and amorphous "freedom" toward responsibility and commitment within structured assignments and roles. Neither the major leaguer nor the little leaguer thinks for one moment that play is supposed to mean being non-accountable; the modality of playing has been socialized, but play has not necessarily been denied.

The perfection of performance is another factor defining the essence of sport. But whereas Knute Rockne based his coaching on a plea for "sacrifice," the promise of "pay-off" is more prevalent today. There is no doubt that "excellence" is both a social and sport value; enduring and contemporaneous. But the social modes of striving and perseverance as valuable processes have, perhaps, been supplanted by the notion that means and ends are different and unrelated, and the process is evaluated by the outcome. The essence of sport, as the struggle toward perfection and the giving of one's best even in a losing effort, has been modified by a society that measures performance only by the highest standard. The individual, even the best performer, loses the essence of sport as performance in a world of super-stars and super-bowls, for sport as experiencing is negated. In this sense, the modality of meaning is non-personal, and that refutes meaningfulness. Some of the effects of the increasing concern with the "products" of sport performance are seen in the ways in which performance is evaluated. More and more, there is an effort to objectify the measurement of sport, to control the conditions of performance, and to use all of the technological devices that dehumanize by dichotomizing the human from his own body and its efforts. When training, team selection, strategy choices and, of course, outcomes are programmed or predicted by computers, the mode of experiencing the essence of the struggle toward perfection and victory has been altered.

The contexts and structure of sport have changed with perceptions of performance as a non-personal essence of sport. The non-personal modality permits the use of drugs or any other substance to improve performance and even transcend human abilities if such were possible. The necessity for scientific testing to determine the sex of competitors is apparent testimony to the importance of the ends of victory or medals and willingness to separate that achievement even from one's own sexual identity. Somehow, all the necessary testing of racehorses, though not consistent with beliefs about the essence of sport as excellence of performance, is not as striking as such testing of human competitors would seem, perhaps because the personal meaning of striving and effort are understood.

The structure of sport, then, is descriptive of its own essential characteristics and the processes of socialization by which these are experienced. If it is assumed that society imposes its meanings on sport to increasingly greater degrees, then sport will simply become more and more like society. There is another possibility, however. Areas of human actualization which are most frustrated by a culture can become a society's most cogent needs. Because of the separate and symbolic nature of sport, the modes of experiencing it are just as likely to derive from these needs or aspirations of society as from social realities. It has already become obvious that some sport cultures are resisting organized and complex structures and affirming open and personal contexts for the pursuit of these sports. The sport modalities, then, are still socialized, but express the choice of sport for its potential actualization of dispositions which are not pervasive in social experience.

Philosophy on the Bleachers*

GEORGE SANTAYANA

In this early summer there is always an answer ready for the man who asks you, "Why do you go to games, why do you waste your time upon the bleachers?" The balm of the air, the lazy shadows of the afternoon, when it is too warm for a walk and too early for dinner, the return of the slack tide between lectures and examinations—all form a situation in which the path of least resistance often leads to Holmes Field. But although these motives lie ready as an excuse, and we may find them plausible, there remains a truer and less expressible interest behind. Motives are always easy to assign, unless we wish to get at the real one. Those little hypocrisies of daily life by which we elude the evils of self-analysis can blind us to our most respectable feelings. We make ourselves cheap to make ourselves intelligible. How often, for instance, do people excuse themselves, as it were, for going to church; the music is so good, the parson such an old friend, the sermon so nearly a discourse of reason. Yet these evasions leave untouched the ultimate cause why churches exist and why people go to them—a cause not to be assigned without philosophy. And it seems to me that similarly in this phenomenon of athletics there is an underlying force, a power of human nature, that commonly escapes us. We talk of the matter with a smile as of a fad or a frolic, a meaningless pastime to which serious things are in danger of being sacrificed. Towards the vague idea of these "serious

* From *Harvard Monthly*, XVIII (July, 1894), 181-190.

things," which might upon inspection be reduced almost without a remainder to the getting of money, we assume an attitude of earnest concern, and we view the sudden irruption of the sporting spirit with alarm and deprecation, but without understanding. Yet some explanation of the monster might perhaps be given, and as I have here a few pages to fill and nothing of moment to communicate, I allow my pen to wander in the same direction as my feet, for a little ramble in the athletic field.

If it is not mere indolence that brings the spectators to our games, neither is it the mere need of healthy exercise that brings the players. The least acquaintance with them or their spirit is enough to convince one of this truth; and yet both friends and enemies of athletics are sometimes found speaking of them as a means of health, as an exercise to keep the mind clear and the body fit for work. That is a function which belongs rather to gymnastics, although the training for games may incidentally accomplish it. If health was alone or chiefly pursued, why should we not be satisfied with some chest-weights in our bedroom, a walk, or a ride, or a little swimming in summer? What could be gained by organized teams, traditional rivalries, or great contests where much money is spent and some bones possibly broken? It is amusing to hear people who are friendly to athletics by instinct or associations labouring to justify them on this ground. However much one may love buoyancy and generosity, and hate a pinched and sordid mind, one cannot help yielding the victory to the enemy when the battle is waged upon this utilitarian ground. Even arguments like those which the *New York Nation,* a paper often so intelligent, propounded not long ago on the subject of football, might then seem relevant, and if relevant conclusive. We should be led to believe that since athletics outrun the sphere of gymnastics, they have no sphere at all. The question why, then, they have come to exist would then pertinently occur, and might lead to unexpected results; but it is a question which the *Nation* and those of like mind need not answer, since to be silent is an ancient privilege of man of which the wise often avail themselves.

Now athletics have a higher function than gymnastics and a deeper basis than utility. They are a response to a natural impulse and exist only as an end in themselves. That is the reason why they have a kind of nobility which the public is quick to recognise, and why "professionalism" is so fatal to them. Professionalism introduces an alien and mercenary motive; but the valetudinarian motive is no less alien, and only harmless because so limited in scope. When the French, for instance shocked at the feeble health and ugliness of their school-boys, send commissioners to England and America to study athletics and the possibility of introducing them into France, the visitors return horrified at the brutality of Anglo-Saxon youth, and recommend some placid kind of foot-ball or some delightful form of non-competitive rowing, as offering all the advantages of fresh air and exercise, without the dangers and false excitements of the English practices. Any gymnastics, with or without pink tights, the French may easily introduce; they are no whit inferior to other nations in this field, as the professional circus can testify. But to introduce athletics into France there must be more than a change of ministry; there would have to be a change of ancestry. For such things are in the blood, and the taste and capacity for them must be inborn or developed by national experiences.

From a certain point of view we may blame athletic enthusiasm as irrational. The athletic temper is indeed not particularly Athenian, not vivacious, sensitive, or intelligent. It is rather Spartan, active, courageous, capable of serious enthusiasm and more ready to endure discipline than to ask for an ultimate reason for that devotion. But this reproach or irrationality ultimately falls upon every human interest, since all in the last analysis rest upon an instinct and not upon a rational necessity. Among the Greeks, to be sure, games had a certain relation to war; some of the contests were with weapons, and were valued for developing martial qualities of soul and body. The relation of athletics to war is intimate, but it is not one of means to end, but more intrinsic, like that of the drama to life. It was not the utility of athletics for war that supported the Greek games; on the contrary, the games arose from the comparative freedom from war, and the consequent liberation of martial energy from the stimulus of necessity, and the expression of it in beautiful and spectacular forms. A certain analogy to war, a certain semblance of dire struggle, are therefore of the essence of athletics. Like war, they demand an organization of activities for the sake of victory. But here the victory is not sought for the sake of any further advantage. There is nothing to conquer or defend except the honour of success. War can thus become a luxury and flower into artistic forms, whenever the circumstances of life no longer drain all the energy native to the character. For this reason athletics flourish only among nations that are comparatively young, free, and safe, like the Greek towns and those American and Australian communities which, in athletics as distinguished from private sport, bid fair to outdo their mother country.

The essential distinction between athletics and gymnastics may help us to understand some other characteristics of our sports. They must, for instance, be confined to a few. Where so much time, skill and endurance are required, as in great athletic contests, the majority is necessarily excluded. If we were dealing with an instrument of health, a safety-valve or balance wheel to an overstrained system, the existence of an athletic aristocracy would be an anomaly. But the case is otherwise. We are dealing with an art in which only the few, the exceptionally gifted, can worthily succeed. Nature must be propitious, circumstances must be favourable, patience and inspiration must not fail. There is an athletic aristocracy for the same reason that there is one of intelligence and one of fashion, because men have different endowments, and only a few can do each thing as well as it is capable of being done. Equality in these respects would mean total absence of excellence. The analogy of moral and practical things would mislead us in this sphere. Comfort or happiness would seem to lose nothing of their value if they were subdivided, and a proportional fraction given to each individual: such an equal distribution of them might even seem a gain, since it would prevent envy, and satisfy a certain sense of mathematical justice. But the opposite happens in the arts. The value of talent, the beauty and dignity of positive achievements, depend on the height reached, and not on the number that reach it. Only the supreme is interesting: the rest has value only as leading to it or reflecting it. Still, although the achievement is rare, the benefit of it is diffused; we all participate through the imagination in the delight and meaning of what lies beyond our power of accomplishment. A few moments of enjoyment and intuition, scattered throughout our lives, are what lift the whole of it from vulgarity. They form a background of comparison, a standard of values, and a magnet for the estimation of tendencies, without which all our thought would be perfunctory and dull. Enthroned in those best moments, art, religion, love, and the other powers of the imagination, govern our character, and silently direct the current of our common thoughts.

Now, in its sphere, athletic sport has a parallel function. A man whose enthusiasm it has stirred in youth, has one more chamber in his memory, one more approach to things, and a manlier standard of pleasures and pains. An interesting task for somebody with adequate knowledge of antiquity would be to trace the influence which athletics had among the Greeks; I fancy it might be shown to permeate their poetry, to dominate their sculpture, and strangely to colour their sentiment. And this influence would come not chiefly from the practice but from the spectacle of games, just as the supposed brutalizing tendency of bull fighting is not conceived to stop with the performers within the ring, but to cross the barrier and infect the nation. Athletic sports are not children's games; they are public spectacles in which young men, carefully trained and disciplined, contend with one another in feats of strength, skill, and courage. Spectators are indispensable, since without them the victory, which should be the only reward, would lose half its power. For as Pindar, who knew, tells us:

> Success
> Is half the prize, the other half renown.
> Who both achieves, he hath the perfect crown.

A circumstance which somewhat perplexes this whole matter is the prevalent notion that athletics have a necessary relation to colleges. They have, indeed, a necessary relation to youth, because the time of greatest physical pliability and alertness is soon over; and as those of our youth who unite leisure with spirit are generally at some university, it happens that universities and colleges have become the centres of athletic interest. But this is an accident; a military or local organization of any sort would be as natural an athletic unit as a college. That athletic teams should bear the name of an institution of learning, and materially influence its reputation and fortune, is at first sight very strange; but the explanation is not far to seek. The English academic tradition, founded upon the clerical life of the middle ages, has always maintained a broad conception of education. All that an aristocratic family might wish to provide for its boys, that the schools and colleges provided. They contained the student's whole life, and they allowed a free and just development to all his faculties. The masters' province did not stop in the schoolroom, nor the professors' in the lecture hall. When possible they shared in the social and athletic life of the boys, and when not possible they at least gave it their heartiest support, making every reasonable concession to it; or, rather, not feeling that such friendliness was a concession at all, since they did not undertake merely the verbal education of their pupils, but had as broad an interest in their pursuits as the pupils themselves, or their parents. I remember a master at Eton, a man of fifty and a clergyman, running along the towpath in a sweater to watch the eight, a thing considered in no way singular or beneath his dignity. On the same principle, and on that principle alone, religious teaching and worship fall within the sphere of a college. To this system is due that beauty, individuality, and wealth of associations which make English colleges so beloved and venerable. They have a value which cannot be compensated or represented by any lists of courses or catalogues of libraries,—the value of a rounded and traditional life.

But even in England this state of things is disappearing. If we renounce it in this country, we need not suffer a permanent loss, provided the interests which are dropped by the colleges find some other social embodiment. Such a division of functions might even conduce to the efficiency of each; as is observed in the case of the German universities which, as compared with the English, are more active in investigation and more purely scientific in spirit, precisely because they have a more abstract function and minister to but one side of the mind. The real loss would come if a merely scientific and technical training were to pass for a human one, and a liberal education were conceived to be possible without leisure, or a generous life without any of those fruits of leisure of which athletics are one. Plato, who was beginning to turn his back upon paganism and held the un-Greek doctrine that the body should be cultivated only for the sake of the mind, nevertheless assigns in his scheme of education seven years to the teacher of the arts and seven to the athletic trainer. This equality, I fancy, would seem to us improper only because the study and cultivation of bodily life is yet a new thing among us. Physically we are barbarians, as is proved by our clothes, our furniture, and our appearance. To bathe was not Christian before this century. But the ascetic prejudice which survives in some of our habits no longer governs our deliberate judgments. Whatever functions, then, we may wish our colleges to have we shall not frown long upon athletic practices altogether. The incoherences of our educational policy cannot permanently alter our social conditions or destroy the basis which athletics have in the instincts of the people.

Into physical discipline, however, a great deal can enter that is not athletics. There are many sports that have nothing competitive in them. Some of them, like angling, involve enough of mild excitement and of intercourse with nature to furnish good entertainment to the lovers of them, although not enough to amuse a looker-on. The reason is that angling is too easy; it requires, no doubt, a certain skill, but the effort is not visible and glorious enough, it has no relation to martial or strenuous qualities. The distinction between athletics and private sport is that between an art and an amusement. The possibility of vicarious interest in the one and its impossibility in the other are grounded on the meaning which athletics have, on their appeal to the imagination. There is in them a great and continuous endeavour, a representation of all the primitive virtues and fundamental gifts of man. The conditions alone are artificial, and when well combined are even better than any natural conditions for the enacting of this sort of physical drama, a drama in which all moral and emotional interests are in a manner involved. For in real life the latter are actually superposed upon physical struggles. Intelligence and virtue are weapons in life, powers that make, as our Darwinian philosophy has it, for survival; science is a plan of campaign and poetry a cry of battle, sometimes of one who cheers us on, sometimes of one who is wounded. Therefore, when some well-conceived contest, like our foot-ball, displays the dramatic essence of physical conflict, we watch it with an interest which no gymnastic feat, no vulgar tricks of the circus or of legerdemain, can ever arouse. The whole soul is stirred by a spectacle that represents the basis of its life.

But besides the meaning which athletic games may have as physical dramas, they are capable, like other tragedies, of a great aesthetic development. This development they have not had in modern times, but we have only to conceive a scene at Olympia, or in a Roman amphitheatre, to see what immense possibilities lie in this direction. Our own games, in which no attention is paid to the aesthetic side, are themselves full of unconscious effects, which a practiced eye watches with delight. The public, however, is not sufficiently trained, nor the sports sufficiently developed, for this merit to be conspicuous. Such as it is, however, it contributes to our interest and helps to draw us to the games.

The chief claim which athletics make upon our respect remains yet unmentioned. They unite vitality with disinterestedness. The curse of our time is industrial supremacy, the sacrifice of every spontaneous faculty and liberal art to the demands of an overgrown material civilization. Our labour is servile and our play frivolous. Religion has long tended to change from a consolation into a puzzle, and to substitute unnatural checks for supernatural guidance. Art sometimes becomes an imposition, too; instead of delight and entertainment, it brings us the awful duty of culture. Our Muse, like Donna Inez, makes

Her thoughts a theorem, her words a problem,
As if she deemed that mystery would ennoble
   'em.

One cannot read verse without hard thought and a dictionary. This irksome and cumbrous manner in the arts is probably an indirect effect of the too great prevalence of practical interests. We carry over into our play the principles of labour. When the stress of life and the niggardliness of nature relax a little and we find it possible for a moment to live as we will, we find ourselves helpless. We cannot comprehend our opportunity, and like the prisoner of Chillon we regain our freedom with a sigh. The saddest effect of moral servitude is this atrophy of the spontaneous and imaginative will. We grow so accustomed to hard conditions that they seem necessary to us, and their absence inconceivable, so that religion, poetry, and the arts, which are the forms in which the soul asserts its independence, languish inwardly in the midst of the peace and riches that should foster them most. We have regained political and religious liberty, but moral freedom—the faculty and privilege of each man under the laws to live and act according to his inward nature—we scarcely care to have. The result is that while, in Greece, Sparta could exist beside Athens, Socrates besides Alcibiades, and Diogenes beside Alexander, we have in the United States seventy millions of people seized with the desire of absolutely resembling one another in dress, speech, habits, and dignities, and not one great or original man among them, except, perhaps, Mr. Edison.

It may seem a ridiculous thing, and yet I think it true, that our athletic life is the most conspicuous and promising rebellion against this industrial tyranny. We elude Mammon only for a few years, which the Philistines think are wasted. We succumb to him soon after leaving college. We sell our birthright for a mess of pottage, and the ancestral garden of the mind for building lots. That garden too often runs to seed, even if we choose a liberal profession, and is overgrown with the thistles of a trivial and narrow scholarship. But while we are young, and as yet amount to nothing, we retain the privilege of infinite potentiality. The poor actuality has not yet taken its place, and in giving one thing made everything else for ever unattainable. But in youth the intellectual part is too immature to bear much fruit; that would come later if the freedom could be retained. The body alone has reached perfection, and very naturally the physical life is what tends to occupy the interval of leisure with its exuberances. Such is the origin of our athletics. Their chief value is that they are the first fruits of that spontaneous life, of which the higher manifestations are not suffered to appear. Perhaps it is well that the body should take the lead, since that is the true and safe order of nature. The rest, if it comes, will then rest on a sounder basis.

When I hear, therefore, the cheering at our great games, when I watch, at Springfield or at New London, the frenzy of joy of the thousands upon one side and the grim and pathetic silence of the thousands upon the other, I cannot feel that the passion is excessive. It might seem so if we think only of what occurs at the moment. But would the game or the race as such be capable of arousing that enthusiasm? Is there not some pent-up energy in us, some thirst for enjoyment and for self-expression, some inward rebellion against a sordid environment, which here finds inarticulate expression? Is not the same force ready to bring us into other arenas, in which, as in those of Greece, honour should come not only to strength, swiftness, and beauty, but to every high gift and inspiration? Such a hope is almost justified by my athletic philosophy, which, with little else, perhaps, to recommend it, I herewith submit to the gentle reader. It may help him, if he receives it kindly, to fill up the waits at a game, while the captains wrangle, and to see in fancy greener fields than Holmes's from the bleachers.

Seeing "t'United" Play*

J. B. PRIESTLEY

These caps have just left the ground of the Bruddersford United Association Football Club. Thirty-five thousand men and boys have just seen what most of them call "t'United" play Bolton Wanderers. Many of them should never have been there at all. It would not be difficult to prove by statistics and those mournful little budgets (How a Man May Live—or rather, avoid death—on Thirty-five Shillings a Week) that seem to attract some minds, that these fellows could not afford the entrance fee. When some mills are only working half the week and others not at all, a shilling is a respectable sum of money. It would puzzle an economist to discover where all these shillings came from. But if he lived in Bruddersford, though he might still wonder where they came from, he would certainly understand why they were produced. To say that these men paid their shillings to watch twenty-two hirelings kick a ball is merely to say that a violin is wood and catgut, that *Hamlet* is so much paper and ink. For a shilling the Bruddersford United A.F.C. offered you Conflict and Art; it turned you into a critic, happy in your judgment of fine points, ready in a second to estimate the worth of a

well-judged pass, a run down the touch line, a lightning shot, a clearance kick by back or goalkeeper; it turned you into a partisan, holding your breath when the ball came sailing into your own goalmouth, ecstatic when your forwards raced away towards the opposite goal, elated, downcast, bitter, triumphant by turns at the fortunes of your side, watching a ball shape Iliads and Odysseys for you; and what is more, it turned you into a member of a new community, all brothers together for an hour and a half, for not only had you escaped from the clanking machinery of this lesser life, from work, wages, rent, doles, sick pay, insurance cards, nagging wives, ailing children, bad bosses, idle workmen, but you had escaped with most of your mates and your neighbours, with half the town, and there you were, cheering together, thumping one another on the shoulders, swopping judgments like lords of the earth, having pushed your way through a turnstile into another and altogether more splendid kind of life, hurtling with Conflict and yet passionate and beautiful in its Art. Moreover, it offered you more than a shilling's worth of material for talk during the rest of the week. A man who had missed the last home match of "t'United" had to enter social life on tiptoe in Bruddersford.

* Excerpt from *The Good Companions,* Vol. I. New York: Harper & Brothers, 1929.

BIBLIOGRAPHY ON SPORT AS A MEANINGFUL EXPERIENCE

Alvarez, A. "I Like to Risk my Life." *Saturday Evening Post,* 240 (September 9, 1967), 10-12.

Banham, Charles. "Man at Play." *Contemporary Review,* 207 (August, 1965), 61-64.

Bannister, Roger. "What Makes the Athlete Run?" *The Australian Journal of Physical Education,* (March, 1964), 31-36.

———. "The Meaning of Athletic Performance." *International Research in Sport and Physical Education.* Edited by E. Jokl and E. Simon. Springfield, Illinois: Charles C Thomas, 1964.

Beisser, Arnold R. "Psychodynamic Observations of a Sport." *Psychoanalytic Review,* 48 (Spring, 1961), 69-76.

———. *The Madness in Sports.* New York: Appleton-Century-Crofts, 1967.

Blumenfield, Walter. "Observations Concerning the Phenomenon and Origin of Play." *Philosophy and Phenomenological Research.* I (June, 1941), 470-478.

Coomaraswamy, A. K. "Play and Seriousness." *Journal of Philosophy,* XXXIX (September, 1942), 550-552.

Davis, John Eisele. "The Utilization of Play in the Construction of Healthy Mental Attitudes." *Mental Hygiene,* 20 (January, 1936), 49-54.

Desmonde, William H. "The Bull-Fight as a Religious Ritual." *American Imago,* 9 (June, 1952), 173-195.

"The Difficult Art of Losing." *Time,* 92 (November 15, 1968), 47-48.

Doherty, J. Kenneth. "Why Men Run." *Quest,* II (April, 1964), 61-66.

———. "Motivation in Endurance Running" in *Modern Training for Running.* New Jersey: Prentice-Hall, 1964.

Felshin, Jan. "Sport and Modes of Meaning." *Journal of Health, Physical Education, and Recreation,* 40 (May, 1969), 43-44.

Furlong, William. "Danger as a Way of Joy." *Sports Illustrated,* 30 (January 27, 1969), 52-53.

Genasci, James E. and Klissouras, Vasillis. "The Delphic Spirit in Sports." *Journal of Health, Physical Education, and Recreation,* 37 (February, 1966), 43-45.

Gerber, Ellen W. "Identity, Relation and Sport." *Quest,* VIII (May, 1967), 90-97.

Gilbert, Bil. "When Games Were for Fun." *Sports Illustrated,* 31 (November 24, 1969), E7-10.

Gregg, Jearald Rex. "A Philosophical Analysis of the Sports Experience and the Role of Athletics in the Schools." Unpublished Ed.D. dissertation, University of Southern California, 1971.

Harper, William A. "Man Alone." *Quest,* XII (May, 1969), 57-60.

Houston, Charles S. "The Last Blue Mountain." *Why Man Takes Chances.* Edited by Samuel Z. Klausner. New York: Anchor Books Edition, 1968.

Houts, Jo Ann. "Feeling and Perception in the Sport Experience." *Journal of Health, Physical Education, and Recreation,* 41 (October, 1970), 71.

Huizinga, Johan. *Homo Ludens.* London: Routledge & Kegan Paul, 1950.

Kahn, Roger. "Intellectuals and Ballplayers." *American Scholar,* 26 (Summer, 1957), 342-349.

Kenyon, Gerald S. "Sport Involvement: A Conceptual Go and Some Consequences Thereof." *Aspects of Contemporary Sport Sociology.* Proceedings of C.I.C. Symposium on the Sociology of Sport. Edited by Gerald S. Kenyon. Illinois: The Athletic Institute, 1969.

Klausner, Samuel Z., Ed. *Why Man Takes Chances.* New York: Anchor Books Edition, 1968.

Kleinman, Seymour. "The Significance of Human Movement: A Phenomenological Approach." National Association for Physical Education of College Women. *Report of the Ruby Anniversary Workshop.* Interlochen, Michigan, 1964.

———. "Sport as Experience." Unpublished paper presented at the Annual Convention of the American Association for Health, Physical Education, and Recreation, Seattle, Washington, April, 1970.

Kretchmar, R. Scott and Harper, William A. "Why Does Man Play?" *Journal of Health, Physical Education, and Recreation,* 40 (March, 1969), 57-58.

Lorenz, Konrad. "Avowal of Optimism" in *On Aggression.* New York: Harcourt, Brace & World, 1966.

McMurty, John. "Philosophy of a Corner Linebacker." *The Nation,* 212 (January 18, 1971), 83-84.

Metheny, Eleanor. *Connotations of Movement in Sport and Dance.* Iowa: Wm. C. Brown, 1965.

———. "The Symbolic Power of Sport." Unpublished paper presented at the annual convention of the Eastern District Association for Health, Physical Education, and Recreation, Washington, D.C., April 26, 1968.

———. *Movement and Meaning.* New York: McGraw-Hill, 1968.

Miller, David L. *Gods and Games: Toward a Theology of Play.* New York: World Publishing Company, 1970.

Norbeck Edward. "Human Play and its Cultural Expression." *Humanitas,* V (Spring, 1969), 43-55.

Parker, Franklin. "Sport, Play and Physical Education in Cultural Perspective." *Journal of Health, Physical Education, and Recreation,* 36 (January, 1965), 29-30.

Pavlich, Mary. "The Power of Sport." *Arizona Journal of Health, Physical Education, Recreation,* 10 (Fall, 1966) 9-10.

Pieper, Josef. *In Tune With the World: A Theory of Festivity.* Translated by Richard and Clara Winston. New York: Harcourt, Brace & World, 1965.

Priestley, J. B. "Seeing 't' United' Play" in *The Good Companions,* Vol. I. New York: Harper & Brothers, 1929.

Rahner, Hugo, S. J. *Man at Play*. New York Herder and Herder, 1967.

Riezler, Kurt. "Play and Seriousness." *Journal of Philosophy*, XXXVIII (September, 1941), 505-517.

Rupp, Adolph. "Defeat and Failure to Me are Enemies." *Sports Illustrated*, 9 (December 8, 1958), 100-106.

Santayana, George. "Philosophy on the Bleachers." *Harvard Monthly*, VIII (July, 1894), 181-190.

Slovenko, Ralph and Knight, James A., Eds. *Motivations in Play, Games and Sports*. Springfield, Illinois: Charles C Thomas, 1967.

Slusher, Howard S. *Man, Sport and Existence*. Philadelphia: Lea & Febiger, 1967.

———. "To Test the Waves is to Test Life." *Journal of Health, Physical Education, and Recreation*, 40 (May, 1969), 32-33.

Stewart, Mary Lou. "Why Do Men Play?" *Journal of Health, Physical Education, and Recreation*, 41 (November-December, 1970), 14.

Stone, Roselyn Elizabeth. "Meanings Found in the Acts of Surfing and Skiing." Unpublished Ph.D. dissertation, University of Southern California, 1970.

Tiger, Lionel. "A Note on Sport" in *Men in Groups*. New York: Random House, 1969.

Vernes, Jean-René. "The Element of Time in Competitive Games." Translated by Victor A. Velen. *Diogenes*, 50 (September, 1965), 25-42.

Weiss, Paul. *Sport: A Philosophic Inquiry*. Carbondale: Southern Illinois University Press, 1969.

Wenkart, Simon. "The Meaning of Sports for Contemporary Man." *Journal of Existential Psychiatry*, 3 (Spring, 1963), 397-404.

———. "Sports and Contemporary Man." *Motivations in Play, Games and Sports*. Edited by Ralph Slovenko and James A. Knight. Springfield, Illinois: Charles C Thomas, 1967.

SPORT AND VALUE-ORIENTED CONCERNS

Sport and Value-Oriented Concerns

INTRODUCTION

Many philosophical questions are somewhat abstract and seem not actually to touch upon the life of an individual. However, the subject of values is relevant to every thinker. Since each person has his or her own idea of what is good, discussion about the value of any subject such as sport often is nothing more than a series of statements of beliefs and attitudes. This, in fact, has been the approach used by many philosophers. They have conceived of their role as the setting forth of a recommended system of values, i.e. a coherent set of beliefs and attitudes which suggested attendant behaviors. Moral philosophy has been, to some, the most important branch of the discipline in that it deals with recognizable and practical issues.

This modus operandi is not as didactic as might first appear. Philosophers base their value systems on their views of reality and truth; this enables them to answer the most immediate and consequential question: "What is the ultimate source of human values?" Depending upon one's philosophical view, the answer might be God, the physical or natural world, society, eternal or classical truths, or the individual. For instance, those who believe that the world of material objects is the real world tend to think that value derives from natural law. Thus Herbert Spencer, a scientist and philosopher who tried to extend the theory of evolution to other spheres, chose to justify amusements by the famous "surplus energy theory." In "The Ethics of Pleasure" it is easy to see the justification of sports based upon ethical principles stemming from Spencer's in-terpretation of the importance of the physical world.

Josiah Royce, on the other hand, was *the* leading American idealist of his time. He was most definite in stating that "the rational solution of moral problems rests on the principle: Be loyal." (p. 247) In his article he values physical training, i.e. sports, because he believes it tends to train people to be loyal. Delbert Oberteuffer and Gus Turbeville assume that certain values, logically pursued through the sport situation, are part of the heritage of mankind. Richard Calisch makes similar assumptions, though he questions the role of competitive athletics in furthering the cause. Richard McCormick's article is a classical treatment of applying "an immutable moral principle" (p. 271) to a current question.

Tom Tiede and Ira Berkow in their observations on "Our Changing Morality" express a social derivation of values; the changing behavior of athletes is, to them, a reflection of changing values.

These articles have in common the authors' basic belief that certain ideas, attitudes or behaviors are right or good. Although they differ in designating the source of these values, they agree on their existence. In this context, sportsmanship, group loyalty, unselfishness, and honesty are assumed to be unquestionable normative standards. Sport, as a particularly significant aspect of human behavior, is expected to play a role in assisting individuals to learn and to behave in accordance with these previously formulated values.

More contemporary philosophical viewpoints

241

are not concerned with recommending or asserting certain value positions. The existentialists, for example, reject the notion that the individual should act in accordance with some preset system of values. They maintain that each individual chooses what he or she values in accordance with his or her being. Ironically, this has led to the development of existentialist values, in that authenticity, being oneself, doing one's own thing, etc. have become "universal" existential values. In "Morality as an Intimate of Sport," Howard S. Slusher points to the ways in which sport and values juncture in an existentialist mode.

Analytical philosophers refuse to deal with values in the usual normative manner. They assert that the role of the philosopher is to analyze propositions to determine their *necessary* implications. Unlike a moral principle, which is true only in accord with a previously accepted value system, an analytical proposition is inherently true. That which is inherent, is necessary; that which is contingent, is a choice. For example, the statement that "basketball is a team game" is an inherently true proposition, while the statement that "basketball should be a cooperative endeavor" is an ethical principle. The article by John Rawls is illustrative of this type of axiological reasoning. Rawls' rules of practice are constitutive rules that constitute and regulate forms of activity, such as sport, the existence of which is logically dependent on the rules. Therefore, to agree to play the game is to agree to abide by the rules because they are an inherent part of the game. Rawls concludes, on the above grounds, that it is immoral to disobey the rules. In an interesting challenge to Rawl's central thesis, Anthony Ralls argues that such a premise implies acceptance of the morality of keeping a promise (to play the game). He puts forth his own proposition relating to rules-keeping. The article by B. J. Diggs is an attempt to clarify the moral position of sport rules by focusing on the necessary relation of game rules to utilitarian game goals. In a completely different vein, but using a similar philosophical technique, James Keating attempts to demonstrate analytically that sportsmanship is a quality inherent to sports and sportsmen.

One of the contradictions which arises in any discussion on morality is the apparent difference between operant and conceived values, the difference, for example, in believing in brotherly love and in practicing it. Does the coach who conceives of the use of sport to teach obedience to social rules (conceived value), contradict himself when he orders his players to "foul for profit" (operant value)? Or, is this merely a good example of the hierarchical nature of values? In other words, the value of winning may be higher on the coach's hierarchy than the value of teaching ethical principles. Since most modes of behaving involve a choice between various action possibilities, inevitably choices are made in accordance with values held to be *most* important.

Many philosophers have attempted to classify the basic value systems exhibited by mankind. One categorization that has some appropriateness for sport distinguishes between the scientific, the human, and the artistic. What happens in a sport situation if the teacher or coach chooses scientific rather than human values? For example, if team efficiency is considered to be more important than human needs, what effect does this have on the players' experience? Furthermore, what happens if the players' values come in conflict with those of the coach or spectator?

Other questions relating to sport and value-oriented concerns come easily to mind. Perhaps first in importance is the question: is sport inherently good? Is sport good for people? Is it good to have to learn various sports? Is that good more important than the good accruing to freedom of choice? Are each or any of the practices associated with sport, good? Which ones and according to what source of values? Is it better to play well or to win? Are there right and wrong ways to play sports?

The numerous writings which connect sport and ethics do not really answer these questions. The authors' attempts have usually been directed toward explicating the values to the individual that accrue from participating in sport, or toward asserting the ethical principles that are inculcated in the participant during the course of the sport experience. Unfortunately, most of the articles are written about sport as it was in nineteenth-century England, rather than as it is in twentieth-century America.

In 1962 the American Association for Health, Physical Education, and Recreation held a conference which attempted to delineate comprehensively the values of sport. Others who wrote in a similar vein include Kellor (1906), Banham (1965) and Powell (1971). Many articles in Section IV of this book, "Sport as a Meaningful Experience," also stress the positive benefits derived from sport. Tunis (1928), Montague (1962), Scott (1971), and McMurty (1971) take a somewhat opposite view, possibly because they choose to examine sport as they perceive it to really be, rather than in its idealized form.

Proceeding from the assumption that ethics and sport go hand in hand, some writers have emphasized the great potential of sport to teach certain moral principles, including particularly, sportsmanship, loyalty and the virtue of discipline. Writings by Hoben (1912), Hosmer (1914), Kennedy (1931), and the "Symposium of Sportsmanship" undertaken by the *Physical Educator* (1949), each underscore this point.

Another dimension of the subject of sportsmanship includes the empirical studies that have attempted to ascertain the concepts of, and attitudes towards, sportsmanship held by various populations. Among these reported studies are Bovyer (1963), Deatherage (1964) and Richardson (1962).

There remains much study to be done about sport and ethical situations. First of all, the relationship between sport and ethics is badly in need of clarification. The assumption that the two subjects are inherently linked together must be examined. The values from sport need definition, particularly with reference to specific kinds and levels of sport. The kind of ethical principles taught through sport, again with reference to various types of sport experiences, needs delineation. In this case, the conclusions derived from philosophical analysis can and should be subjected to empirical testing. And finally, the connection of sport values with social practices, a sensitive area, must be strictly evaluated.

Ethics, as an aspect of philosophy and sport, has been allowed to remain a jumbled bag of assertions which have not been subjected to either philosophical or empirical analysis. It is a subject worthy of the attention of those who love sport, and also of those who are its critics.

The Ethics of Pleasure*

HERBERT SPENCER

To the great majority, who have imbibed more or less of that asceticism which, though appropriate to times of chronic militancy and also useful as a curb to ungoverned sensualism, has swayed too much men's theory of life, it will seem an absurd supposition that amusements are ethically warranted. Yet unless, in common with the Quakers and some extreme evangelicals, they hold them to be positively wrong, they must either say that amusements are neither right nor wrong, or, they must say that they are positively right—are to be morally approved.

That they are sanctioned by hedonistic ethics goes without saying. They are pleasure-giving activities; and that is their sufficient justification, so long as they do not unduly interfere with activities which are obligatory. Though most of our pleasures are to be accepted as concomitants of those various expenditures of energy conducive to self-sustentation and sustentation of family; yet the pursuit of pleasure for pleasure's sake is to be sanctioned, and even enjoined, when primary duties have been fulfilled.

So, too, are they to be approved from the physiological point of view. Not only do the emotional satisfactions which accompany normal life-sustaining labours exalt the vital functions, but the vital functions are exalted by those satisfactions which accompany the superfluous expenditures of energy implied by amusements: much more exalted in fact. Such

satisfactions serve to raise the tide of life, and taken in due proportion conduce to every kind of efficiency.

Yet once more there is the evolutionary justification. In § 534 of *The Principles of Psychology*, it was shown that whereas, in the lowest creatures, the small energies which exist are wholly used up in those actions which serve to maintain the individual and propagate the species; in creatures of successively higher grades, there arises an increasing amount of unused energy: every improvement of organization achieving some economy, and so augmenting the surplus power. This surplus expends itself in the activities we call play. Among the superior *vertebrata* the tendency to these superfluous activities becomes conspicuous; and it is especially conspicuous in Man, when so conditioned that stress of competition does not make the sustentation of self and family too laborious. The implication is that in a fully-developed form of human life, a considerable space will be filled by the pleasurable exercise of faculties which have not been exhausted by daily activities.

. . . .

Throughout the foregoing class of pleasures, resulting from the superfluous excitements of faculties, the individual is mainly passive. We turn now to the class in which he is mainly active; which again is subdivisible into two classes—sports and games. With sports, ethics has little concern beyond graduating its degrees of reprobation. Such of them as involve the direct infliction of pain, especially on fellow-

* From *The Principles of Ethics*, Vol. I. New York: D. Appleton and Company, 1910.

beings, are nothing but means to the gratification of feelings inherited from savages of the baser sort. That after these thousands of years of social discipline, there should still be so many who like to see the encounters of the prize-ring or witness the goring of horses and riders in the arena, shows how slowly the instincts of the barbarian are being subdued. No condemnation can be too strong for these sanguinary amusements which keep alive in men the worst parts of their natures and thus profoundly vitiate social life. Of course in a measure, though in a smaller measure, condemnation must be passed on field-sports—in smaller measure because the obtainment of food affords a partial motive, because the infliction of pain is less conspicuous, and because the chief pleasure is that derived from successful exercise of skill. But it cannot be denied that all activities with which there is joined the consciousness that other sentient beings, far inferior though they may be, are made to suffer, are to some extent demoralizing. The sympathies do, indeed, admit of being so far specialized that the same person who is unsympathetic towards wild animals may be in large measure sympathetic towards fellow-men; but a full amount of sympathy cannot well be present in the one relation and absent in the other. It may be added that the specializing of the sympathies has the effect that they become smaller as the remoteness from human nature becomes greater; and that hence the killing of a deer sins against them more than does the killing of a fish.

Those expenditures of energy which take the form of games, yield pleasures from which there are but small, if any, drawbacks in the entailed pains. Certain of them, indeed, as football, are as much to be reprobated as sports, than some of which they are more brutalizing; and there cannot be much ethical approbation of those games, so-called, such as boat-races, in which a painful and often injurious overtax of the system is gone through to achieve a victory, pleasurable to one side and entailing pain on the other. But there is ethical sanction for those games in which, with a moderate amount of muscular effort, there is joined the excitement of a competition not too intense, kept alive from moment to moment by the changing incidents of the contest. Under these conditions the muscular actions are beneficial, the culture of the perceptions is useful, while the emotional pleasure has but small drawbacks. And here I am prompted to denounce the practice, now so general, of substituting gymnastics for games—violent muscular actions, joined with small concomitant pleasures, for moderate muscular actions joined with great pleasures. This usurpation is a sequence of that pestilent asceticism which thinks that pleasure is of no consequence, and that if the same amount of exercise be taken, the same benefit is gained: the truth being that to the exaltation of the vital functions which the pleasure produces, half the benefit is due.

Of indoor games which chiefly demand quickness of perception, quickness of reasoning, and quickness of judgment, general approval may be expressed with qualifications of no great importance. For young people they are especially desirable as giving to various of the intellectual faculties a valuable training, not to be given by other means. Under the stress of competition, the abilities to observe rapidly, perceive accurately, and infer rightly, are increased; and in addition to the immediate pleasures gained, there are gained powers of dealing more effectually with many of the incidents of life. It should be added that such drawbacks as there are, from the emotions accompanying victory and defeat, are but small in games which involve chance as a considerable factor, but are very noticeable where there is no chance. Chess, for example, which pits together two intelligences in such a way as to show unmistakably the superiority of one to the other in respect of certain powers, produces, much more than whist, a feeling of humiliation in the defeated, and if the sympathies are keen this gives some annoyance to the victor as well as to the vanquished.

Of course, such ethical sanction as is given to games, cannot be given where gambling or betting is an accompaniment. Involving, as both do, in a very definite way, and often to an extreme degree, the obtainment of pleasure at the cost of another's pain, they are to be condemned both for this immediate effect and for their remote effect—the repression of fellow-feeling.

Before passing to the altruistic aspect of amusements, there should be noted a less familiar egotistic aspect. Unless they have kept up during life an interest in pastimes, those who have broken down from overwork (perhaps an overwork entailed on them by imperative duties) usually find themselves incapable of relaxing in any satisfactory way: they are no longer amusable. Capacities for all other pleasures are atrophied, and the only pleasure is that which business gives. In such cases recovery is, if not prevented, greatly retarded by the lack of exhilarating occupations. Frequently dependents suffer.

This last consideration shows that these, like other classes of actions which primarily concern the individual, concern, to some extent, other individuals. But they concern other individuals in more direct and constant ways also. On each person there is imposed not only the peremptory obligation so to carry on his life as to avoid inequitably interfering with the carrying on of others' lives, and not only the less peremptory obligation to aid under various circumstances the carrying on of their lives, but there is imposed some obligation to increase the pleasures of their lives by sociality, and by the cultivation of those powers which conduce to sociality. A man may be a good economical unit of society, while remaining otherwise an almost worthless unit. If he has no knowledge of the arts, no aesthetic feelings, no interest in fiction, the drama, poetry, or music—if he cannot join in any of those amusements which daily and at longer intervals fill leisure spaces in life—if he is thus one to whom others cannot readily give pleasure, at the same time that he can give no pleasure to others; he becomes in great measure a dead unit, and unless he has some special value might better be out of the way.

Thus, that he may add his share to the general happiness, each should cultivate in due measure those superfluous activities which primarily yield self-happiness.

Physical Training and Moral Education*

JOSIAH ROYCE

The rational solution of moral problems rests on the principle: _Be loyal_. This principle, properly understood, involves two consequences. The first is this: Have a cause, choose a cause, give yourself over to that cause actively, devotedly, whole-heartedly, practically. Let this cause be something social, serviceable, requiring loyal devotion. Let this cause, or system of causes, constitute a life-work. Let the cause possess your senses, your attention, your muscles,—all your powers, so long as you are indeed active and awake at all. See that you do not rest in any mere sentiment of devotion to the cause. Act out your loyalty. Loyalty exists in the form of deeds done by the willing and devoted instrument of his chosen cause. This is the first consequence of the commandment: _Be loyal._ The second consequence is like unto the first. It is this: _Be loyal to loyalty._ That is, regard your neighbor's loyalty as something sacred. Do nothing to make him less loyal. Never despise him for his loyalty, however little you care for the cause that he chooses. If your cause and his cause come into some inevitable conflict, so that you indeed have to contend with him, fight, if your loyalty requires you to do so; but in your bitterest warfare fight only against what the opponent does. Thwart his acts where he justly should be thwarted; but do all this in the very cause of loyalty itself, and never do anything to make

*Excerpted from _Some Relations of Physical Training to the Present Problems of Moral Education in America._ Boston: The Boston Normal School of Gymnastics, _ca._ 1908.

your neighbor disloyal. Never do anything to encourage him in any form of disloyalty. In other words, never war against his loyalty. From these consequences of my central principle follow, as I maintain, all those propositions about the special duties of life which can be reasonably defined and defended. Justice, kindliness, chivalry, charity,— these are all of them forms of loyalty to loyalty.

Even while I have set forth this sketch of a general ethical doctrine, I have intentionally illustrated my views by some references to your professional work. But at this point I next have briefly to emphasize the positive relations which physical education may have and should have to the training of the loyal spirit. Here I shall simply repeat what others, more expert than I am, have long since, in various speech, set forth.

The first way in which systematic physical training of all grades and at all ages may be of positive service in a moral education is this: Loyalty, as we have seen, means a willing and thoroughgoing devotion of the whole active self to a chosen cause or to a chosen system of causes. But such devotion, as we have also seen, is a motor process. One must be in control of one's powers, or one has no self to give to one's cause. One must get a personality in order to be able to surrender this personality to anything. And since physical training actually has that relation to the culture of the will which your leaders so generally emphasize, while some physical expression of one's personality is an essential accompaniment of the existence of every human personality,—for both of these reasons, I say, the training of physical strength and skill is one important preparation for a moral life. There is indeed a great deal else in moral training besides what physical training supplies; but the physical training can be a powerful auxiliary. Here I come upon ground that is familiar to all of you, and that I need not attempt to cover anew with suggestions of my own. The positive relation of good physical training to the formation of a sound will is known to all of you. The only relatively new aspect of this familiar region that may have been brought to light by the foregoing considerations is this: Loyalty, as you see, on its highest levels involves the same general mental features which are present whenever a physical activity, at once strenuous and skilful, is going on. As a skilful and difficult physical exercise demands that one should keep his head in the midst of efforts that, by reason of the strain, or of the excitement,—by reason of the very magnitude and fascination of the task, would confuse the untrained man, and make him lose a sense of what he was trying to do, even so the work of the effectively loyal person is always one which requires that he should stand in presence of undertakings large enough to threaten to cloud his judgment and to crush his self-control, while his loyalty still demands that he also should keep his head despite the strain, and should retain steady control of his personality, even in order to devote it to the cause. Loyalty means hard work in the presence of serious responsibilities. The danger of such work is closely similar to the danger of losing one's head in a difficult physical activity. One is devoting the self to the cause. The cause must be vast. For its very vastness is part of what gives it worth. I cannot be loyal to what requires of me no effort. But the consciousness of the vastness and difficulty of one's cause tends to crush the self of the person who is trying to be loyal. And a self crushed into a loss of self-possession, a self no longer aware of its powers, a self that has lost sight of its true contrast with the objects about it, has no longer left the powers which it can devote to any cause. Mere good will is no substitute for trained self-possession either in physical or in moral activities. And self-possession is a necessary condition for self-devotion. When the apostle compared the moral work of the saints to the running of a race, his metaphors were therefore chosen because of this perfectly definite analogy between the devotion of the trained organism to its physical task and the devotion of the moral self to its

cause. In both classes of cases, in loyal devotion and in skilful and strenuous physical exercise, similar mental problems have to be solved. One has to keep the self in sight in order to surrender it anew, through each deed, to the task in hand. Meanwhile, since the task is centred upon something outside of the self, and is a serious and an imposing task, it involves a tendency to strain, to excitement, to a loss of a due self-possession, to disturbance of the equilibrium of consciousness. The result is likely to be, unless one is in a state of physical or of moral training, just a primary confusion of self-consciousness, accompanied by fear or by a sense of helplessness. Against such a mood the mere sentiment of devotion is no safeguard. To hold on to one's self at the moment of the greatest strain, to retain clearness, even when confronted by tasks too large to be carried out as one wishes, to persist doggedly despite defeats, to give up all mere self-will and yet to retain full self-control,—these are requirements which, as I suppose, appear to the consciousness of the athlete and to the consciousness of the moral hero in decidedly analogous ways. And in both cases the processes involved are psycho-physical as well as psychical, and are subject to the general laws of physiology and of psychology.

. . . .

The second way in which physical training may serve the purposes of moral training is a more direct way. It is the one which Dr. Luther Gulick had in mind when he lately asserted in a paper in the *School Review* that "athletics are primarily social and moral in their nature." Dr. Gulick is well known to you as one of the protagonists in the cause of the moral importance of physical education; and you know his main argument. Social training, in boys about twelve years of age, naturally takes the form of the training which gangs of boys give to their members. A gang of boys with nothing significant to do may become more or less of a menace to the general social order. A gang of boys duly organized into athletic teams, in the service of schools, and of other expressions of wholesome community activity, will become centres for training in certain types of loyalty. And this training may extend its influence to large bodies of boys who, as spectators of games or as schoolmates, are more or less influenced by the athletic spirit. *Mutatis mutandis*, the same considerations apply to the socially organizing forces that belong to college athletics. The plans of those who are engaged in physical education may therefore well be guided, from the first, by a disposition to prepare young people to appreciate and to take part in such group activities as these. Thus both the physiological and the intellectual aspects of physical training would appear to be subordinate, after all, to the social, and in this way to the moral, aspects of the profession. In speaking of these moral aspects, one would not even emphasize, as much as many do, the central significance of the self-denial, of the personal restraints and sacrifices, of the morally advantageous physical habits, which attend athletic training. One would rather more centrally emphasize the view that athletic work is not merely a preparation for loyalty, but that in case of the life of the organized athletic teams, and in case of any physical training class of pupils who work together, the athletic work *is* loyalty itself,—loyalty in simple forms, but in forms which appeal to the natural enthusiasm of youth, which are adapted to the boyish and later to the adolescent phases of evolution, and which are a positive training for the very tasks which adult loyalty exemplifies; namely, the tasks that imply the devotion of a man's whole power to an office that takes him out of his private self and into the great world of real social life. The social forms of physical training in classes or in teams require, and so tend to train, loyalty.

. . . .

The third positive relation of physical training to moral training is suggested by what I have said about the need of an enlightened form of loyalty. Merely blind loyalty may do mischief; but it does so, we have said, not because it is loyalty, but because it is blind. It turns into enlightened loyalty in so far as it reaches the stage of loyalty to loyalty,—the stage where one certainly does not tend merely to take over into one's own life and directly to adopt the special cause that one's neighbor has happened to choose as his own, but where one regards the spirit of loyalty, the willingness to devote the self to some cause, as a precious common moral good of mankind,—a good that we can indeed foster in our neighbors even when their individual causes are not, or are even, by accident, opposed to our own. I can respect, can honor, I can help, my neighbor's family loyalty without in the least wishing to become a member of his family. And just so I can be loyal to any aspect of my neighbor's loyalty without accepting his special cause as my own. He may be devoted to what I cannot and will not view as my individual cause; and

still, in dealing with him, I can be loyal to his loyalty.

Now I have already pointed out that the spirit of loyalty to loyalty is finely exemplified by the spirit of fair play in games. For true fair play does not merely mean conformity to a set of rules which chance this season to govern a certain game. Fair play depends upon essentially respecting one's opponent just because of his loyalty to his own side. It means a tendency to enjoy, to admire, to applaud, to love, to further that loyalty of his at the very moment when I keenly want and clearly intend to thwart his individual deeds, and to win this game, if I can. Now in the complications of real life it is hard to keep the spirit of loyalty to loyalty always alive. If my passions are aroused and if I hate a man, it is far too easy to think that even his faithful dog must be a mean cur, in order to be able to be so devoted to his master as he is. And real life often thus confuses our judgment through stirring our passions. But it is a very precious thing when you can keep your head so clearly as to be able to oppose even to the very death, if needs must be, your enemy's cause, even while you are able to love his loyalty to that cause, and to honor his followers for their devotion to their leader and his friends for their fidelity to him.

Now it is just such loyalty to loyalty that can be trained in true sport very much more readily than in real life, because, in sport, the social situation is simple. And because the spirit of fair play, in an athletic sport, can constantly express itself by definite physical deeds, and because the passions aroused by wholesome athletic contests ought never to be as blind, as violent, or as enduring, as those which real life unhappily so often fosters, the training in fair play ought to be much easier in the world of athletic sports than the training of loyalty to loyalty is in our daily life,—much easier, much simpler, and much more definite. Hence, if games were in all cases rightly conducted, if confusing passions were properly kept from unnecessary interference with the joyous devotion of the players to their respective sides, if the general physical training of all those who are to engage in school and in college sports were conducted from the first by teachers who had a serious interest in the moral welfare of their classes,—well, if these conditions were realized, physical education ought to contribute its important share to what we have now seen to be the very crown of human virtue; namely, to the spirit of loyalty to loyalty,—to the spirit that honors and respects one's very enemies for their devotion to the very causes that one assails. The result should be the spiritual power to appreciate that common good for which even those who are mutually most hostile are contending. We human beings cannot agree as to the choice of our individual causes. We can learn to honor one another's loyalty.

.   .   .   .

And with these words I am indeed brought to the central problem amongst all those with which this discussion is concerned. I have set forth the three sorts of positively helpful relations that a sound physical training can develop in its bearing upon the work of moral training. First, because skilful and serious physical exercise involves true devotion, a sound physical training can help to prepare the organism and the personality for loyal types of activity. Secondly, physical training, in so far as it is a part of the life of a social group, can more directly aid the individual to learn to be loyal to his group. Thirdly, physical training, in so far as it can be used to give expression to the spirit of fair play, may be an aid towards the highest types of morality; namely, to those which embody that spirit of loyalty to loyalty which is destined, we hope, some day to bring to pass the spiritual union of all mankind. I have pointed out that all these three forms are simply possible forms in which the moral usefulness of physical training may appear. There is nothing that fatally secures the attainment of any of these three results. All depends upon the spirit, the skill, and the opportunities of the teacher, and upon the awakening of the right spirit in the learners. Instead of these good results, a failure to reach any of these three sorts of good results, in any tangible form, is in case of any given pupil or class of pupils perfectly possible. And, as we have just seen, the failure of certain forms of athletic sports to further, in certain well-known cases, the high cause of loyalty to loyalty has of late been far too conspicuous.

On Learning Values Through Sport*

DELBERT OBERTEUFFER

Now, no fair peeking! And thus came to us the first admonition to assure our conformity to the standards of conduct with which games have been played in our land. We were not supposed to peek! Anyone should know that. The game—what was it?—ten steps or hide and go seek—presumed a code of honor mandatory upon us from the first instant we heard the rules. There were to be no exceptions. One simply did not entertain the idea of cheating. One went full-out for one's own honor and later for the honor of one's own school. After all, there were only two fates worse than death, and one was to be caught cheating at games!

With some reason, one might believe that this successful transmission of acceptable or traditional ethical values has been one of the reassuring and remarkable phenomena of our age. One comes to games, whether stickball in Manhattan or duck-on-the-rock in Grand Island with the understanding that there is a way of doing this and one would not, either as a matter of principle, or for self-preservative reasons be one to violate the code. "Play fair," "give him his turn," "I moved my ball in the rough," "I touched the channel marker with the tip of my boom," have become the confessions or commands heard by all and sundry as the standards of gentle folk have been transmitted through the games and sports of our people.

Games have thus been touched with a de-

*From *Quest*, I (December, 1963), 23-29.

served halo of honor. They have become significant in life as experiences a bit different from the market place. When once the gladiator (or marble-shooter, or rope-skipper, or tennis player) sets foot on the field of play the count is assumed to be correct. The "call" will be without favor or advantage, the chips will fall where they will, and if he loses because of the inexorable forces at work he will withhold his tears and his alibi, acknowledge the superiority of his opponent, and, later, join him in a toast and song to the happy days of friendly contest!

Not yet has the cynicism of "nice guys finish last" penetrated *all* of sport and destroyed its virtue. Not yet has the sportsman who plays with honor and with respect in his heart for the traditions of the game and the rights of the opponent disappeared from the scene.

But almost. Games and sports are rapidly losing their simplicity of former days. They command now the attention of millions—of people and dollars. Fortunes are made from them. Reputations built or ruined. The sporting goods industry grosses within the top ten. Organized athletics in schools and communities have moved from the simple pleasures of a Yale-Harvard boat race to the spectacles of Canton-Massillon or the Cotton Bowl. Much is at stake—including the quality of morality which pervades the phenomenon.

And there is cause for alarm. No longer are all the games played on the high plane of respectability. There has crept into the program

251

elements of immorality and greed which bid fair to spoil the fun. And it will take more effort on the part of many people to stem the tide of anti-morality and anti-intellectualism which is presently engulfing sport as it is engulfing many other aspects of our cultural, political and social existence.

Organized effort? Teach ethics—or morality —by organized effort? Well, let's examine the case for it.

How have any of us arrived at our present level of ethical behavior? How have we achieved the values we live by? Mainly by observing example and partly by responding to teaching and the force of law. We can remember being good boys and girls long enough in Sunday School to reflect upon the startling news that "blessed are the meek for they shall inherit the earth." So we were somewhat perplexed and shocked a little when the noted sports authority, Mr. Durocher was quoted as saying that "nice guys finish last."

Nor can we fail to be impressed with Norman Cozens when he points out how casually we regard violence whether it be in games, traffic or war and shows us how we completely repudiate the admonition to turn the other cheek or to love one's enemies in such situations.

It is going to take organized effort because of the great and powerful influences at work today which are bringing games and sports to their knees in a brutal assault to turn them into instruments not useful for perpetuating the gentle skills of friendly intercourse. They now can be powerful media for greed, bribery, and perhaps worst of all the dominating egocentrism of him who would use others not as Kant would have them used—as ends withal— but through the particularly immoral exploitation for ends which are *not* their own. In some quarters, if we hunger and thirst after righteousness it is becoming a little more difficult to be filled.

The case, as I see it, is alarming. Charlie, my neighboring twelve year old is ready with his alibi if he loses a bike race. He must save face. It does not dawn on him that Benny may have been faster. Parents in Little League and high school sport are becoming notoriously poor sports. The coaching from the bench (distinctly against the rules) in big-time football influences thousands in little-time football. A midwestern college athletic director and President *knew* of an All-American's scholastic ineligibility his sophomore year but by duplicity he continued to play until his eligibility was used up two years later! The cynicism of players, coaches, commissioners, and newsmen associated with tournaments, and championships invariably increases in volume as the gate swells and the audience enlarges. "Amateur" college athletics have all but disappeared leaving only the tears of a lamented Whitney Griswold or an irate Lewis Morrill. Bowl games multiply. To deny one leads to a display of bad temper on the part of the aggrieved press, alumni and students whose ethical standards are no higher than will allow them to throw bottles through the windows of the building where the faculty had voted to deny the darlings a chance to win—and thus gloat.

It is not a pretty picture.

But it ought not be surprising that it is not pretty. Because the decline in morality in sports, the abandonment of those sweet virtues of our polite childhood, are all related to the major transition taking place in the character of our culture.

Richard Holfstadter in that realistic tome "Anti-intellectualism in American Life" (1) traces this disease through our religious institutions, our politics, business, and education. He traces the beginning of the decline of the respect for the gentleman to the attacks on Thomas Jefferson, and he makes it clear that the learned man or woman, the nobleman and his principles of conduct, the gentility of the aristocrat has given way to standards of the mob and the slob. None of us has escaped, and some of us are bruised from this tidal wave of anti-morality which holds our schools suspect of everything from the teaching of the doctrine of racial equality (of all things) to dealing realistically with the true nature of the democratic process!

To stem this tide is the greatest challenge confronting us all in education—and surely it confronts us in physical education. Where better than on the playing fields and in the gymnasiums of our schools and colleges can we demonstrate and evaluate the dynamics of ethical judgment? Our rules of the games *do not* and *can not* govern human conduct completely. Any more than can legislation guarantee equality of opportunity among men. As Martin Buber would put it the demands of authentic existence mean that man cannot blindly follow the prescripts of law but must accept an "ethic of responsibility," in which moral action is a response to what the situation demands at a given time.

I wonder, for example, if we have not misread completely the "competitive spirit" as it flows so brightly in our culture. Competition has made us great—competition with nations, with nature, and with our fellow man. But we seem to have confused the uses of competition as between war and sport. To be sure of it we frequently compare the two by speaking of the invaluable training for sport one gets out of combat or, by claiming as one famous athletic figure did, that the best combat officers come from the ranks of letter winners in college! Maybe so, but there is a discrepancy. Competition in modern war holds no place of honor for the opponent. He is to be killed by the silent means of a missile or a bomber high overhead in a conspiracy of silence of which Nietzsche would have approved because it gave no hint of its actual aim or purpose.

Games are getting like that. We hold secret practice, we hold secret meetings. We learn to hit 'em hard and where they are weak and if we don't exploit the other's tender feelings we miss a bet. All this is, as Mencken would say, because we are fatally insecure, so uncertain of the outcome of the game, so fearful that we may lose that we have no honor to display because honor is predicated upon a feeling of absolute security.

But competition can have another quality. It is, after all, not an end in itself but merely a means. Being a means it must never become so useful as to over-shadow the need for developing mutual respect among men. If the very essence of the democratic way is not respect for personality—then what is it? And any device or practice that teaches the young to hate, to spit upon, or to paint his library needs examination to determine whether the means have grown more important than the ends. Competitive sport can be a fine tool for teaching of democratic morality, or it can, with equal facility, become destructive of it. To paraphrase Rousseau: those who would treat sport and morality apart will never understand the one or the other.

There are many violent critics of sports and of the vehicle which so often carries sport through the academic portals—the program of physical education. Why does Robert M. Hutchins so tartly oppose any effort to make a learning experience out of these activities? Why would Bestor, or Fadiman, or Mayer hold little respect for the attempt to claim educational virtue for modern physical education? Why does even a blue-chip educational statesman like James Bryant Conant find a place for physical education in the curriculum only because there is allegedly a body-building influence involved somewhere therein?

Could these phenomena possibly have resulted from the most effective effort at self-destruction any group of well-meaning educators have engaged in in this century? It seems actually that there has been a conspiracy *not*

to conduct sport programs upon an educational level, *not* to teach seriously the ethical aspects of sports but to deny the educational implications of physical education in face of a single concentration upon values in exercise alone.

Perhaps it is, in the long run impossible for people in the field of physical education to deal with more than one value at a time—and, if forced to choose, the value of strength and sweat, being the easiest attainable will be the most widely advertised.

With such a single value as the only one in view then the impresarios of games are free to conduct them at any level they wish ethically and educationally. As long as the illusory value of "physical fitness" is sought no other standards need to be met. Neither personal satisfaction, nor social competence nor continuous participation need to be sought. The anti-intellectual has taken over completely.

Perhaps games will never be returned, even in part, to those who play them or to those who see them as instruments for educational development but will remain forever in the hands of the one who gets the best price he can out of the schedule. Perhaps there is no end to the wild distortion of purpose. Consider, for example, the sorry plight of our modern interpretations of "amateurism." If we had any respect for the English language (and for our moral effect upon the young) we would understand clearly that probably only five percent of high school and college athletes of today are "amateurs" in any decent interpretation of the word. The rank anti-ethic involved constrains the athletic administrator piously to claim amateur status for the subsidized athlete and suggests that there still may be a social or academic stigma to the professional!

In this day of subsidy? What nonsense! Let's face it morally, not in some pseudo-legal "amateur code." A boy or girl who gets as much as a free meal "on the house" is no longer an amateur but may and usually does remain a splendid gentleman or lady. Let's abandon this immoral make-believe of piety with which we color our concept of "amateur athletics."

Perhaps the academic eye-brow is raised at sport, and its badly named family physical education, because of the internally generated confusion relative to the discerned ends of its efforts. This confusion is patently self-destructive. Right now the popular theme song is physical fitness. This is the fourth time in this century programs of physical education have been captured by this popular theme and bent to fit its illusions. A demigod comes out of the southwest with eloquent credentials in folklore but with knowledge of neither need nor know-how and asks us all to exercise and sweat and thus save the nation, or at least its youth, from devastation and desuetude. Bludgeoned by a Presidential plea for physical fitness we reluctantly test and exercise, push up, pull up and run-walk 600 yards thus chasing a biological end which not only has no relation to the educative process but which has a built-in rejection factor which dooms the program to failure in our kind of society.

For years physical education programs had been moving rather steadily towards accent on the noun. They had been exploring the ways experience in vigorous movement could be used for total development, to recapitulate the culture of our land, to bring the individual into possession of himself and his powers. The exploration was mainly in the area of social and psychological development because these were relatively unexplored fields and the biological virtue of exercise has been well known for years. Exercise is important to life and living. It is here to stay. Only academic fools are oblivious to that.

But what we needed in physical education was full blown research and clinical experience in the relation of movement to the teaching of ethics and morality, to the improvement of psychological states, and the cultivation of social gain between people and groups. These we need and these we are not getting because of the immoral stand we take of being glad to cultivate the sound body as the babysitter to the sound mind! We must follow the leader, sweat profusely, walk fifty miles, do our push-ups, patronize Vic Tanney and Bonnie Prudden, and thus will our population be made strong. Morally? Psychologically? Ethically? Socially? Or just muscularly? What are the great needs for successful life in our society? What kind of man-power does our society need for its preservation? This is the compelling question from the standpoint of national need and people in physical education had better have an answer or they will be lost in the oceans of sweat recommended by the muscle-building anti-intellectual.

But who was John Dewey? To refer to him is risky business in today's world of the Far Right, and the dynamometer! He once said that "The serious threat to our democracy is not the existence of foreign totalitarian states. It is the existence within our own personal attitudes and within our own institutions of conditions similar to those which have given a victory to external authority, discipline, uniformity, and dependence upon The Leader in foreign countries" (2:49).

It is within the repudiation of those idols that we will find the ultimate and eternal strength of free men in a free society. The individual to be educated is a social individual. He lives not alone as a recluse but in a society which is an organic unit of individuals. If we eliminate this social factor we are left with only a pulsating mass of protoplasm sans direction, sans purpose, sans reason for being.

No wonder Hutchins and his group snobbishly advise parents to avoid colleges where physical education is required. He knows that as likely as not the students may be asked to climb ropes ad nauseum or respond seriously to the pseudo-intellectual "fitness" expert who prepares the tables of "fitness" from dynamometers and rope climbs. No wonder. This sort of thing has about the same relation to the educational program as fertilizing the soil with worms does to raising flowers. It may have a part to play but it is a small one and a dubious one at that!

What we in physical education must come soon to understand is that no one, but no one, will take us seriously until we begin to take ourselves seriously and become truly intelligent about exploring the contribution which the world of sports, games, and dance can have to the *education* of man.

Can this world have a bearing upon the Christian ethic? Or any other ethic? Is it to be taken seriously as a means by which the accepted moral standards of the group are to be passed on? Can it be an effective experience in the enrichment of judgment about relative values? Can it help in decision making?

Well, it always *has* had a bearing on these things since man first taught the young through the game and the dance. But right now—when we have organized a program we call physical education, brought it into the school, used motor movement as it means and media, we need to get down to the business of teaching the behaviors this society of ours expects if it is to survive. We need to eliminate the casualness of the "Oh, I say Old Boy, that's not done" approach. We need to get serious about a search for our *total* potential, not merely our muscular.

This country is not going to be saved—or destroyed—by muscle. But by the quality of its moral fibre. What greater challenge can programs of physical education rise to meet?

REFERENCES

1. Hofstadter, Richard. *Anti-Intellectualism in American Life.* New York: Knopf, 1963.
2. Dewey, John. *Freedom and Culture.* New York: G. P. Putnam's Sons, 1939.

On Being Good Sports in Sports*

GUS TURBEVILLE

The 1965 major league baseball season was not very far along when the first "beanball" incidents occurred. John Orsino of the Baltimore Orioles claimed that Phil Ortega of the Washington Senators was throwing at him, and Walter Bond of the Houston Astronauts made a similar accusation against Jim Bunning of the Philadelphia Phillies. A few weeks later, several members of the San Francisco Giants maintained that Don Drysdale of the Los Angeles Dodgers was trying to hit them with the ball, and the star pitcher of the Giants, Juan Marichal, threatened to "get" Drysdale the next time the two teams met.

It must be understood that the pitcher's mound is only 60½ feet from where the batter stands at home plate. A good fastball pitcher, such as Ortega, Bunning, Drysdale, or Marichal, can throw a baseball almost 100 miles an hour. It doesn't take much imagination to realize the damage that a ball thrown from that distance can do to a batter. Although only one player in major league history, Ray Chapman of the Cleveland Indians who was struck by a pitch by Carl Mays of the New York Yankees in 1920, has been killed after a "beaning," numerous minor league and sandlot players have met their demise in this fashion.

Essentially the inside pitch or "duster" is the pitcher's weapon of terror to undermine the batter's confidence. Numerous ballplayers have had their careers ended or considerably diminished after being struck by thrown balls.

The late Mickey Cochrane, a Hall of Fame catcher with the Detroit Tigers, was unable to play baseball again after being beaned by Bump Hadley of the Yankees. A great outfielder, Joe Medwick of the old Brooklyn Dodgers, never again became the feared slugger of old after Bob Bowman of the St. Louis Cardinals "put one in his ear," as Leo Durocher would say.

These incidents are recounted to point out that the game as played should be called a war rather than a sport. When the object is to maim the opponent and to terrify him, true skill and ability are discounted in value—and the bully tends to rise to the top of the heap. Is this the purpose of sports? I think not.

Sports are a form of recreation, a way, literally, of recreating ourselves. They should enable us to relax and enjoy ourselves, to find new meanings in life, to get a different perspective on our jobs, our families, and the things we think are important. They should encourage us to participate and keep our own bodies ("a temple in which resides the soul") healthy, lean, and firm.

But when winning becomes the important thing, yea the only thing, these purposes are lost. Organized athletics become restricted just for the physically gifted, those who need them least. Participation no longer is for fun, but for winning—and mayhem is all right, even encouraged, if it helps achieve the goal.

Coaches have been known to tell their teams that the most important thing they will ever do in their lives is to beat Notre Dame, or

* From *Vital Speeches of the Day*, 31 (June 15, 1965), 542-544.

255

Tennessee, or Southern Cal, or Harvard on a particular day. Nonsense. As a matter of fact, beating a certain team is probably one of the least important things they will ever do in their lives. With a troubled peace constantly being violated, with several million people unemployed in this country, with half of the world's 3,400,000,000 inhabitants going to bed hungry at night, with delinquency, suicide, divorce, insanity, and drug addiction on the rise, who can say that winning a ballgame is so important?

But the coaches say it is, the fans do, and the players believe it. Numerous athletes, such as Bill Russell of the Boston Celtics, actually throw up before a big game. And after a crucial contest has been lost, many of the performers on the losing team will cry like babies. And the sportswriters will say that this is good —that it proves that the athletes played their hearts out. No one wants a good loser on his team. The ideal player is one who throws a tantrum when he loses and tears up the dressing room. Sometimes the manager, such as Gene Mauch of the Philadelphia Phillies, will show the players how it is done, as his performance in Houston several years ago will attest.

According to most historians, Abraham Lincoln was one of our truly great presidents. Yet virtually his whole career was marred by one defeat after another. He lost in love, he lost most of the public offices for which he ran, and he lost two of his young sons. Sometimes his melancholy became so great that his friends were concerned about his sanity. But suppose he had won at love, had been elected to all the public offices for which he aspired, and had not lost his sons? Would he have been the great human being he was? Or did the series of almost overwhelming setbacks temper his character, help him develop humility, compassion, and kindness, and give him a sense of historical perspective on what was really important in life? To ask the question is to answer it.

To win constantly, to always be successful, and never meet with failure are almost sure ways of developing arrogance, coldness, and hardness. What wretched creatures we should be if we didn't know how to experience defeat! Without the shadows, who could appreciate the sunlight? Without cold, who would enjoy warmth? Without the valleys, who would love the mountains? Without defeat, who would savor victory?

This is not to say that one should not try to win the games in which he participates. It's fun to win, but only if one's opponent is making an honest effort. But the game's the thing, and it should be an enjoyable and renewable experience, win or lose. And one should realize that heaven and earth don't depend on the outcome of a particular athletic contest. Of course, it is realized that the professional athlete is in a special category, and if he does not meet with a particular degree of success he will have to look for a new profession.

In our obsession with winning at all costs, the game officials have taken an almost unbelievable beating. Virtually every call adverse to the home team evokes a chorus of boos, and when a close decision is instrumental in the final result, the officials often need police protection. At one time, booing the officials was restricted largely to professional sports, but now this regrettable phenomenon extends to almost every kind of athletic contest at about every level—even the Little League! Sports create good sportsmanship? Whom are we trying to kid?

Some psychologists have attempted to explain the booing syndrome by suggesting that symbolically we associate the officials with our parents. We don't dare openly attack our parents for the authority they hold over us, so we take out our frustration and aggression on the officials whose responsibility it is to tell us what is right and wrong (with the game).

Others advance the thesis that unconsciously we feel guilty that we are mere spectators instead of participants in this leading way of proving one's manhood. But if we can boo the officials and the star players, such as Mickey Mantle, Dean Chance, Wilt Chamberlain, Sonny Liston, Jack Nicklaus, Jim Taylor, and Bob Hayes, we are proving our own superiority to these mere mortals who make mistakes on the playing arena. From our comfortable and safe seat, we always make the proper strategy, always homer with the bases loaded, invariably strike out the opposition, never make an error, never miss a free throw or a long goal attempt, knockout the opponent in boxing, pin him (quickly!) in wrestling, make 18 straight holes-in-one, shake off would be tacklers as though they were children, down the opposing runner for a big loss on a bone-shattering (his!) tackle, run the mile in three minutes, and the 100 yard dash just a bit faster than a greyhound. In bowling we have nothing but strikes, and in tennis our ace serve is never returned, but our opponent's is knocked down his throat, poor lad.

Booing at basketball games has become so rampant that many spectators in disgust have given up attending. It's bad enough to hear the catcalls in a huge open air stadium but to hear them in an enclosed arena is deafening. It is felt by many knowledgeable observers that although the overwhelming majority of officials are completely honest, unconsciously the crowd reactions make them partial to the home team. This may help account for the big advantage that a home court is in basketball.

As is true at most schools, the booing at Notre Dame basketball games had gotten out of hand, and some opposing teams were avoiding trips to South Bend. The new basketball coach, Johnny Dee, decided that something should be done to rescue the reputation of the Fighting Irish for good sportsmanship. In appearances before the student body, he asked them to refrain from booing either the officials or the opposing players. He urged them to cheer good plays of either team, and to remember always that they were ambassadors of Notre Dame. Happily it can be reported that a marked transformation for the better took place in the behavior of the fans at the Notre Dame basketball games. This illustrates what can be done when a responsible authority at an institution decides to take action to curb fan abuse. Are you listening in Starkville, Lexington, Ann Arbor, Palo Alto, Austin, Princeton, Evansville, etc., etc.?

Recently the storied Amos Alonzo Stagg passed to his reward, but the reputation he left behind will endure so long as the men record events on this planet. Although he achieved fame as a result of the successful football teams he developed at the University of Chicago (ante Hutchins) and is credited with numerous innovations involving the forward pass, the lateral, the T-formation, etc., his greatest moment in sports had nothing to do with strategy or prowess, but with integrity.

In a football game his halfback broke away on an end run for some 75 yards and an apparent touchdown. Those who saw the contest will never forget the picture of Mr. Stagg running on to the field shouting, "No, no, it wasn't a touchdown. You (the official) couldn't see it because your view was blocked, but he stepped on the chalk line just past the line of scrimmage." The play was called back, and although the University of Chicago was denied the touchdown, there are those today who say that was her greatest moment in sports.

One of my greatest vicarious sports thrills was having lunch one day at the Avco Corporation with Earl "Red" Blaik, erstwhile great Army football coach and now an executive

with Avco. I asked him what was his most unusual experience as a coach. He replied, "That's an easy one to answer. It happened back in 1940 when I was coaching at Dartmouth, a great school scholastically, but not known for its powerhouse football teams.

"We'd had a mediocre season having already lost four games, when we faced the Big Red of Cornell, undefeated and untied for 18 straight games, and ranked number one in the nation. It was the next to the last game of the season, and the odds on Cornell were prohibitive. It was assumed that we didn't have a chance, and to tell you the truth, I wasn't sure we did either.

"To make a long—and an exciting—story short, going into the last seconds of the game we were holding on to a precarious 3-0 lead. If we could hold Cornell for one more down, we'd get the ball and time would run out within one play. We batted down a pass in the end zone, and pandemonium broke loose both in the stands and on our bench. Our players were ready to call a play to run out the clock when the referee, "Red" Friesell, held up his hand to signal that it was fourth down coming up. He had lost count, later explaining that he thought there had been a double-offside penalty on a previous play, and was giving Cornell an extra down. We protested, but to no avail.

"On the next or fifth play, Cornell scored when Walter Scholl passed to Bill Murphy, and thereby won the game 7-3. Of course everybody there but the officials knew that the touchdown had been scored on an illegal down, but there wasn't anything we could do about it.

"On the following Monday the President of Cornell Dr. Ezra Day, viewed the game films and when he saw that his team had scored its touchdown on a fifth down, he and coach Carl Snavely immediately announced that Dartmouth had won the game and that the score would be officially entered in the records as 3-0."

Naturally the students, alumni, and fans of Cornell were stunned by this decision which denied the team a perfect season and its number one rating. But in retrospect Cornell won more good will and fame as a result of its good sportsmanship than it could possibly have gained from an undefeated season achieved by an official's error.

The dramatic moment in football is the 100 yard run; in baseball, the 400 foot home run; in basketball, the long goal; in golf, the hole-in-one; in boxing, the K.O. But in the last analysis all athletic contests are games of inches. How many long touchdown runs were not made because the runner missed evading a tackler by an inch? How many homeruns were missed by an inch? How many goals in basketball? Holes-in-one in golf? How many K.O.'s were not made in boxing because of the lack of another inch of leverage?

This leads us to one of the really significant contributions sports have to make to our lives. Except for individualized sports, such as boxing and wrestling, athletics involve teamwork. There is no room for selfishness or egotism. The welfare of the team comes first, and when a player puts his own desires first he is cheating on his teammates. Thus when a performer overeats and thus slows himself a step, he is cheating. When he smokes and thereby cuts down on his wind,[1] he is cheating. When he drinks and put added pressure on his entire system, both physically and psychologically, he is cheating. When he doesn't get the sleep his system requires, he is cheating. When he fails to do his calisthenics and lets his body get soft and out of condition, he is cheating.

All of these examples of putting one's own pleasures and indulgences first can mean the inch separating the successful athlete and team from the unsuccessful. No chain is stronger than its weakest link, and in many ways this is true of sports as well. A well disciplined, well trained team in the peak of condition can account for many inches of success during the course of a season. The participant who doesn't care enough for his teammates to keep in proper condition is anything but a good sport.

In this connection, I have always been bothered by the fact that the broadcasts of so many sporting events are sponsored by breweries and tobacco companies whose products have cut innumerable inches from the performances of the players. One would think that at least the colleges and universities would have the courage to refuse that kind of sponsorship of their athletic contests, but unfortunately they have been more concerned with their revenues than with their social responsibilities.

In sports where all the emphasis has been on winning, there has been tremendous pressures on the coaches or managers to win at

[1] According to Dr. W. C. Shafer, physician and scientist at Astronautics in San Diego, "A man who smokes a pack of cigarettes a day breathes as though he were between 5,000 and 8,000 feet high, even if he is standing on the seashore. *Smoke Signals,* May 1965, p. 1.

all costs. Every year in the big leagues, many of the managers lose their jobs because their teams did not win often enough—and then they frequently are hired by another team which fired their manager for the same reason. Sort of a game of musical chairs. When Alvin Dark was managing the Giants he said that when he was hired he knew that inevitably the day would come when he would be fired. He made that statement after his team had won the pennant in 1962 and his job looked safe, but incredibly, two years later he was fired on the last day of the season. It's not enough to win; you have to keep on winning year after year.

The number of great football coaches who have been fired or who were compelled to resign is legion. Such immortal names as Jess Hill, Lynn Waldorf, Bernie Bierman, and Harry Stuldreher immediately come to mind. Every sports fan has read of the shocking abuse that Murray Warmath took at Minnesota before he produced some great teams that went to the Rose Bowl. Not only was he repeatedly hanged in effigy, but also garbage was scattered on his lawn, and he and his family were subjected to abusive telephone calls from "courageous" anonymous fans. Sports writers, such as the late Reider Lund of the Ridder papers, constantly criticized his strategy, his system of recruitment, his scheduling of opponents, *ad infinitum, ad nauseum.* Today some sports writers in the Minneapolis area claim that in Warmath they have the finest football coach in America. It's amazing how much he learned while listening to the abusive fans, the wailing alumni, and the carping sportswriters.

There is a place for sportsmanship in sports, both amateur and professional. The object of the game is to win, but not to exterminate. And it is a game, not a war, as some would have us believe. When Fred Haney took over in 1956 as manager of the Milwaukee Braves, the team immediately went on a long winning streak. It was snapped after eleven straight when the Phillies' great Robin Roberts beat them. After the game Haney shook hands with Roberts and congratulated him on a fine pitching performance. Instead of commenting favorably on this fine example of good sportsmanship, *The Sporting News* (the national baseball weekly) editorialized against Haney!

It wasn't too many years ago that one of the football coaches in the Southwest Conference became enraged at his players because several of them on leaving a game shook hands with their opponents. Other coaches have taught their players to look at the opponents as enemies and to do nothing to help them. Don't pick up the catcher's mask for him, don't help an opposing player off the ground, never congratulate him on a good performance, and if you get a chance, work on his trick knee or shoulder and get him out of the game. When this situation comes to pass, can we call the game a sport? Just witness the beating that a Wilt Chamberlain or a Jim Taylor takes in an average contest, although neither of these stellar performers is known for turning the other cheek.

Far more important than winning any athletic contest is coming out victorious in the great game of life. In this day of cynicism, of winning at all costs, and pursuit of the fast buck, it may sound a little corny to quote Grantland Rice's most famous lines, but their truth is as great now as ever before:

For when the One Great Scorer comes
To write against your name,
He marks—not that you won or lost—
But how you played the game.

The Sportsmanship Myth*

RICHARD CALISCH

Does athletic competition aid in the forming, in youth, of ideals of sportsmanship and fair play? Do competitive athletics actually build sportsmanship? Is it possible that interscholastics do more harm than good in this field?

All of these questions can be answered either *yes* or *no*. Coaches will answer one way; teachers of physical education may answer another; referees and officials may give either answer; as may spectators and participants. But no matter who answers the questions, the answers depend upon some concrete definition of the term sportsmanship.

WHAT IS SPORTSMANSHIP?

Definitions given in literature and in school courses range all the way from "Obeying the rules of the game," to "Acting at all times as you would act in your own home." Neither of these definitions is completely adequate because of one overlooked, yet obvious, fact; *sportsmanship is not a set of rules, it is a code of living*. It includes not only play and athletics, but business, home life, social relations, and all the other myriad activities which make up our lives, and it manifests itself differently in each place. Sportsmanship, or its lack, is as much a part of life as food or its lack; with it we flourish, without it we degenerate.

Do competitive athletics contribute to forming of a desirable, consistent, and acceptable code of living, applicable to all phases of life? If so, then interscholastics have an important *raison d'etre*, aside from the obvious justifica-

* From *Physical Educator*, X (March, 1953), 9-11.

tions concerning physical fitness, social benefits, and health.

If not, then one of our most prized and lauded reasons for including interscholastic athletics in our programs must be discarded, and rightly so, for if we make false claims we are apt to be judged by them, and it is obvious that this can be dangerous, especially to a profession which is forced to be on the defensive most of the time anyway.

Another question, equally important and equally thought provoking, is this: *if interscholastics do not actively contribute to the building of sportsmanship do they actually deter the growth of this desired quality?* If the answer here is *yes,* then no matter how valuable competitives are in other respects, it is they that must be discarded. By destroying the capacity for fair play and decency, which is what sportsmanship means, competitives would be tearing at the roots of society and deterring the normal and healthy growth of the participants in those competitives.

First let us examine some cases purely within the area of athletics, to see if there is any contribution made by competitives to the forming of a desirable, consistent, and acceptable code of living, within the phase of life which we are most interested in, namely athletics themselves. In other words, does participation in one phase of athletics build up good sportsmanship in other phases?

SOME EXAMPLES

This author has recently had the opportunity to observe high school physical education classes for a period of six weeks. The school observed was known for its fine football team, and its reputation as an athletic power was well established. The coaches were men respected in their field, and popular with students and parents alike. The school athletic plant was completely adequate.

Physical education classes in this school were built almost entirely around competition, a situation which gives rise to many instances in which sportsmanship, or lack of it, could be easily observed. Varsity athletes, whose training was such as to render them conscious of sportsmanship and its accompanying behavior patterns, were excused from physical education during the season of their sports. The following instances all occurred within three weeks of the return of the football players to gym classes.

> In a round robin basketball game, the captain of one squad was sent from the game for unsportsmanship like conduct. His action during the game was observed by the referee to be deliberately unfair. His deliberate fouls were penalized by the awarding of the customary two free shots, but the boy was left in the game until, after his fourth personal foul, he lost his temper and threw the ball at the referee in anger. This boy was an all-league quarterback on the league championship football team.
> A freshman basketball player was beaten up by three senior football players, for allegedly bothering the girl friend of one of them. Upon examination the story turned out to be false. The girl stated the freshman had done nothing. No other reason could be found for the incident.
> In an activity class one boy, a non-athlete, was kept from playing in tourney competition by his squad captain, a football team member, for several days. The boy finally reported the action to his teacher in spite of the pressure exerted by the team captain and his friends.

LITTLE CARRY-OVER

Although these examples are merely isolated cases, and in no way conclusive proof of anything, they will probably be familiar to most teachers of physical education, and for that reason may be indicative of the fact that *there is probably little transfer of sportsmanship from one athletic situation to another.*

If a boy is a good sport in football will he be a good sport in basketball? Many factors must be considered in answering this question: home training, the type of coach in each sport, the boy's ability, etc. No answer can be given based alone on the fact that the boy is a good sport in football. It is these other factors which

cause or prevent carry over, the actual competitive sport has little or nothing to do with the transfer.

A boy taught to perform on the piano cannot, because of this training, operate a typewriter, although the skills are somewhat similar; similarly a boy who has been taught the elements of sportsmanship on the basketball floor, will not automatically be a sportsman on the tennis court. A boy may come under the influence of the finest coach in the land, he may learn sportsmanship along with his fundamentals, but if he goes, after practice, to a home where the golden rule is unknown, the coaches' work is all for nothing, because of the overwhelming influence of the home environment.

The home, the school, the playground each have a separate kind of behavior code, a distinct pattern of sportsmanship which is consistent within its own area. These patterns have some similar elements, yes, but they are not identical, and it is probably wise to say that little if any transfer is possible from one phase of life to another if these phases are not almost identical. However, it is probably safe to say that a general attitude may be transferred from one activity to another, making a certain boy "sportsmanship prone" or not "sportsmanship prone."

A businessman does not treat his employees as he treats his family, and no one expects him to do so. A basecketball player, similarly should not be expected to act the same at home as he does on the court, but *he is* expected to do so. *Why?* Because of the popular sportsmanship myth which states that athletes are automatically good sports. This myth was conceived, born, nurtured, raised, and is being perpetuated by those who should be its worst enemies, the physical educators. How often do we see lists of objectives for programs in which "development of sportsmanship" is listed. This is humbug. Athletics develop not *sportsmanship* but football sportsmanship or basketball sportsmanship; not *fair play*, but fair play in wrestling or fair play in soccer; *not honesty*, but honesty in golf or honesty in tennis. Sportsmanship must be learned in specifics.

Again let us examine the key question.

Do competitive athletics contribute to the forming of a desirable, consistent, and acceptable code of living, applicable to all phases of life?

Applicable to all phases of life? Definitely not; unless the phases are, as has been said, identical or unless one has such an overwhelming influence that it rules the behavior of the boy, i.e., the home. For instance, there is little transfer of behavior patterns from the basketball floor to the home, or to the automobile. Yet, there is transfer from the home to the basketball floor because of the obvious, yet too often over looked fact that the boy has spent a long fourteen years at home before he puts on his gym shoes and plays basketball.

So powerful is the influence that a boy from a sportsmanlike home will carry over an attitude which will make him *apt* to behave as he does at home. The same is true of a boy from a home where fair play is unknown. And if we examine the situation we find that the automobile is looked upon by most boys as a special thing, outside and beyond his ordinary life (probably because his parents treat it as such when he asks for it for an evening), and he treats it that way, relating it in no manner to things he has learned outside of the car.

So, let us say that there is little if any justification for the claim that a boy engaged in competitive athletics is receiving anything in the way of sportsmanship education that the non-athlete is not receiving except where that education refers specifically and exactly to the phase of athletics under perusal, i.e., football, basketball and so on.

Do competitive athletics contribute to the forming of a desirable, consistent and acceptable code of living, applicable to all phases of life?

Acceptable? This is a word which means many things; what is perfectly acceptable in Maine, may be heartily despised in Alabama. In order for a thing, be it idea, concept, plan, or philosophy, to be acceptable it must be consistent with social dogma. Yet, in order for it to be desirable, (another of the definition words), it, the concept, idea, or philosophy, often must transcend currently accepted social dogma. Many times what is accepted is not desirable and vice versa.

So it is with sportsmanship. In some areas it is not considered acceptable that all races participate in athletics together; yet this is certainly not a desirable situation as it exists. In spite of all the claims about competitives developing sportsmanship, we may have a situation within the framework of those very competitives which is acceptable to those who live with it, yet which is certainly not desirable.

Once more we can discard a phrase from the definition. *Acceptable* and *desirable* are both to be put aside because many times they cannot exist together, and often a boy will learn in competitive athletics behavior patterns which are desirable, but will be forced to lay them aside to conform to accepted standards. We have only the word *consistent* left.

Is the type of sportsmanship taught by competitive athletics consistent? Probably the answer is *yes,* but *yes* only within the phase of athletics in which it is taught. A boy who learns the why and wherefore of the no-clipping rule in football will not resort to clipping in a game. But that definitely does not imply that he will be a more sportsmanlike automobile driver, or will be a more cooperative citizen.

All learning is consistent within its own scope, but very little will carry over consistently, always the same, into other fields. Sportsmanship, as it is taught through the medium of athletics, has a very limited type of carry over. There can be no justification for any claim that competitives make better citizens, build greater sportsmen, or form finer people; what they do is to make better athletic sportsmen, build greater athletes and form finer people only as those people can be made finer in their actual participation in the athletics.

What we are doing by fostering the claim that athletics build sportsmanship is driving another "nail" into the "coffin" of athletics. The lay public has come to believe our myth, and expects all people who have engaged in athletics to be perfect sportsmen at all times. This is ridiculous; yet, when the myth falls apart who takes the blame? Physical educators do; sports do; coaches do.

When people see and hear of athletes who do not act as the myth states they should, they cannot, believing it as they do, blame the myth. They blame the sports or the teacher. The perpetuation of this fabulous myth may hurt and perhaps eventually kill these sports.

Let us therefore quickly cast aside this false objective and baseless claim before we are stuck with it. By asking people to believe it we are asking them to judge athletics and athletes on a criterion which has not only no basis in fact, but which is a lie from start to finish.

There are enough valid criticisms of our field at present; let us not incur another which, though invalid, may be more powerful than the others. Let us kill the sportsmanship myth.

Sportsmanship as a Moral Category*

JAMES W. KEATING

Sportsmanship, long and inexplicably ignored by philosophers and theologians, has always pretended to a certain moral relevancy, although its precise place among the moral virtues has been uncertain. In spite of this confusion, distinguished advocates have made some remarkable claims for sportsmanship as a moral category. Albert Camus, Nobel prize winner for literature in 1957, said that it was from sports that he learned all that he knew about ethics.[1] Former President Hoover is quoted as saying: "Next to religion, the single greatest factor for good in the United States in recent years has been sport."[2] Dr. Robert C. Clothier, past president of Rutgers University, paraphrased the words of Andrew Fletcher and commented: "I care not who makes the laws or even writes the songs if the code of sportsmanship is sound, for it is that which controls conduct and governs the relationships between men."[3] Henry Steele Commager, professor of history at Columbia University, has argued that it was on the playing fields that Americans learned the lessons of courage and honor which distinguished them in time of war. Commager sums up: "In one way or another, this code of sportsmanship has deeply influenced our national destiny."[4] For Lyman Bryson, of Columbia University, sportsmanship was of extraordinary value:

> The doctrine of love is much too hard a doctrine to live by. But this is not to say that we

have not made progress. It could be established, I think, that the next best thing to the rule of love is the rule of sportsmanship. . . . Some perspicacious historian will some day write a study of the age-old correlation between freedom and sportsmanship. We may then see the importance of sportsmanship as a form of enlightenment. This virtue, without which democracy is impossible and freedom uncertain, has not yet been taken seriously enough in education.[5]

Pope Pius XII, speaking of fair play which is widely regarded as an essential ingredient of sportsmanship, if not synonymous with it, has said:

> From the birthplace of sport came also the proverbial phrase "fair play"; that knightly and courteous emulation which raises the spirit above meanness and deceit and dark subterfuges of vanity and vindictiveness and preserves it from the excesses of a closed and intransigent nationalism. Sport is the school of loyalty, of courage, of fortitude, of resolution and universal brotherhood.[6]

Charles W. Kennedy was a professor of English at Princeton University and chairman of its Board of Athletic Control. His small volume, *Sport and Sportsmanship*, remains to this day probably the most serious study of sportsmanship conducted in America. Kennedy's commitment to sportsmanship was not merely theoretical and scholarly. As chairman of Princeton's Board of Athletic Control, he severed athletic relations with Harvard when unsportsmanlike conduct marred the relationship.[7] For

Kennedy it was not sufficient that sportsmanship characterize man's activities on the athletic field; it must permeate all of life.

> When you pass out from the playing fields to the tasks of life, you will have the same responsibility resting upon you, in greater degree, of fighting in the same spirit for the cause you represent. You will meet bitter and sometimes unfair opposition. . . . You will meet defeat [but] you must not forget that the great victory of which you can never be robbed will be the ability to say, when the race is over and the struggle ended, that the flag you fought under was the shining flag of sportsmanship, never furled or hauled down and that, in victory or defeat, you never lost that contempt for a breach of sportsmanship which will prevent your stooping to it anywhere, anyhow, anytime.[8]

Similar eulogies by other distinguished men with no professional or financial interest in sport or athletics could be multiplied without difficulty, but perhaps the point has already been made. The claims for sportsmanship as a moral category deserves some investigation. It is surprising that the experts in moral theory, the philosopher and the theologian, have seen fit to ignore so substantial an area of human conduct as that occupied by sport and athletics.

Three interrelated problems will be considered in this study: (1) the source of the confusion which invariably accompanies a discussion of sportsmanship and the normal consequences resulting from this confusion; (2) the essence of genuine sportsmanship, or the conduct and attitude proper to sport, with special consideration being given to the dominant or pivotal virtues involved; (3) sportsmanship as applied to athletics—a derivative or analogous use of the term. Once again special attention will be directed to the basic or core virtues which characterize the conduct and attitude of the well-behaved athlete.

THE SOURCE OF CONFUSION AND ITS CONSEQUENCES

What is sportsmanship? William R. Reed, commissioner for the Big Ten Intercollegiate Conference, is most encouraging: "It [sportsmanship] is a word of exact and uncorrupted meaning in the English language, carrying with it an understandable and basic ethical norm. Henry C. Link in his book 'Rediscovery of Morals' says, 'Sportsmanship is probably the clearest and most popular expression of morals.' "[9] Would that this were the case. Reed, however, does not define sportsmanship or enumerate the provisions of its code, and the briefest investigation reveals that he is badly mistaken as to the clarity of the concept. The efforts of no less a champion of sportsmanship than Amos Alonzo Stagg presage the obscurities which lie ahead. In addition to a brilliant athletic career at Yale and forty years as head football coach at the University of Chicago, Stagg did a year of graduate work in Yale's Divinity School and would thus seem to have the ideal background of scholarly training in moral theory and vast practical experience to discuss the problem. Yet his treatment leaves much to be desired. He defined sportsmanship as "a delightful fragrance that people will carry with them in their relations with their fellow men."[10] In addition, he drew up separate codes of sportsmanship, or Ten Commandments of sport, for the coach and for the football player and held that both decalogues were applicable to the business world as well. The second, and by far the most unusual, commandment contained proscriptions seldom found in codes of sportsmanship. "Make your conduct a worthy example. Don't drink intoxicants; don't gamble; don't smoke; don't use smutty language; don't tell dirty stories; don't associate with loose or silly women."[11] Stagg's position is undoubtedly an extreme one, but it calls attention to a tendency all too common among the champions of sportsmanship—the temptation to broaden the concept of sportsmanship until it becomes an all-embracing moral category, a unique road to moral salvation. As always, there is an opposite extreme. Sportsmanship, when not viewed as the pinnacle of moral perfection, can also be viewed as a moral minimum—one step this side of criminal behavior. "A four point program to improve sportsmanship at athletic events has been adopted by the Missouri State High School Activities Association."[12] The first and third provisions of bylaw No. 9 detail penalties for assaults or threats upon officials by players or fans. Such legislative action may be necessary and even admirable, but it is a serious error to confuse the curtailment of criminal activities of this sort with a positive promotion of sportsmanship.

What, then, is sportsmanship? Another approach is by way of the dictionary, everyday experience, and common-sense deductions. Sportsmanship is conduct becoming a sportsman. And who is a sportsman? One who is interested in or takes part in sport. And what is sport? Sport, Webster tells us, is "that which diverts and makes mirth"; it is an "amusement, recreation, pastime." Our problem, then, is to determine the conduct and attitude proper to this type of activity, and this can be done only after a more careful consideration of the nature of sport. Pleasant diversion? Recreation? Amusement? Pastime? Is this how one would describe the World Series, the Masters, the Davis Cup, the Rose Bowl, the Olympic Games, or a high-school basketball tournament? Do the "sport" pages of our newspapers detail the pleasant diversions and amusements of the citizenry, or are they preoccupied with national and international contests which capture the imaginations, the emotions, and the pocketbooks of millions of fans (i.e., fanatics)? It is precisely at this point that we come face to face with the basic problem which has distorted or vitiated most discussions of sportsmanship. Because the term "sport" has been loosely applied to radically different types of human behavior, because it is naïvely regarded as an apt description of (1) activity which seeks only pleasant diversion and, on the other hand, (2) of the agonistic struggle to demonstrate personal or group excellence, the determination of the conduct proper to a participant in "sport" becomes a sticky business indeed. Before proceeding with an analysis of sportsmanship as such, it is necessary to consider briefly an all-important distinction between sport and athletics.

Our dictionary definition of sport leans upon its root or etymological meaning. "Sport," we are told, is an abbreviation of the Middle English *desport* or *disport,* themselves derivatives of the Old French *desporter,* which literally meant to carry away from work. Following this lead, Webster and other lexicographers indicate that "diversion," "recreation," and "pastime" are essential to sport. It is "that which diverts and makes mirth; a pastime." While the dictionaries reflect some of the confusion and fuzziness with which contemporary thought shrouds the concept of athletics, they invariably stress an element which, while only accidentally associated with sport, is essential to athletics. This element is the prize, the *raison d'être* of athletics. Etymologically, the various English forms of the word "athlete" are derived from the Greek verb *athlein,* "to contend for a prize," or the noun *athlos,* "contest," or *athlon,* a prize awarded for the successful completion of the contest. An oblique insight into the nature of athletics is obtained when we realize that the word "agony" comes from the Greek *agonia*—a contest or a struggle for victory in the games. Thus we see that, historically and etymologically, sport and athletics have characterized radically different types of human activity, different not insofar as the game itself or the mechanics or rules

are concerned, but different with regard to the attitude, preparation, and purpose of the participants. Man has probably always desired some release or diversion from the sad and serious side of life. This, of course, is a luxury, and it is only when a hostile environment is brought under close rein and economic factors provide a modicum of leisure that such desires can be gratified. In essence, sport is a kind of diversion which has for its direct and immediate end fun, pleasure, and delight and which is dominated by a spirit of moderation and generosity. Athletics, on the other hand, is essentially a competitive activity, which has for its end victory in the contest and which is characterized by a spirit of dedication, sacrifice, and intensity.

When this essential distinction between sport and athletics is ignored, as it invariably is, the temptation to make sportsmanship an all-embracing moral category becomes irresistible for most of its champions. In 1926 a national Sportmanship Brotherhood was organized for the purpose of spreading the gospel of sportsmanship throughout all aspects of life, from childhood games to international events.[13] Its code consisted of eight rules:

1. Keep the rule.
2. Keep faith with your comrades.
3. Keep yourself fit.
4. Keep your temper.
5. Keep your play free from brutality.
6. Keep pride under in victory.
7. Keep stout heart in defeat.
8. Keep a sound soul and a clean mind in a healthy body.

The slogan adopted by the Brotherhood to accompany its code was "Not that you won or lost—but how you played the game." In giving vigorous editorial support to the Sportsmanship Brotherhood, the *New York Times* said:

> Take the sweet and the bitter as the sweet and bitter come and always "play the game." That is the legend of the true sportsmanship, whether on the ball field, the tennis court, the golf course, or at the desk or machine or throttle. "Play the game." That means truthfulness, courage, spartan endurance, self-control, self-respect, scorn of luxury, consideration one for another's opinions and rights, courtesy, and above all fairness. These are the fruits of the spirit of sportsmanship and in them . . . lies the best hope of social well-being.[14]

Dictionaries that have suggested the distinction between sport and athletics without explicitly emphasizing it have remained relatively

free from this type of romantic incrustation and
moral exaggeration in their treatment of sportsmanship. Beginning with nominal definitions
of sportsmanship as the conduct becoming a
sportsman and of the sportsman as one who
participates in sport, they proceed, much more
meaningfully, to characterize the sportsman by
the kind of conduct expected of him. A sportsman is "a person who can take loss or defeat
without complaint or victory without gloating and who treats his opponents with fairness,
generosity and courtesy." In spite of the limitations of such a description, it at least avoids
the inveterate temptation to make sportsmanship a moral catch-all.

THE ESSENCE OF GENUINE SPORTSMANSHIP

Sportsmanship is not merely an aggregate
of moral qualities comprising a code of specialized behavior; it is also an attitude, a posture,
a manner of interpreting what would otherwise
be only a legal code. Yet the moral qualities
believed to comprise the code have almost
monopolized consideration and have prolifer-
ated to the point of depriving sportsmanship of
any distinctiveness. Truthfulness, courage,
spartan endurance, self-control, self-respect,
scorn of luxury, consideration one for another's
opinions and rights, courtesy, fairness, magnanimity, a high sense of honor, co-operation,
generosity. The list seems interminable. While
the conduct and attitude which are properly
designated as sportsmanlike may reflect many
of the above-mentioned qualities, they are not
all equally basic or fundamental. A man may
be law-abiding, a team player, well conditioned, courageous, humane, and the possessor
of *sang-froid* without qualifying as a sportsman. On the other hand, he may certainly be
categorized as a sportsman without possessing spartan endurance or a scorn of luxury.
Our concern is not with those virtues which
might be found in the sportsman. Nor is it
with those virtues which *often* accompany the
sportsman. Our concern is rather with those
moral habits or qualities which are essential,
which characterize the participant as a sportsman. Examination reveals that there are some
that are pivotal and absolutely essential; others
peripheral. On what grounds is such a conclusion reached? Through the employment of
the principle that the nature of the activity
determines the conduct and attitudes proper
to it. Thus, to the extent that the conduct and
attitudes of the participants contribute to the
attainment of the goal of sport, to that extent

they can be properly characterized as sportsmanlike. The primary purpose of sport is not
to win the match, to catch the fish or kill the
animal, but to derive pleasure from the attempt to do so and to afford pleasure to one's
fellow participants in the process. Now it is
clear that the combined presence of such laudable moral qualities as courage, self-control,
co-operation, and a spirit of honor do not, in
themselves, produce a supporting atmosphere.
They may be found in both parties to a duel
or in a civil war. But generosity and magnanimity are essential ingredients in the conduct
and attitude properly described as sportsmanlike. They establish and maintain the unique
social bond; they guarantee that the purpose
of sport—the immediate pleasure of the participants—will not be sacrificed to other more
selfish ends. All the prescriptions which
make up the code of sportsmanship are
derived from this single, basic, practical
maxim: Always conduct yourself in such a
manner that you will increase rather than detract from the pleasure to be found in the
activity, both your own and that of your fellow participants. If there is disagreement as
to what constitutes sportsmanlike behavior,
then this disagreement stems from the application of the maxim rather than from the
maxim itself. It is to be expected that there
will be differences of opinion as to how the
pleasurable nature of the activity can best be
maximized.

The code governing pure sport is substan-
tially different from a legalistic code in which
lawyers and law courts are seen as a natural
and healthy complement of the system. In fact,
it is in direct comparison with such a system
that the essence of sportsmanship can best be
understood. In itself, sportsmanship is a spirit,
an attitude, a manner or mode of interpreting
an otherwise purely legal code. Its purpose is
to protect and cultivate the festive mood
proper to an activity whose primary purpose
is pleasant diversion, amusement, joy. The
sportsman adopts a cavalier attitude toward
his personal rights under the code; he prefers
to be magnanimous and self-sacrificing if, by
such conduct, he contributes to the enjoyment
of the game. The sportsman is not in search of
legal justice; he prefers to be generous whenever generosity will contribute to the fun of the
occasion. Never in search of ways to evade
the rules, the sportsman acts only from unquestionable moral right.

Our insistence that sport seeks diversion,
recreation, amusement does not imply that the
sportsman is by nature a listless competitor. It

is common practice for him, once the game is under way, to make a determined effort to win. Spirited competitor that he often is, however, his goal is joy in the activity itself and anything—any word, action, or attitude—which makes the game itself less enjoyable should be eliminated. He "fights" gallantly to win because experience has taught him that a determined effort to overcome the obstacles which his particular sport has constructed, adds immeasurably to the enjoyment of the game. He would be cheating himself and robbing the other participants of intense pleasure if his efforts were only halfhearted. Yet there is an important sense in which sporting activity is not competitive but rather co-operative. Competition denotes the struggle of two parties for the same valued object or objective and implies that, to the extent that one of the parties is successful in the struggle, he gains exclusive or predominant possession of that object at the expense of his competitor. But the goal of sporting activity, being the mutual enjoyment of the participants, cannot even be understood in terms of exclusive possession by one of the parties. Its simulated competitive atmosphere camouflages what is at bottom a highly co-operative venture. Sport, then, is a co-operative endeavor to maximize pleasure or joy, the immediate pleasure or joy to be found in the activity itself. To so characterize sport is not to indulge in romantic exaggeration. It is indisputable that the spirit of selfishness is at a very low ebb in genuine sport. Gabriel Marcel's observation concerning the relationship of generosity to joy may even have a limited applicability here. "If generosity enjoys its own self it degenerates into complacent self-satisfaction. This enjoyment of self is not joy, for joy is not a satisfaction but an exaltation. It is only in so far as it is introverted that joy becomes enjoyment."[15] In comparison with sport, athletics emphasize self-satisfaction and enjoyment; sport is better understood in terms of generosity, exaltation, and joy.

Although there is no acknowledgment of the fact, the concern which has been shown for sportsmanship by most of its advocates has been almost exclusively directed to its derivative meaning—a code of conduct for athletes. To the extent that the Sportsmanship Brotherhood was concerned with athletics (and their code of conduct would indicate that was their main concern), their choice of a slogan seems singularly inappropriate. "Not that you won or lost—but how you played the game." Such a slogan can be accommodated in the world of sport, but even there the word "enjoyed" should be substituted for the word "played." Application of this slogan to athletics, on the other hand, would render such activity unintelligible, if not irrational.

"SPORTSMANSHIP" IN ATHLETICS

Careful analysis has revealed that sport, while speaking the language of competition and constantly appearing in its livery, is fundamentally a co-operative venture. The code of the sportsman, sportsmanship, is directed fundamentally to facilitating the co-operative effort and removing all possible barriers to its development. Mutual generosity is a most fertile soil for co-operative activity. When we move from sport to athletics, however, a drastic change takes place. Co-operation is no longer the goal. The objective of the athlete demands exclusive possession. Two cannot share in the same victory unless they are team mates, and, as a result, the problems of competition are immediately in evidence. "Sportsmanship," insofar as it connotes the behavior proper to the athlete, seeks to place certain basic limitations on the rigors of competition, just as continual efforts are being made to soften the impact of the competitive struggle in economics, politics, international relations, etc. But we must not lose sight of an important distinction. Competition in these real-life areas is condoned or encouraged to the extent that it is thought to contribute to the common good. It is not regarded as an end in itself but as the only or most practicable means to socially desirable ends. Friedrich A. Hayek, renowned economist and champion of competition in economics, supports this position:

> The liberal argument is in favor of making the best possible use of the forces of competition as a means of co-ordinating human efforts, not an argument for leaving things just as they are. It is based on the conviction that, where effective competition can be created, it is a better way of guiding individual efforts than any other. It does not deny, but even emphasizes, that, in order that competition should work beneficially, a carefully thought-out legal framework is required and that neither the existing nor the past legal rules are free from grave defects. Nor does it deny that, where it is impossible to create the conditions necessary to make competition effective, we must resort to other methods of guiding economic activity.[16]

A code which seeks to mitigate the full force of the competitive conflict can also be desirable in athletics. While an athlete is in essence a prizefighter, he seeks to demonstrate his excellence in a contest governed by rules which acknowledge human worth and dignity. He mistakes his purpose and insults his opponent if he views the contest as an occasion to display generosity and magnanimity. To the extent that sportsmanship in athletics is virtuous, its essence consists in the practice of fairness under most difficult conditions. Since the sportsman's primary objective is the joy of the moment, it is obvious from that very fact that he places no great emphasis on the importance of winning. It is easy for him to be modest in victory or gracious in defeat and to play fair at all times, these virtues being demonstrated under optimum conditions for their easy exercise. The strange paradox of sportsmanship as applied to athletics is that it asks the athlete, locked in a deadly serious and emotionally charged situation, to act outwardly as if he were engaged in some pleasant diversion. After an athlete has trained and sacrificed for weeks, after he has dreamed of victory and its fruits and literally exhausted himself physically and emotionally in its pursuit—after all this—to ask him to act with fairness in the contest, with modesty in victory, and an admirable composure in defeat is to demand a great deal, and, yet, this is the substance of the demand that "sportsmanship" makes upon the athlete.

For the athlete, being a good loser is demonstrating self-control in the face of adversity. A festive attitude is not called for; it is, in fact, often viewed as in bad taste. The purists or rigorists are of the opinion that a brief period of seclusion and mourning may be more appropriate. They know that, for the real competitor, defeat in an important contest seems heartbreaking and nerve-shattering. The athlete who can control himself in such circumstances demonstrates remarkable equanimity. To ask that he enter into the festive mood of the victory celebration is to request a Pagliacci-like performance. There is no need for phony or effusive displays of congratulations. A simple handshake demonstrates that no personal ill-will is involved. No alibis or complaints are offered. No childish excuses about the judgment of officials or the natural conditions. No temper tantrums. To be a good loser under his code, the athlete need not be exactly gracious in defeat, but he must at least "be a man" about it. This burden, metaphorically characterized as sportsmanship, bears heavily upon all athletes—amateur or professional. But there are added complications for the professional. Victories, superior performances, and high ratings are essential to financial success in professional athletics. Too frequent defeat will result in forced unemployment. It is easy,

therefore, for a professional athlete to view his competitors with a jaundiced eye; to see them as men who seek to deprive him of his livelihood. Under these circumstances, to work daily and often intimately with one's competitors and to compete in circumstances which are highly charged with excitement and emotion, while still showing fairness and consideration, is evidence of an admirable degree of self-mastery.

Attempts have been made to identify sportsmanship with certain games which, it is contended, were the private preserve of the gentleman and, as a result, reflect his high code of honor.

> Bullying, cheating, "crabbing" were all too common in every form of sport. The present movement away from muckerism probably should be attributed in large measure to the growing popularity of golf and tennis. Baseball, boxing, and many of our common sports trace their origin to the common people who possessed no code of honor. On the other hand, golf and tennis, historically gentlemen's games, have come down to us so interwoven with a high code of honor that we have been forced to accept the code along with the game. . . . The effect of the golf code upon the attitude of the millions who play the game is reflected in all our sports.[17]

It is true that in England the terms "gentleman," "sportsman," and "amateur" were regarded as intimately interrelated. The contention that the common people, and consequently the games that were peculiarly theirs, had no comparable code of honor may be correct, but it awaits the careful documentation of some future social historian. One thing is certain, however, and that is that there is nothing in the nature of any game, considered in itself, that necessarily implies adherence to a moral code. Some games like golf and tennis in which the participants do their own officiating provide greater opportunity for the practice of honesty, but if a high code of honor surrounds the "gentleman's games," it is due principally to the general attitude of the gentleman toward life rather than to anything intrinsic to the game itself. The English gentleman was firmly committed to sport in the proper sense of that term and eschewed the specialization, the rigors of precontest preparation, the secret strategy sessions, and professional coaching which have come to be regarded as indispensable for the athlete. "The fact that a man is born into the society of gentlemen imposes upon him the duties and, to some extent, the ideas of his class. He is expected to have a broad education, catholic tastes, and a multiplicity of pursuits. He must not do anything for pecuniary gain; and it will be easily seen that he must not specialize. It is essentially the mark of the bourgeois' mind to specialize."[18] Moreover, "too much preparation is contrary to all English ethics, and secrecy in training is especially abhorrent. Remember that sport is a prerogative of gentlemen. And one of the ear-marks of a gentleman is that he resort to no trickery and that he plays every game with his cards on the table— the game of life as well as the game of football."[19]

It is the contestant's objective and not the game itself which becomes the chief determinant of the conduct and attitudes of the players. If we take tennis as an example and contrast the code of conduct employed by the sportsman with that of the athlete in the matter of officiating, the difference is obvious. The sportsman invariably gives his opponent the benefit of the doubt. Whenever he is not sure, he plays his opponent's shot as good even though he may suspect that it was out. The athlete, however, takes a different approach. Every bit as opposed to cheating as the sportsman, the athlete demands no compelling proof of error. If a shot seems to be out, even though he is not certain, the athlete calls it that way. He is satisfied that his opponent will do the same. He asks no quarter and gives none. As a result of this attitude and by comparison with the sportsman, the athlete will tend toward a legal interpretation of the rules.

The athletic contest is designed to serve a specific purpose—the objective and accurate determination of superior performance and, ultimately, of excellence. If this objective is to be accomplished, then the rules governing the contest must impose the same burdens upon each side. Both contestants must be equal before the law if the test is to have any validity, if the victory is to have any meaning. To the extent that one party to the contest gains a special advantage, unavailable to his opponent, through an unusual interpretation, application, or circumvention of the rules, then that advantage is unfair. The well-known phrase "sense of fair play" suggests much more than an adherence to the letter of the law. It implies that the spirit too must be observed. In the athletic contest there is a mutual recognition that the rules of the game are drawn up for the explicit purpose of aiding in the determination of an honorable victory. Any attempt to disregard or circumvent these rules must be viewed as a deliberate attempt to

deprive the contest of its meaning. Fairness, then, is rooted in a type of equality before the law, which is absolutely necessary if victory in the contest is to have validity and meaning. Once, however, the necessary steps have been taken to make the contest a true test of respective abilities, the athlete's sole objective is to demonstrate marked superiority. Any suggestion that fair play obliges him to maintain equality in the contest ignores the very nature of athletics. "If our analysis of fair play has been correct, coaches who strive to produce superior teams violate a fundamental principle of sportsmanship by teaching their pupils, through example, that superiority is more greatly to be desired than is equality in sport. . . . But who today would expect a coach to give up clear superiority—a game won —by putting in enough substitutes to provide fair playing conditions for an opposing team?"[20] Thus understood, sportsmanship would ask the leopard to change its spots. It rules out, as illegitimate, the very objective of the athlete. Nothing shows more clearly the need for recognition of the distinction between sport and athletics.

CONCLUSION

In conclusion, we would like to summarize our answers to the three problems set down at the outset.

1. The source of the confusion which vitiates most discussion of sportsmanship is the unwarranted assumption that sport and athletics are so similar in nature that a single code of conduct and similar participant attitudes are applicable to both. Failing to take cognizance of the basic differences between sport and athletics, a futile attempt is made to outline a single code of behavior equally applicable to radically diverse activities. Not only is such an attempt, in the nature of things, doomed to failure but a consequence of this abortive effort is the proliferation of various moral virtues under the flag of sportsmanship, which, thus, loses all its distinctiveness. It is variously viewed as a straight road to moral perfection or an antidote to moral corruption.

2. The goal of genuine sport must be the principal determinant of the conduct and attitudes proper to sporting activity. Since its goal is pleasant diversion—the immediate joy to be derived in the activity itself—the pivotal or essential virtue in sportsmanship is generosity. All the other moral qualities that may also be in evidence are colored by this spirit of generosity. As a result of this spirit, a determined effort is made to avoid all unpleasantness and

conflict and to cultivate, in their stead, an unselfish and co-operative effort to maximize the joy of the moment.

3. The essence of sportsmanship as applied to athletics can be determined by the application of the same principle. Honorable victory is the goal of the athlete and, as a result, the code of the athlete demands that nothing be done before, during, or after the contest to cheapen or otherwise detract from such a victory. Fairness or fair play, the pivotal virtue in athletics, emphasizes the need for an impartial and equal application of the rules if the victory is to signify, as it should, athletic excellence. Modesty in victory and a quiet composure in defeat testify to an admirable and extraordinary self-control and, in general, dignify and enhance the goal of the athlete.

NOTES

1. *Resistance, Rebellion and Death* (New York: Alfred A. Knopf, Inc., 1961), p. 242.
2. In Frank Leahy, *Defensive Football* (New York: Prentice-Hall, Inc., 1951), p. 198.
3. "Sportsmanship in Its Relation to American Intercollegiate Athletics," *School and Society,* XLV (April 10, 1937), 506.
4. Henry Steele Commager, in *Scholastic,* XLIV (May 8-13, 1944), 7.
5. Lyman Bryson, *Science and Freedom* (New York: Columbia University Press, 1947), p. 130.
6. Pope Pius XII, *The Human Body* (Boston: Daughters of St. Paul, 1960).
7. "Athletic Relations between Harvard and Princeton," *School and Society,* XXIV (November 20, 1926), 631.
8. Charles W. Kennedy, *Sport and Sportsmanship* (Princeton, N.J.: Princeton University Press, 1931), pp. 58-59.
9. William R. Reed, "Big Time Athletics' Commitment to Education," *Journal of Health, Physical Education, and Recreation,* XXXIV (September, 1963), 30.
10. Quoted in J. B. Griswold, "You Don't Have To Be Born with It," *American Magazine,* CXII (November, 1931), 60.
11. *Ibid.,* p. 133.
12. "Sportsmanship," *School Activities,* XXXII (October, 1960), 38.
13. "A Sportsmanship Brotherhood," *Literary Digest,* LXXXVIII (March 27, 1926), 60.
14. *Ibid.,* pp. 60-61.
15. Gabriel Marcel, *The Mystery of Being,* Vol. II: *Faith and Reality* (Chicago: Henry Regnery Co., 1960), pp. 133-34.
16. Friedrich A. Hayek, *The Road to Serfdom* (Chicago: University of Chicago Press, 1944), p. 36.
17. J. F. Williams and W. W. Nixon, *The Athlete in the Making* (Philadelphia: W. B. Saunders, 1932), p. 153.
18. H. J. Whigham, "American Sport from an English Point of View," *Outlook,* XCIII (November, 1909), 740.
19. *Ibid.*
20. Frederick R. Rogers, *The Amateur Spirit in Scholastic Games and Sports* (Albany, N.Y.: C. F. Williams & Son, 1929), p. 78.

Is Professional Boxing Immoral?*

RICHARD A. McCORMICK, S.J.

Professional boxing is a part of us. Yet every now and then a tragedy (such as the recent death of Benny Paret) shocks us into enquiry. It revives and reveals the morality of professional boxing as a legitimate question. This is in some ways unfortunate. The outbursts surrounding tragedy tend to obscure the real issue by focusing exclusively on fatalities. They also provoke us to continue to think with our hearts rather than our heads. Rarely has morality been clarified in such an atmosphere.

Boxing can be and has been defined as a giving and parrying of light blows with no intention of striking the opponent severely. If no one has ever questioned the morality of this type of thing, neither has anyone ever thought it a realistic definition of modern professional boxing. Recent moral theologians who have reflected on the matter wisely restrict their considerations to "professional boxing as it is today." When the theologian says *as it is today*, he is trying to highlight an existing situation, perhaps not an inevitable one. Some, possibly many, elements of professional boxing could be radically altered, in which case it is quite conceivable that a different moral evaluation of the sport would have to be made.

By using the phrase *professional boxing as it is today* the theologian does not mean to concentrate on the fight-for-pay element which distinguishes amateur from professional; his intention is to emphasize the characteristics of professional boxing once the distinction has

* Reprinted by permission from *Sports Illustrated*, 17 (November 5, 1962), 70-82. © 1962 Time Inc.

been made. He is trying to paint a picture in a single phrase. Among these characteristics there is the element of a career involving a whole series of fights with cumulative effects. There is the admitted effort of most professionals to win by a KO—or at least a TKO—rather than by decision. There is the medical report of injury, particularly to the brain. There is the synthetic notion of courage wherein confession of injury followed by retirement from a fight invites derision by a crowd that enjoys a beating, clamors for the kill and lustily boos evasive tactics. There are the undeniable benefits that boxing has brought to the lives of many individuals. There are television contracts which create severe scheduling demands; there are boxing commissions and control groups. Finally, there is a specific set of rules. Professional boxing involves more and longer rounds, lighter gloves and sometimes different scoring criteria. These are the things the moralist attempts to evoke with the phrase *professional boxing as it is today*. It is not an individual fight that is his immediate concern. Individual fights may not contain the elements widely present in the sport as a whole. Nor is his concern boxing at the level of the Golden Gloves, the CYO and the private club. Still less is it a judgment of the individual fighter and his motives. It is a whole institution as it touches human conduct.

The defenders of professional boxing regard boxing as a science demanding skill, strength and discipline. In boxing there is splendid opportunity for physical development, alertness, poise, confidence, sportsmanship, initiative and character-building in general. Statistically professional boxing is, they point out, far less dangerous than auto racing, college football and several other sports. Furthermore, the game has given underprivileged youngsters a chance to better themselves. In summary, the advantages outweigh the disadvantages.

With an eye to these claims, some earlier moral evaluations of professional boxing were at times relatively tolerant. In fairness to these earlier views, it must be pointed out that they were formulated before widespread publication of pertinent medical findings. In fairness to professional boxing, however, it should be said that even those who now regard the sport as immoral concede the above advantages. Their objections are elsewhere.

The application of immutable moral principle will vary with the variation of concrete fact or its understanding. Thus in the past 20 years or so there has been a growing consensus among theologians that the sport will not survive moral scrutiny. The three most recent American studies (Hillman, Bernard, Laforet) conclude that the current version of professional boxing is immoral. Most moral theologians would endorse and defend this position, not as the official position of the Catholic Church (the Church has never spoken officially on the matter) but as their own conviction after thoughtful application of their principles to the facts as they see them. If they have been less than enthusiastic about publicizing their conviction it is not because of reluctance to take publicly an unpopular stand. That would be cowardice. Rather it is because the conviction has matured slowly and painfully and because even now some uncertainties still cling to it. But as the subject receives intensified study, it is increasingly difficult to find defenders of the sport among theologians.

Professional boxing is unique among the sports. It is admittedly the only sport whose primary objective toward victory is to batter and damage an opponent into helplessness and the incapacity to continue. In a sport where the infliction of damage is rewarded, one would expect a wide variety of injuries.

Ophthalmic injury is far from unknown, even to the extent of actual blindness. Maxillofacial and aural trauma, including damage to the jaw, teeth, nose and hearing apparatus, are more common. Boxer's nose and cauliflower ear are commonplaces. There is also the possibility of renal damage. Studies (*Journal of Urology*, 1954) have concluded that acute kidney trauma occurs in 65% to 89% of boxers during a fight and is manifested by postbout hematuria. A more recent study (*The Journal of the American Medical Association*, 1958), however, shows these symptoms to be innocent, transitory and painless. The long-term effects in terms of kidney scar and permanent impairment do not seem to exist.

While these and other types of injury do occur, it is craniocerebral injury that recently has engrossed the attention of the medical world. Because of the premium placed on the KO and the TKO, the head has always been the prime target in professional boxing. Blows directed to the head or face comprise about 85% of all blows delivered in the ordinary bout. Body blows are principally diversionary tactics to lay open this prime target. The injuries caused by head blows have provided excellent opportunity for medical investigation because, as noted in *The Lancet* (1937), "unlike accidents these injuries are caused by traumas almost always of the same kind and acting with almost laboratory exactness."

Scientists indicate that the human brain weighs about three pounds. It is fluid-packed but not secured within the skull. A blow to the head causes it to wobble, slide and bounce back and forth inside its cranial container. If a moderate blow can bang the brain against its sidewall, a more severe blow can bring it into contact with the bony sphenoidal ridge to produce selective damage to the frontal lobes, either bleeding or bruising. Where there is destruction of nerve cells the damage is permanent and, when repeated, cumulative.

Medical scientists also call attention to another injury not infrequently suffered by boxers: the punctate (small) hemorrhages in the pons and medulla, probably caused by the jamming of cerebrospinal fluid. Again, where such hemorrhages destroy nerve tissue the damage is permanent, though this need not imply that malfunction of the brain ensues. Such a symptom would be a matter of extent and degree. The possibilities for brain damage appear to be as multiple as the organ is delicate.

What are the noticeable results of brain injury? The most sensational, if not the most tragic, is death, generally associated with hemorrhage. Depending on how one reads statistics, will one conclude with Dr. Arthur H. Steinhaus, former chief of the Division of Physical Education and Health Activities of the U.S. Office of Education, that "professional boxing is 83 times more deadly than high school football and 50 times more deadly than college football"? Or with T. A. Gonzales that "32 years of boxing competitions . . . have produced fewer deaths in proportion to the number of participants than occur in baseball or football"? The point is not clear.

But if death is a relative rarity, the same does not seem to be true of brain damage. In 1928 H. S. Maitland concluded his discussion of the punch-drunk syndrome with the statement that 50% of fighters will develop the condition in mild or severe form if they stay in the game long enough, and that this "seems to be good evidence that some special brain injury due to their occupation exists." Dr. Edward J. Carroll Jr., who came to know fighters intimately through professional and nonprofessional contacts, estimated that after five years of boxing 60% of the boxers will develop mental and emotional changes which are obvious to people who know them. He stated (*American Journal of The Medical Sciences*, 1936) that "no head blow is taken with impunity and . . . each knockout causes definite and irreparable damage. If such trauma is repeated for a long enough period, it is inevitable that nerve cell insufficiency will develop ultimately . . . ." The recent work of La Cava in Italy and Pampus in Bonn tends to substantiate these claims. Findings such as these received fresh emphasis by sparring partner Ben Skelton's report (SI, Sept. 24) that Liston's left jab is so hard "that for a week after being hit with it I was taking pills to kill the pain."

Dr. Steinhaus has been so impressed with the medical evidence concerning brain damage in boxing that he feels a second foul line must be created at the shoulder. He cites a noted brain surgeon with wide experience with boxers as contending that every head-pommeling is likely to leave some small portion of the brain tissue permanently damaged, even though this may not be noticed for some time. The treacherous aspect of such injury is that it apparently does not manifest itself clinically until rather late in the degenerative process. Furthermore, there are obvious reasons why professional fighters would be reluctant to report symptoms of brain damage.

When one reads these statements—and there are many more of the same—one has an indefinable sense of uneasiness, of inconclusiveness. There is almost the sense of being in the presence of a crusader. Is it really this bad? Could it be that the admirable tendency of the doctor to regard *any* disease or injury as *too much* has expanded these statements? H. A. Kaplan (*The Journal of the American Medical Association*, 1959) contends that "a blow from a human being with a padded gloved fist probably is not forceful enough to produce any direct damage to the brain." In an area such as this, the theologian admits to hopeless incompetence. To complete his understanding of professional boxing he must rely completely on medical specialists. With this in mind I submitted the following statement, attributed to a prominent brain specialist, to 10 of the top neurosurgeons in the U.S. and Canada: "The brain is so constructed that it cannot suffer a series of head blows over the years in boxing without certainly or at least very probably incurring thereby some permanent injury." These experts agreed that the statement could be endorsed as a general statement. One was at pains to indicate that the statement, while it is probably correct, is poorly written. He could not accept the inference in it that malfunction of the brain follows brain damage. Such a symptom would be a matter of degree.

If these specialists are incorrect in their estimate about brain damage, then the moral theologian would desire to reexamine certain aspects or emphases of his argumentation, as we shall see. But it is this type of evidence that makes one take a long second look at the words of Abe Simon, former heavyweight contender: ". . . jarring of the brain. That's what causes the trouble—my headaches and those of every fighter who has taken punishment. It's not a single punch; it's the constant jarring. . . . [The fighter] is always soothed by the falsehood that he will be just as good as new after a short rest. He never is, and no fighter living today who has had 50 or more reasonably hard fights can honestly make the claim."

Such a medical review was necessary preparation for a moral estimate. Since everyone familiar with the sport concedes its advantages, the moral discussion boils down to this: Are the arguments against professional boxing conclusive? Of the many moral objections one hears, the most serious are reducible to three.

1) *The knockout.* It is simply unrealistic to deny that most professional fighters aim for a knockout. This is regarded as the most decisive and impressive way to win a fight. It is what the fighter wants and very often what the fans want. The long climb to contender status or the comeback often hinges on it. As Nat Fleischer wrote in *The Heavyweight Championship* of Louis' comeback tour after his 1936 loss to Max Schmeling: "There was only one way to do that—to roll up victory after victory over the knockout route."

Not a few moral theologians find it difficult to admit that the knockout is justifiable. They frequently formulate this as follows: directly and violently to deprive oneself or another of the use of reason is morally reprehensible except for a sufficient cause. It is the rational faculties, intellect and free will that distinguish man from the brute. Directly to deprive man of these faculties without a sufficient reason is to dehumanize. These theologians are reluctant to admit that sport, money, fame qualify as sufficient reason. If such violent deprivation of higher controls is reprehensible, then the intent to do so is equally reprehensible. Hence a sport in which this intent plays such an integral role must be condemned.

Is the argument convincing? I do not believe it is. First of all, the knockout is understood in the rather limited sense of "rendering unconscious." This is not a necessary sense of the word. A knockout is, more realistically, beating a fighter to the point where he is physically incapable of continuing. This is what the ordinary professional desires. Deprivation of the use of reason is not essential to this. Hence, practically, it is hard to show how the knockout in this limited sense is an essential aim of most fighters. Second, even if it were the fighter's aim, it would be difficult to show how the knockout of itself (independent of injury) is sufficient to condemn the sport. It can be argued that, generally, deprivation of the use of reason lasts only a few seconds at most (8 to 10 usually) and that this is so little as to be negligible. If this were the only thing at stake, it is highly doubtful that there would be as much objection to boxing as there seems to be.

2) *The intent of injury.* If the argument concerning the knockout is not satisfying, the objection from injury is much more arresting. Professional boxing is the only sport where the immediate objective is to damage the opponent. A puffed or cut eye, a lacerated cheek, a bleeding nose—these are signals for an intensified attack on the vulnerable area. When Jimmy Doyle died after being knocked out by Sugar Ray Robinson, Robinson was asked if he noticed that Doyle was in trouble. He is widely quoted as answering: "Getting him into trouble is my business." In all other sports the immediate objective is to cross a goal line, tip in a basket, throw a strike. Injury and incapacity to continue are incidental. A knee to the groin, a fist to the face in football, bean balls and deliberate spiking in baseball are penalized and would unhesitatingly be branded as immoral by the theologian. Patterson was simply describing the unique character of professional boxing when he wrote (*Victory over Myself*), after the first Johansson knockout, of his desire

never to be vicious again. "At the same time I know that I must be, because I am in a business of violence." If direct damage to the opponent is immoral in all other sports, why not in this business of violence?

It is here that the medical evidence assumes some importance. Were the injury passing and negligible, theologians might perhaps mitigate their judgment. But if the specialists are right in their claims about injury, particularly brain injury, this must give us pause. The sport as now practiced tends directly to inflict this damage. When injury to the cranium and its contents occurs, it is, as Blonstein and Clarke note (*British Medical Journal*, 1954), "a direct product of boxing and not an accident as in all other sports." Since this is true, then these effects are also the direct object of the fighter's intention. This is not to say that the fighter explicitly desires to maim or cause lasting damage. Few would be that inhuman. As a rule, the fighter's only explicit desire is to win as decisively as possible. But the means he chooses are means that are damaging. Hence he implicitly intends this damage as a means. How could he disown it? The point might seem a bit fine, but can one choose to pound and sink a nail and yet disown the hole in the wood?

At this point professional boxing encounters the disapproving frown of many a moralist. Man, they argue, does not possess the right directly to inflict damage on himself or another in this way. He is not the absolute master of his person with the power to destroy or mutilate as he wishes. Absolute dominion over man's integrity is possessed by God alone. As a creature, man is an administrator charged with the duty and privilege of reasonable administration. His ability directly to mutilate himself is severely limited.

This is a cardinal principle of sound moral thought. If there is indecisiveness here, there will inevitably be ambiguity or error in the evaluation of many aspects of modern living. Once the limit on man's ability to mutilate himself is obscured, the condemnation of suicide, euthanasia, reckless medical experiment, useless surgery and so on tends to lose rational defense. The novelist knows that the first chapters profoundly affect the outcome of the final chapters of his book. Similarly moral theology is jealous of her basic principles because they contain the germ of practical conclusions.

Applying these principles, theologians believe that when a man pounds another into helplessness, scars his face, smashes his nose, jars his brain and exposes it to lasting damage, or when he enters a contest where this could happen to him, he has surpassed the bounds of reasonable stewardship of the human person. Surely there are equally—or more—effective ways for men to learn the art of self-defense.

Does the fact that this is done for money affect the moral analysis? Certain medical experiments on the human body, even if done for money, would remain objectionable. In fact, is there not a legitimate sense in which it is true to say that the greater the spoils, the more objectionable the whole business? For as the cash at stake increases, so does the danger of viewing the integrity of the human person as salable at a price. Money can be overvalued. When it is, something else is undervalued. If this something else happens to be the integrity of the human person, have we not made a wrong turn somewhere?

3) *Fostering of brutish instincts.* Man is a delicate combination, midway between animal and angel, with a bit of both in him. His characteristic balance is achieved when he harmonizes these elements. When he fosters one to the neglect of the other, he tends to become either a disengaged dreamer or a savage. Thomas Aquinas knew nothing of professional boxing; but with an unerring knowledge of human nature he pointed out that to take pleasure in the unnecessary sufferings of another man is brutish.

Anyone who has watched professional fights will know what Aquinas was talking about. The crowd too often has come for blood and the knockout. The knockout is the touchdown pass, the home run of boxing. The nearer it is, the more frenzied the howling of the crowd. As Nat Fleischer said simply of the first Patterson-Johansson fight: "The crowd, sensing the kill, went wild." We occasionally hear the referee urge the boys to mix it up, give the fans their money's worth. When a boy is being mauled around the ring, the arena comes alive and emotions run high. The fighter is goaded by the crowd; his own fury further stimulates them. The brutish instinct is in command. At this pitch the finest moves in boxing are missed or—worse—greeted by a chorus of hissing and booing. Tunney was so disgusted with this type of thing in one of his fights that he created the phrase, "the bloodthirsty yap of the mob." The modern prizefight is increasingly the canonization of brute force—and that at a time when we are struggling with all our might to understand the meaning of force in the world.

Is not man too weak a creature to unleash and give free play to these forces with impunity? Does he not tend to grow in the image of that which he cheers? If this is true, how long can he cheer these exhibitions without acting at variance with the demands dictated by his own rational nature? To many, this is the strongest indictment of professional boxing, an objection sufficient in itself as a stricture of the game.

These arguments are not frivolous. Any discussion of professional boxing which ignores them is playing the ostrich. They are drawn from natural law; whatever validity they have would surely be intensified by the Christian revelation through which man becomes conscious of an even more startling personal dignity. It was probably arguments such as these that led the Vatican Radio to announce its conviction that professional boxing is objectively immoral. *L'Osservatore della Domenica* insinuated the same thing. Informed Catholics, however, are rightly distressed at the implications in the assertion that these views are "semiofficial" ecclesiastical positions.

The Catholic Church has not condemned professional boxing. Many have wondered why not. The eager expectation of ecclesiastical intervention could easily contain a distorted notion of the function of the Church. While she jealously guards the purity of morals, it does not follow that condemnations do or should issue from her at the slightest provocation—if for no other reason than that this discourages intellectual effort in the ranks by seeming to render it unnecessary. We stand to learn a great deal from this controversy.

Many reasons suggest themselves in explanation of the Church's official silence on the matter. First of all, and most important perhaps, the matter simply is not clear to her. While the Church speaks frequently on changeless moral principles, she is generally quite content to leave the application of these to her theologians. But theological opinion has been, possibly still is, somewhat divided, or at least hesitant. Most of the serious writing has been unfavorable to boxing, but there are many voices yet to be heard.

Second, professional boxing is largely, but not exclusively, a local American problem. The U.S. champion is the world champion, the big gate is here and the big fights are generally here. If public statements are called for, it is reasonable to think that this would be left to local bishops.

Finally, even should the Church desire to take a strong stand, there is the difficulty of formulating a statement which will avoid the impression that all boxing is being censured. It is foolish to lump the pillow fights of the sixth grader with the hard smashes of the professional. And even at the professional level the differences between individual fighters are tremendous. There are those in superb condition who fight once or twice a year to defend a title—and these are the champions who are hit the least. Then there are those who all but drag themselves into the ring to have their brains rattled on a month-to-month basis. To group these together in a single sweeping rejection would be unrealistic and hazardous.

Not only is the central moral issue challenging; there are also many fringe problems no less tantalizing. One that is increasingly aired: Is the victorious fighter guilty when his opponent dies as a result of blows received in the ring? Though boxing is different from other sports in its direct aim (the infliction of damage), death is such a departure from the average that its occurrence should be regarded as an undesired byproduct of the sport. Morally it is an accident.

Problematic too are the possibilities involved in allowing a man with a past to contend for the crown (SI, Feb. 12). The issue is scarcely one of Christian forgiveness or rehabilitation. Surely we can hope that we are both humble enough and large enough for this. The problem is rather the defenselessness of our children against their own hero-worshiping simplicity. On the other hand, a clear break with an unfortunate past might actually provide a very helpful example to youngsters. What ever the answer may be, there is a moral dimension even here.

The question of professional boxing is a vexing one. The issues seem clear. Defenders of the sport insist that the advantages outweigh the disadvantages. Those who censure it, while admitting the advantages, believe that the moral discussion must begin with the sport itself, not only its circumstances. They see the sport as directly injurious and as one which tends unduly to foster the instinct of brutality in all concerned. Perhaps this is not *necessarily* true; there are many laudable attempts being made to supervise the sport more thoroughly (SI, April 23). Nor is it *factually* true of all professional fights; but it is too *generally* true of the sport today. Thus the majority vote among those who have written on the moral question is unfavorable.

Unless the arguments leveled at professional boxing as it is today can be answered, I believe the sport would have to be labeled immoral. I realize that other theologians may take a different point of view. It could be that not all the facts are in. Perhaps, too, we have a great deal to learn about our own principles. Premature conviction slams the door to enlightenment as effectively as refusal to face the moral issue.

If there remain some uncertainties to haunt us, the general implications of our sincere and honest interest are clear. For, regardless of what answer we come up with, it is both a sign and guarantee of our abiding spiritual health to face issues at their moral root. It is never easy to question the moral character of our own pleasure and entertainment. Since, however, moral issues are not defined by the convenient and inconvenient, the pleasant and the annoying, but reach to the division between good and evil, they are too important to receive less than an earnest, but calm and dispassionate, treatment. Failure to do this would be a collective shrug-of-the-shoulder at moral values and, as such, a threat to the spiritual goods upon which we have built our dignity and freedom.

Our Changing Morality*

TOM TIEDE AND IRA BERKOW

Athletes have always had to combat psychological castration by the fawning public.

The athlete has become an object, a "thing" for the public, detached, nonhuman like the gods of primitive mythology.

If his motor is running well, the athlete is applauded and he likes this. If his wind-up is winding down, he is booed and hissed, and he is at once angry and confused.

"It took me about five years after retirement," said former New York Yankee infielder Gil McDougald, "to finally start liking people again."

So the athlete, usually unwilling and unable to be himself in public, has adopted a role of noninvolvement.

Now, as we enter the 1970s, the trend toward the so-called "New Morality" is changing all this.

Morality has to do with that elusive and vague term, "values." War in Vietnam, The Pill, the Youth Revolution, the Race Revolution, increased liberalization of sex in thought and action and arts have changed our concept of what we are and what we should be. All this has affected sports and sports heroes.

John Pont, football coach at Indiana University, has said that you cannot divorce football from the rest of our society. Pont found out first-hand when a group of black players "struck" his team because of varied grievances relating to the campus black movement. The black players became "involved."

* From *The Springfield Union*, February 24, 1970, p. 17. Reprinted by permission of Newspaper Enterprise Association.

The black college athletes are just one group asserting themselves. On campuses from Indiana to Wyoming to Oregon, black and white athletes have taken stands for independence. Issues have included the length of curls in the hair, to the form of dress ranging from dashikis to blue jeans.

Athletes in college are bridling at the hypocrisy of recruiting techniques, of false promises. To some, the pennant-waving at a college football game is as repugnant an example of provincialism as flag-waving at an American Legion convention. This is not to say that there is anything wrong with loving one's school or nation, but to feel yours is superior because it's yours is "immoral" in the "New Morality."

In professional athletics, heavyweight boxing champion Muhammed Ali (better known as Cassius Clay) is best known for his stand, though the courts so far have taken an opposite tack.

Ali has refused to be drafted by the United States Army because, among other reasons, "them Cong never did nothin' to me."

Once Mayor Jimmy Walker publicly asked Babe Ruth to "reform" because of his evil influence on the "dirty-faced kid in the streets." And thenceforth Ruth followed his gaudy appetites only in private.

Today, however, a Joe Namath declares that he will not hide what he is like from the public because he is his own man and the "dirty-faced kid in the street" should not be fed a lie.

And surface changes—attempts at symbolic psychic changes—have been manifested by a

Bill Russell and his goatee, by a Ken Harrelson and his frilly-front pink shirts, by a Namath and his mink coat, by a Joe Frazier and his motorcycles.

The change in the idea of what money means has been dramatically shown by Curt Flood. Flood, the former St. Louis Cardinal outfielder, has refused to be traded without his consent and is suing baseball, disputing its reserve clause contract. He was making a yearly salary of nearly $90,000 from the Cardinals. Yet Curt, alleging that he's being treated as a "slave," wants to be able to bargain for his talents on the open market. There have been few slaves in history, from the Pharoah's days to Nat Turner's days, who have been paid $90,000 a year.

This is a new day, and money may not have the same value in moral terms as it once had.

It is interesting and innovative that the paragons of masculinity, the athletes, are now proclaiming, "I am a man."

Morality as an Intimate of Sport*

HOWARD S. SLUSHER

Working within the structure of *personal concern* the morality decisions that face man in sport are most personal. They provide the *intimate* fiber of communication between man and the activity. In order to actualize the ethic man must ask where he *is* within the totality of the sport experience. For all of life begins and ends with what he experiences in existence. If one espouses the thesis that you "treat your opponent as you would desire to be treated," then the *meaning of the truth* of that statement is a dependent variable. Its validity is determined by the *intimateness* of man to the experience.

The word "intimate" is being used to connote that which is beyond human thought. The value is not achieved, *really*, if man just *thinks* that is the way to act. Or even if he says that is the way I would like to be treated. This quality of the "intimate" goes into the depths of existence and certainly extends itself beyond modern Christian Ethic. The implication is that man *cares*, not merely intellectually, but with an involvement that extends to the very root of his personhood. If man is not treated in this manner, one is not *just* disappointed, he becomes *nauseated*. He *suffers* because his involvement was more than what was stated—it was *all* of life. Sport is, generally, an act of initial volition. Man participates with *all* of his complexities. This completeness leads to a seriousness of involvement. Only too often the "intermediate" goal of victory blinds man from

seeing the eventuation of his participation. To become intimate is to initiate morality. Real morality cannot be achieved until man is willing to *risk* his self in the sport experience.

In achieving this morality man cannot treat man according to usual role expectancy. One does not treat one as an umpire, bowler, boxer, jockey, skier, or basketball player. One is treated *intimately*, as an *individual*. Too often, in our complicated and mass culture of mechanization, we forget that man is not a collective noun. He is a person with a unique identity. Sport must be wary that, in its zest for *ends* and results that are indicated on the scoreboard, man is not relegated to a *mean*. Again, I trust this thought is in keeping with Buber's moral imperative:

> One cannot treat either an individual or a social organism as a means to an end absolutely, without robbing it of its life substance. . . . One cannot in the nature of things expect a little tree that has been turned into a club to put forth leaves.[1]

The *intimate* relationships of sport provide the raw material for the most "humane" of all ethical structures. However, one must wonder if the potential is being realized or prostituted. The question is not one of the normal means/ends dichotomy. No matter how good or bad is either the means or ends, man is *immoral* if he attempts to structure any form of dualism

* From *Man, Sport and Existence.* Philadelphia: Lea & Febiger, 1967.

[1] Martin Buber. *I and Thou.* Translated by Ronald Gregor Smith. (Edinburgh: T. & T. Clark, 1953), p. 17.

279

which segments, and thereby injures, the authentic existence of man. Our experiences and our goals need be one. Our dreams and our realities need be fused. To say they *are* not is to admit *reality*. To say they *cannot* is to admit *defeat*. We might make choices that are less than what we would hope them to be. But we must not close our eyes and our hearts to those that are *not* chosen. An ethic of *existence* is personal; it is intimate. In sport man can free himself *in* the closeness of another: in his relations with man, in his empathy for skill development, in his appreciation of dedication. All these qualities *bring* him closer to the door of being. Whether he *enters* into life or stays behind a closed partition is a matter of *choice*. A choice of none less than life or death, for man and sport.

In making the choice we cannot run away from the obvious question. Is the authentic life both "good" and "right"? When man is trying to find *real* self in the world of sport, does the *sport* itself encourage man in a world of good and right? In talking about modern sports, The Rev. Edward Hildner, who at ninety-three years of age is the sole surviver of the first basketball game, said, "There are too many whistles, too many interruptions because some silly little rule is broken. The same is true about baseball—all that baloney that makes the game too long."[2] Well the game may now be "right." But is it "good"? Is this what James would call a difference that makes no difference and therefore it makes no difference? I think not. Man does not find any sure and clear roads to follow in journeying toward the *real* life. The subtle differentiation between "right" and "good" affords insights into the sport situation as an arena for the development of *being*. Choices are difficult to make when the scope of the question is clear. But in the complexity of the sport world we are talking of another issue. It is easy to see how man could "settle" for a world of absolutes. When life becomes intimate, man needs to deal with the "gray areas." Black and white will not do. The importance of *relatives* becomes both obvious and terrifying. But now the decisions cannot be avoided. They are close. They are intimate. How do you regulate between the good of the team and the rightness of man? It might be right for man to hunt (the deer will be injured due to overpopulation is the usual reason that is given); but few would say it is good to kill a defenseless animal. Hopefully the reader is not expecting any type of ethical

[2] "Scorecard." *Sports Illustrated*, 25 (1966), p. 22.

panacea. The only answer I know is that man must do what *he* feels is good. Values and ethics, as moral derivatives, need be unclouded so that man can act with a decisiveness that indicates position and reflection. But this is only the start. For the more immediate and intimate man becomes to sport, the greater will be the effort to reach the zenith.

Physical Fitness as a Moral Quality. To talk of *physical* fitness as an aspect of sport is to be obviously and almost hopelessly out of date. Obviously man needs some form of physical tonus to engage in all activities of life. But in sport it is all the more imperative. Yet to talk of *physical* fitness is to relate to an "old" concept. Now the vogue is *total* fitness. But really one can't help but hear the intonations of a guilty dualistic culture giving mouth service to those elements that *also* compose man.

Fitness is basically a survival technique. It is necessary for day-to-day living and receives special attention during a period of increased stress. War and sport have been special modes of human life that have stressed the demands of fitness. To talk of the importance of fitness to any individual concerned with survival is much like "bringing coals to Newcastle." But to see fitness receive extensive stress is to recognize the moral structure of survival.

Since fitness is necessary for survival, we can understand that fitness is a desired *means* for the achievement of a specific end. Accordingly, it becomes a *relative* dimension of morality. How fit should one be for football? How fit should one be for squash? Is the same type of fitness required for sailing as mountain climbing? Obviously, the answer to the dimensions of fitness are dependent upon the *ends*. What is your aim? Obviously the end is not mere participation. Nor is it victory. Somewhere, someplace we come to recognize there is *more* to life than the obvious. We have not forgotten fulfillment, righteousness and self-realization. All this indicates that when we conceive of fitness for the purposes of a sport we are saying it is a *means for a means*. The question that needs to be asked deals with the end to which fitness is an appropriate mean. Is fitness a moral quality, serving as a handmaiden, of sport?

Darwinism has established the principle of survival of the fittest. But the "fit" in sport are not those with qualities of concern, love, empathy, care, passion and respect for personhood. To survive in the world of sport man better *not* have these qualities. To be hard, to be tough, to be strong and to be rough—these are the qualities that pay dividends. Again, the accent is in different kinds of strength or relative values. The truth of the matter is that the Bible would not have a chance against the likes of Darwin in a war or in sport.

Now the preceding conversation begins to haunt us. It might be "right" to develop a level of fitness that enables man to conquer; but is it good? Is it good for *mankind?*

Much is often said of the *social values* of sport. Certainly such moral structures facilitate our social life. About this there can be no complaint. Love, warmth and kindness assist man in his attempt to be human. Yet the qualities of fitness lead man to anything but a social life. They serve as a means, not to the ends of actualization, but rather toward achieving a conquering soul. I think few would deny the apparent necessity for fitness in sport. In so demanding we must readily see that the original choice commits us to further choice. We select sport. We must choose fitness. When we select fitness, we commit ourselves to a "war-like" environment. From this choice little in the way of "tender loving care" can emerge. Morality assists us toward social awareness and compatibility. Fitness facilitates our preparation for war. Since social harmony and war are opposites, it follows that morality and fitness are also at polar extremes. I cannot go quite as far as some who insist fitness is *immoral* (since it is nonsocial). But, from the immediate discussion, it is obvious that I can *almost* go that far.

The morality of man is a consequence of the *existing* social order. Alter the order and you possibly alter the morality. This does not necessitate that the morality be recognized by the social order at the time it existed. To be there is to demonstrate its existence. If it is "right" and "good," it will activate the society toward the appropriate end. But it never will be right for all.

The preceding has demonstrated the social dimension of morality; however, basically, morality is a personal and individual matter. In this regard sport gives man the choice of participating in "individual" activities such as golf, riding, swimming, bowling and skiing. If man desires the social setting, he turns his attention to team sports such as baseball, basketball, football, volley ball, hockey and soccer. It is interesting to note that no matter whether man participates in individual or team activities the social code continues to dictate. Officials, umpires, referees are employed to make certain the "just" receive their due. They are a symbol of the rules. In essence they represent what is *right*. Although they have little direct con-

cern with the *good*, at times they temper their decisions *with what ought to be*. It is quite frequent for an official to "miss" a foul (not right) when it does not affect the direct play of the game (the good). When this action becomes repeated, it soon becomes an expected tradition or custom of the game. Thus, as the social order changes, sport, and the concept of right and good, makes similar modifications. While morality is not completely a servant to changing times, one could hardly deny the rightful effect of the environment upon the morality of any given time.

Allowing for the Existing Morality

Morality is directly related to its environment. However, this does not mean the social matrix always affords assent to the expressed value. Since the realm of sport is atypical from many other endeavors of life—one would expect a varied ethic. That is to say, it is hard to believe that one would even dream that the sport participant would exhibit the same value structure on the gridiron as he does when visiting friends. Each situation calls for its own judgments. This is not to say that this system of relatives is right or wrong. But it does say that it is internally consistent with prior analysis. We might not like ourselves for making certain value decisions. Nevertheless, man makes the choice. Yet, it has been my impression that educators, laymen, sportswriters, and sometimes even coaches act surprised and even shocked when a value is demonstrated that is contrary to the Judea-Christian Ethic. All of this in spite of the accepted thesis of situational ethics.

This expressed horror is not naiveté. In fact, it is more probably a reflection of associated guilt which is manifested in another. Any individual who has been around football for any period of time knows that "elbows fly" on the first play from scrimmage. This is when each man tells his opponent "who is boss." Yet let a player get "caught" for punching and everyone exhibits great shock. "How could such a nice boy do a thing like that? Why he goes to church every Sunday." Yes. But this is Saturday. And on Saturday the name of the game is *kill*. Do we really expect him to practice the Ten Commandments in front of 60,000 people? I think not. We might *like* him to. But we don't *expect* him to. Yet overtly we give the impression that the morality of sport is identical to the morality of the choir. It seems it is high time we either change the nature of sport (which is highly unlikely), or stop the hypocrisy and *admit* to ourselves the existing ethic. To condone, covertly, and punish, overtly, is not my idea of authenticity.

Our expressed purpose and preference in sport is clear. It is not comradeship, self-discovery or aesthetics. I don't care what the "level" of participation is—be it six-year-olds or sixty-year-olds—man plays to succeed. And success is measured by pushing the other guy down, just a little, so that you, as you harness the forces of nature, climb a little higher. Each time we climb a little higher. Each child learns that some day if he works hard and is lucky (but he also learns he has to *make* his own "breaks"), he might grow up to be the champion.

The athlete *knows* the acceptable moral code; however, within this frame he might make many varied value decisions. While he might select to play professional baseball as opposed to seeking a college education, it is not an unethical decision. It is simply an expressed preference. This is what he *likes*. Values are *not* moral imperatives. Since man is *not*, in any sense, forced into action, it would seem wise that we make room for the values we locate in sport. Again, no one is saying this is what we *want*. All that is being said is this is what *is*. Let us not make the mistake of so many who preceded us. Let us recognize *situations* in sport as they exist; and let us stop in the game of self-deception. No life could be more immoral than where one refuses to be aware of his own existence.

The Practice Conception of Rules*

JOHN RAWLS

The other conception of rules I will call the practice conception. On this view rules are pictured as defining a practice. Practices are set up for various reasons, but one of them is that in many areas of conduct each person's deciding what to do on utilitarian grounds case by case leads to confusion, and that the attempt to coordinate behavior by trying to foresee how others will act is bound to fail. As an alternative one realizes that what is required is the establishment of a practice, the specification of a new form of activity; and from this one sees that a practice necessarily involves the abdication of full liberty to act on utilitarian and prudential grounds. It is the mark of a practice that being taught how to engage in it involves being instructed in the rules which define it, and that appeal is made to those rules to correct the behavior of those engaged in it. Those engaged in a practice recognize the rules as defining it. The rules cannot be taken as simply describing how those engaged in the practice in fact behave: it is not simply that they act as if they were obeying the rules. Thus it is essential to the notion of a practice that the rules are publicly known and understood as definitive; and it is essential also that the rules of a practice can be taught and can be acted upon to yield a coherent practice. On this conception, then, rules are not generalizations from the decisions of individuals applying the utilitarian principle directly and independently to recurrent par-

* Excerpted from "Two Concepts of Rules." *The Philosophical Review*, 64 (January, 1955), 3-32.

ticular cases. On the contrary, rules define a practice and are themselves the subject of the utilitarian principle.

To show the important differences between this way of fitting rules into the utilitarian theory and the previous way, I shall consider the differences between the two conceptions on the points previously discussed.

1. In contrast with the summary view, the rules of practices are logically prior to particular cases. This is so because there cannot be a particular case of an action falling under a rule of a practice unless there is the practice. This can be made clearer as follows: in a practice there are rules setting up offices, specifying certain forms of action appropriate to various offices, establishing penalties for the breach of rules, and so on. We may think of the rules of a practice as defining offices, moves, and offenses. Now what is meant by saying that the practice is logically prior to particular cases is this: given any rule which specifies a form of action (a move), a particular action which would be taken as falling under this rule given that there is the practice would not be *described as* that sort of action unless there was the practice. In the case of actions specified by practices it is logically impossible to perform them outside the stage-setting provided by those practices, for unless there is the practice, and unless the requisite proprieties are fulfilled, whatever one does, whatever movements one makes, will fail to count as a form of action which the practice specifies. What one does will be described in some *other* way.

One may illustrate this point from the game of baseball. Many of the actions one performs in a game of baseball one can do by oneself or with others whether there is the game or not. For example, one can throw a ball, run, or swing a peculiarly shaped piece of wood. But one cannot steal base, or strike out, or draw a walk, or make an error, or balk; although one can do certain things which appear to resemble these actions such as sliding into a bag, missing a grounder and so on. Striking out, stealing a base, balking, etc., are all actions which can only happen in a game. No matter what a person did, what he did would not be described as stealing a base or striking out or drawing a walk unless he could also be described as playing baseball, and for him to be doing this presupposes the rule-like practice which constitutes the game. The practice is logically prior to particular cases: unless there is the practice the terms referring to actions specified by it lack a sense.[1]

2. The practice view leads to an entirely different conception of the authority which each person has to decide on the propriety of following a rule in particular cases. To engage in a practice, to perform those actions specified by a practice, means to follow the appropriate rules. If one wants to do an action which a certain practice specifies then there is no way to do it except to follow the rules which define it. Therefore, it doesn't make sense for a person to raise the question whether or not a rule of a practice correctly applies to *his* case where the action he contemplates is a form of action defined by a practice. If someone were to raise such a question, he would simply show that he didn't understand the situation in which he was acting. If one wants to perform an action specified by a practice, the only legitimate question concerns the nature of the

[1] One might feel that it is a mistake to say that a practice is logically prior to the forms of action it specifies on the grounds that if there were never any instances of actions falling under a practice then we should be strongly inclined to say that there wasn't the practice either. Blue-prints for a practice do not make a practice. That there is a practice entails that there are instances of people having been engaged and now being engaged in it (with suitable qualifications). This is correct, but it doesn't hurt the claim that any given particular instance of a form of action specified by a practice presupposes the practice. This isn't so on the summary picture, as each instance must be "there" prior to the rules, so to speak, as something from which one gets the rule by applying the utilitarian principle to it directly.

practice itself ("How do I go about making a will?").

This point is illustrated by the behavior expected of a player in games. If one wants to play a game, one doesn't treat the rules of the game as guides as to what is best in particular cases. In a game of baseball if a batter were to ask "Can I have four strikes?" it would be assumed that he was asking what the rule was; and if, when told what the rule was, he were to say that he meant that on this occasion he thought it would be best on the whole for him to have four strikes rather than three, this would be most kindly taken as a joke. One might contend that baseball would be a better game if four strikes were allowed instead of three; but one cannot picture the rules as guides to what is best on the whole in particular cases, and question their applicability to particular cases as particular cases.

3 and 4. To complete the four points of comparison with the summary conception, it is clear from what has been said that rules of practices are not guides to help one decide particular cases correctly as judged by some higher ethical principle. And neither the quasi-statistical notion of generality, nor the notion of a particular exception, can apply to the rules of practices. A more or less general rule of a practice must be a rule which according to the structure of the practice applies to more or fewer of the kinds of cases arising under it; or it must be a rule which is more or less basic to the understanding of the practice. Again, a particular case cannot be an exception to a rule of a practice. An exception is rather a qualification or a further specification of the rule.

It follows from what we have said about the practice conception of rules that if a person is engaged in a practice, and if he is asked why *he* does what *he* does, or if he is asked to defend what he does, then his explanation, or defense, lies in referring the questioner to the practice. He cannot say of *his* action, if it is an action specified by a practice, that he does it rather than some other because he thinks it is best on the whole.[2] When a man engaged in a practice is queried about his action he must assume that the questioner either doesn't know that he is engaged in it ("Why are you in a hurry to pay him?" "I promised to pay him today") or doesn't know what the practice is. One doesn't so much justify one's particular

[2] A philosophical joke (in the mouth of Jeremy Bentham): "When I run to the other wicket after my partner has struck a good ball I do so because it is best on the whole."

action as explain, or show, that it is in accordance with the practice. The reason for this is that it is only against the stage-setting of the practice that one's particular action is described as it is. Only by reference to the practice can one *say* what one is doing. To explain or to defend one's own action, as a particular action, one fits it into the practice which defines it. If this is not accepted it's a sign that a different question is being raised as to whether one is justified in accepting the practice, or in tolerating it. When the challenge is to the practice, citing the rules (saying what the practice is) is naturally to no avail. But when the challenge is to the particular action defined by the practice, there is nothing one can do but refer to the rules. Concerning particular actions there is only a question for one who isn't clear as to what the practice is, or who doesn't know that it is being engaged in. This is to be contrasted with the case of a maxim which may be taken as pointing to the correct decision on the case as decided on *other* grounds, and so giving a challenge on the case a sense by having it question whether these other grounds really support the decision on this case.

If one compares the two conceptions of rules I have discussed, one can see how the summary conception misses the significance of the distinction between justifying a practice and justifying actions falling under it. On this view rules are regarded as guides whose purpose it is to indicate the ideally rational decision on the given particular case which the flawless application of the utilitarian principle would yield. One has, in principle, full option to use the guides or to discard them as the situation warrants without one's moral office being altered in any way: whether one discards the rules or not, one always holds the office of a rational person seeking case by case to realize the best on the whole. But on the practice conception, if one holds an office defined by a practice then questions regarding one's actions in this office are settled by reference to the rules which define the practice. If one seeks to question these rules, then one's office undergoes a fundamental change: one then assumes the office of one empowered to change and criticize the rules, or the office of a reformer, and so on. The summary conception does away with the distinction of offices and the various forms of argument appropriate to each. On that conception there is one office and so no offices at all. It therefore obscures the fact that the utilitarian principle must, in the case of

actions and offices defined by a practice, apply to the practice, so that general utilitarian arguments are not available to those who act in offices so defined.[3]

Some qualifications are necessary in what I have said. First, I may have talked of the summary and the practice conceptions of rules as if only one of them could be true of rules, and if true of any rules, then necessarily true of *all* rules. I do not, of course, mean this. (It is the critics of utilitarianism who make this mistake insofar as their arguments against utilitarianism presuppose a summary conception of the rules of practices.) Some rules will fit one conception, some rules the other; and so there are rules of practices (rules in the strict sense), and maxims and "rules of thumb."

Secondly, there are further distinctions that can be made in classifying rules, distinctions which should be made if one were considering other questions. The distinctions which I have drawn are those most relevant for the rather special matter I have discussed, and are not intended to be exhaustive.

Finally, there will be many border-line cases about which it will be difficult, if not impossible, to decide which conception of rules is applicable. One expects border-line cases with any concept, and they are especially likely in connection with such involved concepts as those of a practice, institution, game, rule, and so on. Wittgenstein has shown how fluid these notions are.[4] What I have done is to emphasize and sharpen two conceptions for the limited purpose of this paper.

[3] How do these remarks apply to the case of the promise known only to father and son? Well, at first sight the son certainly holds the office of promisor, and so he isn't allowed by the practice to weigh the particular case on general utilitarian grounds. Suppose instead that he wishes to consider himself in the office of one empowered to criticize and change the practice, leaving aside the question as to his right to move from his previously assumed office to another. Then he may consider utilitarian arguments as applied to the practice; but once he does this he will see that there are such arguments for not allowing a general utilitarian defense in the practice for this sort of case. For to do so would make it impossible to ask for and to give a kind of promise which one often wants to be able to ask for and to give. Therefore he will not want to change the practice, and so as a promisor he has no option but to keep his promise.

[4] *Philosophical Investigations* (Oxford, 1953), I, pars. 65-71, for example.

The Game of Life*

ANTHONY RALLS

1. ON PLAYING THE GAME

I wish to continue the discussion of the question *Ought I to be moral and if so why?*, and to do so by referring to a metaphor, analogy or example that has been used occasionally in the contemporary literature, that of *playing a game*. The point of the metaphor, analogy or example is roughly this: if you are playing a certain game (usually it's baseball, although a recent article makes a similar point about chess) you *can't* break the rules. Analogously, if you are playing the moral game, the Game of Life, then you've got to stick to the rules. Now it is obvious that the compulsion to adhere to the rules of a game is not, or not normally, physical; but it is alleged that there is some kind of compulsion or necessitation involved, and that this, rightly understood, will illumine the nature of morality and moral discourse.[1] In addition to its occurrence in the literature, it is clearly an analogy that is, or has been, entrenched in English moral language, as in the Lifeboy motto To PLAY THE GAME, the expression "It's not cricket," and the significantly famous verses of Rudyard Kipling about the Great Scorer.

* Excerpted from "The Game of Life." *The Philosophical Quarterly*, 16 (January, 1966), 23-34.
[1] See, e.g., John Rawls: "Two Concepts of Rules," *Philosophical Review*, 1955, esp. pp. 25 ff; John Searle: "How to Derive 'Ought' from 'Is'", *Philosophical Review*, 1964, esp. p. 56; Max Black: "The Gap between 'Is' and 'Should'", *Philosophical Review*, 1964, pp. 165-181 *passim*.

In this paper I want to raise doubts about the premises that this form of argument requires, namely *that so-and-so is playing the game*, and *that playing the game necessitates keeping the rules*. I consider what justifications these premises themselves require, and in this context I discuss the suggestion made in several quarters recently, that by virtue of the performative nature of moral utterances, all persons, or all members of society, or all language-users, are committed to a moral point of view, or to some moral position in particular. I try to turn the force of this argument against its supporters, and finally consider again some reasons why one might hold that everyone ought to be moral, and just how one could avoid this conclusion. The upshot is that talking of morality as a kind of super-game does not serve the purpose intended, for it does not show us why we *should* play *that* game.

2. ON GETTING OUT OF THE GAME

Consider an argument of the form:
> If you are playing a game, you must keep the rules of that game;
> So-and-so is playing a game;
> THEREFORE so-and-so must keep the rules of that game.

Such an argument is plainly valid provided that the modal 'must' is properly kept within the consequent of the major premiss, and that we can avoid a *Quaternio Terminorum*. But if we are to accept the conclusion, we must first be convinced of the truth of the premises.

Now in the case of the games of cricket, base-ball and the like, it is normally a voluntary matter whether one decides to play or not. And if I agree to play cricket, it would not *be* cricket for me to give up playing half way through, or to break the rules and refuse to accept the consequences as specified in the Laws of Cricket. But you can avoid having to keep the rules, by the simple expedient of not playing; and *this* expedient is supposed not to be available when the question at issue is, Ought I to keep the rules of the Game of Life, that is, to be moral?

Why can I not avoid playing the Game of Life?

One answer need be mentioned only to be dismissed. I mean the claim that I ought to keep the rules, i.e. to be moral, because all men, including me, are proper subjects for making moral judgments *about*. This claim is either question-begging or irrelevant. It is question-begging in that, in making the claim, there is presupposed what is at stake, namely that moral rules are rules to which all men, including me, ought to subscribe. It is irrelevant in that, no matter how many people judge me morally, *I* am not thereby committed to judging myself.

More pertinent might be the contention that everyone plays *some* game, since everyone has some guiding principles or other. But unless it could be shown that to have some guiding principles or other is, *eo ipso*, to be moral, this would not show that everyone is playing the moral game; and even if they were, how would this show that they ought to be doing so, and therefore must keep the rules? I return to this point later.

For the present I observe that the clear inadequacy of these moves seems to be what drives some philosophers into producing allegedly empirical grounds for saying that everyone is actually playing the Game of Life. These moves represent it as a plain *fact*, or a consequence of a plain fact, that everyone plays that game. It would follow that refusing to obey the rules would be inconsistent with the acceptance of some obviously true statement which it would be absurd not to accept; and thus that the refusal to obey the rules would itself be absurd. There are at least three such obviously true statements:

(a) Everyone speaks some language;
(b) Everyone is a member of some community;
(c) Everyone is a human being.

Schematically, I would argue concerning any such general statement, first, that it carries no weight unless regarded *ascriptively;*[2] that is, unless we *already* accept some moral viewpoint which gives moral weight to that feature of the human condition. Secondly, that either such a statement is not universal or not necessarily universal, and so does not or need not bind everyone, or that it *is* necessary, in which case it does not *morally* bind anyone, since a necessarily true statement can have no prescriptive force of itself.

These retorts are expressed in terms too general to carry conviction, and the arguments are better dealt with in particular. I propose to deal at some length with an argument of Searle's which will illustrate these points; but shall first examine the major premiss of the Games argument, in order to narrow down the point at issue.

3. ON KEEPING THE RULES

The major premiss needed to substantiate the conclusion *that everyone must keep the rules* would be the major premiss of the argument in (2), namely *that if you are playing a game, you must keep its rules.* I think this is always intended to be analytically true (it certainly is by Searle); it is worth noticing that it serves no purpose if it is not analytic. Treating it as a synthetic statement it presumably amounts to one of two possible claims. The first might be:

If you are playing a game, then it'll be a bad thing, a poor show, not cricket, if you don't keep the rules.

But this is itself a piece of explicitly moral reasoning, which of course substantiates a moral conclusion, but not in the manner desired. If we question the conclusion, of course we'll question this premiss too.

The alternative reading of this premiss might be:

If you are playing a game, then it'll be the worse for you, you'll catch it, if you don't keep the rules.

The first comment on this claim must be, that if it is genuinely factual it is hard to see how it could be substantiated. The second, hardly less obvious, comment is, that this alleged fact is strictly irrelevant to establish-

[2] I have tried to say something about *ascriptive judgments* in "The Ascription of Personal Responsibility and Identity," *Australasian Journal of Philosophy*, 1963, esp. pp. 347-8, developing a feature of ascription which is implicit in Hart's account (H. L. A. Hart, "The Ascription of Responsibility and Rights," in *Logic and Language* (1st series), ed. Antony Flew, Oxford, 1951).

ing the moral conclusion desiderated. For no matter how certainly it is demonstrated that acting thus will be in my interests, will achieve what I really want to have or avoid what I really want not to have, the question necessarily remains to be asked: Should I act thus? Should I consider my own interests here? Indeed it is hard to see what is left to 'should' if we exclude the possibility of setting 'I want' over against 'I should.' So that while it may be the case that in fact what I want to do is always what I should do, or even that what everybody wants to do is always what everybody should do, this has to be shown; hence this version of the major premiss won't support by itself the conclusion that one should or that one must obey the rules, but stands in need of support.

I think we are left with the analytic reading of the major premiss as the only one possible, but the consequences of this are almost equally disastrous. It might go somewhat as follows:

If you are playing a game, then you cannot without self-stultification, or self-contradiction, not keep its rules.

But this, which still seems to be saying something interesting, in fact only amounts to this:

If you are to be said to be playing a game, then you must (among other things) be keeping its rules.

This makes keeping the rules a necessary condition of playing the game, with the inevitable consequence that the fact that you are playing the game cannot be adduced as *a reason why* you must keep the rules. It immediately follows that the alleged argument, from the consideration of which this paper got going, is quite insubstantial. If the analytic account of the major premiss is correct, persuading people to play the game is the same thing as, and therefore not logically prior to, persuading them to keep the rules. If 'everyone is playing the game' is to be true, it *must* be true that everyone must keep the rules.

Rules and Utilitarianism*

B. J. DIGGS

I

The first kind of rule which I shall describe belongs to a large class of rules which I call "instrumental." All rules in this large class are adopted or followed as a means to an end, in order to "accomplish a purpose" or "get a job done." The simplest of these rules is the "practical maxim" which one ordinarily follows at his own pleasure, such as "Be sure the surface to be painted is thoroughly dry" or "Do not plant tomatoes until after the last frost."[1]

The instrumental rule to which I call attention is more complex. On many occasions when one wants a job done, either he is not in a position or not able or not willing to do the job himself. If he is in a position of power or authority, or if he has money, he may simply order or hire others to "do the job" and leave it to them. In numerous cases, however, he himself lays down rules of procedure, and establishes "jobs" or "roles" in the institutional sense. A "job" in this latter sense is not a job to be "done," but a job to be "offered to" or "given" to a person. If a person "takes" or is "assigned" "the job" then we often think of him as under an obligation to "do his job," and this partly consists in his following rules. Instrumental rules of this

* Excerpted from "Rules and Utilitarianism." *American Philosophical Quarterly*, I (January, 1964), 32-44.
[1] Cf. Max Black, "Notes on the Meaning of 'Rule'," *Theoria*, vol. 24 (1958), pp. 121-122; reprinted in his *Models and Metaphors* (Ithaca, N.Y., 1962), pp. 95-139.

kind, unlike practical maxims, have a social dimension: It *makes sense* to ask whether a job-holder (or role-taker) is *obligated* to follow a particular rule, or whether this is one of his *duties*, and the penalty attaching to a breach of the rules does not consist simply in his not "getting the job done."

Rules of this kind are found in very different institutions. Some are rules of a "job" in the ordinary sense. Others apply to anyone who voluntarily assumes a "role," such as "automobile driver." Others characterize a position which one is obliged to take by law, for example, that of private in the army. The goals which the rules are designed to serve may be ordinary products of labor, such as houses, steel beams, etc.; or fairly specific social goals such as "getting vehicles to their destinations safely and expeditiously"; or goals as general as "the national defense." In some cases the rules, differing from job to job, mark a division of labor, as the rules which say what factory workers, or the members of a platoon, are to do. In other cases, the same rules apply more or less equally to all as in the case of (at least some) rules regulating traffic.

Notwithstanding their variety, these rules can be classified together because they share two fundamental characteristics: (1) The rules prescribe action which is thought to contribute to the attainment of a goal. This is the "design" of such rules, at least in the sense that if the prescribed action does not effectively contribute to the attainment of the goal, for the most part, then the rule itself is subject to criticism. (2) The rules are "laid down" or "legislated" or "made the rule" by a party which has power or authority of some kind; one cannot learn "what the rules are" simply by determining what general procedures most effectively promote the goal. This latter characteristic sharply differentiates these rules from what I have called practical maxims, although both share the first characteristic and are "instrumental."[2]

. . . .

III

Rules of common competitive games, such as baseball, chess, and the like, say how a game is to be played. They state the "object of the game," "the moves," "how the counting should go," etc. Often they are stated in "rule books," and sometimes they are enforced by referees appointed by an acknowledged authority. These formalities, however, are not at all necessary. The rules must be "laid down" or "adopted" in some sense, but all that is required (in the case of those games being discussed) is that a group of players "agree" on a

[2] Practical maxims should not be dismissed, however, as "mere rules of thumb" on the one hand, or as "simply stating relations between means and ends" on the other. When one follows a maxim the rule *directs* action and is a *criterion* of certain kinds of rightness and wrongness in acting.

In passing note that Rawls's "summary conception," as a whole, does not properly apply to practical maxims, although several features of this conception do apply. Rawls's analysis, admirable as it is, is very apt to mislead. For the "summary view," as he calls it, is a blend of two quite distinct conceptions: In part it is a confused conception or a misconception of a rule, as a summary or report. In other respects it is an accurate conception of what I have called a practical maxim. This may account for an ambivalence in Rawls's article: Cf. ". . . it is doubtful that anything to which the summary conception did apply would be called a *rule*." [(p. 23) "Two Concepts . . ."] with "Some rules will fit one conception, some rules the other; and so there are rules of practice (rules in the strict sense), and maxims and 'rules of thumb'." (p. 29). The point is that maxims are rules in a *different* sense from other kinds of rules, whereas no rule, *qua rule*, is a summary or report.

The importance of this point is that there are two possible confusions here, not one: A person may conceive moral rules as summaries or reports, or he may conceive moral rules on the model of maxims. The texts of Austin and Mill, which Rawls cites, together with Rawls's discussion, suggest that the latter, more than the former, was their mistake. V., however, note 13 below.

set of rules. This agreement may consist simply in their following and enforcing rules which they all have learned: Think, for example, of a group of small boys playing baseball, and think of the difference between one's knowing the rules and playing the game. In such cases there is no formally agreed-upon authority; each player—in principle—is both rule-follower and rule-enforcer. No player has the authority to modify the rules at will, but the players together can change them in any way they see fit. As one should expect, there are many variations.

In the latter respects game rules of this kind are quite like the rules in (I). These game rules, however, noticeably lack the first major characteristic of those rules: They are not designed to yield a product. More precisely, they are not adopted to promote the attainment of a goal which, in the senses indicated earlier, is "over and beyond" the rules.[3] They do not serve a goal which is "logically independent" of the game which they define.

3.1.1 Of course people who play games do so with various motives, and some of the goals which motivate them are logically independent of the game; for example, exercise, recreation, the opportunity to talk to friends or make a conquest. Undoubtedly games are popular because they serve so many ends. Nevertheless, motives and goals of this kind are not essential. Many players participate (so far as can be determined without psychoanalyzing them) "just because they want to" or simply "from love of the game." Actually this kind of motive, even if it is not typical, is that which is most distinctive of players: One who "loves a game" commonly regards another, who lacks the motive, as poorly appreciating "the quality of the game." This is apt to be missed just because games have been turned into instruments, for exercise, diversion, etc., to such a great degree. The point is, they *need* not be.

Moreover, games *qua* games do not seem to have a design or goal *different* from the motives of the rule-followers, in the way rules of jobs commonly do. What is this goal? One who most appreciates a game speaks about it rather as if it were an aesthetic object, worth playing on its own account and apart from any product or result; and if he is asked to justify his claim that it is good, he seems to have a problem analogous to that of justifying an aesthetic

[3] Some games have become instruments to such a considerable degree, and some instrumental activities have become so much like games, that no description will prevent the intrusion of dubious and borderline cases.

judgment.[4] Sometimes, to be sure, the rules of games are changed, and in particular instances violated, in order to change the consequences. Many official rules, for example, have been changed in order to lessen player injuries; and particular persons may find a game played by the official rules too strenuous, or pursuit of the ball after a bad drive too troublesome. These facts, however, do not imply that the rules are designed to produce consequences, such as the right amount of exercise or exertion, or the good health of the players. Changes of the kind mentioned simply indicate that the rules of a game, like the rules of a job, are adopted in a context by persons who have many desires and many obligations other than "to play the game" and "follow its rules." Games are often altered to make them harmonize better with such contextual features. It is true, of course, that persons who have turned games into instruments change or violate the rules more readily. As we say, these people do not take the game as seriously.

Some philosophers are inclined to say that even when one plays a game "just because he wants to" or "for love of the game," the game is still an instrument—to "his enjoyment" or "pleasure." This stand depends for its cogency on our being able to describe this pleasure or enjoyment without referring to the game, which should be possible if the pleasure or enjoyment really were something separate from playing the game. However, although it is clearly possible to play a game and not enjoy it, the converse does not appear plausible. To be sure, one sometimes says that he gets about the same enjoyment from one game as another, especially when the two are similar. But this is apt to mean that he has no strong preference for one game over another, that he likes one as well as the other, not that there is a kind of pleasurable feeling which in fact results from both, more or less equally, and which *conceivably* could be had from very different activities or even from being acted *on* in some way. (Similarly, when one says that he "likes to talk to one person about as much as another," this clearly does not mean that talking to the two persons produces the same kind of pleasure in him.) Moreover, when we speak of getting about the same enjoyment from two

games, sometimes the "enjoyment" does not appear to be, strictly speaking, the enjoyment "of playing the game," but rather the enjoyment of exercising, talking to friends, etc. I do not deny, however, that games can become instruments. I want to argue that they need not be, often are not, and that in calling them games we do not imply that they are instruments.

The kind of goal the pursuit of which to some degree *is* essential to the playing of the game is the "object of the game," as defined by the rules, and the various sub-goals which promote this object according to the rules. Such goals as these, for example, "to score the most runs," "to get the batter out at second base," obviously are not logically independent of the rules of the game—if there were no rules it would be logically impossible to try to do these things. It is just nonsense to speak of changing the rules so that one can better attain the object of the game.

3.1.2 Since the action within a game is designed to attain goals defined by the rules, the action as well as the goal logically depends on the rules: In important respects a move in the game has the consequences it has because the rules say it has; *in these respects* the rules define the consequences and determine the character of the action.[5] Since the character of instrumental action is fixed at least partly by the goal which the action is designed to serve, the action can be described in this essential respect, as a "trying to get the goal," without refering to or presupposing rules. In the case of play in a game, unless the game has become an instrument, this is not possible; if one describes the action in a game apart from the rules, as a "trying to catch a ball," he leaves out the design. On account of this difference one may feel inclined to say that whereas rules of the kind described in (I) *may* be used to describe an action, game rules by defining new kinds of action just constitute "forms of life."[6]

3.2 However, this is but one side of the story, and if it were the only one it is not likely that the two kinds of rules would be confused. To see the other side, which is equally important, one should attend to the fact that the play in a game is not wholly defined by the rules of the game. "The kind of game he plays" ordinarily does not refer to the game as defined by the rules; "to play a game" ordinarily means more than following

[4] This reminds one of the ancient distinctions between "doing" and "making," and between (what the medievals called) "immanent" and "transitive" activity. I do not mean to deny that some jobs are worth doing "on their own account," but even when "one enjoys a job," there is a discernible purpose which it is designed to promote.

[5] This is the point which Rawls emphasized.

[6] Cf. A. I. Melden, "Action," *Philosophical Review*, vol. 65 (1956), pp. 523-541.

the rules. The point is that although the object of the game is defined by the rules, since the action in a game normally consists in "trying to attain that object," and since the game rules do not determine success in this respect, the action in *this* respect is instrumental. Players often develop tactics and strategies and skills in playing. Sometimes they follow what I have called practical maxims, and at other times they follow team rules agreed on among themselves or laid down by the "manager." The latter are, of course, examples of the rules described in (I). Obviously they should not be confused with rules of games, as I have described them. For one can be said to play a game without his following any particular set of instrumental rules.

The point of greatest importance here is that although game rules are not themselves instruments, they support, as it were, a considerable amount of instrumental activity, much of which logically could not be carried on without them. To play a game is typically to follow the rules of the game *and* engage in this instrumental activity; a "good player" does more than just follow the rules. Even one who "loves the game for its own sake" derives his satisfaction from the kind of *instrumental* activity which the rules of the game make possible. Games make new goals, new pursuits, and new skills available to men.

In this situation it is not surprising that some should regard games themselves as instruments. To regard them in this way, however, would be to confuse their function.

BIBLIOGRAPHY ON SPORT AND VALUE-ORIENTED CONCERNS

American Association for Health, Physical Education, and Recreation, Division for Girls and Women's Sports and Division of Men's Athletics. *Report of a National Conference on Values in Sports.* Interlochen, Michigan, June 17-22, 1962.

Asinof, Eliot. "1919: The Fix Is In." in *The Realm of Sport.* Edited by Herbert Warren Wind. New York: Simon and Schuster, 1966.

"Athletics and Morals." *Atlantic Monthly,* CXIII (February, 1914), 145-148.

Banham, Charles. "Man at Play." *Contemporary Review,* 207 (August, 1965), 61-64.

Beisser, Arnold R. *The Madness in Sports.* New York: Appleton-Century-Crofts, 1967.

Bend, Emil. "Some Functions of Competitive Team Sports in American Society." Unpublished Ph.D. dissertation, University of Pittsburgh, 1970.

Bovyer, George. "Children's Concepts of Sportsmanship in the Fourth, Fifth, and Sixth Grades." 34, (October, 1963), 282-287.

Bowen, Wilbur P. "The Evolution of Athletic Evils." *American Physical Education Review,* XIV (March, 1909), 151-156.

Calisch, Richard. "The Sportsmanship Myth." *Physical Educator,* X (March, 1953), 9-11.

Chryssafis, Jean E. "Aristotle on Physical Education." *Journal of Health and Physical Education,* 1 (January; February; September, 1930), 3-8, 50; 14-17, 46-47; 14-17, 54-56.

Clifton, Marguerite. "Values Through Sports." Unpublished paper presented at the annual convention of the Eastern District Association for Health, Physical Education, and Recreation, Philadelphia, Pennsylvania, March 18, 1963.

Comer, G. "Relationships Between Sport and Mental Health." *Physical Education,* 60 (November, 1968), 83-86.

Coon, Roger. "Sportsmanship, A Worthy Objective." *Physical Educator,* 21 (March, 1964), 16.

Deatherage, Dorothy. "Factors Related to Concepts of Sportsmanship." Unpublished Ed.D. dissertation, University of Southern California, 1964.

Diggs, B. J. "Rules and Utilitarianism." *American Philosophical Quarterly,* I (January, 1964), 32-44.

Graves, H. "A Philosophy of Sport." *Contemporary Review,* 78 (December, 1900), 877-893.

Hartman, Betty Grant. "An Exploratory Method for Determining Ethical Standards in Sports." Unpublished Ph.D. dissertation, The Ohio State University, 1958.

Hoben, Allan. "The Ethical Value of Organized Play." *Biblical World,* XXXIX (March, 1912), 175-187.

Hogan, William R. "Sin and Sports." *Motivations in Play, Games and Sports.* Edited by Ralph Slovenko and James A. Knight. Illinois: Charles C Thomas, 1967.

Hosmer, Millicent. "The Development of Morality through Physical Education." *Mind and Body,* 21 (June, 1914), 156-163.

Johnson, George E. "Play and Character." *American Physical Education Review,* XXXI (October, 1926), 981-988.

Keating, James W. "Sportsmanship as a Moral Category." *Ethics,* LXXV (October, 1964), 25-35.

————. "The Heart of the Problem of Amateur Athletics." *Journal of General Education,* 16 (January, 1965), 261-272.

————. "Athletics and the Pursuit of Excellence." *Education,* 85 (March, 1965), 428-431.

Kehr, Geneva Belle. "An Analysis of Sportsmanship Responses of Groups of Boys Classified as Participants and Non-Participants in Organized Baseball." Unpublished Ed.D. dissertation, New York University, 1959.

Kellor, Frances A. "Ethical Value of Sports for Women." *American Physical Education Review,* XI (September, 1906), 160-171.

Kennedy, C[harles] W. "The Effect of Athletic Competition on Character Building." *American Physical Education Review,* XXXI (October, 1926), 988-991.

―――. *Sport and Sportsmanship.* New Jersey: Princeton University Press, 1931.

Laughter, Robert James. "Socio-Psychological Aspects of the Development of Athletic Practices and Sports Ethics." Unpublished Ph.D. dissertation, The Ohio State University, 1963.

Lee, Joseph. *Play in Education.* New York: Macmillan, 1920.

McAfee, Robert A. "Sportsmanship Attitudes of Sixth, Seventh, and Eighth Grade Boys." *Research Quarterly,* 26 (March, 1955), 120.

McBride, P. *The Philosophy of Sport.* London: Heath Cranton, 1932.

McCormick, Richard A., S. J. "Is Professional Boxing Immoral?" *Sports Illustrated,* 17 (November 5, 1962), 70-82.

McMurty, John. "Philosophy of a Corner Linebacker." *The Nation,* 212 (January 18, 1971), 83-84.

Massengale, John Denny. "The Effect of Sportsmanship Instruction on Junior High School Boys." Unpublished Ed.D. dissertation, The University of New Mexico, 1969.

Montague, Ashley. "Play or Murder" in *The Humanization of Man.* New York: World Publishing, 1962.

Muhammad, Elijah. "On Sport and Play" in *Message to the Blackman in America.* Illinois: Muhammad Mosque of Islam No. 2, 1965.

Nash, Jay B. "The Aristocracy of Virtue." *Journal of Health, Physical Education, and Recreation,* 20 (March, 1949), 157, 216-217.

"Now Ike's Golf is Legal." *Sports Illustrated,* 12 (January 18, 1960), 24.

Oberteuffer, Delbert. "On Learning Values Through Sport." *Quest,* I (December, 1963), 23-29.

Oberteuffer, Delbert, Michielli, Donald and Carlson, Joseph. "Sportsmanship—Whose Responsibility?" *Anthology of Contemporary Readings.* Edited by Howard S. Slusher and Aileene S. Lockhart. Iowa: Wm. C. Brown, 1966.

Potter, Stephen. *The Theory and Practice of Gamesmanship.* New York: Bantam Books, 1965. (First published New York: Holt, Rinehart and Winston, 1948.)

Powell, John T. "Culture, Countries and Sport." Unpublished paper presented at the annual convention of the American Association for Health, Physical Education, and Recreation, Detroit, Michigan, April 3, 1971.

Ralls, Anthony. "The Game of Life." *Philosophical Quarterly,* 16 (January, 1966), 23-34.

Rawls, John. "Two Concepts of Rules." *Philosophical Review,* 64 (January, 1955), 3-32.

"Requiem for a Friend [Pope Pius XII on sport]." *Sports Illustrated,* 9 (October 20, 1958), 27.

Richardson, Deane E. "Ethical Conduct in Sport Situations." *Proceedings of the Sixty-Fifth Annual Meeting of the National College Physical Education Association.* San Francisco, California, 1962.

Roberts, Terry. "The Fiction of Morally Indifferent Acts in Sport." Unpublished paper presented at The First Canadian Symposium on The Philosophy of Sport and Physical Action, Windsor, Ontario, Canada, May 3, 1972.

Rogers, Frederick Rand. *The Amateur Spirit in Scholastic Games and Sports.* Albany, New York: C. F. Williams & Son, 1929.

Royce, Josiah. *Some Relations of Physical Training to the Present Problems of Moral Education in America.* Boston: The Boston Normal School of Gymnastics, *ca.* 1908.

Rupp, Adolph. "Defeat and Failure to Me Are Enemies." *Sports Illustrated,* 9 (December 8, 1958), 100-106.

Scott, Jack. *The Athletic Revolution.* New York: Free Press, 1971.

―――. "Ethics in Sport: The Revolutionary Ethic." Unpublished paper presented at the annual convention of the American Association for Health, Physical Education, and Recreation, Houston, Texas, March 28, 1972.

Shaw, John H. "The Operation of a Value System in the Selection of Activities and Methods of Instruction in Physical Education." *Proceedings of the Fifty-Ninth Annual Meeting of the College Physical Education Association,* Daytona Beach, Florida, 1956.

Shriver, Sargent. "The Moral Force of Sport." *Sports Illustrated,* 18 (June 3, 1963), 30-31, 62-63.

Slusher, Howard S. *Man, Sport and Existence.* Philadelphia: Lea & Febiger, 1967.

―――. "Ethics in Sport: The American Ethic." Unpublished paper presented at the annual convention of the American Association for Health, Physical Education and Recreation, Houston, Texas, March 28, 1972.

Spencer, Herbert. "Amusements" in *The Principles of Ethics,* Vol. I. New York: D. Appleton and Company, 1910.

Stearns, Alfred E. "Athletics and the School." *Atlantic Monthly,* CXIII (February, 1914), 148-152.

Stewart, C. A. "Athletics and the College." *Atlantic Monthly,* CXIII (February, 1914), 153-160.

Suits, Bernard. "Is Life a Game We Are Playing?" *Ethics,* 77 (April, 1967), 209-213.

"Symposium of Sportsmanship." *Physical Educator,* VI (October, 1949), 1-15.

Tiede, Tom and Berkow, Ira. "Our Changing Morality," Part 3. *The Springfield Union,* February 24, 1970, p. 17.

Tunis, John R. "The Great Sports Myths" in *$port$: Heroics and Hysterics.* New York: John Day, 1928.

Turbeville, Gus. "On Being Good Sports in Sports." *Vital Speeches,* 31 (June 15, 1965), 542-544.

Ulrich, Celeste. "Ethics in Sport: The Christian

Ethic." Unpublished paper presented at the annual convention of the American Association for Health, Physical Education, and Recreation, Houston, Texas, March 28, 1972.

Underwood, John. "The True Crisis [Is Sport Crooked?]." *Sports Illustrated,* 18 (May 20, 1963), 16-19, 83.

UNESCO. *Sport, Work, Culture. Report of the International Conference on The Contribution of Sports to the Improvement of Professional Abilities and to Cultural Development.* Helsinki, Finland, August 10-15, 1959.

Weiss, Paul. *Sport: A Philosophic Inquiry.* Carbondale: Southern Illinois University Press, 1969.

Wilton, W. M. "An Early Consensus on Sportsmanship." *Physical Educator,* 20 (October, 1963), 113-114.

Woods, Sherwyn M. "The Violent World of the Athlete." *Quest,* XVI (June, 1971), 55-60.

Zeegers, Machiel. "The Swindler as Player." *Motivations in Play, Games and Sports.* Edited by Ralph Slovenko and James A. Knight. Illinois: Charles C Thomas, 1967.

SPORT AND AESTHETICS

Sport and Aesthetics

INTRODUCTION

Aesthetics as a branch of philosophy coexists with ethics in the general category of axiology. Whereas ethics deals with the question of what is good, aesthetics is concerned with what is beautiful. Questions concerning beauty, taste, and the nature of the aesthetic experience, are among the most complex of philosophical issues.

Much of aesthetic inquiry centers around the appreciation and evaluation of artificial art—that is, objects deliberately created to be beautiful, to catalyze an aesthetic experience. Nevertheless, most people have had the pleasure of experiencing beauty in a natural setting, with no artist intervening. In fact many artists have devoted their work to attempting to re-create or capture scenes of natural beauty. Somewhere between the natural and the created art object is the structure created for utilitarian purposes, such as a building, which also happens to be beautiful and invokes an aesthetic experience.

Sport may be an example of the latter category, or it may be considered a phenomenon of natural beauty. In either case, it should be realized that whatever their artistic merits, most sports cannot be compared to a painting or other deliberately created art object. The exceptions, of course, are the "form" sports: diving, gymnastics, figure skating, aquatic art, and riding. However, these activities are transitory, they exist as objects d'art only momentarily and are therefore a unique form of art.*

* Refer to Maheu (1963) for an excellent discussion of this point.

The question of what is art hinges upon the more fundamental problem of what is beauty. As with all other philosophical issues, there are various points of view roughly corresponding to the major philosophical schools of thought. Opinions include the beliefs that beauty is the idealized representation of nature (a concept held by the classical Greeks, for example), and the often-quoted statement that "beauty is in the eye of the beholder." In either case, certain criteria are applied, either those which correspond to the dictates of nature, or those which the individual chooses to apply. The admission of the latter possibility has led aestheticians to question the validity of assuming that art is a subtopic of the theory of beauty. While a person may have an aesthetic response to beauty, a similar reaction may occur when confronted with the ugly or violent or even, if contemporary pop artists are to be taken seriously, with the merely ordinary.

Still another complex question is the problem of aesthetic quality. Much of traditional art criticism has been based upon the assumption that certain principles of aesthetics have been established, either classically or in a given time and society. The evaluation of a work of art is then made in conformity to these accepted principles. A competing viewpoint is the notion that basic to quality in art is the object's ability to evoke an emotional response, a reaction, an "experience," a moment of communication between the viewer and the artist via the art object. Although stated in much more sophisticated terms today, the root of this is in the pleasure theories exposited by men like Herbert Spencer in the late nineteenth century. Then the aesthetic response was described in terms of the viewer's enjoyment, a primarily emotional response. However, with the development of aesthetic theories which regard art as deliberately symbolic, as non-verbal language, cognitive responses are also considered to be a part of the aesthetic experience. Meaning, relevance, communication, insight are all terms used in connection with the aesthetic experience. As with the word beauty, the connotations of the term pleasure have been much expanded.

Sport has long been considered a worthy subject for artists. In other words, its potential as an object of beauty to be represented in some created art form has been recognized. Sporting art has been shown to be meaningful, capable of evoking an aesthetic experience. Some of the best examples come from the ancient Greeks who gave particular representation to sport and sportsmen in art. Lawrence Toynbee's article on "Artists and Sports" offers reasons for this long-term fascination.

Perhaps more important than the representation of sport *in* art, is the belief that sport itself *is* an *art* form. As a form of cultural expression, it fits the criteria applied to other art forms such as painting and sculpture. The origin of this idea is generally credited to the German romantic philosopher Friedrich von Schiller. He contended that the ideal of beauty is represented in the play-instinct; play, which is the expression of man at his most complete, can be the highest form of aesthetic culture. Karl Groos, in his classic work *The Play of Man*, expresses a similar point of view.

Schiller and Groos established the relationship between play and aesthetics on the basis of similarities between them. For example, they are both nonproductive and, in a biological sense, removed from the acts of man necessary for survival. More recent speculations have gone further in attempting to demonstrate that the sport experience is inherently an aesthetic experience. The articles by Eugene Kaelin and Marjorie Fisher both analyze the aesthetic qualities of sporting events, though Kaelin limits his discussion to sport from the view of the spectator. Fisher is interested in the separate experiences of both the spectator and athlete, and in the objective qualities of sport as an art form.

One can accept the assumption that sport is an art form, that participating in the sport experience as either player or spectator is potentially an aesthetic experience. But the overriding question in art is when does a phenomenon have the quality to be considered a work of art? In other words, what is the difference between a child's drawing and a Picasso painting? What is the qualitative difference between the action of a Willie Mays and that of a young sandlot player? Is every sport experience an aesthetic experience? When does one's athletic experience transcend the ordinary and become an aesthetic occasion? Does awareness of aesthetic qualities enhance the sport experience?

The literature on sport and art does not even attempt to answer these questions; generally, it has been concerned with attempting to demonstrate the existence of a relationship between sport and art. A number of writers have exposited Schiller's original theories, modifying or expanding them in accord with some philosophical justifications. The articles by Seward (1944) and Hein (1968) are examples of this type of analysis. Two excellent selections which discuss sport as art in cultural terms, are those by Maheu (1963) and Jokl (1964). Metzl (1962) analyzes a number of art pieces which take sport as their subject. An interesting paper by Lowe (1971) attempts to set the parameters of the issues relating to sport and aesthetics.

With such a sparse treatment of the subject, there is much room for further research. Most needed are standards for evaluating the quality of movement. Those standards already established in sports such as diving, might be re-examined in terms of their faithfulness to artistic principles. Similarly, artistic criteria for games might be developed. A comparison of the art form sport with other art forms might be undertaken with a view to delineating sport's special place within the realm of art. Empirical evidence might be gathered in support of the contention that the sport experience is, in fact, an aesthetic experience according to accepted criteria.

Such analyses may be subject to the criticism that they are an attempt to exalt sport beyond its simple importance as a source of pleasure and meaning to its millions of participants and spectators. But it is part of man's desire to appreciate the value of his works, that leads to the discipline of aesthetic criticism.

Play and Beauty*

FRIEDRICH VON SCHILLER

I approach continually nearer to the end to which I lead you, by a path offering few attractions. Be pleased to follow me a few steps further, and a large horizon will open up to you, and a delightful prospect will reward you for the labor of the way.

The object of the sensuous instinct, expressed in a universal conception, is named Life in the widest acceptation; a conception that expresses all material existence and all that is immediately present in the senses. The object of the formal instinct, expressed in a universal conception, is called shape or form, as well in an exact as in an inexact acceptation; a conception that embraces all formal qualities of things and all relations of the same to the thinking powers. The object of the play instinct, represented in a general statement, may therefore bear the name of *living form;* a term that serves to describe all aesthetic qualities of phenomena, and what people style, in the widest sense, *beauty.*

Beauty is neither extended to the whole field of all living things nor merely enclosed in this field. A marble block, though it is and remains lifeless, can nevertheless become a living form by the architect and sculptor; a man, though he lives and has a form, is far from being a living form on that account. For this to be the case, it is necessary that his form should be life, and that his life should

* "Letter XV" from *Essays and Letters.* Vol. VIII. Trans. by A. Lodge, E. B. Eastwick and A. J. W. Morrison. London: Anthological Society, 1882.

be a form. As long as we only think of his form, it is lifeless, a mere abstraction; as long as we only feel his life, it is without form, a mere impression. It is only when his form lives in our feeling, and his life in our understanding, he is the living form, and this will everywhere be the case where we judge him to be beautiful.

But the genesis of beauty is by no means declared because we know how to point out the component parts, which in their combination produce beauty. For to this end it would be necessary to comprehend that *combination itself,* which continues to defy our exploration, as well as all mutual operation between the finite and the infinite. The reason, on transcendental grounds, makes the following demand: There shall be a communion between the formal impulse and the material impulse—that is, there shall be a play instinct—because it is only the unity of reality with the form, of the accidental with the necessary, of the passive state with freedom, that the conception of humanity is completed. Reason is obliged to make this demand, because her nature impels her to completeness and to the removal of all bounds; while every exclusive activity of one or the other impulse leaves human nature incomplete and places a limit in it. Accordingly, as soon as reason issues the mandate, "a humanity shall exist," it proclaims at the same time the law, "there shall be a beauty." Experience can answer us if there is a beauty, and we shall know it as soon as she has taught us if a humanity can exist. But neither reason nor experience can tell us how beauty can be and how a humanity is possible.

We know that man is neither exclusively matter nor exclusively spirit. Accordingly, beauty as the consummation of humanity, can neither be exclusively mere life, as has been asserted by sharp-sighted observers, who kept too close to the testimony of experience, and to which the taste of the time would gladly degrade it; nor can beauty be merely form, as has been judged by speculative sophists, who departed too far from experience, and by philosophic artists, who were led too much by the necessity of art in explaining beauty; it is rather the common object of both impulses, that is of the play instinct. The use of language completely justifies this name, as it is wont to qualify with the word play what is neither subjectively nor objectively accidental, and yet does not impose necessity either externally or internally. As the mind in the intuition of the beautiful finds itself in a happy medium between law and necessity, it is, because it divides itself between both, emancipated from the pressure of both. The formal impulse and the material impulse are equally earnest in their demands, because one relates in its cognition to things in their reality and the other to their necessity; because in action the first is directed to the preservation of life, the second to the preservation of dignity, and therefore both to truth and perfection. But life becomes more indifferent when dignity is mixed up with it, and duty no longer coerces when inclination attracts. In like manner the mind takes in the reality of things, material truth, more freely and tranquilly as soon as it encounters formal truth, the law of necessity; nor does the mind find itself strung by abstraction as soon as immediate intuition can accompany it. In one word, when the mind comes into communion with ideas, all reality loses its serious value because it becomes *small;* and as it comes in contact with feeling, necessity parts also with its serious value because it is *easy.*

But perhaps the objection has for some time occurred to you. Is not the beautiful degraded by this, that it is made a mere play? and is it not reduced to the level of frivolous objects which have for ages passed under that name? Does it not contradict the conception of the reason and the dignity of beauty, which is nevertheless regarded as an instrument of culture, to confine it to the work of being a mere play? and does it not contradict the empirical conception of play, which can coexist with the exclusion of all taste, to confine it merely to beauty?

But what is meant by a *mere play*, when we know that in all conditions of humanity that very thing is play, and *only* that is play which makes man complete and develops simultaneously his twofold nature? What you style *limitation*, according to your representation of the matter, according to my views, which I have justified by proofs, I name *enlargement*. Consequently I should have said exactly the reverse: man is serious *only* with the agreeable, with the good, and with the perfect, but he *plays* with beauty. In saying this we must not indeed think of the plays that are in vogue in real life, and which commonly refer only to his material state. But in real life we should also seek in vain for the beauty of which we are here speaking. The actually present beauty is worthy of the really, of the actually present play-impulse; but by the ideal of beauty, which is set up by the reason, an ideal of the play-instinct is also presented, which man ought to have before his eyes in all his plays.

Therefore, no error will ever be incurred if we seek the ideal of beauty on the same road on which we satisfy our play-impulse. We can immediately understand why the ideal form of a Venus, of a Juno, and of an Apollo, is to be sought not at Rome, but in Greece, if we contrast the Greek population, delighting in the bloodless athletic contests of boxing, racing, and intellectual rivalry at Olympia, with the Roman people gloating over the agony of a gladiator. Now the reason pronounces that the beautiful must not only be life and form, but a living form, that is, beauty, inasmuch as it dictates to man the twofold law of absolute formality and absolute reality. Reason also utters the decision that man shall only *play* with beauty, and he *shall only play* with *beauty.*

For, to speak out once for all, man only plays when in the full meaning of the word he is a man, and *he is only completely a man when he plays*. This proposition, which at this moment perhaps appears paradoxical, will receive a great and deep meaning if we have advanced far enough to apply it to the twofold seriousness of duty and of destiny. I promise you that the whole edifice of aesthetic art and the still more difficult art of life will be supported by this principle. But this proposition is only unexpected in science; long ago it lived and worked in art and in the feeling of the Greeks, her most accomplished masters;

only they removed to Olympus what ought to have been preserved on earth. Influenced by the truth of this principle, they effaced from the brow of their gods the earnestness and labor which furrow the cheeks of mortals, and also the hollow lust that smoothes the empty face. They set free the ever serene from the chains of every purpose, of every duty, of every care, and they made *indolence* and *indifference* the envied condition of the god-like race; merely human appellations for the freest and highest mind. As well the material pressure of natural laws as the spiritual pressure of moral laws lost itself in its higher idea of necessity, which embraced at the same time both worlds, and out of the union of these two necessities issued true freedom. Inspired by this spirit the Greeks also effaced from the features of their ideal, together with *desire or inclination*, all traces of *volition*, or, better still, they made both unrecognizable, be-

cause they knew how to wed them both in the closest alliance. It is neither charm, nor is it dignity, which speaks from the glorious face of Juno Ludovici; it is neither of these, for it is both at once. While the female god challenges our veneration, the godlike woman at the same time kindles our love. But while in ecstasy we give ourselves up to the heavenly beauty, the heavenly self-repose awes us back. The whole form rests and dwells in itself—a fully complete creation in itself—and as if she were out of space, without advance or resistance; it shows no force contending with force, no opening through which time could break in. Irresistibly carried away and attracted by her womanly charm, kept off at a distance by her godly dignity, we also find ourselves at length in the state of the greatest repose, and the result is a wonderful impression for which the understanding has no idea and language no name.

Play From the Aesthetic Standpoint*

KARL GROOS

While it is true that undue emphasis of the overflow of energy reduces play to self-indulgence, at the same time it is unfair to art to make too prominent its kinship with play. This is just the position of Guyau in his aesthetic writings; yet he is far from denying the kinship, and I think that he would have concurred to a great extent in Schiller's view if he could have convinced himself of the biological and sociological importance of play by adequate investigation of its phenomena. I at least have been confirmed in my conviction of the close connection between play and aesthetics by the perusal of his book, and there, too, my view stated in the very outset—namely, that this connection obtains in a higher degree than does that between play and artistic production —is also supported by his more thoroughgoing investigation of the facts.

The following points present themselves as the most general results of our observation of aesthetic enjoyment. We have found that all sense organs display numerous impulses to activity, and consequently enjoyment of the response to stimuli is a universal basis of play, varying as to conditions and the quality of the stimuli. Now, since every aesthetic pleasure (except the appreciation of poetry) is connected with sense-perception, we find in it a genuine source of enjoyment, depending on the origin and quality of such perception. Observation merely for its own sake is the lowest

* From *The Play of Man*. New York: D. Appleton and Company, 1901.

form of aesthetic enjoyment, and is so far identical with sensuous play.

On this foundation arises enjoyment of special stimuli. Confining ourselves to sensory play, we can distinguish two groups—namely, sensuously agreeable stimuli and intensive ones. The former, provided higher aesthetic observation does its work of personification, finds its sole object in beauty. Pleasure in intense stimuli is strong enough to subdue the pain which is commonly associated with it, and forms an introduction to enjoyment of what is grotesque, striking, and tragic. It is especially prominent in the trancelike state so common in movement-play as well as in aesthetic enjoyment.

Before going further we must pause to consider the idea so often advanced that such enjoyment is peculiarly the prerogative of the higher senses. Is the pleasure which I feel when I inhale a perfume as much aesthetic as is the perception of beautiful colour? I think the case is like that of the common idea of play. From a psychological standpoint we recognise as such any act that is practised purely for its pleasurable effect, and sham occupation in the higher forms of play may be subjective. Therefore we can affirm that pleasure in perception as such, and not necessarily in agreeable perception, grounds it, and to this extent no one can demur if the beautiful colour is classed with the pleasant odour. For the utmost aesthetic satisfaction, however, more than this is requisite—first, definite form, and second, richer spiritual effect—and since these are perceptible only to the higher senses, it becomes their exclusive prerogative to take in the utmost effects of artistic effort.

To resume our review, we observe that aesthetic enjoyment is not merely a playful sensor experience, but manifests as well the higher psychic grounds of perception. What we said of the pleasure of recognition, the stimulus of novelty, and the shock of surprise need not here be repeated. Illusion remains the most certain mark of higher aesthetic enjoyment, and the important psychological problem connected with it which was referred to in the preceding section has its application here as in other illusion play. The first thing to notice about it here is that it consists partly in the transference of thought from the copy to an original,[1] and that sympathy and the borrowing of qualities which are connected with imitation have also their parts to play. Bearing all this in mind, we are in a position to put the question next in order, What is the principal content of illusion?

Thus we arrive at a point similar to that reached in our study of sensory plays. As the pleasure in stimulus as such surpasses the pleasure in any particular form of stimulus, so here the subjective activity of inner imitation as such is a source of pleasure quite apart from the qualities inherent in the thing copied. Lipps says, in his notice of my Einleitung in die Aesthetik, that for me the aesthetic value of the object under observation and personification is not that it is personified, but that it is I who personify it. Part III of the book proves the injustice of this to my general view, yet I do maintain that inner imitation is as such accompanied by pleasurable feelings,[2] and consequently that aesthetic satisfaction possibly finds its first limit when any painfulness connected with the subject outweighs the enjoyment derived from inner imitation.

If, then, the act of inner imitation is in itself pleasurable, it strikes me as self-evident that the degree of satisfaction attained must be proportional to the value of its object. This is clearly illustrated by the highest character of aesthetic intuition, the impression of vital and mental completeness; and inner imitation

shows this, for it delights to act in response to the functions of movement, force, life, and animation. Therefore Lotze is right when he says, after approving the limitations which we have pointed out, "No form is too chaste for the entrance and possession of our imagination." On the other hand, it is evident that the value of this indwelling depends essentially on the peculiarities of the subject. If, for instance, I transform myself into a shellfish and enter into its sole method of enjoyment, opening and shutting its shell, I experience a far narrower sort of aesthetic satisfaction than when I feel with a mother who is caressing her child. It is just because inner imitation is involved that the value of the aesthetic effect is determined by the qualities of the object. But what are the qualities, it may be asked, which augment or detract from this effect? An exhaustive and satisfactory answer to this question is impossible here; such is the extraordinary variety of the contributory factors. It properly belongs, too, to specialized aesthetics. In general, however, it is safe to say that we enjoy imitating what produces agreeable and intense feelings, and we thus find again on higher ground the same conditions which we encountered in sensory play. This distinction is clearly brought out by Lipps in his article on the impression made by a Doric column: "The mechanical effects which are 'easily' attained remind us of such acts of our own as are accomplished without effort or impediment, and likewise the powerful expenditure of active mechanical energy recalls a similar output of our will power. In the first case a cheerful feeling of lightness and freedom results; in the other no less agreeable sensations of our own vigour."[3] In other spheres the value of such indwelling seems to me to be chiefly in the two directions which Schiller has indicated in his comparison of "grace" and "dignity." I would refer again in this connection to what has been said about the importance of poetic enjoyment; if we are right in assigning love and conflict as its chief motives, then here too enjoyment of agreeable and intense stimuli is prominent.

If we ask, finally, how aesthetic enjoyment extends its sway beyond the entire sphere of play, we encroach on the ethical bearings of art. With the introduction of an element of moral elevation and profound insight into life, aesthetic satisfaction ceases to be "mere" play and transcends our present subject. But we must be careful to maintain that it is trans-

---

[1] Lange has treated of the contrary case where Nature is regarded as a work of art. I do not think, however, that it has the significance that belongs to the conversion of appearance into reality.

[2] "À la vue d'un objet expressif," says Jouffroy, "qui me jette dans un état sympathique de soi-même désagréable, il y a en moi un plaisir qui résulte de ce que je suis dans cet état."—*Op. cit.,* 270.

[3] Raumästhetik, p. 6.

cendence and not exclusion, for even when
(as is possible to a Shakespeare and a Schiller)
the intent toward moral elevation and profound
insight is prominent, our enjoyment remains
aesthetic only so long as these effects are developed and set forth in connection with playful sympathy.

Our second leading question is that of the
relation between play and artistic production.
Let us set out by announcing at once that the
latter, especially in highly developed art, is
further removed from play than is aesthetic
enjoyment. This is implied in the fact that,
for the genuine artist, practical application
of his aptitude is, as a rule, his life's calling; not necessarily his only means of support, of course, but sufficiently absorbing to
force the man of creative ability to devote
most of his life to an end which to the mass
of mankind seems unworthy of serious effort.
In such a case art ceases to be playful. But
this transformation is not unique. That absorption in an apparently useless form of activity
which is so incomprehensible to the average
man, but which easily lures its votaries to rapt
enthusiasm for their art, is displayed in many
forms less exalted than the striving for an
ideal. Plays not connected with art hold des-
potic sway over their victims. Many devote
their life's best effort to some forms of sport,
and others to mental contests, such as those of
chess, whist, etc. E. Isolani says that when
Zuckertort was a medical student in Berlin he
accidentally became a witness of a match game
between two fine chess players, and, although
unfamiliar with the rules, he detected a false
play. This interested him in the game, and
he became a pupil of Anderson. Soon chess
instead of medicine became his chief business
in life; he thought of nothing but how to improve his play. It kept him awake at night, or,
if fatigue overcame him, its problems pursued
him in dreams. At twenty-four he was a worn-
out man. The demoniac power with which art
drives a man so predisposed resides in other
games as well; and in this both activities cease
to be pure play.

Another basis for our subject is found in the
fact that art presupposes a useful field of application for technical skill whose acquirement
and improvement are no longer ends in themselves. The acquisition is often a long and
painful process, with little that is playful about
it. But this is common enough in other play as
well when the technical side of any sport is
made the subject of serious study and effort.

Our third ground is to be sought in a very
real aim, which is ever beckoning to the artist.

It may be designated in a general way as the
sympathetic interest of others, manifested in
admiring recognition and appreciation of the
powers displayed, or in subscribing to the con-
victions, views, and ideals of the artist. In so
far as this is an effective motive, art is no
play. Strictly artistic temperaments are especially liable to its influence at the beginning
of their career. Indifference, when sincere, is
usually a later development, the product of
experience.

Having thus fortified our position against
misconstruction, we are prepared to proclaim
the proper relationship between artistic production and play. It seems to me to be more and
more conspicuous as we approach the springs
of art. The primitive festival, combining as it
did music and poetry with dancing, had indeed
a tremendous effect on its witnessers, and its
manifestations were essentially playful. Skill
acquired in childhood through playful practice
was playfully exhibited with original variations.
The epic art, too, was playfully employed by
the primitive recounter, with no indication of
toilsome preparation or serious treatment, and
the case is not widely different with what we
know of the beginnings of pictorial art. So
long as primitive sculpture served no religious
purpose, simple delight in its use was much
more prominent, since all inherited the capacity, and none was opposed to the mass as the
exponent of a specialty. We meet the same
conditions in studying the child's artistic efforts;
his poetic and musical efforts as well as those
in drawing are essentially playful. The idea
of making an impression on others does appear,
but it is still very much in the background;
enjoyment of his own productive activity pre-
dominates in the infantile consciousness. Although highly developed art does so transcend the sphere of play, it too is rooted in
playful experimentation and imitation, and we
can detect their later growth of joy in being
a cause in the work of full-fledged artists of
our own day. Indeed, it is present in all creative activity, gilding earnest work with a
sportive glitter. In artistic production, however,
it has the special office of differentiating it
from ordinary toil and making appreciation of
the thing created go hand in hand with its
production. Each new-found harmony of tone
or colour or outline appealing to criticism of
its creator causes him intense enjoyment all
through the progress of its production, and the
indifference sometimes felt toward the finished
work results from frequent repetition which
has dulled the edge of appetite.

Artists and Sport*

LAWRENCE TOYNBEE

The idea that there might be quite a close relationship between popular sport and the arts may seem rather absurd. By popular sport I mean the various ball games now in vogue, and athletics, and racing, not the field sports which have long been associated with paintings of a certain type and which have of themselves a sort of romance. To most people these games to which I refer would seem to be the antithesis of art—the simplest form of public entertainment to be appreciated by ordinary simple people with no pretensions to intellectual interests, and typified in their players and adherents by a cheerful philistine outlook on life.

I consider any such ideas of incompatibility between everyday sports and the arts to be untrue. Good artists do have a very profound respect for the art they practice, but just because they are practitioners it is part of their everyday life and in many cases—particularly with painters—very dependent upon it. Even in our present era when so many varied and contradictory views are held about the purpose and significance of painting it cannot be denied that the vast majority of great European painters since the 14th century have used as a means of expression a convention based on the observation of the world around them and of their own personal visual experience of it. Furthermore a very great number of painters have based their work very deeply in direct observations and their visual, emotional and

* This article first appeared in *New Society*, 6 (November 8, 1962), 28, the weekly review of the social sciences, 128 Long Acre, London WC 2.

psychological reaction to it. Since the acceptance of the Impressionists it has become widely understood that a painter may in fact find inspiration and interest in any subject he may see in the life he knows and enjoys: the simplest landscape by Pissarro or the sleaziest cafe by Toulouse-Lautrec. But such motifs still preserve a certain traditional romantic aura: natural beauty, the night life of Paris; even horse racing because the dignity and innate beauty of thoroughbred horses is again a recognized thing. But if everyday experience and the visual knowledge and understanding of the sights and events around them are the raw materials of a great many painters then there is no reason why they should be confined just to those aspects of life that have been used by many painters before and which are generally considered traditional and "artistic." Nor, of course, is there any reason why new and original artists should not find the stimulus they need in subjects which are not in themselves new or original.

There is no real reason, then, why games should not be a fruitful source of inspiration for a painter—or for a writer, a poet, a dancer or a musician. In fact I think there are reasons why athletic activities may prove to be a particularly sympathetic and stimulating source of inspiration to artists.

Qualities which are demanded of all athletes are sense of balance and timing and control of the mind and body in rapid movement. In addition team games such as Association Football, Rugby Football, Hockey, and even Cricket demand of their exponent a sense of positional play, or one might say of pattern and design in movement, flowing and continuous, though often interrupted and changed, but still basically creative and alive. It was this creative moving element which made the great World Cup Final between Real Madrid and Eintracht such an exciting and satisfying experience, and which captivates those who see Tottenham Hotspur at their best. It is this that one hopes for in open Rugby: the swooping, darting, forward-running and backward-passing pattern of the attack pitting itself against the more staccato overlapping tackling of the defence. It is the same quality which illuminates the stick work and complex inter-passing of first class hockey players.

This sense of design is there too in more individual actions: the relationship of the squash player both spatially and in movement to the four static walls of the court and to the movements of his opponent and the ball: the inevitability of the great batsman's integration of his stroke with the type of ball he is bowled and the position of the fieldsman and the situation of the game. One could quote many other examples in other games and sports, and I think it is clear that in them all—especially where real skill is displayed—these elements of balance, controlled movement, and inter-related and inter-dependent patterns of action exist. I have referred to these already as qualities of design, and I believe them to be very much the same as some of the qualities of design which are searched for by an artist.

But this purely formal rapport between sport and art is not all. The similarity between the abstract movements and complex relationships of games players to the underlying abstract construction and theme of a work of art is enriched by the intense humanity of sport of this sort. It is a distillation of the basic struggle between human beings elevated to a civilized plane, and inspired by human genius at times just as it is frequently modified by human error. One of the themes which fascinate a painter is the apparently paradoxical combination in the visual world of the general and the particular, the abstract timeless norm and the living ephemeral variation on it. A haystack is always a haystack yet each haystack is differ-ent from every other, and each haystack is different each time it is seen at a different time and in a different light. In games exactly the same thing is found. Each match played to the same rules by different teams, or the same team at different times, or even between the same teams on the same ground on different days, contains the same timeless elements and yet the human beings playing it create an intense individuality, sometimes of greatness, sometimes of bathos, but whether memorable and stirring or not, each match is different from every other, each pattern and design is unique. Each match can therefore provide an entirely new and special experience for the artist as well as the more universal one I have discussed already.

Finally there are the opportunities provided by games to observe and admire the human figure at full stretch. The figure no longer holds the supreme position as a motif for painters that it held in the past, but it still remains of absorbing interest to many as being the most complex and mysterious of all creations, and the aesthetic possibilities of the figure in action have been explored by artists ever since the cave-painting of Lascaux. Modern ball games and athletics, and horse and greyhound racing, must provide a far wider range of physical activity than has ever before been available. A game like Rugby combining as it does running, jumping, kicking, wrestling, thunderous forward rushes, and delicate, balanced handling and sidestepping by the backs, in itself provides examples of the human body employing its various skills and abilities in almost all ways. Other games may be less complete but in them all the body is trained and driven toward perfection of movement and achievement in one way or another. So the oldest and possibly most universally interesting of all subject matter is presented to the artist by contemporary sports.

These are just some of the reasons why I consider that there is a close relationship between sport and the arts. They do in fact involve those who follow them in the same sort of endeavour and problem, they do both demand intense skill and extra awareness and control, and possibly in fact as our society develops they are drawing even closer together.

The Well-Played Game: Notes Toward an Aesthetics of Sport[*]

E. F. KAELIN

When, under the chancellorship of Robert Maynard Hutchins, the University of Chicago "de-emphasized" its commitment to intercollegiate football, reactions to the defection of the Maroons were various. Some critics, recalling the legendary remark of the youthful chancellor—no iron man this—that whenever the desire for physical activty manifested itself, he immediately lay down until it passed off, uttered a resigned "What can you expect?" Others, more rationalistic if less philosophical, pointed out the poor showing of Chicago's gladiators in recent Big-10 competition as sufficient reason for the radical step: better to save face by quitting than to continue bringing up the rear. Both views tended to ignore the corresponding re-emphasis on intramural sport activities intended to keep those egg-heads screwed on to functioning bodies, and not all of them could know of the Manhattan Project developing under the abandoned bleachers of Alonzo Stagg Field. You win some and you lose some; and as all cynics know only too well, if you are the coach and you lose too many, you chance to lose your job as well. Rather than looking for another coach and another site for experimenting on atomic fission, the Chicagoans ended their embarrassment by copping out. The chancellor's tirades against the growing professionalism of the college game were never really heard.

No one was surprised, and only the avid

fans of big-time football mourned the passing of an American institution. The case was different when, about ten years later, the University of Notre Dame made a similar decision. Here was a bigger institution yet. The Fighting Irish with the Polish names were one of the principal reasons for the very existence of South Bend, Indiana. Who were these religious men who decided that a university could be run without the attendant big business of football? Were their souls so hardened that they could no longer respond to the demand of winning one for the Gipper? What else is there to do in the Midwest on a fall Saturday afternoon? No one was naive enough to believe that the lack of distracting spectacles—cultural or otherwise—that is our Mid-western civilization would induce our football-deprived students to pass their time with the books. Thus, not succeeding in their idealism—not even that could make the alumni accept an 8-2 season for the Fighting Irish, where the "8" refers to the number of losses in one season—ND's administration decided to face up to reality: they needed a new coach, someone like Rockne and Layden and Leahy, someone who knew how to win; but they also needed an increased budget to float the necessary football scholarships. The rest of the story is known: they found both, only to have their most recent siege on the national championship fended off by the appearance of another national power. Oh, the horror of it: Michigan State Univer-

* From *Quest*, X (May, 1968), 16-28.

sity, which fills in the beef on its line with the culturally disadvantaged youth of the Southland and which hires its professors to foment counterrevolution in such places as Viet Nam, forced the Irish to play for a tie. They should have done as well in South Vietnam. Who was to console the despondent spirit of the Gipper now? Not Parseghian. He played this one out for his boys who played too hard for too long to accept second place in what turned out to be the only truly national championship competition in college football during recent times. Evidently we build character in our student athletes only by teaching them to win —or at least not to lose—with grace.

Who is to fault such a decision? Shall we repeat it? "It matters not . . . , it's how you play the game. And no one plays for a tie." The desire to win is a necessary part of all competitive sport, as, unfortunately, are the economics and consequently the politics of American universities—always on the make— engaged in big-time football. The question is: does such a mass of interlocking institutions possess a component which is distinctively sporting and distinctively aesthetic? Some of us, spectators and lovers of competitive sports we cannot engage in and participators in those suited to our physical characteristics, claim there is. What we need is a method of inquiry to make clear what we find happening in sport.

I propose to begin my inquiry with some observations on the nature of spectator sports in our American culture. In an affluent society the question of bread is for the most part guaranteed; and where it is not, bread can always be procured if only one is strong enough, agile or skilled enough to perform in the community circus. And there are many circuses in which to perform. Baseball, which lays the oldest and perhaps most fraudulent claim to being America's national pastime, was never played before as great a collective audience as basketball, once it was discovered that an outsized ball could be thrown through a peach basket placed at a suitable height from the floor. Every town in the country has its high school team; every junior college, college, and university that is too small to compete with bigger institutions for the honors of semi-professional football can and does produce basketball teams of acceptable caliber; and some of them rank with the best teams playing anywhere.

But if this were not enough to challenge baseball's claim to supremacy, along came television, which propelled collegiate and professional football into the national consciousness as never before. Where audiences in the stadia, gymnasia, and field houses across the nation were limited to the hundreds of thousands, the new audience for a single performance is currently being measured in the millions. And if the greedy moguls of professional football do not kill the goose that lays this golden egg by overexposing her, the growing trend of football fanship will make it quite plain even to the most rabid of baseball's fans that football is indeed the currently reigning national sport. Are sport appreciators fickle in their affections? Or is there a deeper reason for the rising disaffection with the game played with a bat?

Yes, Virginia, there is. But it is not the greater violence of football, that, appealing to some dark neurotic drive of the spectators, makes it more popular than nine innings of baseball played in the sun or under the lights. Violence it may be which makes the term "gladiator" more applicable to the participant in the contact sport; after all, the original gladiators fought to the death to appease the neuroses of the Roman citizens. But if the greater popularity of football were attributed to this sort of appeal, then ice hockey or lacrosse or boxing should be more popular than football. Violence, even the vicarious experience of violence on the part of the sports fan, is not what makes it a moral equivalent of war, as were the jousts and tournaments of bored knights. The value of violence in sport to both participant and spectator is not in its expression per se, but in its control toward the achievement of a contested end. Where violence may be sufficient to generate interst in an activity, its control is necessary to sustain our continued interest in its expression.

One of the factors which has worked to reduce interest in the game of baseball, moreover, has been precisely the introduction of more violence. When it was discovered that fans were willing to pay to see home runs instead of closely fought ball games, the era of the king of swat was very swiftly changed to that of the rabbit ball, band box ball parks, and the .260 hitter. Violence in this game was thus found to be one of the factors working toward its undoing as an aesthetic phenomenon and hence as a satisfying spectator sport. Pitchers were converted in this unnatural process into throwers, and their opponents in the struggle for survival into bottle bat bombers whose very cheapness has killed interest in an otherwise intriguing game. Perhaps the game was meant for the Latin Americans and the Japanese after all.

If not the violence of the action, then perhaps the continuity of action, or the lack of it, is the secret of baseball's apparent demise. Consider the experience of introducing a European to the delights of night baseball. Brought up on soccer, in which team, coach, and spectator are all satisfied to win the game by a single goal, 1-0 or 2-1 after a continuous hour's struggle—heaven help the goalie that allows three scores in a single game—our bemused European visitor finds nine innings of walks, hit basemen, home runs, and lengthy rhubarbs an interminable bore. True, it takes some time for him to perceive that the main tension of the game pits the pitcher's power and skill against those of each succeeding batter and that these may be slightly modified by the tension created between the speed of a runner and the "arm" of a defensive fielder; but even when brought to a recognition of these niceties, he can hardly be led to perceive the qualitative character of the game itself. And character discrimination is the essence of aesthetic perception.

In all but a very few instances baseball fails to generate any kind of dramatic unity. Occasionally the loyal fan may wait for the proverbial last inning stand in which the home team overcomes a lead ineptly allowed the visitors in earlier frames, but even this drama is experienced more for itself than as the culmination of many meaningful events leading up to this singular climax of controlled violence. The lack of continuity between the preparation and the climax is all too apparent, and it becomes even more so as viewed on television. Contrast it with a goal line stand in the final seconds of a football game. Who will forget that quarterback sneak of Bart Starr in the last NFL championship game, played on a frozen field, after two prior attempts had failed? Kramer found footing and blocked his man, allowing Starr to penetrate by the distance of half a yard. Twenty-two men were involved in the single action that capped the previous fifty-nine minutes of continuous struggle. The game would have been as beautiful had Dallas's line held; only the irrational support of one team over the other could have changed the character of that game, but then the heroes and the goats would have changed names.

If my observations, though limited, are sufficient to point out one of the differences in appeal between baseball and football (that the action of the one game is diffuse, badly articulated, and rarely climaxing as opposed to the continuous, tightly structured, and usually climaxing action of the other), some **ground** would have been gained for understanding

the greater spectator appeal in the more dramatic game. I propose in what follows to treat my subject from another point of view. I should like to examine the conditions under which the game itself is a vehicle of creative physical activity, akin to that expended in the production and experience of any bona fide work of art.

Such terms as the "superior dramatic action" of the football game over the baseball game may lead one to suspect that the aesthetic properties of athletic contests are to be explained by metaphor or, what amounts to the same thing, by application of a model taken from another context—here, dramatic literature—where the use of the terms is more clearly understood. Such was not my intent. I have referred to the "dramatic action" of competitive sport only to assert for those who have not yet perceived it that the action of organized sports is capable of highly dramatic action. True fans, who are aware of the dramatic content of their sporting events, need no such explanation. What they may lack is a clear understanding of the manner in which those memorable games have achieved the aesthetic character which made them memorable. It is to those fans I now address my efforts.

If I were to use a model of a completely developed aesthetic activity which is understood on its own terms, my choice would not be of a totally dissimilar medium, such as dramatic literature, which works its wonders by the articulation of words and by their meanings, but by the similar medium of dance: human effort expended in kinaesthetic response to the growing needs of a physical situation. In dance, of course, the situation and the responses are mutually determinant and self-contained. My argument will be that competitive sport is capable of the same kind of development, that the sporting event, at its best, is the one which achieves the same sort of mutual determinancy and self-containedness as the most abstract of dance. The "drama" of the sport may indeed produce a more effectively expressive vehicle than what is usually achieved in dance.

The effect of dance, like that of any other art form, is the effect of abstraction. This means only that to make a work of art one needs a medium. Music became an art when sounds were controlled to produce meaningful sequences; painting, when line was used to delineate a form and colored pigments were used to create space tensions. The artwork appears when someone perceives the effects of moving such physical things as sounds, marks, and color pigments out of one context, where they are aesthetically insignificant, into another where they achieve a new interest to perception in a freely created, purely aesthetic context. That the dance itself is rather poorly understood as an art medium is easily grasped, because of the difficulty in our perceiving the abstraction. The dancer moves his body, but so do street walkers and ball players; he uses the gestures and movements of his physiological and kinesiological substructure which are already implicit in the acts of walking or swimming or running. If the balletic gesture does nothing more than incorporate our basic bodily movements without an added significance to its occurrence in the aesthetic context, the choreographer or the performing dancer has failed in his task of successful abstraction. For the moment it is sufficient to understand that the medium of the dance and the medium of the sporting event are the same. That is the reason for their comparison.

In another place[1] I have attempted to show the continuous abstraction of human movement from its everyday context, such as walking, stretching, and the like, into the "pure" movements of a creative dance. The abstractive hierarchy runs as follows: at the base is our bodily presence in the natural environment, in which we always move from here to there. The "here" is defined as the center of our own bodily schemata; the "there" may be anything: an object to be grasped or avoided. Under the impulse of our own needs and desires we may wish to kick it, caress it, or merely move it out of the way. Given the necessary sensory-motor coordination we can ordinarily do any of these things. But even at this rather mundane level of human locomotor experience, we may effectuate an abstraction. Having learned to walk to achieve our ends of living, we may begin to play with our motor responses. Here, rather than achieving an end, the activity itself may be changed from means to end. I may walk because I enjoy walking, or I may walk in such a way as to develop a distinctive style of walking.

Whereas walking for the pleasure of walking may develop my muscles or keep them in tone, walking for a distinctive style may develop what traditional aestheticians have always called "grace." It is the abortion of this ideal in the provocative woman's walk which makes her rolling bottom appear obscene, not its invitation to carnal knowledge, which cannot be obscene. When grace is reduced to provocation, the movement is no longer a successful abstraction, being a call to the achievement of another kind of concrete goal. As long as we merely

contemplate the move without entering into its enticement, it may retain the discriminable aesthetic quality I have already named; it is merely provocative. But even they who are incapable of the necessary "aesthetic distance" and accept the proffered gambit to engage in the act of love may yet achieve successful aesthetic abstraction. It suffices to separate the act from its normal consequences, an immediate pleasure or pain and the procreation of the race, to find oneself in possession of a "new" artistic medium, the gentle art of coupling, than which no medium is more powerful in the creation and release of psychic tension, climaxing into a moment of peace. It matters little whether we refer to the medium as the art of making love or as the dance of life; the beauty of it is already apparent in the courting gyrations of birds.

The rhythms of sexual gymnastics would be an odd place to look for a model of sporting aesthetics. Not even the bad joke of referring to lovemaking as America's most popular indoor sport could make the comparison profitable. More to the point, however, is the manner in which the creation and release of psychic tension becomes qualitatively one; or, to put the matter in another way, how man's need for violent activity is expressed in a context in which the partner is not destroyed, but edified in and through the experience. The conventionality or the artificiality added to the natural context allows this expression and develops what is distinctively human. I have already referred to the controlled expression of violence as "the moral equivalent of war," and we are constantly being reminded of this fact by all those protest buttons proclaiming that one ought to "Make LOVE not WAR." The slogan makes sense, but how can you get the generals to see that it does? Or the country parsons, for that matter?

Starting with basic human movements engaged in to achieve a natural goal or end, we may come to understand that the order of significance achievable in this way is "natural"; it grows out of the coordination of our bodies to the achievement of natural ends. Developing grace and learning to experience the aesthetics of love are merely two low-order abstractions on this kind of movements, and man possesses this ability in common with all other natural life forms.

A higher order of significance is reached when physical coordination is related to artificially set goals. Here the significance is "conventional." Man has developed a real taste for playing with his motor responses—for distraction, for the maintenance of physical well-being, or for the moral and aesthetic experiences which play, in its most successful forms, affords. We all know the story: terrains are laid out, rules adopted, equipment standardized. The aim is to perform a physical act with the highest possible degree of efficiency. Significance is attained relative to the attainment of the goal.

Unfortunately for many of our aesthetic interests, this significance is often measured in quantitative terms, and thus in terms of winning or losing. So many points conventionally assigned to the prescribed ways of scoring have often led to ignoring the qualitative aspects of the experience itself. But win or lose, the players must perform their allotted tasks in a specific manner; and all the niceties of movement over and above the strict necessity of scoring—and thus of winning or losing—have come to be called "form." Consider the judging of divers or figure skaters; consider also the graceful movements of a powerful batter—Ted Williams was one—who always looks good with a bat in his hands, even while striking out. This same sort of grace can become the object of the physical performance, as it does in synchronized swimming and team calisthenics. In addition to providing the controlled release of violence, such sports as the latter are capable of producing elaborate visual and spatial configurations of no mean attraction.

Dance is merely the last of the hierarchic series of abstractive human movements. The context created is still artificial, yet not conventional (except for the ballet, which never really achieved its independence from music). I prefer to call the meaning of the dance "auto-significance," intending that expression to refer to the fact that any movement of the dance which achieves any kind of significance at all does so by virtue of the relationship it bears to other movements in the context, considered as both means and end of the kinaesthetic expression. All the significance of the dance is internal to the dance. It may englobe many gestures imitative of everyday human locomotive patterns and even subhuman as well; but the significance of such representational elements is seriously modified for their incorporation into the balletic context. It is not sufficient, for example, for a choreographer to tell his performers to go out and make like a bird or to imitate the actions of a child playing hop-scotch; it is the total dance which determines the significance of each of the parts.

Can this model of the self-contained, auto-significant balletic context be applied to our previous understanding of the aesthetic effect of athletic contests? Two considerations are necessary in order to grasp my contention that it can. First, the winning or the losing of the game is irrelevant to its aesthetic evaluation. An honest tie—one which results from an attempt on the part of opposing teams to win—is not therefore an absolute indicator of the failure to achieve aesthetic quality in the performance. Coaches like Parseghian of Notre Dame and Peterson of Florida State had something else in mind when they decided to play for a tie instead of for victory. Fans with an aesthetic interest can only be disappointed by the calculated decision to accept the tie; even though there is some doubt about the kicker's ability to make the field goal, the decision to go for it instead of for the touchdown which would win the game (as Florida State did against Penn State in last New Year's Gator Bowl) is always an anti-climax.

Even when the kicker succeeds, the game itself merely peters out into insignificance. With that decision, the "drama" of the game was lost even if the game itself was not. Thus, although the winning or losing of the game is aesthetically irrelevant, the desire to win is never aesthetically irrelevant.

Besides, the game is made an aesthetic event by the opposition of strength in the wills to win. But desire itself is not sufficient for the highly dramatic sporting event. In any game defined by the opposition of power, skill, and determination in its players, the power and skill cannot be lacking. Expansion teams of professional football and baseball are not aesthetically effective because they can offer no successful competition to the older, more established teams in their respective leagues. They may, of course, succeed in compensating for a lack of power and skill by a superabundance of determination and still participate effectively in the production of an aesthetically meaningful contest of purpose. Worth is still measured in terms of "how you play the game." Playing for a tie is cheating the public.

The second consideration necessary for the understanding of aesthetic quality in sporting events is a point taken from general aesthetic theory. It concerns media and their use to establish significant contexts we call works of art. Someone may have assumed that the previous discussion of abstraction would imply that there are no successful representational art works. This would be a misunderstanding of the process of creation. Some works, and very good ones at that, are highly representational.

But no matter how imitative certain of the discriminable elements within the aesthetic context happen to be, the worth of that work is not measurable in terms of the accuracy of representation. If this were the case, the best painting would be the one which most effectively pictured the events of nature and hardly any so-called "serious" music could be considered beautiful at all.

The truth of the matter is that all works of art are abstract in the sense indicated above—that their significance is perceivable only in the context in which they appear, in spite of the fact that the artist must artificially construct this context out of what he already knows and feels about the things he must work with as a medium and, if he chooses to represent objects of nature, about them as well. All his knowledge and skill, all the materials and technological means of expression at his disposal constitute the initial context from which he is to abstract his significance by manipulating the materials of his craft. Whence the term "transformation"[2] to describe the activity of the artist; he creates by transforming existing materials into something uniquely significant.

Dances too may be non-objective, producing no recognizable natural movement or object; or they may be interpretative and include them. We call the first "surface" expressions; the second "depth" expressions. The term "surface" refers to the organized sensuous features of the experience; and "depth" to recognizable images, ideas, or objects represented in the organization of the surface patterns. Since the value of the depth expressions is not to be found in the accuracy of representation, it can be found only in the tense relationship between expressing surface and expressed depth. Call that "tension" or "total expressiveness" of the artwork in question.

Making aesthetic judgments on works of art, then, proceeds from our attempts to perceive the qualitative relatedness of surface or of surface and depth "counters" (anything discriminable within the context). When we feel the expressiveness of the related counters, we are experiencing the expressive quality of the piece in question. Such judgments are made daily on creative dances. Can the same be done for our perception of the qualitative uniqueness of games?

The answer is obvious: yes, if we can isolate the relevant counters of the experience. And this is a matter of perceiving the tensions where they occur. In baseball it is the continuing struggle between pitcher and successive batters, which mounts with runners on the bases and

is qualified by the intermittent tensions between runners and throwers. But, as pointed out before, these tensions fund into qualitative uniqueness slowly, discontinuously, and hardly ever in a meaningful climax. The game of baseball is at best a summation of innings in which the change of offensive and defensive strategies tends to break the continuity of the action. This is possible in football too. But the rules of the game have been set up to maintain aesthetic quality—and hence spectator interest. A change from defensive to offensive strategy in football is allowed by the interception of passes, in which the defensive player himself assumes the offensive; in the recovery of fumbles; and in effective punting, which may put a whole offensive squad on the defensive if the ball may be downed within the five-yard line. The tempo and rhythm of the game are defined in terms of the building up and the release of dynamic tensions, created ultimately by the opposition of equally capable teams.

Controlled violence in which the opponent is not destroyed, but only defeated, and yet somehow morally edified—such is the essence of competitive sport. It reaches its aesthetic heights when the victor narrowly surpasses a worthy opponent. The game itself considered as an aesthetic object is perceived as a tense experience in which pressure is built up from moment to moment, sustained through continuous opposition, until the climax of victory or defeat. The closer this climax occurs to the end of the game, the stronger is our feeling of its qualitative uniqueness. Sudden death playoffs—and perhaps extra-inning games—are as close as a sport may come to achieving this aesthetic ideal.

We are now in a position to evaluate the possibilities of sport to produce aesthetic experiences. To make the point we may summarize the way in which "significance" is achieved within the levels of abstraction discernible in distinctively human locomotive contexts.

At the most basic level, significance is achieved merely by ordering our bodily existence in accordance with the ends imposed upon it by the natural environment and dominated by biological necessity. We have all learned to walk, run, or swim to increase our control of the conditions of our existence, which is often eked out against a hostile environment. Thus, sometimes with the help of the physical environment and sometimes against its tendency to thwart our growth, we learn to fulfill our vital needs. At this level of experience the possibilities of aesthetic perception are already multiple: we may abstract from the necessity to achieve a particular goal and focus on the movement pattern employed in its achievement, thereby developing "natural" grace. This is recognized as much for its maximum efficiency—the greatest amount of result for the least effort—as for the "beauty" of its execution. The feeling of being at one with nature, using it to fulfill our own aims with consummate ease, is a direct aesthetic response of the mover to his motion.

But there is another mode of abstraction possible even at this level of human experience. I have used the provocative walk to illustrate the point. He who gives in to the provocation is once again acting to fulfill a basic human and biological need. We may once more abstract from the naturally imposed end—the propagation of our species or the experience of pleasure as the outcome of the act—and concentrate upon the pattern of significance which develops between the dynamic tensions in the sexual drama, which would remain totally devoid of meaning without the building up and release of psychic tension through mutually determinant masculine and feminine movement sequences. Any pleasure which is not just attendant upon the act must be the consciousness of the many kinaesthetic gestures funding to make up the act. Each act of love is qualitatively unique and aesthetically recognizable for the manner in which it creates tensions, releases them, and terminates in ultimate peace. In their intimate dance of life, the partners to the act create a new human entity: the couple, which is still the basis for the continued existence of our species.

Dissatisfaction with their respective roles in the creation of this entity—due in part to inadequate physical and mental preparation, but in part as well to the failure to perceive its aesthetic aspects—has led many a married person to seek its artificial dissolution in divorce. Because of the religious and moral prejudices placed upon the significance of the act of love, we may never as educators be allowed to participate in any form of physical instruction devised to maximize the attainment of this sort of aesthetic value. Older, more primitive societies do, and their members are quite obviously better adapted to the sexual conditions of life.

My aim, in the pursuit of this example, was not to shock or even to astound, but rather, to point out that even at this level of abstraction the process of humanly-directed, conscious bodily movements is capable of a high degree

of aesthetic perfection in which the performers and the performance cannot be differentiated.

The same, of course, is true of the dance, which is not less dramatic for being less sexual in explicit expression. Competitive sporting events are somewhat like the dance and somewhat like an act of love. Like the dance, the athletic competition is defined in terms of the artificiality of its goals; like an act of love, the athletic competition represents an expression of human violence undergone under conditions of control in which the partner or opponent is not destroyed, but morally or humanly edified. Unlike the dance, however, the athletic medium is not "pure." The game does not create its own goals as kinaesthetic responses unfold; rather, these are imposed upon the participants by the rules of the game. To be an aesthetic event, therefore, the athletic contests must within the limits of the rules set down for the game become a unique context of dramatically significant tensional wholes. This it does by building up tension, sustaining and complicating it, and ultimately releasing the percipient into the state of peace. Well-played, i.e., successfully played, games and they alone succeed in this aesthetic ideal.

To abstract from the conventional goal of the game—to win—means only that the manner of playing the game is aesthetically predominant; and skill, power, and desire to win are the factors determining the manner in which the game is played. Thus it has been truthfully said (at least from the aesthetic point of view) that "It matters not whether you win or lose; it's how you play the game."

Unlike the dance, however, the medium of the sporting event cannot be totally abstracted from a pre-existent aim. The dancer or choreographer creates his end in making the dance, within which the performers (their activities) and the performance are one. The form of the game is always more concrete in that, although winning or losing may be irrelevant to its aesthetic significance, the desire to win may never be excluded as one of the determinants of the action. It is for this reason that aesthetic connoisseurs look down their noses at coaches like Notre Dame's Parseghian and Florida State's Peterson. In their calculated decisions to play for ties, they, on one occasion at least, have put the requirement of not losing over the aesthetic ideal of the well-played game.

Lastly, in order to motivate my phenomenological reading of the essence of sporting aesthetics, I have speculated that the declining popularity of baseball in face of the growing interest in football is explicable in aesthetic terms—that the game (or aesthetic product of the one) is inferior in marshalling the aesthetic interest of its viewers.

One point in the foregoing description remains all too sketchy. I refer to the ontological and psychoanalytical commitments in such phrases as "the psychic and moral edification" of the participants in sporting events. For the necessary connections between our existential concept of the body, or consciousness-body, as a "bodily schema" or "bodily image" and the self-creation of the human personality, I can do no better than refer the interested reader to the phenomenological psychoanalytical work of Eugène Minkowski. Two of his central notions, the creative imagination and spontaneity of movement, are contained in articles translated as "Imagination?" and "Spontaneity (. . . spontaneous movement like this!)" found in a recent anthology of readings in existential phenomenology.[3] His point of view on the creation of personality through movement would be necessary for a complete account of aesthetic creation through sensory-motor coordination. We need only keep in mind that any creative artist forms his own personality *qua* artist by transforming his experiences, through significant abstraction, into works of art; and in the arts utilizing human movement as a medium of expression, there is no distinction between the performer and his performance. But a complete account of the communication of aesthetic value through a sporting event was deemed too extravagant a task to be placed upon this author, who chose merely to explain the nature of the aesthetic qualities of a sporting event.

Minkowski's method as well as my own is distinctively phenomenological. His remarks are relevant to an understanding of the way in which the creative locomotor event is performed; mine, to the way in which the sensitive viewer responds to the event as performed. The middle ground, of course, is the event itself. I have only interpreted the rising and falling fortunes of two of our professionalized sports, along with the disgust on the part of some recent football fans at recurring decisions on the part of collegiate coaches to play a game for a tie. Both of these phenomena are meaningful in view of the description given the aesthetic ideal of sporting events, that of the "well-played game."

The beauty of motion referred to as "grace" in the descriptions above is possible at all levels of human motility. For the higher purposes of expressiveness in the dance or of maximal tension in competitive sports it is usually considered of only secondary interest: it represents the exploitation of skill for skill's sake alone. Like the virtuosity of a musical performer, however, that sport technique is the best which is noticed the least.

Give us more coaches who are willing to put their jobs and reputations on the line by going for the well-played game. Let us at least try to go out and win one for the Gipper, who has become in spite of the legend a symbol of the aesthetically dissatisfied sports fan.

NOTES

1. See my "Being in the Body" in the NAPCEW Report *Aesthetics and Human Movement* (Washington, D. C., 1964), pp. 84-103.
2. Cf. its use by Roger Fry in *Transformations* (Garden City, N. Y.: Doubleday Anchor Books, 1956).
3. See Lawrence and O'Connor, eds., *Readings in Existential Phenomenology* (Englewood Cliffs, N. J.: Prentice-Hall, 1967), pp. 75-92, 168-177.

Sport as an Aesthetic Experience

MARJORIE FISHER

INTRODUCTION

As is true of almost any of man's endeavors, "sport has provided an inspiration to artists." (29:28) In 1959, this was the primary reason for the establishment of a National Art Museum of Sport.

> The founders of this Museum hope that the combination of these two exacting fields of human endeavor will create a bond of excitement and pleasure to be shared by devotees of each, enlarging the appreciation of all. . . . We believe that an enhanced understanding of the functions of art and sport in life will provide a renewed inspiration for all. . . . (14:47)

This statement of purpose serves to point out the problem to be considered within this paper—the relationship of sport to art. Sport and art are generally thought of as two separate entities. Rene Maheu regards sports as one of "culture's modes of expression, . . . as a companion phenomenon to culture itself." (18:10-11) And Adrian Stokes considers sport to be a substitute for art, a parallel recreation. (28:389) But, very little consideration has been given to sport as a vehicle of aesthetic experience, or as an art form in and of itself. Thus, the purpose of this work is to explicate a theory of art appropriate to the conditional assumption that sport is a legitimate art form. In order to view sport as an art or as an "aesthetic situation," (40:349) it will be necessary to consider the athlete and the spectator also.

In this attempt, the use of the terms "sport" and "aesthetics" must be clarified. Sport is, above all, a human activity. It is a physical activity, undertaken with an eye to a specific outcome. The means by which this outcome is reached may be highly organized, structured by means of standard rules, or rules which have been agreed upon, defining the objectives of the activity and the limits of human behavior. Or, the activity may be loosely organized with few or no rules at all. Sport involves a challenge of some sort which may or may not be competitive in nature. (23:2) Most definitions also include a statement concerning the temporal and spatial aspects of sport; and, to be sure, the dimensionality of it, as of anything of this world, is unquestionable, but these aspects will be discussed later in an aesthetic context.

The meaning of the term "aesthetics" to be used in the context of this paper is derived from the Greek.

> The word 'aesthetics' (from the Greek *aisthanesthai,* to perceive; aisthetica, things perceptible) was introduced into philosophical terminology about the middle of the eighteenth century by Alexander Gottlieb Baumgarten, . . . and it is because of the odd use to which he put the word that the branch of philosophy which is concerned with investigation into the nature and principles of beauty now bears this incongruous name. (27:15)

In essence, this demonstrates the connotative aspect of the word. Popularly, what is considered as a thing of aesthetic worth, is considered to be a thing of beauty. For this paper the literal translation of the Greek—relating aesthetics to perception and thereby vastly broadening its use—is more relevant because in some cases, what may qualify as a valid aspect

315

of the aesthetic experience may not necessarily be "beautiful."

Two particular works have been chosen as sources for the theory to be applied to sport. James Joyce's *A Portrait of the Artist as a Young Man* is used as a pivotal work for the reason that within the story, a theory of art is explained. And Arturo Fallico's *Art and Existentialism* provides a source for expanding Joyce's theory.

A THEORY OF ART

In *A Portrait of the Artist as a Young Man,* James Joyce, through the character of Stephen Daedalus, propounds a particular theory of art. The primary condition necessary for the art-object to be considered as such is one that Joyce terms the "esthetic stasis." He states that there are two types of emotions—one static, the other kinetic.

> The feelings excited by improper art are kinetic, desire or loathing. Desire urges us to possess, to go to something; loathing urges us to abandon, to go from something. These are kinetic emotions. The arts which excite them, pornographical or didactic, are therefore improper arts. The esthetic emotion is therefore static. The mind is arrested and raised above desire and loathing. (12:205)

That is to say, the kinetic emotion implies that in the appreciation of "improper" art, the appreciator is moved towards some end to which the "art"-work is a means. He is not arrested, but moved.

Another way in which to view the "esthetic stasis" is in the terms of Martin Buber's "relation." In this context, the appreciation of the art work may be likened to the I-Thou relation. Buber says:

> The relation to the *Thou* is direct. No system of ideas, no foreknowledge, and no fancy intervene between *I* and *Thou*. . . . No aim, no lust, and no anticipation intervene between *I* and *Thou*. . . . Every means is an obstacle. Only when every means has collapsed does the meeting come about. (4:11-12)

Thus, one may conclude that in relation there is stasis, or in stasis there is relation; but if there is any intervention of irrelevancies, such as emotion or aim, there is no relation, the effect is kinetic.

To further explicate this idea, Fallico states that "there is never in the aesthetic any pretense at knowing and possessing;" (8:70) that there is a "pre-reflective directness" (8:87) inherent in the aesthetic.

The notion of esthetic stasis leads directly to a second phase in this theory—a notion which is perhaps the one universally accepted aspect of art—that is, that art is non-utilitarian in nature. James Joyce implies this when he speaks of "improper art" and the kinetic emotions which result. Fallico states specifically that "the aesthetic enactment or presence as such has, of course, no use. In itself, art has no use or purpose. . . ." (8:148) It is, however, as is anything that is done, a purposive activity; but:

> . . . Art is a purposiveness without a purpose, a purposing freed from all projects which must be such that the end to be achieved antecedes, or can be distinguished in thought from the means and process of achieving it. (8:42)

That is, the art-work exists as the completed object, and, as such, is useless.

In light of Buber's philosophy, in accepting the assumption that the aesthetic moment is a moment of relation," it is, by definition, distinguished from "experience." Experience connotes divergence, a turning outward, accumulating information about the object; whereas, the world of relation is self-contained, all that one needs to know about the art object is present at the moment of encounter—it may be put to no use, and there is nothing more to be known about it.

This leads directly into the aesthetic notion of "presentness" and the relation of art to time. "With art, the now is everything." That is, art exists as a presence—"Which carries its past and future entirely within itself." More explicitly, Fallico states that: "All art is contemporaneous in its very nature: it is always *now* by the fact that its being is to be nothing else but presence." (8:80-81)

In essence, this is the same as Benedetto Croce's view "that art is a universal manifestation of the human spirit and hence outside the category of time." (6:310) The work of art is always the same work no matter when it is viewed. This is not to say it is always viewed the same way—it never is. It merely implies that the work of art is what it is—always.

Another aspect of this aesthetic theory is the concept that the art object is a work of pure possibility. Fallico states:

> . . . There are rare occasions when we experience an overwhelming awareness, not of things that are possible, but pure possibility *qua* possibility, nameless and unincorporated. It neither springs from nor is directed at a particular hope or despair in our life experience. We cannot pin it down except to say that what we are feeling is the presence of infinite possibility which is not directed from, toward, or for-the-sake-of anything. (8:52-53)

For Fallico, it is the work of art which stands as a representation of this possibility. It might be said that the work of art does not merely have possibilities, it is its possibilities, it exists as pure possibility. From Martin Buber comes the phrase: "the endless possibility that is offered up on the altar of form." (4:10) This not only supports the aesthetic notion of "pure possibility," but also introduces the view that what is perceived as art, is perceived as form. He speaks of moments

> . . . Of silent depth in which you look on the world-order fully present. Then in its very flight the note will be heard. . . . These moments are immortal, and most transitory of all; no content may be secured from them. . . . (4:31)

In essence, the world of art "is a world that is intended to be nothing else but surface play; it is a world in which form is impressed upon things with imperceptible, spontaneous effort. There is a sense of 'waiting for something to happen'." (8:126) That is, the encounter with pure possibility.

Thus, to summarize, it has been shown that the art object produces an "esthetic stasis," and in so doing, implies the non-functional aspect of art. Art is seen as the result of spontaneity, aesthetically it exists purely as form, to be encountered in its presentness, divorced from time, as pure possibility.

It is now necessary to return to James Joyce to consider his essential qualities of the aesthetic. "Three things are needed . . ., wholeness, harmony, and radiance." (12:212) In attempting to explain this to his companion, Stephen says:

> In order to see that basket, your mind first of all separates the basket from the rest of the visible universe which is not the basket. . . . The esthetic image is first luminously apprehended as self-bounded and self-contained upon the immeasurable background of space or time which is not it. You apprehend it as one thing. You see it as one whole. You apprehend its wholeness. That is *integritas*. (12:212)

Martin Buber makes a statement which seems to paraphrase Joyce.

> The Thou appears, to be sure, in space, but in the exclusive situation of what is over against it, where everything else can be only the background out of which it emerges, not its boundary and measured limit. It appears, too, in time, but in that of the event which is fulfilled in itself; it is not lived as a part of a continuous and organised sequence, but is lived in a "duration" whose purely intensive dimension is definable only in terms of itself. (4:30)

Thus the art object is seen as one thing, taken out of the context in which it has been set; everything else, which is not the object, becomes irrelevant and goes unnoticed.

The second "phase of apprehension" is harmony, or *consonantia*.

> Then, said Stephen, you pass from point to point, led by its formal lines; you apprehend it as balanced part against part within its limits; you feel the rhythm of its structure. In other words the synthesis of immediate perception is followed by the analysis of apprehension. Having first felt it is *one* thing, you feel now that it is a *thing*. You apprehend it as complex, multiple, divisible, separable, made up of its parts, the result of its parts and their sum, harmonious. That is *consonantia*. (12:212)

It is felt that the implication here is not that the art object is a "thing" to be "experienced" in Buber's sense of the word, but that the internal structure of the work is essential in evolving the "indissoluble unity" of the artwork.

The last of the three phases of apprehension is that of radiance. Stephen says:

> The radiance . . . is the scholastic *quidditas*, the whatness of a thing. This supreme quality is felt by the artist when the esthetic image is first conceived in his imagination. . . . The clear radiance of the esthetic image is the luminous silent stasis of esthetic pleasure. . . . (12:213)

It is the essence of the art-work, "the moment of truthfulness par excellence." (8:87) Berenson, in his view of the "aesthetic moment," also explains what is meant by the notion of radiance.

> In visual art the aesthetic moment is the flitting instant, so brief as to be almost timeless, when the spectator is at one with the work of art he is looking at, or with actuality of any kind that the spectator himself sees in terms of art, as form and colour. He ceases to be his ordinary self, and the picture or building, statue, landscape, or aesthetic actuality is no longer outside himself. The two become one entity; time and space are abolished and the spectator is possessed by one awareness. When he recovers workaday consciousness it is as if he had been initiated into illuminating, exalting, formative mysteries. In short, the aesthetic moment is a moment of mystic vision. (3:84-85)

To summarize, it may be said that it has been primarily the work of art (as form, as spontaneity, as a purposiveness without a purpose, as a presence) and the perception of the spectator (in terms of stasis and the phases of apprehension, and in relation) with which this section has been concerned. However, there is one final aspect of the "aesthetic situation" which must be considered—namely, the artist. According to Joyce, "the artist, like the God of creation, remains within or behind or beyond or above his handiwork, invisible, refined out of existence, indifferent, paring his fingernails." (12:215) This directly refers to the objectivity of the artist; aesthetically, what is most important is the relation between the art-object and viewer. And the artist, in having completed his work, "as a purposer . . . is stripped of his purposes, and thus capable of a unique kind of objectivity." (8:13) Once the art-work is complete, the artist becomes disengaged from the process and views the product disinterestedly.

THE AESTHETIC EXPERIENCE IN SPORT

The emphasis of the ensuing section is based on the assumption that sport is an art form. The direction that this chapter will take is derived from R. F. Racy's view of the "aesthetic situation." That is, for this particular situation to exist, three things are necessary—an artist, a work of art, and a spectator. (25) The parallel with sport is obvious.

The purpose of the first phases will be to determine the sources of the aesthetic experience in sport for both the "fan" and the athlete. At times, this will be done by comparison to their counterparts in the "art world," and, at times, directly from their comments. The last phase will be concerned with making the case for assuming sport to be a legitimate art form. Again, it will be primarily through comparison and specific reference.

The Spectator

For the spectator, the aesthetic experience develops in many ways. The attempt at this point will be to demonstrate what the sources of art may be for the spectator, and why, possibly, particular sports may have greater aesthetic value.

The determination of artistic merit is a matter of individual perception, and where it is found is a function of selectivity. Whether or not a spectator is caught up in the aesthetics of a sport situation depends on a number of things. Relation must come about, and by the nature of relation, the necessity of the spectator is established. Stasis occurs, time is frozen, becoming a "real, filled present." The work (or game) is apprehended as a unity—in wholeness and harmony. It is accepted as such—no judgment precedes, and none comes after. And

finally, radiance is realized, the spectator has become one with the work of art.

From the spectator's point of view, the aesthetic experience may come from any of three sources in sport—from the human form in action, from a single action, or from the action of the whole game at one moment. Where it comes from is a function of the spectator's selective perceptions.

The human form has long been considered an aesthetic entity. John McCormick, speaking of the Spanish bull-fighter, Cayetano, said: "Reliable witnesses speak of his grace, naturalness, . . . which, linked to his spontaneity, made him exciting and interesting to watch." (21:58) Actually, little need be said about the aesthetic value of the human form, particularly in action. There is form, rhythm, grace, spontaneity, tension; there is the stamp of the personal, the form in its uniqueness. From any one, or from all of these, the spectator may be caught up in the aesthetic moment—having experienced all that that implies.

The other aspects of sport provide sources of aesthetic encounter for the spectator. They are a particular action or the action as a whole within the framework of the game. Bill Russell, in considering basketball aesthetically, said that it is the "most graceful of all our major sports. . . . The jump shot opened it up, made it more fluid, . . . it is close to an art form." (26:88) Here, there are numerous sources to be considered. Again, there is the human form —hanging in the air, frozen in time and space. There is the form of the action as a whole, from the beginning of the jump to the flight of the ball. There is no reason not to consider this as a source of aesthetic possibilities. It is the spectator and his manner of perception, or relation, if you will, that determines whether or not aesthetic encounter comes about.

Finally, there is to be considered the third source of the aesthetic experience for the spectator. This lies in the "big picture"—a consideration of all the action taking place before him. Again, using the example of basketball, Willard Manus says:

> Sports Illustrated once described the essence of basketball as a "fluid rhythm with the underlying mathematical symmetry of a fugue by Johann Sebastian Bach. What to the spectator may seem merely hectic anarchy is designed to be a smoothly integrated pattern demanding dexterity, endurance, fine timing and continuous split second appraisal of percentages and alternatives." (20:436)

There is a wholeness to be found—it is the action of one scene, by nature bounded from what is not it. There is harmony—every player and every movement is a necessary part of the whole. There is radiance—the realization by the spectator of what, in the scene before him, is "over against him." There is also a certain spontaneity in the game pattern, and there is the presentation of pure possibility.

Another aspect of the aesthetic situation of the spectator falls into the category of the appreciation of violence, or of the "ugly." Both Dave Meggyesy and Chip Oliver take issue with the violence and dehumanizing aspects of football, and are concerned with the effect on the spectator. And Bannister refers to "an unhealthy element among spectators in many of these (high-risk) sports that is disturbing. In motor-racing how many spectators are attracted . . . by the morbid anticipation of disaster . . .?" (2:71)

The psychology of this type of spectator would, no doubt, be most interesting; but, aesthetically, all that need be said is that: "Beauty is in the eye of the beholder." The major point to be made is that the spectator's perceptions are selective and subjective. Almost anything could serve as a source of art—to bring about stasis, apprehension, and understanding in relation. And, sport provides abundant aesthetic possibilities for the spectator.

The Athlete

In this section, the athlete will be conceived of as artist. At times, he is a spectator, and he may also be considered a work of art in his own right, but both views are irrelevant to this discussion.

One spelunker who found a virgin room in a new cave filled with tall stalagmite formations was not primarily impressed with the beauty of it all. "What really excited me was the floor of the room. There wasn't a print in the sand. I was the first human ever to set foot there." (23:3)

The aesthetic experience in this instance does not come from natural beauty; that is a seemingly unimportant aspect of it. Instead, it lies in the mere fact of entrance. Stasis occurs with his entering the room. Wholeness and harmony are inherent in the scene before him, as aspects of nature. Radiance, however, comes with the recognition of the essence of the experience—he is the *first*, there has been no one else. The spelunker is, in a sense, both artist and appreciator. The work of art is the fact (the "thing done") of entrance, and thus, the man is an artist. His objectivity is apparent in his perception. He stands outside what he has done in order to realize it.

This situation is somewhat similar to an experience involving Ricky Grigg.

One day at Waimea, Ricky was taking off on a huge wave, well over fifteen feet high, when he suddenly got so jazzed over the beauty of the curling monster that he ran to the nose of his board, screamed with delight and then unexpectedly dove off the nose of his board. He landed prone down the face of the wave in a body-surfing position and kept on going. Fred Van Dyke . . . remembers seeing the whole thing. . . . "I retrieved his board and asked him why. 'Aw gee, Fred, the wave was so beautiful that I just couldn't do anything else.'" (7:85-86)

Here, a source of the aesthetic experience may be seen in the wave itself, just as Ricky saw it. The wave is nature-made, providing one level of artistry. A second level is in the act of the surfer. He has a feeling (from his perception of the wave), and from it, he makes an image; that is, he expresses his feeling—he literally becomes "one with the wave." This passage also demonstrates the spontaneity inherent in the creation of art.

Joseph Conrad states:

I would illustrate my idea of fidelity between man and ship as between the master and his art. . . . The genuine masters of their craft . . . have thought of nothing but doing their very best by the vessel under their charge. To forget one's self, to surrender all personal feeling in the service of that fine art, is the only way for a seaman to faithfully discharge his trust. . . . (5:155)

This gives reason to draw further parallels between the athlete and artist, and it also hints at the objectivity of the artist—the artist who must be "refined out of existence," (12:215) who "surrenders all personal feeling."

This does not rule out the personal element; the athlete marks his performance with his own unique style. But once he has done one particular thing, has been an artist in one instant, he moves on, literally and figuratively. The thing he has done stands alone, perhaps in the mind's eye, perhaps on film; but, nevertheless, the "artist" has gone.

Karl Groos has another way in which to view this objective aspect of the artist. The work of art "causes him intense enjoyment all through the progress of its production, and the indifference sometimes felt toward the finished work results from frequent repetition which has dulled the edge of appetite." (9:395) This serves as an apt explanation for the staleness sometimes experienced by the athlete; but, in the context of the game, the athlete must move on of necessity, bored or otherwise.

Spontaneity is another aspect of the artist-athlete. It has already been mentioned once in relation to Ricky Grigg. Jack Kramer also supports this notion. He feels "there is not time to think on a tennis court. . . ." (16:615) Therefore, he must act spontaneously.

One final way in which the athlete may be viewed, once it has been established that he is an artist, is to consider him, from among the various categories of artistry, a primary artist. That is to say, that in dance, the dancer is one step removed from the dance in that it is the choreographer's creation. As a performer, he is an artist in his own right, but he is also attempting to express the choreographer's artistry. The same is true of the actor in a play. However, he is even further removed in that his artistry comes after that of the director's, whose artistry comes after that of the playwright. (10:382) The athlete, however, is his own man; which, incidentally, makes him all the more spontaneous. The coach may send in plays, or the natural sportsman may have a plan in mind, but neither can cope with all the possibilities inherent in even a moment's activity. Thus, the artist-athlete must find his own way. He may be guided, but what he does is his own.

So, to conclude this section, it is definitely evident that sources of aesthetic experience may be found in sport. The action itself, the human form, or both considered at once, also provide for artistic perceptions. The patterns of play, inherent in a game, provide still another source.

When it is said that the surfer "becomes one with the wave," or that a skier "becomes one with the mountain," it is implied that the athlete has perceived nature in a special way, has accepted it as he sees it, and responds accordingly "in his own way." That is, he enters into relation with nature by surfing it, by skiing it, by sailing it; he enters into relation as an artist. He has been considered as a primary artist, a creator—of a single action, or as a part of a larger aesthetic whole—the game.

Sport as Art

Up to this point, sport has been discussed as a source providing aesthetic possibilities for the athlete and the spectator. It now remains to look at sport itself to determine, if indeed, it is an art form. Rene Maheu believes that sport and the arts have the same origin—that of leisure; and that sport "fulfills the same function as culture, for it too dignifies those hours and that energy not absorbed by our utilitarian work." (18:11) In other words, neither sport nor art have any utilitarian value.

This idea leads directly to the notion that sport is essentially a purposiveness without a purpose. Inasmuch as it is a human activity,

it is, by its very nature, a purposive activity. However, it may be concluded that since sport has no use, it is then, a purposiveness without a purpose.

Maheu goes on to say that sport is, as is culture, a creator of aesthetic impressions.

In the action and rhythm which testify to mastery of space and time, sport becomes akin to the arts. . . . No athlete can accomplish a genuine feat without such perfect physical control, in time and space, that his movements and the rhythm of their timing are not to be differentiated from the finest ballet, the most splendid passages of prose or verse, the most glorious lines in architecture or sculpture or the loveliest harmonies of light and colour. Lastly, in art as in sport, we find in the protagonist the same inimitable assertion of personality which we call style. (18:14)

D. W. J. Anthony, in discussing various views of the relationship of sport to art, states:

Toynbee describes the sense of balance, the timing, the control of mind and body in rapid movement—the qualities of the athlete. Games, he writes, "demand a sense of positional play, a pattern of design in movement (be it a single movement or the action of the game as a whole), flowing and continuous, but basically creative and alive." As, to an artist, a haystack is always a haystack yet each one is different, so in sport "each match pattern and design is unique." Moore and Williams claim that in modern football, "space, creativity, effort and rhythm" are major factors. . . . Laurent describes the affinity of feeling between the athlete and the artist. The athlete, "in modelling his body by repeated drilling," shares the feelings of the artist, concerned as he is, "with the need to correct a faulty line, to attenuate a corpulence. . . ." (1:1)

Thus, Maheu and the writers discussed by Anthony attribute the elements of the art-work to sport; and the athlete is compared to the artist—not only in attempting to create of his human form a work of art, but, with repeated practice, in attempting to perfect the forms of the game. And, while recent studies show that those engaged in natural sports in no way aspire to mastery, they strive for expression, (24: 46-47) an uncontestable aspect of the artist.

To further compare sport and art, on the basis of the previous quotation (by Maheu), wholeness and harmony are found in the "match pattern," the "space," and the "rhythm." Each pattern is unique, it is one thing. It takes place in an area, sometime specifically designated, sometimes not, from which everything which is not a part of sport is kept separate. "That is *integritas*." Harmony may be discerned in the creative use of space and rhythm in both individual movements and in the action as a whole, in the patterns of the game.

Somewhat related to this is the conception of art as mere form. Susanne Langer discusses an aspect of what she calls "living form," in which movement provides form, i.e., the "form of motion." (17:48) This aspect as related to sport is particularly apparent in competitive team games where patterns of play are run, but it is also apparent in free-form activities where movement also provides form.

Radiance is more difficult to pin down. It is the "qualitative character" of the game of which Kaelin speaks. (13:19) And the determination of this essence is the sole province of the spectator and his manner of perception.

The "present" or timeless aspects of sport can be discussed in various ways. In the context of Buber's relation, it may be said that sport constitutes a "real, filled present." Inasmuch as it is purely form, everything that need be known about it is present—and, hence, outside the category of historic time—in essence, timeless. A particularly good example of this comes from one man's experiences in parachuting—a free-form activity. As a part of the aesthetic experience, he states: "There is no sound. . . . No sensation. . . . The flatness far below, frozen in time and space . . . time itself has ground to a halt." (15:174) The essence of his experience is his "real, filled present." Robert Jones also had a way of expressing this. Of his Peace Pentathalon, he said: "I run up the mountain. I flow down the mountain. In time with the moment." (11:50) What matters to him is Now. —

The final aspect to be discussed is that of sport as an expression of pure possibility. Who can know the outcome? Who can know how that outcome may be reached? Therein lies the essence of sport's possibilities. Man himself, as Fallico states, "is his possibilities." (8:53) And, sport provides man a context of illimitable possibilities in which he may express himself, as his possibilities. Jay Wright speaks of the ballplayer who will always be trying "to transcend by the perfection of his craft, the limitations that are inherent in it, and in himself." (31:39) Here the idea of transcendence is introduced. Man is a creature bound by physical limitations, but within that framework there are no limits to his possibilities. A prime example is that of Bob Beamon's phenomenal long-jump. In the 1968 Olympics, Beamon jumped 29' 2½''; almost two feet further than the previous record jump. It was "as if there never was a 28' barrier to fool with. . . ." (30:22) Thus it may justifiably be said that sport, in providing man as his possibilities,

with its own infinite possibilities, is an expression of "pure possibility."

CONCLUSION

The purpose of this paper was to view sport as an aesthetic situation, a situation characterized by three essential facets—a spectator, and artist, and a work of art. A theory of art was derived from James Joyce's *A Portrait of the Artist as a Young Man,* and expanded through the use of Arturo Fallico's *Art and Existentialism* with the specific intent of applying it to the sport situation.

It has been determined that whether or not the spectator is caught up in aesthetic relation is a function of his selective perceptions. The athlete has been equated with the artist by means of appropriate comment and comparison. And thus, it is certain that sport provides an unlimited source for the experiencing of aesthetic possibilities. And finally, while sport demonstrates aesthetic elements in its creation and in its perception, it has also been shown that sport includes those elements which are characteristic of an art work and, thus, is an art form.

REFERENCES

1. Anthony, D. W. J. "Sport and Physical Education as a Means of Aesthetic Education." *Physical Education,* 60 (March, 1968), 1-6.
2. Bannister, Roger. "The Meaning of Athletic Performance." *International Research in Sport and Physical Education.* Edited by E. Jokl and E. Simon. Springfield, Illinois: Charles C Thomas, 1964, 64-73.
3. Berenson, Bernard. *Aesthetics and History in the Visual Arts.* New York: Pantheon Books Inc., 1948.
4. Buber, Martin. *I and Thou.* Second edition. Translated by Ronald Gregor Smith. New York: Charles Scribner's Sons, 1958.
5. Conrad, Joseph. "The Fine Art." *The Realm of Sport.* Edited by Herbert Warren Wind. New York: Simon and Schuster, 1966, 152-157.
6. De Gennaro, Angelo A. "Benedetto Croce and Herbert Read." *Journal of Aesthetics and Art Criticism,* 26 (Spring, 1968), 307-310.
7. Dixon, Peter. *Men Who Ride Mountains.* New York: Bantam Books Inc., 1969.
8. Fallico, Arturo B. *Art and Existentialism.* Englewood Cliffs, N.J.: Prentice-Hall, Inc., 1962.
9. Groos, Karl. *The Play of Man.* New York: D. Appleton and Co., 1901.
10. Hein, Hilde. "Performance as an Aesthetic Category." *Journal of Aesthetics and Art Criticism,* 28 (Spring, 1970), 381-386.
11. Jones, Robert F. "The World's First Peace Pentathalon." *Sports Illustrated,* 32 (May 11, 1970), 50-60.

12. Joyce, James. *A Portrait of the Artist as a Young Man*. New York: The Viking Press, 1966.
13. Kaelin, E. F. "The Well-Played Game: Notes Toward an Aesthetics of Sport." *Quest*, X (May, 1968), 16-28.
14. Kent, Norman. "Art in Sports." *American Artist*, 32 (March, 1968), 45-47.
15. Kittinger, Capt. Joseph W., Jr. *The Long Lonely Leap*. New York: Ed Dutton and Co., Inc., 1961.
16. Kramer, Jack. "Some Thoughts on the Big Game and Other Matters." *The Realm of Sport*. Edited by Herbert Warren Wind. New York: Simon and Schuster, 1966.
17. Langer, Susanne K. *Problems of Art*. New York: Charles Scribner's Sons, 1957.
18. Maheu, Rene. "Sport and Culture." *International Research in Sport and Physical Education*. Edited by E. Jokl and E. Simon. Springfield, Illinois: Charles C Thomas, 1964, 9-22.
19. "Man in Sport." *Print*, 22 (January-February, 1968), 28-32.
20. Manus, Willard. "Basketball." *Motivations in Play, Games, and Sports*. Edited by Ralph Slovenko and James A. Knight. Springfield, Illinois: Charles C Thomas, 1967, 435-442.
21. McCormick, John. "Perhaps Not Great, But Hardly Gutless." *Sports Illustrated*, 32 (June 29, 1970), 58-59.
22. McLuhan, Marshall. *Understanding Media: The Extensions of Man*. New York: A Signet Book, 1964.
23. Progen, Jan. "Man, Nature, and Sport." Unpublished Paper, University of Massachusetts, 1970.
24. ———. "The Achievement Motivation of College Women and Their Sport Preferences." Unpublished Honors Thesis, University of Massachusetts, 1971.
25. Racy, R. F. "The Aesthetic Experience." *The British Journal of Aesthetics*, 9 (October, 1969), 345-352.
26. Russell, William F. "Success is a Journey." *Sports Illustrated*, 32 (June 8, 1970), 80-93.
27. Saw, Ruth and Osborne, Harold. "Aesthetics as a Branch of Philosophy." *Aesthetics in the Modern World*. Edited by Harold Osborne. New York: Weybright and Talley, 1968, 15-32.
28. Stokes, Adrian. "The Development of Ball Games." *Motivations in Play, Games, and Sports*. Edited by Ralph Slovenko and James A. Knight, Springfield, Illinois: Charles C Thomas, 1967, 387-397.
29. Toynbee, Lawrence. "Artists and Sport." *New Society*, 6 (November 8, 1962), 28.
30. Underwood, John. "A High Time for Sprinters —and Kenyans." *Sports Illustrated*, 29 (October 28, 1968), 16-27.
31. Wright, Jay. "A Diamond-Bright Art Form." *Sports Illustrated*, 30 (June 23, 1969), 33-39.

BIBLIOGRAPHY ON SPORT AND AESTHETICS

Aldrich, Virgil C. "Art and the Human Form." *Journal of Aesthetics and Art Criticism*, 29 (Spring, 1971), 295-302.

Anthony, D. W. J. "Sport and Physical Education as a Means of Aesthetic Education." *Physical Education*, 60 (March, 1968), 1-6.

Brown, Margaret C. "Sculpture and Physical Education." *Physical Educator*, I (October, 1940), 3-4.

Groos, Karl. *The Play of Man*. New York: D. Appleton and Company, 1901.

Hein, Hilde. "Play as an Aesthetic Concept." *Journal of Aesthetics*, 27 (Fall, 1968), 67-71. [Reprinted in *Humanitas*, V (Spring, 1969), 21-28.]

———. "Performance as an Aesthetic Category." *Journal of Aesthetics and Art Criticism*, 28 (Spring, 1970), 381-386.

Jokl, Ernst. "Sport and Culture" in *Medical Sociology and Cultural Anthropology of Sport and Physical Education*. Illinois: Charles C Thomas, 1964.

Kaelin, E. F. "The Well-Played Game: Notes Toward an Aesthetics of Sport." *Quest*, X (May, 1968), 16-28.

Kent, Norman. "Art in Sports." *American Artist*, 32 (March, 1968), 45-47, 55.

Kovich, Maureen. "Sport as an Art Form." *Journal of Health, Physical Education, and Recreation*, 42 (October, 1971), 42.

Lowe, Benjamin. "The Aesthetics of Sport: The Statement of a Problem." *Quest*, XVI (June, 1971), 13-17.

Maheu, Rene. "Sport and Culture." *Journal of Health, Physical Education, and Recreation*, 34 (October, 1963), 30-32, 49-50, 52-54.

Metzl, Ervine. "Art in Sports." *American Artist*, 26 (November, 1962), 31-37.

"The Poetry of Football." *The Arts of Sport and Recreation*. Edited by Derek Stanford. London: Thomas Nelson and Sons, 1967. (Reprinted from *The Times*, October 23, 1962).

Rau, Catherine. "Psychological Notes on the Theory of Art as Play." *Journal of Aesthetics and Art Criticism*, 8 (June, 1950), 229-238.

Schiller, Friedrich von. *Essays and Letters*. Volume VIII. Translated by A. Lodge, E. B. Eastwick and A. J. W. Morrison. London: The Anthological Society, 1882.

Seward, George. "Play as Art." *Journal of Philosophy*. XLI (March, 1944), 178-184.

Smith, Hope M. "Movement and Aesthetics." *Introduction to Human Movement*. Edited by Hope M. Smith. Massachusetts: Addison-Wesley, 1968.

Spencer, Herbert. "Aesthetic Sentiments." *Background Readings for Physical Education*. Edited by Ann Paterson and Edmond C. Hallberg. New York: Holt, Rinehart and Winston, 1965.

Sweeney, James Johnson. "Contemporary Art: The Generative Role of Play." *Review of Politics*, 21 (April, 1959), 389-401.

Toynbee, Lawrence. "Artists and Sport." *New Society*, 6 (November 8, 1962), 28.

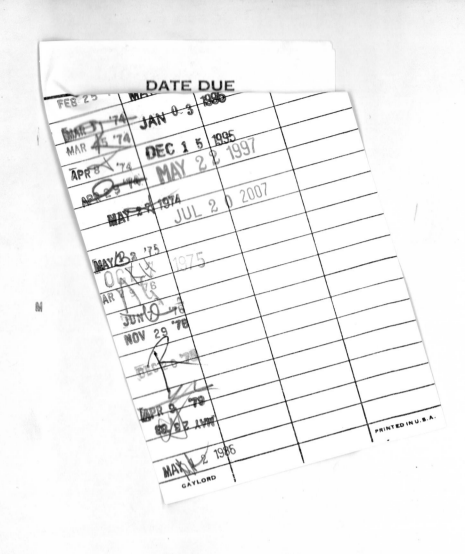

DATE DUE

FEB 25			
MAR 1 '74 JAN 0 3 1995			
MAR 15 '74 DEC 1 5 1995			
APR 8 '74 MAY 2 2 1997			
APR 29 '74			
MAY 2 8 1974 JUL 2 0 2007			
MAY 2 2 '75 1975			
OCT			
MAR '76			
JUN 0 '76			
NOV 29 '76			
DEC			
APR 9 '79			
MAY 2 2 '80			PRINTED IN U.S.A.
MAR 1 2 1986			
GAYLORD			